D1589516

KEY MATHS 7[1]

First edition published in 1995 by:
Stanley Thornes (Publishers) Ltd
Second edition 2000

Reprinted in 2002 by:
Nelson Thornes Ltd
Delta Place
27 Bath Road
CHELTENHAM
GL53 7TH
United Kingdom

02 03 04 / 10 9 8 7 6 5

A catalogue record for this book is available from the British Library

ISBN 0-7487-5524-1

Illustrations by Maltings Partnership, Mark Dunn, Clinton Banbury and Mike Gordon
Page make-up by Tech Set Ltd

Printed and bound in China by Dah Hua Printing Press Co. Ltd.

Acknowledgements
The publishers thank the following for permission to reproduce copyright material: Ace Photo Agency, spine, p. 216 (Anthony Price); Aerofilms, p. 266; British Museum, p. 283; British Shoe Council, p. 363; Buxton Micrarium, p. 41 (bottom); Collections/Brian Shuel, p. 231; Colorsport, p. 358; Genesis Space Photo Library, pp. 280, 344 (NASA); George Wimpey PLC, p. 367; Images, p. 31; Lincolnshire County Council, p. 38; Mary Evans Picture Library, p. 167; Ordnance Survey, p. 266 (top right – reproduced from 1990 Ordnance Survey 2 cm to 1 km West London area map with the permission of the Controller of Her Majesty's Stationery Office © Crown Copyright); OSF, p. 273 (top left – G I Bernard, top middle – Barry Walker, bottom right – Mark Hamblin); Paul Smith, pp. 172, 173, 174, 175; Sally and Richard Greenhill, p. 192; Science and Society Picture Library, p. 239; Science Photo Library, pp. 124, 266 (bottom left – Claude Nuridsany and Marie Perennou); Tony Stone Images, front cover, back cover (Lori Adamski Peek); Zefa, pp. 41 (top), 145, 273 (top right – Mehner, bottom left – Reinhard).
All other photographs by Martyn F Chillmaid.

The publishers have made every effort to contact copyright holders but apologise if any have been overlooked.

KEY MATHS 7[1]

David Baker
The Anthony Gell School, Wirksworth

Peter Bland
Huntingdon School, York

Paul Hogan
Fulwood High School, Preston

Barbara Holt
Churchdown School, Gloucester

Barbara Job
Christleton County High School, Chester

Renie Verity
Pensby High School for Girls, Heswall

Graham Wills
The Dyson Perrins CE High School, Malvern

Contents

1 Statistics: about our school

CORE

1 **Surveys**

2 **Pie-charts**

3 **Tallying in groups**

4 **Location**

5 **Scatter diagrams**

QUESTIONS

EXTENSION

SUMMARY

TEST YOURSELF

The size of your school is measured by the number of pupils.
These pie-charts give information about secondary schools in the UK.

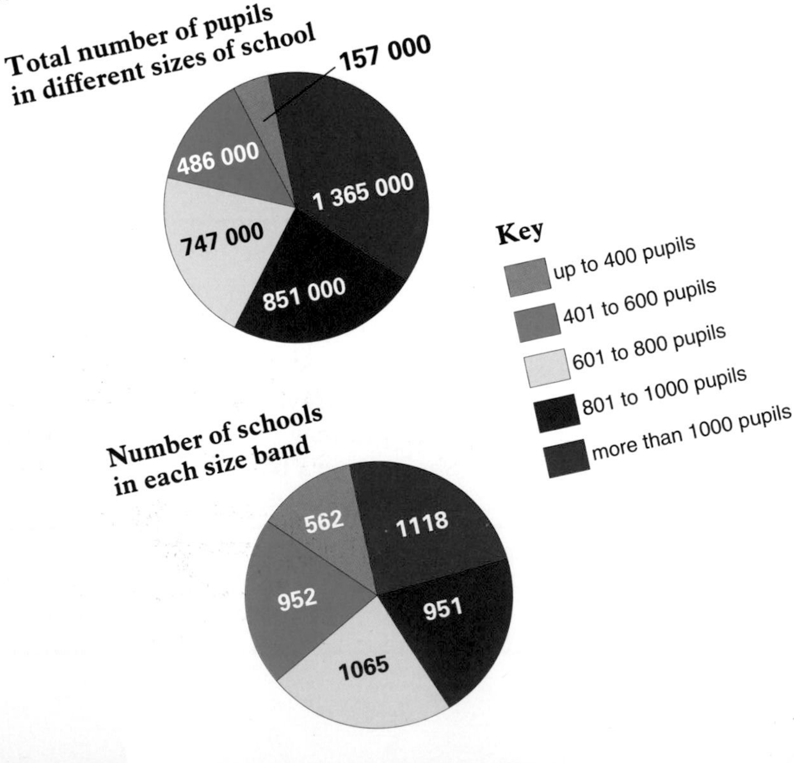

1 Surveys

In a **survey** we collect information. This information is also called **data**. The data can be sorted and shown on a diagram.

Statistics

The study of facts about numbers is called **statistics**. Governments were the first collectors of statistics. (The name statistics came from the word **states**.) They counted things like the number of people who should pay taxes.

Exercise 1:1

Sarah is doing a survey. She is asking her friends how they come to school. Is it by car, bus, train or bike, or do they walk?
Numbers on their own may look dull. Sarah wants to show her results in a diagram. She can use a bar-chart, a pictogram or a pie-chart.

Bar-chart

A **bar-chart** is a diagram made up of bars.
Each bar **represents** part of the data.

1 Sarah has drawn a bar-chart.

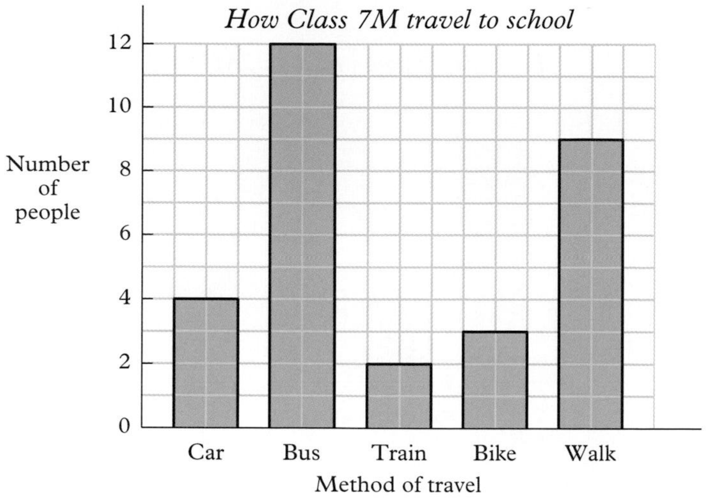

a How many children walk to school?
b What is the most common way to travel? How can you tell this from the bar-chart?
c How many children are in this class?

2 Andrew has one brother and one sister. This means that there are three children in his family.
He has done a survey for his class to find the number of children in each family.

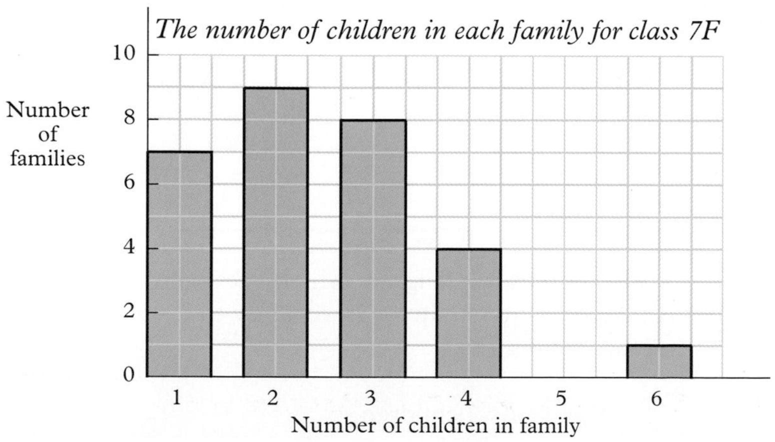

a How many families have just one child?
b Which is the most popular number of children for a family to have?
c How many families have five children?
d How many families were in the survey?

3 Kevin has done a survey on favourite colours.

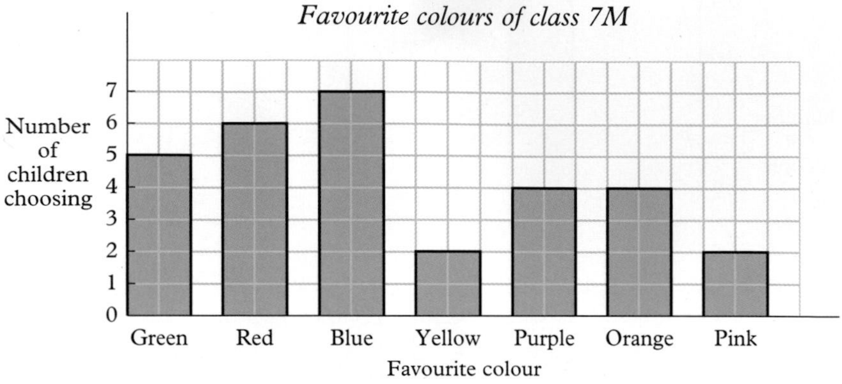

a What is the most popular colour?
b How many pupils chose red?
c How many pupils were in Kevin's survey?

Pictogram
Key

A **pictogram** is a diagram which uses pictures instead of bars. A pictogram must always have a **key** to show what each small picture represents.

Example

 represents 2 children.

 represents 1 child.

 represents 2 + 2 + 2 + 1 = 7 children.

4 Liam has drawn a pictogram. This is part of Liam's pictogram.

How Class 7M travel to school

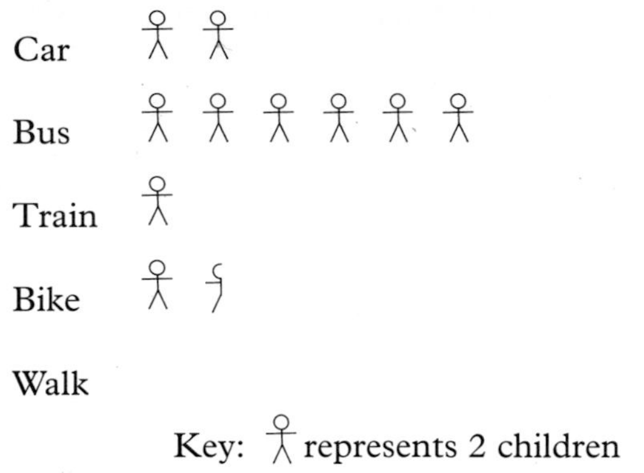

a How many children came by bus?
b How many children came by bike?
c Nine children walk to school.
Draw the missing line for Liam's pictogram in your exercise book.

5 Here are the results of a survey on where people went on holiday:

England	Scotland	Wales	Ireland	France	Spain	Other
9	4	5	1	5	4	1

Jaswinder has drawn a pictogram:

Jaswinder's pictogram is not very good.
Write down two things which you think are wrong.

6 Draw a correct pictogram for the results in Question **5**.

7 **a** Draw a bar-chart for Jaswinder's survey in Question **5**.
b Did you find the pictogram or the bar-chart easier to draw?
c Write down your reasons.

8 Alix has done a survey. She asked the girls in Year 7 which primary school they used to attend.
She used **tally marks**. Tally marks are done in groups of 5. The fifth tally mark goes across the other four. This makes them easier to count.

School	Tally	Total
St Bridget's	𝍸 𝍸 ||	12
Mill Junior	𝍸 𝍸 𝍸 𝍸 |||	
Canal Road	𝍸 𝍸 𝍸 ||||	19
Church Junior	𝍸 𝍸 ||	
Other	𝍸 |	6
	Total	_____

a How many Year 7 girls went to Mill Junior?
b How many went to Church Junior?
c What is the total number of girls in the survey?

Some surveys are difficult to do.
Would it be difficult to do a survey of hair colour or of eye colour?
What problems might you find?

Exercise 1:2

1 **a** Choose a subject for your own survey.
b Look at the tally-table in Question **8** above. You will need a tally-table like that for your own survey.
c Decide who you are going to ask in your survey. These are the people in your **sample**.
Do not ask the same person twice. You could keep a record of names to help you.
You could get a friend to help.
d Draw a pictogram and then a bar-chart to show your results.
e Write about what you did. Say who you asked.
Write about any problems you had.
f At the end put the heading **Conclusions**.
Say what you found out:
What was the most common?
What was the least common?
Did you notice anything else?

2 Pie-charts

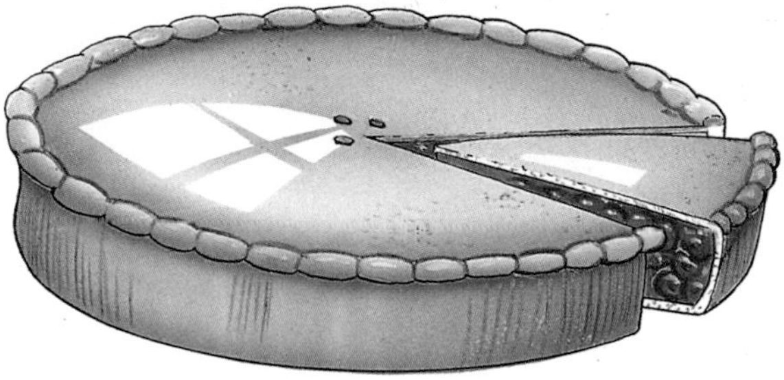

Pie-chart Another type of diagram is a **pie-chart**. The **angle** of the slice represents the number of items.

Exercise 1:3

1 7B had a choice of lunchtime clubs.
The pie-chart shows how they chose.
Seven chose the computer club.
a Write down the fraction of the pie-chart that is the computer club.
b Write down the number of pupils in 7B.

Lunchtime clubs in 7B

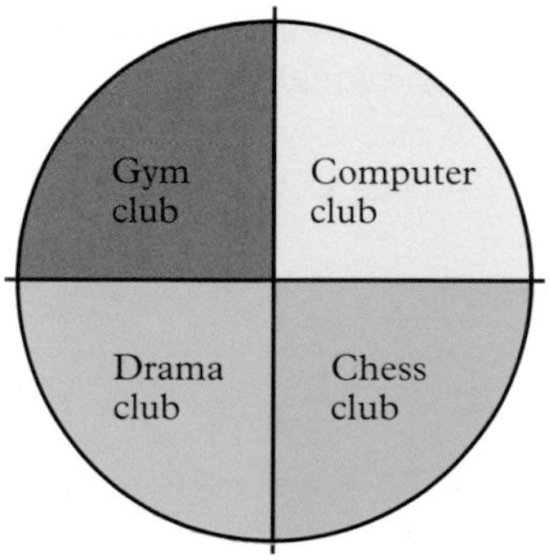

2 Pritti in 7B has drawn a pie-chart. It shows which girls wear a school blazer.
Pritti asked 8 girls.
a Write down the number of girls who wear a blazer.
b Write down the number of girls who don't wear a blazer.

Girls who wear blazers

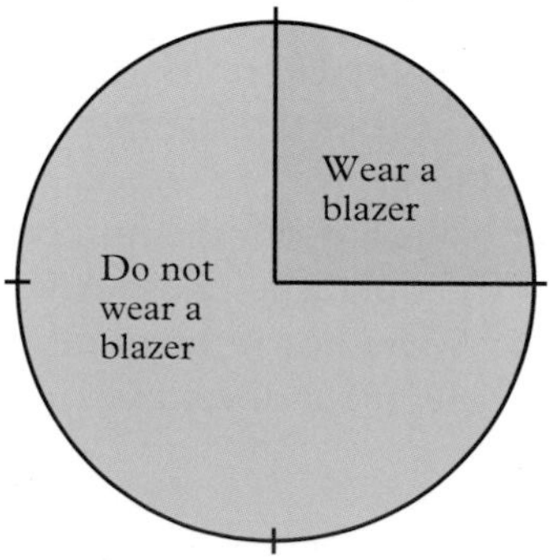

3 Hitesh has drawn a pie-chart.
He asked boys in 7R whether they preferred diet cola or ordinary cola.
There are 16 boys in 7R.

a Write down the number of boys who prefer ordinary cola.

b Write down the number of boys who prefer diet cola.

7R's choice of cola

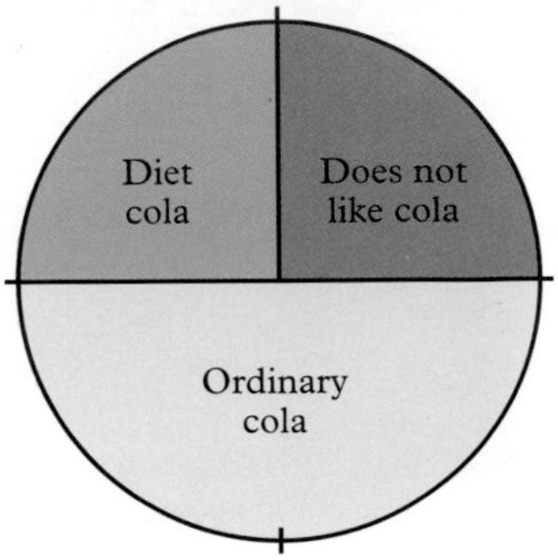

4 This pie-chart shows how 7D have lunch.

a Write down the largest slice of the pie-chart.

b Write down the fraction of the class that has sandwiches.

c Eight pupils in 7D have sandwiches.
Write down the number of pupils in the class.

How 7D have lunch

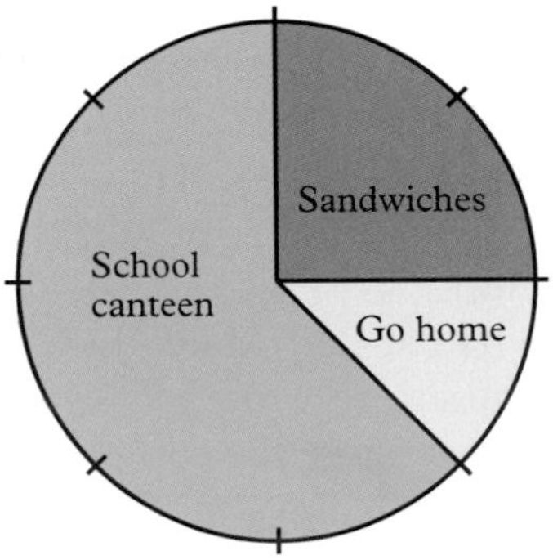

● **5** Chantelle's pie-chart for 7B shows favourite subjects.
14 people chose Maths.

a Write down the most popular subject.

b Write down the number of people who chose Art.

c Write down the number of people in the survey.

Favourite subjects

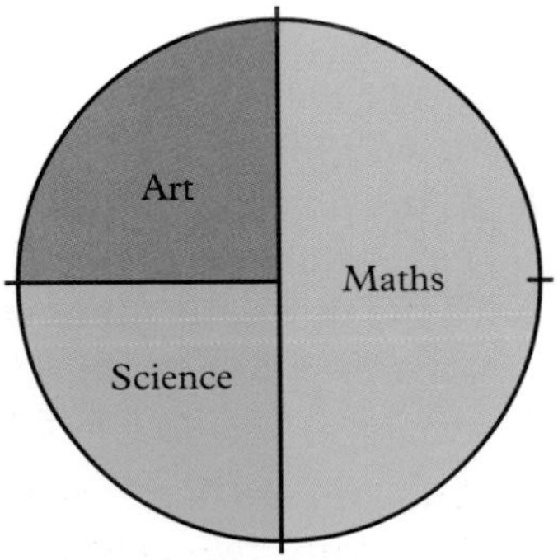

- **6** This pie-chart shows how 7T get their lunch.
  There are 32 pupils in 7T.

How 7T get their lunch

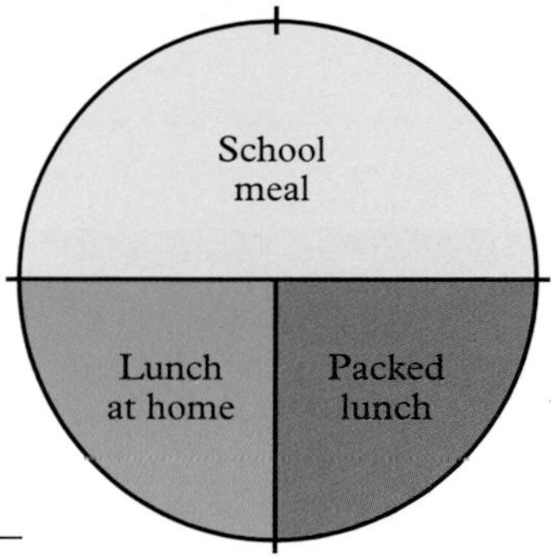

Copy this table and fill it in.

7T at lunch	Lunch at home	Packed lunch	School meal
Number of pupils			

7 **a** Ask eight people in your class to choose their favourite colour.
Make a note of the results.

b Get a blank piece of paper. Draw a large circle. Cut out the circle.

c (1) Fold the circle in half.
(2) Then fold it in half again.
(3) Then fold once again.
(4) Unfold your circle. It should have eight 'slices'.

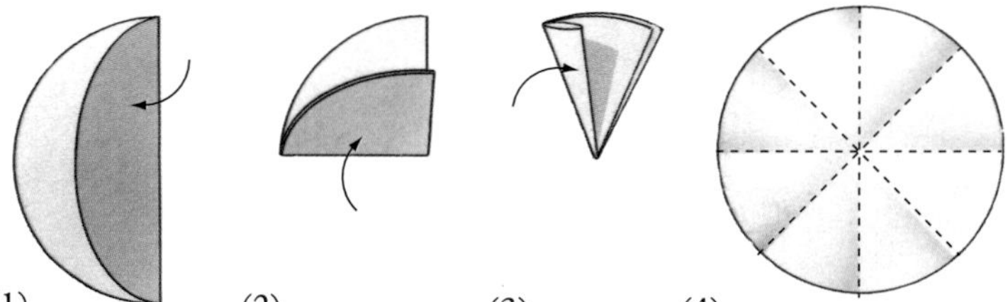

d Colour the slices to match the favourite colours.
If two people chose the same colour, red for example, put the red slices next to each other.

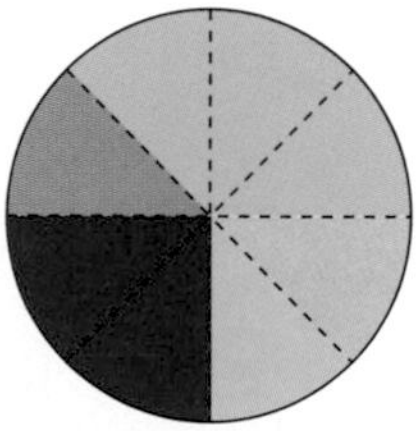

You have now drawn a pie-chart.

e Glue the pie-chart next to your copy of the results.
Give your pie-chart a title: *Favourite colours of eight people in my class*

3 Tallying in groups

How long did it take you to get to school this morning? Was it five minutes, half an hour or even longer?

Suppose we wanted to put the times for the whole class on a tally-table. A table showing every minute would be too long.

This sort of data needs to be tallied in **groups**.

Groups

Bar-charts for **groups** have their *bars touching*. A bar-chart for groups might look like this:

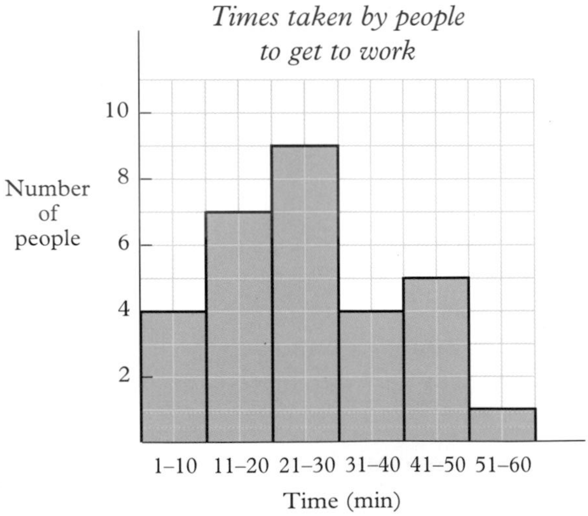

Exercise 1:4

1 Here are the times the pupils in 7M took to get to school this morning.
The times are in minutes, correct to the nearest minute.

15	5	8	22	12	10	30	25	27	22
35	8	18	17	22	15	44	35	45	55
12	28	35	48	48	30	40	19	25	50

a Copy the tally-table.
Fill it in by tallying the times.

Time (min)	Tally	Total
1–10		
11–20		
21–30		
31–40		
41–50		
51–60		
	Total	

b Write down the group that has the most pupils in it.

c Copy the axes on to squared or graph paper.
Draw a bar-chart. Remember not to leave gaps between the bars.

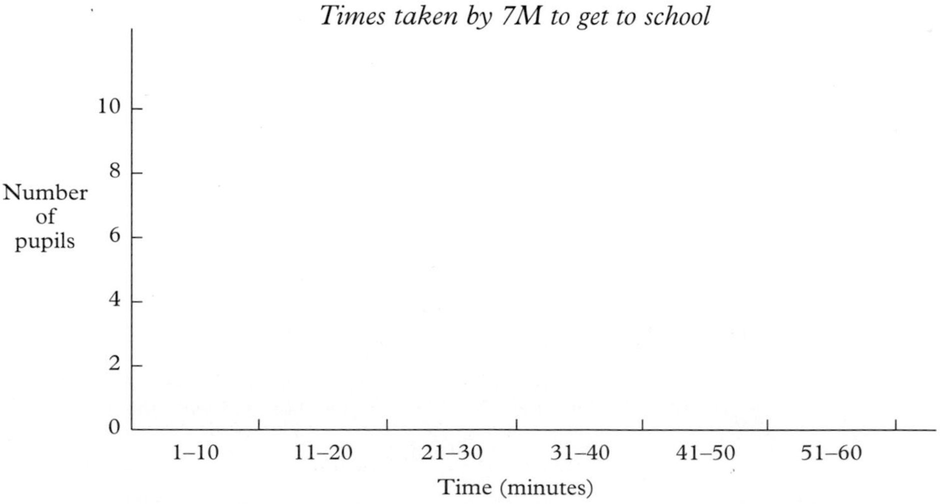

2 A class measured their armspans from fingertip to fingertip.
Here are their results. The measurements are in centimetres, correct to the nearest centimetre.

132	129	147	127	128	124	134	139
138	136	144	143	133	141	139	130
142	143	140	137	148	136	146	151
123	131	135	135	130	140	138	133

a Copy the tally-table and fill it in.

Armspan (cm)	Tally	Total
120–124		
125–129		
130–134		
135–139		
140–144		
145–149		
150–154		
	Total	____

b Copy the axes on to squared or graph paper.
Draw a bar-chart of the results.

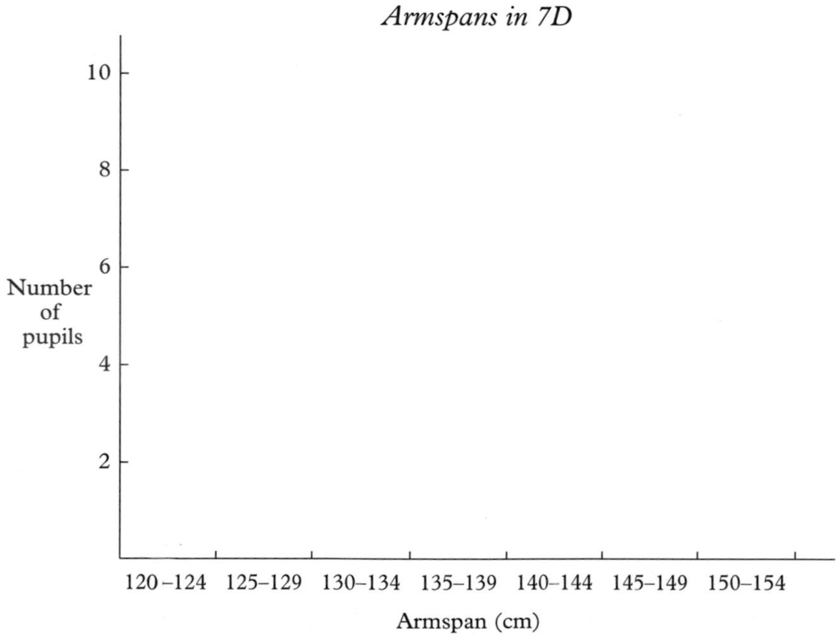

c Write down the group of results that has the most people in it.

● **3** Class 7F collect for charity.
Here are the amounts collected for the first half term.

21p	48p	87p	40p	76p	35p	25p	18p	0	2p
6p	59p	30p	67p	11p	55p	37p	53p	31p	20p
36p	46p	51p	7p	32p	65p	97p	42p	84p	69p
15p	60p	81p	33p	44p	9p	75p	0	34p	20p

a Copy the tally-table and fill it in.

Amount (pence)	Tally	Total
0 19		
20–39		
40–59		
60–79		
80–99		

Total ____

b Draw a bar-chart of the results.

4 Do a survey of your own. Try this idea.
a Choose a book or magazine of your own.
b Count the number of words in each of the first 50 sentences.
c Make a tally-table like this:

Number of words in a sentence	Tally	Total
1–5		
6–10		
11–15		
16–20		
21–25		
26–30		
31–35		
36–40		
Over 40		

Total ____

d Use your tally-table to record your results.
e Draw a bar-chart of your results.
f What can you say about your results?
g Compare your results with the results of a friend.
Which book do you think is easier to read? Give reasons for your answer.

4 Location

Have you travelled on a train? People often book seats on long train journeys. You get a card with a letter and a number on it. The coaches have letters on them and the seats have numbers.
The card tells you where to sit.

Have you flown in an aeroplane? You are given a boarding card with a letter and a number. This tells you where your seat is.

In a theatre the rows are given letters and the seats have numbers.

This is a ticket for *Phantom of the Opera*.
You would be in row D, seat number 4.

Exercise 1:5

1 The diagram shows the seats in a theatre.
There are six rows, A to F. Each seat is numbered.
Mrs Ellis and her two small children have seats A7, A8 and A9.

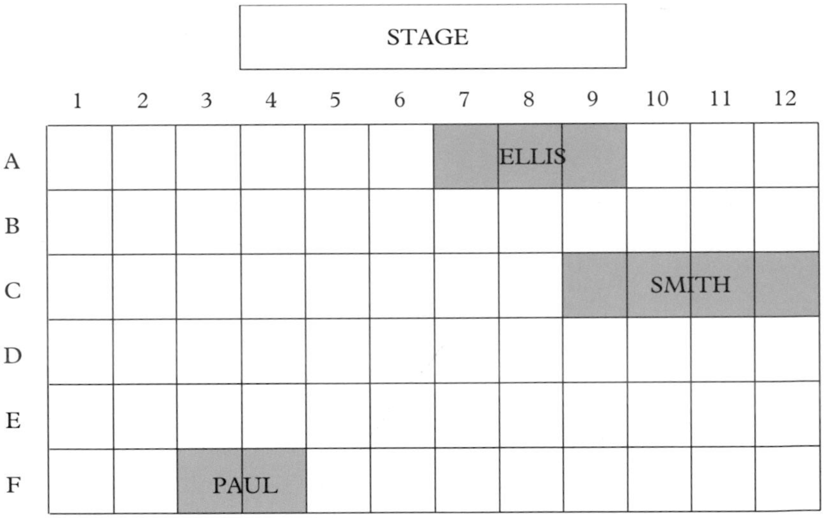

a Mr Smith has bought four seats for his family.
Write down his seats.

b Paul has bought two seats in the back row.
Write down his seats.

Co-ordinates
***x* axis**
***y* axis**

In maths, we need to mark the positions of things at points. We use two numbers. These numbers are called **co-ordinates**.

We draw a horizontal line and a vertical line known as **axes**. The horizontal line is called the ***x* axis**. The vertical line is called the ***y* axis**.

The ***x* co-ordinate** (across number) is given **first**. The ***y* co-ordinate** (up number) is given **second**.

In the diagram, A has co-ordinates (3, 2). B has co-ordinates (1, 0).

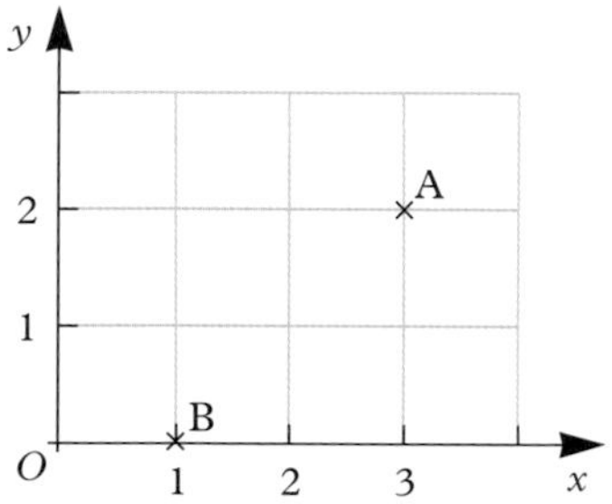

2 List the co-ordinates of the vertices (or corners) of these shapes:

a the square ABCD
b the rectangle PQRS
c the triangle LMN

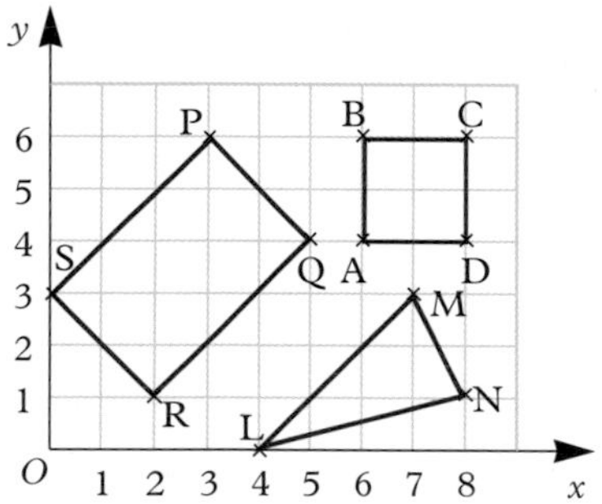

W **3** For each part, **a**, **b** and **c** draw a pair of axes as shown. Use squared paper.
Plot the points. Join them in order as you go.

a A (2, 0) (2, 1) (0, 1)
(2, 3) (1, 3) (3, 5)
B (3, 5) (5, 3) (4, 3)
(6, 1) (4, 1) (4, 0)

b A (1, 0) (0, 1) (6, 1) (5, 0)
B (0, 2) (2, 6) (6, 2) (0, 2)
C (2, 1) (2, 2)

c A (2, 0) (2, 1) (1, 1) (1, 2)
(2, 2) (1, 3) (1, 4) (0, 4)
B (0, 4) (1, 5) (1, 7) (4, 7)
(5, 6) (5, 0)
C (2, 4) (2, 5) (3, 4) (2, 4)

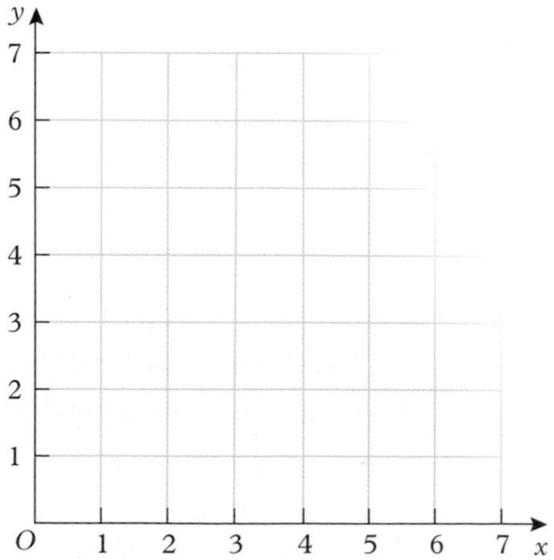

5 Scatter diagrams

Bill has taken a job as an ice cream man.

When will he sell the most ice cream?

Bill expects it will be on a hot day. On a cooler day he will sell less. Bill will sell very little ice cream on a very cold day. Bill calls that common sense.
In maths it is called **correlation**.

Correlation

A hot day means a lot of ice cream sold. A lot of ice cream sold means a hot day. It works both ways.
There is **correlation** between the two.

A graph showing Bill's correlation looks like this:

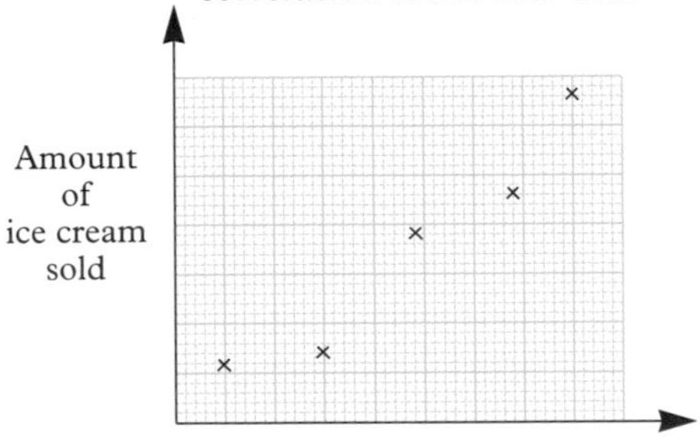

No correlation looks like this:

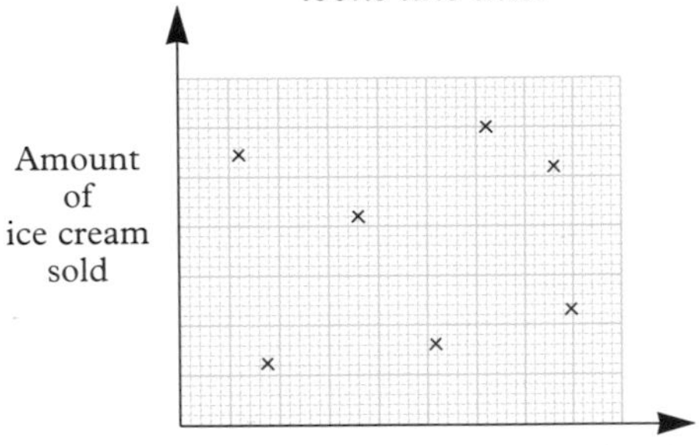

Scatter diagrams

Graphs like these are called **scatter diagrams**.
The points are scattered about.

Big hands often go with big feet.
Little hands often go with little feet.
That sounds like **correlation**.

Exercise 1:6

1 **a** Collect the hand length (to the nearest half centimetre) and the shoe size of people in your class.
Write them in a table like the one below.

You do not have to collect from everybody. About twelve people should be enough.

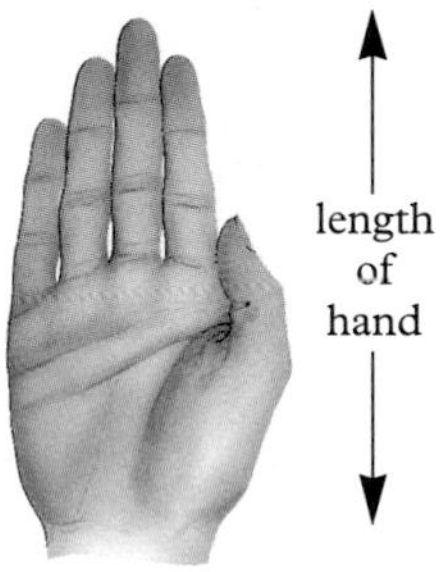

Name												
Shoe size												
Hand length (cm)												

b Plot your results on graph paper.
Use axes as shown. You may need to make them larger.

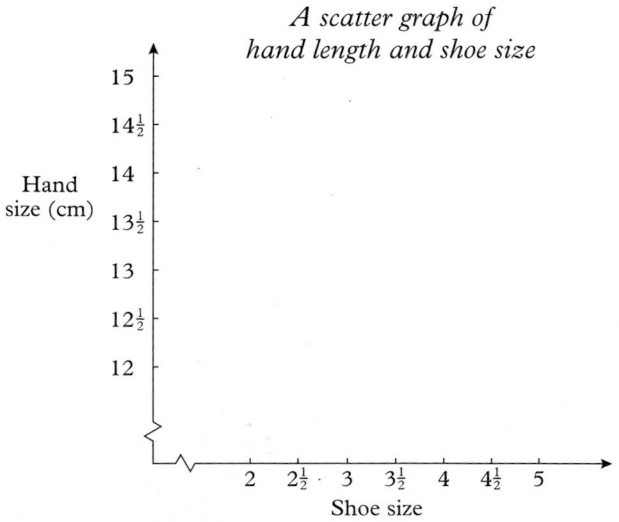

c Write down what you notice.

1 Vicky has done a survey. She asked each pupil in 7W their favourite fruit. Here is a bar-chart of her results:

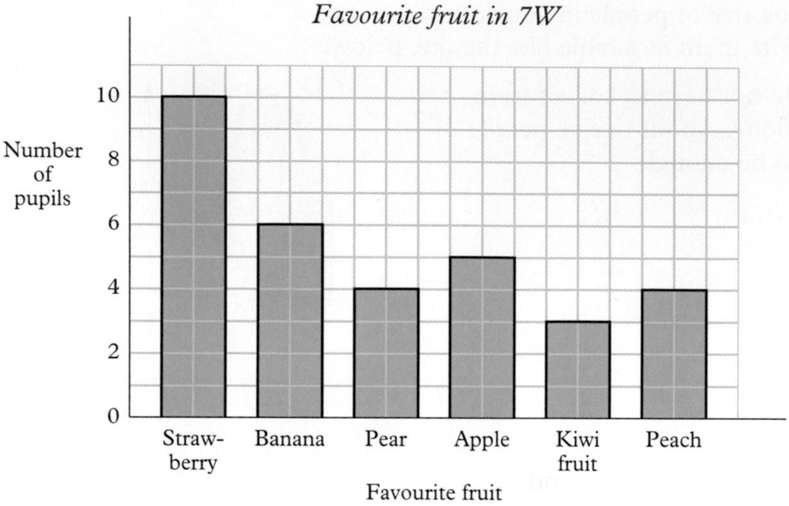

a Write down how many pupils chose bananas.
b Write down how many chose apples.
c Write down the most popular choice.
d Write down how many pupils took part in the survey.

2 Copy the pictogram frame below on to graph paper or squared paper.

Draw a pictogram of the survey on fruit in Question **1**.

Use  represents 2 pupils

Favourite fruit in 7W

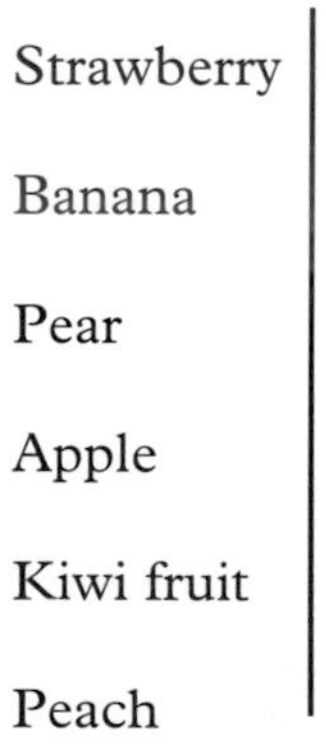

Key:  represents 2 children

3 The table shows the shoe sizes of the 27 pupils in 7R.

Shoe size	3	$3\frac{1}{2}$	4	$4\frac{1}{2}$	5	$5\frac{1}{2}$	6	$6\frac{1}{2}$
Number of people	1	0	4	6	7	5	3	1

a Draw a bar-chart of the results in the table.
b Write down the most common shoe size.
c Explain how the most common size shows up on your bar-chart.

4 Here are the results of a Maths exam for two Year 7 classes. The marks are out of 100.

63	84	62	37	54	56	64	57	66	62
71	73	79	91	72	75	87	76	78	80
50	54	61	58	65	45	67	51	84	74
74	49	68	55	52	66	59	61	34	81
59	77	64	60	69	65	63	48	93	53

a Copy the tally-table and fill it in.

Marks	Tally	Total
31–40		
41–50		
51–60		
61–70		
71–80		
81–90		
91–100		
	Total	

b Write down the group of marks with the most students in it.
c Draw a bar-chart from your tally-table.
Remember to make the bars touch.

5 Paul has drawn a pie-chart. It shows when pupils like to do their homework.
a Write down the most popular time.
b Write down the fraction that like to do their homework after tea.

There are 20 pupils in the survey.
c Write down the number that like to do their homework before tea.
d Write down the number that choose lunchtime.

Favourite homework times

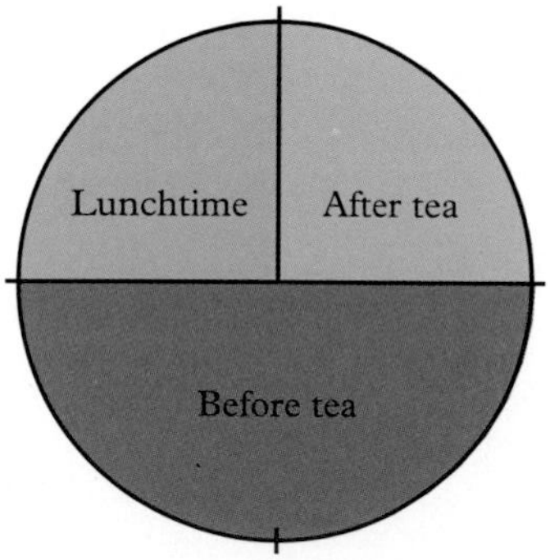

6 For each part **a**, **b**, **c** and **d** draw a pair of axes as shown.
Use squared paper.
Plot the points for each part. Join them in order as you go.

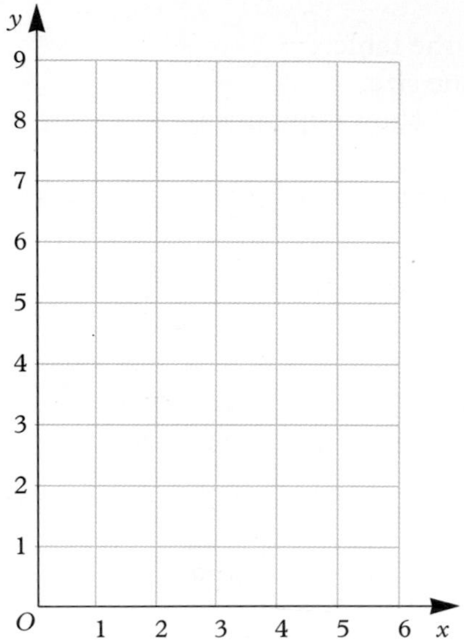

a A (1, 0) (1, 4) (2, 4) (2, 5) (1, 5) (1, 7)
B (1, 7) (2, 9) (2, 7) (3, 7) (3, 9) (4, 7)
C (4, 7) (4, 5) (3, 5) (3, 4) (4, 4) (4, 1) (5, 1) (5, 0)

b A (1, 0) (1, 5) (3, 9) (5, 5) (5, 0)
B (2, 0) (2, 2) (3, 2) (3, 0)
C (3, 3) (3, 5) (4, 5) (4, 3) (3, 3)

c A (1, 0) (3, 3) (5, 0)
B (3, 3) (3, 6) (2, 6) (2, 8) (4, 8) (4, 6) (3, 6)
C (1, 3) (3, 5) (5, 3)

d A (2, 0) (2, 2) (1, 2) (1, 6)
B (4, 0) (4, 2) (5, 2) (5, 6)
C (0, 6) (2, 8) (4, 8) (6, 6) (0, 6)
D (2, 3) (4, 3)
E $(2, 4\frac{1}{2})$ $(2\frac{1}{2}, 4\frac{1}{2})$
F $(3\frac{1}{2}, 4\frac{1}{2})$ $(4, 4\frac{1}{2})$

1 The school tuck shop has done a survey of Year 7. They want to know the most popular flavours of crisps.
Here are the results.

Flavour	Ready salted	Cheese and onion	Salt and vinegar	Barbecued beef	Prawn cocktail
Number of pupils	25	40	35	45	20

a Write down the most popular flavour.
b Work out the number of Year 7 pupils who took part in the survey.
c Draw a bar-chart of the survey results.
Number the axis which goes up the page 5, 10, 15, …, up to 50.

2 **a** Draw a pictogram for the survey results in Question **1**.
Use  represents 5 pupils.
b Pictograms can be hard to draw.
What would be the problem if 38 and not 35 chose salt and vinegar?

3 Sian has asked her class, 7D, what sort of bikes they have.
There are 32 children in the class.
a Write down the most popular sort of bike.
b Write down the number of children who do not have a bike.

Choice of bike in my class

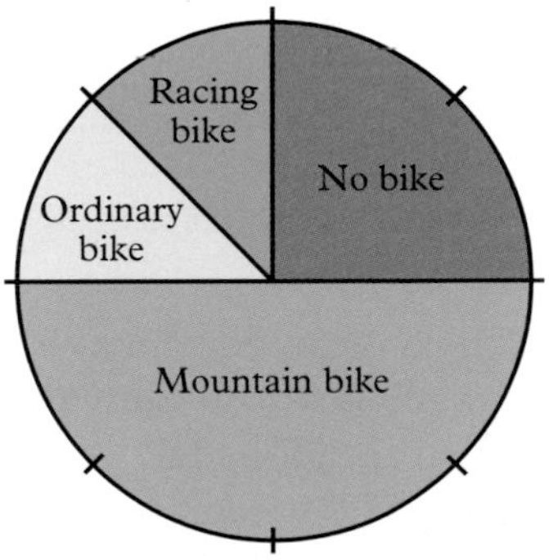

c Copy this table and fill in the numbers of pupils.

Bike	Mountain	Racing	Ordinary	None
Number of pupils				

4 Class 7M decided to see how good they were at estimating one minute. They shut their eyes and counted. They opened their eyes on the count of 60 and wrote down what they saw on the clock.
The results, in seconds, are given below.

72	70	52	48	52	48	63	71	63	70
61	62	59	62	50	64	46	65	69	65
58	64	61	48	63	68	67	73	55	51

a Make a tally-table. Count in fives starting with 46–50.
Go up to 71–75.

Time (sec)	Tally	Total
46–50		
51–55		
56–60		

b Draw a bar-chart of the results.
c How good do you think they were at estimating?

5

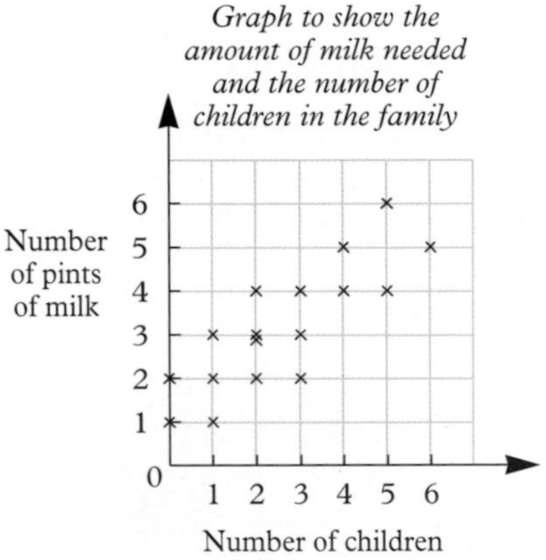

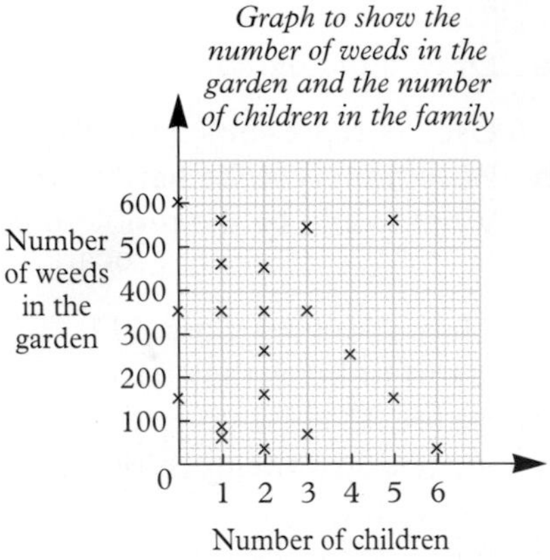

a Which of these graphs shows correlation?
Explain how you can tell from the patterns of the crosses.
b If you had done the surveys, would you have expected the graphs of the results to look like this? Explain your answer.

6 Some Year 7 pupils had been studying statistics. They each did a survey and wrote about their results. They also had a test.
The marks for the survey and the test are shown in the table. All marks are out of 20.

Test	16	12	18	15	6	14	18	4	16	8	13	16
Survey	14	13	15	15	8	12	19	6	17	5	11	19

a Draw axes on graph paper or squared paper.
Make both axes go from 0 to 20.
Label the axes and give the graph a title.
b Plot the points.
c Is there correlation? Explain your answer.

S U M M A R Y

- Data is collected in a survey.
Tally marks are used to record data.
Data can be represented in diagrams.
Pictures are used to represent data in a pictogram.
Pictograms should have a key.
Bars are used to represent data in a bar-chart.
All diagrams should have a title.

School	Tally	Total
St Bridget's	𝍸 𝍸 ||	12
Mill Junior	𝍸 𝍸 𝍸 𝍸 |||	23
Canal Road	𝍸 𝍸 𝍸 ||||	19
Church Junior	𝍸 𝍸 ||	12
Other	𝍸 |	6
	Total	72

- Angles are used to represent data in a pie-chart.

- Some data is tallied in groups.
Bar-charts for groups are drawn with their *bars touching*.

- Co-ordinates are used to locate a point.
The x co-ordinate is written first, then the y co-ordinate.
Co-ordinates must always be put inside a pair of brackets.
A is (3, 2)
B is (1, 0)

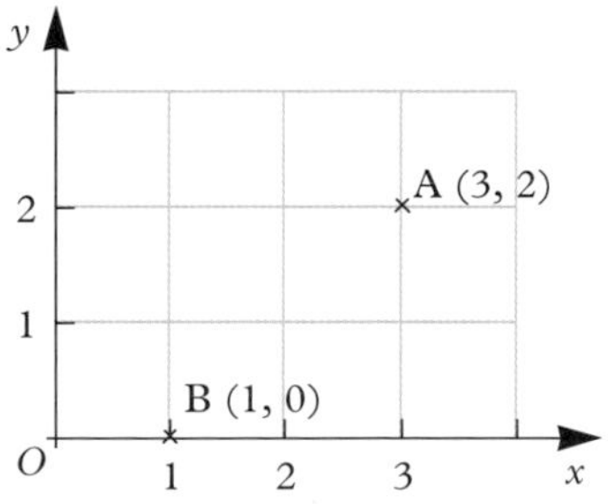

- Scatter diagrams compare two sets of data.
Scatter diagrams can show correlation.

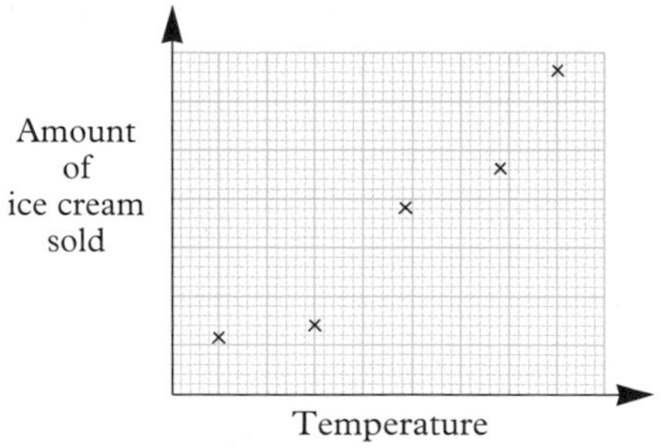

1 The pie-chart shows where the 28 pupils in 7P spent their holidays.
Copy the table and fill it in.

7P on holiday	UK	USA	Europe
Number of pupils			

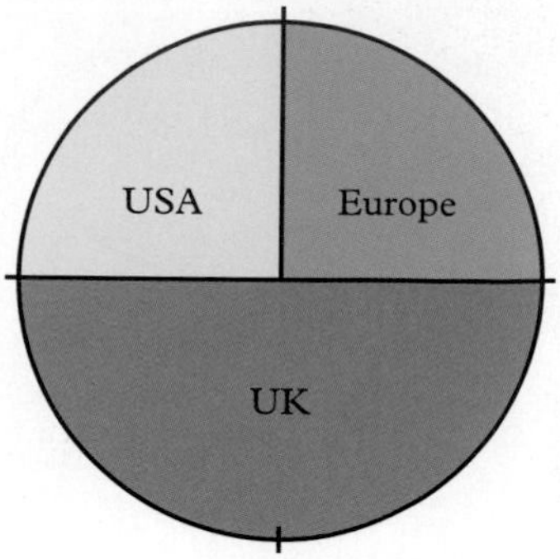

7P on holiday

2 Draw a pictogram of the survey in Question **1**.
Use  to represent 2 pupils.

3 The tally-chart shows pupils' results in a school science exam.

Results	Tally	Total
1–20	𝍸 |	
21–40	|||	
41–60	𝍸 𝍸	
61–80	𝍸 |||	
81–100	𝍸	
	Total	

a Copy the table and fill it in.
b Draw a bar-chart from the table.

4 Write down the scatter graphs that show correlation.

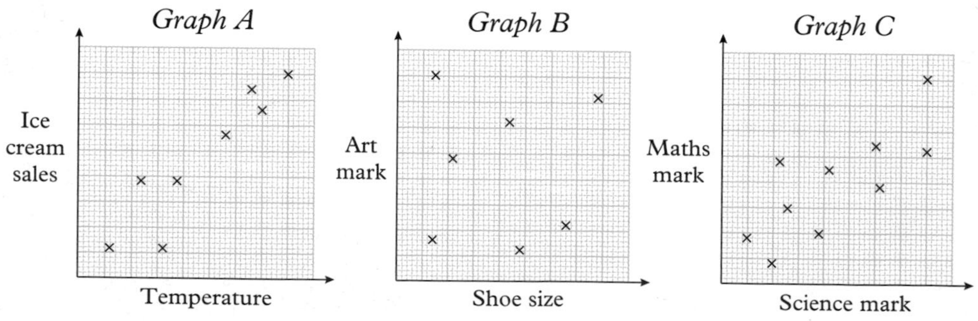

2 Symmetry

CORE

1 Lines of symmetry

2 Symmetry in everyday life

3 Turnings

4 Rotational symmetry

QUESTIONS

EXTENSION

SUMMARY

TEST YOURSELF

1 Lines of symmetry

This picture of a house has a line of symmetry. It can be split down the middle so that one half is the reflection of the other.

Line of symmetry	A **line of symmetry** divides a shape into two equal parts. Each part is a reflection of the other. If you fold the shape along this line, each part fits exactly on top of the other.

Exercise 2:1

1 **a** Copy the shapes on the next page on to 1 cm squared paper.
b Cut them out.
c Fold them along the dotted line to check that this is a line of symmetry.
d Stick them into your exercise book like this:

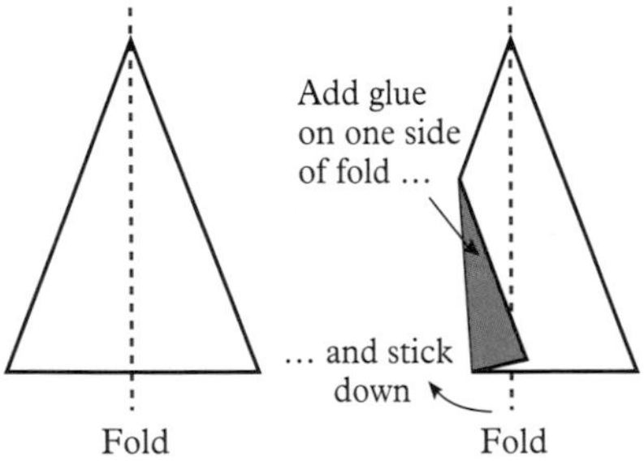

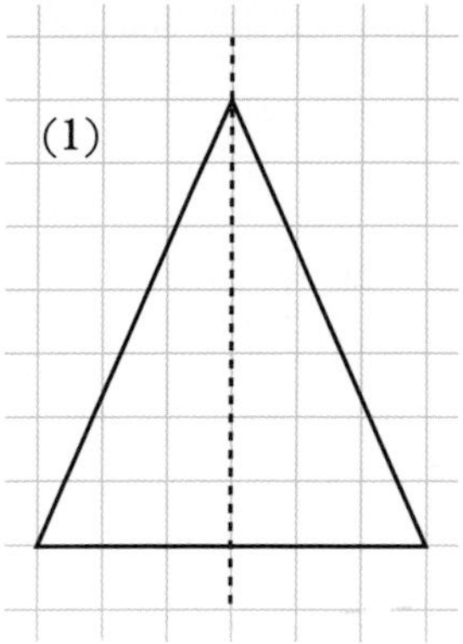

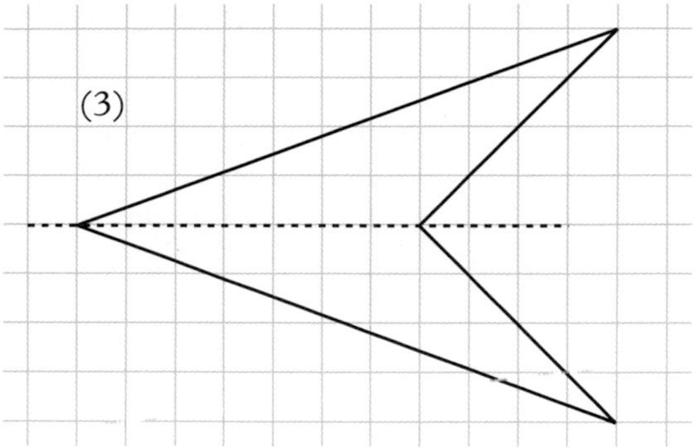

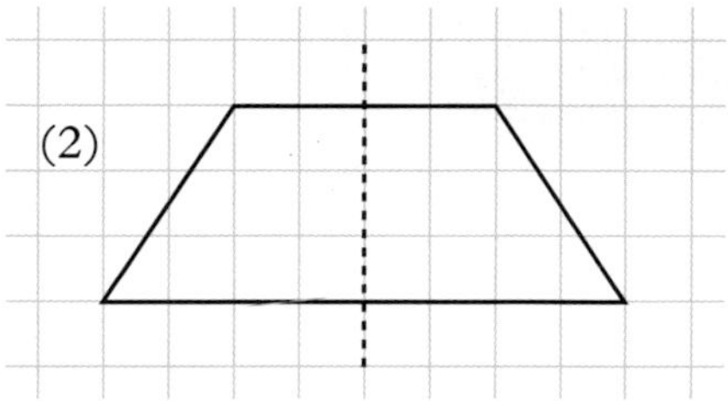

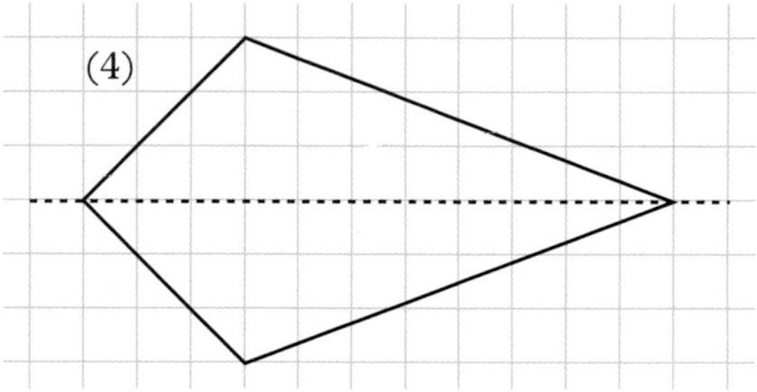

Some shapes have more than one line of symmetry. We usually show all the lines on one diagram.
A square has 4 lines of symmetry.

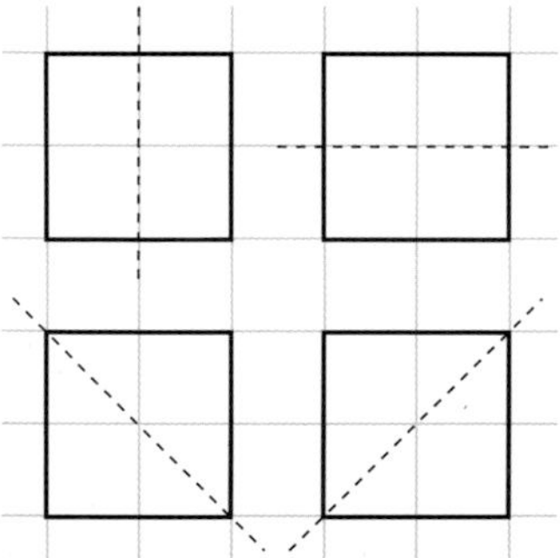

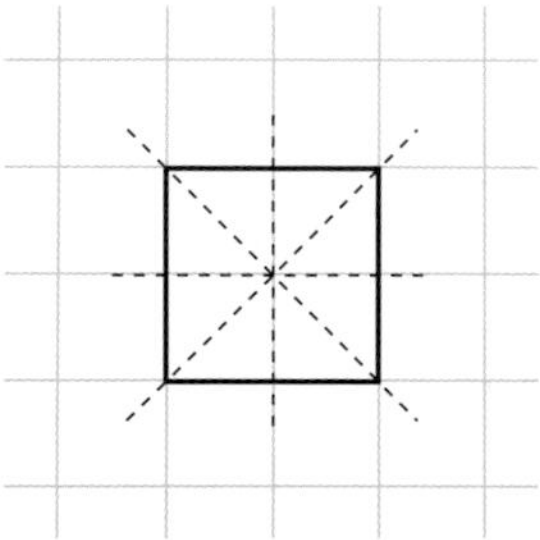

Exercise 2:2

1 **a** Copy these shapes on to squared paper.
b Mark on **all** the lines of symmetry using dotted lines.
c Cut out each shape.
d Fold the shapes along your broken lines to check that they are lines of symmetry.

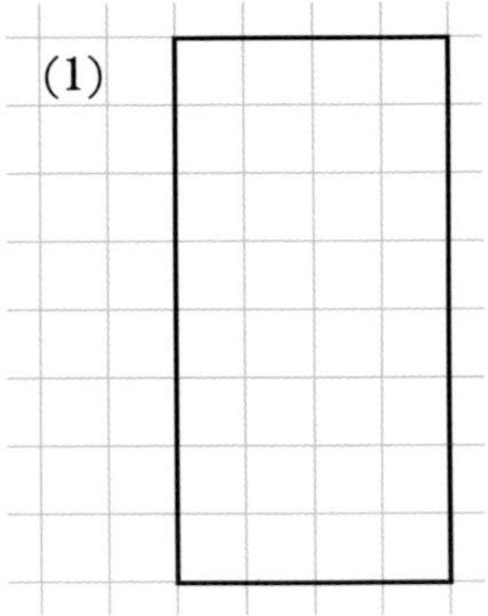

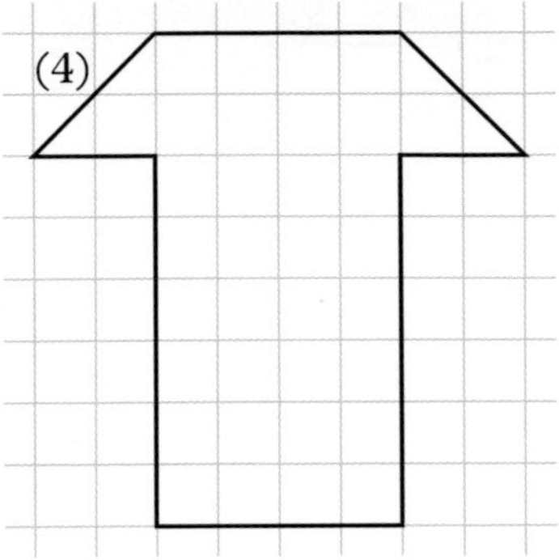

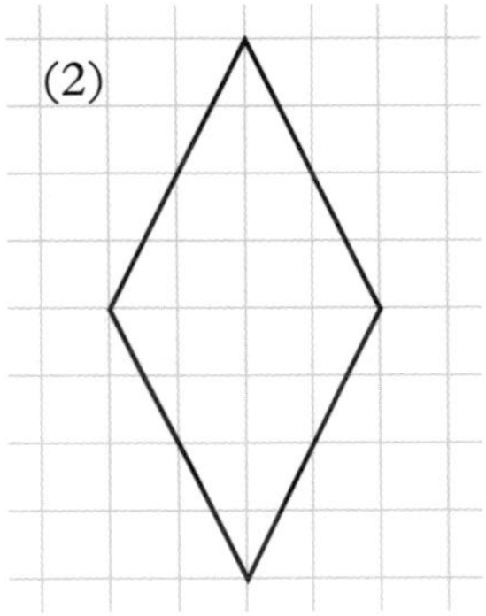

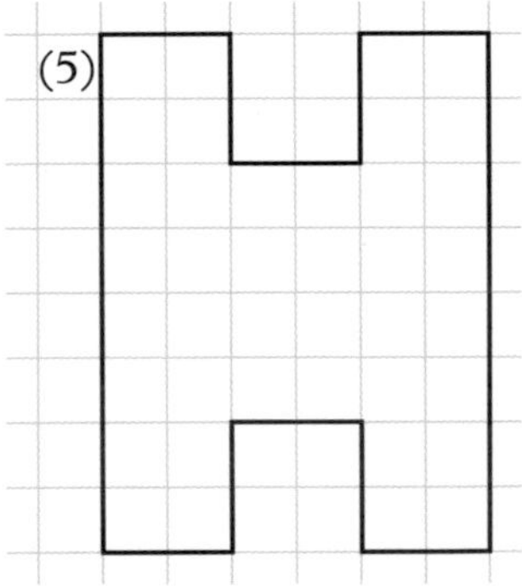

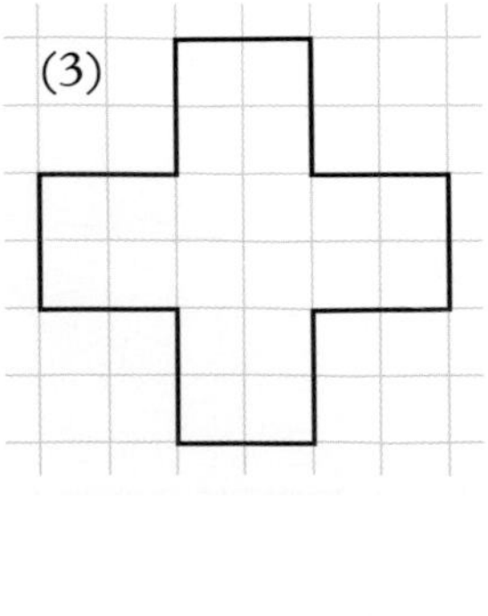

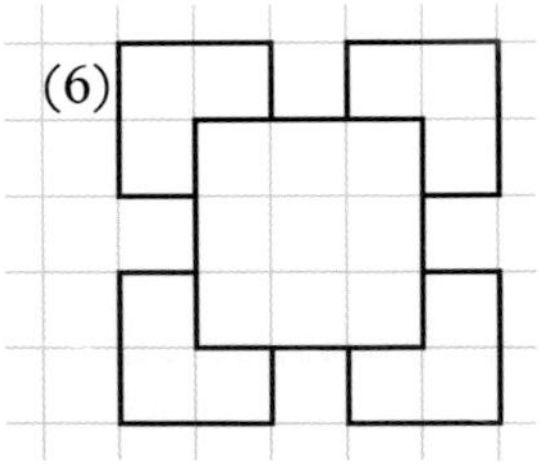

You can only see half of this shape:

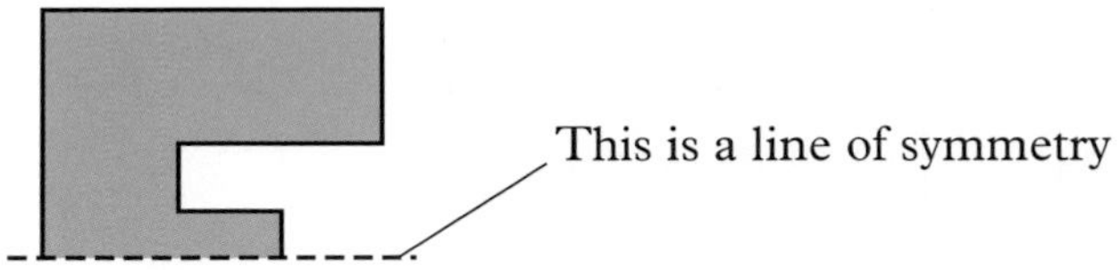
This is a line of symmetry

We can use the line of symmetry to complete the shape.
It now looks like this:

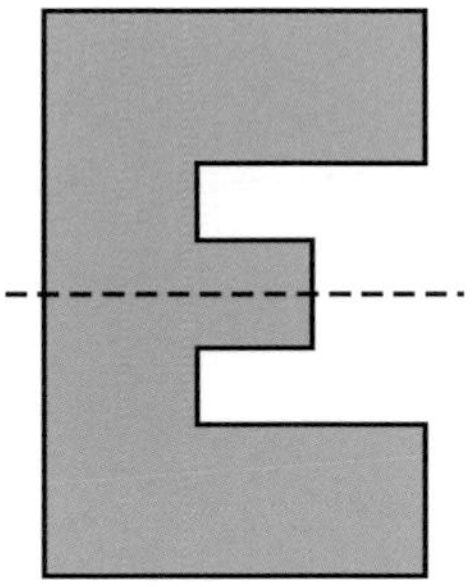

Place a mirror along the line of symmetry.
The reflection completes the shape.

Mirror line A line of symmetry is often called a **mirror line**.

Exercise 2:3

1 Copy this diagram *and* diagrams **b** and **c** on the next page on to squared paper.
Draw their reflections in the line of symmetry.

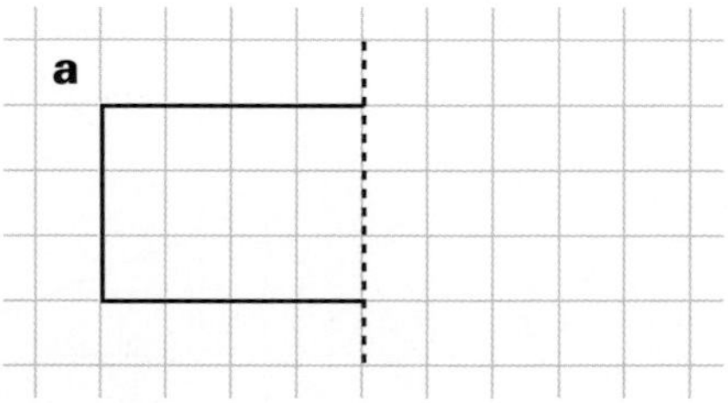
a

b

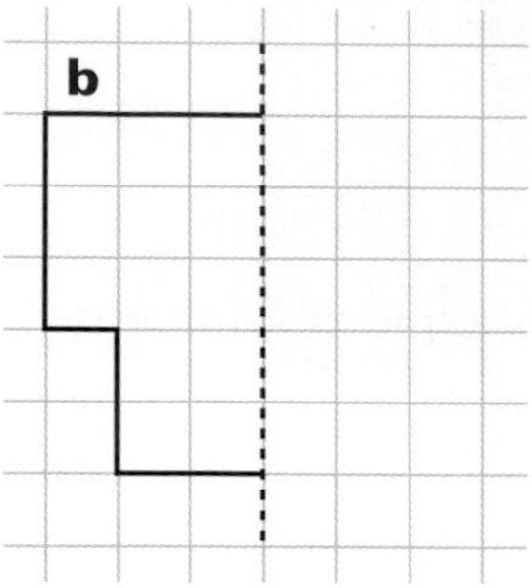

c

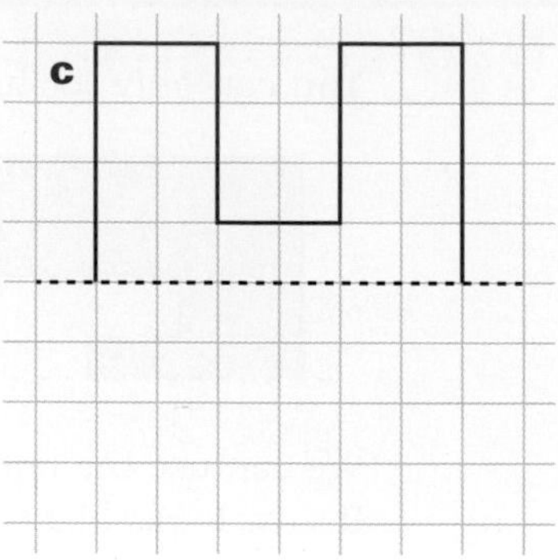

2 Copy these diagrams on to squared paper.
Draw their reflections in the line of symmetry.

a

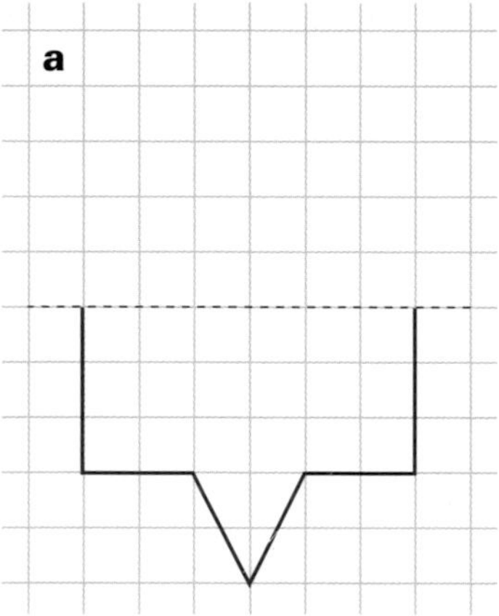

c

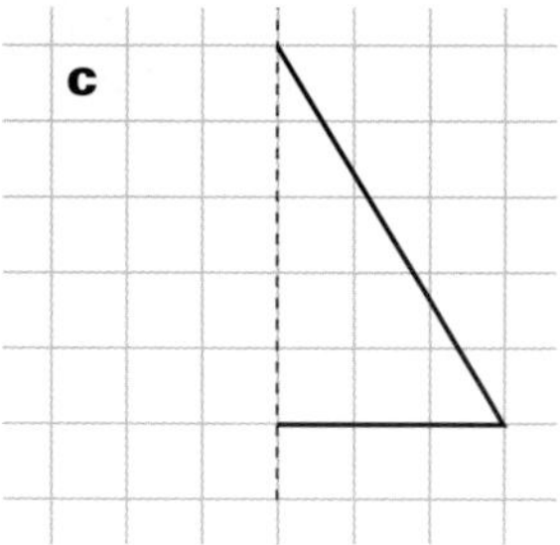

● d

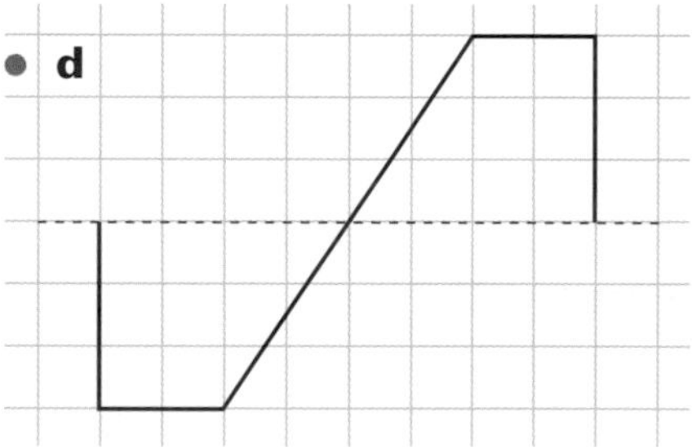

b

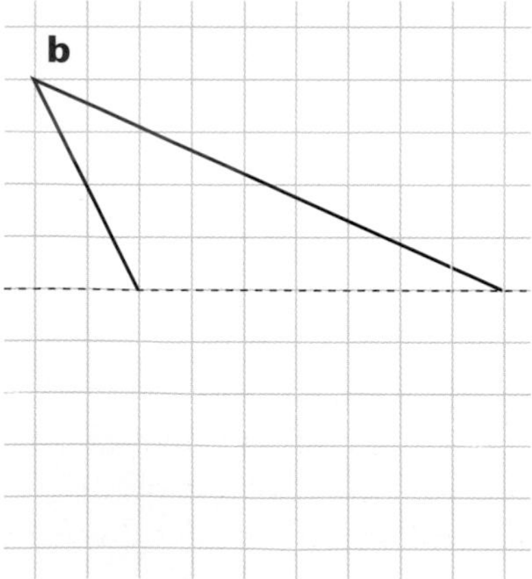

e

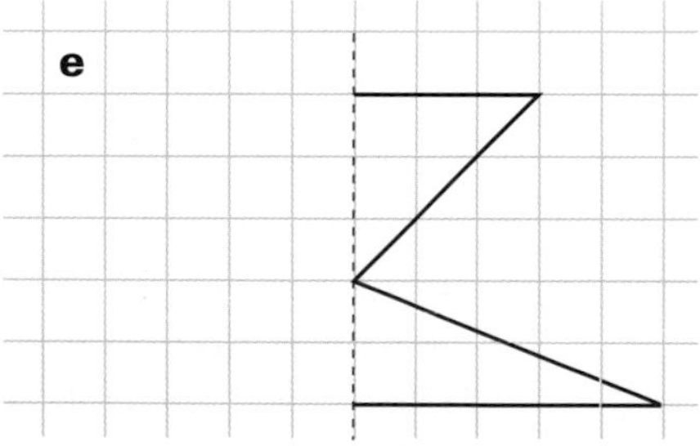

2 Symmetry in everyday life

Here are some letters of the alphabet. We have marked their lines of symmetry.

The letter **A** has a **vertical** line of symmetry

The letter **C** has a **horizontal** line of symmetry

The letter **X** has a vertical **and** a horizontal line of symmetry

The letter **P** has no line of symmetry.

Exercise 2:4

1 Here are some letters of the alphabet:

H A D M I U B C E X Y

Copy out the letters and mark on the lines of symmetry.

a Write down the letters that have a vertical line of symmetry.

b Write down the letters that have a horizontal line of symmetry.

c Write down the letters that have a vertical **and** a horizontal line of symmetry.

2 This word has a line of symmetry

Write down two other words that have a line of symmetry.

On black and white television a pattern looked like this:

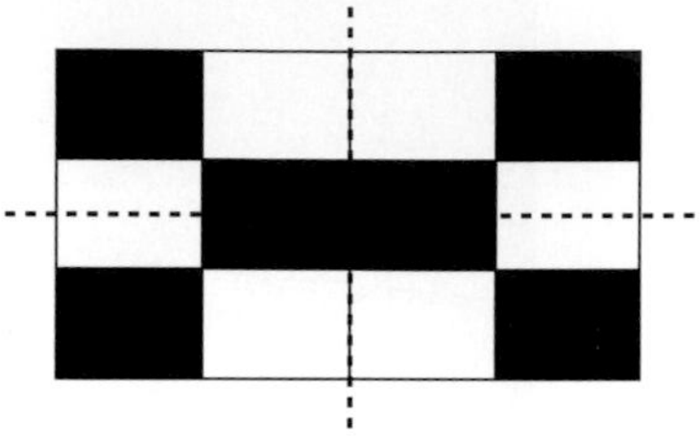

It has two lines of symmetry.

On colour television the same pattern looked like this:

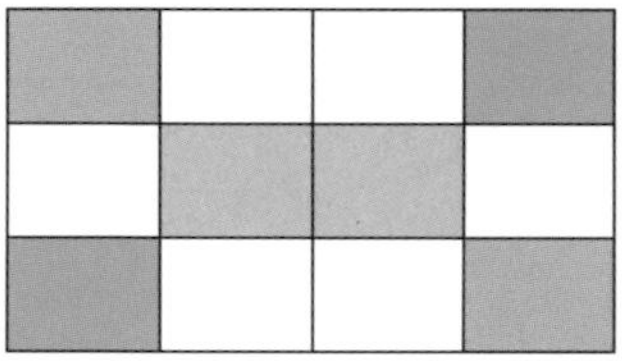

In colour the pattern has no lines of symmetry.

Colour can affect symmetry.

Exercise 2:5

1 Look at these flags.
Copy and complete the table on the next page.
Write 'yes' or 'no' in each box.

a

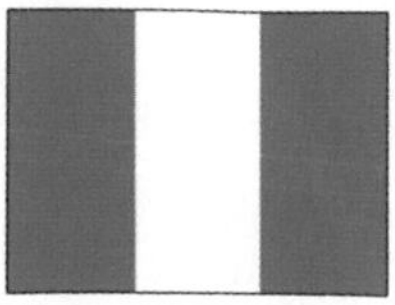

Nigeria

b

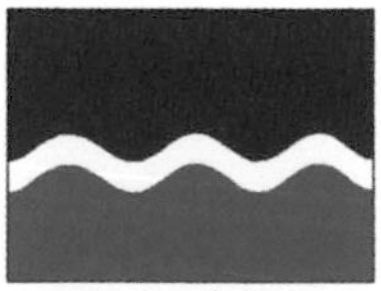

Seychelles

c

São Tomé-Principe

d

District of Columbia

Flag	Horizontal line of symmetry	Vertical line of symmetry
a		
b		
c		
d		

2 How many lines of symmetry do these road signs have?
Write down your answers.

a

b

c

d

3 These symbols are called logos. You see them on cars.
They have line symmetry.

a **b** **c** **d** **e**

Sketch the logos and mark on the lines of symmetry.

4 Words are sometimes shown by symbols.
Write down the numbers of lines of symmetry for each symbol.

a

c

e

b

d

• **5** **a** Copy these four tiles on to squared paper.

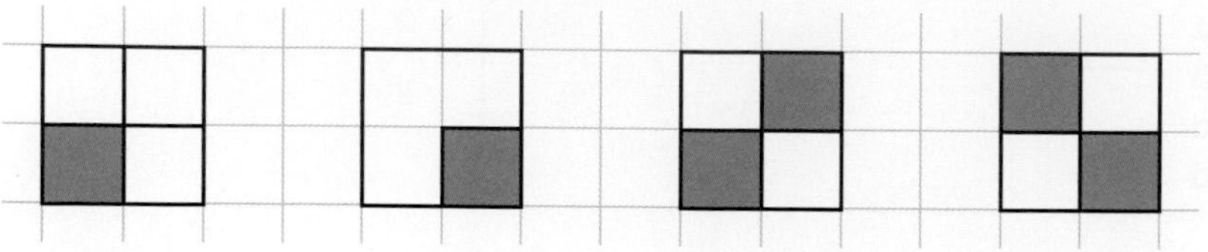

b Cut out the tiles.

c Put the tiles together to make a larger tile.
For example:

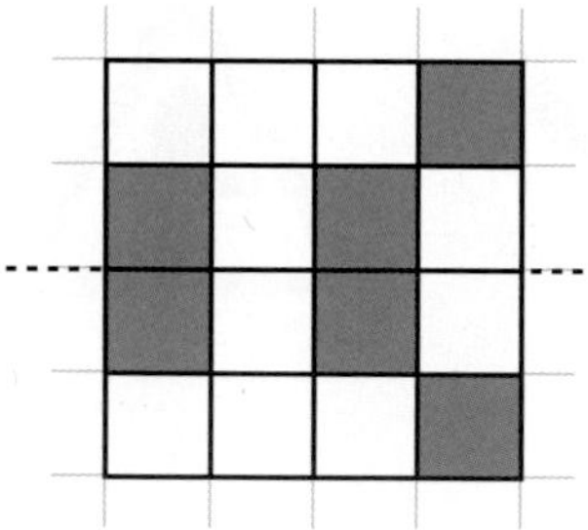

d Copy your new tile on to squared paper.
Mark the lines of symmetry.

e Make five more patterns that have vertical symmetry or horizontal symmetry.
Copy each of your patterns on to squared paper.
Draw in the lines of symmetry.

f Make two patterns that have a diagonal line of symmetry.

• **6** The outlines of leaves can show symmetry.
Bring in to school a collection of different leaves.
Which leaves have outlines with lines of symmetry?

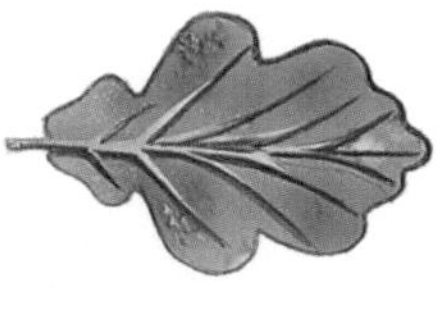
Oak

Ash

Horse chestnut

3 Turnings

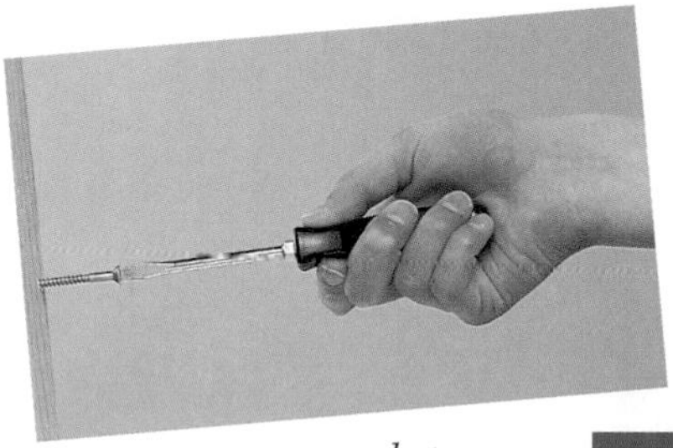

'Tighten the screw another half turn'

'Turn right at the crossroads'

'The wind changed, turning from North to North-East'

Turn

We use the word **turn** to describe something that moves round in a circle.

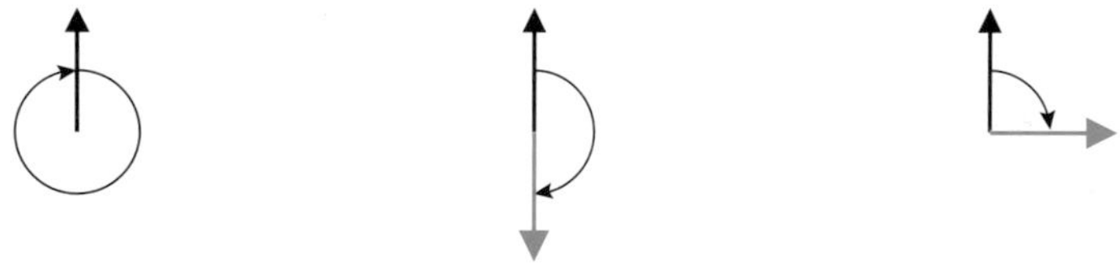

1 full turn　　Half turn　　Quarter turn

Clockwise Anti-clockwise

We use **clockwise** and **anti-clockwise** to say which way to turn.

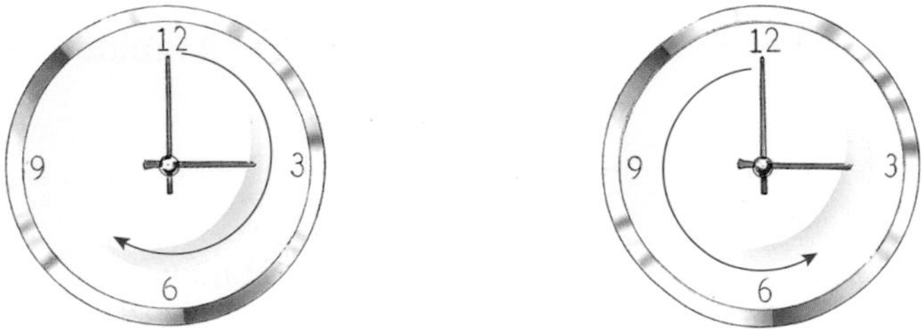

Clockwise　　Anti-clockwise

Exercise 2:6

The clock shows 3 o'clock.

The minute hand makes a full turn each hour.

The minute hand makes a quarter turn in 15 minutes.

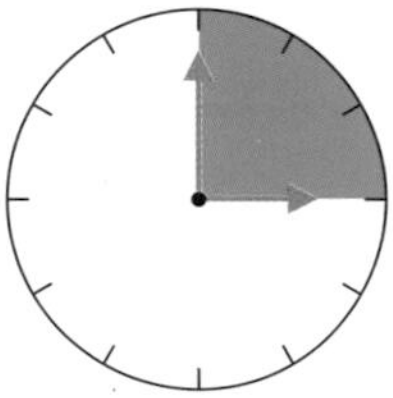

1 What part of a turn does the minute hand make in:

a

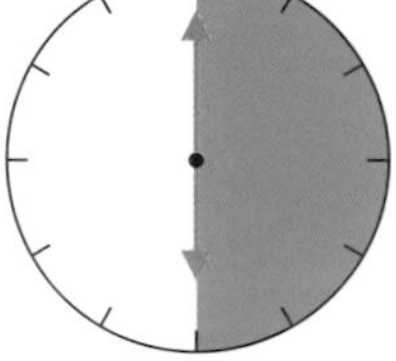

30 minutes?

b

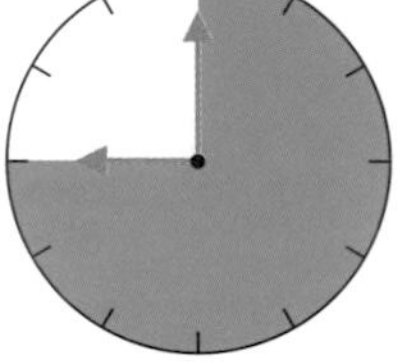

45 minutes?

2 What time passes when the minute hand makes:

a a quarter turn?

b a half turn?

c four full turns?

Points of the compass

The diagram shows the **points of the compass**.

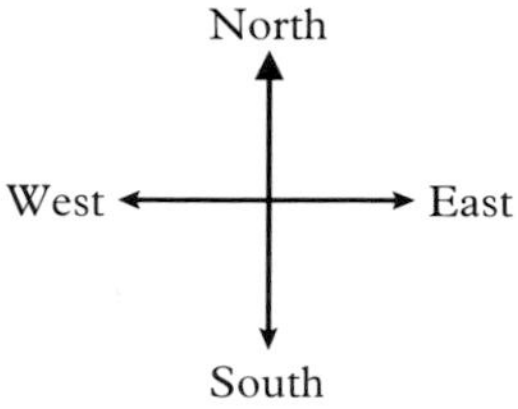

If you face East and make a half turn clockwise

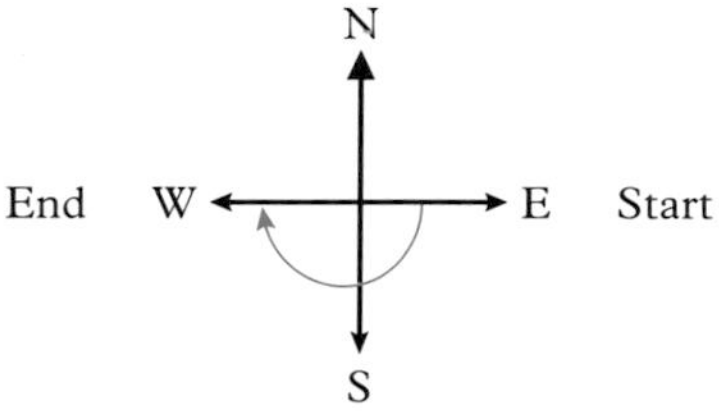

You end up facing West.

3 Copy and complete this table.

Start facing	Turn	Direction	End up facing
N	$\frac{1}{4}$	clockwise	
N	$\frac{1}{2}$	clockwise	
N	$\frac{3}{4}$	clockwise	
S	$\frac{1}{4}$	clockwise	
E	$\frac{3}{4}$	clockwise	
W	$\frac{1}{4}$	anti-clockwise	
S	$\frac{1}{2}$	anti-clockwise	
W	$\frac{3}{4}$	clockwise	
W	$\frac{3}{4}$	anti-clockwise	
S	$\frac{1}{4}$	anti-clockwise	

4 Rotational symmetry

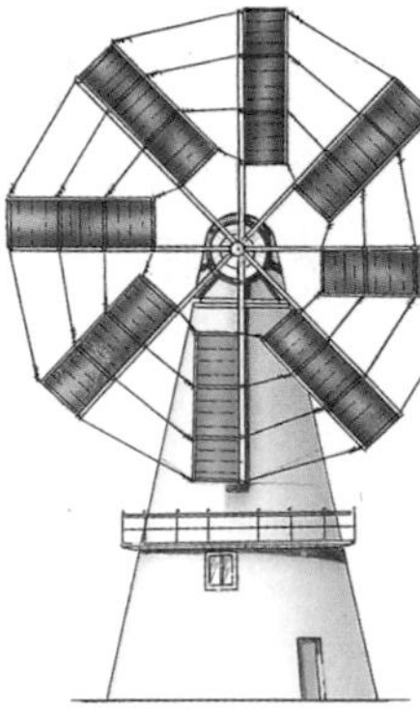

Kelly visited a windmill.
She saw that one sail of the windmill pointed down the line of the windows.

This sail was back at its starting position after 8 equal part-turns.

The diagram shows what Kelly saw.
The green sail is the one that she watched.

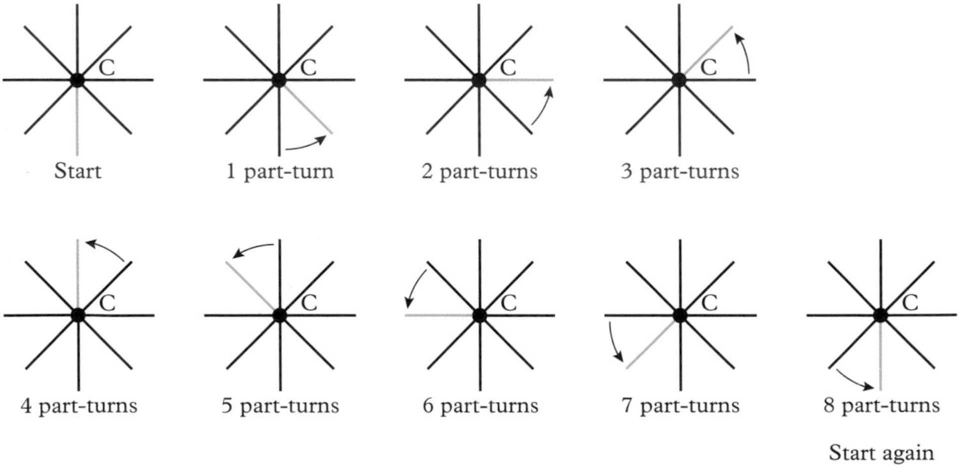

The windmill has **rotational symmetry of order 8 about its centre** (marked C).

Rotational symmetry	A shape has **rotational symmetry** if it fits on top of itself more than once as it makes a complete turn.
Order of rotational symmetry	The **order of rotational symmetry** is the number of times that the shape fits on top of itself. This must be 2 or more. Shapes that only fit on themselves once have no rotational symmetry.
Centre of rotation	The **centre of rotation** is the point about which the shape turns.

Exercise 2:7

1 For each shape:

a Trace the shape.

b Use your tracing to see how many times the shape fits on top of itself in one complete turn.

c Write down the order of rotational symmetry.
If a shape has no rotational symmetry, write 'none'.

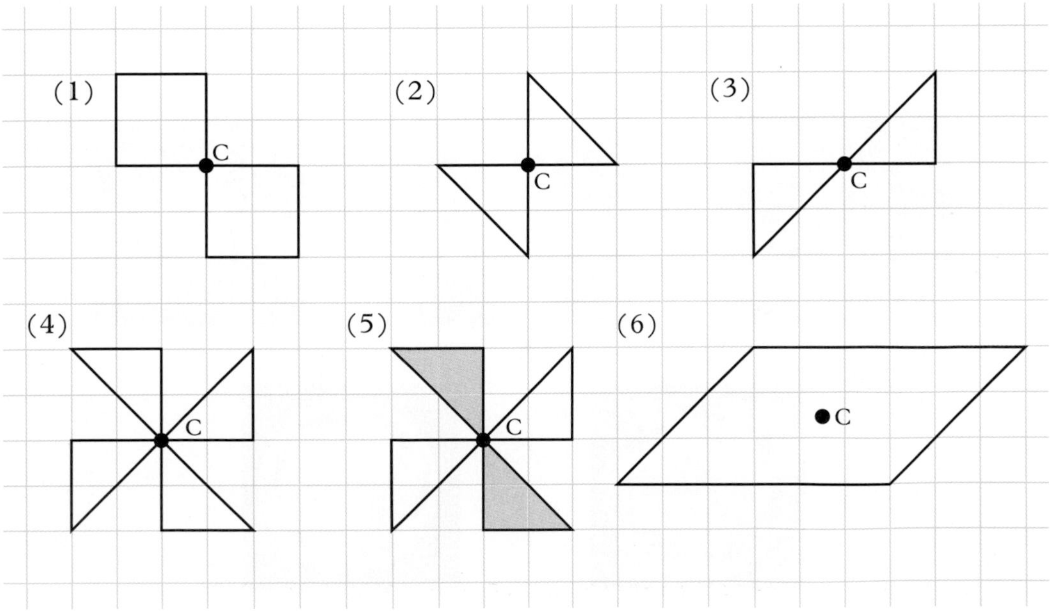

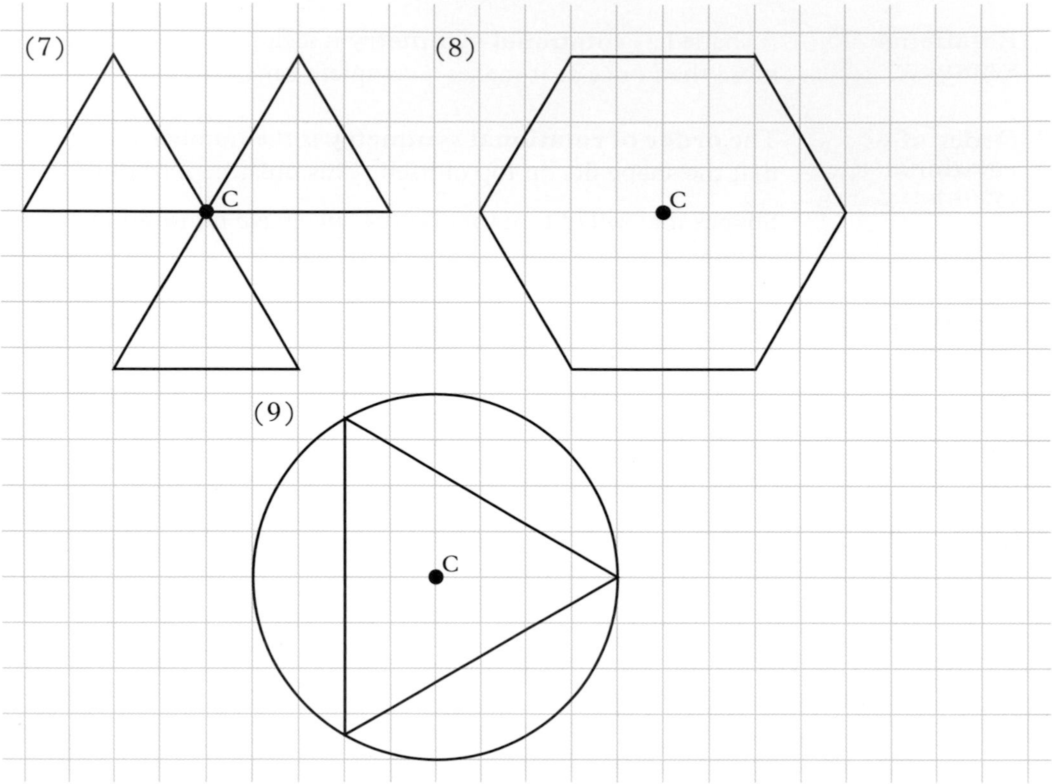

2 Rachel saw that the hubcaps of cars have rotational symmetry.
Write down the order of rotational symmetry of each of these hubcaps.
Ignore the maker's logo in parts **c**, **d** and **e**.

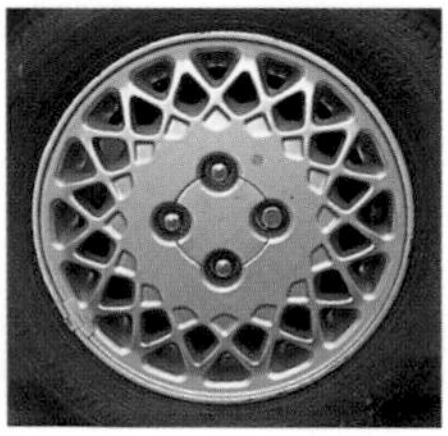

a

b

c

d

e

3 Write down the order of rotational symmetry of these road signs.
If a sign has no rotational symmetry, write 'none'.

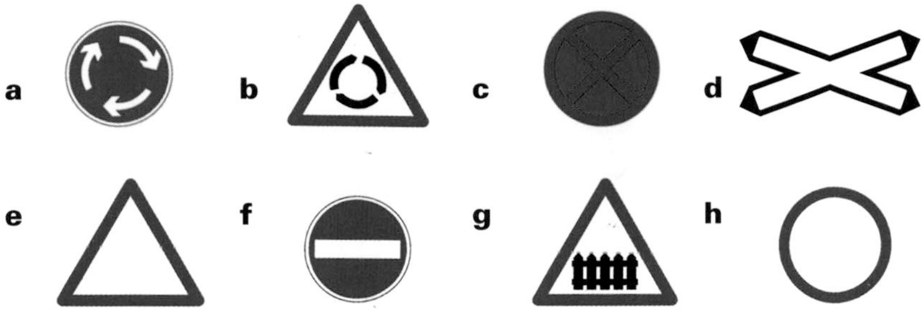

4 These are photographs of snowflakes.
No two snowflakes are the same.
Write down the order of rotational symmetry of each snowflake.

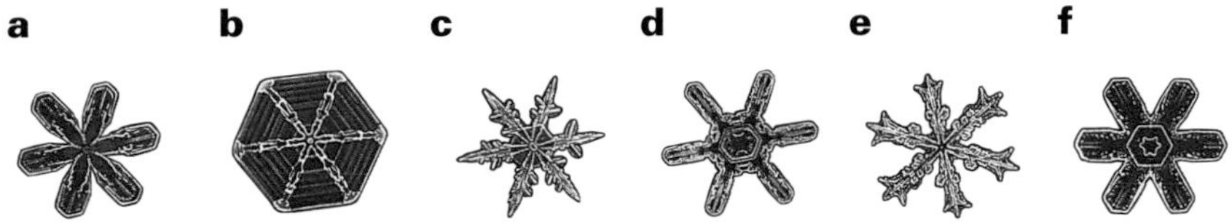

5 Diatoms are tiny cells with beautiful ornate outer shells.

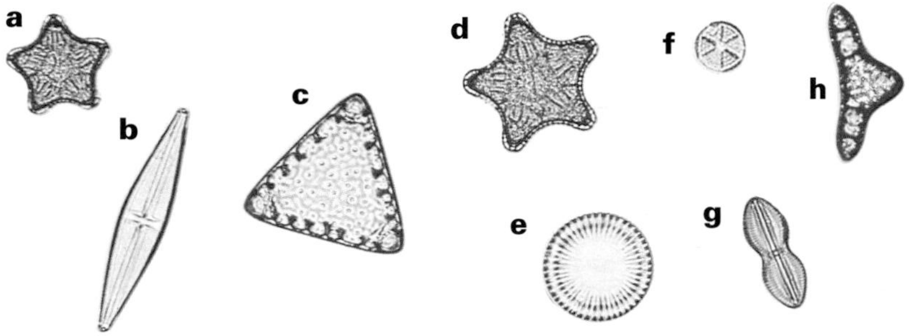

Write down the order of rotational symmetry of each diatom.

1 Copy these shapes on to squared paper.
Mark on **all** the lines of symmetry.

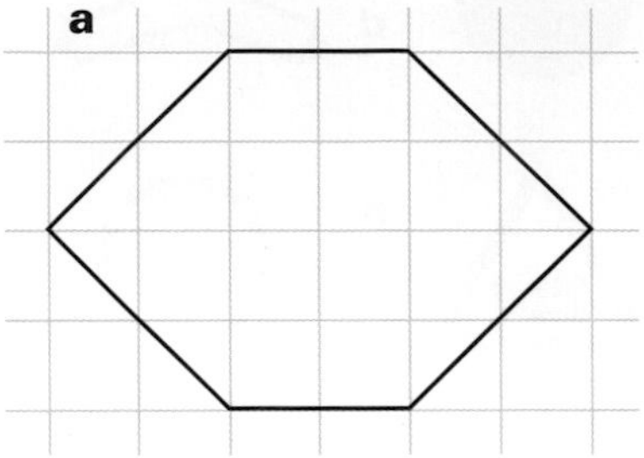

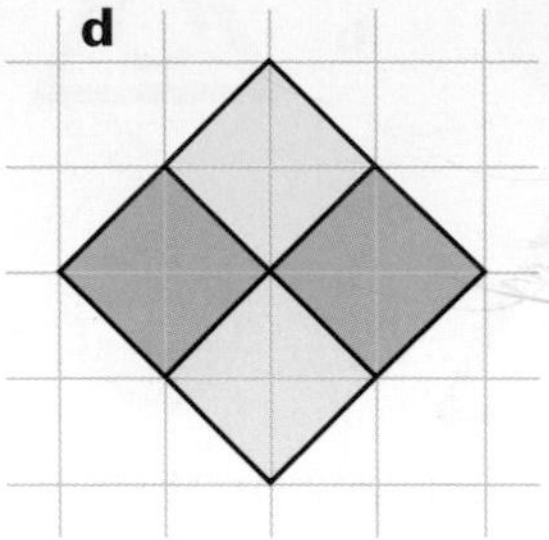

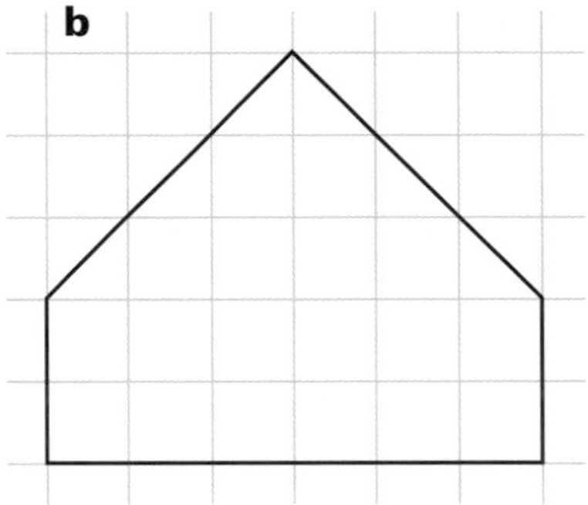

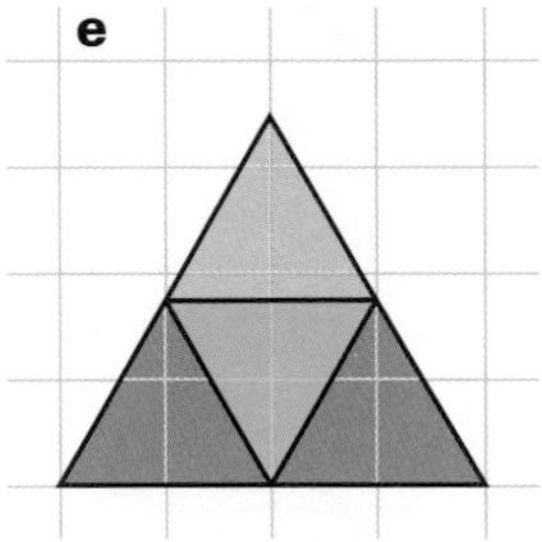

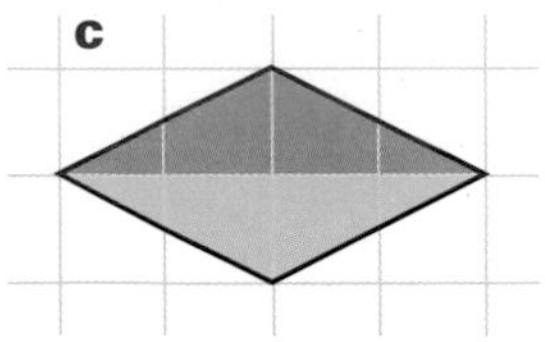

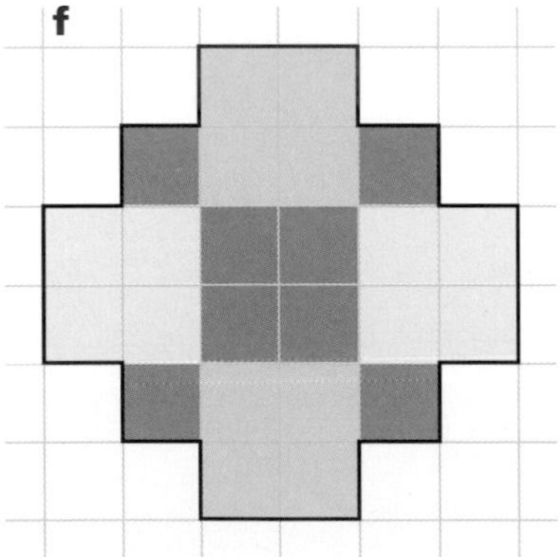

2 Copy these diagrams on to squared paper.
Draw their reflections in the line of symmetry.

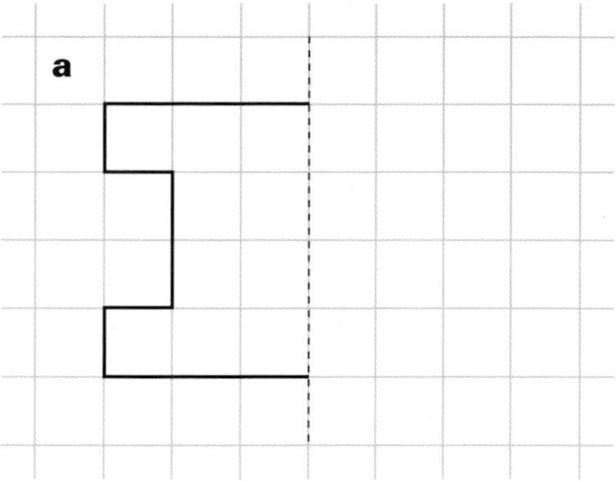

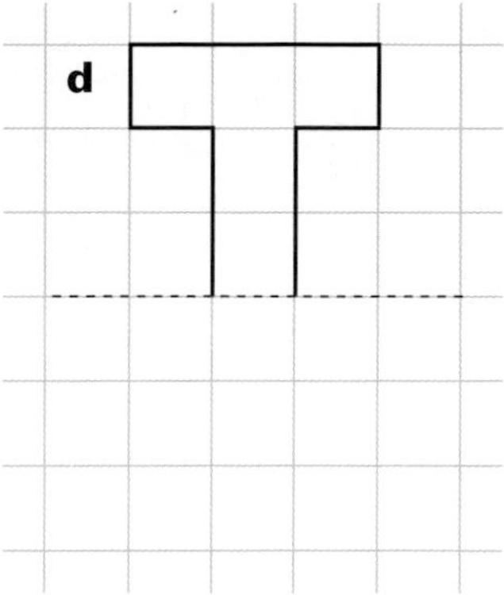

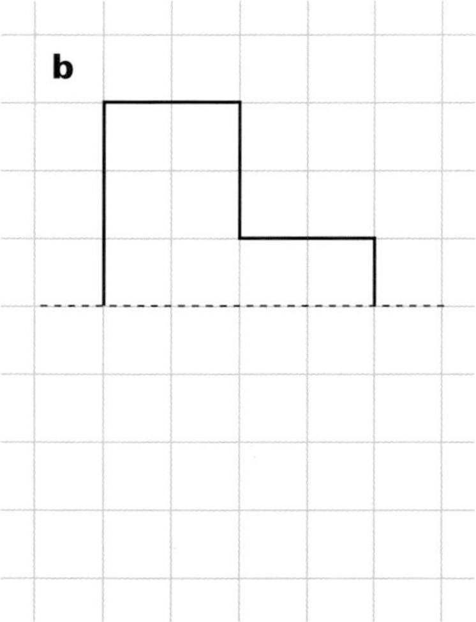

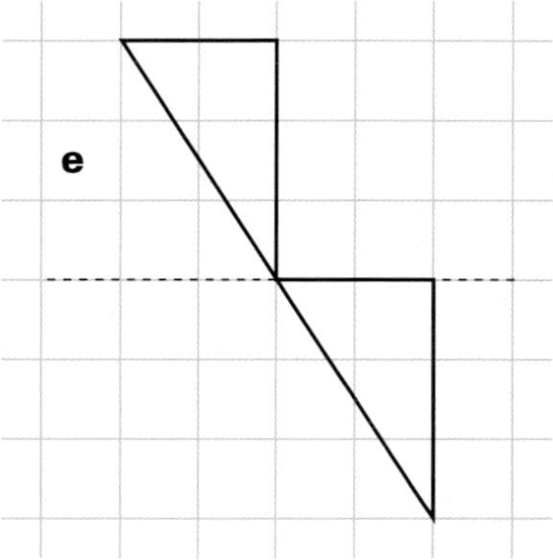

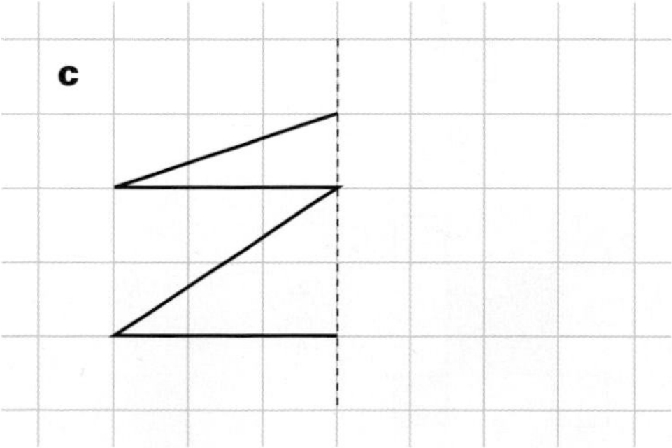

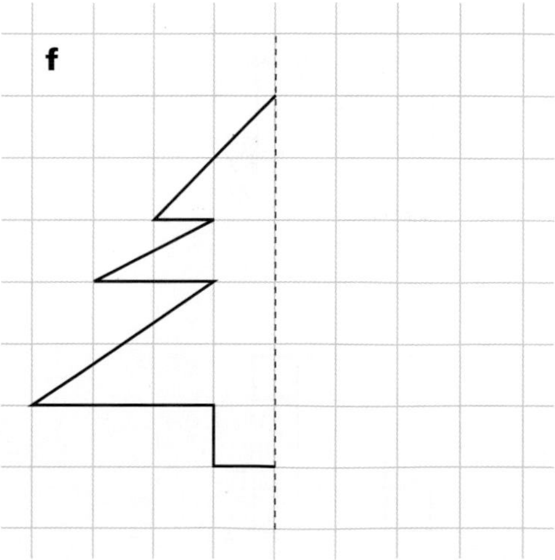

3 Copy and complete this table.

Start facing	Turn	Direction	End up facing
S	$\frac{3}{4}$	clockwise	
W	$\frac{1}{2}$	clockwise	
E	$\frac{1}{4}$	anti-clockwise	
N	$\frac{3}{4}$	anti-clockwise	
W	$\frac{1}{4}$	clockwise	
E	$\frac{3}{4}$	anti-clockwise	
S	$\frac{1}{2}$	anti-clockwise	
	$\frac{1}{2}$	clockwise	S
	$\frac{1}{4}$	anti-clockwise	W
	$\frac{1}{4}$	clockwise	N

4 Write down the order of rotational symmetry of each of these shapes. If a shape has no rotational symmetry, write 'none'.

a

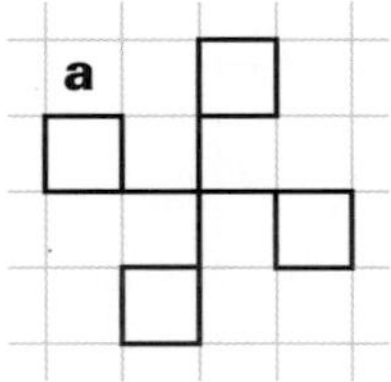

d

b

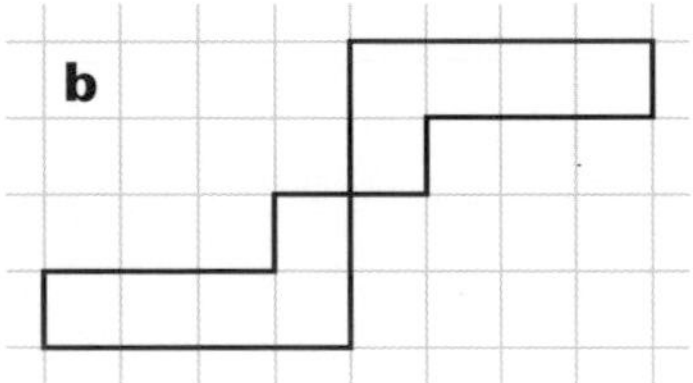

e

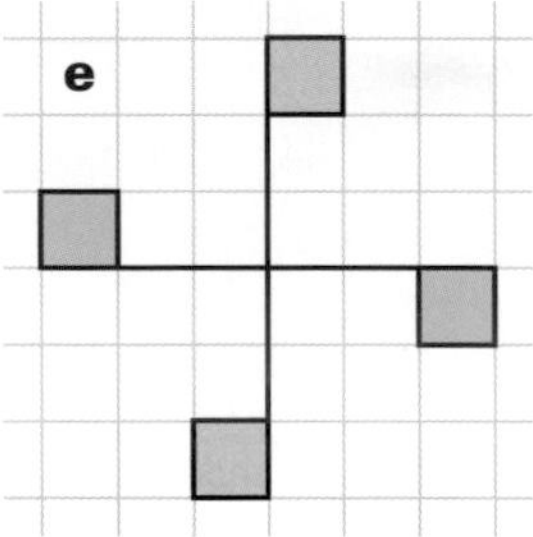

c

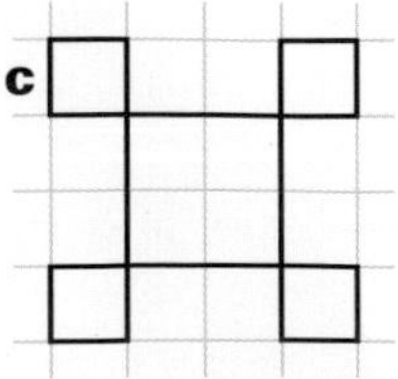

f

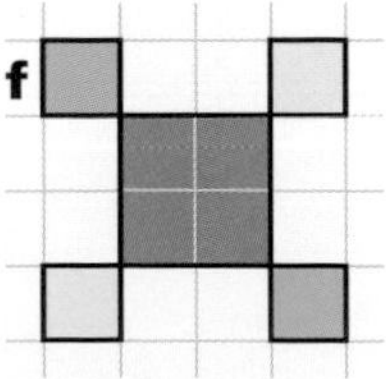

1 Copy these shapes on to squared paper.
Mark on **all** the lines of symmetry.

a

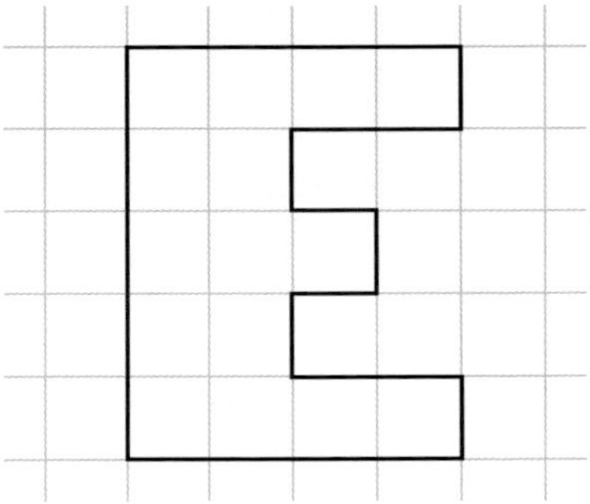

b

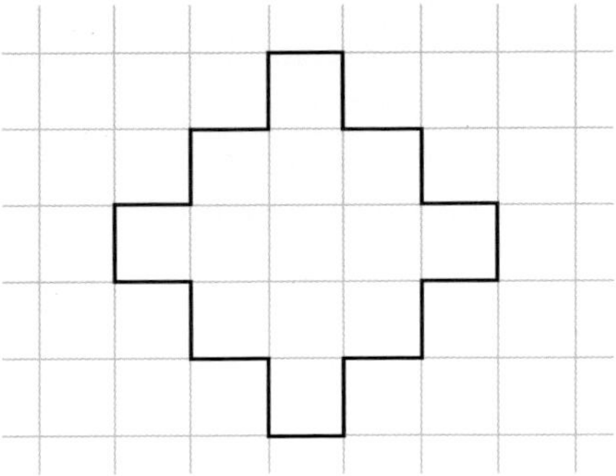

2 Copy these diagrams on to squared paper.
Draw their reflections in the lines of symmetry.

a

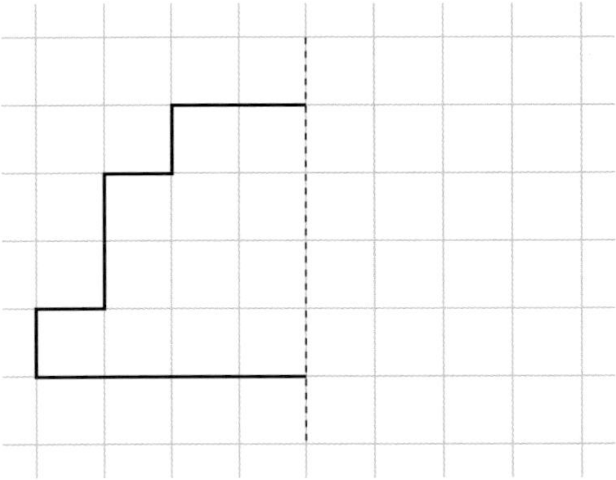

b

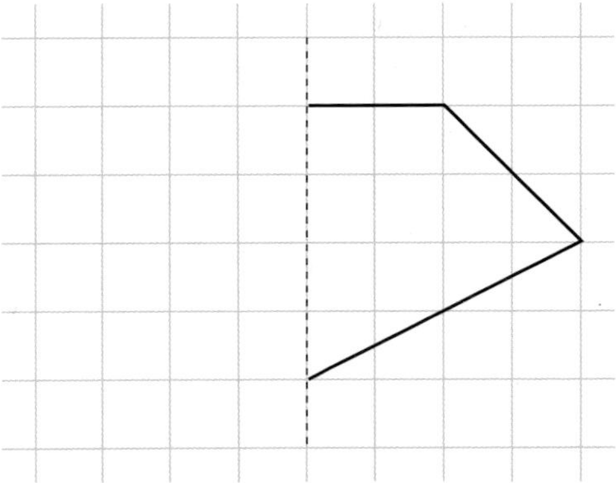

c

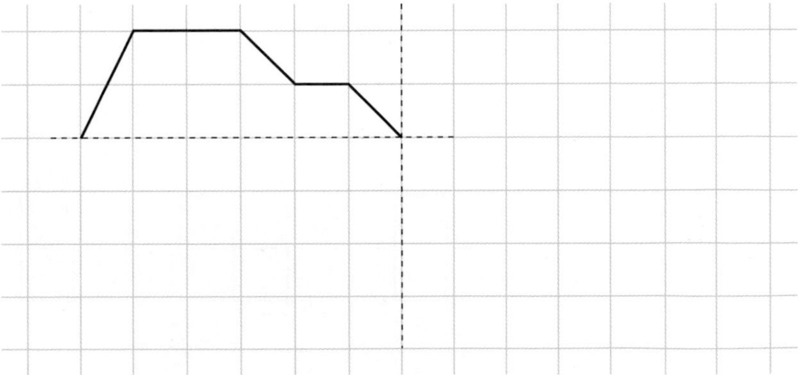

3 **M J A E T V P D**

Write down the letters in the list that have:

a a vertical line of symmetry.

b a horizontal line of symmetry.

4 Write down the number of lines of symmetry for each information symbol.

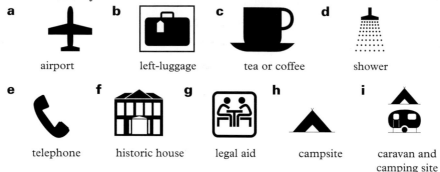

a 

airport

b 

left-luggage

c 

tea or coffee

d 

shower

e 

telephone

f 

historic house

g 

legal aid

h 

campsite

i 

caravan and camping site

5 These are old-fashioned science symbols.

(1) 

Azote

(2) 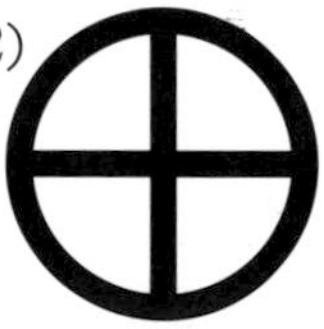

Sulphur

(3) 

Lime

(4) 

Phosphorus

(5) 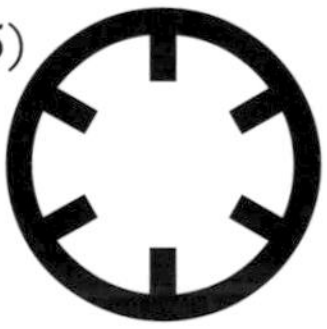

Barytes

a Write down the number of lines of symmetry for each symbol.

b Write down the order of rotational symmetry for each symbol. If a symbol has no rotational symmetry, write 'none'.

6 **a** Copy each of these shapes on to squared paper. Leave plenty of space between them.

b Complete your shapes so that they have rotational symmetry of order 4 about C.

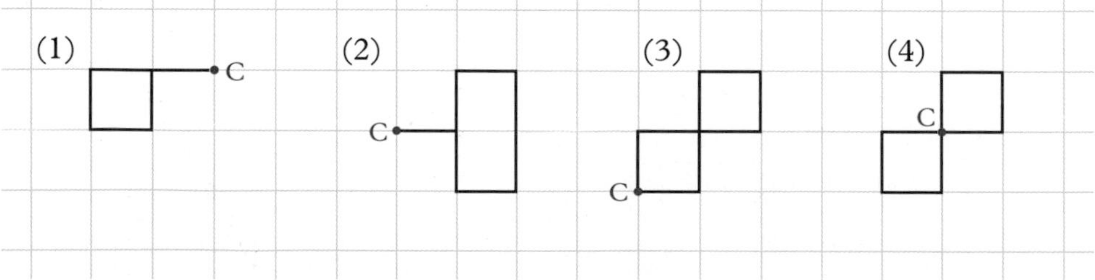

- **Line of symmetry**

  A line of symmetry divides a shape into two equal parts. Each part is a reflection of the other.

  If you fold the shape along this line, each part fits exactly on top of the other.

- Some shapes have more than one line of symmetry.
  A square has 4.

  We usually show all the lines on one diagram:

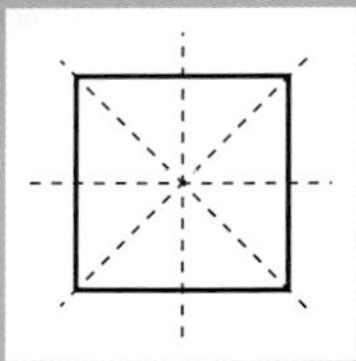

- **Turn**

  We use the word '**turn**' to describe something that moves round in a circle.

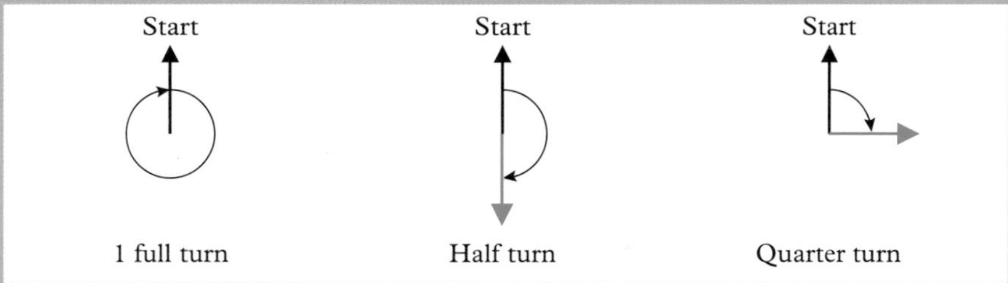

We use clockwise and anti-clockwise to say which way to turn.

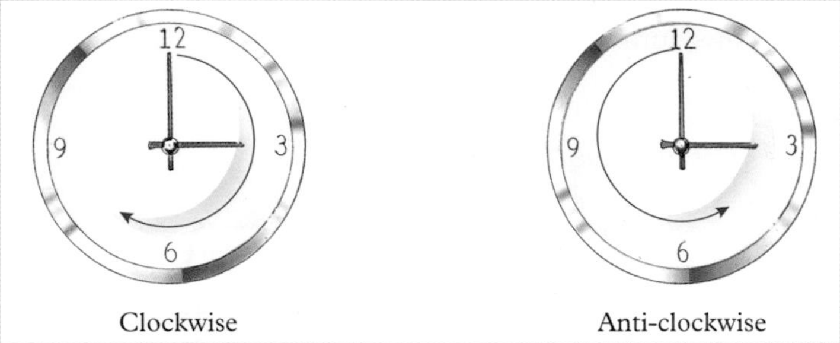

- A shape has **rotational symmetry** if it fits on top of itself more than once as it makes a complete turn.

  The **order of rotational symmetry** is the number of times that the shape fits on top of itself. This must be 2 or more.

  Shapes that only fit on themselves once have no rotational symmetry.

  The **centre of rotation** is the point about which the shape turns.

1 Copy these shapes on to squared paper.
Mark on **all** the lines of symmetry.

a

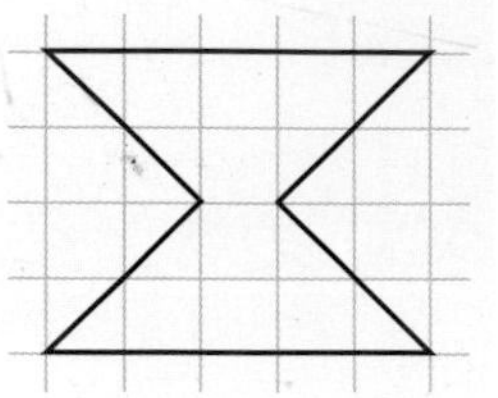

b

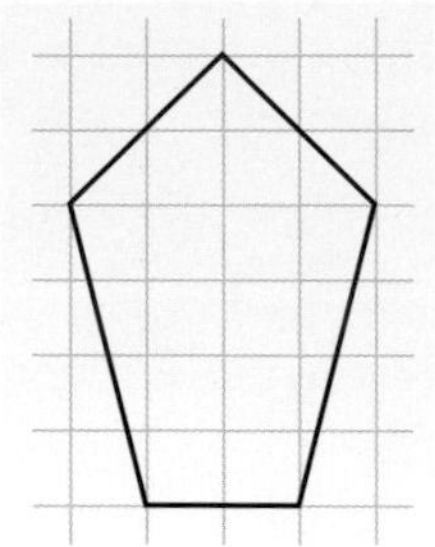

2 Copy these diagrams on to squared paper.
Draw their reflections in the line of symmetry.

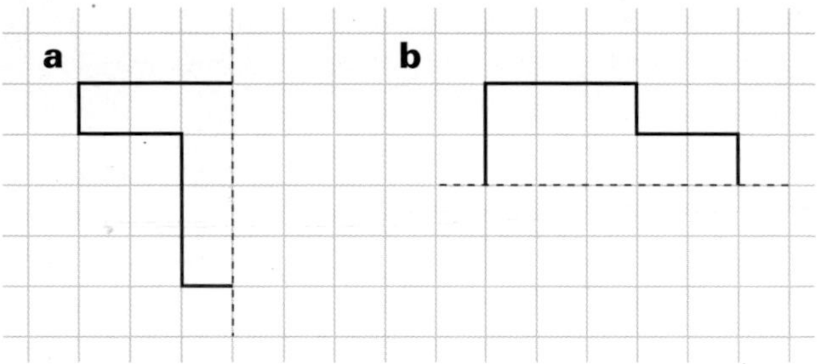

3 **A C W Y D S J**
Write down the letters in the list that have:
a a vertical line of symmetry.
b a horizontal line of symmetry.
c no line of symmetry.

4 Write down which symbols have lines of symmetry.

a

b

c

5 Write down the order of rotational symmetry of these shapes.
If a shape has no rotational symmetry, write 'none'.

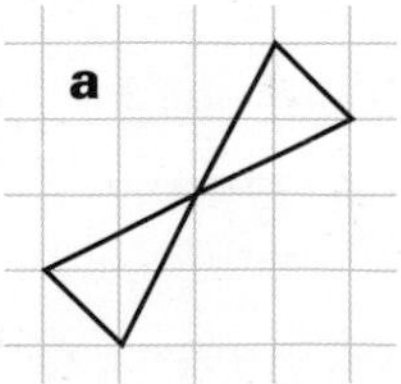

b

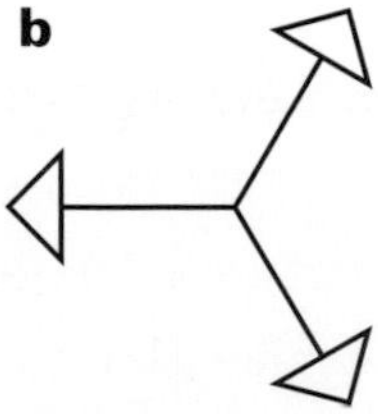

c

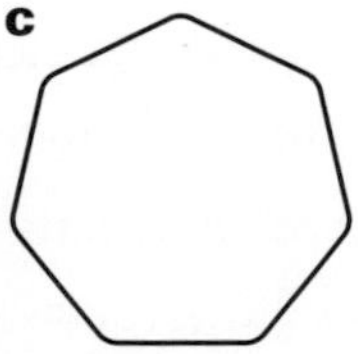

3 Number patterns

CORE

1 **Factors, multiples and primes**

2 **Patterns in number**

3 **Rules and robots**

QUESTIONS

EXTENSION

SUMMARY

TEST YOURSELF

This is a Chinese version of the number pattern known as 'Pascal's Triangle'. It appears in a manuscript dated 1303; Blaise Pascal was born in 1623.

1 Factors, multiples and primes

Sometimes we cannot see any order or pattern.

Sometimes we can see order.

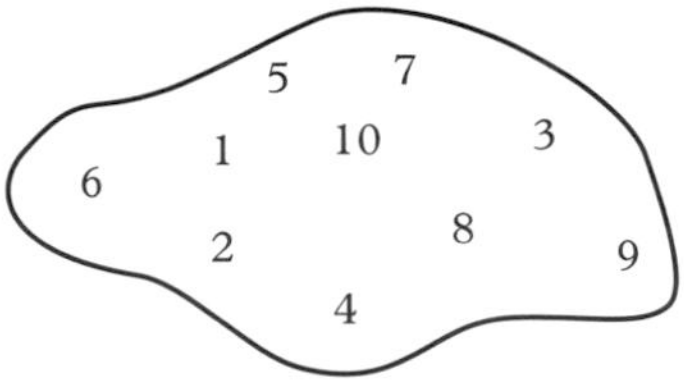

1 2 3 4 5 6 7 8 9 10

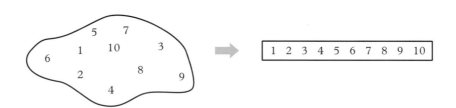

Counting numbers The **counting numbers** are:

1 2 3 4 5 6 7 8 9 10 11 12 …

Odd numbers The red numbers have a pattern. They start the **odd numbers**.

Even numbers The blue numbers also have a pattern. They start the **even numbers**.

The rule is 'add 2' to get the next number.

Exercise 3:1

1 **a** List the even numbers from 20 to 50.
b Copy and complete:
An even number always ends in 0, 2, …, …, …

2 **a** List the odd numbers from 51 to 81.
b Copy and complete:
An odd number always ends in …, 3, …, …, 9

Example

Write down the rule for each of these patterns.
Find the next two terms.

a 1, 4, 7, 10, 13, …
b 22, 20, 18, 16, 14, …

a 1 → 4 → 7 → 10 → 13 → 16 → 19
(+ 3, + 3, + 3, + 3, + 3, + 3)

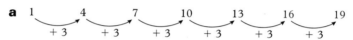

The rule is +3. The next two terms are 16, 19.

b 22 → 20 → 18 → 16 → 14 → 12 → 10
(− 2, − 2, − 2, − 2, − 2, − 2)

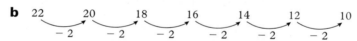

The rule is −2. The next two terms are 12, 10.

---

3 Write down the rule for each number pattern.
Find the next two terms.

a 3, 5, 7, 9, 11, …
b 3, 6, 9, 12, 15, …
c 4, 8, 12, 16, …
d 24, 21, 18, 15, 12, …
e 2, 4, 8, 16, 32, …
f 80, 70, 60, 50, 40, …

4 Copy these number patterns.
Write down the rule for each one.
Use your rule to fill in the missing numbers.

a 1, 5, 9, …, 17, …, 25
b 21, 23, …, 27, …, 31
c 32, 34, 36, …, …, 42
d 7, 12, …, 22, 27, …
e 12, 10, 8, …, 4, …
f 24, 20, …, 12, …, 4

5 Each pattern has a rule and a starting number.
Copy the table.
Fill in the next four numbers in each pattern. The first one has been done for you.

Rule	Starting number	Next four numbers
+5	7	12 17 22 27
+2	11	
+4	3	
−1	15	
−3	20	
×2	3	

If we multiply each counting number by 2 we get

	1 × 2	2 × 2	3 × 2	4 × 2	5 × 2	6 × 2	7 × 2
	↓	↓	↓	↓	↓	↓	↓
or	2	4	6	8	10	12	14

Multiples

The **multiples** of 2 are 2, 4, 6, 8, 10, 12, 14, …

The multiples of 3 are 3, 6, 9, 12, 15, …
The multiples of 4 are 4, 8, 12, 16, 20, …

All numbers are multiples of 1.

Exercise 3:2

1 Copy the table.
Fill in the first five multiples of each number.

Number	×1	×2	×3	×4	×5
5	5	10			
6	6	12			
7					
8					
9					
10					

2 Copy these lists of multiples.
Fill in the missing numbers.

a 3, 6, 9, …, 15, 18, …
b 4, 8, …, 16, 20, …, 28
c 15, 20, …, 30, 35, …, 45
d 21, …, 35, 42, 49, …, 63
e 12, …, 24, 30, …, 42
f 18, …, …, 45, 54, 63

3 Multiples of 2 are even numbers.
Which of these numbers are multiples of 2?
32, 425, 120, 17, 86, 300

4 **a** Write down the first four multiples of 5.
b Copy and complete:
Multiples of 5 always end in … or …
c Which of these numbers are multiples of 5?
35, 87, 170, 58, 600, 115

5 Which of these numbers are multiples of 10?
80, 225, 1000, 110, 40, 305

Factor A number that divides exactly into **another number** is called a **factor** of that number.

Examples

1 $10 = 1 \times 10$
$10 = 2 \times 5$
1, 2, 5 and 10 are the factors of 10.

2 $3 = 1 \times 3$
1 and 3 are the factors of 3.

Exercise 3:3

1 Copy and complete:
$8 = 1 \times 8$
$8 = 2 \times 4$
The factors of 8 are 1, 2, … and …

2 Copy and complete:
$6 = 1 \times ?$
$6 = 2 \times ?$
The factors of 6 are …, …, 3 and …

3 Work out the factors of 14.

4 Find the factors of 5.

5 Find the factors of 9.

● **6** Find the factors of these numbers:
a 11 **b** 12 **c** 15 **d** 16 **e** 18

7 **a** Copy and complete.
$24 = 1 \times \ldots$
$24 = 2 \times \ldots$
$24 = 3 \times \ldots$
$24 = 4 \times \ldots$
b Write down the factors of 24.

● **8** Work out the factors of:
a 40 **b** 100

Exercise 3:4

W **1** You will need a *new copy* of the 1–100 number square for *each part* of this question.

1	2	3	4	5	6	7	8	9	10
11	12	13	14	15	16	17	18	19	20
21	22	23	24	25	26	27	28	29	30
31	32	33	34	35	36	37	38	39	40
41	42	43	44	45	46	47	48	49	50
51	52	53	54	55	56	57	58	59	60
61	62	63	64	65	66	67	68	69	70
71	72	73	74	75	76	77	78	79	80
81	82	83	84	85	86	87	88	89	90
91	92	93	94	95	96	97	98	99	100

a Shade all the squares that contain multiples of 2.
b Shade all the squares that contain multiples of 3.
c Shade all the squares that contain multiples of 5.
d Shade all the squares that contain multiples of 7.
e On another copy of the 1–100 number square:
(1) Cross out number 1.
(2) Circle the numbers 2, 3, 5 and 7.
Do not cross them out.
Cross out all the other numbers you shaded in parts **a, b, c** and **d**.
(3) 2, 3, 5 and 7 have already been circled.
Circle all the other numbers that are not crossed out.
(4) Make a list of all your circled numbers.
They are called **prime numbers**.

Prime numbers **Prime numbers** have only two factors, themselves and 1.

Examples of prime numbers are 2, 3, 11, 19.
1 is not a prime number.

2 There is only one even number that is prime.
Write down this number.

3 Use the list of prime numbers that you made at the end of Question **1**.
- **a** The number 1 is not prime, but many prime numbers end in 1. List the prime numbers up to 100 ending in 1.
- **b** 3 is prime and many prime numbers end in 3. List the prime numbers up to 100 ending in 3.
- **c** 5 is prime. Explain why no other prime number ends in 5.
- **d** 7 is prime. List the prime numbers up to 100 ending in 7.
- **e** (1) Explain why 9 is not prime.
  (2) List the prime numbers up to 100 ending in 9.

W **4** 2, 3, 5 and 7 are the prime numbers less than 10. You shaded their patterns in Question **1**.
Other numbers also make attractive patterns.

You need a new copy of the 1–100 number square for each part of this question.
Shade multiples of:

a 4	**c** 8	**e** 10
b 6	**d** 9	**f** 11

2 Patterns in number

Some number patterns have special names because of the shapes that they make.

Exercise 3:5

1 Copy the square patterns.
Complete the multiplications.

$1 \times 1 = \ldots$ $2 \times 2 = \ldots$ $3 \times 3 = \ldots$

2 Draw the next two patterns.
Write down their multiplications.

Square numbers

1, 4, 9, 16, 25, … are called **square numbers**.

---

3 Write down the next two square numbers after 25.

4 **a** Copy and complete:

$1 = 1$
$1 + 3 = 4$
$1 + 3 + 5 = \ldots$
$1 + 3 + 5 + 7 = \ldots$
$1 + 3 + 5 + 7 + \ldots = \ldots$

b What special numbers are your answers?

Exercise 3:6

1

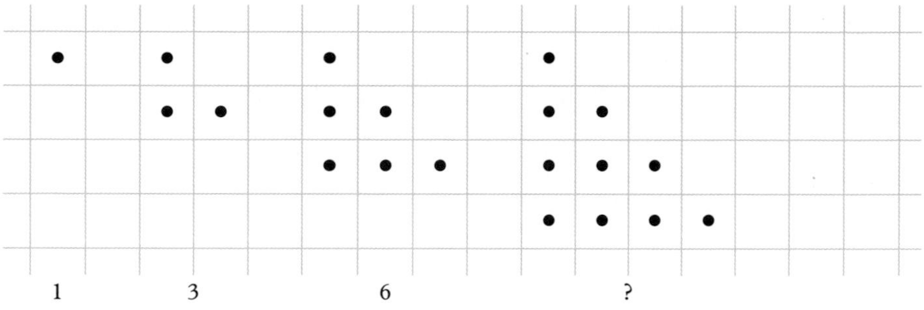

Copy these triangle patterns on to squared paper.

2 Draw the next two patterns.
Count the dots.

Triangle numbers 1, 3, 6, 10, 15, 21, … are called **triangle numbers**.

---

3 **a** Copy and complete:

1 = 1
1 + 2 = 3
1 + 2 + 3 = 6
1 + 2 + 3 + 4 = …
1 + 2 + 3 + 4 + 5 = …
1 + 2 + 3 + 4 + 5 + … = …

b What special numbers are your answers?

Patterns from tables

1 Write out the two times table:

$1 \times 2 = 2$	$6 \times 2 = 12$
$2 \times 2 = 4$	$7 \times 2 = 14$
$3 \times 2 = 6$	$8 \times 2 = 16$
$4 \times 2 = 8$	$9 \times 2 = 18$
$5 \times 2 = 10$	$10 \times 2 = 20$

2 Some of the answers have two digits.
Add these digits together to give a single digit.
This gives the red numbers.

2	2
4	4
6	6
8	8
10	1 + 0 = 1
12	1 + 2 = 3
14	1 + 4 = 5
16	1 + 6 = 7
18	1 + 8 = 9
20	2 + 0 = 2

W **3** Mark 9 equally spaced points around a circle.
Number them 1 to 9.

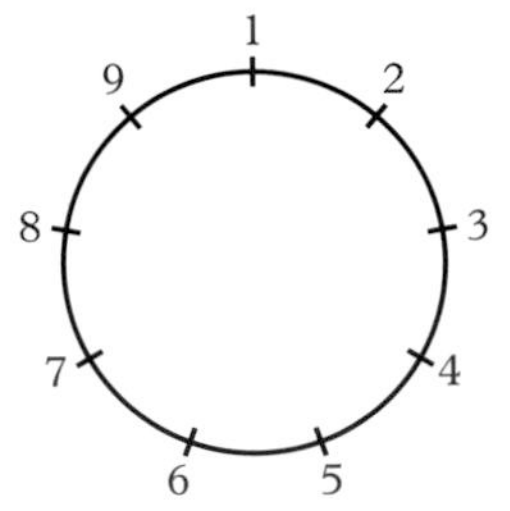

4 Join the points in the order of the red numbers.
Always use a ruler.

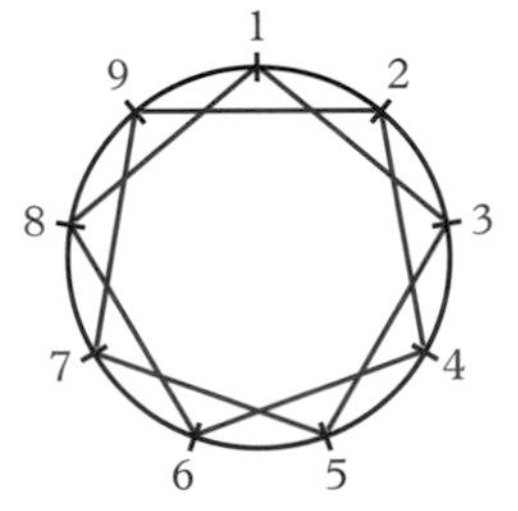

5 Investigate patterns made by other tables.
Are all the patterns different?
Can you group the patterns in some way?
Can you predict which pattern will come from each table?
What will you do with numbers like 7 × 4 = 28 where 2 + 8 = 10?

6 Write a short report on what you have found out.
Explain any patterns that you have found.
Include your diagrams. You could colour them.
You could make a display for your classroom.

3 Rules and robots

Imagine that we have a robot to help us with our patterns.

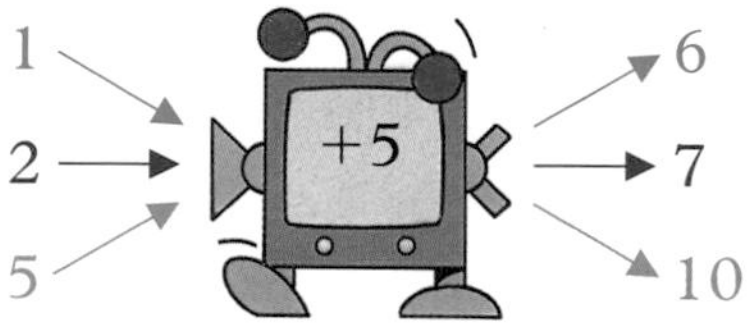

This robot adds 5 to any number.

Example What answers will this robot give?

We only need to draw the robot's screen.

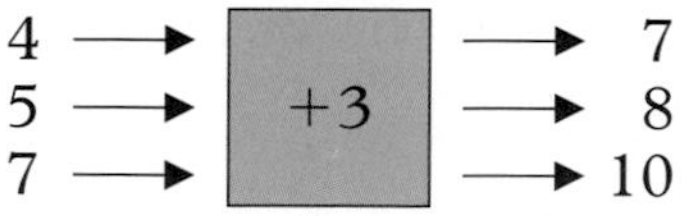

Exercise 3:7

Draw the screen for each robot.
Write down each robot's answers.

1
1 → +2 →
3 → +2 →
5 → +2 →

2
2 → +7 →
4 → +7 →
5 → +7 →

3
3 → +10 →
4 → +10 →
8 → +10 →

4
3 → −1 →
5 → −1 →
10 → −1 →

5
2 → ×2 →
3 → ×2 →
4 → ×2 →

6
2 → ×5 →
3 → ×5 →
5 → ×5 →

7
2 → ×10 →
5 → ×10 →
8 → ×10 →

8
4 → −3 →
6 → −3 →
9 → −3 →

One day, the robot's screen does not work.
What should the robot's screen show?

5 → Normal service will be resumed as soon as possible → 10
10 → → 15
25 → → 30

The robot's screen should show +5.

Exercise 3:8

Write down the rule that belongs on each screen.

1
1 → ? → 5
3 → ? → 7
10 → ? → 14

2
1 → ? → 7
6 → ? → 12
9 → ? → 15

3

5 →	?	→ 3
8 →		→ 6
9 →		→ 7

4

30 →	?	→ 20
50 →		→ 40
90 →		→ 80

5

2 →	?	→ 6
4 →		→ 12
5 →		→ 15

● **6**

6 →	?	→ 3
10 →		→ 5
20 →		→ 10

We can use two robots.

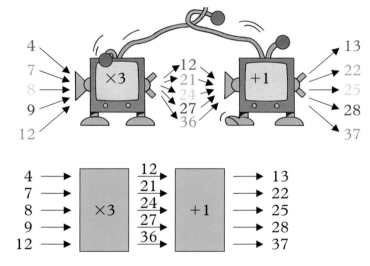

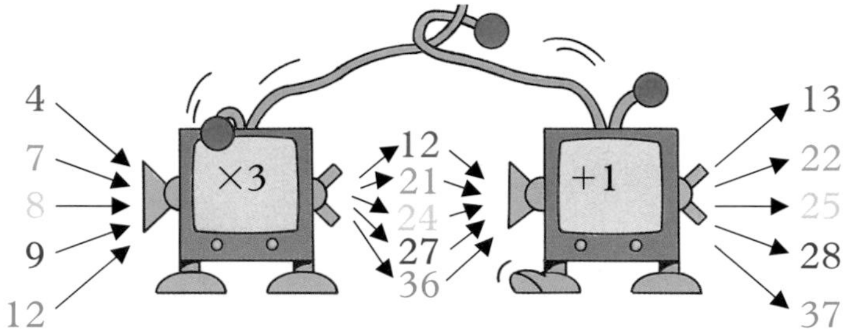

4 →	×3	12 →	+1	→ 13
7 →		21 →		→ 22
8 →		24 →		→ 25
9 →		27 →		→ 28
12 →		36 →		→ 37

Exercise 3:9

1 Copy and complete:

3 →	×2	6 →	+1	→ 7
4 →		? →		→ ?
6 →		? →		→ ?

2 Copy and complete:

2 →	−1	1 →	×3	→ 3
3 →		? →		→ ?
5 →		? →		→ ?

Copy these diagrams.
Write down the robots' answers.

3

2 →	×3	? →	−1	→ ?
3 →		? →		→ ?
4 →		? →		→ ?

4

1 →	+4	→	×2	→
2 →		→		→
4 →		→		→

5

1 →	+3	→	×5	→
3 →		→		→
5 →		→		→

6

2 →	×5	→	+1	→
4 →		→		→
6 →		→		→

7

3 →	+2	→	×3	→
4 →		→		→
7 →		→		→

8

1 →	×5	→	+3	→
3 →		→		→
6 →		→		→

9

1 →	+3	→	×5	→
2 →		→		→
4 →		→		→

10

5 →	+1	→	÷2	→
7 →		→		→
9 →		→		→

Copy these diagrams.
Fill in the rule that belongs on each screen.

• 11

2 →	?	6 →	?	→ 8
3 →		9 →		→ 11
5 →		15 →		→ 17

• 12

2 →	?	0 →	?	→ 0
4 →		2 →		→ 4
5 →		3 →		→ 6

1 Look at these numbers
69, 94, 140, 25, 523, 600, 1037
a List the odd numbers.
b List the even numbers.

2 Copy these number patterns.
Write down the rule for each one.
Use your rule to complete the patterns.
a 4, 7, 10, …, 16, …
b 5, …, 25, 35, …
c 60, 54, …, …, 36
d 50, 43, 36, …, …

3 Each pattern has a rule and a starting number.
Write down the next five numbers in each pattern.

Rule	Starting number	Next five numbers
+4	3	
×2	4	
×5	2	
−2	24	
−10	61	

4

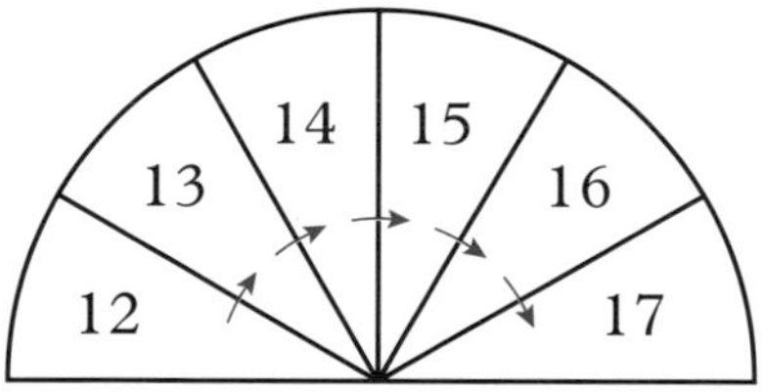

a Write down the rule to move from one number to the next.
b List the prime numbers in the diagram.
c Write down the number that is a multiple of 6.
d 3 is a factor of two of the numbers. Write them down.
e Which number is a square number?
f Which number is a triangle number?

5 Copy and complete:
36 = 1 × …
36 = 2 × …
36 = 3 × …
36 = 4 × …
36 = 6 × …
The factors of 36 are …

6 **a** Write down the factors of each of these numbers:

(1) 7 (2) 13 (3) 19

b What special kind of number are 7, 13, 19?

7 Here are six square numbers:

1, 4, 9, 16, 25, 36.

Two of the numbers add together to make a square number.
Write down the two numbers.

8 Copy these diagrams.
Write down each robot's answers.

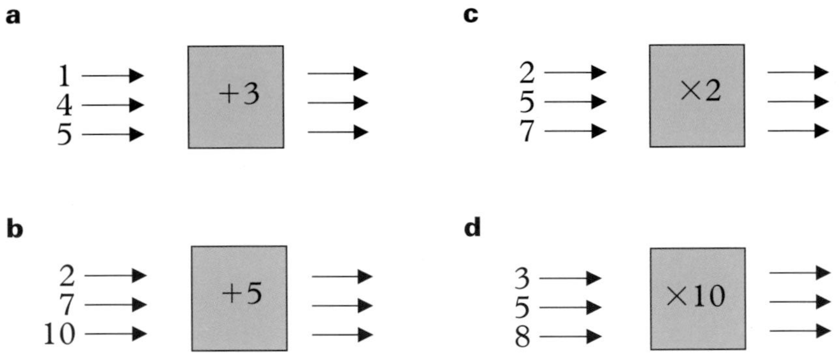

9 Write down the rule that belongs on each screen.

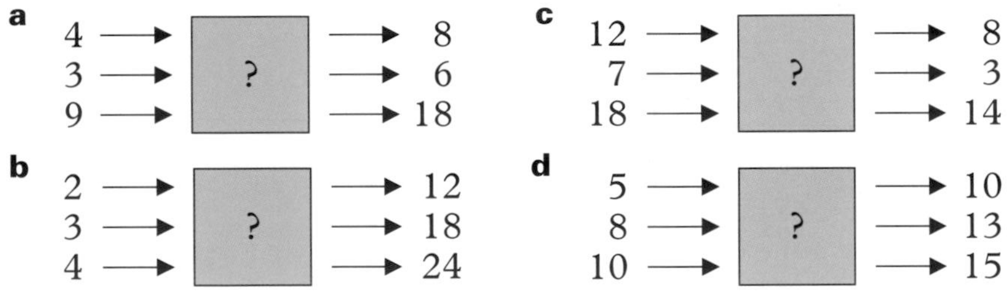

10 Copy the diagrams for each pair of robots.
Write down the robots' answers.

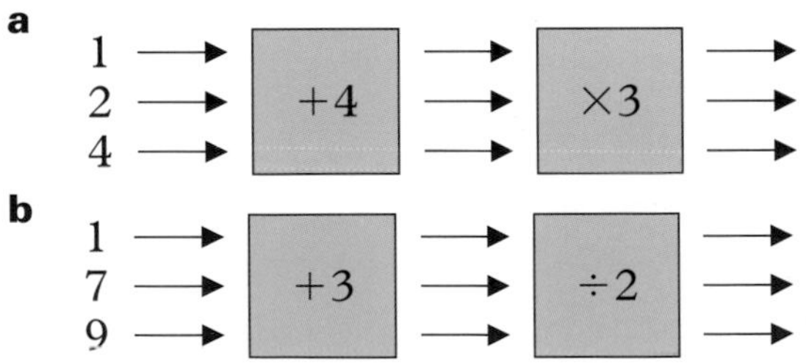

1 Write down the rule for each number pattern.

a 15, 30, 60, 120, 240
b 24, 32, 40, 48, 56
c 45, 38, 31, 24, 17
d 96, 48, 24, 12, 6

2 Copy and complete these patterns.
Write down each rule.

a 7, 14, 21, …, 35, …, …
b 64, 32, …, …, 4, …
c 1, 4, …, 64, 256
d 85, 73, …, 49, …, 25

3 Copy the diagrams.
Write down each robot's answers.

a

Input	Robot	Output
4 →	+11	→
7 →		→
2 →		→

b

Input	Robot	Output
3 →	×7	→
2 →		→
6 →		→

c

Input	Robot	Output
15 →	−13	→
17 →		→
29 →		→

d

Input	Robot	Output
144 →	÷12	→
48 →		→
60 →		→

4 Copy the diagrams.
Write down the robots' answers.

a

Input	Robot 1		Robot 2	Output
3 →	×3	→	+11	→
7 →		→		→
1 →		→		→

b

Input	Robot 1		Robot 2	Output
6 →	÷3	→	+7	→
3 →		→		→
9 →		→		→

c

Input	Robot 1		Robot 2	Output
5 →	+4	→	×3	→
1 →		→		→
0 →		→		→

d

Input	Robot 1		Robot 2	Output
4 →	×4	→	−9	→
8 →		→		→
12 →		→		→

5 Look at these numbers:

1 6 11 16 21 26 31 36

a Write down the rule for this number pattern.
b List the prime numbers in this pattern.
c List the triangle numbers in this pattern.
d List the square numbers.
e List the multiples of 6.
f Write down the number that has 7 as a factor.

6 A number that reads the same backwards as it does forwards is called a **palindromic** number.

323 is a palindromic number.

33, 17, 88, 11, 29, 13, 22, 202

From this list of numbers write down:
a the palindromic numbers.
b the prime numbers.
c the smallest palindromic prime number.

d 1991 was a palindromic year.
By writing down the years that follow 1991, find the next palindromic year.

7

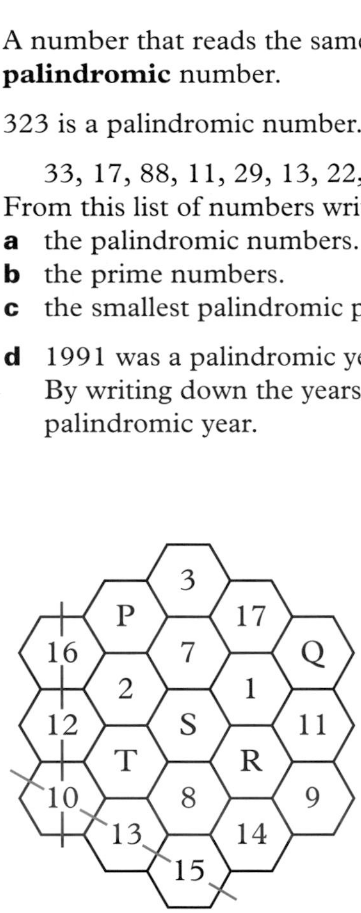

This hexagon puzzle contains the numbers 1 to 19.
Each number is used only once. Some of the numbers are missing.
a Find the sum of the numbers in the red column.
b Find the sum of the numbers in the blue diagonal.

The sum of the numbers in each column and diagonal is the same.
c Write down the numbers that go in the spaces P, Q, R, S and T.

- 1 2 3 4 5 6 7 8 9 10 11 12 …
  The red numbers are **odd**.
  The blue numbers are **even**.
  Odd numbers always end in 1, 3, 5, 7 or 9.
  Even numbers always end in 0, 2, 4, 6 or 8.

- The **multiples** of 2 are 2, 4, 6, 8, 10, 12, …
  The multiples of 3 are 3, 6, 9, 12, 15, …
  The multiples of 4 are 4, 8, 12, 16, 20, …
  All numbers are multiples of 1.

- Numbers which divide exactly into another number are called **factors**.
  1, 2, 5 and 10 are the factors of 10.

- **Prime numbers** have only two factors, themselves and 1.
  Examples of prime numbers are 2, 3, 11, 19.
  1 is not a prime number.

- 1, 4, 9, 16, 25, …
  are called **square numbers**.

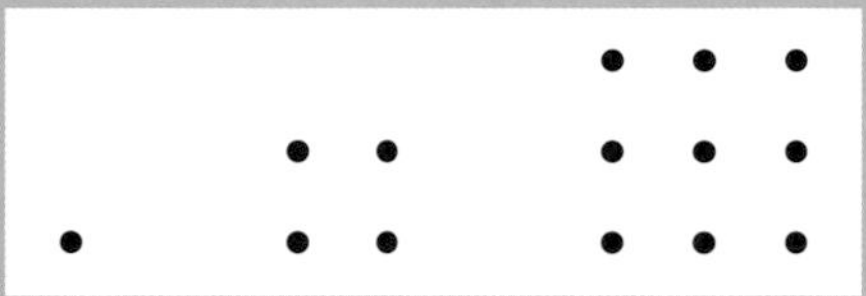

- 1, 3, 6, 10, 15, …
  are called **triangle numbers**.

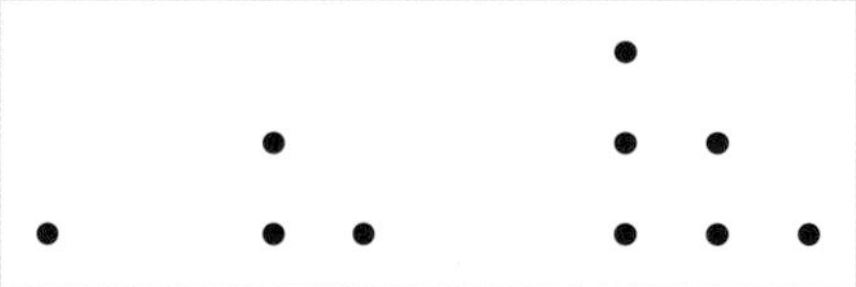

- This robot adds 5 to any number

3 TEST YOURSELF

1 Look at these numbers:
15, 18, 23, 125, 228, 320.

a List the even numbers.

b List the odd numbers.

2 Copy and complete these number patterns.
Write down the rule for each one.

a 8, 10, 12, …, …, 18

b 26, 23, 20, …, 14, …

c 1, 2, 4, …, …, 32

3 List the first six multiples of 4.

4 List all the factors of: **a** 8 **b** 15

5 1, 5, 9, 13, 17, 21, 25

a Write down the rule for this number pattern.

b List the prime numbers.

c List the triangle numbers.

d List the square numbers.

6 Copy these diagrams.
Write down each robot's answers.

a

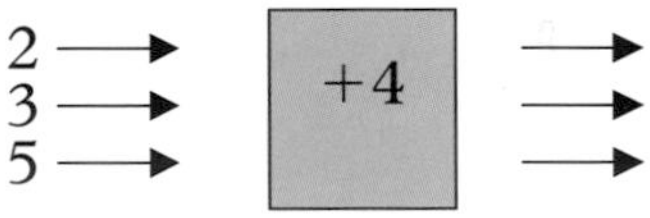

c

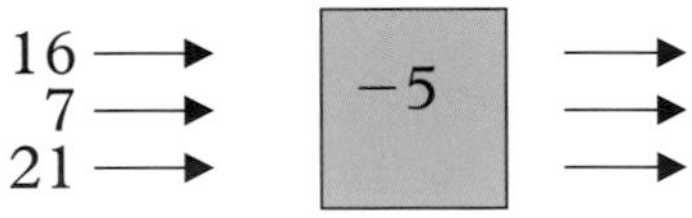

b

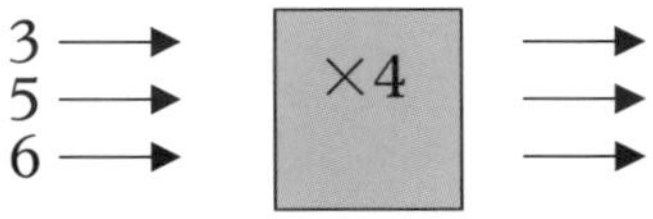

7 Write down the rule that belongs on this screen.

8 Copy the diagram.
Write down the robots' answers.

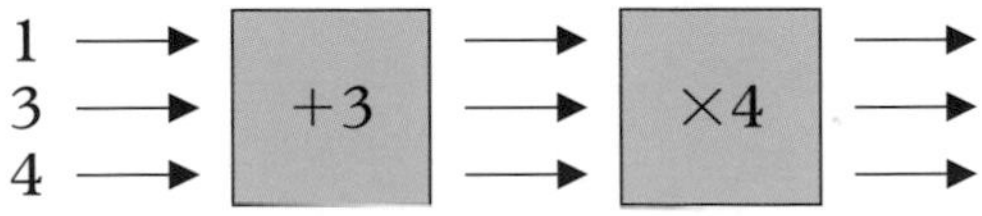

4 Arithmetic and the calculator

CORE

1 **Rounding up and rounding down**

2 **Mental arithmetic**

3 **Estimation**

4 **Priority of operations**

QUESTIONS

EXTENSION

SUMMARY

TEST YOURSELF

John Napier was born in Scotland in 1550.
One of the calculating methods he invented is known as Napier's Bones or Napier's Rods.

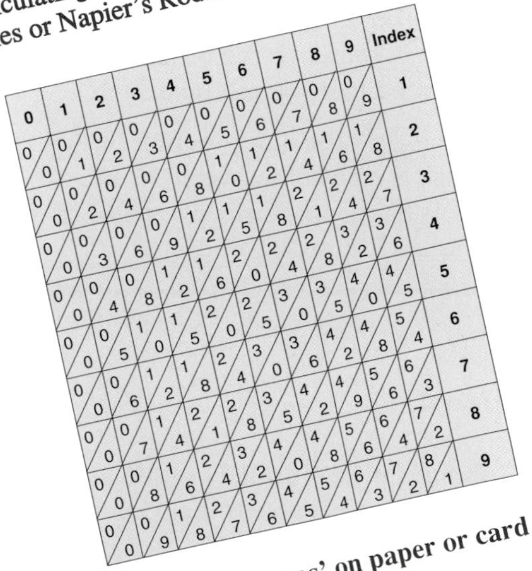

**You can make a set of 'bones' on paper or card like this.
Can you find out how they work?**

1 Rounding up and rounding down

36 000 people attend rock concert

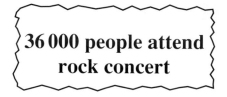

Look at this newspaper headline.
It doesn't mean that exactly 36 000 people attended the concert.
The number who attended might be 35 987 or 36 245.
The exact number has been rounded to the nearest thousand.

We can round numbers to the nearest 10.

Look at this number line. It shows the multiples of 10.

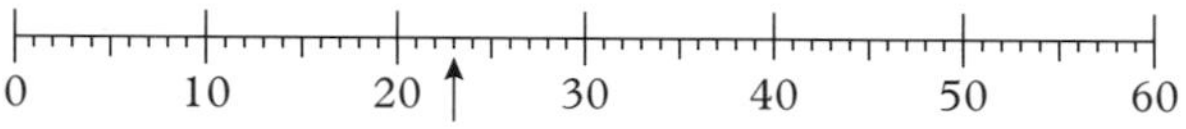

Copy the number line and put a mark on it to represent 23.
The mark is nearer to the 20 than to the 30.
23 is rounded down to 20.

Put a mark on your line to represent 58.
This mark is nearer to the 60 than to the 50.
58 is rounded to 60 to the nearest 10.

Put a mark on your line to represent 35.
This mark is halfway between 30 and 40.
When this happens we always round to the higher number.
35 is rounded up to 40.

Exercise 4:1

Round these numbers to the nearest 10.
Use a number line to help you.

1 49	**4** 65	**7** 124	**10** 672
2 81	**5** 34	**8** 346	**11** 535
3 27	**6** 8	**9** 285	**12** 198

Sometimes we round numbers to the nearest 100.

Look at this number line. It shows the multiples of 100.

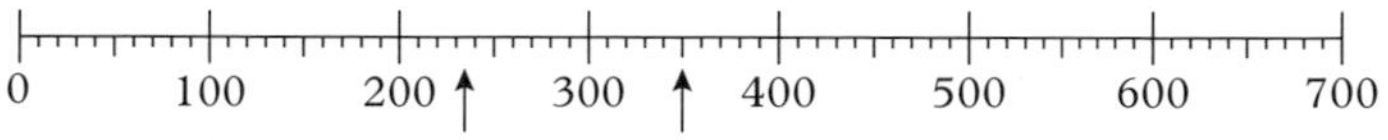

The mark that represents 236 is nearer to the 200 than to the 300.
So 236 is rounded to 200 to the nearest 100.

The mark that represents 350 is halfway between 300 and 400.
It is rounded to the higher number.
350 is rounded to 400.

Exercise 4:2

Round these numbers to the nearest 100.
Use a number line to help you.

1	269	**4**	407	**7**	399	**10**	357
2	617	**5**	850	**8**	563	**11**	88
3	770	**6**	849	**9**	111	**12**	993

Rounding in problems

We sometimes get a remainder when we divide.

Divide 9 by 2. The answer is 4 remainder 1.

Some questions must have a whole number as an answer.
You have to decide whether to round down or round up.

Examples

1 Aniseed balls cost 2 p each.
How many can you buy for 9 p?

$9 \div 2 = 4$, remainder 1.
4 aniseed balls cost 8 p. You are left with 1 p.
You cannot buy half an aniseed ball.
You can only buy 4 aniseed balls.

2 The PE department needs 9 squash balls.
Squash balls are sold in packs of 2 balls.
How many packs will the PE department need to buy?

4 packs contain 8 balls.
The PE department needs 1 more ball.
They will need to buy 5 packs to get 9 balls.

Exercise 4:3

Work through these questions.
Think very carefully whether to round up or down.

1 Chocolate bars cost 10 p each.
How many bars can I buy for 35 p?

Copy and complete this answer.
35 ÷ 10 = … remainder **5**
I can buy … chocolate bars.

2 A lift carries eight people.
Seventeen people are waiting to take the lift to the car park.
How many trips of the lift will it take to get all the people to the car park?

Copy and complete this answer.
17 ÷ 8 = … remainder …
It will take … trips of the lift.

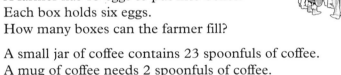

3 A farmer has 13 eggs to put into boxes.
Each box holds six eggs.
How many boxes can the farmer fill?

4 A small jar of coffee contains 23 spoonfuls of coffee.
A mug of coffee needs 2 spoonfuls of coffee.
How many mugs of coffee can be made from this jar?

5 A ferry-boat can carry 50 people at one time.
How many trips must the ferry-boat make to carry 110 people?

6 One tin of paint will cover 2 bikes.
How many tins of paint will be needed to cover 5 bikes?

7 One tin of tuna makes 20 sandwiches.
I need to make 50 sandwiches.
How many tins of tuna do I need to buy?

8 A packet of screws contains 12 screws.
I need 25 screws.
How many packets do I need to buy?

9 It takes 30 beads to make a necklace.
How many necklaces can I make with 75 beads?

• **10** A puppy eats 1 large tin of food every two days.
How many tins of food must I buy to feed the puppy for a week?

2 Mental arithmetic

How well do you know your times tables?

Exercise 4:4

W **1** Use a copy of the multiplication table.
Fill in as many answers as you can in 5 minutes.
Do not use a calculator.

2 Now use a calculator to check your answers.

3 Fill in any empty spaces in a different colour.
You may use a calculator to help you.

Exercise 4:5

Use your multiplication table for this exercise.

1 **a** Copy and complete:
$5 \times 10 = \ldots \quad 7 \times 10 = \ldots \quad 3 \times 10 = \ldots \quad 4 \times 10 = \ldots$

Can you see a pattern? What is it?

b Write down the answers to these.
$8 \times 10, \quad 9 \times 10, \quad 12 \times 10, \quad 15 \times 10$

2 **a** Look at your multiplication table.
Find the answers in the 5 column. They start 5, 10, 15, 20.
Can you see a pattern in these numbers?
What is it?

b Which of these numbers would you find in the 5 column if it was continued?
108 120 155 162 175

• **3** Can you find a line of symmetry for the multiplication table?
Where is it?

Example Look at these number facts:

$5 \times 4 = 20$ $20 \div 5 = 4$
$20 \div 4 = 5$

Exercise 4:6

1 Copy and complete these number facts:

a $3 \times 7 = 21$ $21 \div 7 = \ldots$
$21 \div \ldots = 7$

b $3 \times 8 = 24$ $24 \div \ldots = \ldots$
$24 \div \ldots = \ldots$

Look at your multiplication table.
Find the number 24. It appears twice.
We can get 24 by using 4 and 6 as well as by using 3 and 8.

$4 \times 6 = 24$ $24 \div 6 = 4$
$24 \div 4 = 6$

$3 \times 8 = 24$ $24 \div 8 = 3$
$24 \div 3 = 8$

We have four division facts for 24.

W **2** Look at your copy of the division table.
The division facts for 24 have been entered.
Complete the table on the worksheet.
Remember there may be four division facts for some numbers.
Use your multiplication table to help you.

Some spaces will still be empty. Try to fill these using your calculator.

3 Estimation

Estimating

Wei Yen buys 1 chocolate bar and 1 packet of mints.
Harry adds 28 and 19 and asks for 83 p.
Wei Yen thinks that this is wrong.

Wei Yen can't add 28 p and 19 p in her head.
She does an easier sum. She rounds 28 to 30 and 19 to 20

30 + 20 = 50

Wei Yen knows that Harry has made a mistake because 83 p is not close to 50 p.

To make an estimate:

Step 1: Round the numbers to the nearest 10 or 100.
Step 2: Do the simple sum in your head.
Step 3: Write down your estimate.

Examples

1 Add together 119 and 56.

Estimate: 100 + 60 = 160
160 is the estimate.
Calculation: 119 + 56 = 175

The answer 175 is close to the estimate of 160.
It is probably correct.

2 Find 221 − 135
Estimate: 200 − 100 = 100
100 is the estimate.

Scott does the calculation.
Calculation: 221 − 135 = 26

Scott's answer 26 is not close to the estimate. This tells him the answer 26 is wrong.
Scott must do the calculation again.
221 − 135 = 86

The answer is close to the estimate.
It is probably correct.

Exercise 4:7

1 Copy the table and fill it in.
The first problem has been done for you.

	Problem	Estimate	Correct answer
a	69 + 34	70 + 30 = 100	103
b	73 + 19		
c	29 + 38		
d	269 + 132		
e	67 − 15		
f	491 − 187		
g	508 − 392		

We can make estimates for multiplication sums.

2 Copy the table and fill it in.
Some have been done for you.

Problem	Estimate	Correct answer
28 × 9	30 × 10 = 300	252
13 × 8		
19 × 9		
18 × 8		
56 × 11	60 × 10 = 600	
47 × 11		
35 × 12		

Problem-solving with a calculator

When you are given a problem it is important to read it carefully.

Step 1: Imagine what is happening in the question.
Write down the facts given to you.

Step 2: Decide whether to add, subtract, multiply or divide.

Step 3: Work out an estimate for the answer.

Step 4: Work out and write down the answer.
Check this answer with the estimate.
If it doesn't agree, start again.

Example

Stanthorne High School cricket team scored 29 runs before lunch. After lunch they score another 37 runs.
What is their total score?

Step 1:

37 more runs.

Step 2: We need to add.

Step 3: 29 + 37
Estimate: 30 + 40 = 70 The estimate is 70.

Step 4: 29 + 37 = 66
66 is close to 70.
It is probably correct.

Exercise 4:8

1 Camilla has saved £28.
Her mother gives her another £9.
How much money has she now?

Copy and complete this answer.
Step 2 We need to …
Step 3 28 + 9
Estimate: 30 + 10 = …
Step 4 28 + 9 = …
She now has £…

2 Lucy collected 32 empty cans for recycling.
Paul collected 59 cans.
How many cans did they collect altogether?

3 Malachi has 28 marbles and Carly has 41 marbles.
How many marbles do they have altogether?

4 Add together 182 and 436.

5 Find a number that is 21 more than 12.

6 What is 42 plus 29?

7 Year 7 pupils went to Alton Towers in 2 coaches.
There were 52 pupils on one coach and 43 pupils on the other.
How many pupils were there altogether?

8 Zeta had scored 249 on a pinball machine.
She scored 325 with her next ball.
What was her new total?

Example Melanie has £89 in her Savings Account.
She takes out £37 to buy a personal stereo.
How much does she have left?

Step 1:

A/c no: 75621A/42D		
Paid in	Withdrawn	Balance
		£89

Step 2: We need to subtract.

Step 3: 89 − 37
Estimate: 90 − 40 = 50 The estimate is £50.

Step 4: 89 − 37 = 52
£52 is close to £50.

Exercise 4:9

1 Judy has 28 chocolates.
She eats 9 of them.
How many does she have left?

Copy and complete this answer.
Step 2 We need to …
Step 3 28 − 9
Estimate: 30 − 10 = …
Step 4 28 − 9 = …
She has … left.

2 Rudi had 134 model animals in his collection.
His baby brother broke 19 of them.
How many does he have left?

3 Take 321 from 680.

4 What is the difference between 78 and 35?

5 Theo is 152 cm tall.
Michael is 139 cm tall.
What is the difference in their heights?

6 If I add a number to 63 I get 98.
What is the number?

7 When I add two numbers I get 263.
One number is 142.
What is the other number?

8 A rope is 88 metres long.
A length of 67 metres is cut off.
What length is left?

Example

Kyle has 12 conkers.
Zoë has nine times as many.
How many conkers does Zoë have?

Step 1:

Step 2: We need to multiply.

Step 3: 12×9
Estimate: $10 \times 10 = 100$ The estimate is 100.

Step 4: $12 \times 9 = 108$
108 is close to 100.

Exercise 4:10

1 A pack of playing cards contains 52 cards.
How many cards are there in 8 packs?

Copy and complete this answer.
Step 2 We need to …
Step 3 52×8
Estimate: … × … = …
Step 4 52×8 = …
There are … cards in 8 packs.

2 Rula is 146 cm tall.
She climbs a tree that is seven times as tall as she is.
How tall is the tree?

3 A student was training to run the marathon.
He ran 22 miles every day for 12 days.
How far did he run altogether?

4 Multiply 63 by 21.

5 There are 24 hours in a day.
How many hours are there in 28 days?

6 There are twelve eggs in each box of eggs.
How many eggs are there in 38 boxes?

7 Each box of fireworks costs £18.
How much will 9 boxes cost?

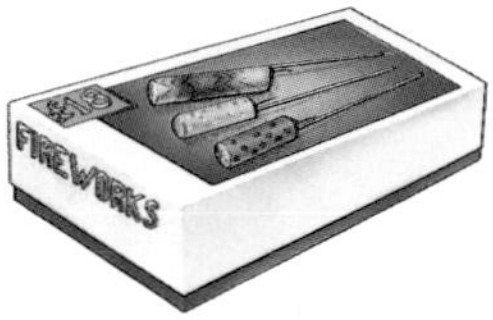

8 There are 18 rows of chairs in the school hall.
Each row contains 24 chairs.
How many chairs are there altogether?

Example There are 12 children at a party.
They share a box of 108 sweets equally between them.
How many sweets does each child get?

Step 1:

12 children

Step 2: We need to divide.

Step 3: 108 ÷ 12
Estimate: 100 ÷ 10 = 10 The estimate is 10.

Step 4: 108 ÷ 12 = 9
9 is close to 10.

Exercise 4:11

1 Nine scouts earned 477p.
How much did each scout earn?

Copy and complete:
Step 2: We need to …
Step 3: $477 \div 9$
Estimate: $\ldots \div \ldots = \ldots$
Step 4: $477 \div 9 = \ldots$
Each scout earned …p.

2 A tray of 121 biscuits is to be shared by eleven boys.
How many biscuits does each boy get?

3 £184 is to be shared equally between eight prize winners.
How much does each get?

4 A 117 cm length of string is cut into pieces of length 13 cm.
How many pieces are there?

5 A roll of ribbon of length 312 cm is cut into twelve pieces.
What is the length of each piece?

6 A farmer has 84 kg of potatoes.
He puts them into bags containing 12 kg.
How many bags does he fill?

7 A shopkeeper has 132 eggs.
She puts them into boxes of 12 eggs.
How many boxes does she fill?

8 How many days (24 hours) are there in 192 hours?

4 Priority of operations

Here are two calculators.

Scientific calculator

Simple calculator

These two calculators work differently.

If you do $2 + 5 \times 3$ on the scientific calculator you get 17.
If you do $2 + 5 \times 3$ on the simple calculator you get 21.

Can you see why?

> The scientific calculator does **5 × 3** first then + **2**.

> The simple calculator does **2 + 5** first then × 3.

We should only have one answer. The simple calculator is wrong.

The rule is:
Always do multiplication and division *before* addition and subtraction.

Examples	**1**	$3 \times 4 + 2$	We do the multiplication first.
		$12 + 2$	Then we do the addition.
		14	The answer is 14.
	2	$7 - 12 \div 3$	We do the division first.
		$7 - 4$	Then we do the subtraction.
		3	The answer is 3.

Exercise 4:12

Copy and complete these questions.
Do the red part first.
The first question has been done for you.

1 $2 \times 3 + 4$
$= 6 + 4$
$= 10$

2 $5 + 2 \times 4$
$= 5 +$
$=$

3 $6 + 4 \times 7$
$=$
$=$

4 $12 \div 6 + 2$

5 $10 - 6 \div 2$

6 $25 - 16 \div 8$

Copy these questions. Underline the part to be done first.
Then work out the answer.

7 $4 \times 3 + 2$

8 $5 + 4 \times 10$

9 $6 + 5 \times 4$

10 $14 \div 2 - 5$

11 $16 \div 4 + 3$

12 $17 - 15 \div 5$

13 $11 \times 5 - 3$

14 $12 - 9 \div 3$

15 $6 \times 7 + 9$

16 $8 \div 4 + 3 \times 5$
$= \dots + \dots$
$=$

17 $12 \times 3 - 8 \div 2$
$= \dots - \dots$
$=$

18 $20 \div 5 + 12 \div 2$

19 $6 \times 2 - 10 \div 5$

20 $14 \div 2 - 2 \times 3$

21 $7 \times 7 + 18 \div 9$

Sometimes we want the addition or subtraction done first.
We use brackets to show this.

The rule is:
Always do the brackets first.

Examples **1**

$6 \times (3 + 4)$ Do the bracket first.
$= 6 \times 7$ Then do the multiplication.
$= 42$ The answer is 42.

2

$(6 + 8) \div (5 + 2) + 10$ Do the brackets first.
$= 14 \div 7 + 10$ Then do the division
$= 2 + 10$ Then do the addition.
$= 12$ The answer is 12.

Exercise 4:13

Copy and complete these calculations.

1 $(3 + 2) \times 4$
$= \dots \times 4$
$=$

2 $(5 + 3) \div 2$
$= \dots \div 2$
$=$

3 $(12 - 4) \times 6$
$=$
$=$

4 $(14 - 8) \times 2$

5 $(6 + 4) \div 5$

6 $12 \div (7 - 4)$

7 $(6 + 4) \div (5 - 3)$

8 $(7 - 4) \times (3 + 5)$

9 $(11 + 5) \div (10 - 2)$

10 $(2 + 6) \times (14 - 12)$

11 $(18 - 6) \div (6 - 3)$

12 $6 + 3 \times 7 - (4 + 5)$

You can use the codeword BODMAS to remind you what to do first.

This reminds you to do	**B**rackets first
then powers	**O**f
Then do	**D**ivision
and	**M**ultiplication
Then do	**A**ddition
and	**S**ubtraction

Powers of

You sometimes have to multiply a number by itself many times
$2 \times 2 \times 2 \times 2 \times 2$

A quick way of writing this is 2^5
The small number 5 is called a **power**.
It tells you how many twos are multiplied together.

Power 4^3 The **power** '3' tells you how many fours are multiplied together.
$4^3 = 4 \times 4 \times 4$

Exercise 4:14

1 Write these numbers using a power.

a $2 \times 2 \times 2$
b 5×5
c $6 \times 6 \times 6 \times 6 \times 6$
d $10 \times 10 \times 10 \times 10$
e $3 \times 3 \times 3 \times 3 \times 3 \times 3 \times 3$

Example Find the value of: **a** 4^2 **b** 2^5

a $4^2 = 4 \times 4$
$= 16$

b $2^5 = 2 \times 2 \times 2 \times 2 \times 2$
$= 32$

2 Use your calculator to find the value of:

a 2^3
b 8^2
c 5^2
d 3^4
e 10^3
f 7^3
g 4^3

1 Round these numbers to the nearest 10.
a 57 **b** 43 **c** 22 **d** 125

2 Round these numbers to the nearest 100.
a 536 **b** 692 **c** 450 **d** 337

3 Lisa had 23 CDs in her collection.
She was given 3 more CDs for her birthday.
How many CDs does she have now?

4 Ben went to town with £5.
He spent £2 on a burger.
How much did he have left?

5 Paula has £4 and Neil has £7.
How much do they have altogether?

6 A piece of wire is 38 metres long.
It is cut into pieces 2 metres long.
How many pieces are there?

7 A sack of potatoes contains 150 kg.
It is used to fill 5 kg bags.
How many bags will be filled?

8 Balraj is cycling to school.
The distance to school is 17 km.
He has already cycled 9 km.
How much further does he have to go?

9 A bag of sugar weighs 2 kg.
How much will 27 bags weigh?

10 A chocolate bar costs 23 p.
How much will 3 chocolate bars cost?

11 Last week I had £129 in my savings account.
This week I withdrew £25 from my account.
How much is still left in my account?

A/c no: 75621A/42D		
Paid in	Withdrawn	Balance
	£25	£129

12 A bus stopped at the bus stop.
12 people got off.
There were now 31 people on the bus.
How many were on the bus before it stopped?

13 Ruth's dogs eat two large tins of dog food between them each day.
Each tin costs 36 p.
How much does it cost to feed the dogs each day?

14 A holiday for 5 people costs £1765.
How much does it cost for one person?

15 A factory makes 270 T-shirts each day.
How many T-shirts will the factory make in 5 days?

16 Do these calculations. Do not use a calculator.

a $7 \times 2 + 5$
b $18 - 2 \times 3$
c $4 + 12 \div 6$
d $10 + 6 \times 4$
e $3 \times (4 + 2)$
f $(10 - 6) \div 2$

17 Use a calculator to do these calculations.

a $14 + 15 \times 12$
b $57 - 360 \div 20$
c $27 \times 23 - 16 \times 12$
d $27 \times (38 - 13)$
e $(7 + 8) \div (21 - 16)$
f $(567 - 245) \times (216 - 188)$

18 Write these numbers using a power.

a $7 \times 7 \times 7 \times 7$
b $4 \times 4 \times 4$
d $2 \times 2 \times 2 \times 2 \times 2$
e $1 \times 1 \times 1 \times 1 \times 1 \times 1 \times 1$

19 Use your calculator to find the value of:

a 6^3 **b** 2^4 **c** 5^3 **d** 9^2

20 Use your calculator to find the value of:

a $2^3 + 3^5$ **b** $4^5 - 2^5$ **c** $3^4 \times 5^3$

1 Copy the table and fill it in.
The first line is done for you.

Number	To the nearest ten	To the nearest hundred
369	370	400
814		
386		
855		
632		
208		
197		
709		
550		
961		

2 Jars of jam are packed in boxes of 36.
How many boxes are needed to pack 972 jars?

3 Eight people won a prize on the football pools.
The prize was worth £125 000.
How much did each person get?

4 Alison bought a second-hand car.
It had done 23 651 miles before she bought it.
After she had driven it for a year it had done 31 258 miles.
How many miles did she drive during that year?

5 The Smith family have just come back from holiday.
They take the films from their camera to the shop for developing.
The table shows how much the shop charges.

Number of exposures	12	24	36
Cost of processing	£3.99	£4.99	£5.99

They have 6 films. One is 36 exposures, three are 24 exposures and two are 12 exposures.

a How much will it cost to have their films processed?
b Which size of film gives the cheapest price per photo?

6 This is a well-known saying:
'Thirty days has September, April, June and November.
All the rest have 31 except February alone.
It has 28 in a normal year and 29 in a leap year'.

How many days are there in:

a August?
b July?
c November and December?
d The first three months of a leap year?
e The third and fourth months?
f March, October and December?
g The last six months?
h The first and seventh months?

7 Do these calculations.

a $2 \times 7 - 5$
b $8 - 2 \times 3$
c $2 \times 12 \div 6$
d $9 \times (8^2 - 6^2)$
e $4 \times 5 - 6 \times 3$
f $18 \div 2 + 6 \times 7$
g $(16 - 7) \times (13 - 4)$
h $(215 - 45) \div (58 - 41)$
i $(316 - 214) \div (64 - 13)$
j $(32 + 14) \times (56 + 12)$
k $(86 + 32) \times (24 - 15)$
l $(6^3 - 2^5) \times (130 - 5^3)$

8 A supermarket sells two brands of cat food, Pussdins and Kittimeat.
Pussdins is 37 p per can and there is a special offer, 'Buy any 5 – get the sixth free'.
Kittimeat is 36 p per can. A set of 12 cans is on offer for £4.20.
Which is the better buy?
Show your working.

9 A DIY shop sells nails at 44 p for 4 oz. A local hardware store sells the same nails for 65 p for 6 oz.

a I want 12 oz of nails.
Which shop should I choose?
How much will the nails cost?

b I want 8 oz of nails.
Which shop should I choose?
How much will the nails cost?

- **Rounding**

To round a number to the nearest 10 we look at a number line. We decide which multiple of 10 it is closer to.
If the number is half-way between two multiples of 10 we always choose the higher one.

To the nearest 10: 24 becomes 20
25 becomes 30
28 becomes 30

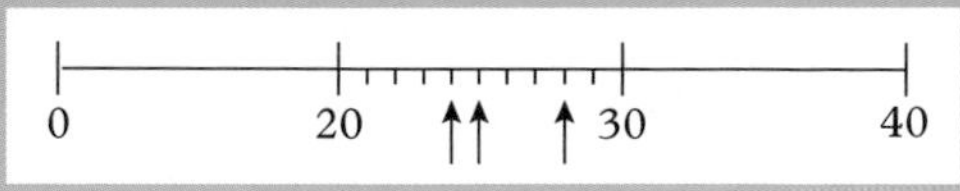

To round a number to the nearest 100 we decide which multiple of 100 it is closer to.
If it is half-way between two multiples of 100 we always choose the higher one.

To the nearest 100: 240 becomes 200
250 becomes 300
280 becomes 300

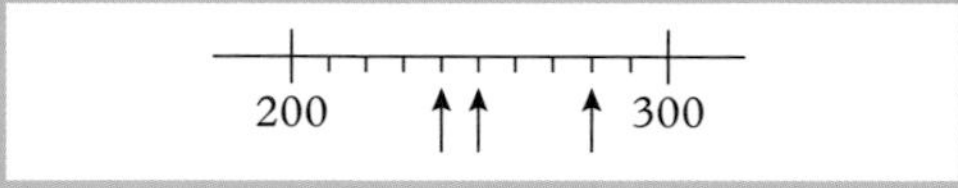

- **Estimating**

The calculator will show the wrong answer if you key in the wrong number by mistake.
You should always make an estimate of the answer in your head.

21×39 Estimate: $20 \times 40 = 800$
Calculation: $21 \times 39 = 819$

- **Power**

4^3 The **power** 3 tells you how many fours are multiplied together.

- **BODMAS**

The codeword BODMAS reminds you what to do first:
Brackets, Powers **O**f, **D**ivide, **M**ultiply, **A**dd, **S**ubtract.

Examples **1** $2 + 7 \times 10 = 2 + 70$ Do the multiplication first.
$= 72$

2 $15 \div 3 - 2 = 5 - 2$ Do the division first.
$= 3$

3 $22 - (6 + 4) = 22 - 10$ Do the bracket first.
$= 12$

4 $5^2 - 3 \times 6 = 25 - 3 \times 6$ Do the power first ($5^2 = 5 \times 5 = 25$)
$= 25 - 18$ Do the multiplication next.
$= 7$

1 Round these numbers to the nearest 10.

a 38 **b** 85 **c** 253

2 Round these numbers to the nearest 100.

a 449 **b** 681 **c** 250

3 **a** Gina had 25 marbles.
She won 3 more.
How many has she got now?

b Justin has 3 boxes.
Each box contains 25 cassettes.
How many cassettes does he have altogether?

4 **a** Peter had £12.
He spent £7.
How much does he have left?

b Grandma sends the twins £24 for their birthday.
How much does each get?

Do these calculations.

5 **a** $20 \div 2 - 8$ **b** $24 + 2 \times 4$ **c** $24 - 2 \times 7$

6 **a** $(5 + 4) \times 2$ **b** $(16 - 11) \times 3$ **c** $60 \div (7 + 5)$

7 **a** $5 \times 6 + 7 \times 8$ **b** $9 \times 3 - 3 \times 5$ **c** $15 + 10 \div 5$

8 **a** 3^3 **b** 5^4 **c** $2^3 + 8^2$

5 Shape and construction

CORE

QUESTIONS

EXTENSION

SUMMARY

TEST YOURSELF

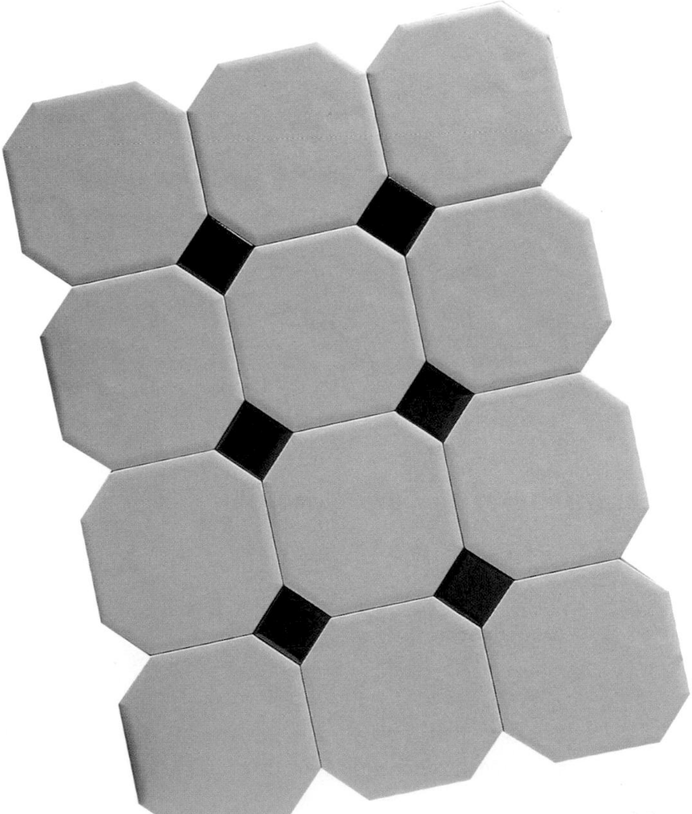

1 Names of polygons

Shapes can be seen everywhere. The design of this building uses shape for decoration.

A clock face has twelve points equally spaced around its edge.

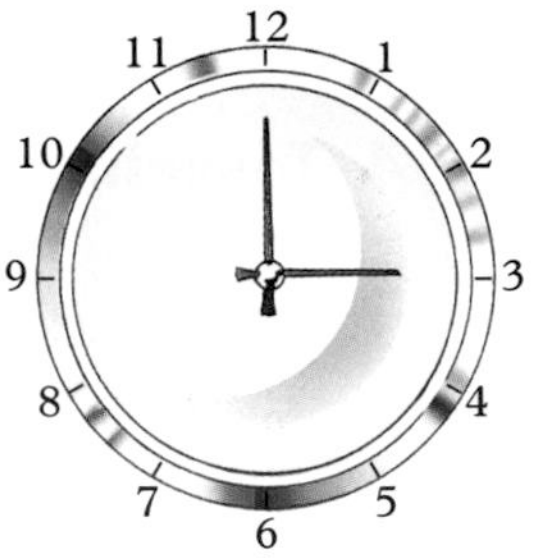

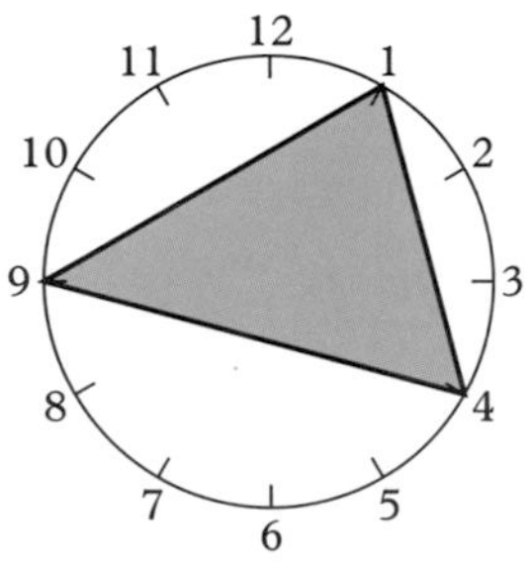

Join the points:
1 → 4 → 9 → 1
to get a triangle.

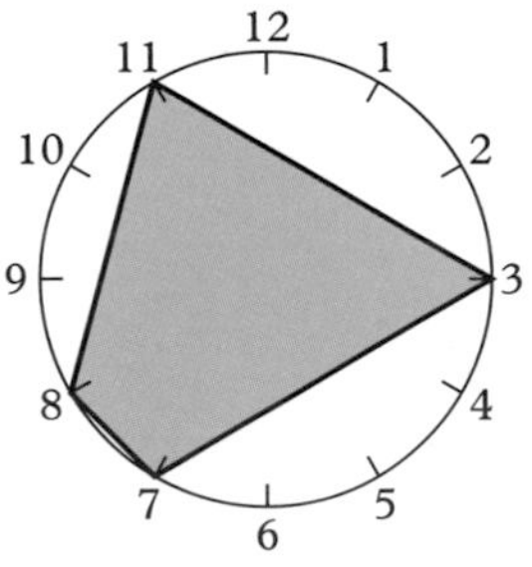

Join the points:
11 → 3 → 7 → 8 → 11
to get a quadrilateral.

Exercise 5:1 Special triangles

W You will need copies of a clock face for this exercise.

1 **a** Join the points:
(1) 12 → 4 → 8 → 12
(2) 1 → 5 → 9 → 1
(3) 3 → 7 → 11 → 3

b What do you notice about the sides of the triangles in part **a**?

c Draw a triangle like those in part **a**. Start at 2.

2 **a** Join the points:

(1) $2 \rightarrow 4 \rightarrow 9 \rightarrow 2$ (3) $11 \rightarrow 1 \rightarrow 6 \rightarrow 11$

(2) $6 \rightarrow 12 \rightarrow 3 \rightarrow 6$ (4) $10 \rightarrow 4 \rightarrow 1 \rightarrow 10$

b What do you notice about the sides of the triangles in part **a**?

Equilateral triangle An **equilateral triangle** has three equal sides.

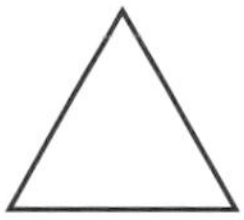

Isosceles triangle An **isosceles** triangle has two equal sides.

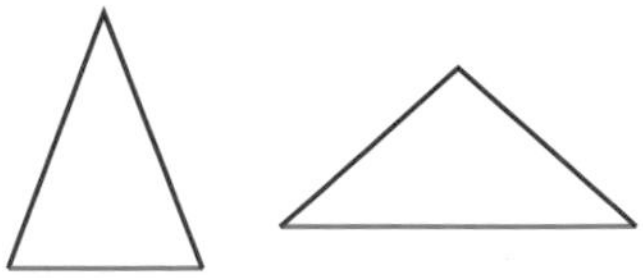

Scalene triangle A **scalene triangle** has no equal sides.

---

3 Use a ruler to measure the sides of these triangles.

a Copy and complete:

a = ? cm
b = ? cm
c = ? cm

The triangle has ? equal sides.

It is an .... triangle.

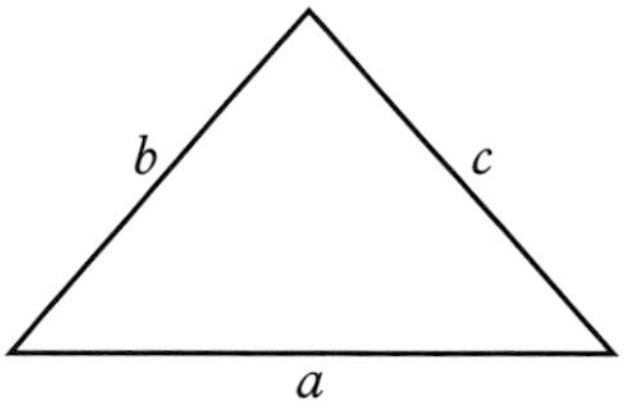

b Copy and complete:

d = ? cm
e = ? cm
f = ? cm

The triangle has ? equal sides.

It is a .... triangle.

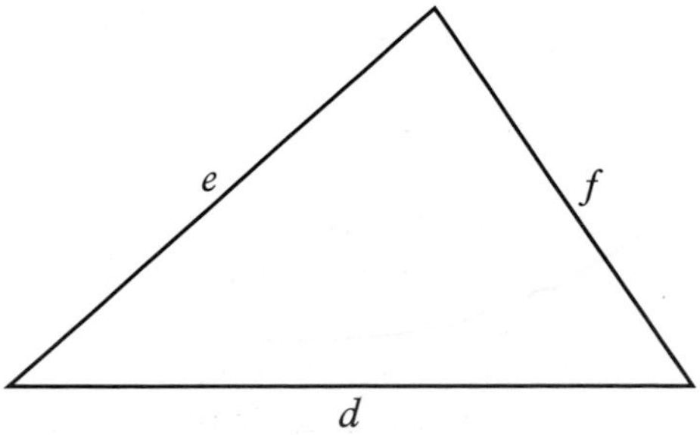

c Copy and complete:

g = ? cm
h = ? cm
i = ? cm

The triangle has ? equal sides.

It is an .... triangle.

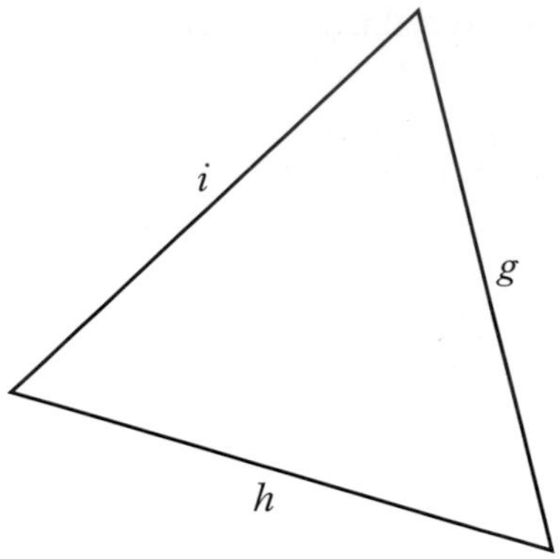

d Copy and complete:

j = ? cm
k = ? cm
l = ? cm

The triangle has ? equal sides.

It is an .... triangle.

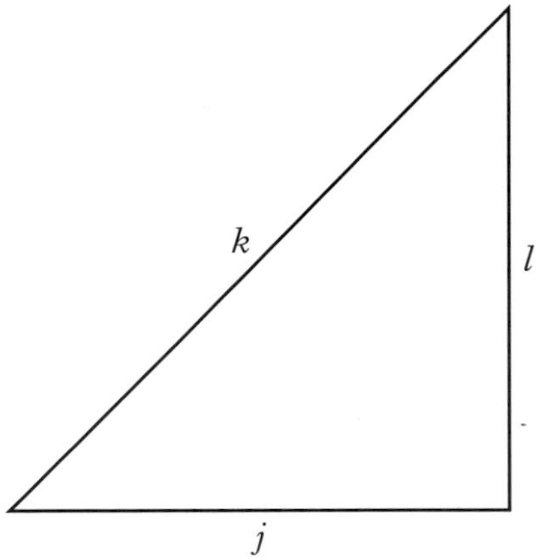

Quadrilateral

A **quadrilateral** has four sides.
Here are some special quadrilaterals.

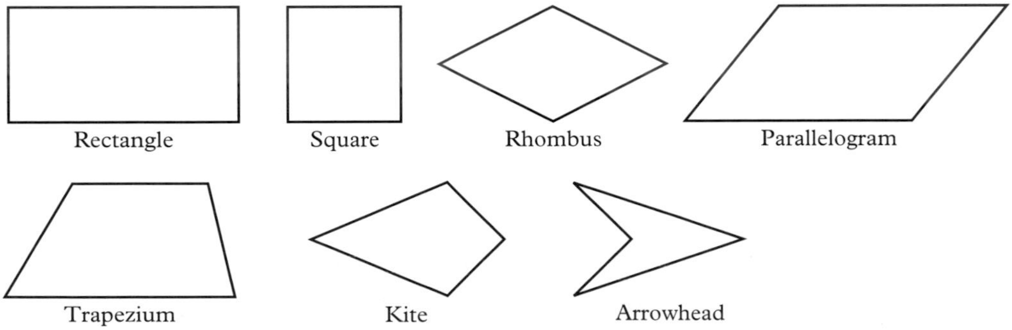

Exercise 5:2 Special quadrilaterals

1 You will need copies of a clock face for this question.

a Join the points:

(1) 2 → 4 → 8 → 10 → 2

(2) 1 → 3 → 5 → 11 → 1

(3) 2 → 6 → 10 → 12 → 2

(4) 12 → 3 → 6 → 9 → 12

(5) 4 → Centre → 8 → 12 → 4

(6) 11 → 1 → Centre → 9 → 11

(7) 10 → 2 → (extend line beyond 2)
4 → 3 → (extend line beyond 3)
4 → 8 → (extend line beyond 8)
10 → 9 → (extend line beyond 9)

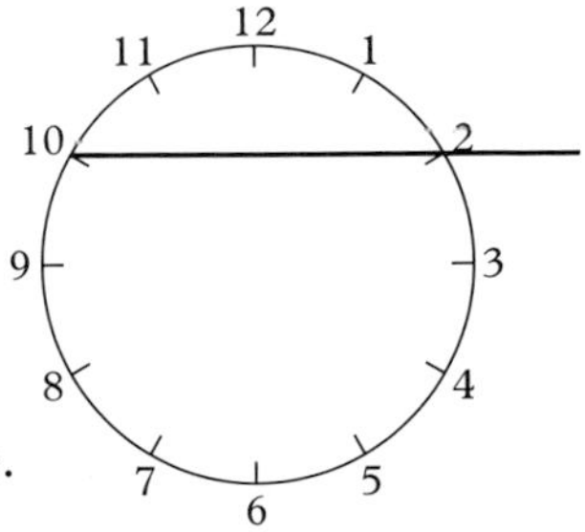

b Label each quadrilateral with its special name.

c The colours on these shapes show equal sides.
Use colours to show equal sides on your shapes.

Parallel

Parallel lines never meet.
They stay the same distance apart.

Parallel lines

Parallel lines on diagrams are shown with arrows.

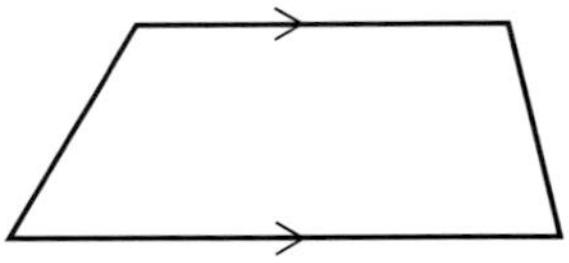

Trapezium

Two pairs of parallel lines need extra arrows.

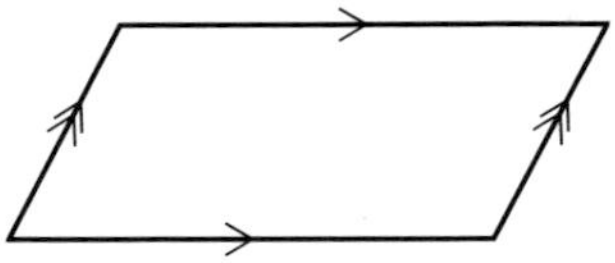

Parallelogram

---

2 Write down which of these pairs of lines are parallel.

a

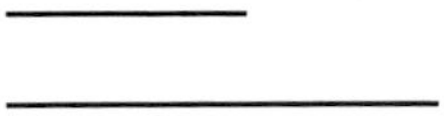

b

c

• **3** You need your answers to question **1** for this question.

a Look at your trapezium and your parallelogram.
Mark their sides with arrows like the examples.

b Find the pairs of parallel lines on other special quadrilaterals.
Mark them with arrows.

c Write down the quadrilaterals that have:
(1) two pairs of parallel sides
(2) one pair of parallel sides
(3) no parallel sides.

Shapes can have more than four sides.

Polygon

A **polygon** is a shape with straight sides.
Triangles and quadrilaterals are polygons.

Some other polygons have special names.

Number of sides	Name of polygon
3	Triangle
4	Quadrilateral
5	Pentagon
6	Hexagon
8	Octagon

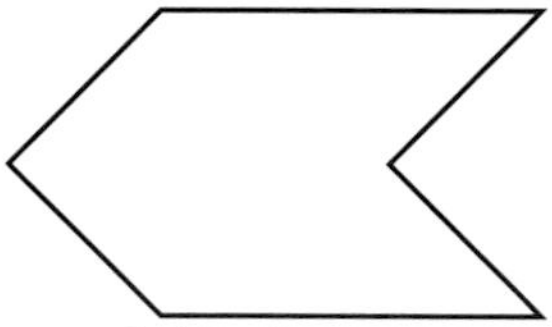

6 sides: hexagon

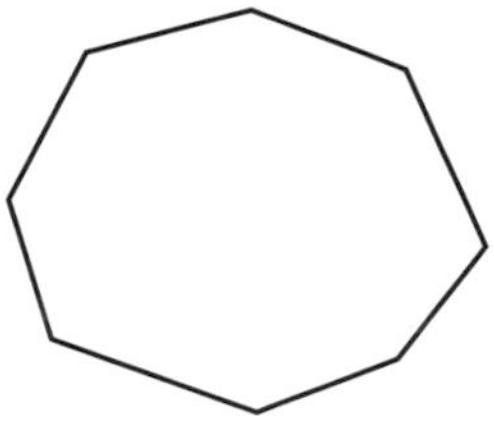

8 sides: octagon

Exercise 5:3

1

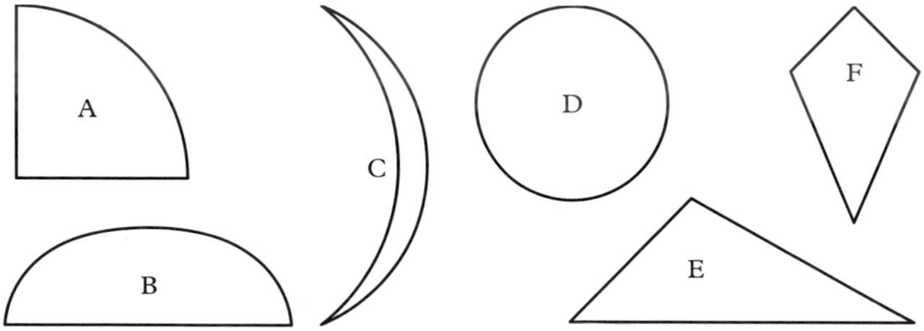

a Write down the shapes that are polygons.

b Write down the shapes that have both curved edges and straight edges.

c Write down the shapes that have only curved edges.

2

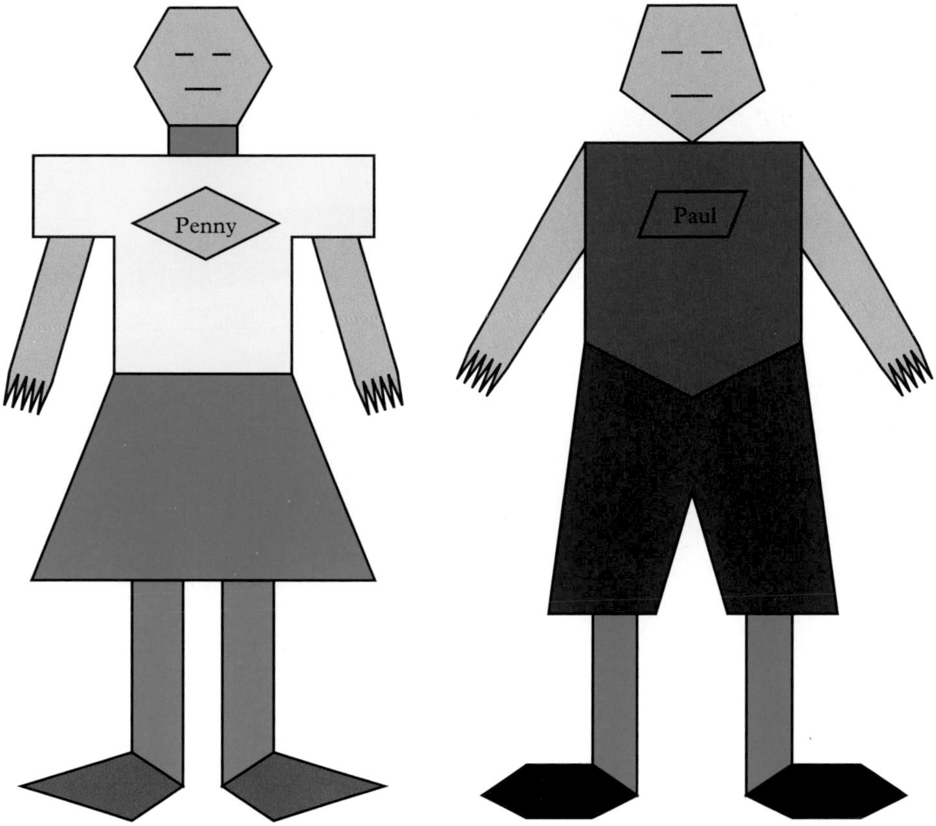

Penny and Paul are made from polygons.
Copy the tables and fill them in.
Give the special names of the quadrilaterals.

a Penny

Description	Number of sides	Name of polygon
(1) Neck		
(2) Head		
(3) T-shirt		
(4) Name badge		
(5) Skirt		
(6) Shoes		

b Paul

Description	Number of sides	Name of polygon
(7) Head		
(8) T-shirt		
(9) Name badge		
(10) Trousers		
(11) Legs		
(12) Shoes		

2 More about polygons

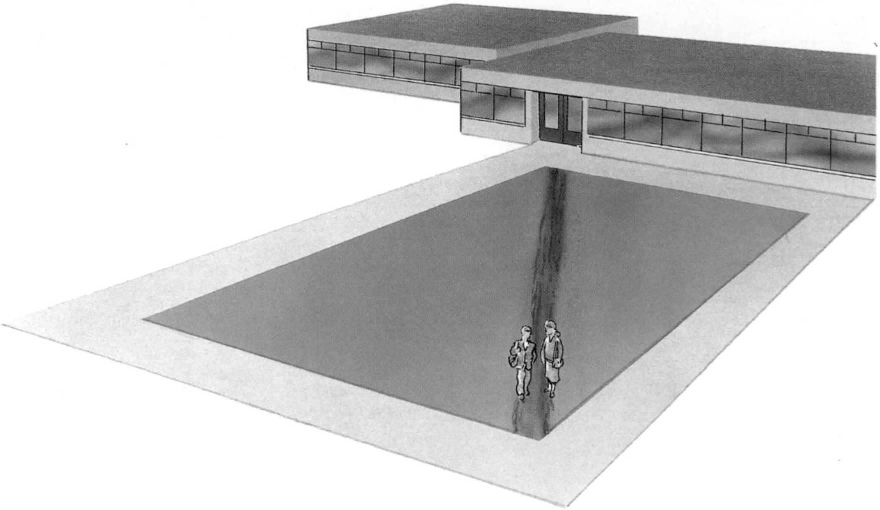

In front of Stanthorne High School is a rectangle of grass.
The pupils should go round the edge.
They like to take a short-cut from one corner to another.

Vertex

Vertices

A point or corner of a shape is called a **vertex**. For more than one point we say **vertices**.

A triangle has three vertices.

Diagonal

A line joining two vertices is a **diagonal**.

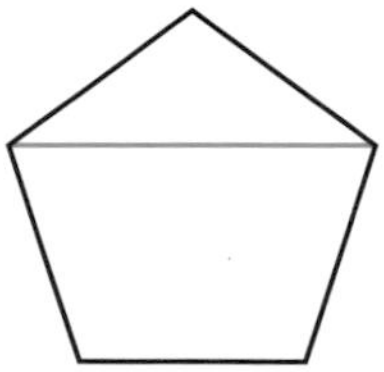

One diagonal is drawn in this pentagon.

Exercise 5:4

1 Trace these shapes:

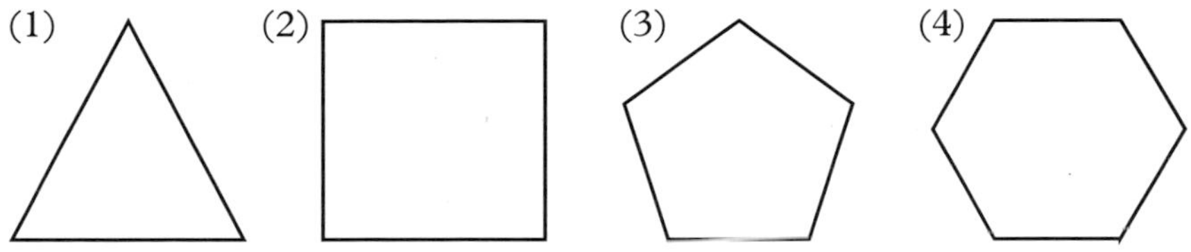

a Draw all the diagonals in each shape.
Make sure each vertex is joined to every other vertex.

b Copy this table and fill it in.

Name of shape	Number of sides	Number of vertices	Number of diagonals
(1)			
(2)			
(3)			
(4)			

● **2** Write down the number of vertices in:
a a rectangle
b an octagon
c a 20-sided polygon.

The shapes in question **1** are all regular polygons.

Regular

Regular polygons have all their sides the same length.
Also all their vertices look the same.

An equilateral triangle and a square are special regular polygons.

---

3 Which of these shapes are regular polygons?

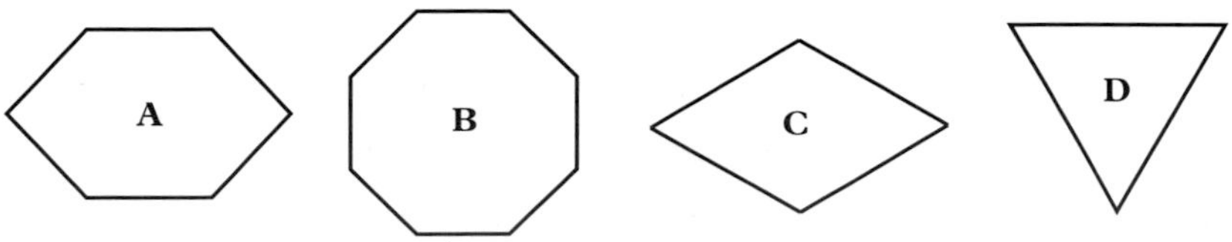

The arrowhead has one of its diagonals outside its shape.
It is concave.

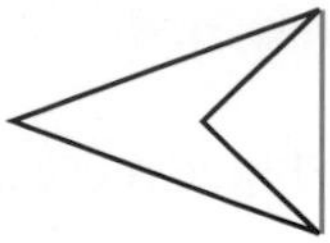

Convex

Concave

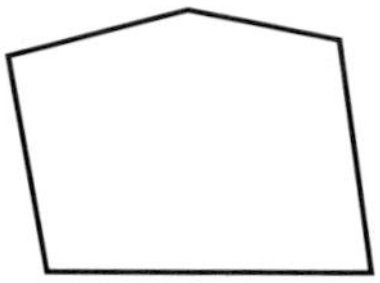

Convex polygon

These sides make this shape **concave**. They go into the shape (like a cave).

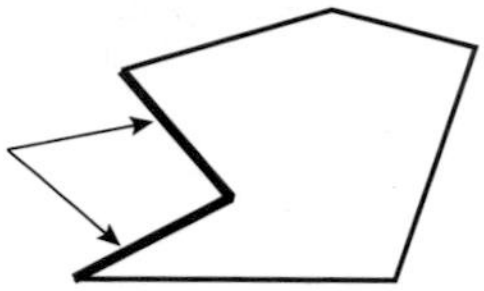

Concave polygon

---

4 Sketch these polygons and label them **concave** or **convex**.

a

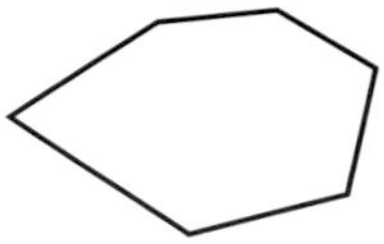

b

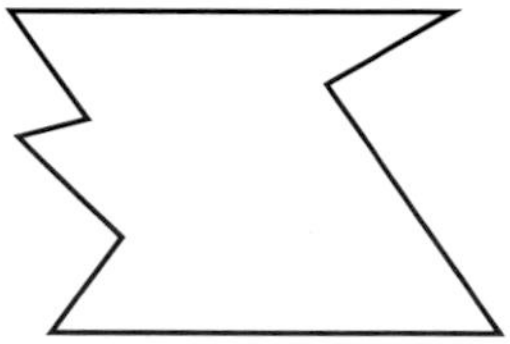

c

Exercise 5:5 Symmetry in polygons

1 Trace these triangles:

(1)

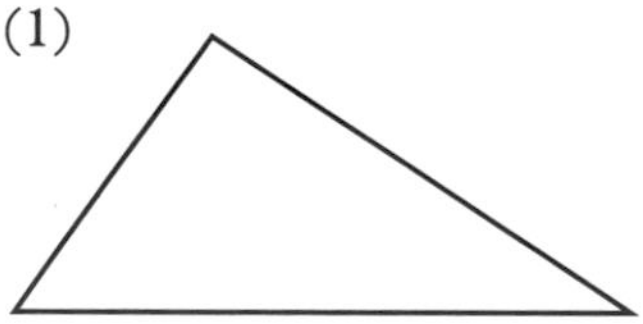

(2)

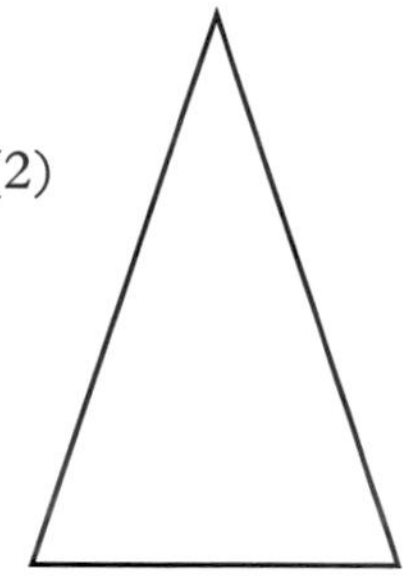

(3)

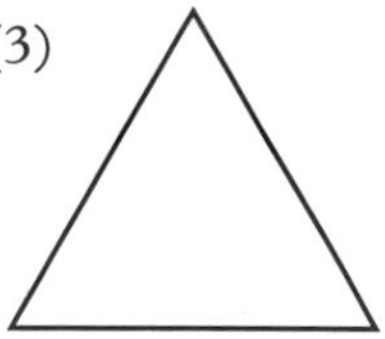

a Draw all the lines of symmetry on the triangles.
b Copy this table and fill it in.

Name of triangle	Number of lines of symmetry
(1)	
(2)	
(3)	

c Is there a triangle with two lines of symmetry?

2 Trace these special quadrilaterals:

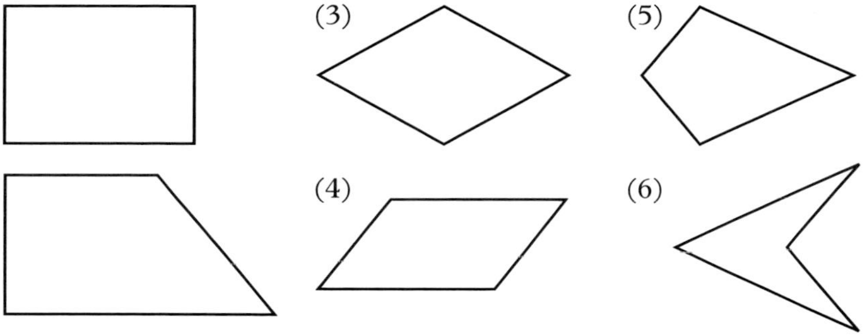

a Draw the diagonals of each special quadrilateral.
b Which of the diagonals are lines of symmetry?
Go over these lines in red.
c Write down the quadrilateral that has equal diagonals.
d The rectangle has lines of symmetry which are not diagonals.
Draw these lines of symmetry.

● **3** Trace the regular polygons in Exercise 5:4 question **1**.
a Draw **all** the lines of symmetry on the regular polygons.
b Polygons can have three kinds of lines of symmetry.

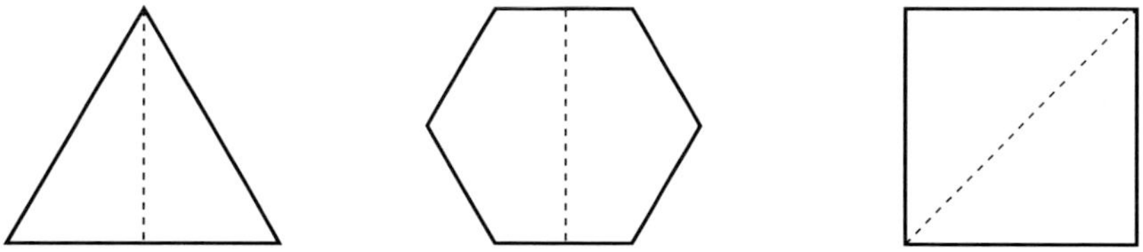

Vertex to side   Side to side   Diagonal

Copy this table and fill it in for your regular polygons.

		Lines of symmetry			
Number of sides	Name of regular polygon	Vertex to side	Side to side	Diagonal	Total
3	Equilateral triangle	3	0	0	3
4					

c Write down the total number of lines of symmetry for a regular octagon.

- **4** Use tracing paper and the regular polygons in Exercise 5:4 question **1**.
  a Write down the order of rotational symmetry of:
  (1) an equilateral triangle
  (2) a square
  (3) a regular pentagon
  (4) a regular hexagon.
  b Write down the order of rotational symmetry of a regular octagon.

This rectangle has its vertices labelled ABCD.

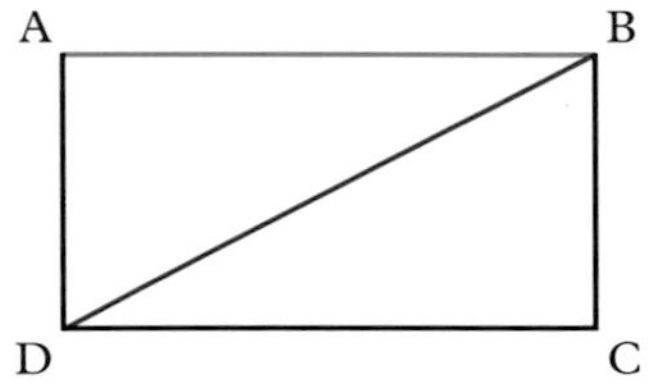

The green side is AB.
The red diagonal is DB.

Exercise 5:6

1 Write down the letter name of:
a the green side
b the blue side
c the red diagonal.

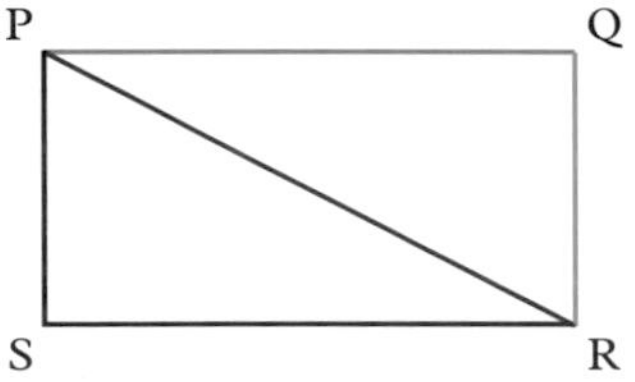

2 Write down the colour of:
a NL
b LM
c JL
d NM

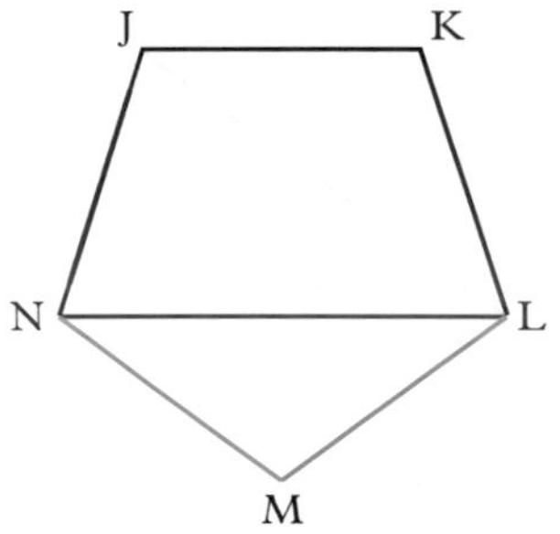

- **3** **a** Write down the special name of this triangle.
  b Write down the letter names of the two equal sides.

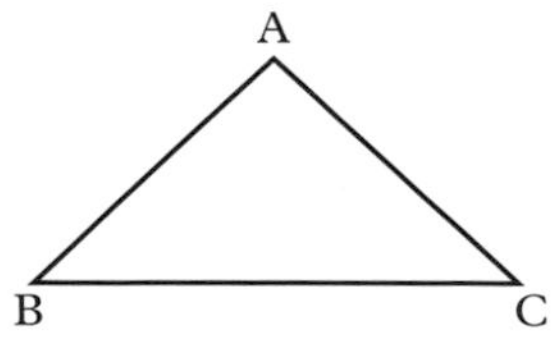

3 Using compasses

There is a legend about King Arthur.
He and his knights lived in Britain long ago.
They all sat at a round table.
The table top was a **circle**.

Parts of a circle have special names.

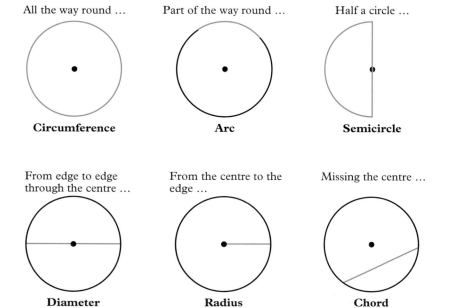

All the way round …

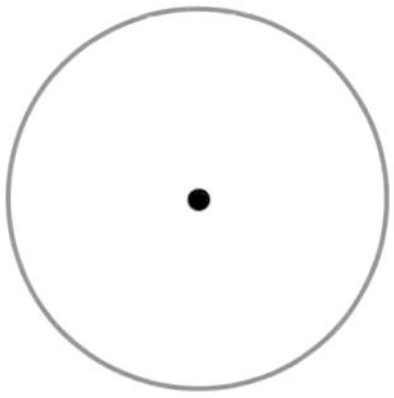

Circumference

Part of the way round …

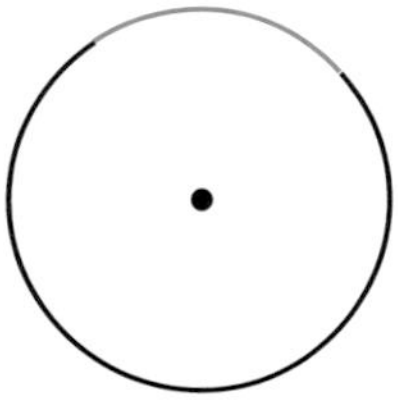

Arc

Half a circle …

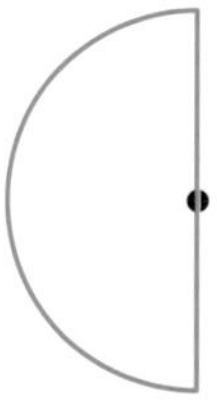

Semicircle

From edge to edge through the centre …

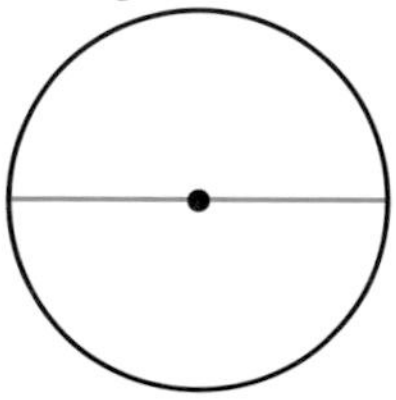

Diameter

From the centre to the edge …

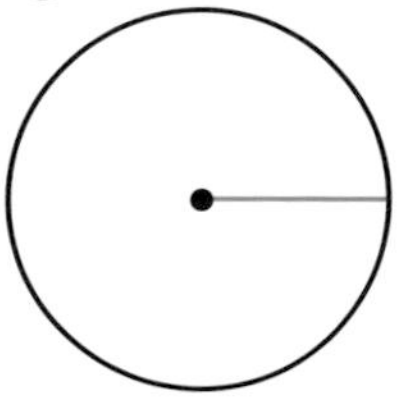

Radius

Missing the centre …

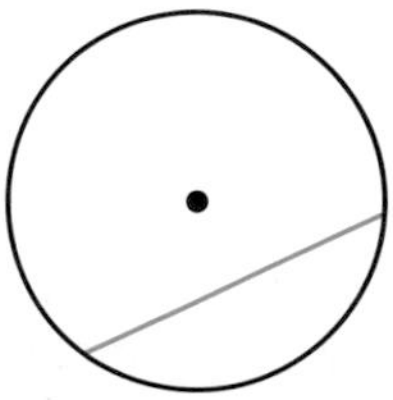

Chord

Exercise 5:7

Use compasses to draw your circles.

1 **a** Draw a circle of radius 4 cm.
b Draw in your circle:
(1) a diameter
(2) a radius
(3) a chord.
c Label these lines with their names.

2 **a** Draw a circle of radius 3 cm.
b Draw a diameter in your circle.
The diameter divides the circle into two semicircles.
c Colour the two semicircles in different colours.
Label one of them 'semicircle'.

3 **a** Draw two circles of radius 2.5 cm.
b Go over the whole edge of the first circle in colour.
Label your coloured edge 'circumference'.
c Go over part of the edge of the second circle in colour.
Label the coloured part 'arc'.

You can use compasses to draw triangles accurately.

Example

Draw triangle ABC.
AB = 7 cm, AC = 5 cm,
BC = 4 cm

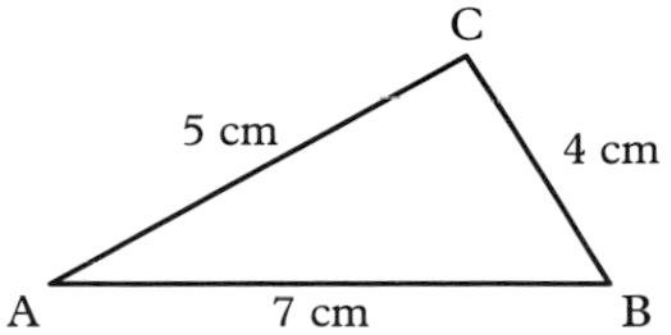

A sketch of the triangle.

1 Draw a line AB, 7 cm long.

2 Open your compasses to 5 cm.
Put the point on A. Draw an arc.

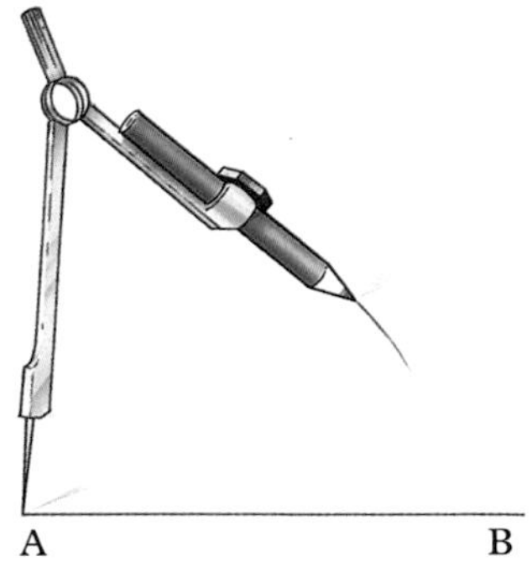

3 Open your compasses to 4 cm.
Put the point on B. Draw an arc.

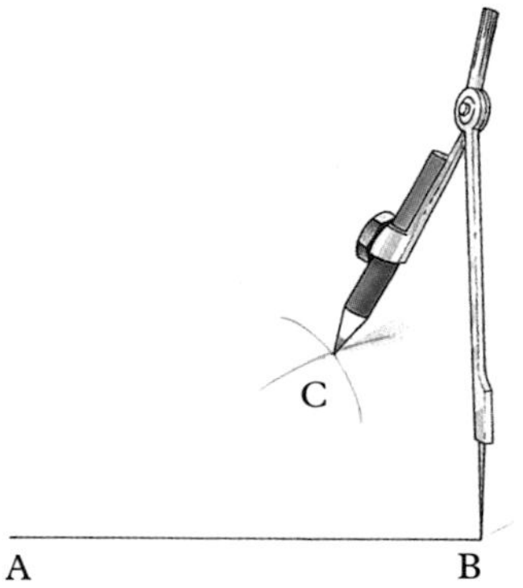

4 Draw in AC and BC with a ruler.
Do not rub out your arcs.

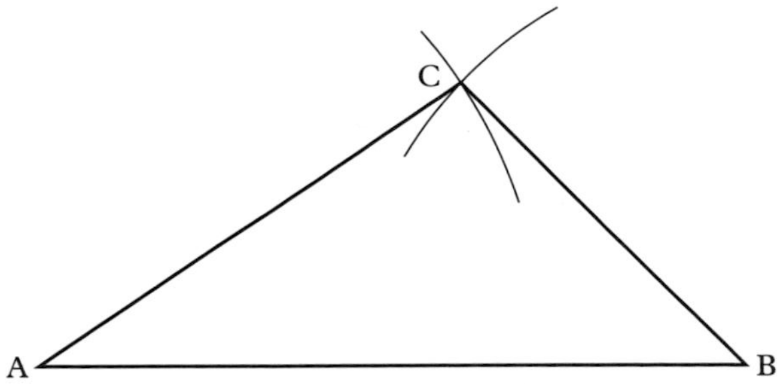

Exercise 5:8

1 Draw the triangle ABC as shown in the example.

2 Triangle PQR has
PQ = 7 cm, QR = 6 cm, RP = 4 cm.

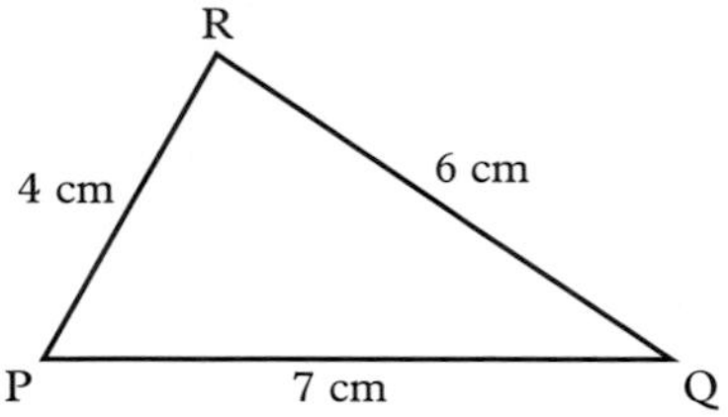

Draw triangle PQR accurately.

3 Triangle XYZ has
XY = 6 cm, YZ = 4 cm, ZX = 4 cm.
a Draw triangle XYZ accurately.
b Write down the special name of triangle XYZ.

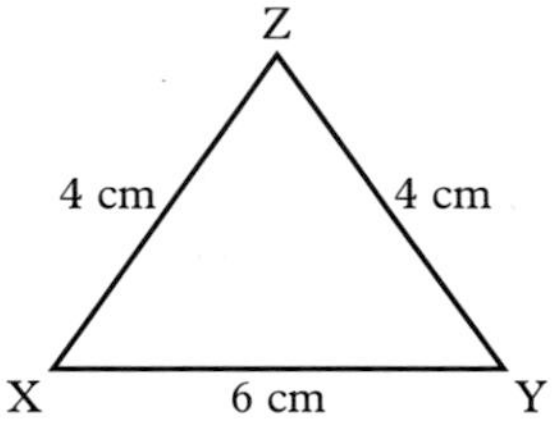

• **4** Triangle DEF is equilateral.
a DE = 5 cm. Write down the lengths of EF and FD.
b Draw triangle DEF accurately.

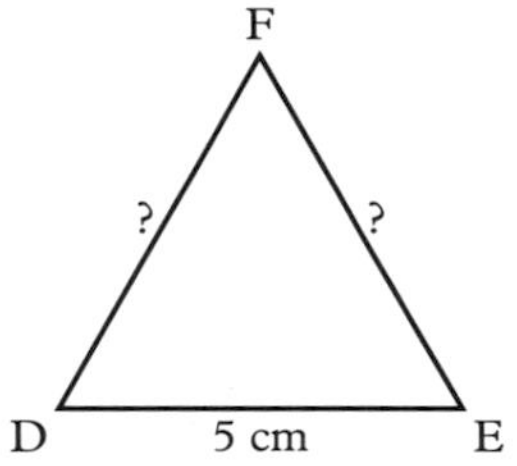

Exercise 5:9 Constructing regular polygons

1 **a** Draw a circle of radius 3 cm.
b Keep your compasses open to 3 cm. Go round the circle making arcs 3 cm apart.

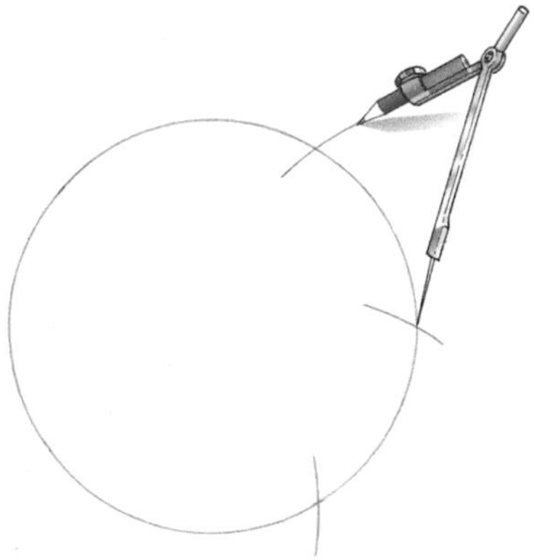

c Join the points where the arcs cross the circle.
d Label your polygon 'a regular ....'.

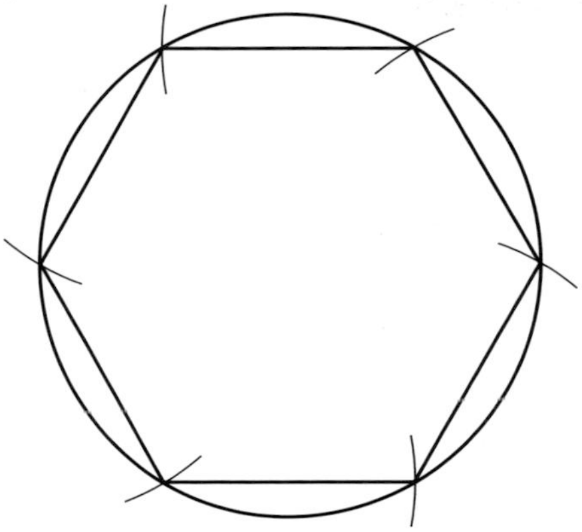

2 **a** Draw a circle of radius 4 cm on plain paper.
Cut out the circle.
(1) Fold the circle in half.
(2) Then fold it in half again.
(3) Then fold once again.
(4) Unfold your circle.

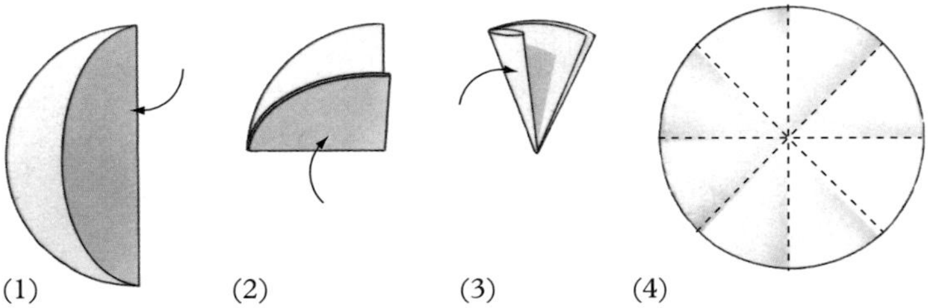

(1) (2) (3) (4)

b Join the points where the folds reach the circumference.

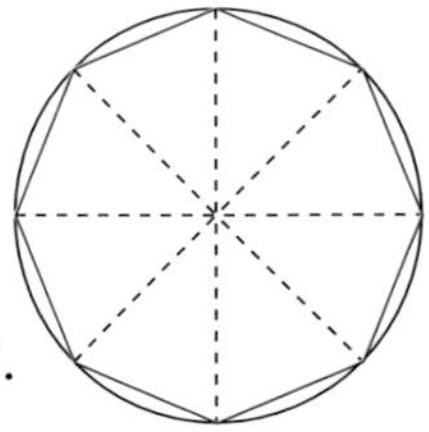

c Label your polygon 'a regular ....'.

3

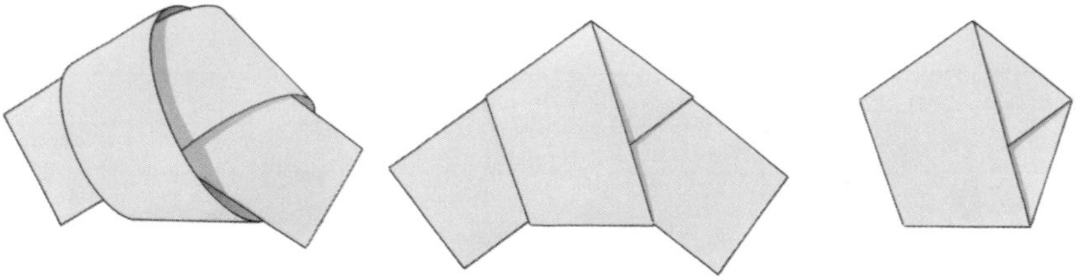

a Cut out a strip of paper 3 cm wide and about 25 cm long.
Tie a knot in this strip.
b Gently pull the knot tight.
Press down until the knot is flat.
c Fold back the spare ends.
Label your polygon 'a regular ....'.

4 Tessellations and congruence

Many patterns are made by repeating the same shape.
Such patterns are often found on floors and walls.

Tessellation

A **tessellation** is a pattern made by repeating the same shape over and over again.
There are no gaps in a tessellation.

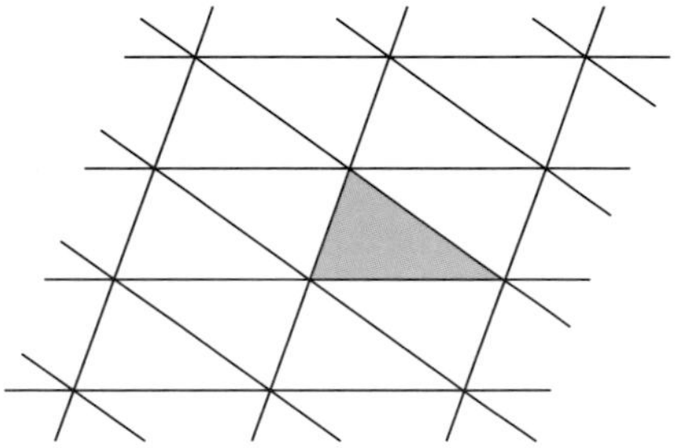

The triangle shape has been repeated over and over again.

Exercise 5:10

Use squared paper for drawing these tessellations.

1 Rectangles tessellate.

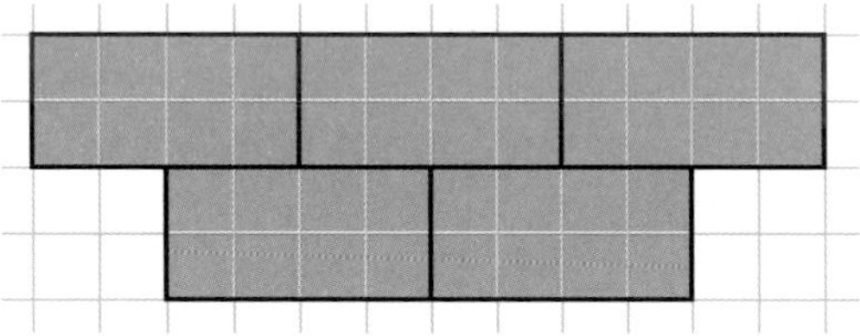

'Brick' pattern

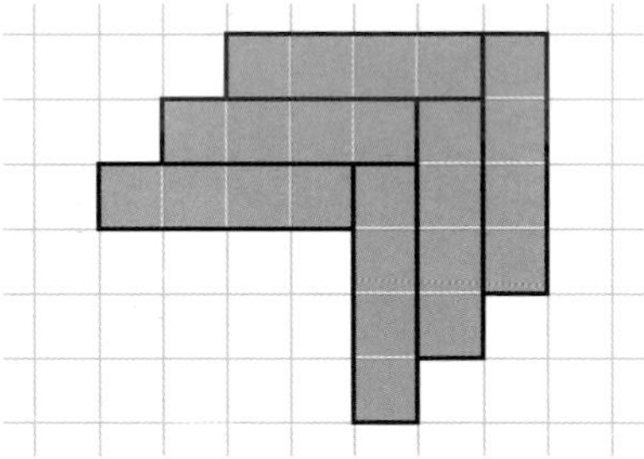

'Herringbone' pattern

Draw a tessellation of rectangles.
Copy one of these tessellations or make up your own.

2 All quadrilaterals tessellate.
Copy one of these tessellations or make up your own.
Use a special quadrilateral.

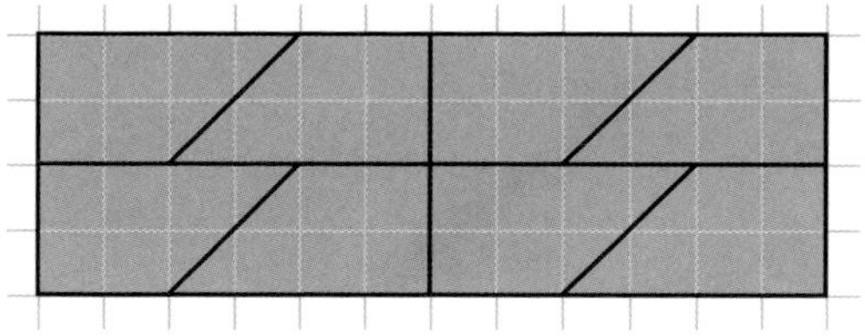

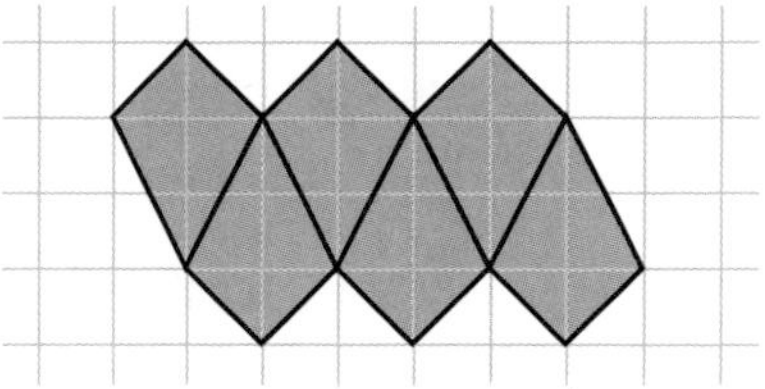

3 All triangles tessellate.
Draw a tessellation of triangles.

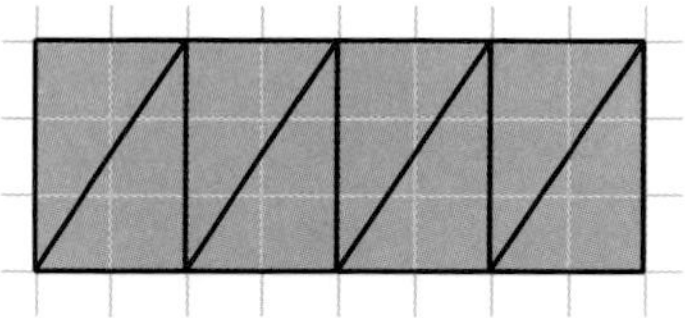

4 Lots of other shapes tessellate.
Experiment with some shapes of your own.

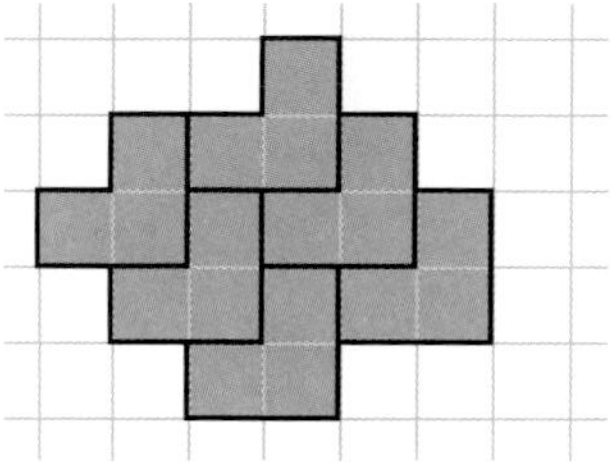

5 **a** (1) Look for tessellations in your school.
Look at the floor, the walls and the ceiling.
(2) Make sketches of the tessellations you find.
Write down where you find them.
b Repeat **a** for tessellations outside school.

A tessellation is made up of many identical shapes.
Identical shapes in maths are called congruent shapes.

Congruent

When shapes are identical we say they are **congruent**.

Congruent shapes can be reflections of each other.

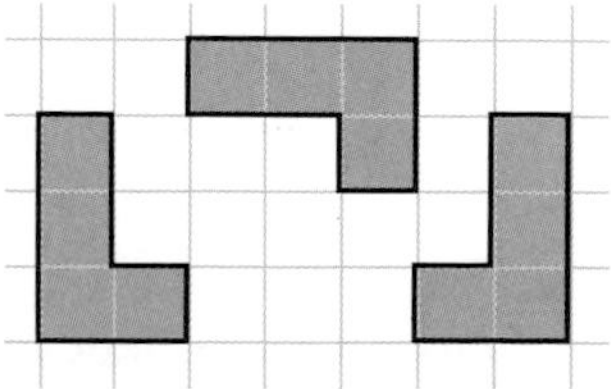

These shapes are congruent.

Exercise 5:11

1 In each of these write down the shape that is not congruent to the others.

a

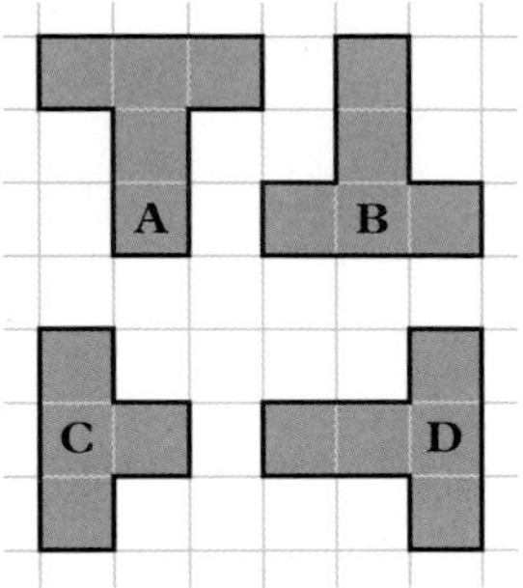

c

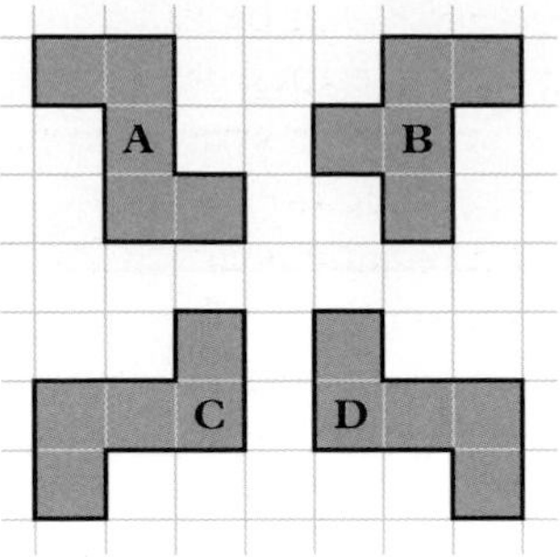

b

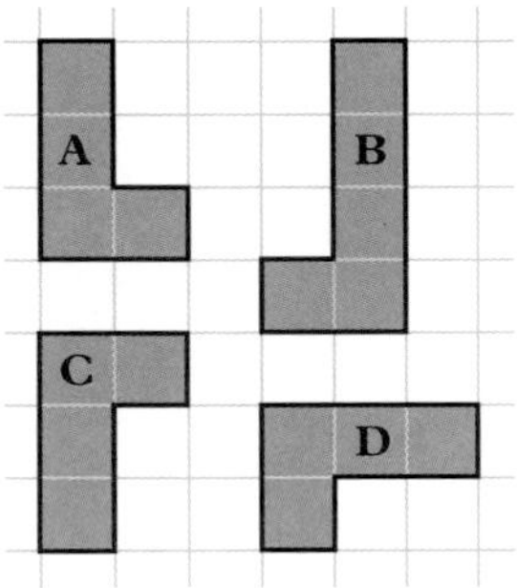

d

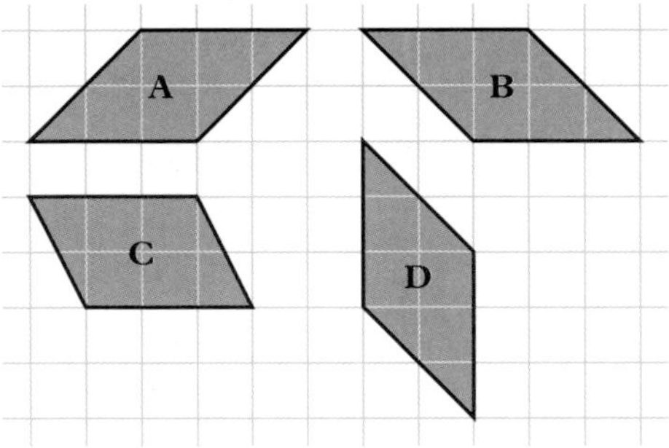

2 **a** Draw a square of side 3 cm.
b Join one diagonal to give two triangles.
c Are the two triangles congruent?
d Join the other diagonal to give four triangles.
e Are the four triangles congruent?

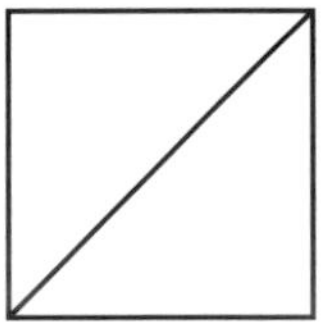

• **3** Trace the special quadrilaterals in Exercise 5:5, question **2**.
Divide each shape into two congruent triangles.

You cannot do this for one shape.
Which is it?

1 Stanthorne High School has tables with trapezium shaped tops.

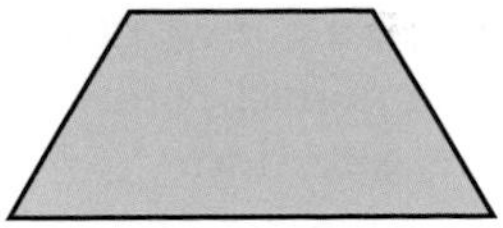

a Two tables can be put together like this.

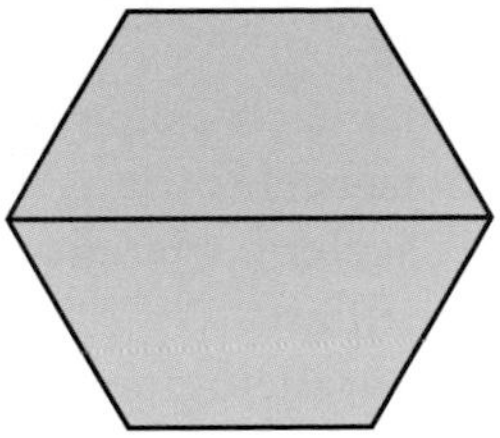

(1) Sketch this arrangement in your book.

(2) The shape is a regular polygon.
Write down its name.

b Sketch two tables together in a parallelogram.

c Sketch two tables together in a concave hexagon.

d Write down the names of other shapes that would make good table tops.

2 Penny and Paul Polygon keep some polygon pets.

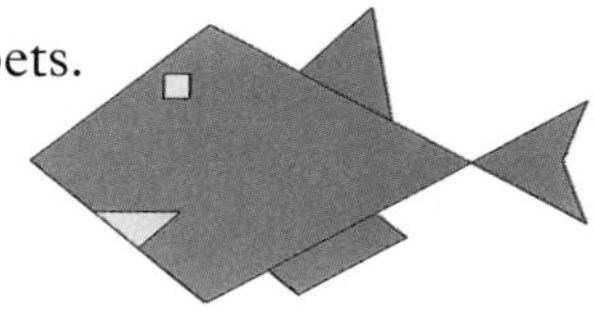

a List the polygons in this pet.

b Draw another polygon pet.
List the polygons you use.

3 **a** (1) Use compasses to draw a circle.
Keep your compasses open at the same radius.
Go round the circle making arcs.
You will make six arcs.

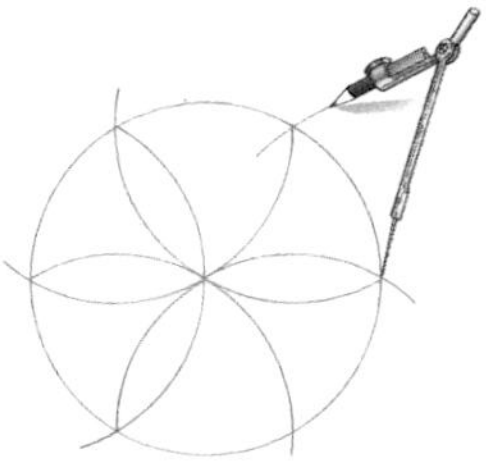

(2) Keep your compasses open at the same radius.
Put the compass point on each mark in turn. Draw an arc.

(3) Complete the pattern to get a flower.

b (1) Start with six marks on a circle.

(2) Join the points with chords.
Complete the pattern to get a star.

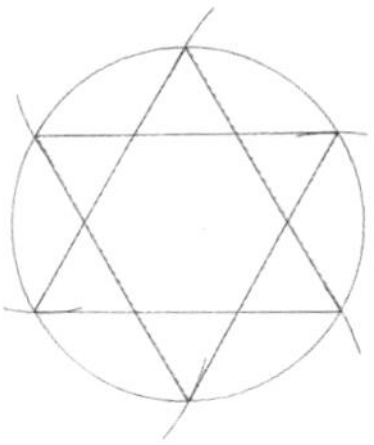

4 Use compasses to construct these triangles:

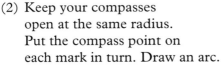

a

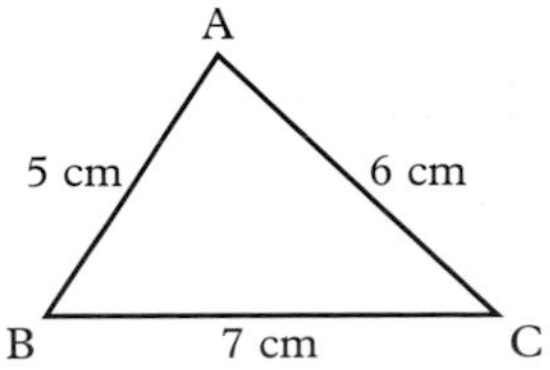

b

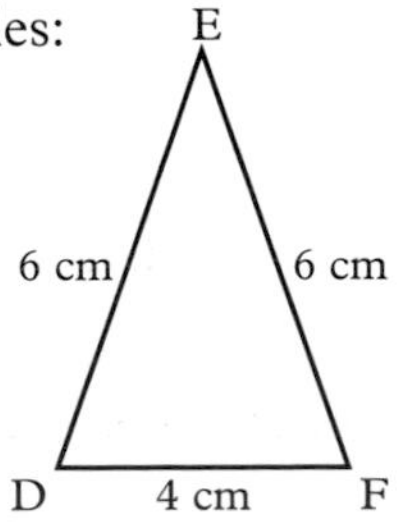

1 Make a copy of this 9-point grid on squared paper for each part of this question.

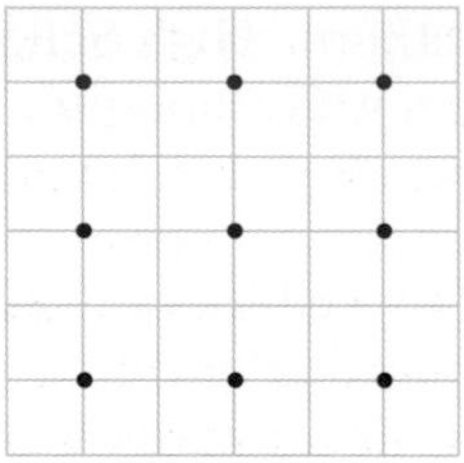

9-point grid

Join dots on your grid to make these.
Label each shape with its name.

a isosceles triangle
b scalene triangle
c square
d parallelogram
e trapezium
f rectangle
g arrowhead
h convex pentagon
i convex hexagon
j concave hexagon

2 **a** Write down the letter names of:
(1) two diameters
(2) two chords
(3) four radiuses
(4) a pair of parallel lines.

b Copy and complete:

Triangle AOB is

....

It is .... to

triangle COD.

Triangle COD is also ....

(choose from: isosceles, congruent)

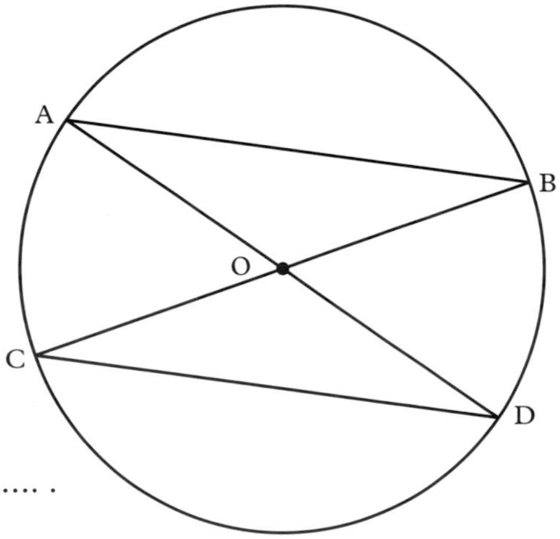

3 **a** Triangle ABC has
AB = 7 cm, AC = 7 cm and BC = 6 cm
(1) Draw a sketch of triangle ABC.
(2) Use compasses to make an accurate drawing of triangle ABC.
(3) Write down the name of triangle ABC.

b Make an accurate drawing of equilateral triangle PQR with sides 6 cm.

4 **a** Draw a circle of radius 4 cm.
b Draw a diameter.
Mark points (1) and (2) 2 cm from the centre.
c With a radius of 2 cm, draw semicircles centre (1) and (2).
d Rub out your diameter.
e Describe the symmetry of your pattern.

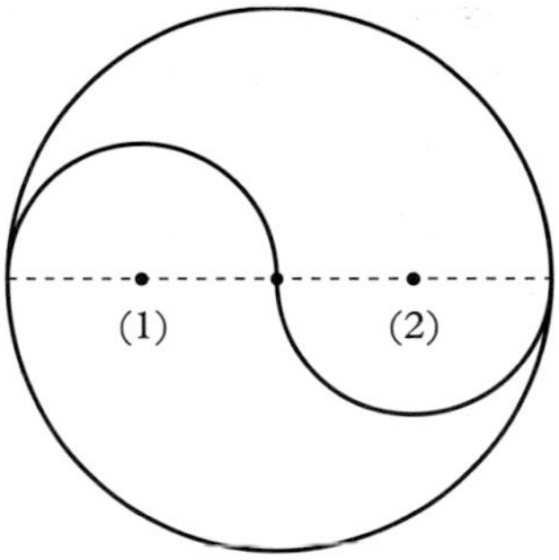

5 **a** Draw round a circular coin.
Shade this circle.
b Use the same coin.
Place it around your shaded circle as shown.
Draw round your coin each time.
c Write down the number of coins you needed to go round the shaded circle.
d Join the centres of the unshaded circles.
Write down the name of the polygon you get.
e Write down the British coins that are **not** circular.
Are these coins polygons?
f Explain why circles do not tessellate.

6 Using triangular grid paper make a tessellation of:
a rhombuses **b** trapeziums **c** hexagons.

7 **a** Write down the shape of most of the rooms in your school.
b Give a reason for the shape of the rooms.

- A **polygon** is a shape with straight sides.
  Triangles and quadrilaterals are polygons.
  A polygon can be **convex** or **concave**.

Number of sides	Name of polygon
5	Pentagon
6	Hexagon
8	Octagon

- An **equilateral triangle** has three equal sides.
  An **isosceles triangle** has two equal sides.
  A **scalene triangle** has no equal sides.

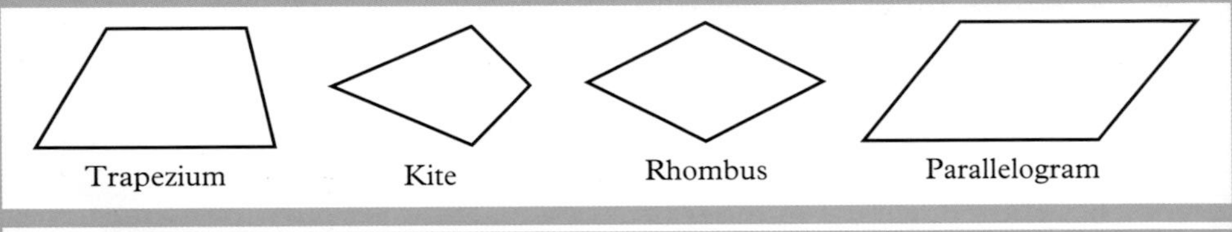

- A point at the corner of a shape is called a **vertex**.
  A line joining two vertices is a **diagonal**.

- **Parallel** lines never meet.
  Parallel lines on diagrams are shown with arrows.
  Two pairs of parallel lines need extra arrows.

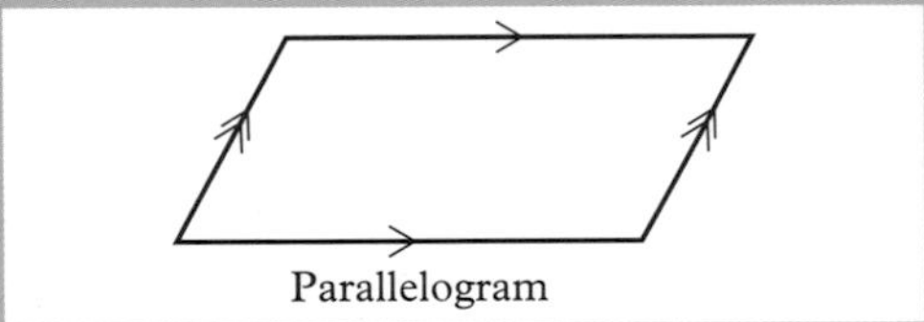

- **Regular polygons** have all their sides the same length.
  Also all their vertices look the same.
  An equilateral triangle and a square are special regular polygons.

- 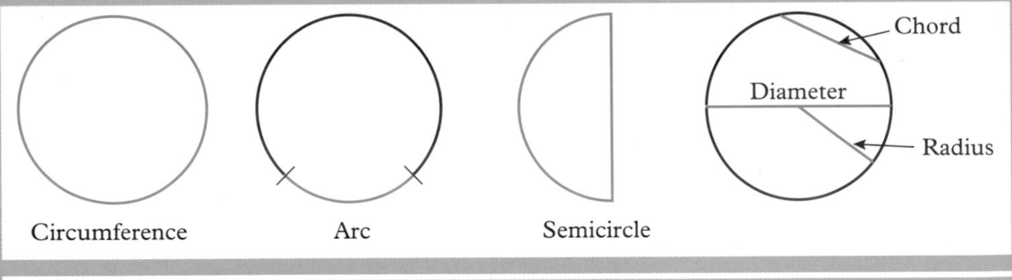

- A **tessellation** is a pattern made by repeating the same shape over and over again. There are no gaps in a tessellation.

  When shapes are identical we say they are **congruent**.
  Congruent shapes can be reflections of each other.

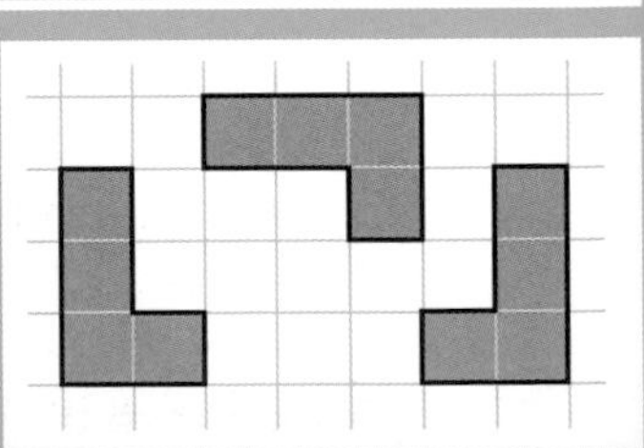

Order ID: 026-9397236-6955556

Thank you for buying from mjs3740 on Amazon Marketplace.

Delivery address:
Naoko Fader
19 Glengall Road
Kilburn
London
NW6 7EL
United Kingdom

Order Date: 20 Aug 2010
Shipping Service: Standard
Buyer Name: Naoko Fader
Seller Name: mjs3740

Quantity	Product Details
1	**Key Maths 7/1 Pupils' Book Revised Edition: Pupil's Book Year 7/1 [Paperback...** **Merchant SKU:** HC-NLCD-B61L **ASIN:** 0748755241 **Listing ID:** 0716EA46OU4 **Order-Item ID:** 58138210361715 **Condition:** Used - Like New **Comments:** IMMACULATE CONDITION INSIDE, few little surface marks to cover. DISPATCHED WITHIN 24 HOURS!

Thanks for buying on Amazon Marketplace. To provide feedback for the seller please visit www.amazon.co.uk/feedback. To contact the seller, please visit Amazon.co.uk and click on "Your Account" at the top of any page. In Your Account, go to the "Orders" section and click on the link "Leave seller feedback". Select the order or click on the "View Order" button. Click on the "seller profile" under the appropriate product. On the lower right side of the page under "Seller Help", click on "Contact this seller".

1

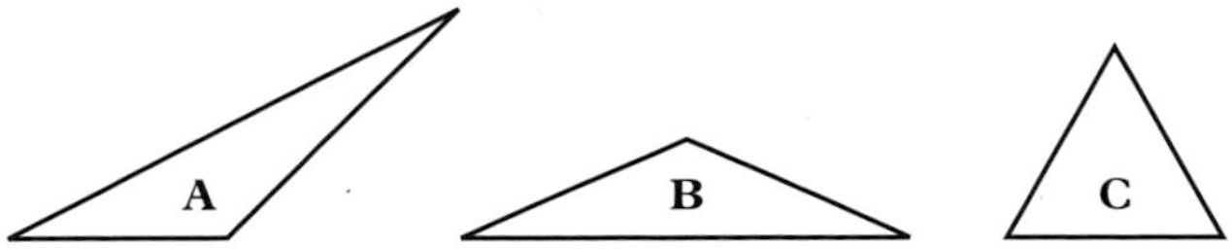

Which triangle is:

a isosceles

b equilateral

c scalene?

2 Write down the name of each special quadrilateral.

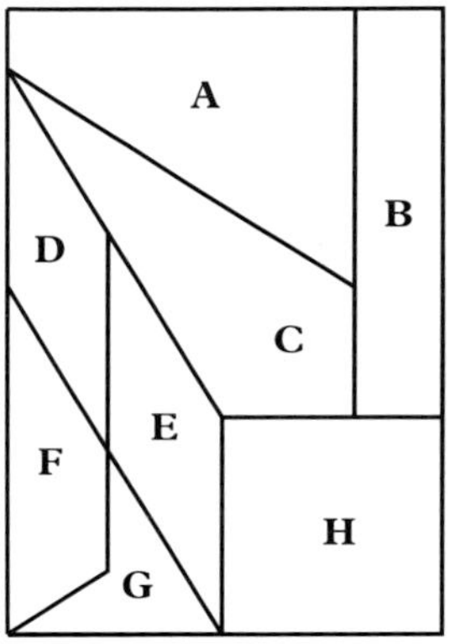

A trapezium

B

C

D

E

F

G

H

3 This parallelogram has the parallel lines marked wrongly.

a Sketch the parallelogram.
Correct the arrows.

b Write down the number of vertices in the parallelogram.

c Draw one diagonal of the parallelogram.

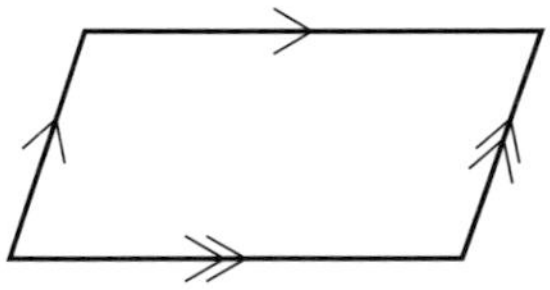

4

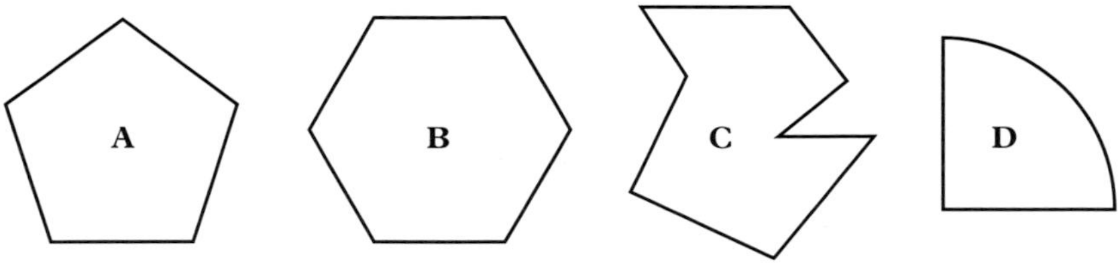

a Write down the shape that is:

(1) regular

(2) convex

(3) concave.

b Write down the shape that is:

(1) an octagon

(2) a pentagon

(3) a hexagon

(4) not a polygon.

5 **a** Write down the letter names of:
(1) a chord
(2) a diameter
(3) a radius.

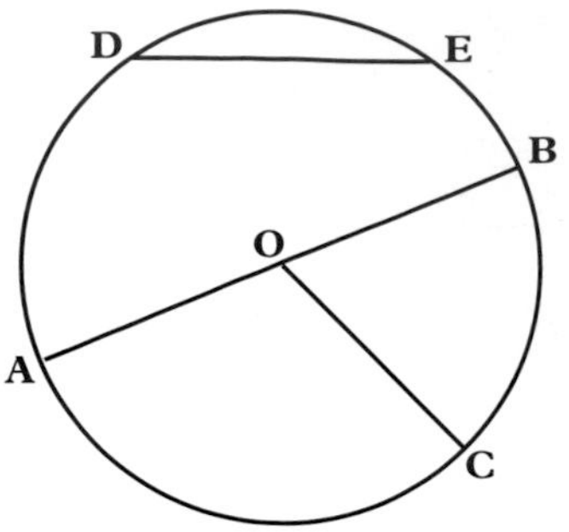

b Choose from:
circumference, semicircle, arc
to complete:

(1) All the way round the outside of a circle is the ....

(2) An .... goes part of the way round the outside.

(3) Half a circle is called a ....

6 Use compasses to draw triangle ABC accurately.

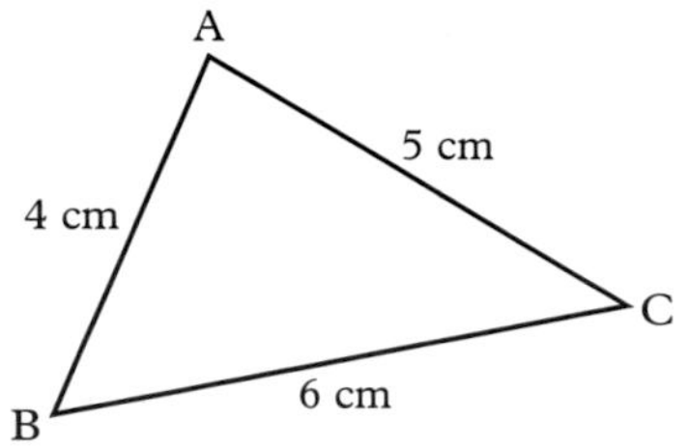

7 **a** In each of these write down the shape that is not congruent to the others.

(1)

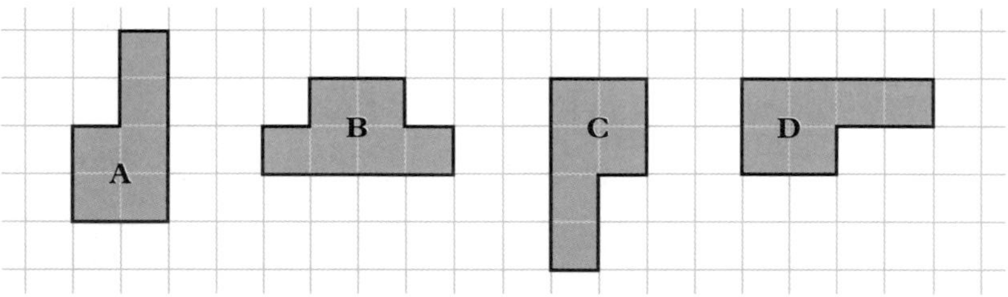

(2)

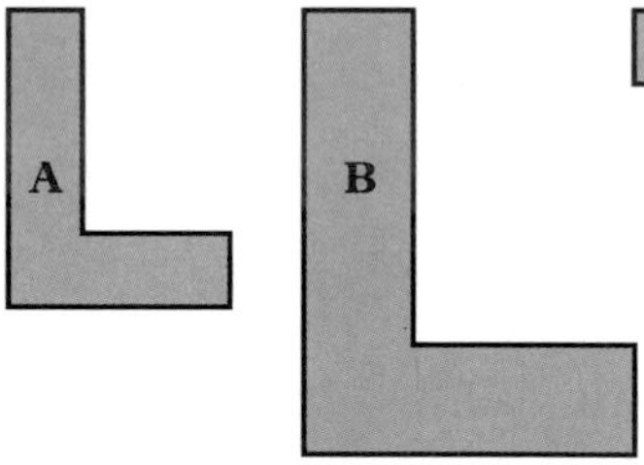

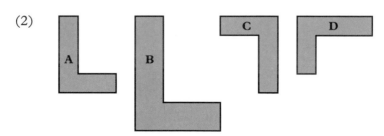

b Use this shape to draw a tessellation.
Use squared paper.

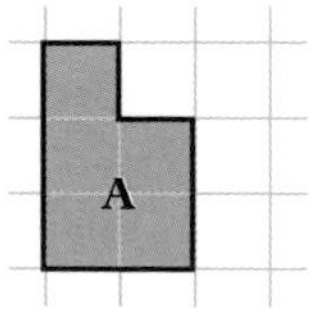

6 Decimals: what's the point?

CORE

1 **Place value in whole numbers**

2 **The decimal point**

3 **Working with decimals**

4 **Problems involving decimals**

QUESTIONS

EXTENSION

SUMMARY

TEST YOURSELF

WHO INVENTED THE DECIMAL POINT?

In different countries mathematicians tried different ways.

Jemshid Al-Kashi, a Persian who died about 1436, wrote 3 142 (the space is for the end of the whole numbers).

Christoff Rudolf, a German, published a book in 1530. He calculated interest on money and wrote 413|4347 (the line is used like our decimal point).

In about 1585 a Flemish mathematician, **Simon Stevin,** published the rules for using decimal fractions. He wrote numbers like this 27(0)8(1)4(2)7(3), meaning 27.847.

Even today people do not agree. The United Kingdom and the United States use a decimal point. In Europe a comma is used.

1 Place value in whole numbers

We can write five hundred and seventy-four as 574 using the figures or **digits** 5, 7 and 4.
457 and 745 can be made from the same digits.
The 7 is in different places in 574, 457 and 745. The 7 has a different **value** each time.
Numbers can be written in columns. The columns have names according to their value.

thousands 1 000s	hundreds 100s	tens 10s	units 1s	
	4	5	7	7 units .... value 7
	5	7	4	7 tens .... value 70
	7	4	5	7 hundreds .. value 700

Exercise 6:1

1 What is the **value** of the red digit in these numbers?

	thousands	hundreds	tens	units
a	3	4	2	1
b		2	4	3
c	4	8	0	4
d	1	9	7	1
e		6	0	5

2 What is the value of the red digit in these numbers?

a 365 **b** 491 **c** 824 **d** 395 **e** 677 **f** 3249

3 **a** Make as many numbers as you can from 5, 3 and 6. 536, 653, …
Use all the digits.

b Which is the largest of these numbers?

c Which number is the smallest?

● **4** 451 has been chosen for this question.

a Write down the number 451.

b Write 451 backwards.

c Which is larger, 451 or 154?

d Subtract 154 from 451.

$$\begin{array}{r} 451 \\ -\ \underline{154} \\ \underline{} \end{array}$$

Write down your answer.

e Write the answer to **d** backwards.

f Add the answers to **d** and **e**.

g Choose your own number. Do the same again.

h Compare your answers with your friend's answers.

When we write large numbers we group the digits in threes.
We write forty-three thousand six hundred and seventeen as 43 617

↑ We leave a small gap

We write five million eight hundred and seventy-four thousand three hundred and nineteen as 5 874 319.

↑ ↑ We leave small gaps

In old books you may see numbers grouped with commas: 43,617
We no longer use a comma.

Exercise 6:2

1 Write these numbers in figures.
- **a** twenty-five
- **b** seven hundred and fifty-six
- **c** two thousand four hundred and eighty-two
- **d** nine hundred and three
- **e** one thousand six hundred and twenty-nine
- **f** thirteen thousand five hundred and twenty
- **g** two million five hundred and ninety-eight thousand two hundred and thirty-one

2 Write these numbers in words.
- **a** 46
- **b** 27
- **c** 103
- **d** 617
- **e** 1 524
- **f** 5 740
- **g** 35 814

Start at the 'units' column. You can add extra columns to the left.

millions	hundred thousands	ten thousands	thousands	hundreds	tens	units
← ×10	← ×10	← ×10	← ×10	← ×10	← ×10	
1 000 000s	100 000s	10 000s	1 000s	100s	10s	1s

Each column is 10 times the one on its right.

Look at the numbers 25, 250, 2500.

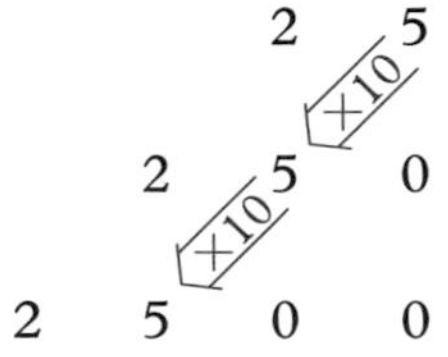

When we multiply by **10** the digits change by **one** column.
When we multiply by **10** × **10** or **100** the digits change by **two** columns.

Exercise 6:3

Copy the table. Complete the missing numbers.

		thousands	hundreds	tens	units
1	3				3
	3 × 10			3	0
	3 × 100				
	3 × 1 000				
2	7				7
	7 × 10				
	7 × 100				
	7 × 1 000				
3	6				
	6 × 100				
	6 × 1 000				
4	2				
	2 × 10				
	2 × 1000				
5	50			5	0
	50 × 10				
	50 × 100				
6	80				
	80 × 10				
	80 × 100				
7	25				
	25 × 10				
	25 × 100				
8	63				
	63 × 10				
	63 × 100				
9	4				4
	4 × ?			4	0
	4 × ?		4	0	0
	4 × ?	4	0	0	0
10	9				9
	9 × ?		9	0	0
	9 × ?	9	0	0	0

2 The decimal point

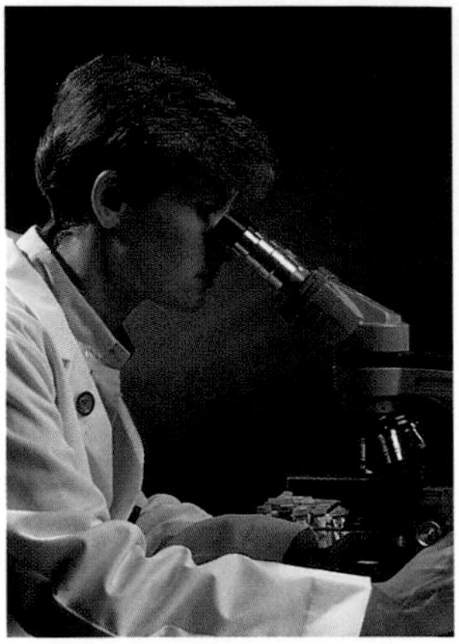

A scientist needs to measure a special screw very accurately.

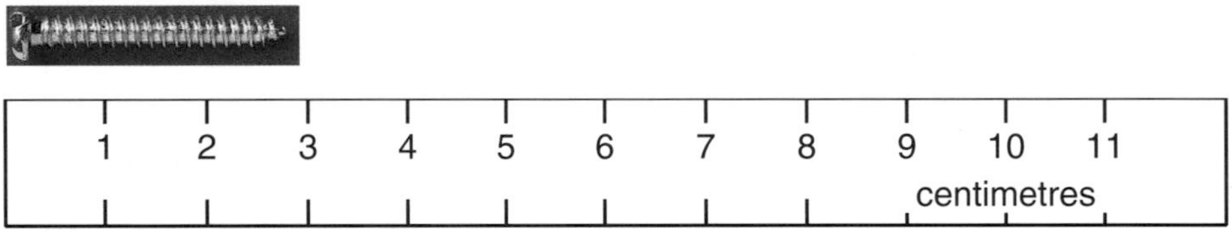

This is part of a simple ruler. The screw measures between 2 and 3 centimetres. This is no good to the scientist.

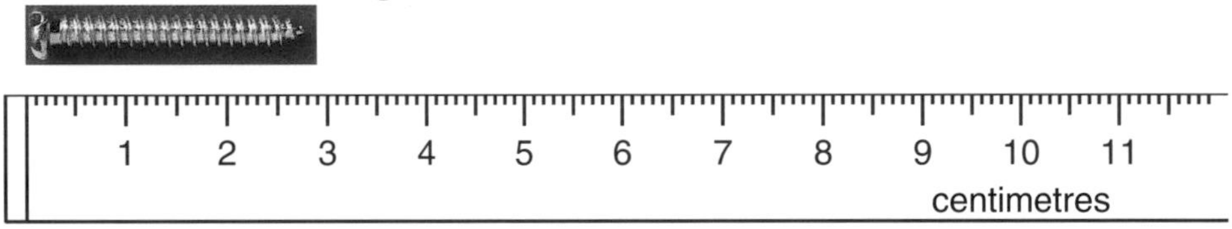

This ruler is better. Each whole centimetre has been divided into **10** equal parts or **tenths**.
The screw looks a little more than 2.**8** cm long.

The dot between the 2 and 8 is called a **decimal point**.

Decimal point

The word **decimal** comes from the Romans' word for 10.
Our number system is based on ten.
The **point** marks where whole numbers end and fractions or parts of numbers begin.
Examples of numbers with decimal points are 2.8 3.145 14.08

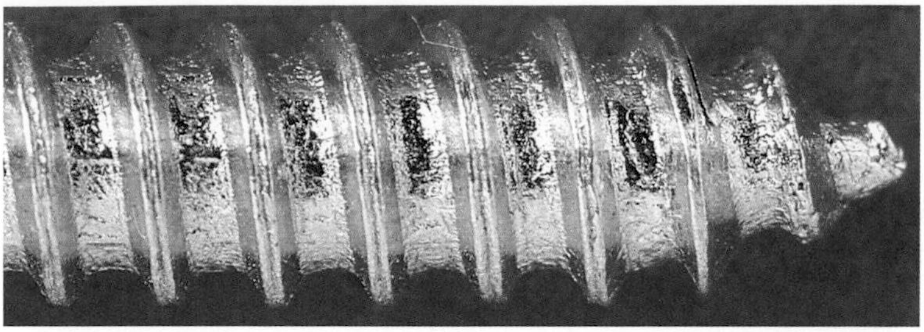

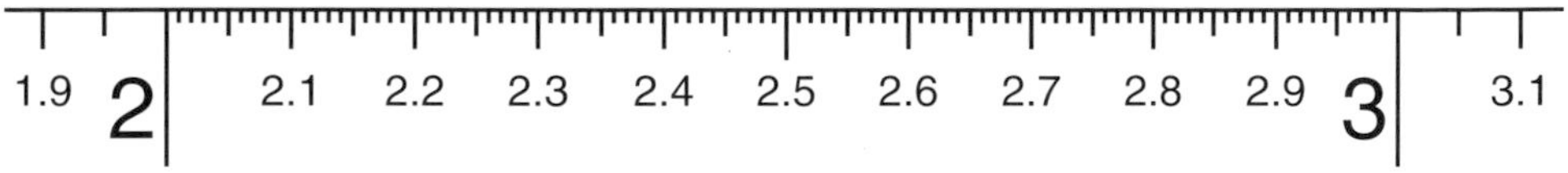

Here is an enlargement of part of the screw and ruler. There are now **100** tiny spaces or **hundredths** between 2 and 3.
The screw is a little more than 2.85 (two point eight five) cm.

We can enlarge the ruler again. There are now **1000** very small spaces or **thousandths** between 2 and 3.
The screw is now too large to be shown. It would end at 2.85**6** (two point eight five six).
To measure this accurately, we would need a special measuring device.

If we used accurate enough ways of measuring, we could add more and more numbers: 2.856 18 … and so on.

Decimals in words

2.**35** in words is two point **three five**.
£4.76 in words is four pounds seventy-six. We really mean four pounds and seventy-six pence.

Exercise 6:4

1 Write these decimal numbers in words.
a 3.29 **b** 4.125 **c** 0.06 **d** 7.302 **e** 5.19

2 Write these numbers in figures.
a Seven point eight
b Nought point three nought four
c Six point nine six
d Five point nought five three
e One point two three five

W **3** Ask your teacher for a copy of 'Labelling number lines' worksheet.

4 In each of these, decide which measurement has been given more accurately.

a 2.458 cm, 2.46 cm
b 3.7 cm, 3.69 cm
c 1.12 m, 1.124 m
d 8.623 ml, 8.6228 ml
e 0.41 mm, 0.406 mm
f 4.7 g, 4.70 g

Exercise 6:5

Copy the column headings and the numbers in the table.

	thousands	hundreds	tens	units	.	tenths	hundredths	thousandths	value of red digit in words
1			3	5	.	6	4	3	six tenths
2		1	1	4	.	7	0	5	five …
3			6	1	.	6	5		five …
4		2	3	0	.	9	2		nine …
5	1	0	3	2	.	6			six …

Add these numbers to your table.

6 253.05
7 4.563
8 0.601
9 12.03
10 4.191
11 125
12 13
13 5.123
14 4210
15 1305.19

Multiplying by powers of 10

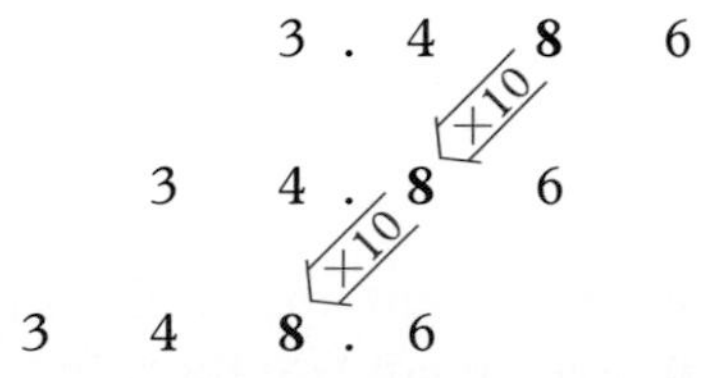

When we multiply by **10**, the digits change by **one** column.
When we multiply by **10** × **10** or **100**, the digits change by **two** columns.

Exercise 6:6

You may need to use a calculator to start.

1 Multiply each of these numbers by 10.

a 4	**e** 2.4	**i** 5.78	**m** 0.3
b 7	**f** 7.1	**j** 6.125	**n** 0.9
c 1.4	**g** 27.3	**k** 4.708	**o** 0.75
d 8.6	**h** 56.9	**l** 12.61	**p** 0.54

2 Multiply each of these numbers by 100.

a 6	**d** 5.4	**g** 17.34	**j** 0.613
b 13	**e** 17.9	**h** 12.54	**k** 0.97
c 7.4	**f** 34.3	**i** 3.245	**l** 0.075

3

a 2.6×10	**e** 80×10	**i** 0.56×100
b 65×10	**f** 6.3×10	**j** 4.1×100
c 0.5×10	**g** 0.04×100	**k** 2.3×100
d 15.6×100	**h** 0.9×100	**l** 0.004×100

Example The column change in division is the opposite way.

a $42 \div 10 = 4.2$

b $36.5 \div 100 = 0.365$

● **4**

a $36 \div 10$	**e** $5060 \div 100$	**i** $5.41 \div 10$
b $7.8 \div 10$	**f** $76.54 \div 10$	**j** $0.762 \div 10$
c $760 \div 100$	**g** $8.9 \div 100$	**k** $1.62 \div 100$
d $4500 \div 100$	**h** $90 \div 100$	**l** $67.125 \div 100$

3 Working with decimals

Robin, Rachel and Mark have to line up in alphabetical order. **M** for **M**ark comes before **R** for **R**obin and **R** for **R**achel.

As Robin and Rachel both start with R, they will have to look at the next letters.
Robin, Rachel: **a** comes before **o** so Rachel is before Robin.
The order is: Mark, Rachel, Robin.

Decimals are put in order in the same way.

Example

Put 4.615, 3.842 and 4.67 in order of size, smallest first.

a 4.615 3.842 4.67
3 is smaller than 4.
3.842 is the smallest number.

b 4.615 4.67
The first figure after the decimal point is the same.

c 4.615 4.67
1 is smaller than 7, so 4.615 is smaller than 4.67.
The numbers in order are: 3.842, 4.615, 4.67.

Exercise 6:7

In questions 1 to 13, put the numbers in order of size, smallest first.

1 2.53, 4.68

2 7.61, 3.2

3 4.57, 4.21

4 7.63, 7.8

5 1.24, 1.27

6 2.54, 3.812, 3.65

7 1.234, 2.34, 1.34

8 7.643, 6.41, 7.65

9 6.4, 6.41

10 5.704, 5.71

11 16.3, 16.29

12 8.094, 8.049

• **13** 2.60, 2.06, 2.161

- **14** These are the longest throws of each person entered in a javelin competition.
Pick out the first, second and third places.

M. Bland	40.66 m	D. Smith	47.91 m
T. Jones	48.05 m	L. George	47.63 m
P. Grant	47.95 m	C. Peters	43.80 m

- **15** Replace ? with < (less than) or > (more than) or =
a 12.75 ? 12.705 **c** 8.424 ? 8.42 **e** 0.607 ? 0.67
b 6.091 ? 6.19 **d** 0.064 ? 0.064

Exercise 6:8

Write down the next four terms in these patterns.
The first one is done for you.

1 **a** 0.1, 0.3, 0.5, 0.7, 0.9, 1.1 (Adding 0.2)
b 0.2, 0.4, … (Adding 0.2)
c 0.3, 0.6, … (Adding 0.3)
d 0.4, 0.8, … (Adding 0.4)
e 0.5, 1.0, … (Adding 0.5)
f 0.25, 0.50, … (Adding 0.25)
g 12.0, 11.5, … (Subtracting 0.5)
h 6.0, 5.8, … (Subtracting 0.2)

2 Check your answers to Question **1**.
The *ans function* on your calculator would be useful.

Calculators are different but most can do patterns.

To get 5, 7, 9, 11, 13, 15, … (adding 2) try:

[5] [=] [+] [2] [=] [=] [=] …

On some calculators you could use:

[5] [+] [+] [2] [=] [=] [=] …

or [2] [+] [+] [5] [=] [=] [=] …

- **3** Complete these patterns.
Write down the rule for each one.
a 4.8, 5.0, …, 5.4, 5.6, 5.8, …
b 7.0, …, 6.0, 5.5, 5.0, …, 4.0
c 12.0, 10.5, 9.0, 7.5, …, …
d 1.05, 1.15, 1.25, …, 1.45, …
e 0.5, …, 2.5, 3.5, 4.5, …
f 16, 8, 4, 2, 1, …, …

Addition and subtraction of decimals

Examples

1 4.52 + 6.851

The decimal points go underneath each other.
Some people find it helps to put in 0s.

$$\begin{array}{r} 4.520 \\ +\ 6.851 \\ \hline 11.371 \end{array}$$

The extra 0s are important when doing subtraction.

2 19.6 − 7.53

$$\begin{array}{r} 19.\overset{5}{\cancel{6}}\overset{1}{0} \\ -\ 7.53 \\ \hline 12.07 \end{array}$$

Here is a mixture of whole numbers and decimals.

3 4 − 1.58

$$\begin{array}{r} \overset{3}{\cancel{4}}.\overset{9}{\cancel{0}}0 \\ -\ 1.58 \\ \hline 2.42 \end{array}$$

Exercise 6:9

1 **a** 2.8 + 4.1

$$\begin{array}{r} 2.8 \\ +\ 4.1 \\ \hline \\ \hline \end{array}$$

b 5.6 + 1.02

$$\begin{array}{r} 5.6 \\ +\ 1.02 \\ \hline \\ \hline \end{array}$$

c 25.6 + 7.56

$$\begin{array}{r} 25.6 \\ +\ 7.56 \\ \hline \\ \hline \end{array}$$

2 **a** 3.7 + 2.06 **c** 4.81 + 2.34 **e** 15.25 + 0.675
b 3.3 + 6.05 **d** 141.6 + 82.71 **f** 13.65 + 29.09

3 **a** 5.38 − 2.16 **c** 12.47 − 6.29 **e** 6.72 − 5.4
b 7.36 − 4.15 **d** 3.68 − 1.74 **f** 8.24 − 6.5

4 **a** 3.6 − 1.42

$$\begin{array}{r} 3.60 \\ -\ 1.42 \\ \hline \\ \hline \end{array}$$

b 7 − 5.3

$$\begin{array}{r} 7.0 \\ -\ 5.3 \\ \hline \\ \hline \end{array}$$

c 5.6 − 2.35

$$\begin{array}{r} 5.6 \\ -\ 2.35 \\ \hline \\ \hline \end{array}$$

d 8 − 2.6 **e** 9.3 − 5.67 **f** 10.4 − 8.52

5 **a** $14 + 35.9$ **c** $7 + 4.97$ **e** $15.7 + 39$
b $5 - 1.8$ **d** $23 - 6.75$ **f** $12.3 - 6.75$

Multiplication of a decimal by a whole number

Examples

1 16.2×3

$$\begin{array}{r} 16.2 \\ \times \quad 3 \\ \hline 48.6 \\ \hline {}_{1} \end{array}$$

2 23.6 by 5

$$\begin{array}{r} 23.6 \\ \times \quad 5 \\ \hline 118.0 \\ \hline {}_{1\,3} \end{array}$$

Exercise 6:10

1 4.2×3

$$\begin{array}{r} 4.2 \\ \times \quad 3 \\ \hline \\ \hline \end{array}$$

2 12.5×5

$$\begin{array}{r} 12.5 \\ \times \quad 5 \\ \hline \\ \hline \end{array}$$

3 6.8×4

$$\begin{array}{r} 6.8 \\ \times \quad 4 \\ \hline \\ \hline \end{array}$$

4 5.72×3

5 12.3×4

6 5.74×2

7 4.56×3

8 40.5×4

9 0.056×5

Division of a decimal by a whole number

Example $23.6 \div 4 =$

$$\begin{array}{r} 5.9 \\ 4\overline{)23.{}^{3}6} \end{array}$$

Exercise 6:11

1 $4.62 \div 2$

$$\begin{array}{r} . \\ 2\overline{)4.62} \end{array}$$

2 $3.42 \div 3$

$$\begin{array}{r} . \\ 3\overline{)3.42} \end{array}$$

3 $5.65 \div 5$

$$\begin{array}{r} . \\ 5\overline{)5.65} \end{array}$$

4 $3.4 \div 2$

5 $4.88 \div 4$

6 $2.13 \div 3$

7 $10.5 \div 5$

8 $11.2 \div 2$

9 $2.16 \div 2$

10 $6.21 \div 3$

11 $17.2 \div 4$

12 $16.5 \div 5$

4 Problems involving decimals

Sometimes we get more numbers after the decimal point than we need.

Aisha has enough beads to make seven necklaces.
She has 290 cm of cord.

She needs to cut the cord into seven equal pieces.

Aisha uses a calculator to work out 290 ÷ 7.
The display gives **41.428571**

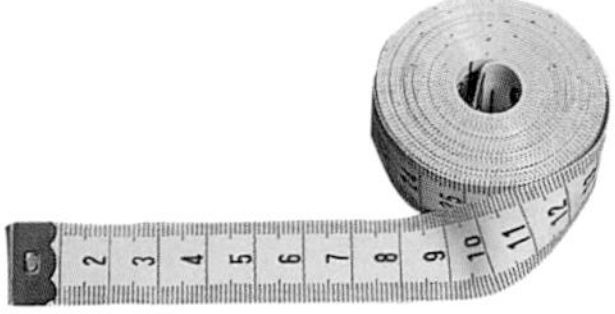

To use this tape-measure Aisha needs only one number after the decimal point.

Aisha looks at the next number as well.

41.428571

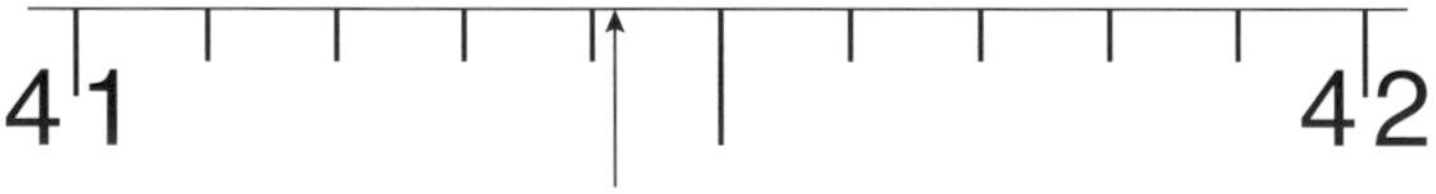

41.42 is nearer to 41.4

The number is **corrected to one decimal place**.

Example Round (a) 5.61 and (b) 5.68 correct to one decimal place.
(a) 5.61 is nearer to 5.6
(b) 5.68 is nearer to 5.7

Exercise 6:12

1 Write these numbers correct to one decimal place.

a 3.71 **e** 5.09 **i** 4.07
b 4.52 **f** 10.37 **j** 8.46
c 5.38 **g** 12.41 **k** 3.65
d 4.69 **h** 15.79 **l** 4.15

Examples

1 Round the number 4.6 correct to the nearest whole number.

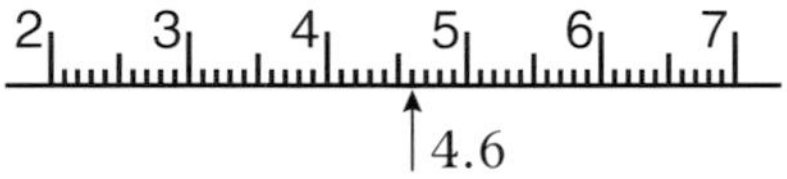

4.6 is closer to 5. It is rounded to 5.

2 3.5 is halfway between 3 and 4.
It is rounded to 4.

---

2 Round these decimals to the nearest whole number.

a 5.6 **g** 4.7
b 2.8 **h** 15.3
c 3.1 **i** 8.5
d 6.2 **j** 20.1
e 7.4 **k** 1.3
f 10.9 **l** 13.5

Example

Write these amounts of money correct to the nearest penny.

1 £7.458 **2** £1.3729 **3** £17.025

We need **two** figures after the decimal point.
Look at the **third** figure
£7.458 is closer to £7.46
£1.3729 is closer to £1.37
£17.025 is halfway, so round up to £17.03

Exercise 6:13

Round these amounts of money correct to the nearest penny.

1 £3.261 **3** £8.599

2 £10.173 **4** £14.1562

5 £23.2491

6 £2.857

7 £17.435

8 £6.318

9 £39.697

10 £4.9996

Example £5.35 × 4
On a calculator we get the display 21.4
We need two figures after the decimal point
Answer £21.40

Exercise 6:14

Write the answers with two figures after the decimal point.

1 £3.24 × 5

2 £23.20 ÷ 4

3 £4.82 + £1.08

4 £12.50 ÷ 5

5 £14 + £1.24 + 86p

6 £15.32 ÷ 8

7 £26.38 − £14.58

8 £24.23 ÷ 4

9 £2.29 − £1.89

10 £56.25 ÷ 4

Exercise 6:15

Answer these problems.

1 The height of a television and stand is 77.9 cm.
The stand is 32.6 cm high.
How high is the television?

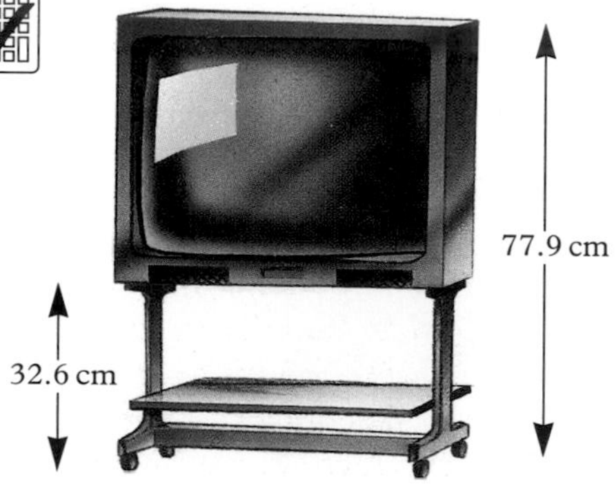

2 A hedge is 1.76 m high.
It is trimmed by 0.21 m.
How high is it now?

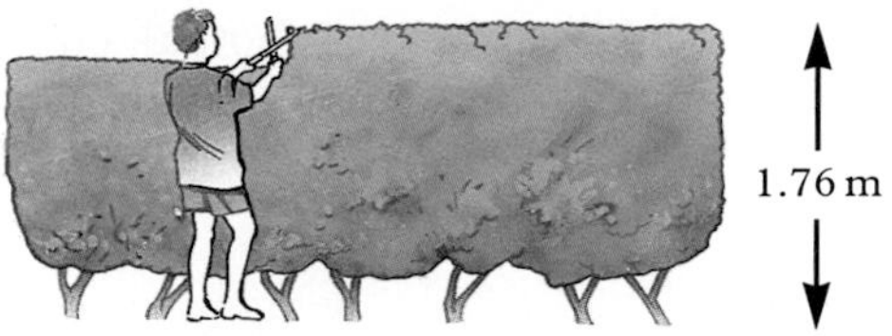

3 Samantha makes a scarf 92 cm long.
She adds a fringe 10.3 cm long to each end.
What is the total length of the scarf?

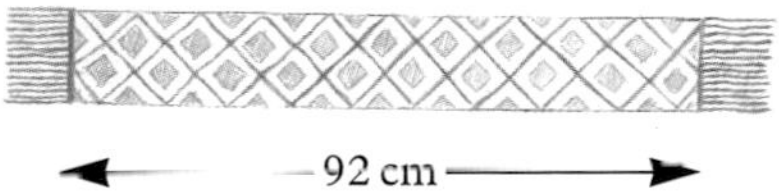

4 Six cassettes fit exactly along a shelf.
Each cassette is 6.9 cm wide.
What is the length of the shelf?

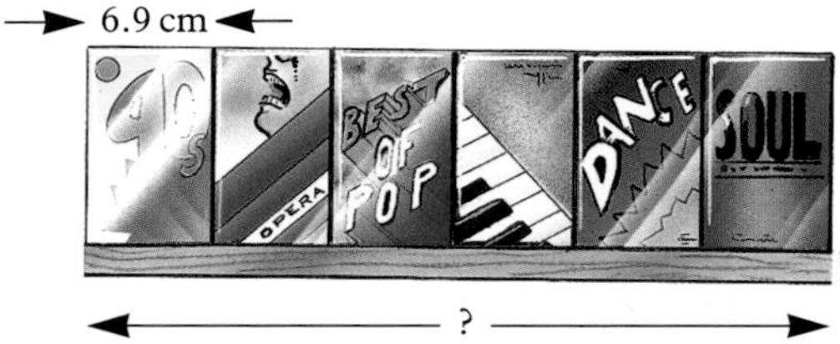

5 In the afternoon Raj cycled 4.8 km to his friend's house.
In the evening he cycled home.
How far did he cycle altogether?

6 Mrs Buckle pays £14.00 for 5 tickets at the cinema.
How much is each ticket?

7 How far is it from the tips of Hannah's fingers to the rim of the basket?

8 Adam wants to find the length of one pace. He takes six even paces which measure 5.82 m.
- **a** Adam works out the length of one pace. What is his answer?
- **b** Find the length of your own pace in this way.

9 Shane is joining the local football club. His uncle offers to buy the training kit and a bag. How much does it cost him?

10 Jolene saves for four weeks. She wants a book which costs £5.50.
Jolene saves: £1.50, £1.10, £2, £1.25.
Jolene adds like this:

$$\begin{array}{r} 1.50 \\ 1.10 \\ 2 \\ +\ 1.25 \\ \hline 3.87 \\ \hline \end{array}$$

Jolene is sad that this is not £5.50.
Jolene has made a mistake.
How much has Jolene saved?

• **11** Kevin has a job in a sweet shop. Mrs Patel buys a box of chocolates costing £2.29.
She pays with three pound coins.
Kevin works out the change

$$\begin{array}{r} 3.00 \\ -\ 2.29 \\ \hline 1.29 \\ \hline \end{array}$$

What has Kevin done wrong?
What should the answer be?

• **12** Baldeep's mother gives him £6 to buy five meat pies.
They cost £1.16 each.
Baldeep works out the cost of the pies on his calculator.

5 × 1.16 = 5.8

Six pounds less five pounds and eight pence is 92p, thinks Baldeep.
What has Baldeep done wrong?
How much is the change?

1 Use all the digits 5, 6 and 8.
a What is the largest number you can make?
b What is the smallest number you can make?

2 **a** Write these numbers in words.
(1) 6.75 (2) 0.503 (3) 2.04 (4) 5.321 (5) 0.002
b Write these numbers in figures.
(1) Three point six two
(2) Seven point five nine five
(3) Ten point one nought five
(4) Nought point nought two seven

3 In each of these, decide which measurement has been given more accurately.
a 1.73 cm, 1.728 cm
b 16.815 m, 16.8 m
c 25.61 kg, 25.607 kg
d 10.5 mm, 10.50 mm

4 **a** Copy the column headings.

thousands	hundreds	tens	units	.	tenths	hundredths	thousandths

b Write these numbers in the correct columns.
(1) 7.133
(2) 1205.4
(3) 4134
(4) 20.032
(5) 814.48
(6) 320
c Give the value of the red digit in words.

5 Give the number between each of these pairs on a number line.
Example 1.23, **1.24**, 1.25.
a 6.7, ..., 6.9
b 4.4, ..., 4.6
c 21, ..., 23
d 15.3, ..., 15.5
e 0.04, ..., 0.06
f 2.76, ..., 2.78
g 1.36, ..., 1.38
h 10.43, ..., 10.45

6 Put these numbers in order of size, smallest first.
a 4.76, 4.345, 3.76
b 1.543, 1.43
c 9.312, 9.32, 8.312
d 2.6, 2.65, 2.556
e 0.519, 0.52
f 0.71, 0.7, 0.703

7 **a** Complete these patterns by finding the next four terms.
(1) 0.3, 0.5, ... (Adding 0.2)
(2) 2.5, 3.0, ... (Adding 0.5)
(3) 6.0, 5.8, ... (Subtracting 0.2)
(4) 2.14, 2.13, ... (Subtracting 0.01)
b Complete these patterns.
Write down the rule in each case.
(1) 10.0, 10.5, ..., 11.5, 12.0, ..., 13.0
(2) 4.36, ..., 4.38, 4.39, ..., 4.41, 4.42
(3) 8.4, 8.3, 8.2, 8.1, ..., ..., 7.8
(4) 1.62, 1.60, 1.58, ..., 1.54, 1.52, 1.50, ...

8 Set these questions out carefully.
a 15.6 + 7.82
b 4.63 + 15.9
c 13.7 + 15
d 3.162 + 4.57

9 Set these questions out carefully.
a 5.94 − 3.6
b 14.42 − 12.61
c 7 − 4.8
d 4.52 − 3.6

10 Set these questions out carefully.
a 3.56 × 2
b 4.13 × 5
c 12.7 × 3
d 14.23 × 4

11 Set these questions out carefully.
a 3.6 ÷ 2
b 4.84 ÷ 4
c 6.42 ÷ 3
d 10.65 ÷ 5

12 Round these decimals correct to the nearest whole number.
a 5.2 **b** 7.3 **c** 10.8 **d** 8.5

13 Round these numbers correct to one decimal place.
a 5.21 **b** 4.37 **c** 14.46 **d** 1.65

14 How high is the television with its stand?

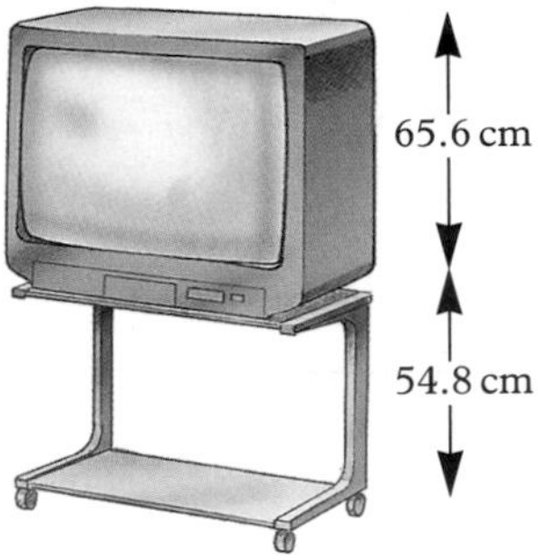

15 Alice has a piece of ribbon 57.5 cm long.
She cuts off a piece 13.8 cm long.
How long is Alice's ribbon now?

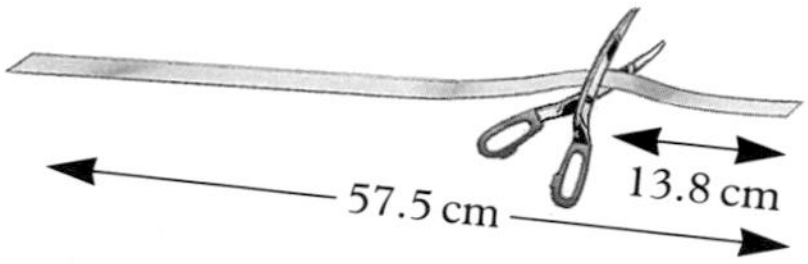

16 Mrs Brown buys three pens for children. The pens are £1.28 each.
How much does Mrs Brown pay altogether?

17 Four friends share a prize of £5.
How much do they each get?

1

Country	Population
Austria	7 526 000
Belgium	9 940 000
Denmark	5 175 000
France	54 414 000
Greece	9 665 000
Italy	56 189 000

This is the information that Craig has been given for homework.

a Which country has the largest population?
b Write the population of Italy in words.

2 Write the value of each red digit in words.

a 123.45 **c** 1457 **e** 140.05
b 61.004 **d** 9.152 **f** 0.607

3 Give the number between each of these pairs on a number line.
Example 4.55, **4.56**, 4.57.

a 3.51, …, 3.53 **c** 1.58, …, 1.6 **e** 0.3, …, 0.32
b 6.9, …, 7.1 **d** 5.6, …, 5.62

4 **a** Put these numbers in order of size, smallest first.
(1) 5.417, 5.42, 5.4 (3) 0.504, 0.541, 0.514
(2) 17.304, 17.34, 17.3 (4) 0.732, 0.7302, 0.73

b These are times of six athletes for a 200 metre race. List the gold, silver, and bronze medal winners.

R. Green	23.67 s	S. Newton	24.43 s
W. Collins	24.90 s	L. Small	24.09 s
T. James	25.01 s	P. Williams	23.85 s

5 **a** Complete these patterns by finding the next four terms.
(1) 0.7, 1.8, … (Adding 1.1)
(2) 3.86, 3.88, … (Adding 0.02)
(3) 10.0, 9.7, … (Subtracting 0.3)
(4) 0.60, 0.54, … (Subtracting 0.06)

b Complete these patterns.
Write down the rule in each case.
(1) 0.08, …, 0.24, 0.32, …, 0.48, 0.56, 0.64
(2) 0.4, 0.7, …, 1.3, 1.6, 1.9, …
(3) 40, 20, 10, 5, …, 1.25, …, 0.3125
(4) 7.5, 7.25, …, …, 6.5, 6.25, 6

6 In each of these add noughts until the division is finished or you get a pattern.

a 7.31 ÷ 2 **c** 7.37 ÷ 4
b 5.62 ÷ 3 **d** 13.6 ÷ 6

7 Sally has rounded 5.649 correct to one decimal place.
Sally's answer is 5.7.
Here is Sally's working:
5.649 rounds to 5.65
5.65 rounds to 5.7

a Give the correct answer.
b Explain where Sally went wrong.

8 These calculator displays show amounts of money in pounds. Write them correctly using £. Round correct to the nearest penny if necessary.

a 6.4 **c** 17.3 **e** 4.752
b 4.317 **d** 53 **f** 16.008

9 Mr. Truman has a shelf 110 cm wide.
Each of his video cases is 3 cm wide.

a How many can he fit on to his shelf?
b What size gap is left?

10 A child walks around the edge of a rectangular lawn. He arrives back at his starting point.
How far has the child walked?

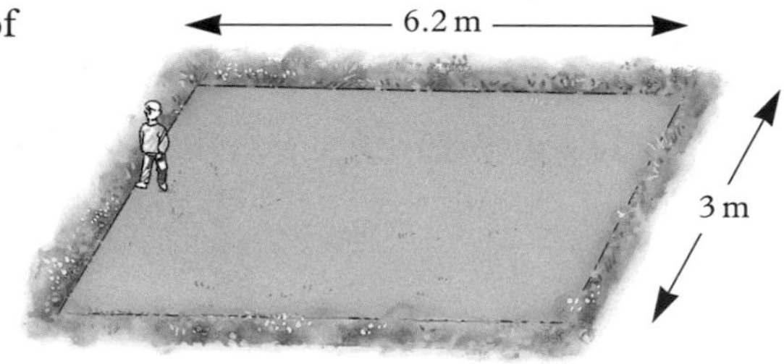

11 Mr Jones bought three packets of sandwiches and two beefburgers. He also bought one tea, one coffee and three colas.
How much was his total bill?

Menu	
Tea	60p
Coffee	80p
Cola	60p
Packet of sandwiches	£1.80
Beefburger	£2.90

12 Kylie was asked to make up a problem for the sum 2.5 + 4.3 = 6.8.
Here is Kylie's answer.
'Andrew had 2.5 sweets. His friend gave him 4.3 sweets. Andrew now has 6.8 sweets.'

What do you think of Kylie's answer?
Make up a better problem for the same sum.

- forty-three thousand six hundred and seventeen 43 617
- **Decimals in words** *Example*: 2.35 is **'two point three five'**
- **Decimal point** The **point** marks where whole numbers end and fractions or parts of numbers begin.
  Examples of numbers with decimal points are:
  2.4 3.145 14.08
-

thousands	hundreds	tens	units	.	tenths	hundredths	thousandths
		2	4	.	3	0	6

The red digit is **three tenths**

- **Place value** The position of a digit in a number affects its **value**. Each column has a value **ten times** the one to the **right** of it.
-

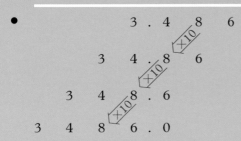

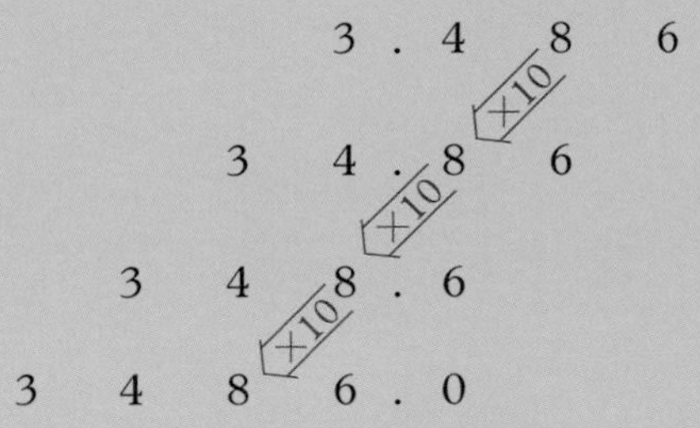

When multiplying by **10**, the digits change by **one** column.
When multiplying by **10 × 10** or **100**, the digits change by **two** columns.

- Putting 4.615 and 4.67 in order of size.
  4.615 4.67 The first figure after the decimal point is the same.
  4.615 4.67 1 is smaller than 7 so 4.615 is smaller than 4.67
-

$$\begin{array}{r} 4.520 \\ +\ 6.851 \\ \hline 11.371 \end{array} \qquad \begin{array}{r} 19.^{5}\!\cancel{6}{}^{1}0 \\ -\ 7.53 \\ \hline 12.07 \end{array} \qquad \begin{array}{r} 16.2 \\ \times\ \ \ 3 \\ \hline 48.6 \\ {}_{1} \end{array} \qquad \begin{array}{r} 5.9 \\ 4\overline{)23.^{3}6} \end{array}$$

- 4.6 rounds to 5. 4.1 rounds to 4.
  3.5 is halfway between 3 and 4. It is rounded to 4.
- To round (a) 5.1679 and (b) 5.6879 to one decimal place.
  (a) 5.6179 5.61 is nearer to 5.6
  (b) 5.6879 5.68 is nearer to 5.7

1 **a** What is 4 multiplied by to give it the value 400?
b By how many columns has the 4 changed?

2 **a** Write the number 5.63 in words
b Write the number nought point nought seven nine in figures.

3 **a** Copy the column headings.

thousands	hundreds	tens	units	.	tenths	hundredths	thousandths

Write these numbers in the correct columns.
(1) 65.319 (3) 7.096 (5) 0.423
(2) 8104 (4) 104.57
b Give the value of the red digit in words.

4 Write the numbers
4.42, 3.42, 4.414
in order of size, smallest first.

5 Complete these patterns.
Write down the rule in each case.
a 3.6, 3.8, …, 4.2, 4.4, 4.6, …
b …, 8.5, 8.0, 7.5, 7.0, …, 6.0

6 Set this question out carefully.
a $4.51 + 6.2$
b $9.5 - 5.38$
c $6.05 + 7$
d $29 - 8.7$

7 Set this question out carefully.
a 3.4×5
b 0.16×3
c $8.4 \div 3$
d $17.2 \div 4$

8 **a** Round these decimals correct to the nearest whole number.
(1) 4.9 (2) 8.5 (3) 13.3
b Round these numbers correct to one decimal place.
(1) 3.79 (2) 4.62 (3) 6.35

9 Here are some amounts of money.
Round them correct to the nearest penny.
a £3.752 **b** £25.609 **c** £0.875

7 3-D work: the extra dimension

CORE

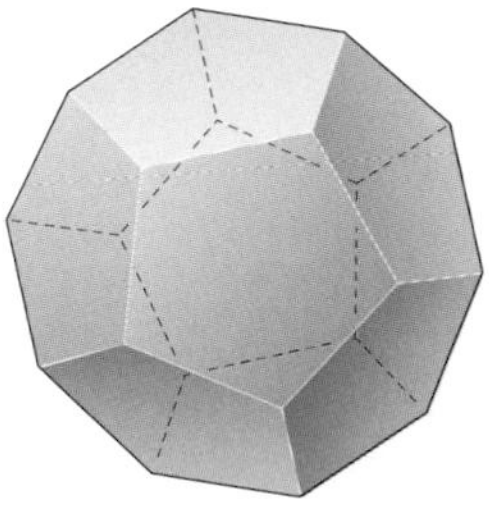

δωδεκάεδρον

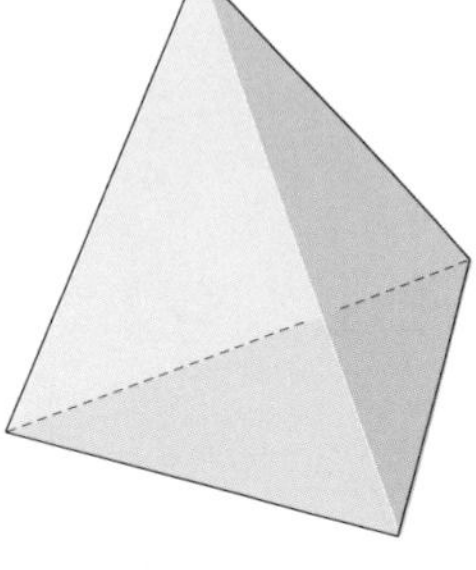

τετράεδρον

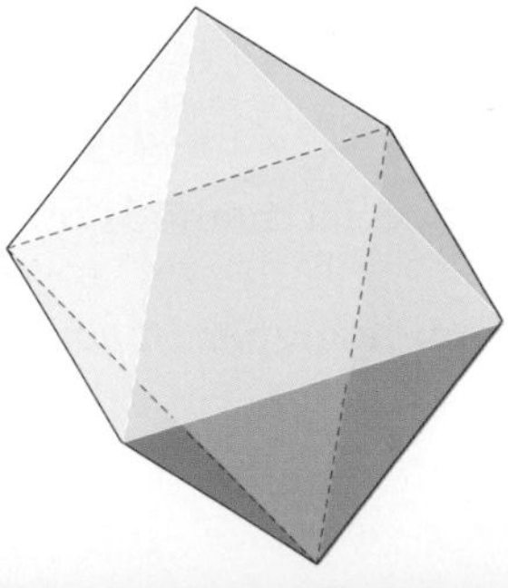

οκτάεδρον

1 Identifying solids

A line has one dimension. We need one number to give a position in one dimension.
A is at the point 4.

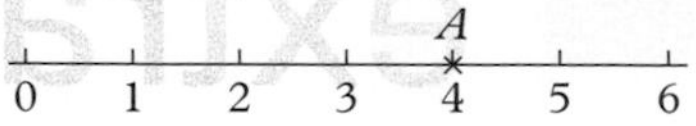

This page has two dimensions.
So does a pair of axes for a graph.
B is at (1, 2).
Its position is given by two numbers.

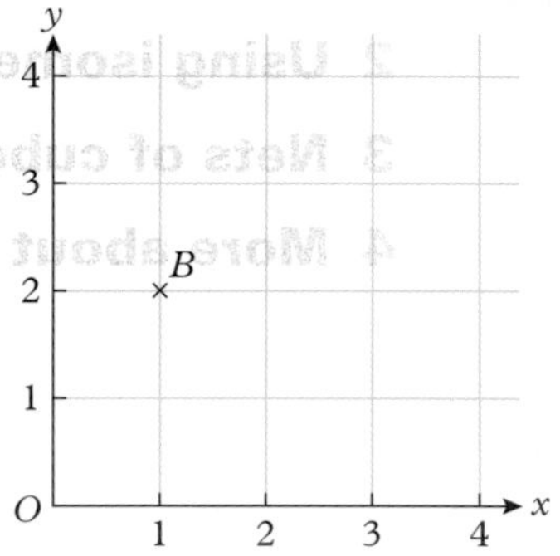

Hold a pencil point about 4 cm above *B*.

We need a third number for the distance upwards. We can then describe where the pencil point is.
We have three dimensions or 3-D for short.

Some books work in 3-D by having 'pop-up' pages.

Most books rely on special methods of drawing 3-D solids on their 2-D pages.
They may also use photographs of actual solid objects.

A jigsaw cat

An ornament cat

A real cat

In mathematics 3-D shapes are drawn in special ways.
Hidden edges are shown by dashed lines.

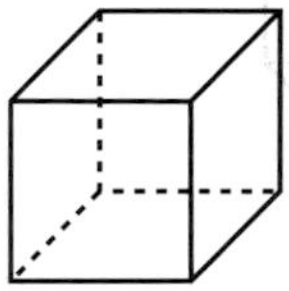
Cube

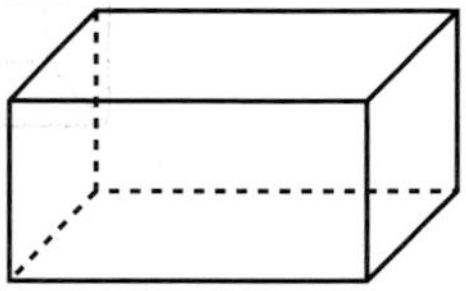
Cuboid

Exercise 7:1

1 Use this method to draw a cube on squared paper.
Use a pencil. Press lightly.

a Start with a square.

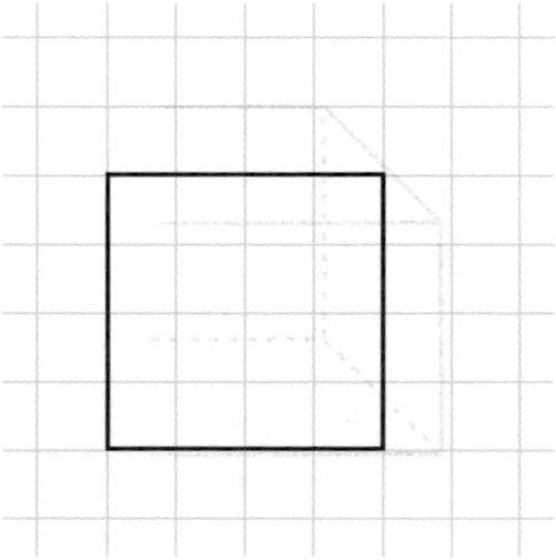

b Draw a second square the same size.

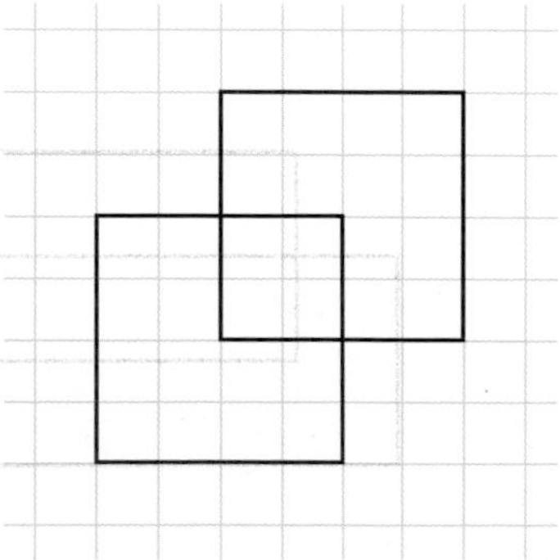

c Join the corners of the squares.

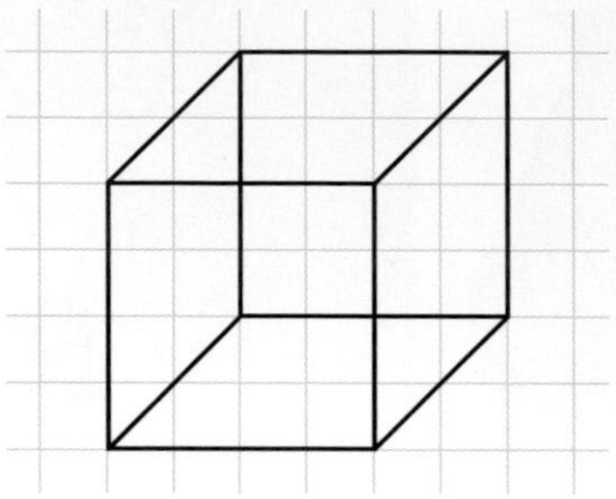

d Rub gaps in three lines. This makes the hidden edges appear dashed.

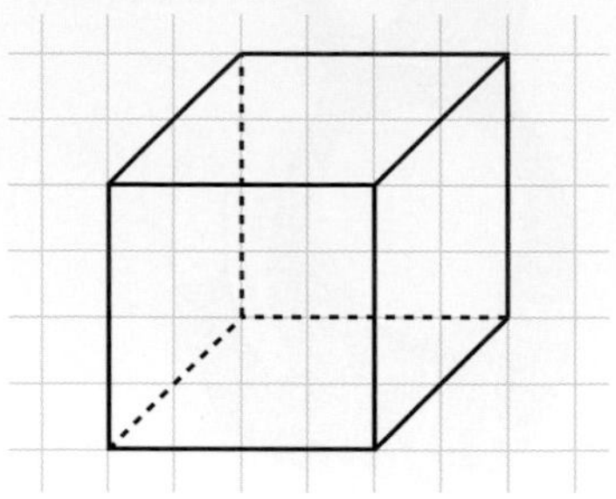

2 Draw two more cubes.

a

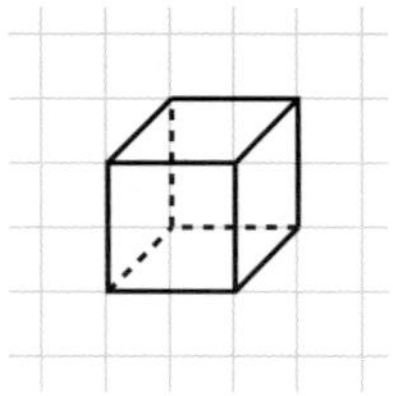

b

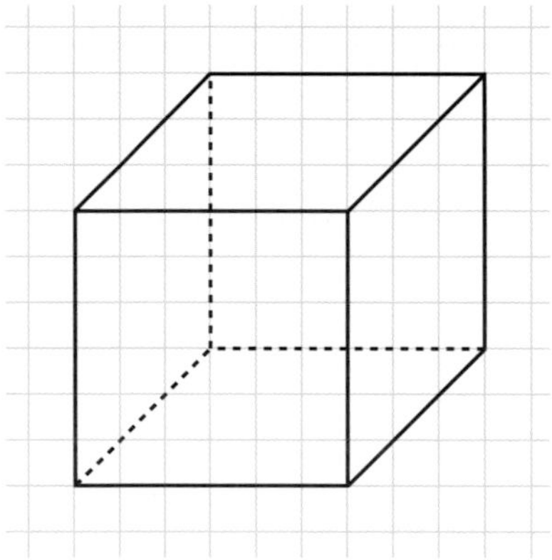

3 a Copy this cuboid (rectangular block).

Start from:

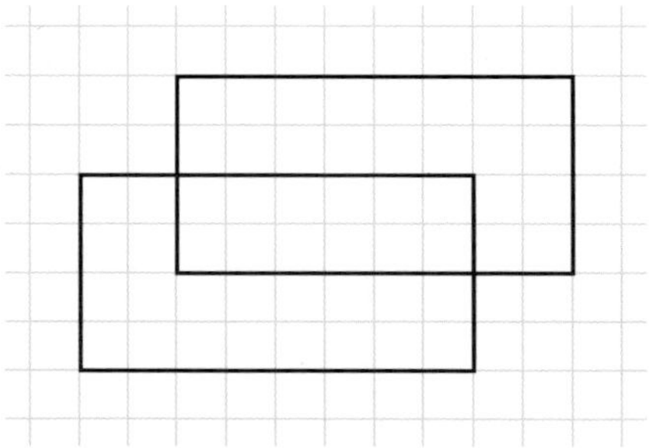

to get:

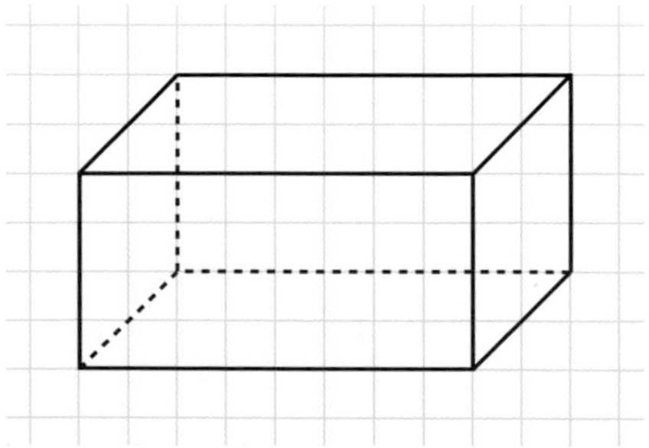

Now copy these cuboids.

b

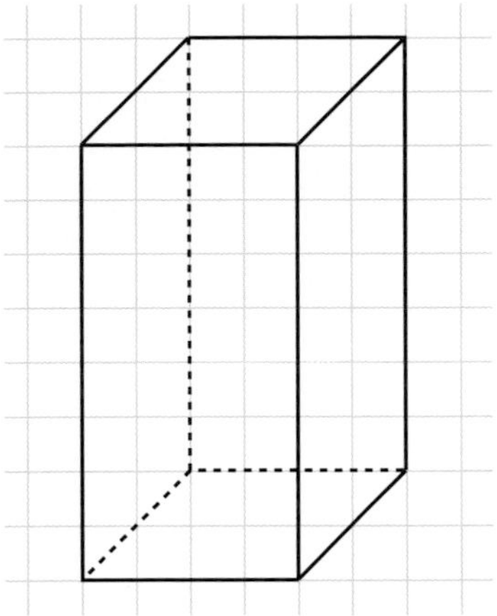

c

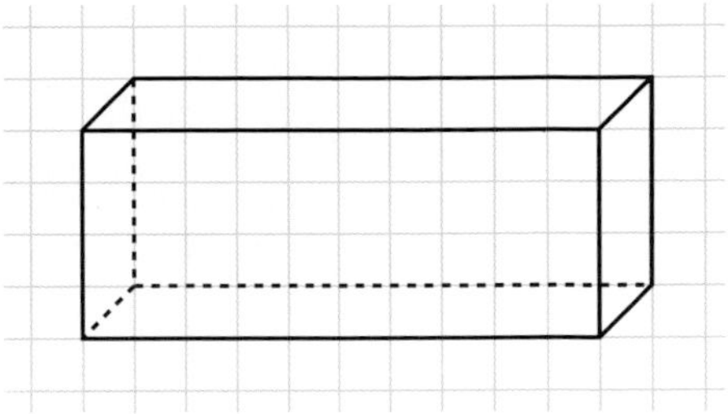

4 Two of the cuboids in Question **3** are the same.
Which two are they?

Prism

A **prism** has the same shape all the way through.
Its sides are parallel. So are its ends.

Cube
Cuboid

A prism takes its name from the shape of its ends.
Some prisms have special names. A **cube** and a **cuboid** are prisms.

The diagram shows a prism with a triangle at its ends.

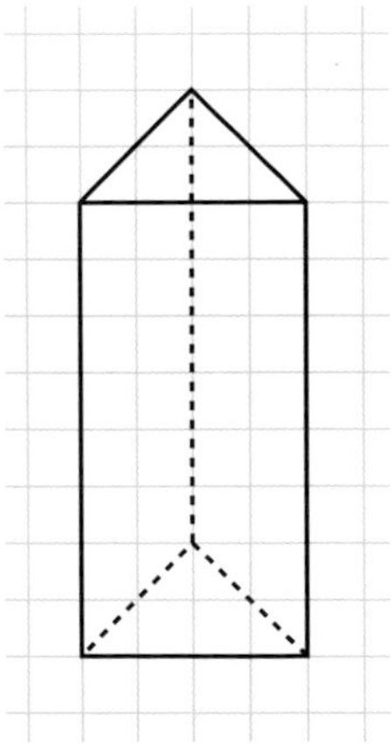

A triangular prism

---

5 Copy the triangular prism and label it.

Pyramid

A **pyramid** is a solid whose side edges meet in a point. All its side faces are triangles.

A pyramid takes its name from the shape of its base.

The diagram shows a pyramid with a square base.

Tetrahedron

A pyramid with a triangular base has a special name. It is called a **tetrahedron**.

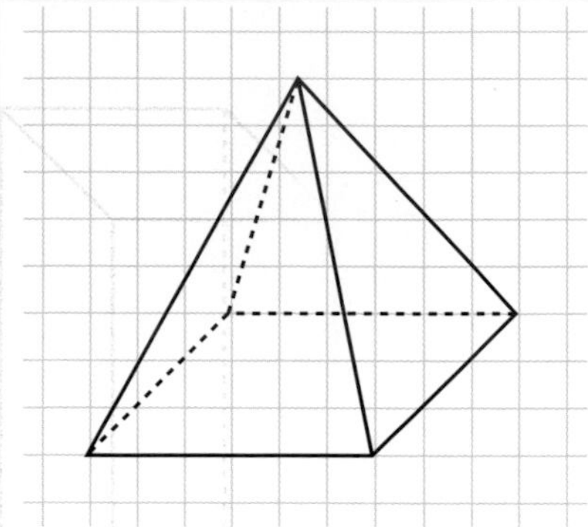

A square pyramid

6 Copy the square pyramid and label it.

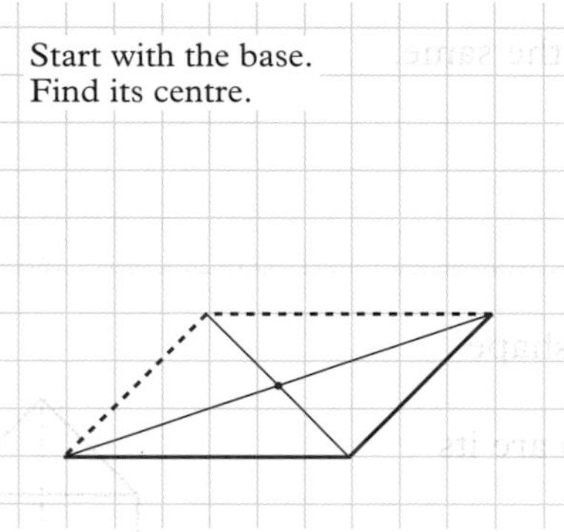
Start with the base.
Find its centre.

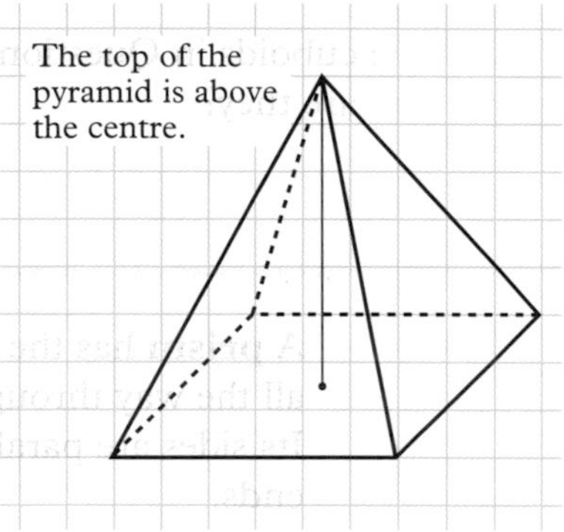
The top of the
pyramid is above
the centre.

● **7** Make a list of the names of these shapes. You do not have to draw them. Choose from: hexagonal pyramid, triangular prism, tetrahedron, pentagonal pyramid, hexagonal prism, square pyramid, pentagonal prism.

a

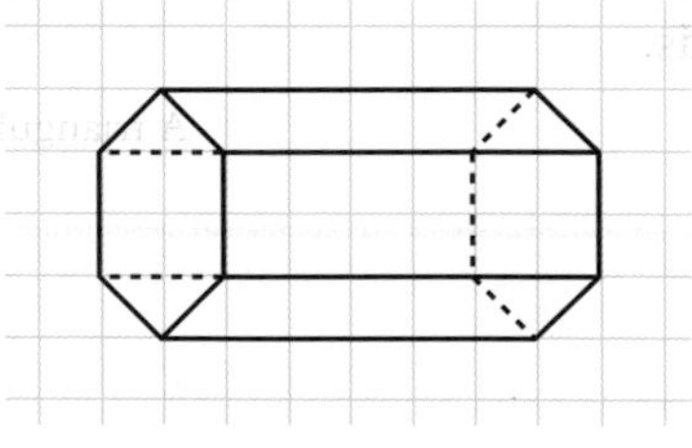

b

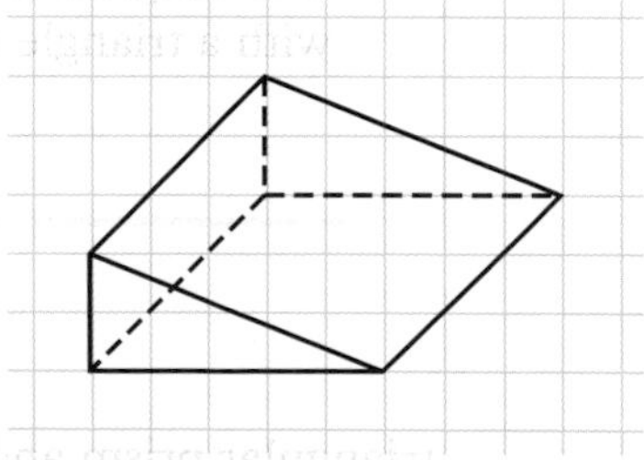

c

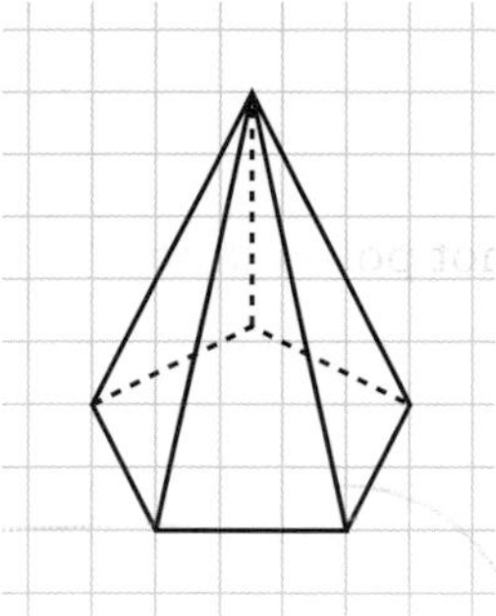

e

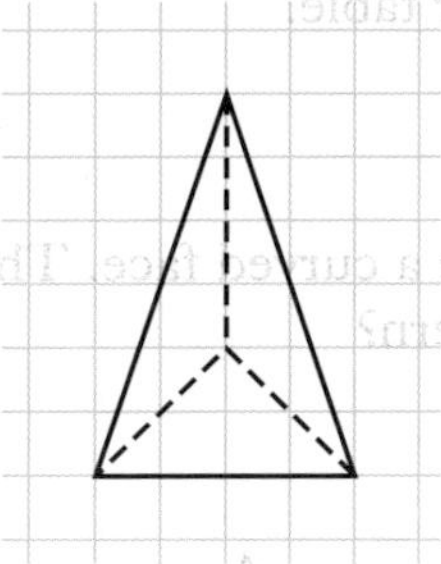

g

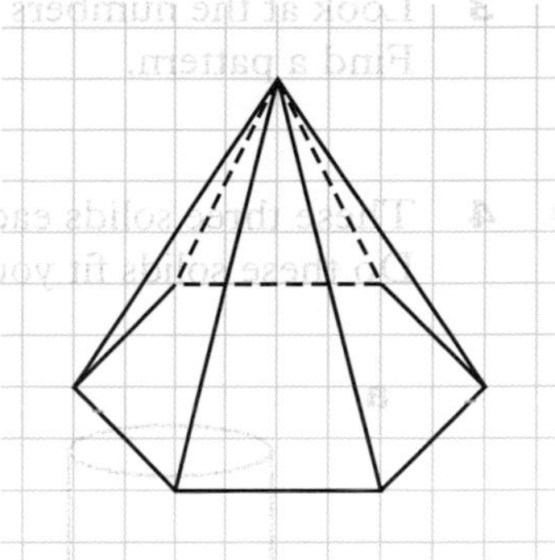

f

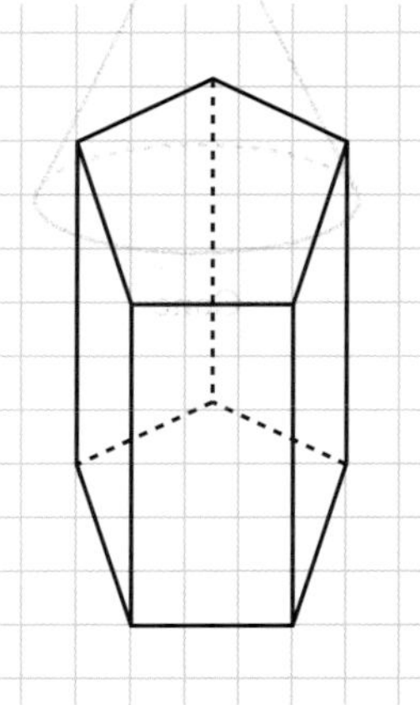

d

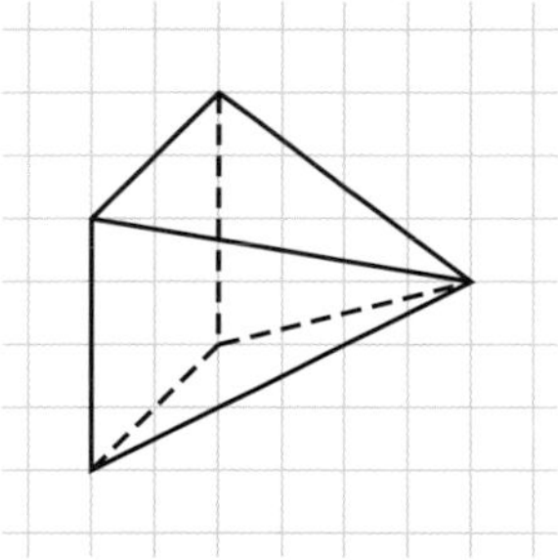

Polyhedron	A **polyhedron** is a solid whose faces are all plane (flat).

Exercise 7:2 Euler's formula

1 Copy the table.

Polyhedron	*F*	*V*	*F* + *V*	*E*
(1) Cube	6	8	14	12
(2) Cuboid				
(3) Triangular prism				
(4) Square pyramid				
(5) Tetrahedron				

2 Complete the table.
F is the number of faces. *V* is the number of vertices (corners).
E is the number of edges.

3 Look at the numbers in your table.
Find a pattern.

● **4** These three solids each have a curved face. They are not polyhedrons.
Do these solids fit your pattern?

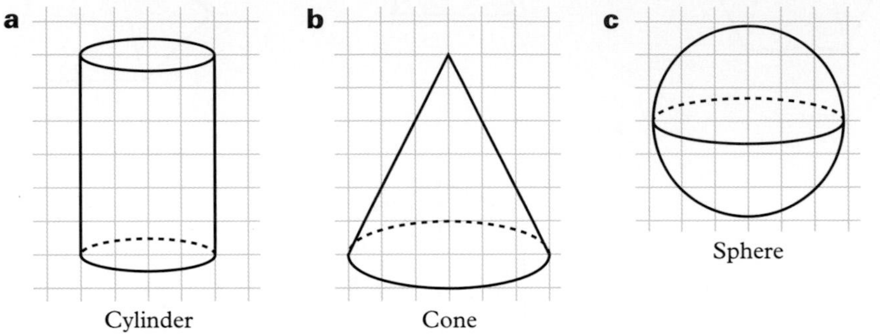

Exercise 7:3

1 Copy the three solids from Exercise 7:2, Question 4.
Label each shape with its name.

2 The cylinder, cone and sphere are common in everyday life.
Make a list or draw some of their uses.

3 Cuboids are very common in everyday life.
Do you know any uses for other prisms or pyramids?

Look for all these shapes outside school.

2 Using isometric paper

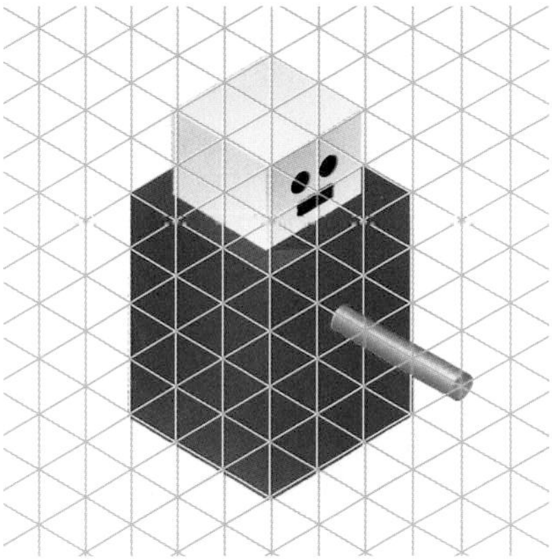

Paper with the pattern printed in triangles is called **isometric** paper.
Isometric means equal measure.
How do you think the paper got its name?

Isometric paper has a right way up.

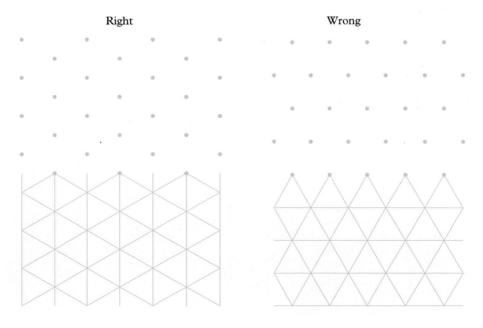

Right

Wrong

A cube or cuboid can be drawn on isometric paper with its edges shown their correct lengths. The dashed lines for the hidden edges are often missed out.

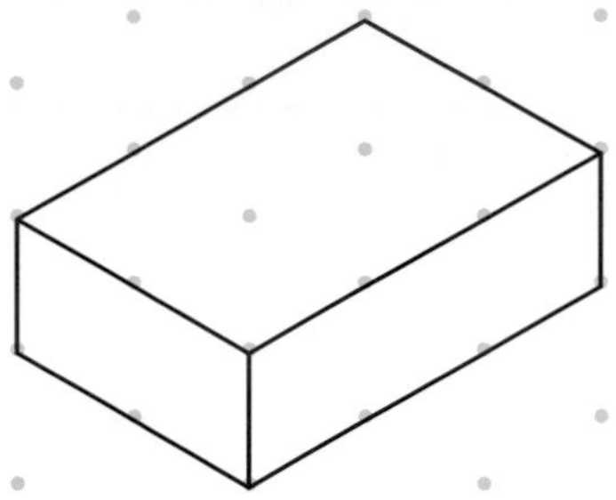

This cuboid has length 3 cm, width 2 cm and height 1 cm.

Exercise 7:4

Here are a cube and some cuboids.

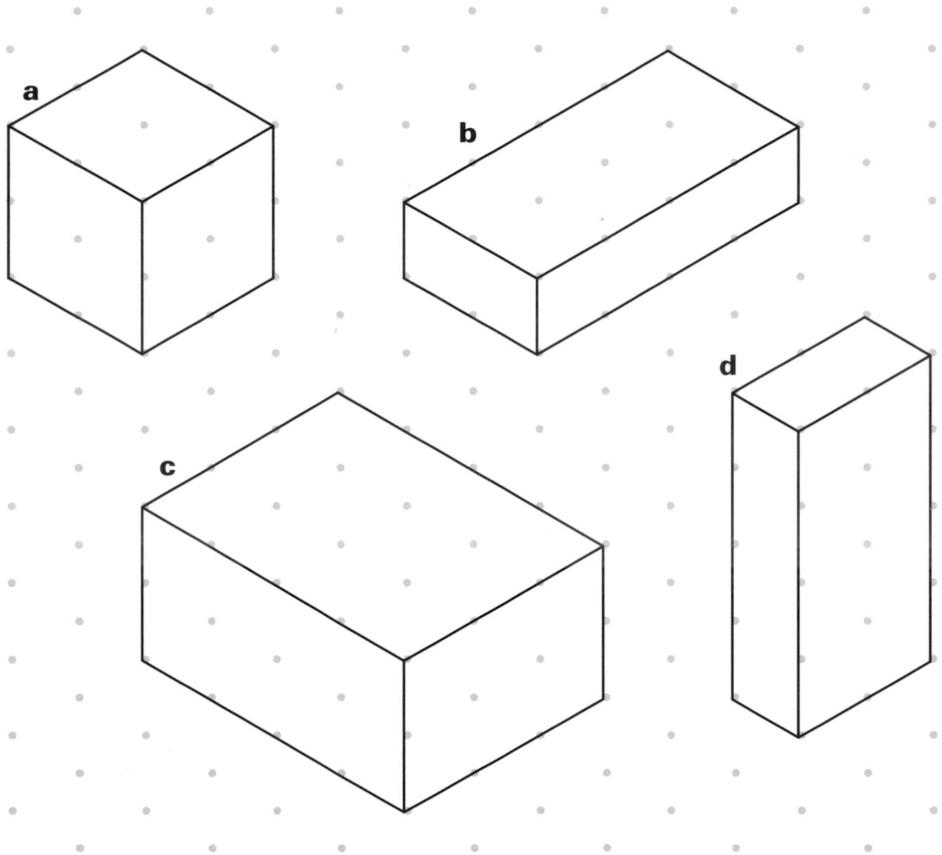

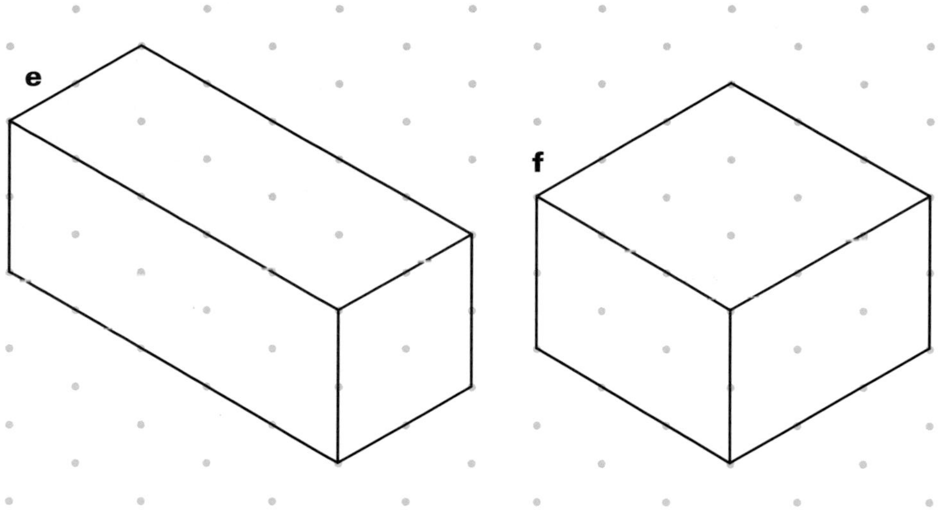

You will need 1 cm isometric paper for this exercise.

1 Copy the cube and cuboids.
For each one, write down the length, the width and the height.

2 Which two drawings show the same cuboid?

● **3** Draw a cube of side 3 cm.

● **4** Draw a cube of side 1 cm.

Exercise 7:5

You will need some cubes and some dotty isometric paper.

1 Join two cubes as shown.
Two cubes can be joined
in only one way.

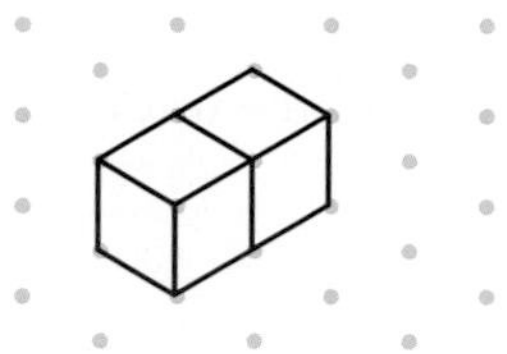

2 Three cubes can be arranged in two ways. Make the two arrangements.

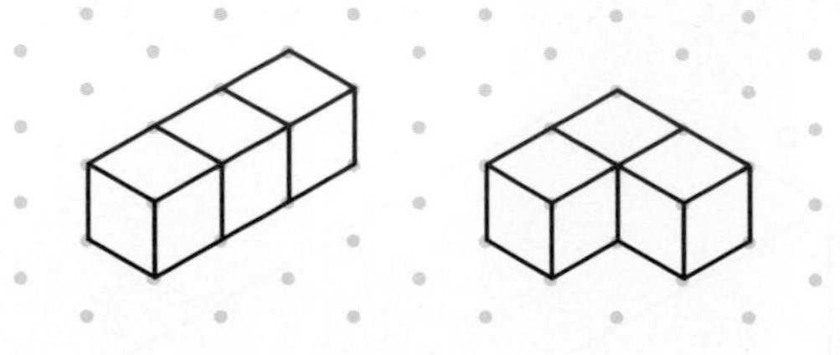

3 Four cubes can be joined in lots of different ways. For each pair of sketches:

a make the pair of arrangements shown.

b decide whether the arrangements are the same.

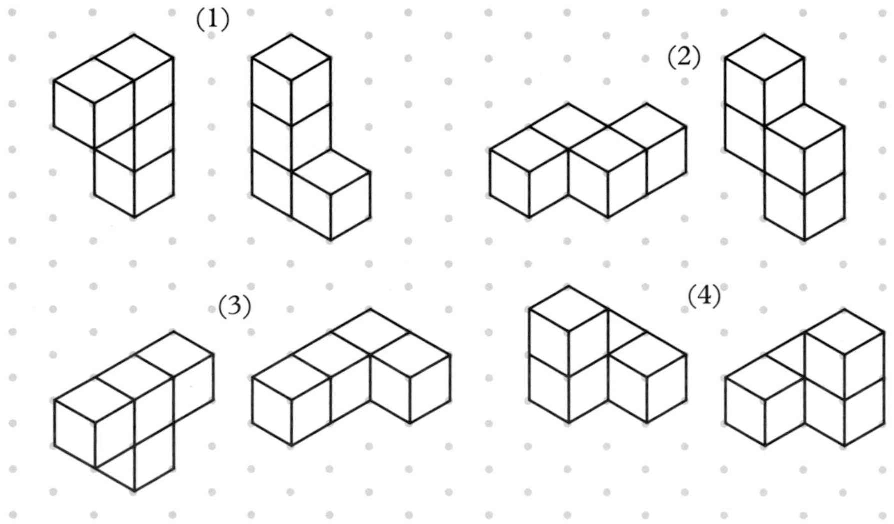

4 Find other ways of joining four cubes.

5 How many different ways of joining four cubes did you find?

6 Draw some of the ways of arranging two, three and four cubes.

3 Nets of cubes and cuboids

Most boxes are cubes or cuboids.
They are cut from flat pieces of card and folded into box shapes.

Net

A **net** is a pattern of shapes on a piece of paper or card.
The shapes are arranged so that the net can be folded to make a hollow solid.

Example

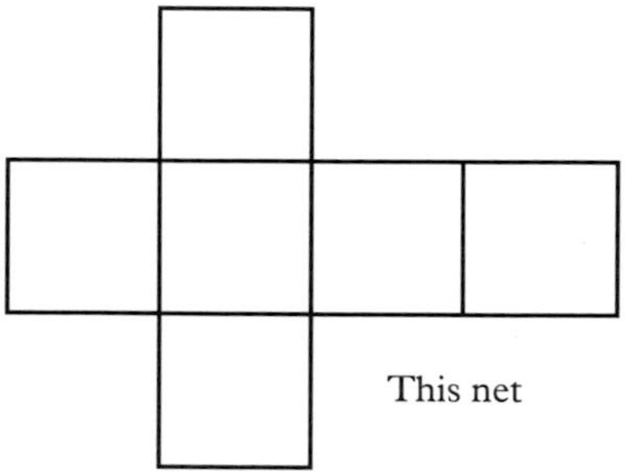

This net

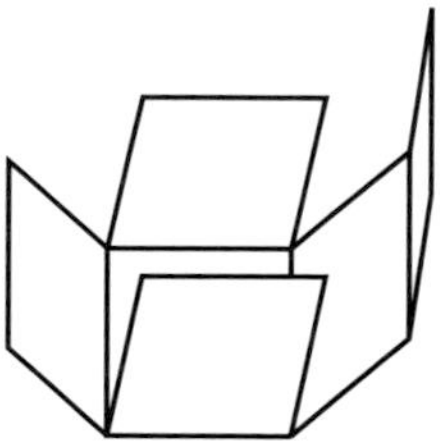

would make

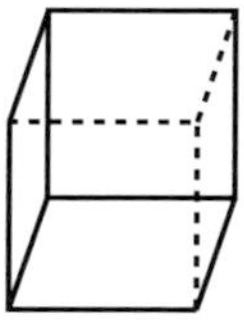

this cube.

Exercise 7:6

1 **a** Copy the net of the cube. Make the sides 3 cm.
b Cut out the net.
Fold it into a cube.
c Stick the net into your exercise book.

2 Here are more patterns. Some are nets of cubes.
- **a** Draw the patterns on squared paper.
- **b** Cut the patterns out.
  Fold them up. See which make cubes.
- **c** Stick the patterns into your book.
  Arrange them in two groups: those that are nets of cubes and those that are not.

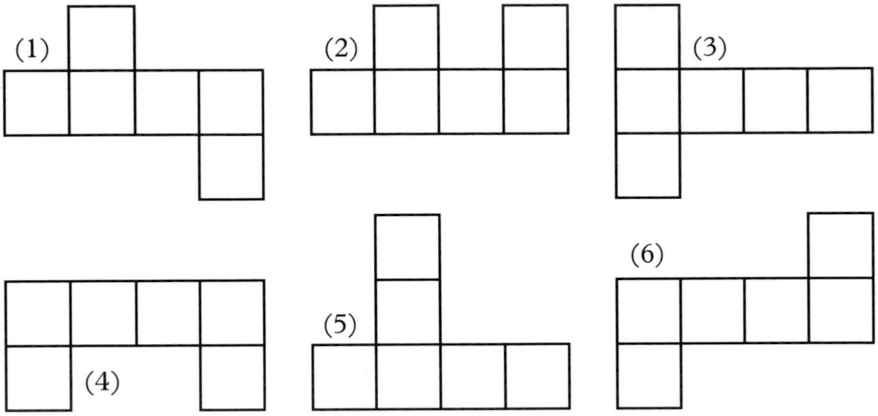

● **3** Six squares joined together as in Question **2** are called **hexominoes**.
- **a** Draw three more patterns of six squares.
- **b** Are your hexominoes nets of cubes?
  Cut them out and test them.
- **c** Stick your hexominoes in your book.

A cuboid also has six faces but they are not all the same size.

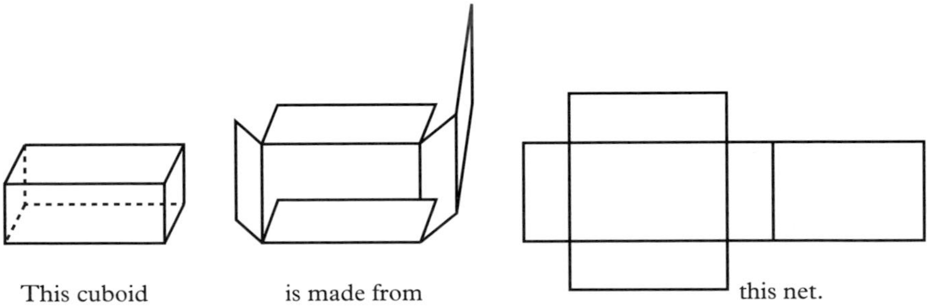

4 This net makes a cuboid 4 cm by 3 cm by 2 cm.

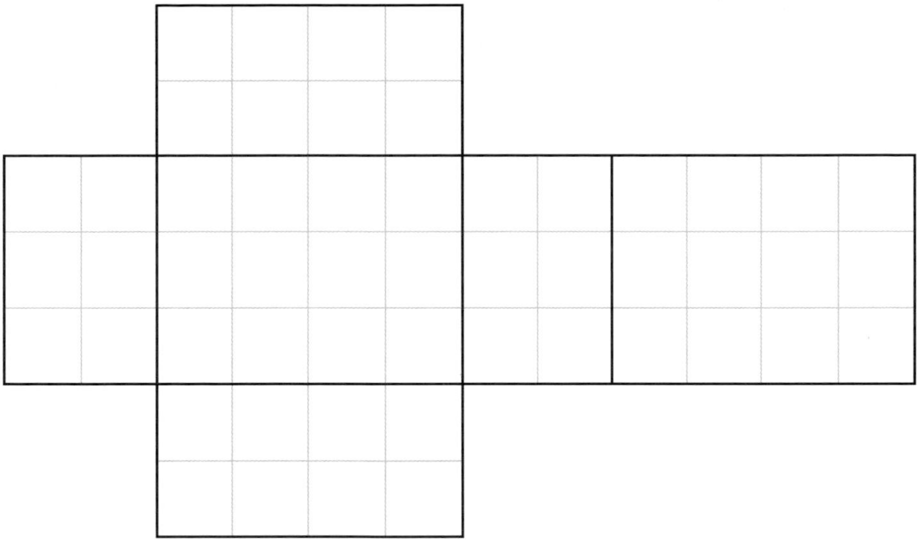

a Copy the net.
b Cut out the net. Fold it into a cuboid.
c Stick the cuboid net into your book.

• **5** Here is a net. It makes a cuboid.
a What is the length of the cuboid?
b What is the width of the cuboid?
c What is the height of the cuboid?
d Make a copy of the net. Fold it to make the cuboid.

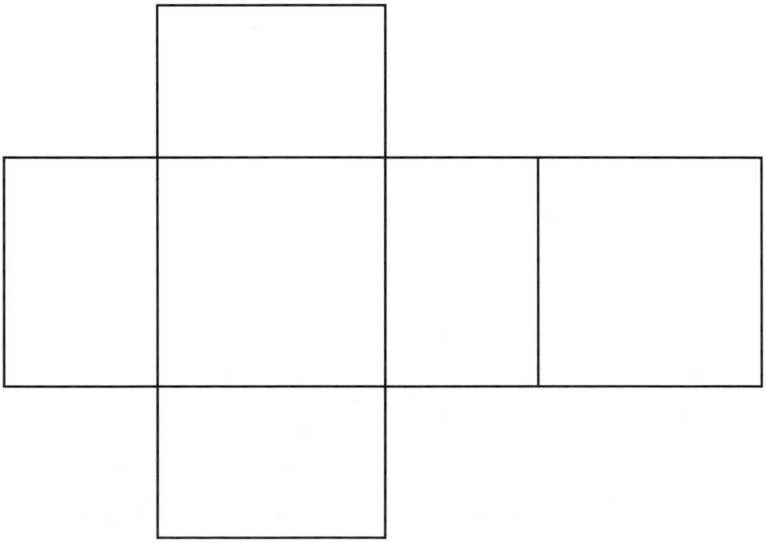

4 More about nets and solids

Exercise 7:7

Different shapes have different nets.

1 You will need some large, lined isometric paper for this question.

a The diagram shows a pattern made by four triangles. Copy the pattern.

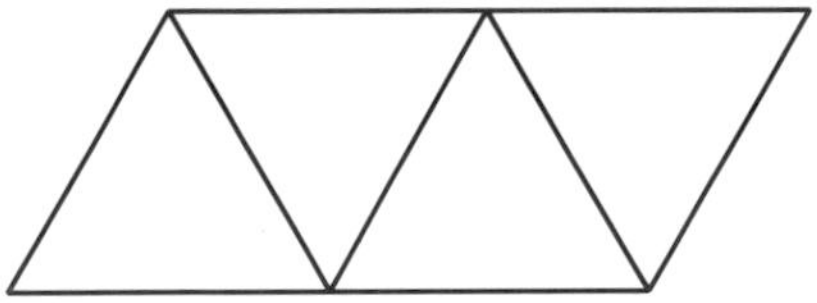

b Find two other patterns of four triangles.

c Look at the patterns.
Which of them are nets of tetrahedrons?
Cut out the patterns to see if you are right.

• **2** The diagram on the next page shows the net of a solid.

a What is the name of the solid?

b Measure the net.
Use compasses and a ruler to draw the net on plain paper.

c Cut out the net.
Fold it to make a solid.

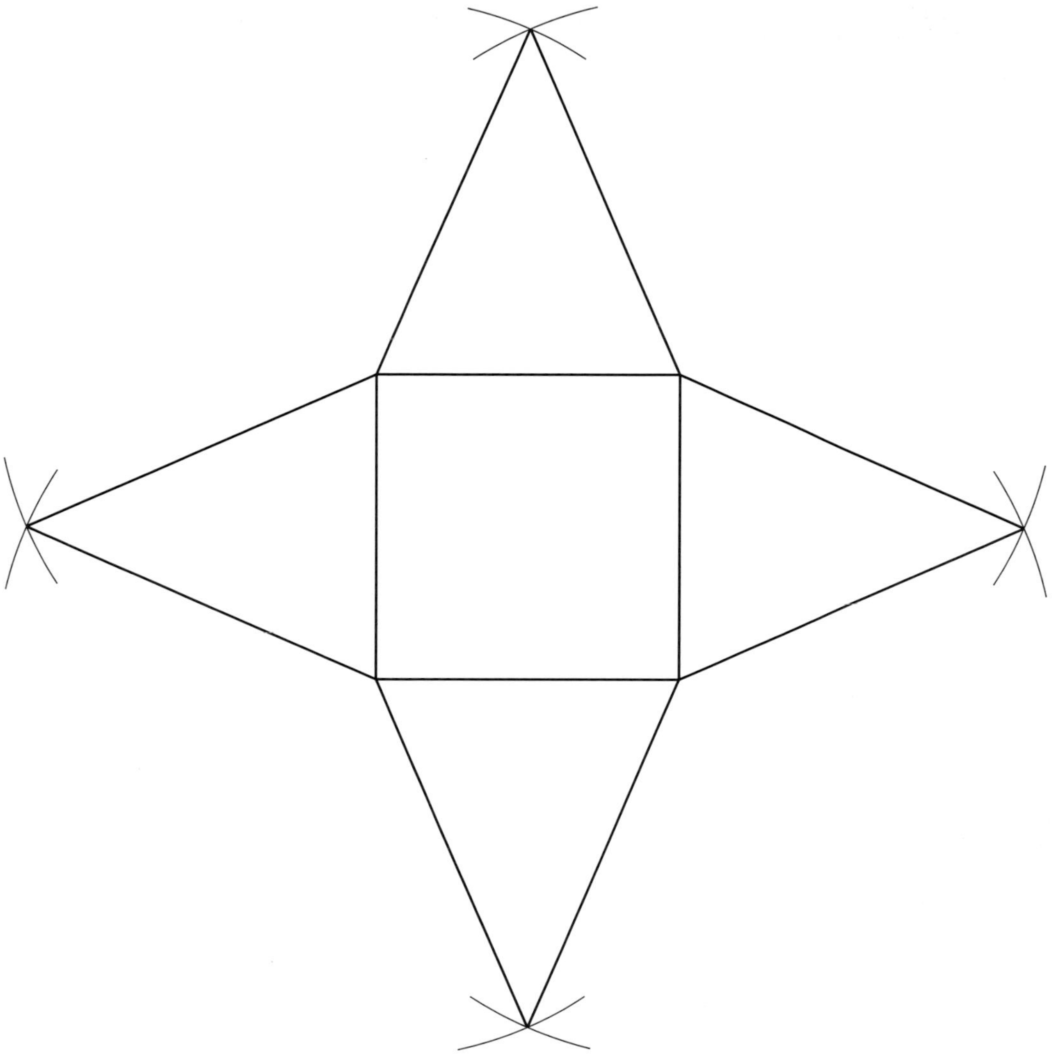

Exercise 7:8

1 A cube has each face painted a different colour.
  a How many colours will be needed?
  b How many colours will meet at any one edge?
  c How many colours will meet at any one vertex?

- **2** Name solids with the following numbers of faces.
  a 4 **b** 5 **c** 6 **d** 7 **e** 8

- **3** The rule for putting spots on the faces of dice is that opposite faces add up to seven.
  This is the net of a dice.
  How many spots would go on faces A, B and C?

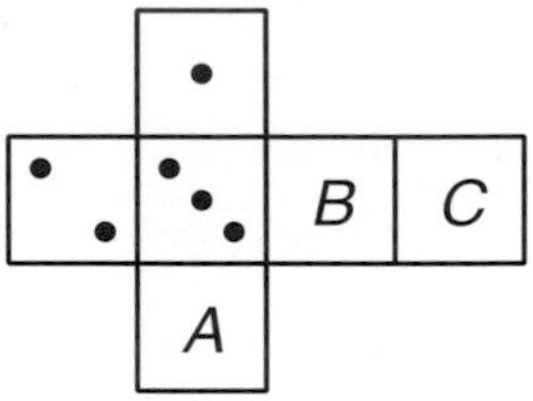

Extra things to do

1 Collect some boxes of different sizes. Open a box out flat.
You will see the net of the box. The net will have extra card.
The extra card is used as **flaps** to stick the box together. It will also make the box stronger.
Open out some of the other boxes. The nets will not all be the same.

2 Copy the net of one of the boxes that you have opened out on to thin card.
Score along the fold lines.
Fold your net and glue it using the flaps.

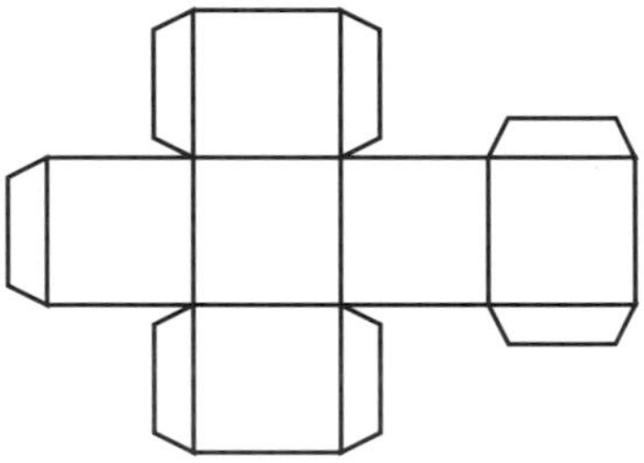

3 Make a cube with flaps like the diagram.
Half the edges of this net have flaps.

4 Make a model from different solids.
Use sellotape instead of flaps and glue.
Here are some ideas.

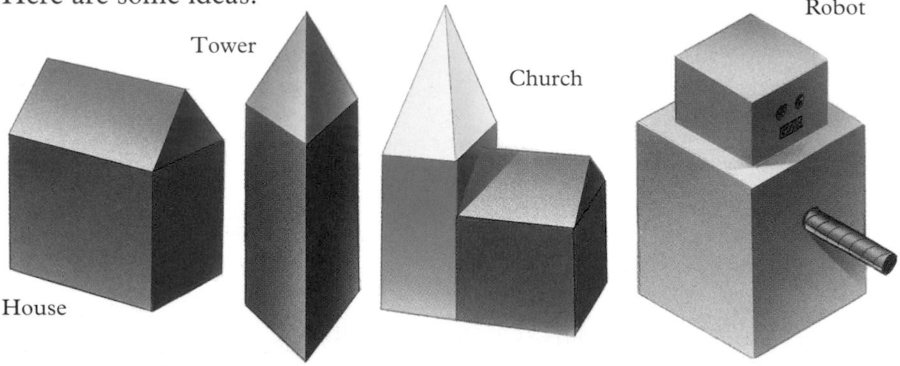

5 Your mathematics room may have a book with nets of solids. You could also look in the school library.

1 **a** This camping site has three unusual tents. What are the names of the shapes of the tents?

b What shape is the flagpole?

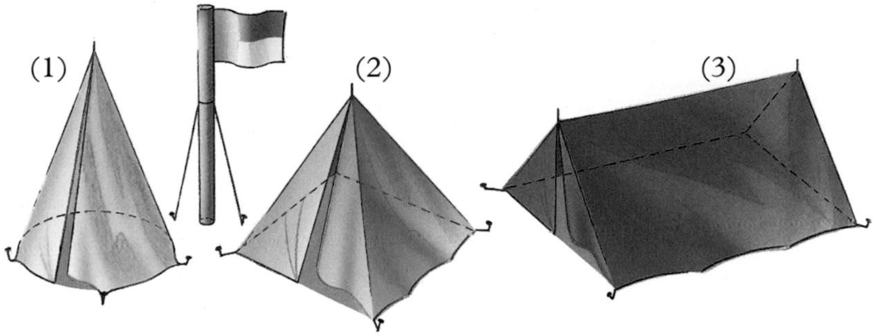

2 Write down the length, width and height of each cuboid.

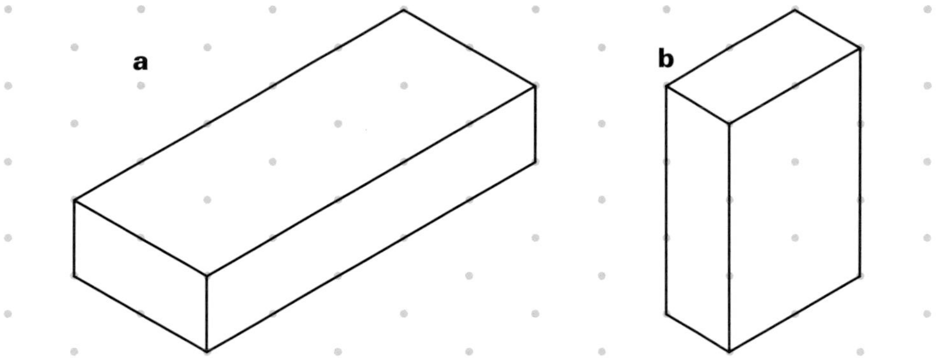

3 What is the least number of cubes you need to make each of these shapes?

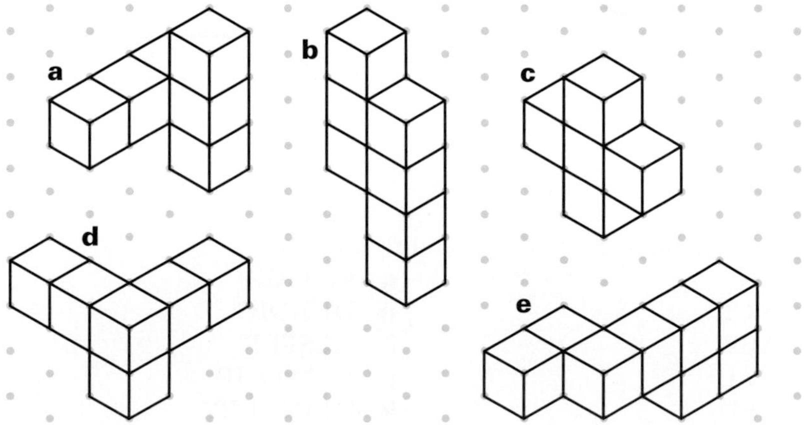

4 Here is a net. It makes a cuboid.

a What is the length of the cuboid?
b What is the width of the cuboid?
c What is the height of the cuboid?

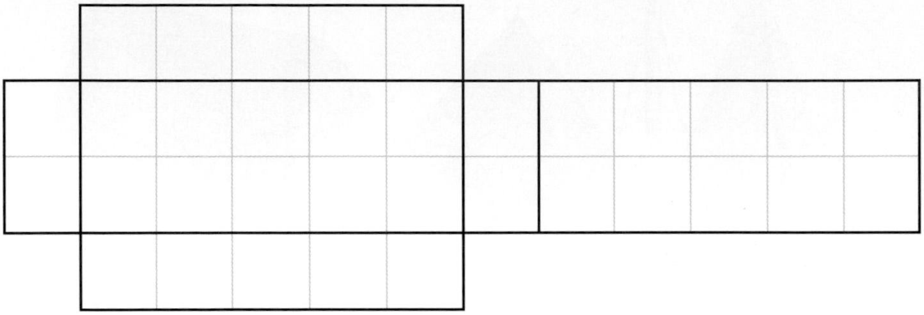

5 Copy the diagram in Question **4**.
Cut it out and fold it to make a cuboid.

6 Write down the names of the solids that can be made from these nets.

a

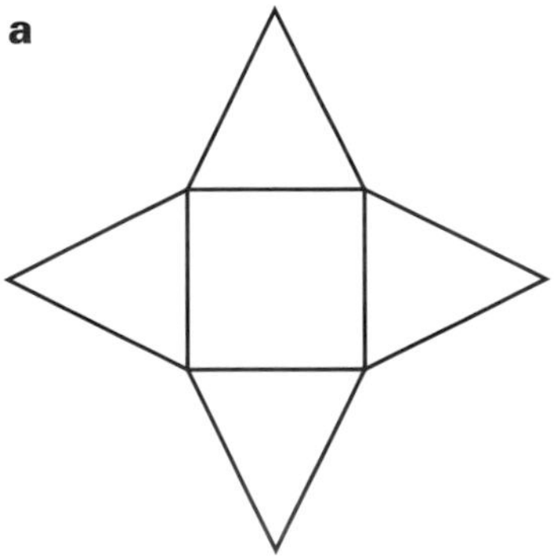

b

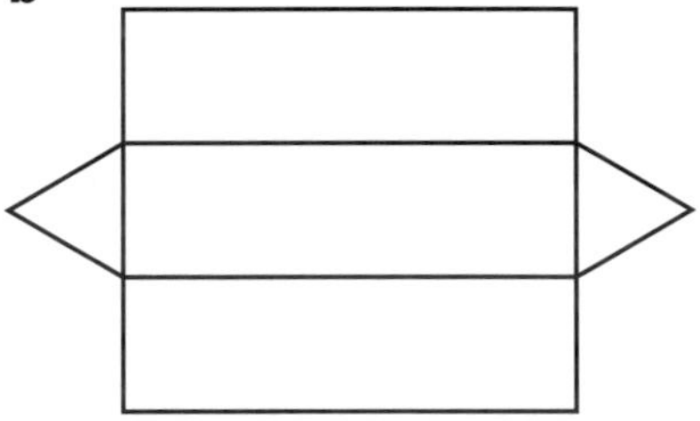

7 Rearrange these to get words from this chapter.

a TEN
b ONCE
c CAFE
d BUCE
e GEED
f MIRPS
g EXTREV
h DUBOIC
i HESPER
j ARMYDIP
k DLINCERY
l SOMERCITI

1 Sapna has stuck two solids together to get this shape.

a What two solids has Sapna used?

b Which of the solids is a prism?

c How many faces, vertices and edges has Sapna's new solid?

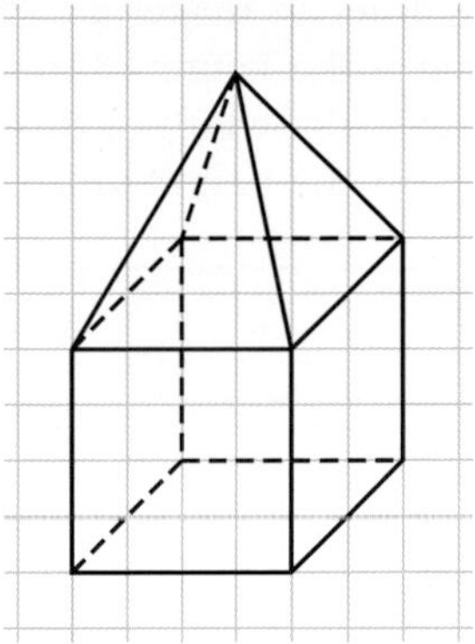

2 Draw these cuboids on 1 cm isometric paper.

a

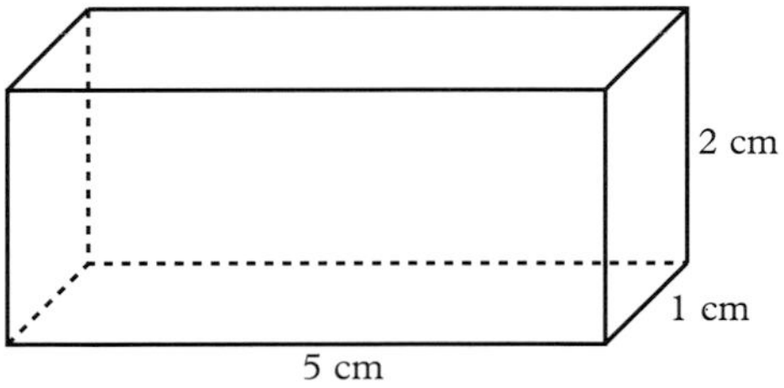

b

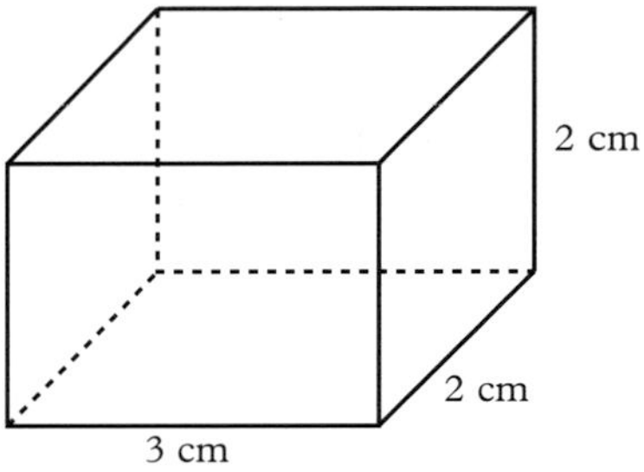

3 Draw nets of the two cuboids in Question 2.

4 The diagrams show four cubes joined together. A fifth cube is joined to each of the green faces in turn.
On isometric paper, draw sketches to show the three different solids.

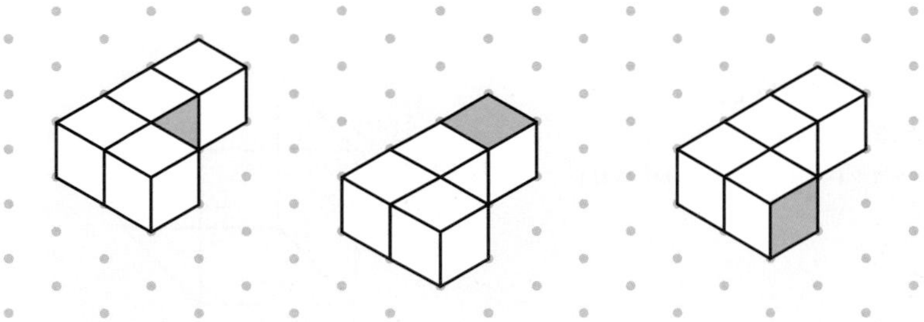

5 Here is a net. It makes a cuboid.
a What is the length of this cuboid?
b What is the width of this cuboid?
c What is the height of this cuboid?

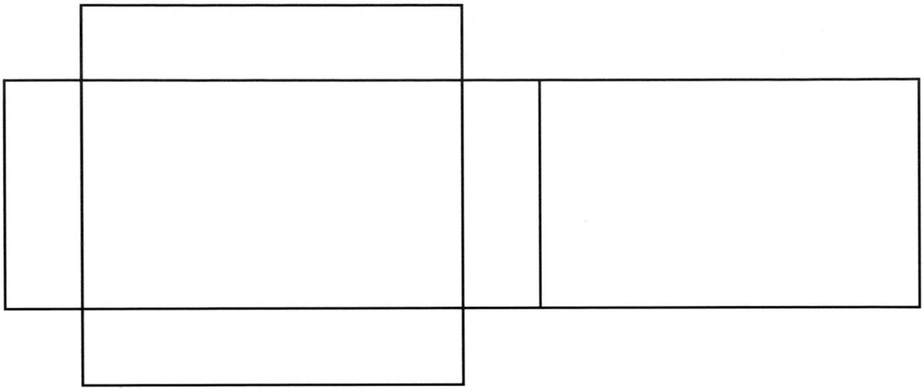

6 Copy the diagram in Question **5** on to paper.
Cut it out and fold it to make a cuboid.

7 Write down the names of the solids that can be made from these nets.

a

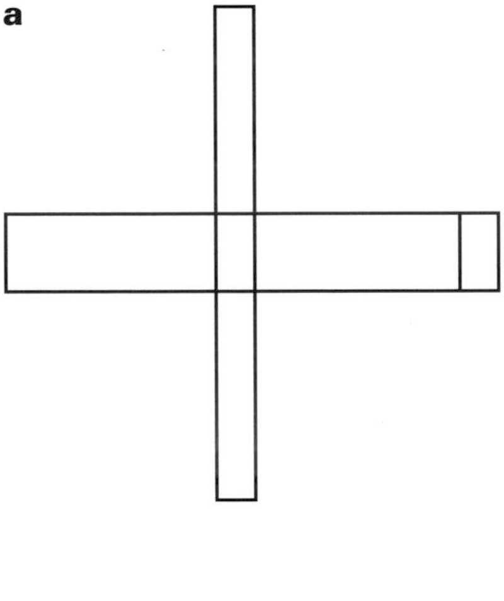

b

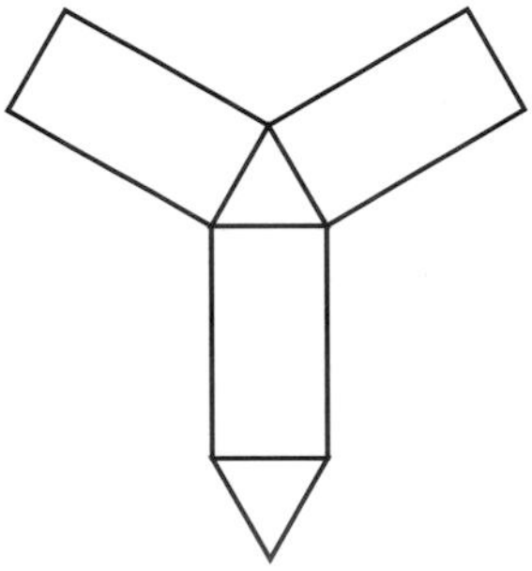

c

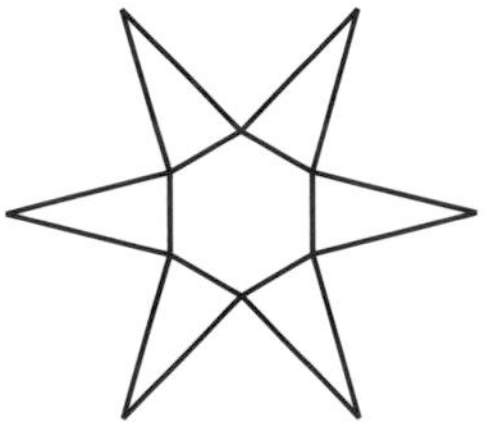

8 This cube is made of wire.
Each edge is 5 cm long.
What is the total length of wire needed?

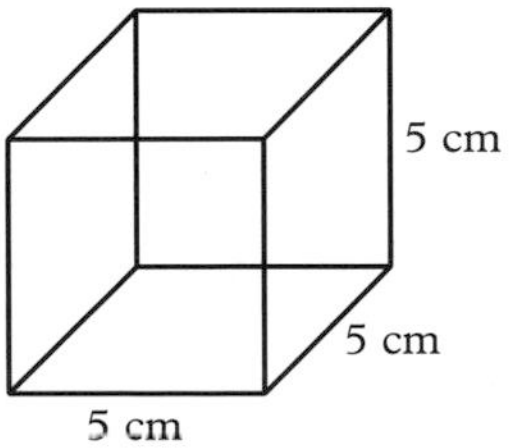

- In mathematics 3-D shapes are drawn in special ways. Hidden edges are shown by dashed lines.

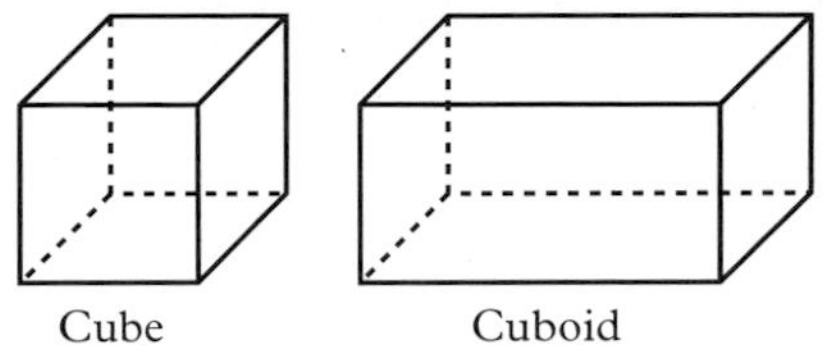

- A **prism** has the same shape all the way through. Its sides are parallel. So are its ends.

  A prism takes its name from the shape of its ends.

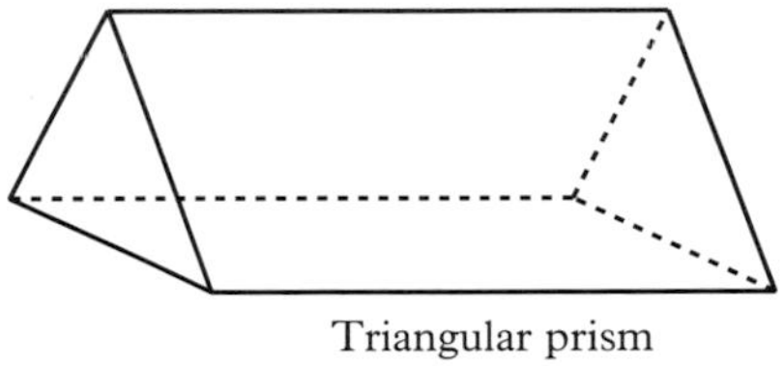

- A **pyramid** is a solid whose side edges meet in a point. All its side faces are triangles.

  A pyramid takes its name from the shape of its base.

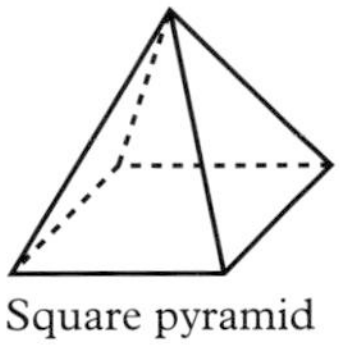

- Shapes with a curved face.

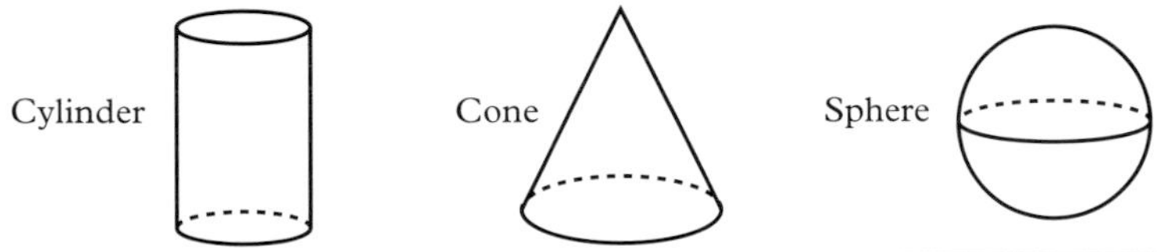

- A cube or cuboid can be drawn on isometric paper with its edges shown their correct lengths.

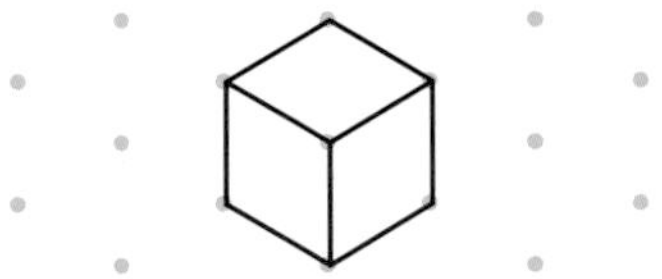

- A **net** is a pattern of shapes on a piece of paper or card. The shapes are arranged so that the net can be folded to make a hollow solid.

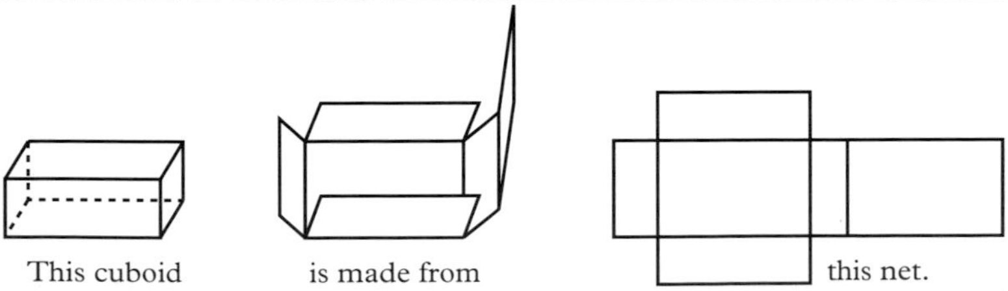

1 **a** How do you tell the difference between a prism and a pyramid?
b What is the name of this solid?
c How many edges does it have?
d How many faces does it have?
e How many vertices does it have?

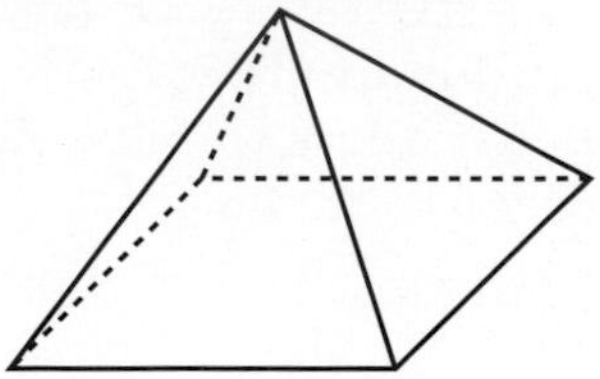

2 **a** Write down the length, width and height of this cuboid.

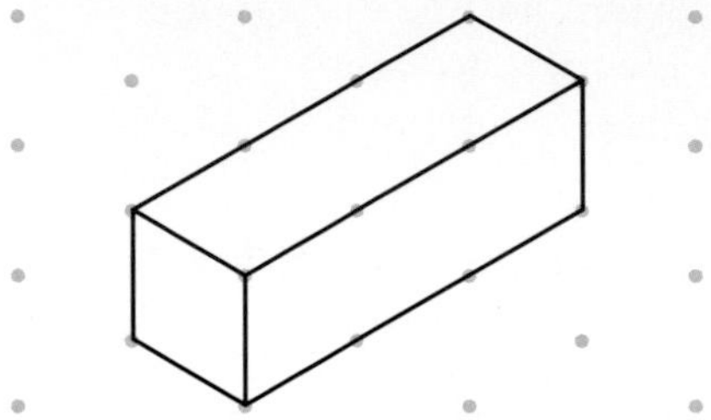

b What is the least number of cubes you need to make each of these shapes?

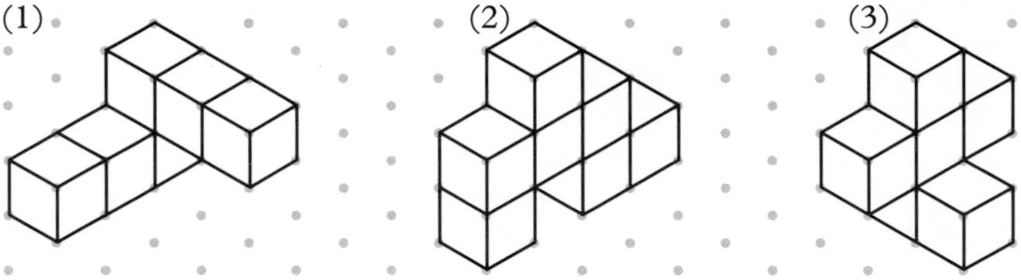

3 Which of these patterns is *not* the net of a cube?

a
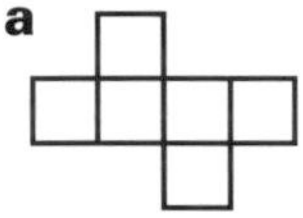
b
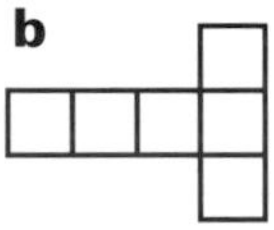
c
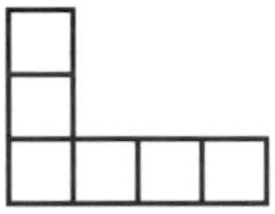

4 **a** Write down the length, width and height of the cuboid you could make from this net.

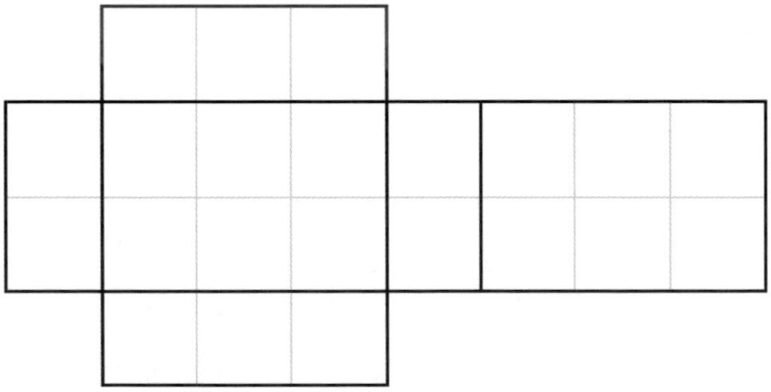

b What solid could you make from this net?

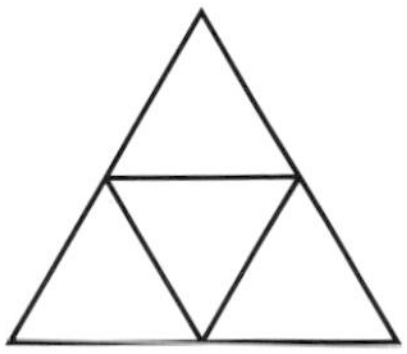

8 Probability

CORE

1 Probability scales
2 How the theory works
3 Experiments and games
4 When the theory doesn't help

QUESTIONS
EXTENSION
SUMMARY
TEST YOURSELF

Jacques Bernoulli

The Bernoulli family produced some of the most famous mathematicians in history.

Two brothers, Jacques (1654–1705) and Jean (1667–1748), were probably the most famous. Jacques did a lot of work on probability.

His main book, called 'The Art of Conjecturing', was the first major book about probability. It was not published until 8 years after his death.

A lot of the work on probability is very recent and has been done since 1945.

1 Probability scales

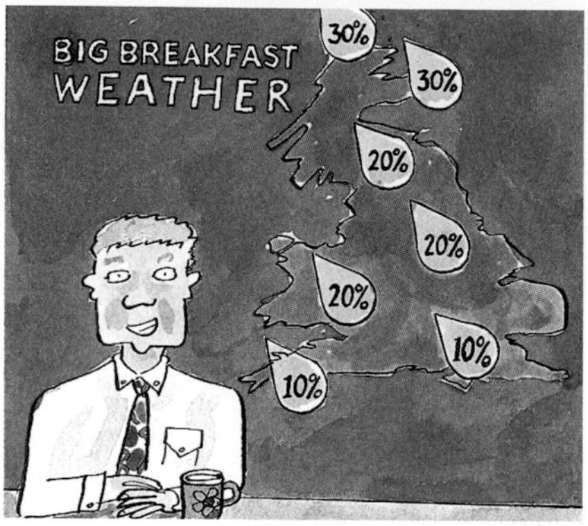

If you watch Breakfast TV you will have seen the weather forecast showing the probability of rain. The presenter may say 'There is a low chance of rain in southern England and a slightly higher chance everywhere else'.

Probability

In maths, **probability** means how likely something is to happen.

Probabilities are often shown on a scale with 'impossible' at one end and 'certain' at the other.

Example

Here is a probability scale.

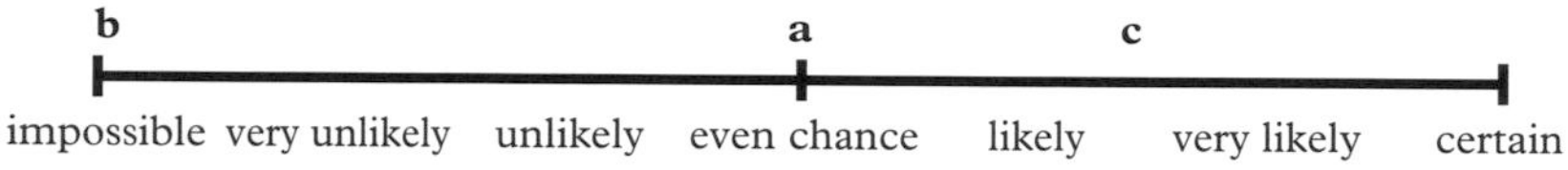

We have shown on the scale

a A newly born baby will be a girl
b You will live to be 200
c The next person to come into the room will be right-handed.

Exercise 8:1

For each question below, draw a probability scale.
Mark on it points **a**, **b** and **c** to show how likely you think each one is.

1 **a** You will go home from school today
b A newly born baby will be a boy
c You will walk from London to Glasgow in one day

2 **a** You will watch TV sometime tonight
b You will be late for school at least once this term
c It will snow on Christmas Day where you live

3 **a** A £1 ticket will win the jackpot in the National Lottery
b A £1 ticket will win £10 in the National Lottery
c You will know the person who wins the jackpot this week

4 **a** A coin thrown in the air will land heads up
b A coin thrown in the air will land tails up
c A coin thrown in the air will land on its edge

Random	If a person is chosen at **random** it means that every person has an equal chance of being chosen.

5 **a** A person chosen at random from your school will be left-handed
b A person chosen at random in your school will own at least one pet
c A teacher chosen at random from your school will be female

To measure probability more accurately we use numbers. We use 0 for 'impossible' and 1 for 'certain'. If something is not certain to happen it must have a probability less than 1.

Probabilities are written as fractions or decimals. Sometimes they are written as percentages. You saw this at the beginning of the chapter.

2 How the theory works

Michelle has bought a ticket for a raffle.
100 tickets have been sold altogether.

Michelle says, 'I have a 1 in 100 chance of winning.'
In maths we write the probability
of Michelle winning as $\frac{1}{100}$.

Joshua bought five tickets.
The probability of Joshua winning is $\frac{5}{100}$.

Exercise 8:2

1 James has bought one ticket for a raffle.
200 tickets were sold altogether.
What is the probability that James wins first prize?

2 What is the probability of rolling a six on an ordinary dice?

3 A letter is chosen at random from the words KEY MATHS.
a How many letters are there to choose from?
b What is the probability that the K is chosen?

4 What is the probability of a 5p coin landing so that it shows
a heads
b tails

5 An ordinary dice has the numbers 1 to 6 on it.

a Copy this table into your book.
Fill it in.

Type of number	Numbers on the dice	How many?
even	2, 4, 6	3
odd		3
prime	2	3
less than 3		

b Write down the probability of rolling
(1) an even number
(2) an odd number
(3) a prime number
(4) a number less than 3
(5) a two

● **6** Pardeep has one 50p coin and two 10p coins in her pocket.
She takes a coin from her pocket at random.
What is the probability that she takes out a 10p coin?

7 This spinner is spun once.

a Copy this table into your book.
Fill it in.

Colour	Number of sectors
red	2
blue	
pink	
green	1
yellow	
Total	8

b Write down the probability of the spinner landing on
(1) green
(2) pink

8 A pencil case contains 15 biros. There are 6 black, 6 blue, 2 red and 1 green. One biro is removed without looking. Find the probability that the biro removed is
- **a** black
- **b** green
- **c** yellow

9 A packet of 15 fruit drops contains 6 strawberry, 4 lime, 3 orange and 2 lemon sweets.
You choose a sweet without being able to see into the packet.
Find the probability that the sweet chosen is
- **a** strawberry
- **b** orange
- **c** lemon
- **d** lime

A pack of playing cards has four suits.
There are two red suits, diamonds ♦ and hearts ♥.
There are two black suits, clubs ♣ and spades ♠.
Each suit has 13 cards.

Here are the hearts:

The jack, queen, king and ace are called picture cards.
A full pack has 16 picture cards and 36 numbered cards, that makes 52 cards altogether.

---

10 In an ordinary pack of 52 playing cards, say how many cards are
- **a** black
- **b** red
- **c** hearts
- **d** spades
- **e** pictures
- **f** fives
- **g** threes
- **h** aces
- **i** red queens
- **j** black fives

11 One card is chosen from a full pack of 52 cards.
Find the probability that it is
- **a** black
- **b** red
- **c** a heart
- **d** a spade
- **e** a picture card
- **f** a five
- **g** a three
- **h** an ace
- **i** a red queen
- **j** a black five

Exercise 8:3 Higher or lower?

This card game is for 2 players.
You will need one suit of cards.

Rules

1 Shuffle the cards.
2 Deal the 13 cards face down in a line.
3 Turn over the first card on the left.
4 Player 1 predicts whether the next card will be higher or lower than the first one.
5 Player 1 turns over the next card and scores 1 point if their guess is right.
6 Player 2 does the same with the next card.
7 Continue until all the cards are face up.
The player with the most points is the winner.

Play the game three times.

Exercise 8:4

William and Stephen are playing 'Higher or lower'.
Each player has a list of the cards.
They cross off the cards that have gone.
The first card turned over is the 5.

William is first. He crosses off the 5 on his list.
2 3 4 ~~5~~ 6 7 8 9 10 jack queen king ace
He counts the cards that are higher than 5.
6 7 8 9 10 J Q K A
There are 9.

He then counts the cards that are less than 5.
2 3 4
There are 3.

He sees that 9 of the 12 cards are higher.
This means that there is a $\frac{9}{12}$ chance of getting a higher card.
He sees that 3 of the 12 cards are lower. So there is a $\frac{3}{12}$ chance of getting a lower card.
He decides to say 'higher'.

The card he turns over is the 10. He scores one point and crosses the card off his list.

2 3 4 ~~5~~ 6 7 8 9 ~~10~~ jack queen king ace

Now it is Stephen's turn.

1 Copy this list with the 5 and the 10 crossed out.

2 Write down a list of all the cards that are less than the 10. Remember that the 5 has gone.

3 Write down a list of all the cards higher than the 10.

4 **a** Write down the probability of getting a card higher than 10. (There are 11 cards left altogether)
b Write down the probability of getting a card lower than 10.

5 What should Stephen say, higher or lower?

6 The card Stephen turned over was the 8. Was his guess correct?

7 Now it is William's turn again.
a Cross out the 8 on your list.
b How many cards left are lower than 8?
c How many cards left are higher than 8?
d What is the probability that the next card will be lower than 8?
e What is the probability that the next card will be higher than 8?
f Should William say higher or lower?

8 William turned over the ace.
The cards now look like this:

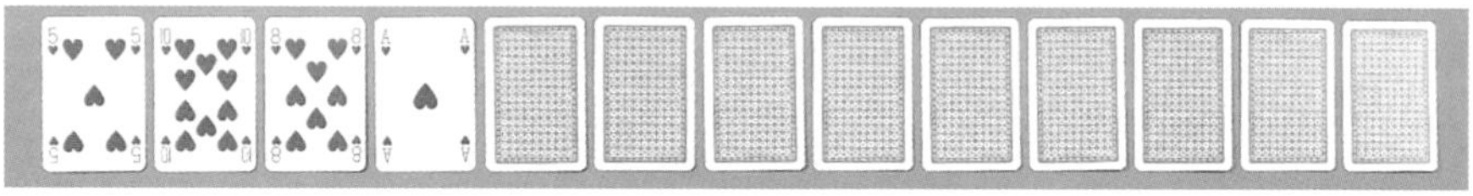

It is Stephen's turn again.
a Cross out the ace on your list.
b How many cards left are higher than the ace?
c How many cards left are lower than the ace?
d What is the probability that the next card will be higher than the ace?
e What is the probability that the next card will be lower than the ace?
f What should Stephen say?

9 The pictures show games of 'Higher or lower'.
For each one:
(1) Write down the list of cards 2 3 4 5 6 7 8 9 10 J Q K A
(2) Cross out the cards that you can see.
(3) Circle the last card that was turned over.
(4) How many cards left are higher than this one?
(5) How many are lower?
(6) How many cards are left altogether?
(7) What is the probability that the next card will be higher?
(8) What is the probability that the next card will be lower?
(9) What would you say, higher or lower?

a
b
c
d

3 Experiments and games

Probability can help you when you are playing games.

In this section you are going to play some games to see how probability is involved.

Game 1 Odds and Evens 1

This game is for two players.
You need an ordinary dice.

One player is Evens and the other player is Odds.
Take it in turns to throw the dice.

Evens throws first. If the dice shows an even number then score one point. If it is odd, score no points.
Odds goes next and only scores a point if the dice shows an odd number.

Tally your score in a table like this:

Game	Evens	Odds	Winner
1	𝍸	𝍷𝍷𝍷	Evens
2	𝍷𝍷𝍷𝍷	𝍸	Odds

The first player to score 5 points wins the game.

Play the game 6 times.

1 How many games did Evens win?

2 How many games did Odds win?

3 Was this what you expected?
Why?

4 What is the probability of scoring an even number on any throw?

5 What is the probability of scoring an odd number on any throw?

Game 2 Two coin chance

This is another game for two players.
You need two coins that are the same.

When you throw two coins, one of three things can happen.
You can get:
2 heads (HH)
or 2 tails (TT)
or 1 head and 1 tail (HT)

Each player should choose one of these three.

Take it in turns to throw the coins.
You only score a point if your choice appears on your throw.

Tally your score in a table like this:

Game	Player 1	Player 2	Winner	Winning choice HH or TT or HT
1				
2				
3				

The first player to score 5 points wins.

Play the game 6 times.
You may change your choice for each game.

1 How many times was HH the winning choice?

2 How many times was TT the winning choice?

3 How many times was HT the winning choice?

4 Was this what you expected?
Why?

Game 3 Odds and Evens 2

This game is a new version of Odds and Evens.

This time if Odds throws an odd number, they score the number shown on the dice.

If Evens throws an even number, they too score the number shown. The first player to score 30 points wins.

1 Do you think that this is a fair game?
Why?

Play the game 6 times.
Record your results in a table.

2 How many times did Evens win?

3 How many times did Odds win?

4 Have you changed your mind about the fairness of the game?

• **5** If you changed the game so that three people were playing, which two numbers would you give to each person so that the game is fair?

• **6** Try out your new game a few times to see if you think it is fair.

Exercise 8:5

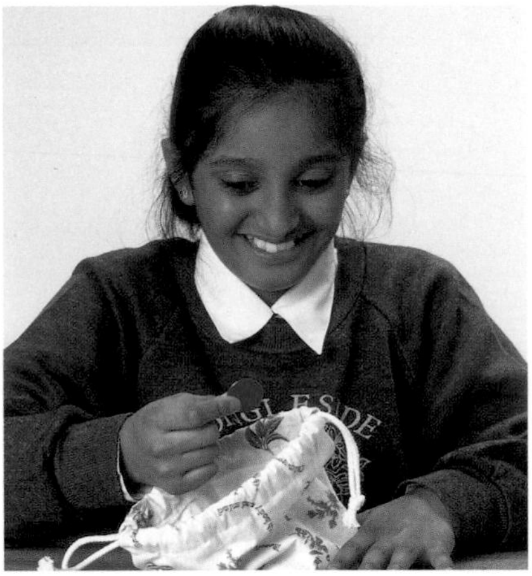

Aisha is planning a probability experiment.

She has 4 red counters and 2 green counters in a bag.

She is going to pick out one counter at random.
She will record its colour. Then she will replace the counter in the bag.

Aisha is going to do this 6 times.
She thinks that she will get 4 red counters and 2 green counters.

1 Aisha picks out a counter 12 times (twice as many as before).
How many red counters do you think she will get?

2 How many green counters do you think she will get?

3 She is going to do the experiment 18 times (three times as many as before). How many of each colour do you think she will get?

4 Copy this table. Fill it in.
Look for patterns in the numbers.

Number of times	Number of red counters	Number of green counters
6	4	2
12	8	4
18	12	6
24		
30	20	10
36		
42		
48		

As Aisha does her experiment she records her results in a tally-table.
She picks out a counter 30 times.
She *expects* to get 20 reds and 10 greens.

Here is her tally-table:

Colour	Tally	Frequency
red	𝍸 𝍸 𝍸 II	17
green	𝍸 𝍸 III	13
		Total 30

The results are not exactly as she expected, but they are close.

5 Do Aisha's experiment for yourself.
Record your results in a tally-table in the same way.

6 Are your results the same as Aisha's?

7 Change your counters so that you now have 5 red and 1 green.
Copy this table and fill it in.
It shows how many reds and greens you would *expect* to get.

Number of times	Number of red counters	Number of green counters
6	5	1
12	10	2
18		
24		
30		
36	30	6

8 Now do the experiment 30 times.
Tally your results in a table.

● **9** Write a sentence comparing your results with what you expected.

● **10** Repeat Questions **7**, **8** and **9** using 3 red counters and 3 green counters.

Spot the bias!

Draw the net of a cube with sides of length 3 cm on thin card.
Don't forget to add flaps!

Mark spots on the net to make it into a dice.
Here is one way of doing this:

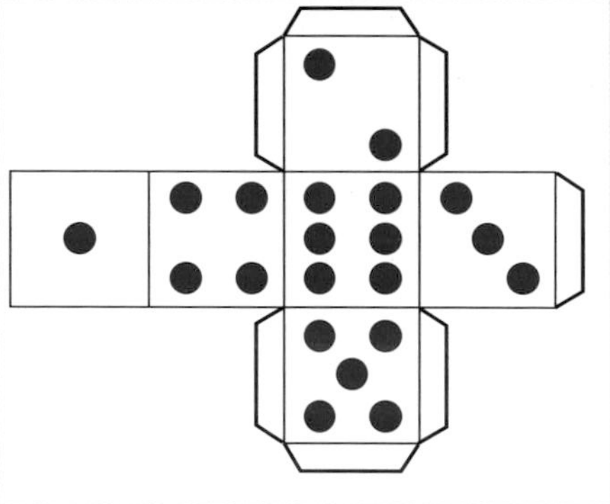

Before you make up the dice, tape a small piece of Blu-tack to the inside of one of the faces.
Write down which face you chose.

Stick the dice together.
You now have a biased dice. This means that it is not fair.

Do an experiment to test the bias of your dice.
Before you start, write down what you expect to happen.

Record your results in a suitable way. Display them using one of the methods you saw in Chapter 1.

Write up your experiment. Include what you expected to happen and whether or not you were right.
Try to explain your results.

When you have finished, swap dice with a partner. Try to find out which face their Blu-tack is on.

4 When the theory doesn't help

Dean is using a biased dice.
He cannot work out the exact probability of each score.

Dean rolls the dice 100 times.
He scores a six 35 times.

Relative frequency

Dean estimates the probability of throwing a six with his dice.

He says that it is $\frac{35}{100}$.

This type of estimate is called a **relative frequency**.

Kirsty has a biased dice.
She throws it 1000 times.

Here are her results:

Score on dice	1	2	3	4	5	6
Frequency	200	300	100	150	75	175

As you can see, this is a very strange dice!

We can use this data to estimate the probability of each score.

Score on dice	1	2	3	4	5	6
Estimate of probability (Relative frequency)	$\frac{200}{1000}$	$\frac{300}{1000}$	$\frac{100}{1000}$	$\frac{150}{1000}$	$\frac{75}{1000}$	$\frac{175}{1000}$

Exercise 8:6

1 Tom throws a dice 500 times.
These are his results

Score on dice	1	2	3	4	5	6
Frequency	25	180	80	70	100	45

Copy this table into your book.
Fill it in.

Score on dice	1	2	3	4	5	6
Estimate of probability	$\frac{25}{500}$				$\frac{100}{500}$	

2 This biased spinner has 4 coloured sections.

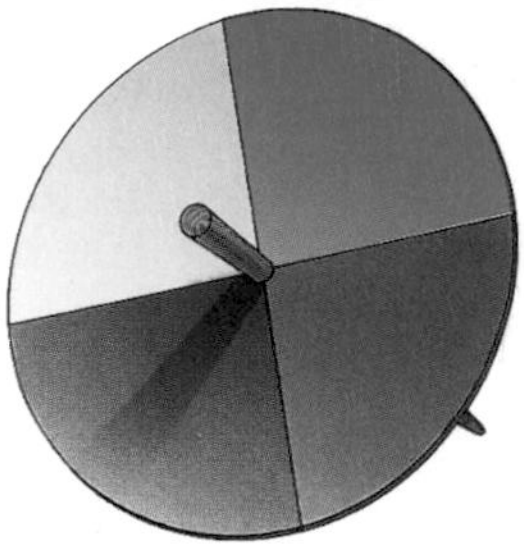

Harpinder wants to know the probability of getting each colour. She spins it 600 times and she records her results.
Here is part of her table:

Colour	blue	green	red	yellow
Frequency	120	200	110	

a How many times did she spin a yellow?
b Copy this table into your book. Fill it in.

Colour	blue	green	red	yellow
Estimate of probability	$\frac{120}{600}$			

Research

Sometimes you may not need to do an experiment or collect data yourself.
You can use data collected by someone else.
The data may have been collected over a number of years, e.g. how often it snows in London on Christmas Day.
Finding data in this way is called **research**.

3 For each of the following questions, say which method you would choose to work out the probability:

Method 1 Collect your own data or do an experiment
Method 2 Research to find data
Method 3 Use theory to calculate it

If you decide to use method 1, then say what you would do.
Also say how much data you would collect or how many times you would repeat the experiment.

a The probability that the next car passing your school will be red.
b The probability that I win a raffle if I buy 5 tickets and 350 are sold.
c The probability that there will be an earthquake somewhere in the world next month.
d The probability that a car will be broken into in Manchester next Saturday night.
e The probability that if someone is chosen at random from your class, their favourite TV programme will be Coronation Street.
f The probability that a shoe pushed off a table will land the right way up.
g The probability of finding Grumpy in a packet of cornflakes if every packet contains one of the Seven Dwarfs.
h The probability that the volcano Mount Etna will erupt in the next year.
i The probability of winning the jackpot on a fruit machine.
j The probability that a drawing pin will land point up if dropped on to a flat surface.

1 These objects are being carried in a plastic carrier bag.
The bag is dropped on to a hard floor.

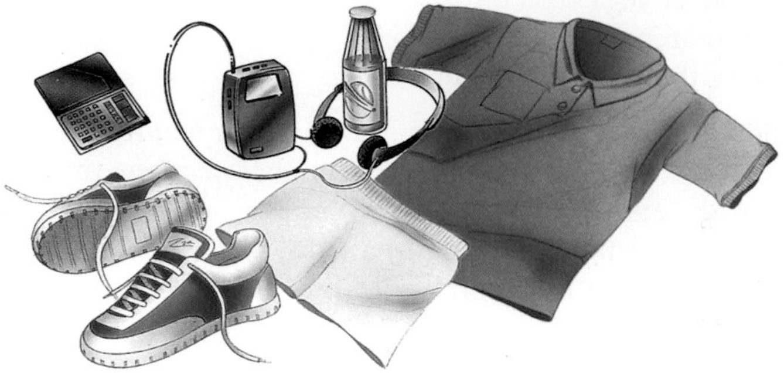

a List the objects in order of how likely they are to break.
Start with the most likely.

b The arrow on the scale shows the probability of the bottle breaking.
Copy the scale and mark on arrows for the other objects.

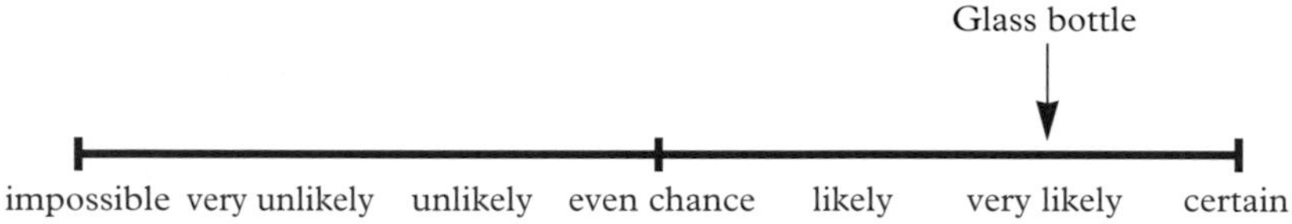

2 For each of the following, write down the probability as a fraction.

a Winning a raffle when you have bought one ticket if 235 are sold.

b Throwing a 3 on an ordinary dice.

c Throwing a 5 on a 12-sided dice numbered 1 to 12.

d Picking the King of Spades from a full pack of cards.

e Picking the blue counter from a bag containing 1 blue counter and 3 red counters.

f Picking the purple counter from a bag containing 1 purple counter, 3 red counters and 2 blue counters.

3 For each of the following, write down the probability as a fraction.

a Winning a raffle when you have bought five tickets if 560 are sold.

b Picking a jack from a pack of 52 cards.

c Picking a spade from a pack of 52 cards.

d Throwing a number bigger than 4 on an ordinary dice.

e Picking a red cube from a bag containing 3 red cubes and 4 black cubes.

f Picking a prize box in a lucky dip which has 10 prize boxes and 60 empty boxes.

4 This spinner is used in a game.
Work out the probability of it landing on each colour.

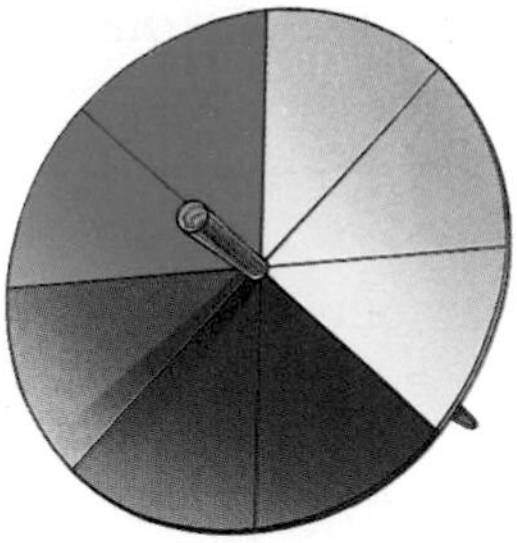

5 Leroy and Joanne are doing a probability experiment.
They have 6 red counters and 5 green counters in a bag.
a How many counters are there altogether?
b What is the probability of picking out a green counter?
c What is the probability of picking out a red counter?

Leroy picks out a counter and Joanne records the colour.
Leroy puts the counter back in the bag.
d Copy this table and fill it in.
It shows how many reds and greens they *expect* to get.

Number of counters	Number of red counters	Number of green counters
11	6	5
22	12	
33		
44		
55		
66		

e They do the experiment 99 times. How many of each colour do you expect them to get?

1 On a probability line like the one below, mark on letters to show the probability of the following:

a December following November next year
b A person chosen at random from your school having brown eyes
c A piece of toast being dropped butter side down
d Throwing a five on a dice
e Snow falling in Sheffield in August

2 Write down the probability of each of the following as a fraction:
a Throwing a 5 on a normal dice
b Dealing a red card from a full pack of cards
c Winning a raffle where you buy 1 of the 300 tickets sold
d Picking out the one bad egg in a box of six eggs
e A person chosen at random from your school having been born on a Sunday

3 Write down the probability of each of the following as a fraction:
a Picking a king from a full pack of cards
b Picking a heart from a full pack of cards
c Throwing an odd number on an ordinary dice
d Throwing an even number on a 10-sided dice numbered 1 to 10
e Winning a raffle with one of your 5 tickets when 300 have been sold
f A letter chosen at random from the alphabet being a vowel
g A number thrown on a 12-sided dice numbered 1 to 12 being a multiple of 3

4 The following pictures were taken in the middle of a game of 'higher or lower', played with one suit of 13 cards.
For each one work out:
(1) The probability of the next card turned over being higher
(2) The probability of the next card turned over being lower
(3) The best answer for the player, higher or lower

a
b
c
d

5 Gavin is doing a probability experiment.
He puts five blue counters and seven orange counters in a bag.
He picks out a counter at random and writes down its colour.
He then puts the counter back into the bag.

a What is the probability of pulling out an orange counter?

b What is the probability of pulling out a blue counter?

c If Gavin did his experiment 12 times, how many blue counters would you expect him to get?

d If Gavin did his experiment 12 times, how many orange counters would you expect him to get?

e If Gavin did the experiment 24 times, how many of each colour should he expect to get?

f If Gavin did the experiment 36 times, how many of each colour should he expect to get?

6 In an experiment, a bag contains three red counters, four blue counters and five yellow counters.

a What is the probability of a counter taken out at random being
(1) yellow (2) blue (3) red (4) orange?

b A counter is chosen at random. Its colour is recorded and then it is replaced in the bag.
If this is repeated 120 times, how many of each colour would you expect to get?

c Would the answers you gave to part **b** be guaranteed to happen?

7 A simple game consists of a wheel split into twelve equal sectors as shown in the diagram.
The wheel is not biased.

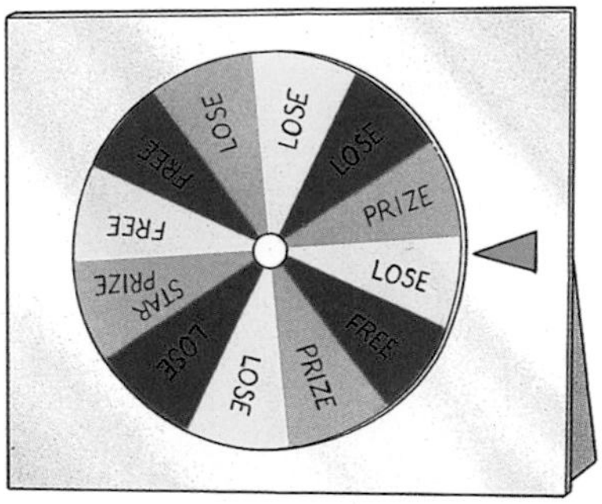

a What is the probability of winning the star prize?

b What is the probability of winning a normal prize?

c What is the probability of getting a free go?

d What is the probability of losing?

e How many times do you think you should spin the wheel in order to win a prize or get a free go?
Explain your answer.

f If the wheel is spun 180 times, how many times would you expect it to fall in each category?

8 SUMMARY

- Probability can be marked on scales.

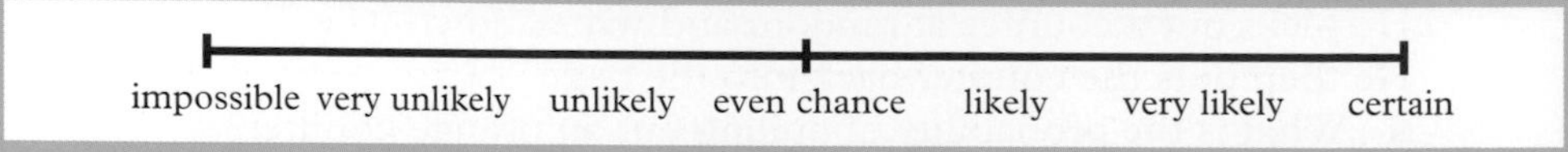

- Probabilities are usually written as fractions.

  probability of throwing a 2 $= \frac{1}{6}$

  probability of choosing a blue counter $= \frac{3}{7}$

- Experiments can be done but they don't always come out exactly as predicted. Experiments repeated several times often produce different results.

- When probability can't be calculated it can be estimated by doing an experiment. You can do this yourself or you can look at data collected by other people.

1 Copy this probability scale. Mark letters on it to show where the following statements should go.

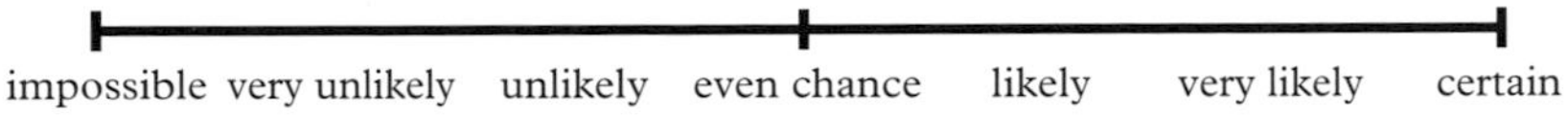

a A page of a book having at least one letter **e** on it
b A page of a book having at least one letter **z** on it
c Throwing an even number on an ordinary dice
d Snow falling somewhere in Scotland in January
e Your maths teacher becoming Prime Minister

2 Write down the probability of each of the following as a fraction.
a Throwing a 4 on an ordinary dice
b Throwing a 6 on an ordinary dice
c Winning a raffle when you have bought one ticket if 325 were sold.
d Winning a raffle when you have bought five tickets if 325 were sold.
e A fair coin landing heads up
f Scoring a six on a 12-sided dice numbered 1 to 12

3 Stefan puts 10 cubes in a bag. There are 3 reds, 2 greens and 5 blues.
He picks out a cube at random, records its colour and puts it back in the bag.
a What is the probability that the cube is red?
b What is the probability that the cube is green?
c What is the probability that the cube is blue?
If Stefan does this 10 times
d How many times would you expect him to get a green cube?
e How many times would you expect him to get a red cube?
f How many times would you expect him to get a blue cube?
If he does this 30 times (three times as many as before)
g How many times would you expect him to get a green cube?
h How many times would you expect him to get a red cube?
i How many times would you expect him to get a blue cube?

4 Gemma throws a dice 600 times.
These are her results.

Score on dice	1	2	3	4	5	6
Frequency	80	110	170	80	70	90

a Copy this table and fill it in.
It shows estimates for the probabilities of scoring each number on this dice.

Score on dice	1	2	3	4	5	6
Estimate of probability	$\frac{80}{600}$				$\frac{70}{600}$	

b How many times would you expect to get each score with a fair dice?
c Do you think that this dice is fair or biased?
Why?

9 Algebra: writing letters

CORE

QUESTIONS

EXTENSION

SUMMARY

TEST YOURSELF

The earliest algebra came from Egypt. It is over 5000 years old, dating from around the time the pyramids were built.

The ancient Egyptians used the word 'aha', meaning 'heap', to mean an unknown number. In the same way, we might use the letter x today. Problems have been discovered which were clearly set as exercises for young mathematicians.

One of these was a problem about houses, cats, mice and grain and was a very early version of our rhyme:

As I was going to St Ives,
I met a man with seven wives;
Every wife had seven sacks,
Every sack had seven cats,
Every cat had seven kits.
Kits, cats, sacks and wives,
How many were going to St Ives?

1 Writing simple formulas

Ellen and Jason are doing a sponsored swim. Ellen's sponsors will pay £2 for each length.

Ellen can work out her total sponsor money like this:
The ***t***otal equals
£2 × number of ***l***engths
In short form this is
$t = 2 \times l$

Jason's sponsors will pay £3 for each length he swims.
Jason's rule is $t = 3 \times l$

Exercise 9:1

Write down the short form of these rules.
Use the red letters and numbers.

1 The ***t***otal money raised in a sponsored swim at £**5** for each ***l***ength.
$t = \ldots \times \ldots$

2 The ***t***otal money raised on a sponsored walk at £**4** for each ***m***ile.
$t = \ldots \times \ldots$

3 The ***t***otal cost of a weekly magazine at £**2** each ***w***eek.
$t = \ldots \times \ldots$

4 The ***t***otal cost of some carpet at £**12** per square ***m***etre.
$t = \ldots \times \ldots$

5 The ***r***ecording time on some video ***c***assettes of **3** hours each.
$r = \ldots \times \ldots$

6 The ***w***ages earned by someone who earns £**6** per ***h***our.
$w = \ldots \times \ldots$

7 The number of ***t***ins of cat food needed by cats who eat **4** tins a ***w***eek.
$t = \ldots \times \ldots$

8 The **t**otal weight of a number of **c**ars weighing **800** kg each.
$t = \ldots \times \ldots$

9 The **t**otal number of children in all the **c**lasses at a school if there are 27 children in each class
$t = \ldots \times \ldots$

10 The **a**mount of money Andy saves if he saves **£2.50** a **w**eek
$a = \ldots \times \ldots$

Algebra

Algebra is a short way of writing mathematical rules. It uses letters and symbols to replace words and numbers.
People from many different countries can understand algebra because there are no words to translate.

Examples

1 Mr Brown's car is 4 m long. He is buying a caravan.
The **t**otal length will be **4** m plus the length of the **c**aravan.
In short form this will be $t = 4 + c$

2 The **m**oney received by **6** children when a **p**rize is shared equally among them.
In short form this would be $m = p \div 6$

Exercise 9:2

Write down the short form of these rules.
Use the red letters and numbers.

1 The **t**otal length of a car **5** m long and a **c**aravan.
$t = \ldots + \ldots$

2 The **t**otal length of a mini **3** m long and a **c**aravan.
$t = \ldots + \ldots$

3 The **t**otal length of a large **6** m car and a **c**aravan.
$t = \ldots + \ldots$

4 The ***l***ength remaining on a **10** m roll of carpet when a ***p***iece has been cut off.

$l = \ldots - \ldots$

5 The number of ***s***weets remaining in a bag of **20** when some have been ***e***aten.

$s = \ldots - \ldots$

6 The ***d***istance left on a **200** mile journey after travelling a number of ***m***iles.

$d = \ldots - \ldots$

7 The ***a***mount each child gets when a ***p***rize is shared equally among **4** pupils.

$a = \ldots \div \ldots$

8 The ***w***eight of each cake when some ***m***ixture is split into **12**.

$w = \ldots \div \ldots$

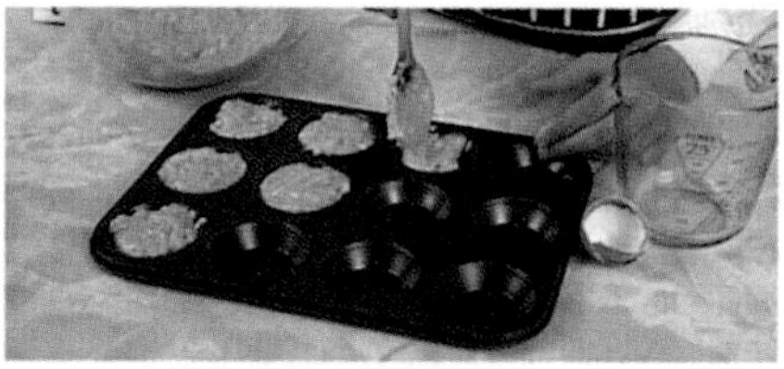

• **9** The ***n***umber of **3** m pieces that can be cut from a ***l***ength of string.

$n = \ldots \div \ldots$

• **10** The ***s***ale price of a CD player with £**10** off the normal ***p***rice.

$s = \ldots - \ldots$

11 The number of ***f***ree seats left in a theatre seating **340** when some seats have been ***b***ooked.

$f = \ldots - \ldots$

12 The total number of ***s***eats in a cinema with **16** seats in each ***r***ow.

$s = \ldots \times \ldots$

13 The ***t***otal cost of a meal for ***f***ood and £**3** for drink.

$t = \ldots + \ldots$

14 The ***t***otal cost of a meal for ***f***ood and £**1.50** for drink.

$t = \ldots + \ldots$

15 The ***m***oney received by **10** children when a ***p***rize is shared equally among them.

$m = \ldots \div \ldots$

• **16** The ***s***ale price of a CD player with £**15** off the normal ***p***rice.

$s = \ldots - \ldots$

Formula A rule written out in algebra is known as a **formula**.

Examples

$t = c \times 4$
$r = p + k$
$c = r - 5$
$w = z \div y$

The formula for the total length of a 3 m car and a caravan is $t = 3 + c$.
The value of **c** can vary but the same formula is used to find the total length.

Example Use the formula $t = 3 + c$ to find the total length of a 3 m car with

a a 4 m caravan.
b a 3.5 m caravan.

a $t = 3 + 4$
$= 7$ **m**

b $t = 3 + 3.5$
$= 6.5$ **m**

Exercise 9:3

1 A formula for the *t*otal length of a 4 m car and a *c*aravan is $t = 4 + c$.
Find the total length if

a The caravan is 5 m long $t = 4 + \ldots$
b The caravan is 7 m long $t = \ldots + \ldots$
c The caravan is 4.5 m long. $t = \ldots + \ldots$

2 The *d*istance left on a **300** mile journey after travelling a *n*umber of miles is $d = 300 - n$.
Find the distance left to travel

a 58 miles $d = 300 - \ldots$
b 120 miles $d = \ldots - \ldots$
c 230 miles. $d = \ldots - \ldots$

3 The *a*mount **5** people get when a *p*rize is shared equally among them is $a = p \div 5$
Find how much each gets when the prize is

a £20 $a = \ldots \div 5$
b £55 $a = \ldots \div \ldots$
c £125 $a = \ldots \div \ldots$
d £165 $a = \ldots \div \ldots$

2 Two-stage formulas

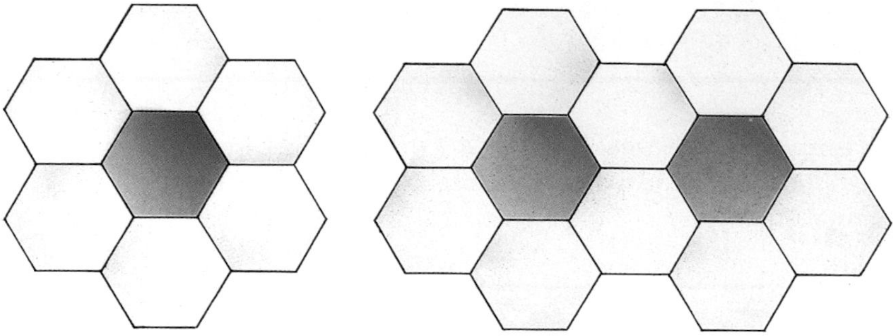

Rod is building a new patio.
He is using red and white slabs. He wants to work out how many white slabs he needs for each red slab.
He works out a formula to help him.

Algebra and formulas can be used to solve mathematical problems.

Exercise 9:4

1 **a** Copy these diagrams.

b Copy this table and fill it in.
Leave 6 more lines to finish the table later.

Number of squares ***S***	Number of blue edges *B*	Number of yellow edges *Y*	Total number of edges *T*
1	2	2	4
2	4	2	6
3	6	2	
4	8	2	

c Look at column ***B***.
Copy and fill in:
To work out the number of blue edges you .... the number of squares by ....

d Look at column ***Y***.
Copy and fill in:
The number of yellow edges is always ....

e Look at column ***T***.
It is found by adding column ***B*** to column ***Y***.
We can put the two parts of the rule together.
Copy and fill in:
To find the ***T***otal number of edges you .... the number of ***S***quares by .... and then add ....

f Write this sentence as a formula. Use the letters ***S*** and ***T***.
T = ...

You could write $T = B + Y$, but this does not tell you how to work out the number of edges from the number of squares.

g Draw the next three patterns.
Use them to fill in lines 5, 6 and 7 of the table.
Check that your rule works for these new lines.

h Fill in the table using 8, 9 and 10 squares without drawing them.
You could draw them to check that you are right.

Exercise 9:5

1 **a** Copy these diagrams.

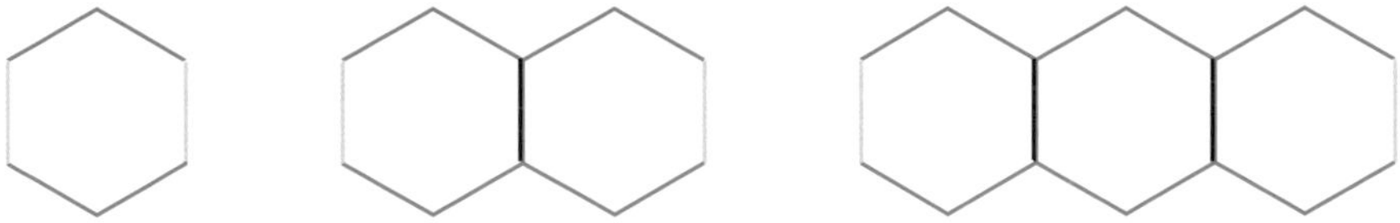

b Copy this table and fill it in.
Leave 6 more lines to finish the table later.

Number of hexagons ***H***	Number of blue edges ***B***	Number of yellow edges ***Y***	Total number of edges ***T***
1	4	2	6
2	8	2	
3	12	2	
4	16	2	

c Look at column ***B***.
Copy and fill in:
To work out the number of blue edges you .... the number of hexagons by ....

d Look at column ***Y***.
Copy and fill in:
The number of yellow edges is always ....

e Look at column ***T***. It is found by adding column ***B*** to column ***Y***.
We can put the two parts of the rule together.
Copy and fill in:
To find the ***T***otal number of edges you .... the number of ***H***exagons by .... and then add ....

f Write this sentence as a formula. Use the letters ***H*** and ***T***.
T = ...
You could write $T = B + Y$, but this does not tell you how to work out the number of edges from the number of hexagons.

g Draw the next three patterns.
Use them to fill in lines 5, 6 and 7 of the table.
Check that your rule works for these new lines.

h Fill in the table using 8, 9 and 10 hexagons without drawing them.
You could draw them to check that you are right.

Exercise 9:6

You will need some cubes.

1 **a** Make these models.

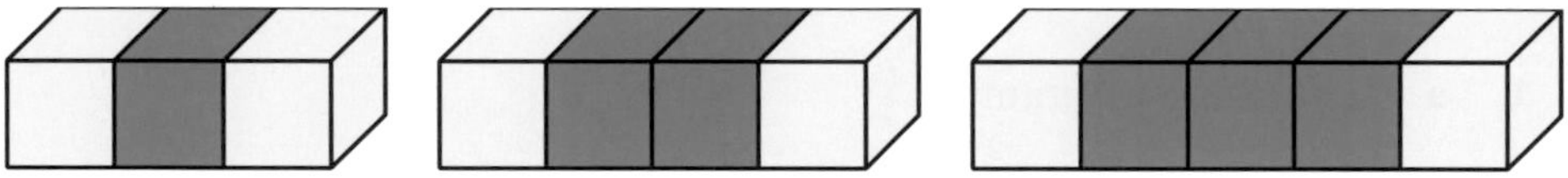

b Copy this table. Leave room for 10 rows altogether.
Fill in the table as far as row 4.

Number of blue cubes *b*	Number of blue faces	Number of yellow faces	Total number of faces *T*
1	4	10	
2	8	10	
3			
4			

c Copy and fill in:
To work out the number of blue faces you .... the number of blue cubes by ....

d Copy and fill in:
The number of yellow faces is always ....

e Copy this. Use your answers to **c** and **d** to fill it in.
To work out the total number of faces you .... the number of blue cubes by .... and then ....

f Write your answer to part **e** as a formula.

g Fill in the rest of the table up to row 10 using cubes or just by using your rule.

3 How to make everyone understand

〔証明〕 かりに $a+b\sqrt{2}$ が無理数でないとすると,

$$a+b\sqrt{2}=p$$

は有理数である. $b\neq 0$ であるから, この式を変形して,

$$\sqrt{2}=\frac{p-a}{b}$$

となるが, a, b, p は有理数であるから, 右辺は有理数となる. 左辺が無理数であるから, これは不合理である.

したがって, $a+b\sqrt{2}$ は無理数である.

There are some simple rules that everyone uses.
Algebra is the same in all languages.
You can see the algebra in this Japanese maths book.

Try to learn these rules and use them from now on.

Rules of algebra

We miss out multiplication signs because they look too much like the letter x.

We write the formula $t = 4 \times C + 3$ as $t = 4C + 3$

$5y$ means multiply 5 by y.
The number is always written first.
We never write $y5$.

Always put the letter you are finding on the left hand side.
Write $t = 4y + z$ not $4y + z = t$

Miss out any units.
You do not put cm in any formulas involving lengths.

Write divide like a fraction.

Write $5 \div y$ as $\frac{5}{y}$

Exercise 9:7

Rewrite each of these formulas.
Use the rules on the previous page.

1 $F = m \times a$

2 $t = w \times 5$

3 $8 + t = p$

4 $y = 6 \div t$

5 $g \times 3 = t$

6 $I \times R = V$

7 $v \div t = r$

8 $y = 5 \times L + 26$

9 $C + 32 = t$

10 $10 \times t = v$

Exercise 9:8

1 Triangles are drawn corner to corner as shown.

a Copy the table and fill it in.

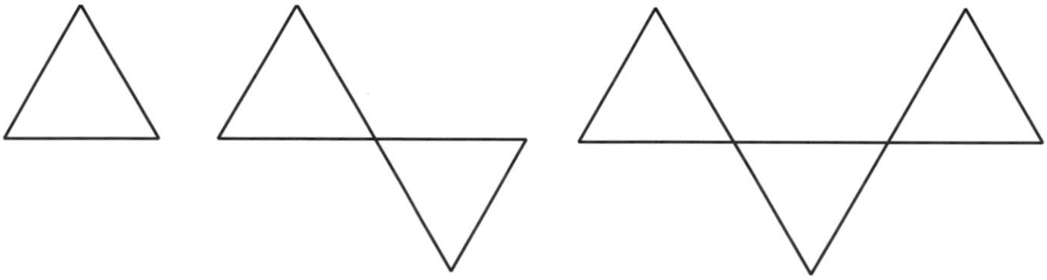

Number of triangles T	Number of sides S
1	3
2	
3	
4	

b Copy and fill in:

To work out the number of sides you ....

c Write this as a formula

$S =$ .... $\times$ ....

d Now write this using the rules of algebra.

2 Squares are made out of matchsticks as shown.

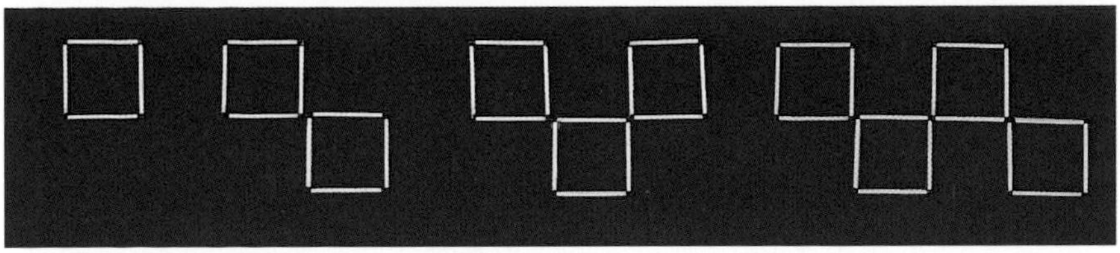

a Copy this table and fill it in.

Number of squares ***S***	Number of sides ***T***
1	4
2	
3	
4	

b Copy and fill in:
To work out the number of sides you ....

c Write this as a formula:
T = ... × ....

d Write this using the rules of algebra.

• **3** Hiring lockers at school costs £3 per term and a £5 deposit for the key.

a Copy this table and fill it in.

Number of terms ***T***	Hire cost	Deposit	Total cost ***C***
1	3	5	8
2	6	5	11
3	9	5	14
4			
5			
6			
7			

b Copy and fill in:
To work out the total cost you .... the number of terms by .... and then ....

c Write this as a formula using the rules of algebra.
C =

● **4** A series of magazines costs £3.50 per week plus £8 for a set of folders.

a Copy this table.
Fill it in to show the total cost for each number of weeks.

Number of weeks ***W***	Cost of magazines (£)	Cost of folders (£)	Total cost ***C*** (£)
1	3.50	8.00	11.50
2	7.00	8.00	15.00
3			
4			
5			
6			

b Write down in words the rule for the total cost.

c Write your rule as a formula.

5 In a shop, the manager is paid £50 a day. Each of the sales staff is paid £30 a day.

a Copy this table and fill it in.

Number of sales staff *n*	Cost of sales staff (£)	Cost of manager (£)	Total cost ***T*** (£)
1	30	50	
2	60		
3			
4			
5			
6			

b Write down a rule for working out the total cost.

c Write your rule as a formula.

4 Collecting terms

Cuisenaire rods are coloured rods which are all different lengths. They come in units of 1 to 10.

Different combinations of rods can be fitted together. They then make the same length as other rods.

You are going to write down your findings using algebra.

Exercise 9:9 Cuisenaire investigation

1 Find a green rod.
Make the same length with three white rods.
You can write
One green rod equals 3 white rods.
In algebra
$g = 3w$ (you do not write a 1 in front of the g)

There is another way to make a green rod. Use 1 red rod and 1 white rod.

a Copy and fill in:
One green rod equals 1 .... and 1 ....

b Write your answer to **a** as a formula.
$g =$ .... + ...

$g = r + w$ and $g = w + r$ mean the same.
There is no point in writing both of them.

2 Take a pink rod. Use two other rods to make this length.

a Copy and fill in:
A pink rod is the same as ....

b Write this as a formula: $p =$ ....

c Make up a pink rod using three other rods.

d Copy and fill in:
A pink rod is the same as ....

e Write this as a formula: $p = \dots\dots\dots$

f Find any other ways you can to make a pink rod.
Write down their formulas.

3 Find as many ways as you can of making a yellow rod.
Write each one you find as a formula.
There are six different formulas.

4 Carry on for some of the other rods.
You will find it easier to draw them as you go along.
Write each one as a formula using algebra.
Count how many different ones you find for each length.

Are you sure that you have found them all?

Katrina and Liam both pay 38 p bus fare each school day.
They work out their totals for the week.

Katrina works like this:

$$\begin{array}{r} 38 \\ 38 \\ 38 \\ 38 \\ +\,38 \\ \hline 190 \\ \hline \end{array}$$

Liam does his like this:

$$\begin{array}{r} 38 \\ \times\;\;5 \\ \hline 190 \\ \hline \end{array}$$

Obviously they get the same total.

In algebra Katrina would write $\boldsymbol{t = b + b + b + b + b}$

Liam would write $\boldsymbol{t = b \times 5}$ or $\boldsymbol{t = 5b}$

Collecting terms

It is quicker to write $b + b + b + b + b$ as $5b$. This is called **collecting terms**.

In the same way $c + c + c = 3c$ $\quad 3d + 4d = 7d$ $\quad$ and $5e - 3e = 2e$

Exercise 9:10

Collect these terms.

1 $a + a + a + a$

2 $g + g + g + g + g + g$

3 $h + h + h + h + h$

4 $k + k$

5 $d + d + d + d$

6 $3s - 2s$

7 $3c - c$

8 $2p + 2p$

9 $5q - 2q$

10 $6d - 5d$

11 $6m - 6m$

12 $4d - 3d$

13 $4c + 3c$

14 $2p + 6p$

15 $b + b + 2b$

16 $c + 2c + c$

17 $2h + 2h + 2h$

• **18** $3g + 2g - g$

• **19** $6k - 4k - k$

• **20** $7p - p - 2p$

Different letters and numbers are collected separately.

Examples

1 $2a + 3b$ cannot be collected.

2 $2a + 4a + 3b = 6a + 3b$

3 $4t + 2 + 3t = 7t + 2$

4 $3g - 2g + 2h + 4h = g + 6h$

Exercise 9:11

Collect these terms.

1 **a** $2s + 3s + 2t + 4t = \dots s + \dots t$
b $3d + d + e + 2e = \dots d + \dots e$
c $5a + 2a + 2b + b$
d $2p + 4p + q + 3q$
e $4y + y + 3z + 2z$
f $3g + 4g + 2h + h$

2 **a** $2d + 4d + 3e = \dots d + \dots e$
b $3r + 2r + 4s = \dots r + \dots s$
c $2a + 3b + 2b$
d $5f + 2g + g$

3 **a** $3k + 2k + 2 + 4 = \dots k + \dots$
b $2 + 3 + 2d + 3d = \dots + \dots d$
c $3 + 4 + 4t + 2t$
d $2s + 3 + 4$

4 **a** $5g + 2h + 3h$
b $2 + 3 + 3w + 4w$
c $4f + 2 + 4$
d $3a + a + 2b + 3b$

5 **a** $2d + 3e + 2d + 2e$
b $3r + 3s + r + 4s$
c $3 + 2f + 4 + 4f$
d $2q + 3 + 4q + 2$
e $2w + 3x + 2w$
f $3 + 2s + 4$

6 **a** $4d - 2d + 5e - 2e$
b $5f - 3f + 4g - g$
c $5r - 3r + 3s$
d $6 + 3 + 4f - 3f$
e $4a + 4 - 2$
f $4d - 2d + 4 + 3$

• **7** **a** $3a - 3a + 4b + b$
b $4c + 2b + 3b + 2c$
c $4a + 3b$
d $3s + 4t + t + 2s$
e $5 + 2w + w + 2$
f $2e + 4f$
g $3a + 4b - 3b$
h $5 - 3 + 3w$

5 Substituting in formulas

You can use algebra and formulas to work out codes.
These codes can be used to write messages.

Here is a simple way of numbering the alphabet.

a	*b*	*c*	*d*	*e*	*f*	*g*	*h*	*i*	*j*	*k*	*l*	*m*
1	2	3	4	5	6	7	8	9	10	11	12	13
n	*o*	*p*	*q*	*r*	*s*	*t*	*u*	*v*	*w*	*x*	*y*	*z*
14	15	16	17	18	19	20	21	22	23	24	25	26

Examples

Using $b = 2$, $c = 3$, $d = 4$ and $e = 5$

$3d = 3 \times d = 3 \times 4 = 12$

$be = b \times e = 2 \times 5 = 10$

$c^2 = c \times c = 3 \times 3 = 9$

Exercise 9:12

Work these out.

1 $3b$

2 $4e$

3 $6c$

4 ce $(c \times e)$

5 bd $(b \times d)$

6 cd

7 $3e$

8 b^2 $(b \times b)$

9 d^2

10 e^2

Example	The numbers can be used as a code to write messages.		
		$c + 5 = 3 + 5$	$2d - f = 8 - 6$
	Use the answers	$= 8$	$= 2$
	to find new letters:	$= h$	$= b$

Exercise 9:13

Here are some messages for you to solve.

A

1 $c + 10$

2 $6 - e$

3 $q + 3$

4 $g + 1$

5 $u - 2$

6 $d + e$

7 $y - f$

8 $k - e$

9 $j + k$

10 $20 - f$

B

1 $7 - d$

2 $2 + s$

3 $22 - c$

4 $5d$

5 $20 - s$

6 $3f$

7 $t - 16$

8 $6a$

9 $5c$

10 $t - 2$

11 $4e$

12 $12 - g$

13 $m - 12$

• **C**

1 $c + t$

2 $j - e$

3 $2j + 3$

4 $3d - 11$

5 bg $(b \times g)$

6 de

7 c^2 $(c \times c)$

8 $\frac{f}{2}$ $(f \div 2)$

9 $\frac{j}{2}$

10 $\frac{i}{3}$

11 cf

12 ae

13 $2d - 7$

14 $3d + 1$

D Use the code to write some messages of your own.

1 Write down the short form of these rules. Use the red letters and numbers.

a The *t*otal money raised in a sponsored cycle ride at £2 a *m*ile.
$t = \ldots \times \ldots$

b The *t*otal cost of a theatre visit at £10 a *s*eat.
$t = \ldots \times \ldots$

c The *t*otal length of a car 4 m long and a *c*aravan.
$t = \ldots + \ldots$

d The *t*otal height of a 15 m tower when a *f*lagpole is put up on the top.
$t = \ldots + \ldots$

e The *t*otal height of a 8 m tree when a *p*iece is cut off the top.
$t = \ldots - \ldots$

f The *w*eight of a 14 ounce cake when a *s*lice has been eaten.
$w = \ldots - \ldots$

g The *a*mount of money each boy receives when a cash *p*rize is shared between 2 brothers.
$a = \ldots \div \ldots$

2 Rewrite each of these formulas. Use the rules of algebra.

a $p = t \times 4$

b $7 + g = h$

c $I = V \div R$

d $M = m \times u$

e $10 \times t = v$

f $v = u + 10 \times t$

g $20 - t = s$

h $S = D \div T$

3 A train has an engine 8 m long. The engine pulls some carriages each 12 m long.
Copy and complete this table.

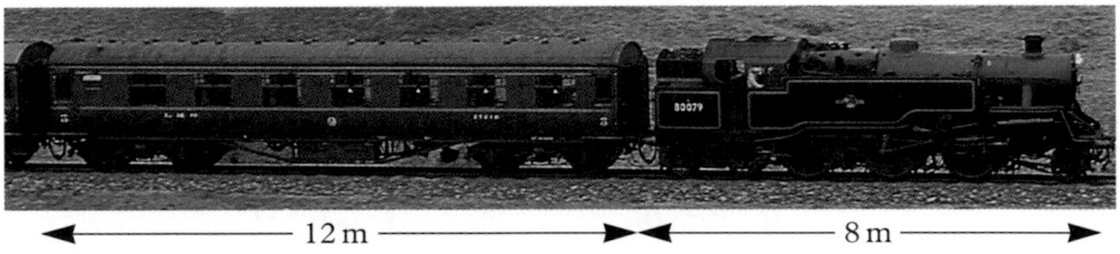

Number of carriages *C*	Length of carriages (m)	Length of engine (m)	Total length of train *T* (m)
1	12	8	
2			
3			
4			
5			

Write down in words the rule for the total length of the train.
Write the rule as a formula. Use the letters *T* and *C*.

4 Pentagons are made of matchsticks as shown.

a Copy the table and fill it in.

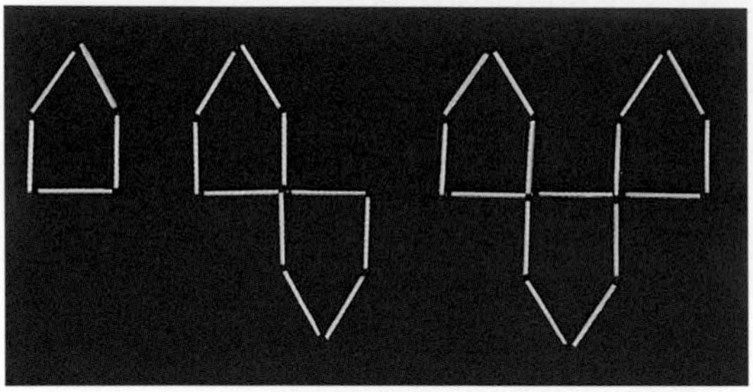

Number of pentagons P	Number of matches M
1	5
2	
3	
4	

b Write in words the rule for finding the number of matches.

c Write the rule as a formula. Use the letters M and P.

5 Simplify these by collecting the terms which are the same.

a $h + h + h + h$

b $g + 2g + g$

c $5c - 2c + 3c$

d $4p + 5p + 3q + 2q$

e $10f + 5f + 3$

f $5 + 3 + 4m + 2m$

g $3s + 2t + 4t + 2s$

h $5v + 2w + 3w + 2w$

i $5y - 2y + 4z - z$

j $6a - 5a + 6 - 3$

6 Work these out using $a = 4$, $b = 2$ and $c = 5$

a $3a$

b bc

c ab

d a^2

e c^2

f $a + c$

g $c - b$

h $a + 4$

i $20 - c$

j $c - 3$

k $3c$

l $a + 7$

m $a - b$

7 The **c**ost of a meal including **f**ood and **d**rink is $c = f + d$
Find c when

a $f = 30$ and $d = 10$

b $f = 40$ and $d = 10$

c $f = 45$ and $d = 15$

d $f = 24$ and $d = 9$

1 Write down the short form of these rules.
Use the red letters and numbers.

a The ***t***otal raised in a sponsored run at £2 a ***m***ile.
b The ***t***otal length of a 4 m car with a ***b***oat trailer.
c The ***h***eight of a 6 ft post after a ***p***iece has been cut off.
d The ***a***mount each receives when 4 friends share a ***p***rize.
e The ***t***otal cost of some ***b***ags of sweets at ***p*** pence a bag.
f The ***n***umber in a form when the ***p***upils in year 7 are divided into ***f*** forms.
g The ***l***ength remaining in a ***b***all of string when a ***p***iece is cut off.
h The ***t***otal length of a building plot for a ***h***ouse and a ***g***arden.

2 Rewrite each of these formulas. Use the rules of algebra.

a $P = m \times g \times h$
b $D \div T = S$
c $m \times v = M$
d $A = b \times h \div 2$
e $S = a \times b + c \times d$
f $A = s \times s$
g $s \times 16 = v$

3 **a** The teachers at Stanthorne High are having a Christmas social. It costs £100 to hire a disco and £4 each person to provide a supper. Write down a formula for the total cost.
(T = total cost, P = number of people)
b A goods train is made up of an engine pulling some trucks. The engine is 7 metres long and the trucks are each 8 metres. Write down a formula for the total length of the train.
(L = total length, t = number of trucks)

4 Collect these terms.

a $b + b + b + b + b$
b $3c + 4c - 2c$
c $3p + 2p + 7q + 3q$
d $4g + 3h + g + 2h$
e $3y + 2y + y + 2z$
f $7j - 5j + 4k - 2k$
g $5a + 4b - b - 3a$
h $8 + 6d + 5 - 5d$
i $7s - 3s + 5t + t - 2t$
j $5f + 4g - 5f - 3g$

5 Work these out using $r = 3$, $s = 4$, $t = 6$

a r^2
b $s^2 + s^2$
c $r + s + t$
d $r + s - t$
e $2t - 3s$
f $\frac{t}{3}$
g $rs + t$
h $rt - 2s$
i $2r + 2s$
j $5t - 5r$
k $3t - 2r$
l $\frac{t}{2}$
m rst
n $2rs$
o $\frac{t}{r}$

6 Solve these problems

a The formula $\boldsymbol{R} = \dfrac{\boldsymbol{H \times P}}{\mathbf{50}}$ can be used to estimate the number of rolls of wallpaper needed to paper a room of height ***H*** feet and perimeter (distance round the room) ***P*** feet.
Find the number of rolls of wallpaper needed to paper a room of height 7 feet and perimeter 100 feet.

b $\boldsymbol{O = 16P}$ is a formula for changing pounds into ounces.
How many ounces are there in 5 pounds?

c $\boldsymbol{E = 10mh}$ is a formula used in science for calculating energy.
Find the energy when $\boldsymbol{m = 2}$ and $\boldsymbol{h = 4}$.

d A formula sometimes used in maths is $\boldsymbol{s} = \dfrac{\boldsymbol{a + b + c}}{\mathbf{2}}$
where ***s*** is the distance half way round a triangle.
Find ***s*** when $\boldsymbol{a}$ **= 5 cm,** $\boldsymbol{b}$ = 7 **cm** and $\boldsymbol{c}$ = **6 cm**.

7 In these problems the formula is written in words.
You can solve the problems using the words but see if you can write the formula in symbols as well.
Use the letters shown in red.

a The ***p***erimeter (distance round the outside) of a regular octagon can be found by multiplying the length of one ***s***ide by eight.
Find the perimeter of a regular octagon of side 5 cm.

b The number of ***t***axis needed to get some ***g***uests to a wedding is found by dividing the number of guests by five.
Work out how many taxis would be needed for 40 guests.

c The number of carpet ***t***iles needed to cover the floor of a room can be found by multiplying the ***l***ength of the room by its ***w***idth and multiplying the answer by four.
Find the number of tiles needed for a room which is 6 metres long and 4 metres wide.

d To estimate the ***d***istance an aeroplane will travel in a given time, multiply the ***s***peed of the plane by the ***t***ime.
How far would a plane travelling at 600 miles per hour travel in 3 hours?

- Algebra is a short way of writing mathematical rules. It uses letters and symbols to replace words and numbers.

- A rule written out in algebra is known as a formula.

- **Rules of algebra**

  We miss out multiplication signs because they look too much like the letter x.

  We write the formula $t = 4 \times C + 3$ as $t = 4C + 3$

  $5y$ means multiply 5 by y.
  The number is always written first.
  We never write $y5$.

  Always put the letter you are finding on the left hand side.
  Write $t = 4y + z$ not $4y + z = t$

  Miss out any units.
  You do not put cm in any formulas involving lengths.

  Write divide like a fraction.
  Write $5 \div y$ as $\frac{5}{y}$

- It is quicker to write $b + b + b + b + b$ as $5b$.
  This is called collecting terms.

  Collect different letters and numbers separately.

  1 $2a + 3b$ cannot be collected.

  2 $2a + 4a + 3b = 6a + 3b$

  3 $4t + 2 + 3t = 7t + 2$

  4 $3g - 2g + 2h + 4h = g + 6h$

- You can use algebra and formulas to work out codes.
  Using $b = 2$, $c = 3$, $d = 4$ and $e = 5$

$3d = 3 \times d$	$be = b \times e$	$c^2 = c \times c$	$c + 5 = 3 + 5$
$= 3 \times 4$	$= 2 \times 5$	$= 3 \times 3$	$= 8$
$= 12$	$= 10$	$= 9$	

1 Write down the short form of these rules. Use the red letters and numbers.

a The *t*otal money raised in a sponsored jog at £4 a *m*ile.

$t = \ldots \times \ldots$

b The *t*otal length of an 8 m ladder with an *e*xtension.

$t = \ldots + \ldots$

c The *a*mount left when a 25 metre roll of sticky tape has a *p*iece cut off.

$a = \ldots - \ldots$

d The *a*mount received by each person when a cash *p*rize is shared by 4 friends.

$a = \ldots \div \ldots$

2 Rewrite each of these formulas. Use the rules of algebra.

a $C = r \times 3$

b $p - w = t$

c $a = b \div c$

d $3 \times r + 4 = h$

3 The hockey team have sent for some shirts from a mail order firm. The costs are £10 a shirt plus £3 postage and packing. Copy this table and fill it in.

Number of shirts S	Cost of shirts (£)	Cost of postage and packing (£)	Total cost T (£)
1			
2			
3			
4			
5			
6			

Write down in words the rule for the total cost.
Write your rule as a formula.

4 Collect these terms if possible.

a $n + n + n + n + n$

b $6g + 5g + 2g$

c $2r + 3s + 4r + 4s$

d $4 + 3e + 2e + 3$

e $2a + 3b$

f $6s - 4s + 5t - 4t$

5 Find the answers to these.
Use $g = 5$ and $h = 2$.

a g^2

b $g + h$

c $g - h$

d gh

e $2g + h$

f $\frac{g}{5}$

10 Angles

CORE

QUESTIONS

EXTENSION

SUMMARY

TEST YOURSELF

The Earth's orbit

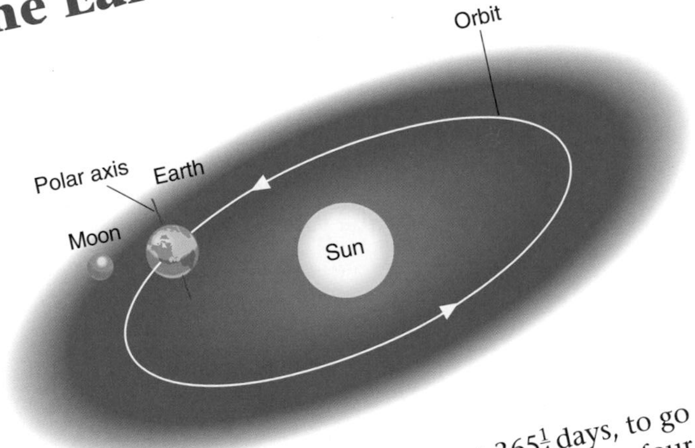

The Earth takes one year, or about $365\frac{1}{4}$ days, to go round the Sun. The $\frac{1}{4}$s add together and every four years make a leap year.

Long ago people thought the Sun went round the Earth. They thought it took 360 days to go round. 360 degrees in a circle probably came from this – one degree for each day.

1 Introducing angles

The pirate ship turns one way.
It then turns back the other way.

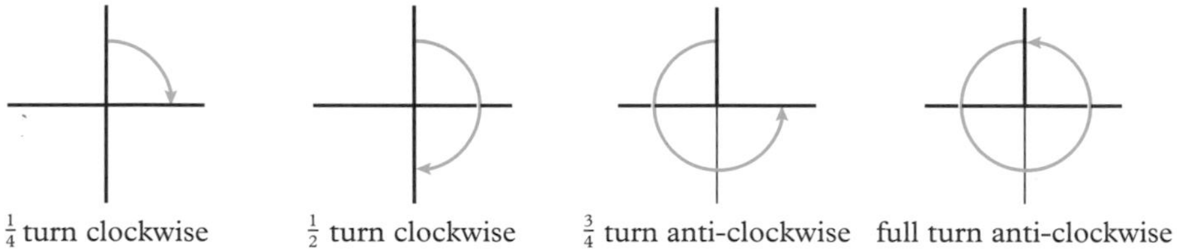

Exercise 10:1

1 For each part write down the fraction of a turn.
Write down if the turning is clockwise or anti-clockwise.

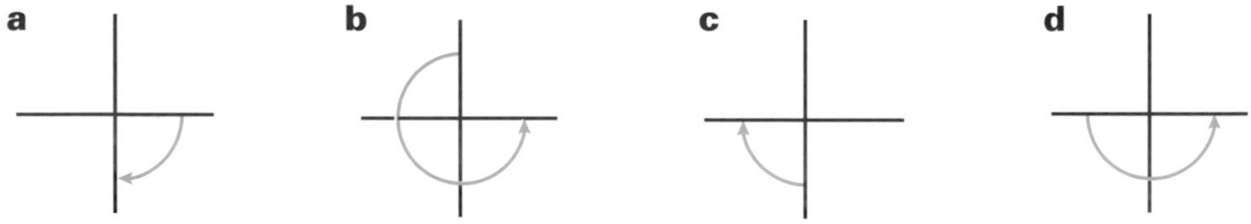

● **2** **a** Copy the map.
b Copy and complete the writing.
Choose from **clockwise** and **anti-clockwise**.
(1) Sally leaves home. She turns ______ to go to school.
(2) Sally turns ______ to go home from school.

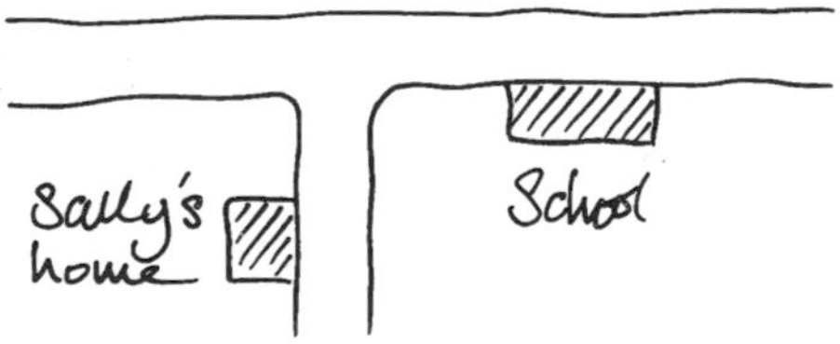

right angle

$\frac{1}{4}$ turn is called a **right angle**.

The corners of squares and rectangles are right angles.

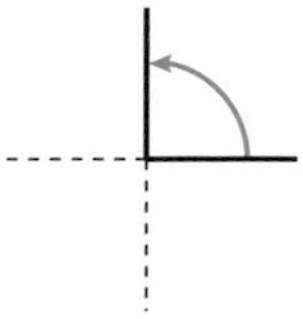

A right angle is often shown like this:

$\frac{1}{2}$ turn makes a straight angle or line.

3 **a** Draw a square of side 4 cm.
b Mark the four corners using the sign for a right angle.

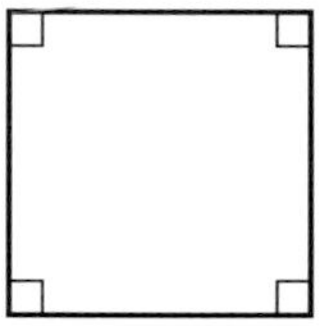

4 Take a piece of rough paper.
a Fold it to make a straight line.
b Fold it again to make a right angle.

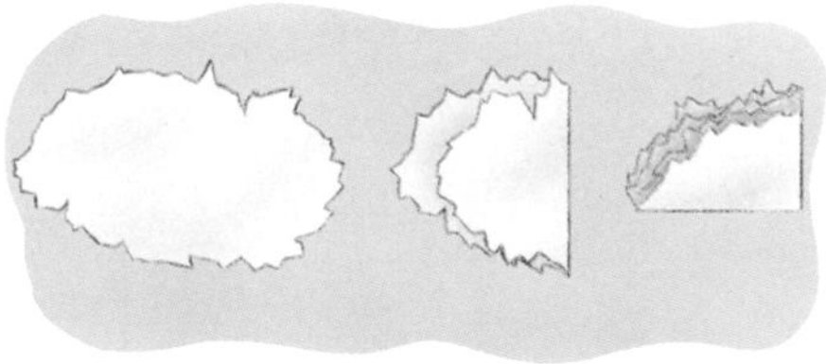

Keep your right angle to use later.

5 Look for right angles in your classroom.
Write down six things with right angled shaped corners.

degree We use degrees (written °) to measure angles.

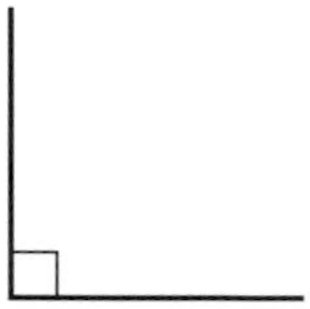

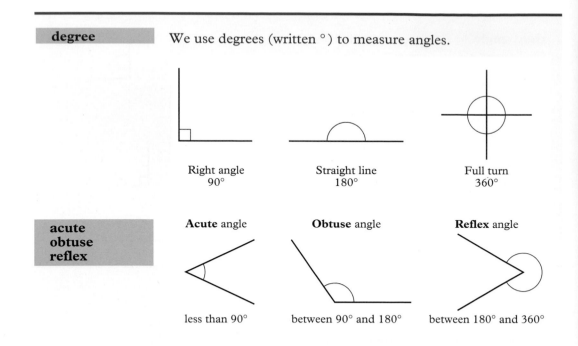

Right angle
90°

Straight line
180°

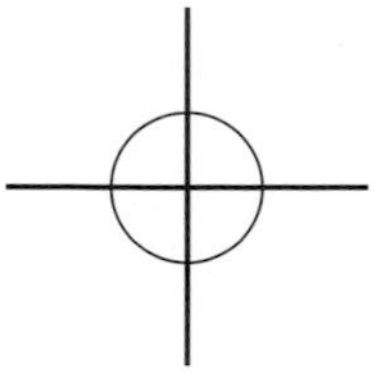

Full turn
360°

acute
obtuse
reflex

Acute angle

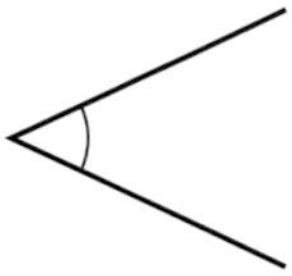

less than 90°

Obtuse angle

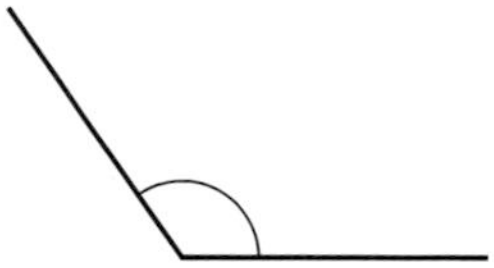

between 90° and 180°

Reflex angle

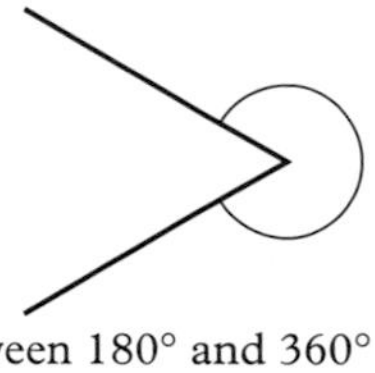

between 180° and 360°

Exercise 10:2

Use your folded right angle to help you with this question.

1 Write down the angles that are:

a right angles
b straight lines
c acute angles
d reflex angles
e obtuse angles.

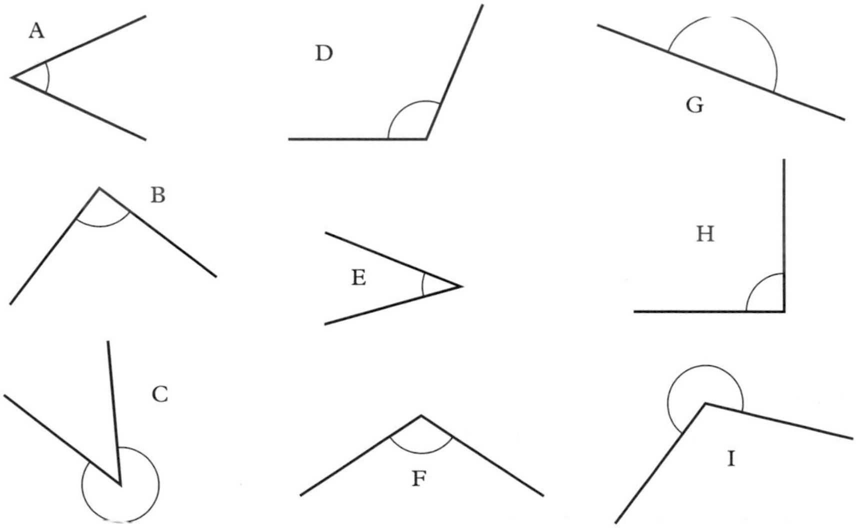

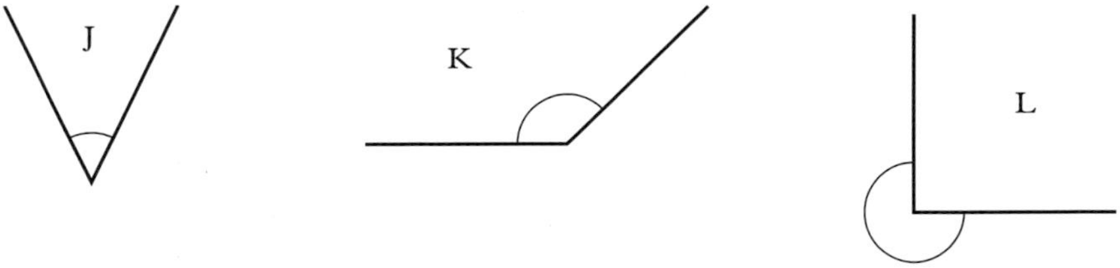

Example Estimate the sizes of these angles.

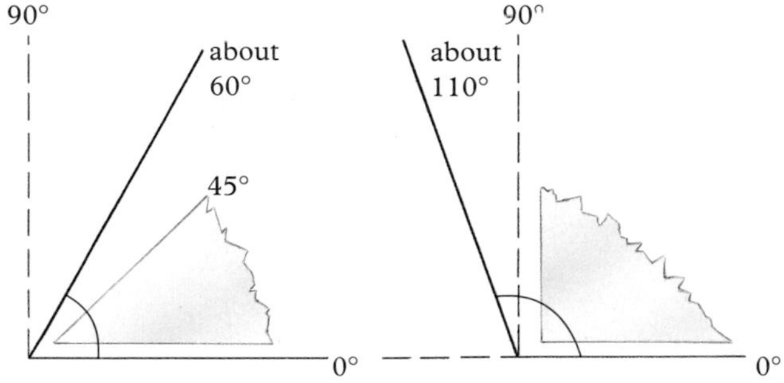

Fold 90° in half to get 45°

Exercise 10:3

Estimate the size in degrees of each of these angles. Use your folded right angle to help you.

Copy this table and fill in your estimates. You will need the 'Actual' column later.

	Estimate	Actual
1		
2		
3		

1

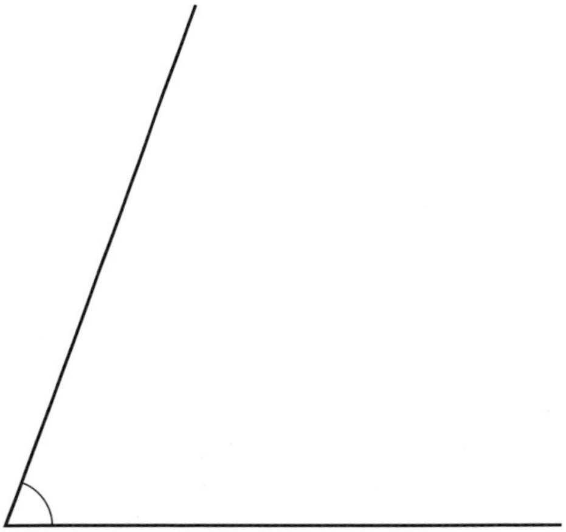

2

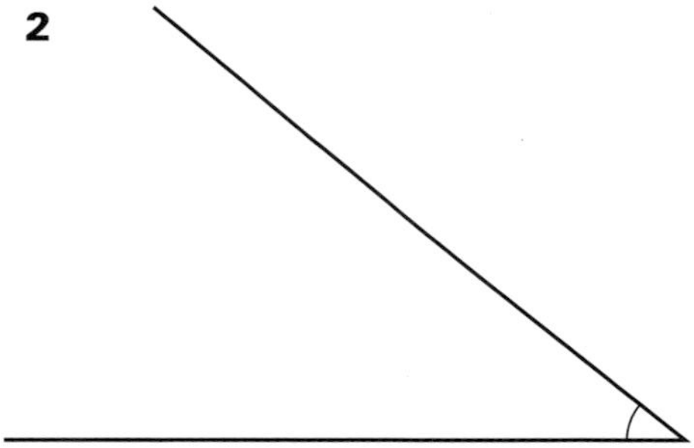

3

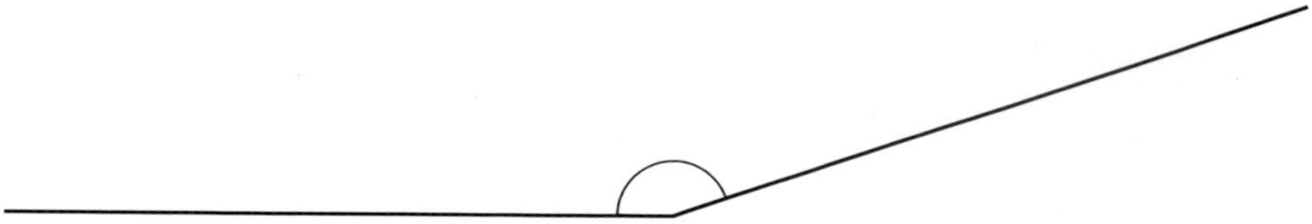

4

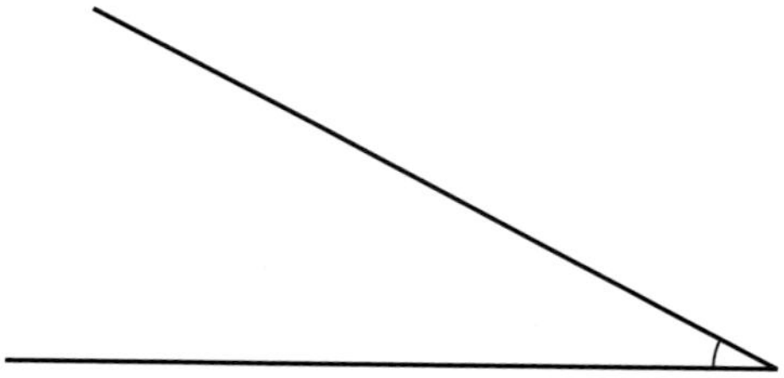

5

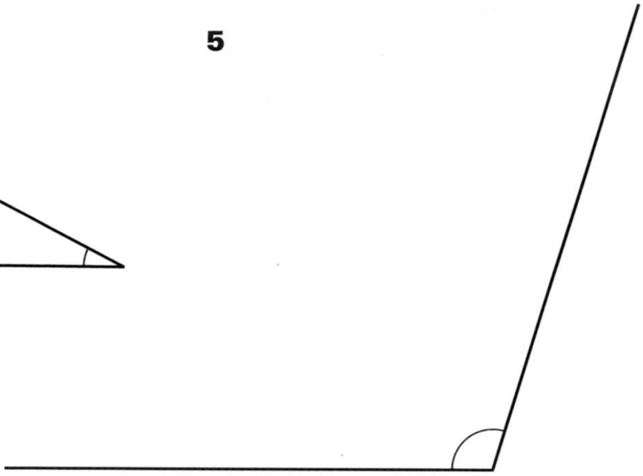

6

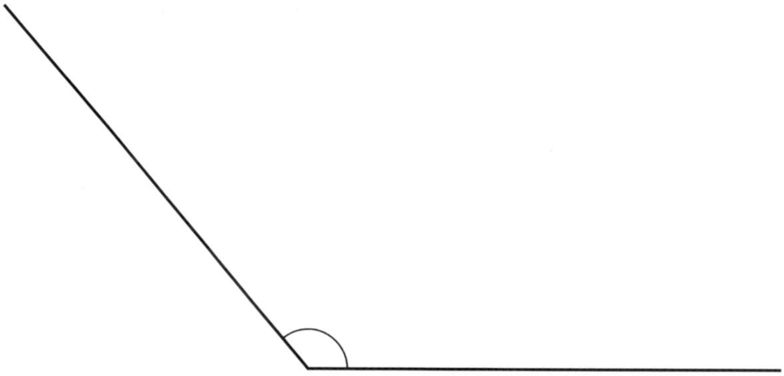

7

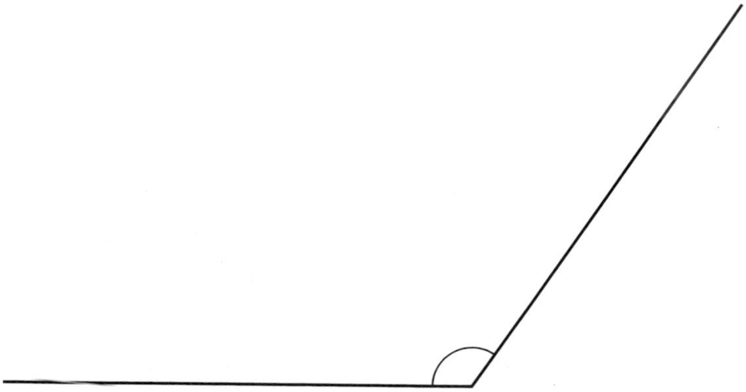

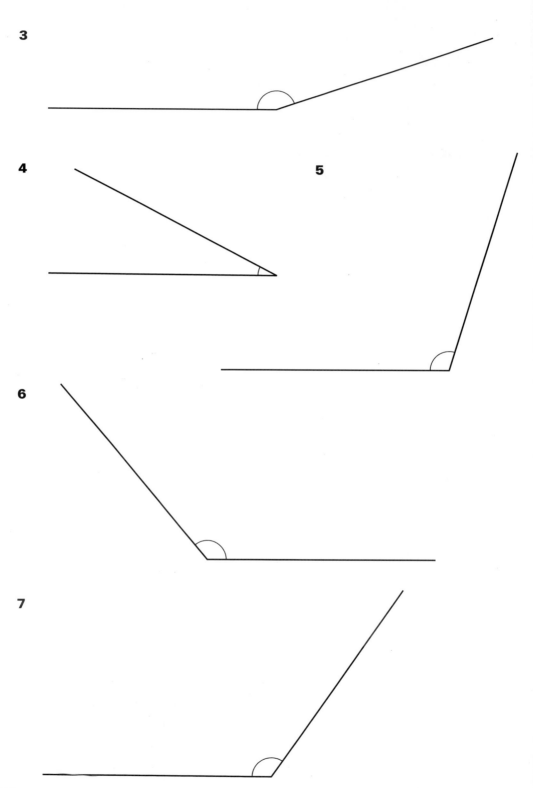

8

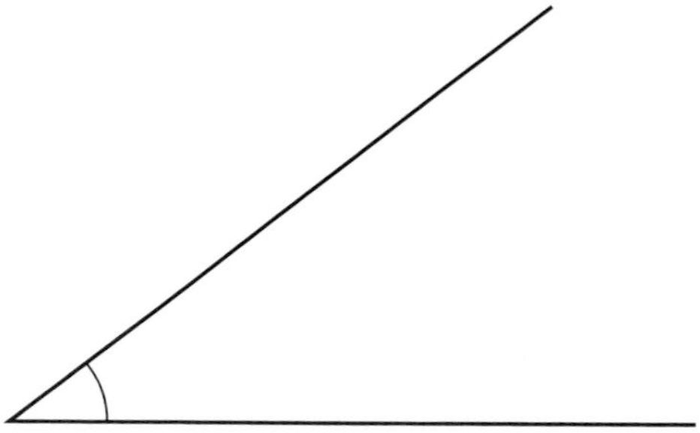

9

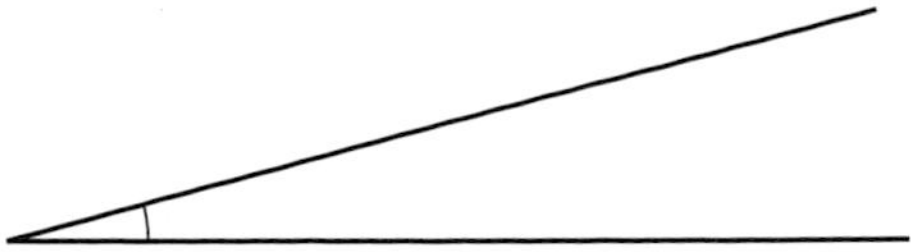

Measuring angles

We use a protractor or angle measurer to measure angles.
This can be in the shape of either a half or full turn.

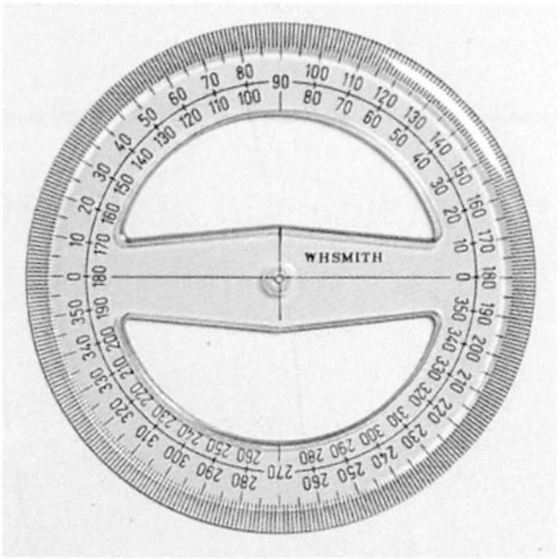

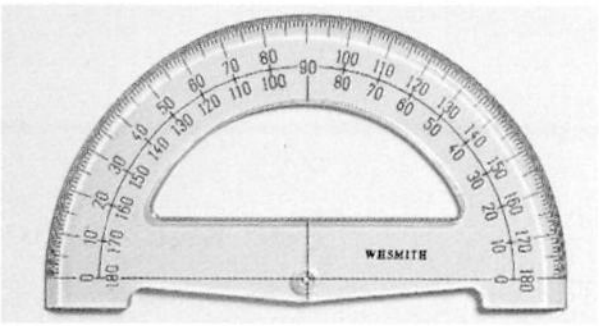

A protractor has a clockwise scale and an anti-clockwise scale.

10 Use your protractor to measure the angles in questions **1–9** accurately.
Write your answers in the 'Actual' column in your table.

Exercise 10:4

Use your protractor to draw these angles.
Label each angle like this:

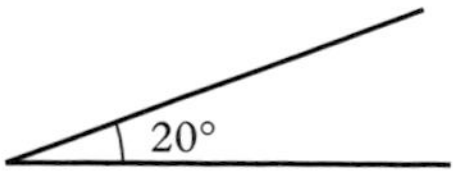

1 60°

2 45°

3 130°

4 145°

5 75°

6 105°

7 57°

8 168°

9 23°

2 Calculating with angles

We do not always find angles by measuring.
We can calculate angles.

The angles on a straight line add up to 180°

Example Calculate angle a

$a = 180° - 80°$
$a = 100°$

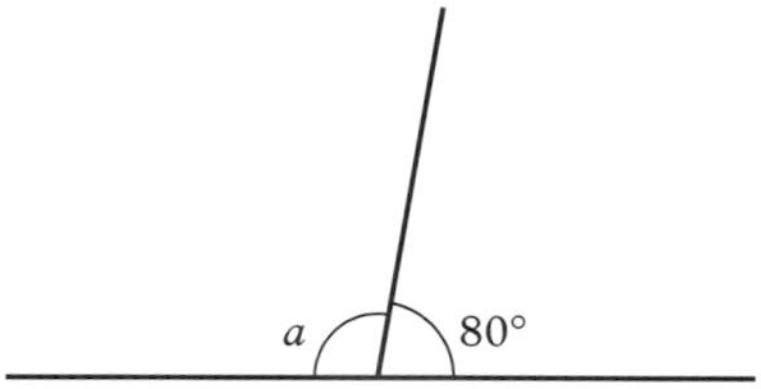

Exercise 10:5

Calculate the angles marked with letters.

1

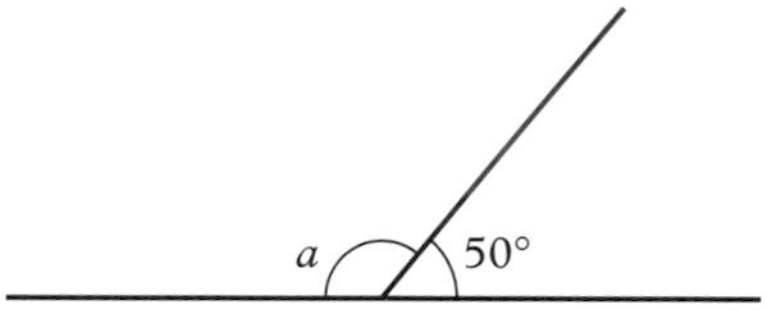

2

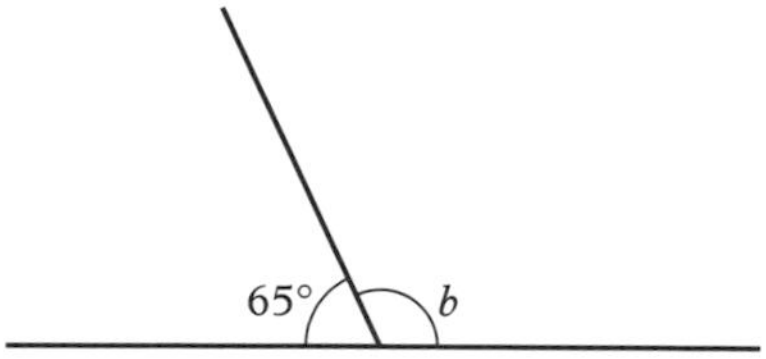

3

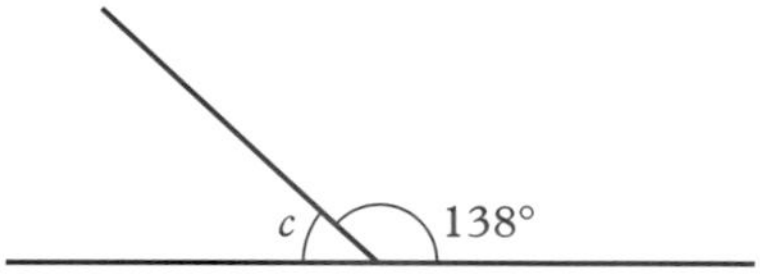

4

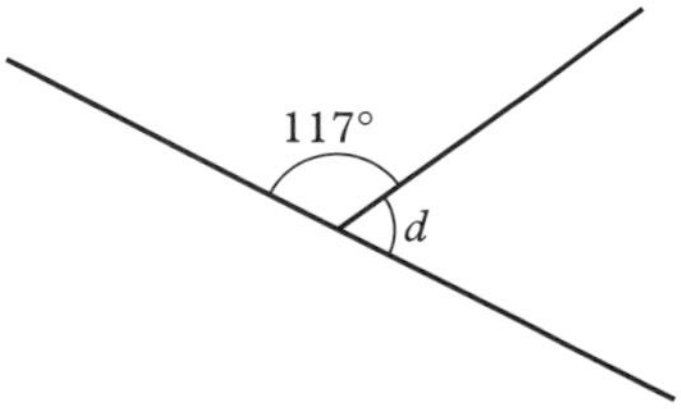

5

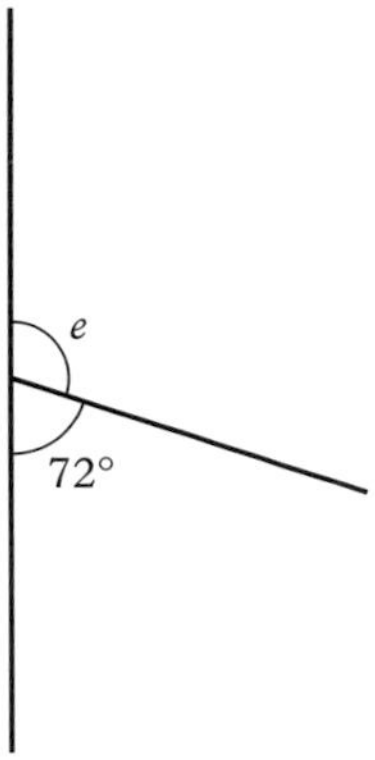

6

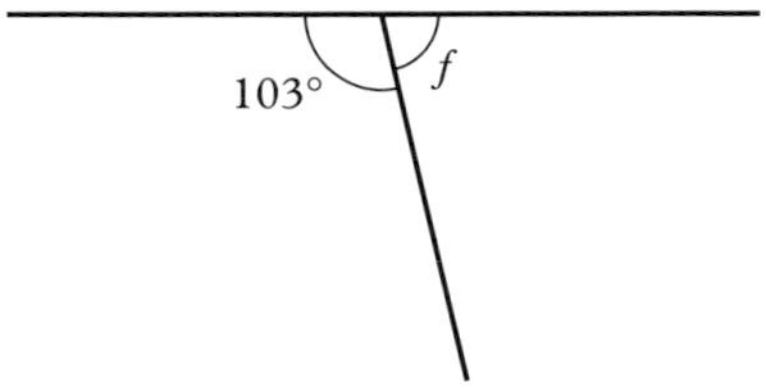

7

8

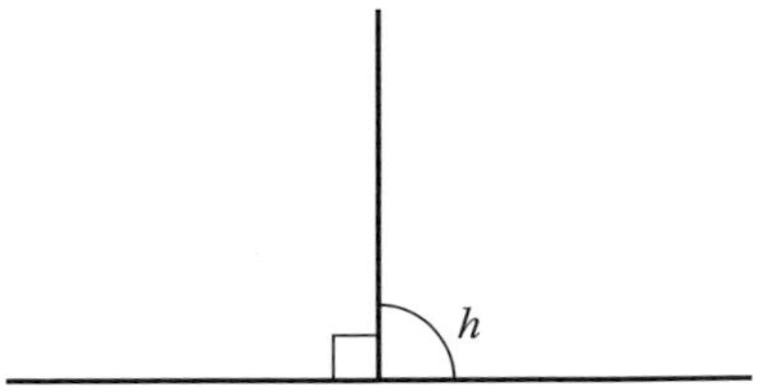

• **9**

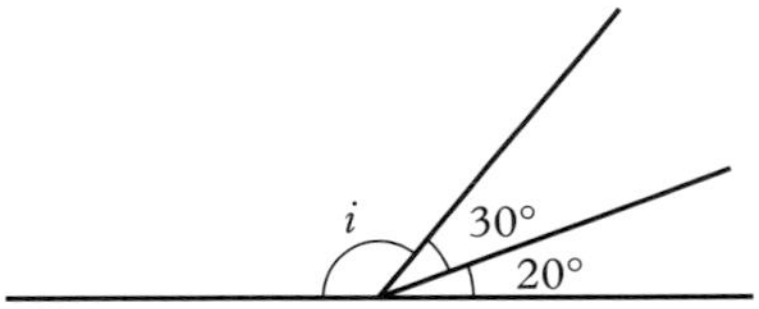

• **10**

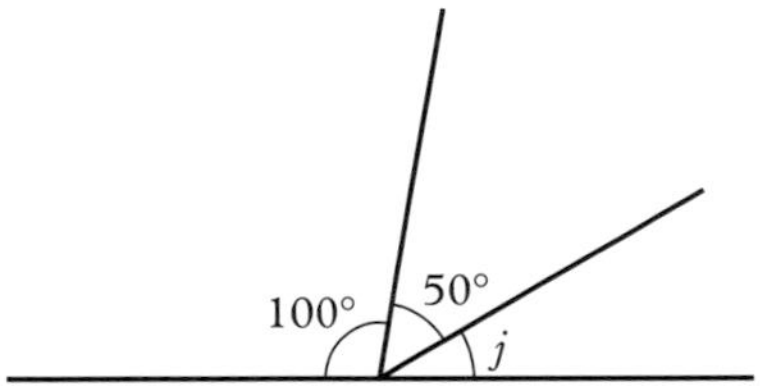

The angles at a point make a full turn.
They add up to 360°

Example Calculate angle a

$a = 360° - 290°$
$a = 70°$

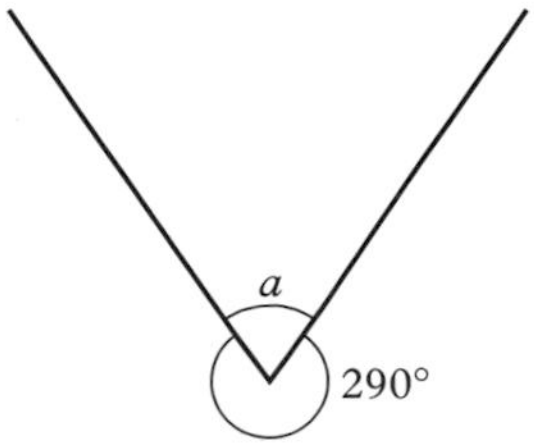

Exercise 10:6

Calculate the angles marked with letters.

1

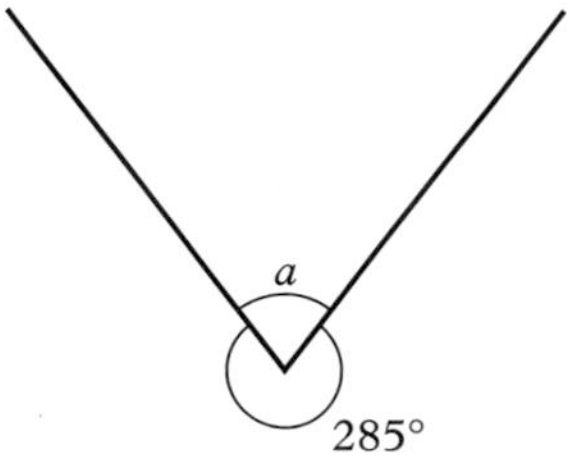

2

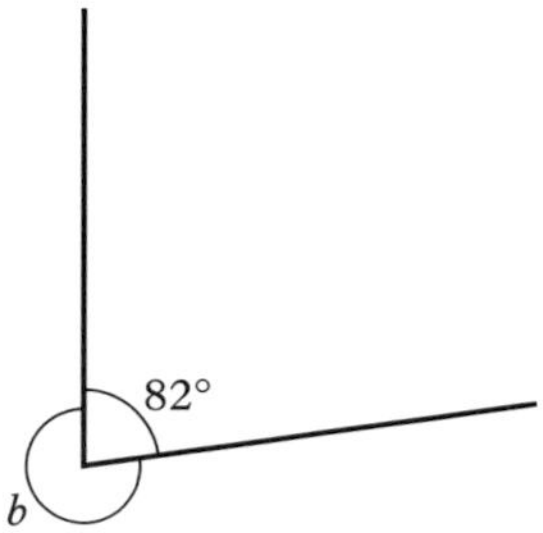

3

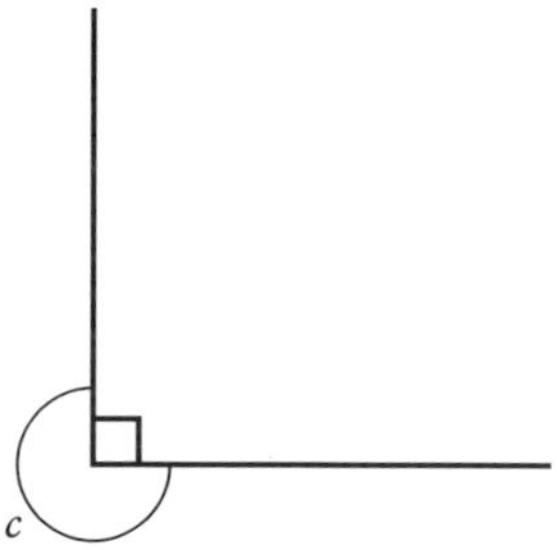

4

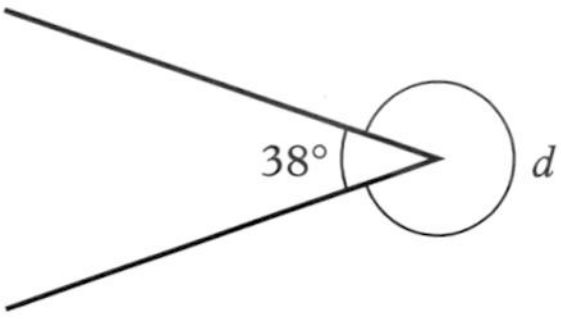

5

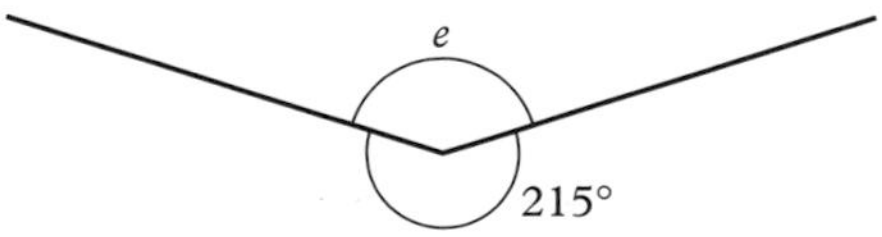

6

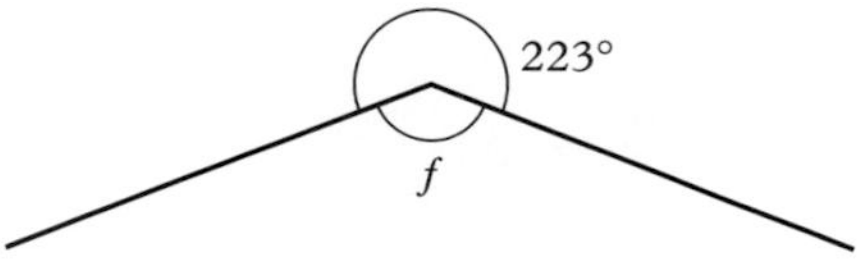

7

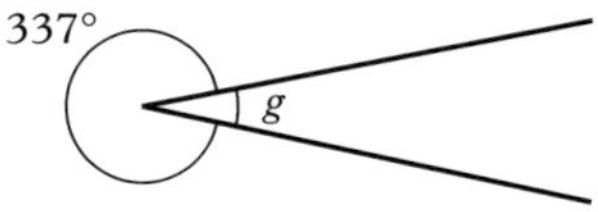

8

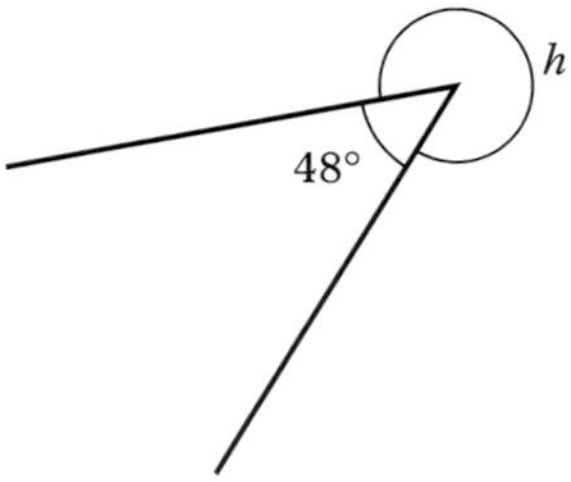

• **9**

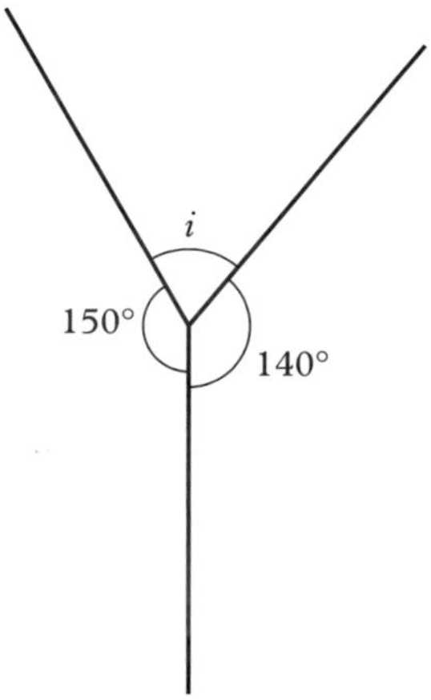

• **10**

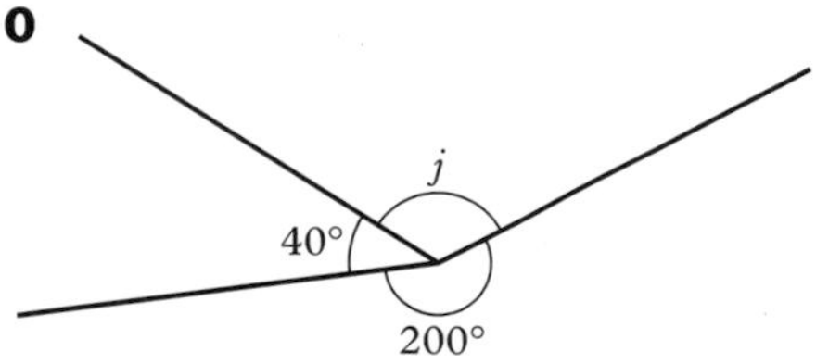

Exercise 10:7

Measure these angles.

1

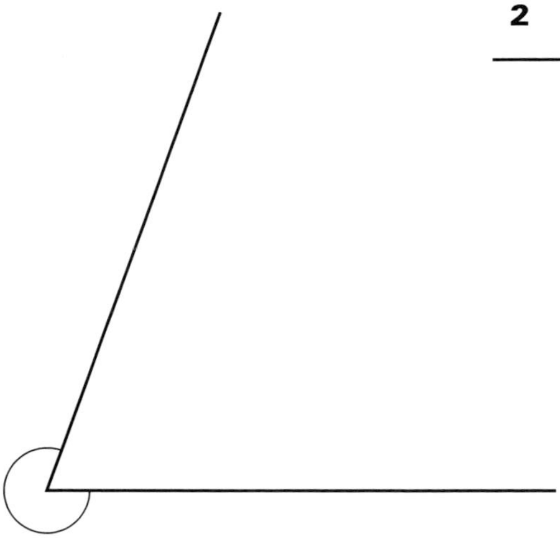

2

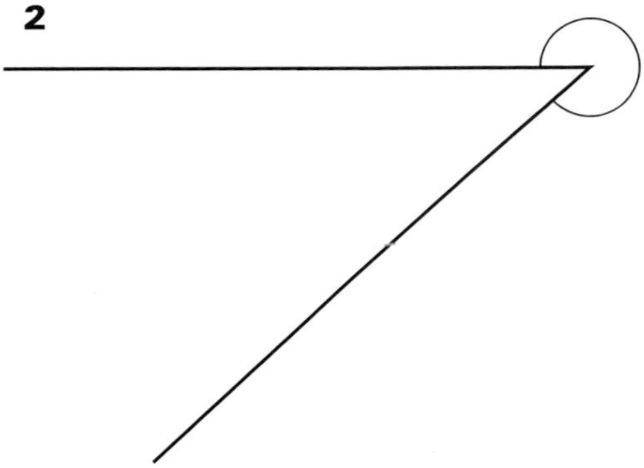

3

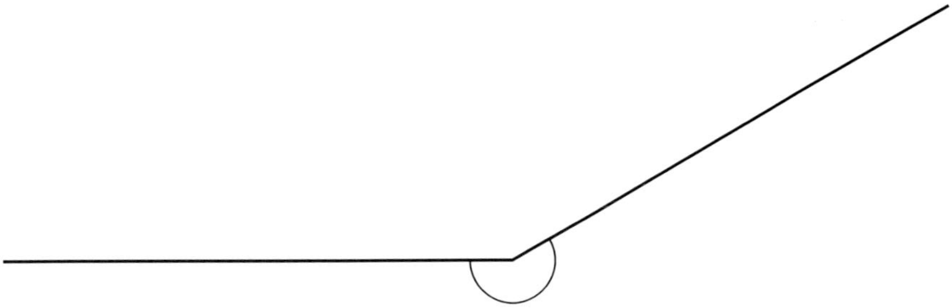

4

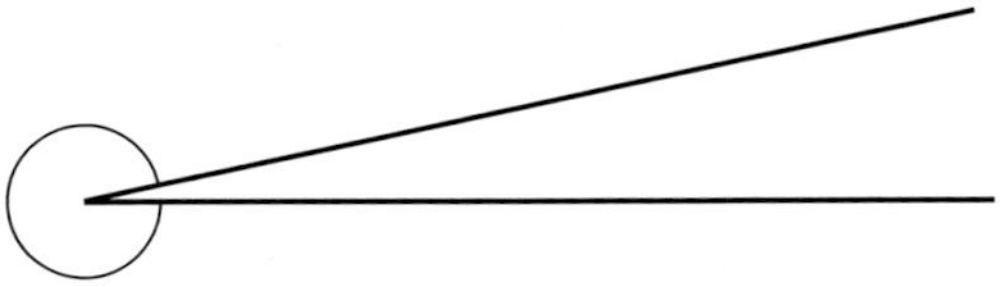

5

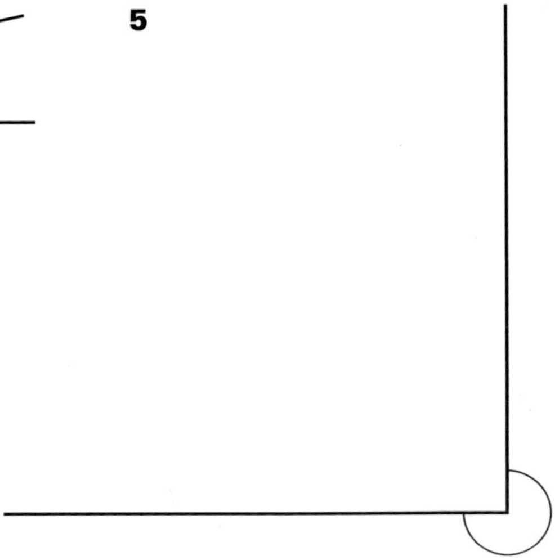

6

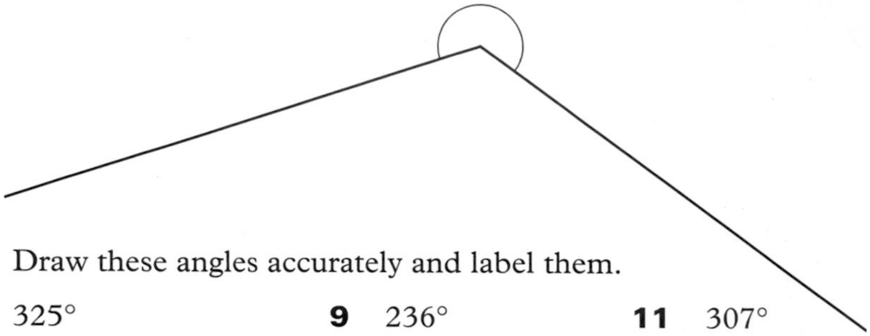

Draw these angles accurately and label them.

7 325°	**9** 236°	**11** 307°
8 190°	**10** 283°	**12** 258°

Opposite angles are equal.

Example Find the angles marked with letters.

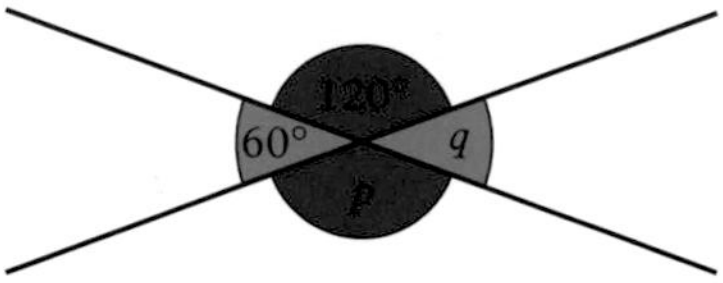

p is opposite 120°
q is opposite 60°
$p = 120°$, $q = 60°$

Exercise 10:8

Find the angles marked with letters.

1

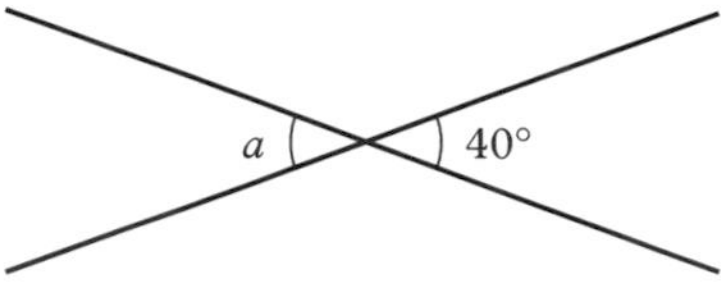

2

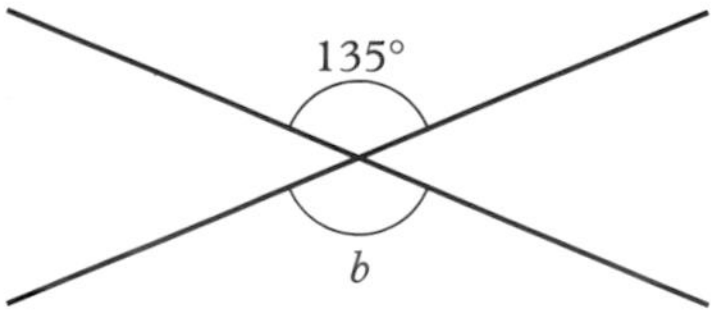

3

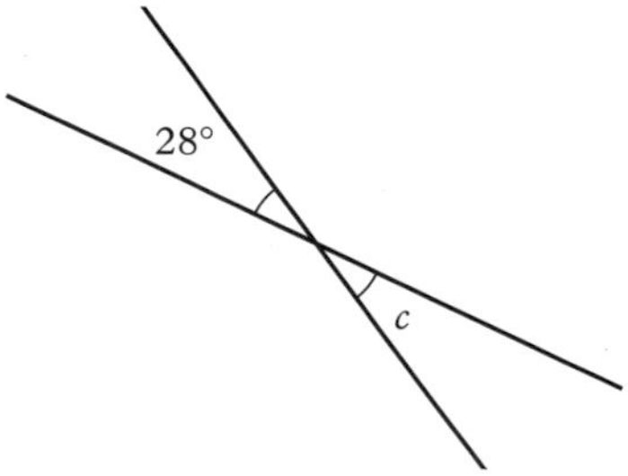

4

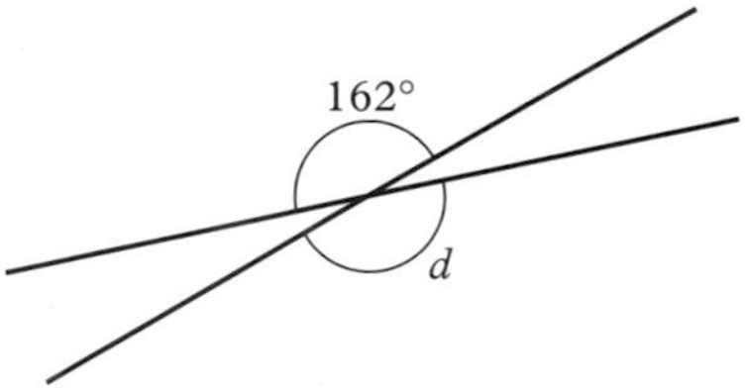

5

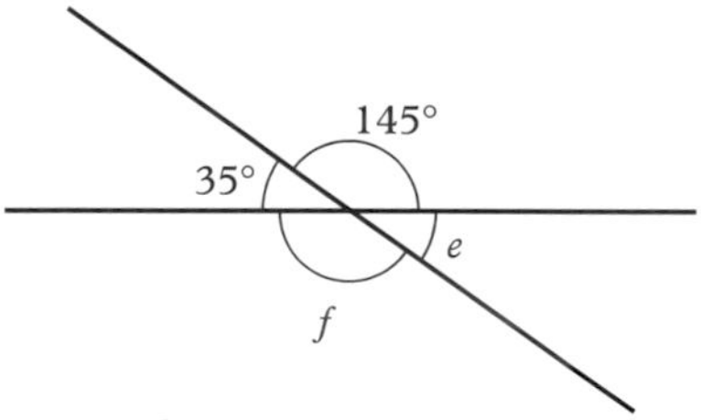

6

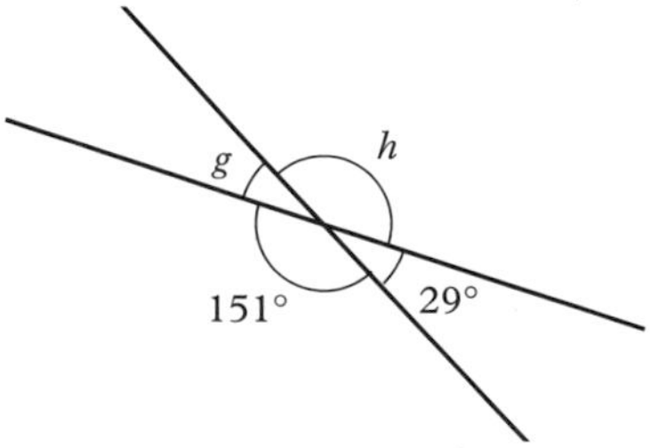

7

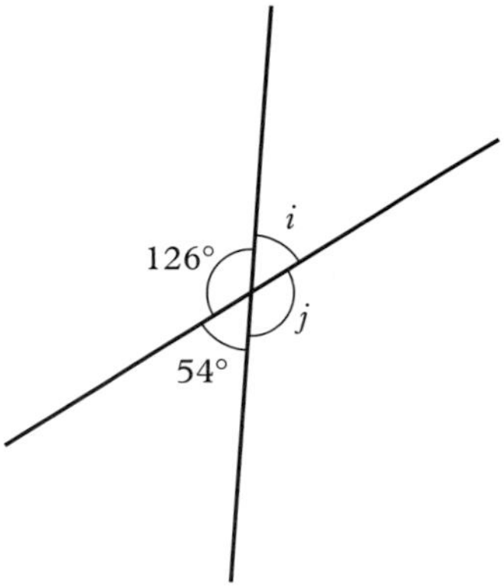

8

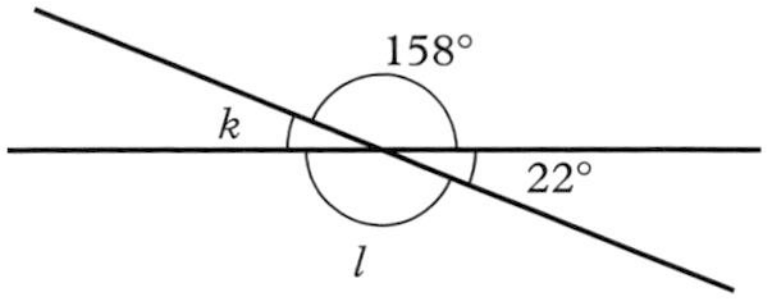

Exercise 10:9

Calculate the angles marked with letters.

1

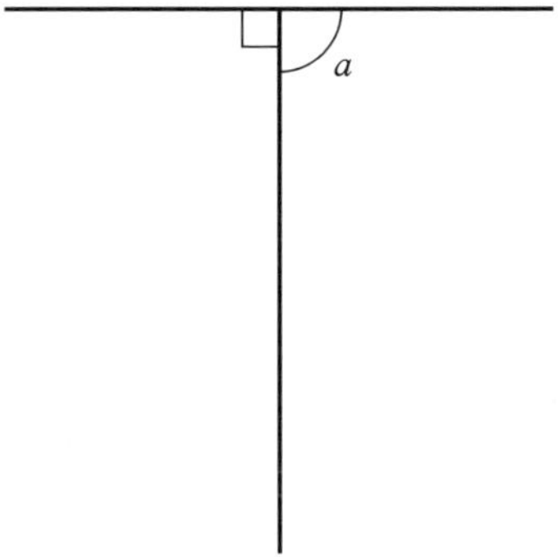

3

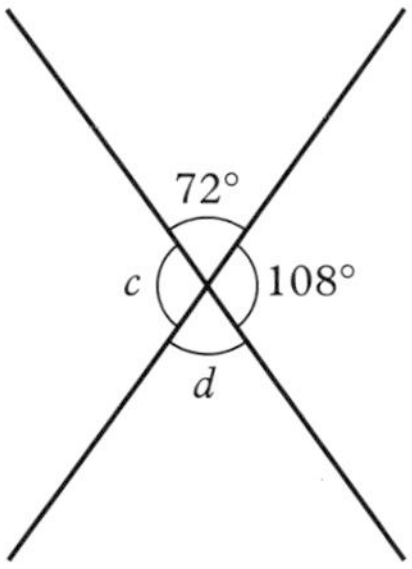

5

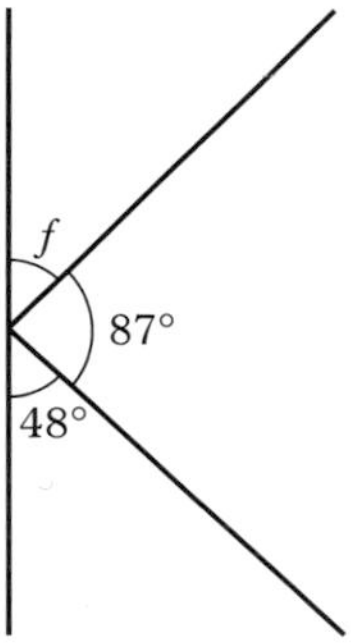

2

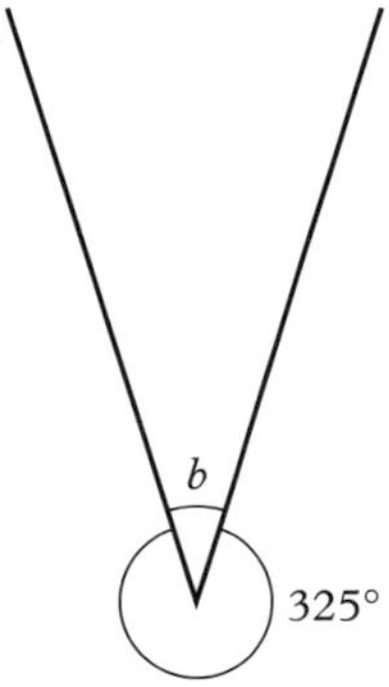

4

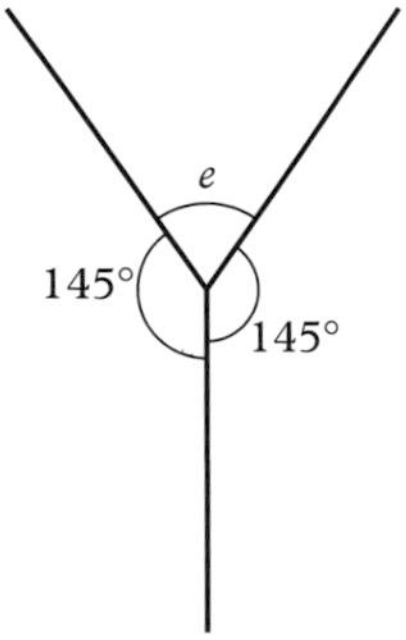

• **6**

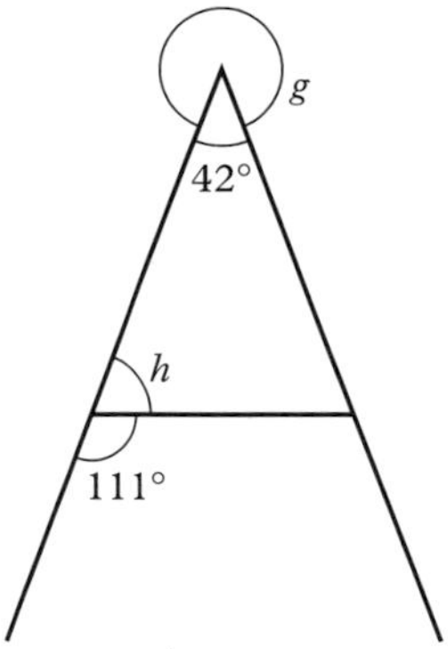

7 Write down the angle between the hands of the clock when the time is:

a 3 o'clock

b 6 o'clock.

3 Angles in triangles

Some sets of geometry instruments contain set squares. Set squares are triangles with special angles to help with drawing.

Exercise 10:10

1 Draw a triangle of your own.
Measure the angles of your triangle.
Find the sum of the angles.

2 **a** Measure the angles of a set square.
Find the sum of the angles.
b Repeat for the other shape of set square.

3 **a** Cut out a large triangle from scrap paper.
b Draw round the triangle in your book.
c Tear the three corners from your triangle.
d Stick the torn triangle inside its outline.
(Keep the three corners and stick them in a straight line.)

The angles of a triangle make a straight line.

The angles of a triangle add up to 180°.

Example Calculate angle a

$a = 180° - 85° - 65°$
$a = 30°$

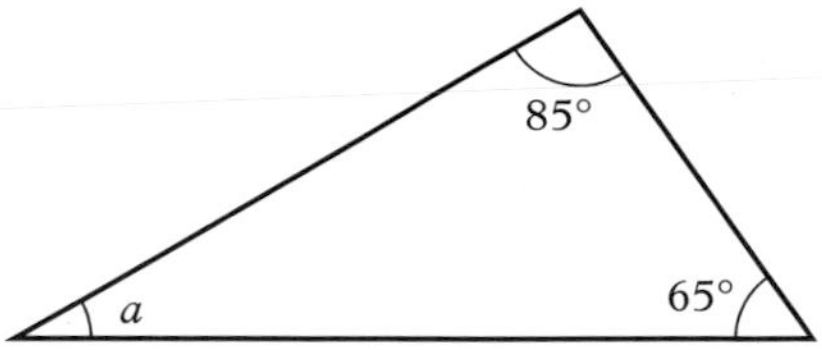

Exercise 10:11

Calculate the angles marked with letters.

1
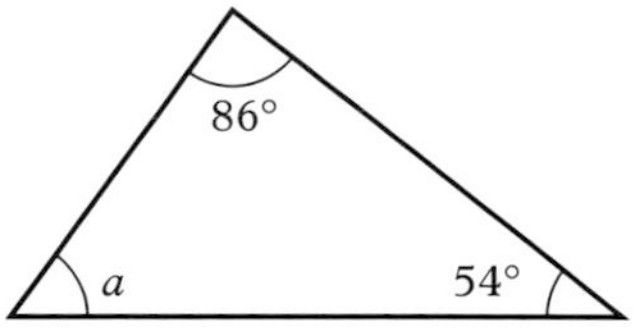

2
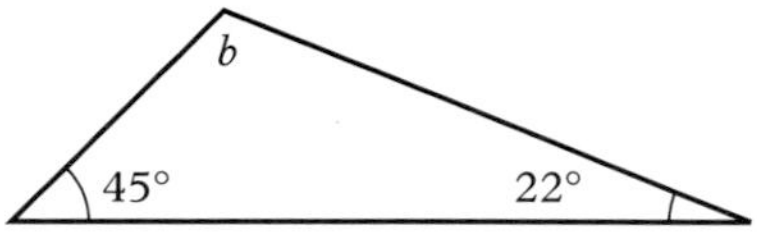

3
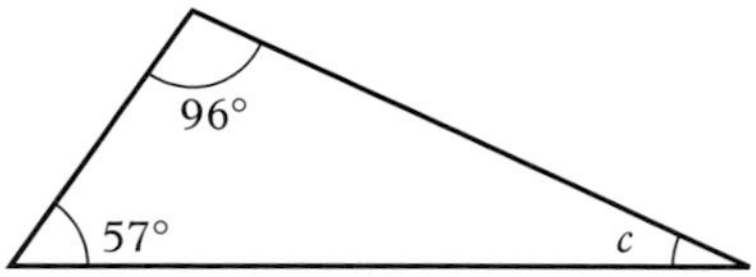

4
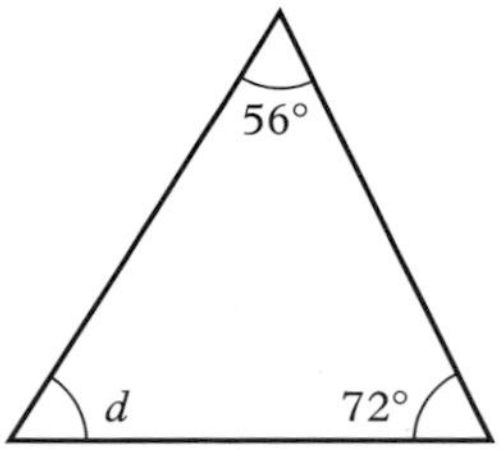

5
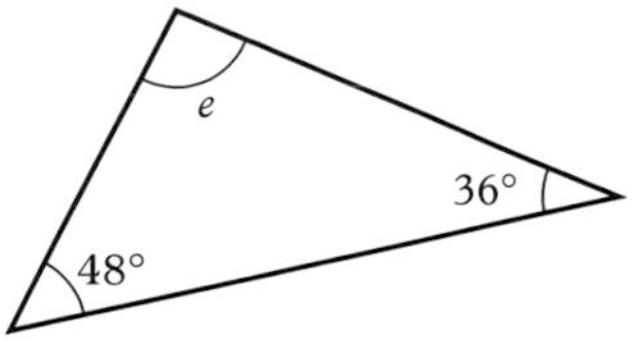

6
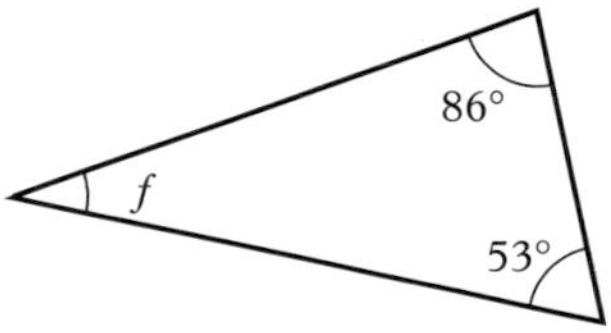

7
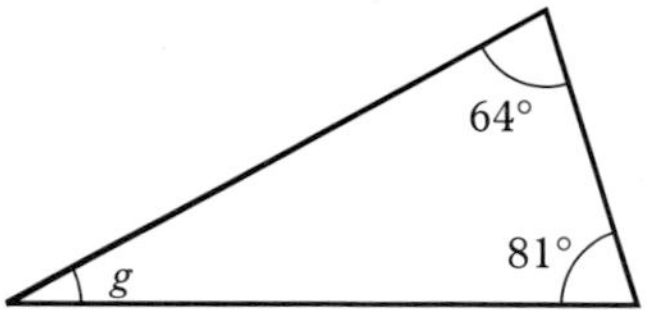

8
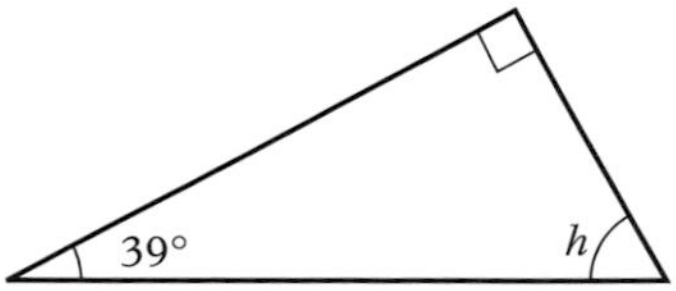

An **isosceles triangle** has two equal angles and two equal sides.

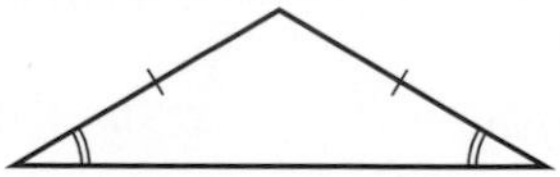

An **equilateral triangle** has three equal angles and three equal sides.

Each angle is 60°.

The same mark on sides or angles means that they are equal.

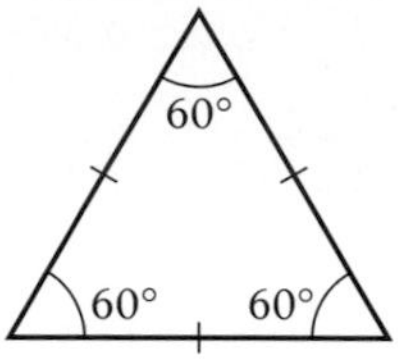

Exercise 10:12

Find the angles marked with letters.

1

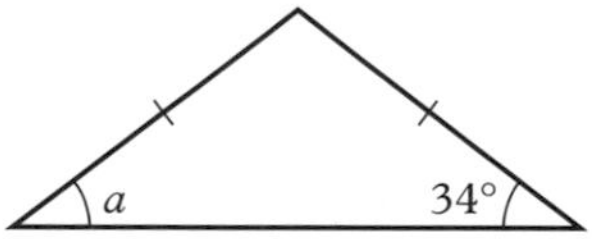

2

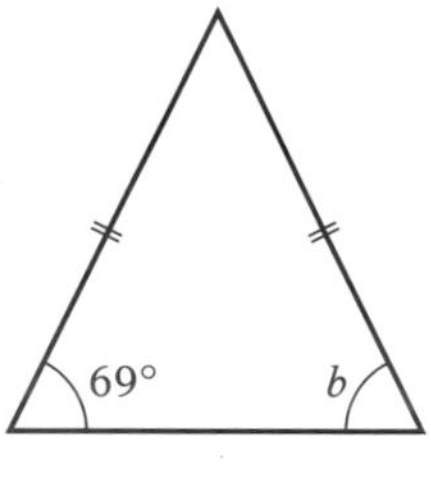

3

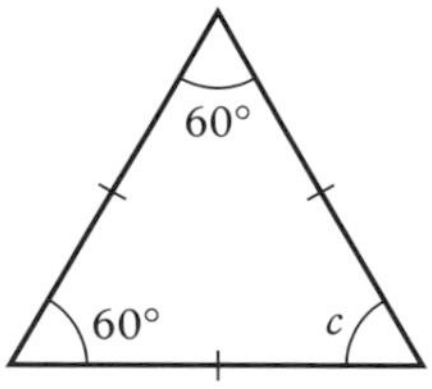

● **4**

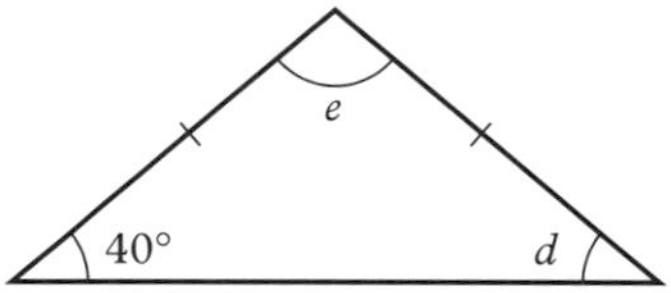

● **5**

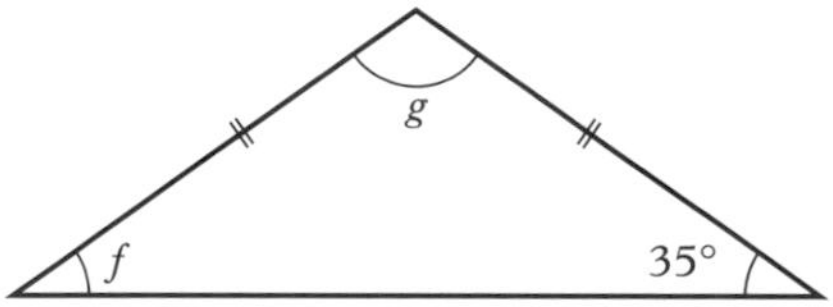

● **6**

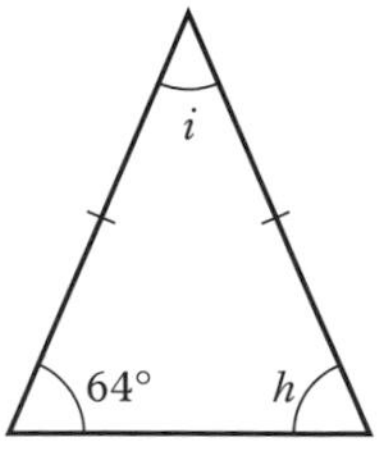

4 Constructions

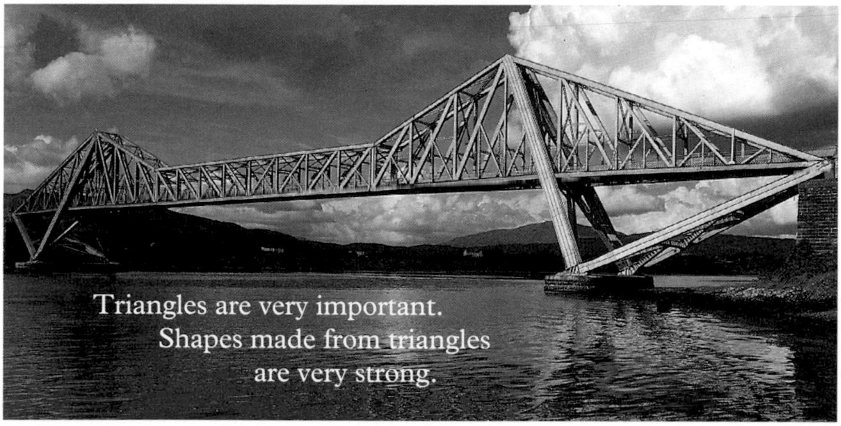

Triangles are very important.
Shapes made from triangles
are very strong.

Example

Construct triangle ABC.

AB = 7 cm ∠A (angle A) = 36° ∠B (angle B) = 58°

1 Start with a sketch.

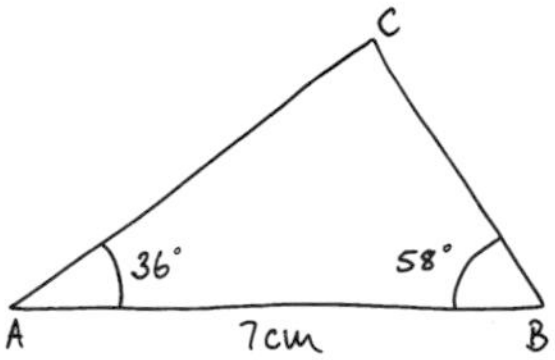

2 Draw a line AB 7 cm long.

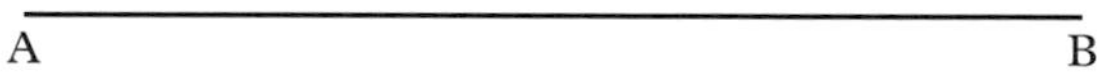

3 Draw an angle of 36° at A.

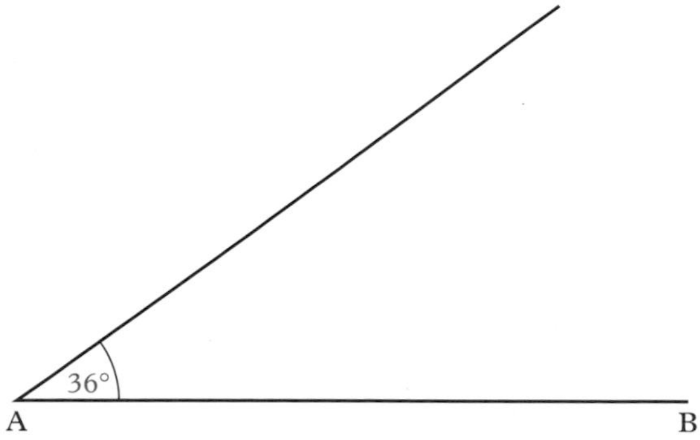

4 Draw an angle of 58° at B.
Label point C.

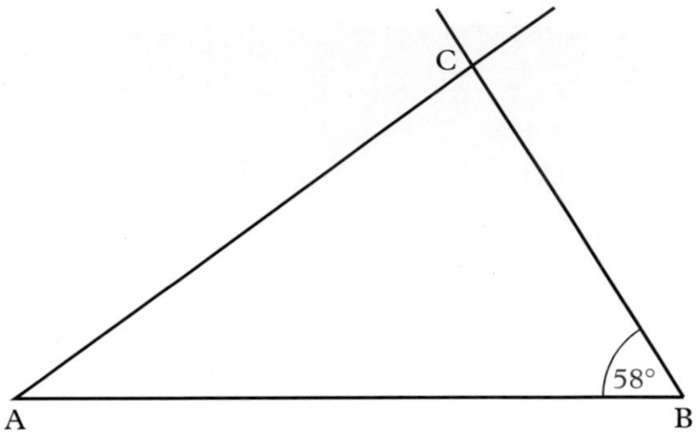

Exercise 10:13

1 Construct triangle ABC as shown in the example.

2 **a** Construct triangle LMN.
LM = 8 cm, ∠L = 47°, ∠M = 32°
b Measure side MN.
Write down its length.

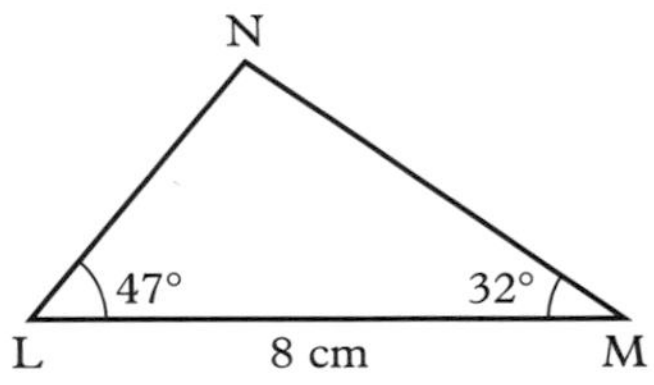

3 **a** Construct triangle PQR.
PQ = 6 cm, ∠P = 28°, ∠Q = 114°
b Measure side PR.
Write down its length.

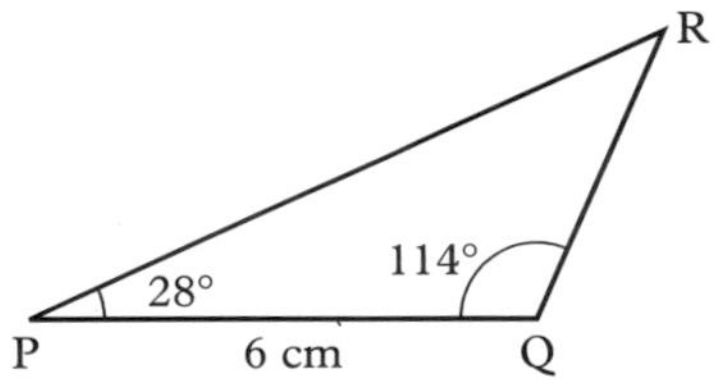

4 **a** Construct triangle XYZ.
XY = 6.2 cm, ∠X = 60°, XZ = 6.2 cm
b Measure side YZ.
c What sort of triangle is XYZ?

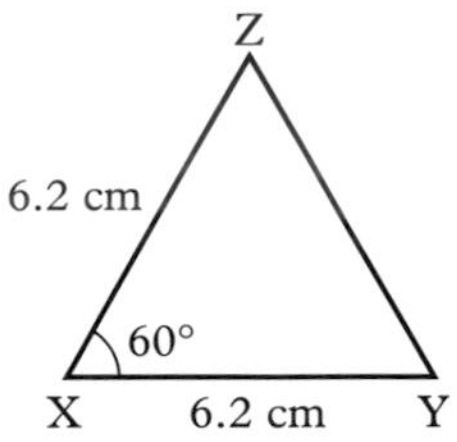

5 **a** Construct triangle DEF.
DE = 5.6 cm, ∠E = 126°, EF = 5.6 cm
b Measure ∠D and ∠F
c What sort of triangle is DEF?

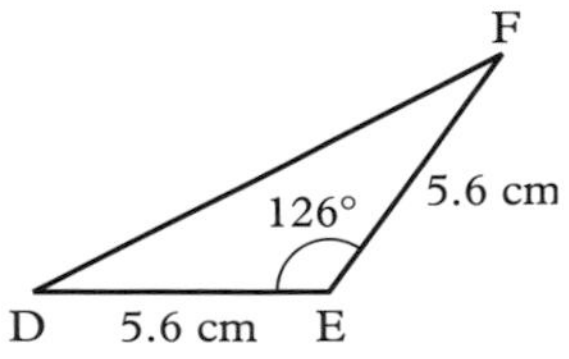

1 Mrs Patel goes from her house to the shop.
Copy the instructions.
Use **clockwise** and **anti-clockwise** to fill the gaps.

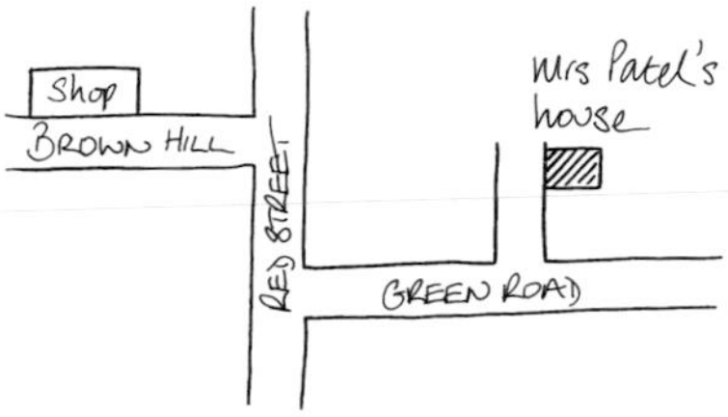

Mrs Patel turns .... into Green Road.
She turns .... into Red Street and .... into Brown Road.

2 Measure angles
a, *b*, *c*, *d*.

Say whether each angle is acute, a right angle, obtuse or reflex.

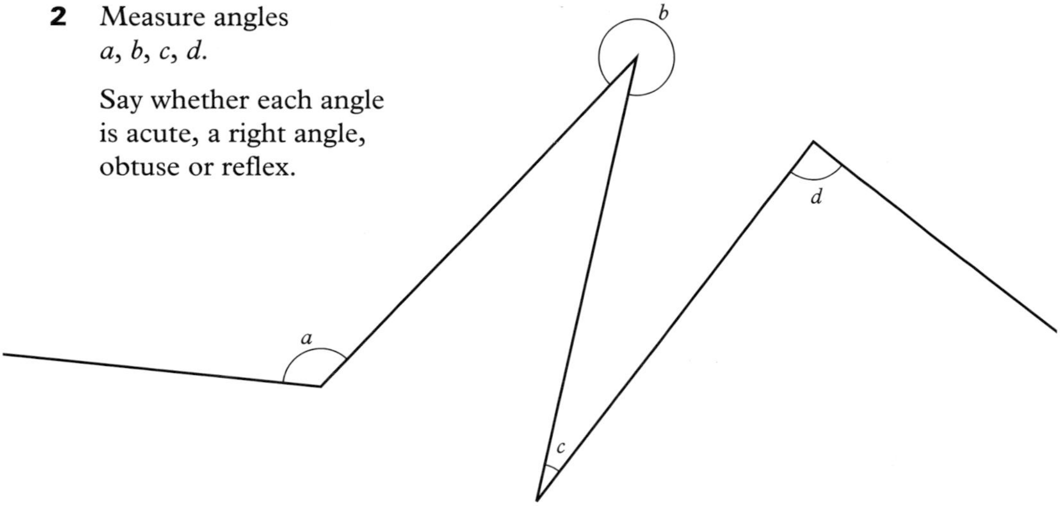

3 **a** (1) Construct triangle ABC.
(2) Measure ∠C.

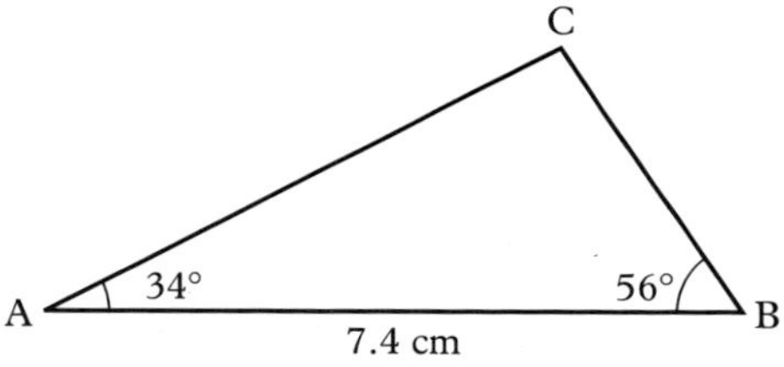

b (1) Construct triangle XYZ.
(2) Measure side YZ.

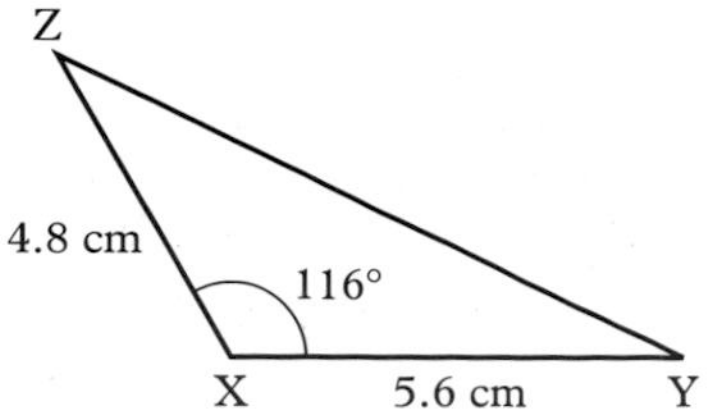

Crossnumber puzzle

Copy the crossnumber.
Find the angles marked x to fill in your crossnumber.

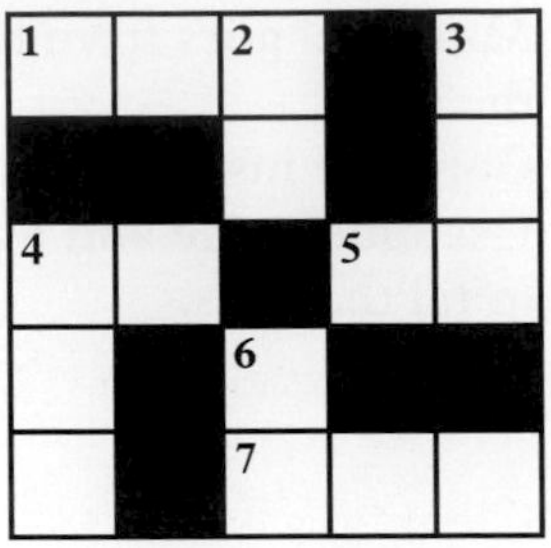

Across

1

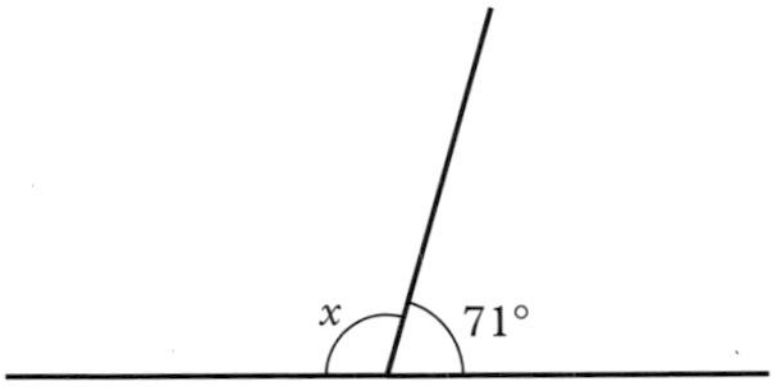

4

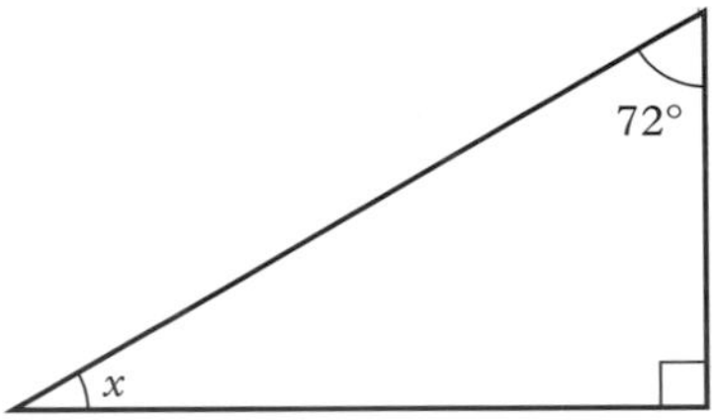

5

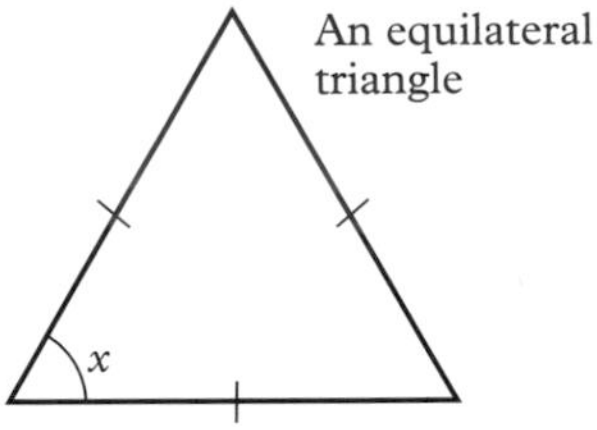

7

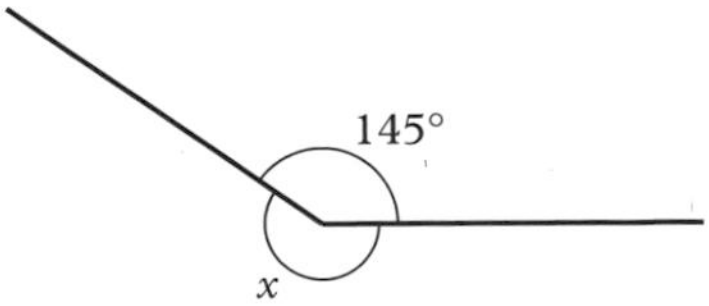

Down

2

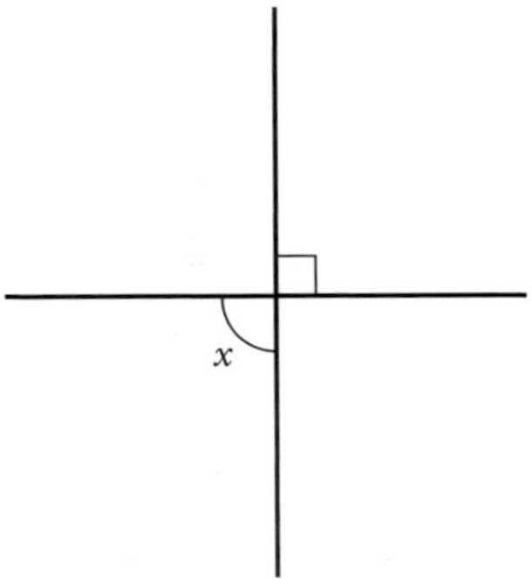

3

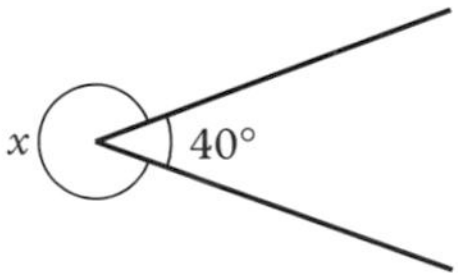

4

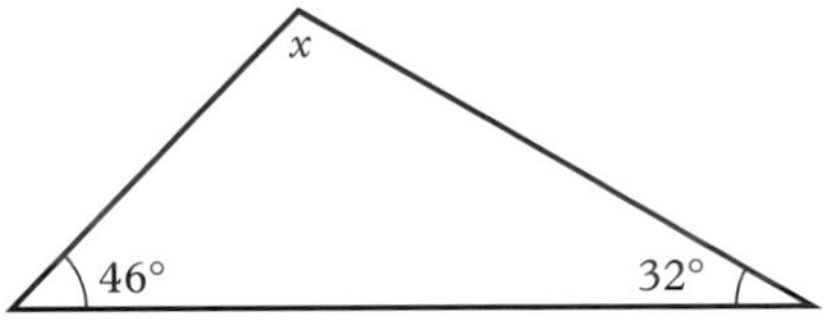

6

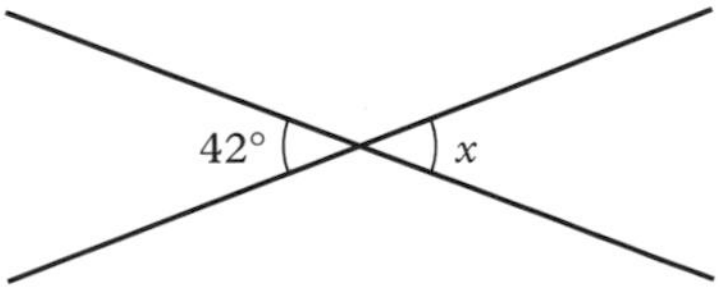

1 **a** Sketch these quadrilaterals:
rhombus, square, parallelogram, rectangle, trapezium, kite.
b Draw in both diagonals in each of your quadrilaterals.
c Which quadrilaterals have diagonals that cross at right angles?

2 **a** Draw a triangle with extended sides.
b Colour the equal opposite angles that are outside the triangle.
c Measure **one** angle of each colour.
d Add your three angles together.
e Repeat parts **a** to **d** for a different triangle.
f Write down what you notice.

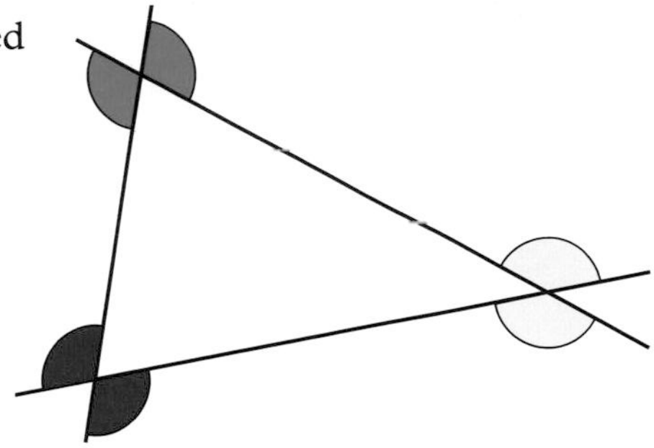

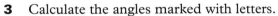

3 Calculate the angles marked with letters.

a The side of a bungalow.

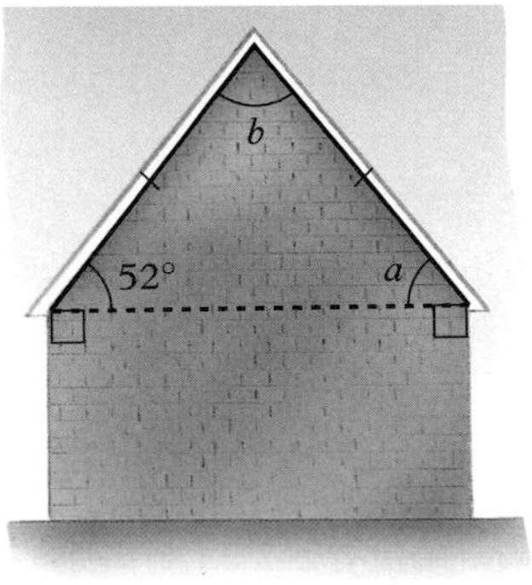

b The front of a nesting box.

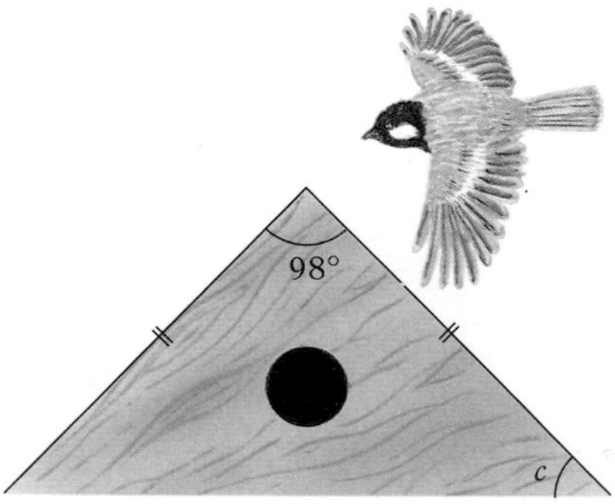

c A garden gate.

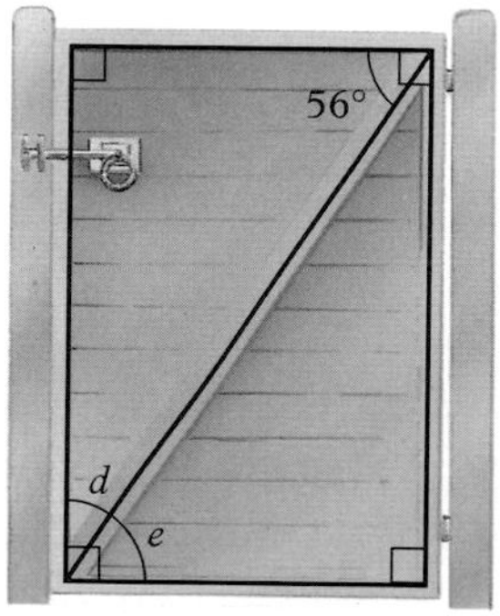

d The support for a wall.

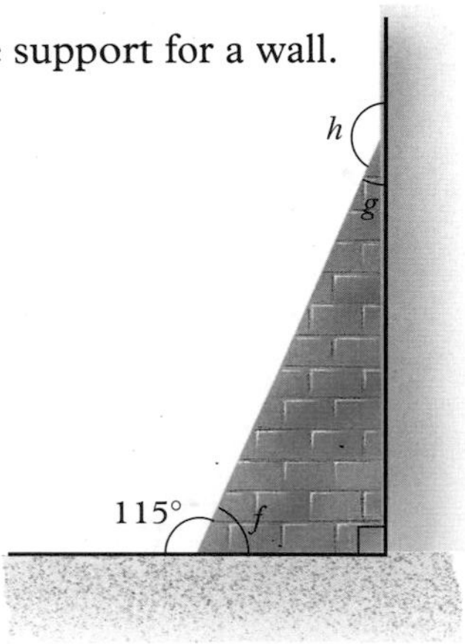

e A picnic hamper.

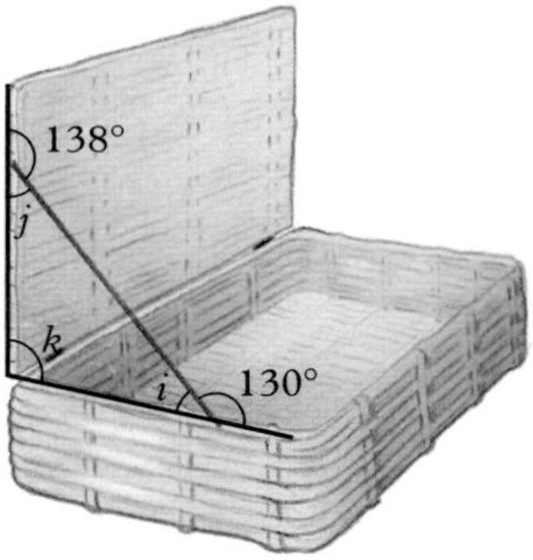

f Part of some stairs.

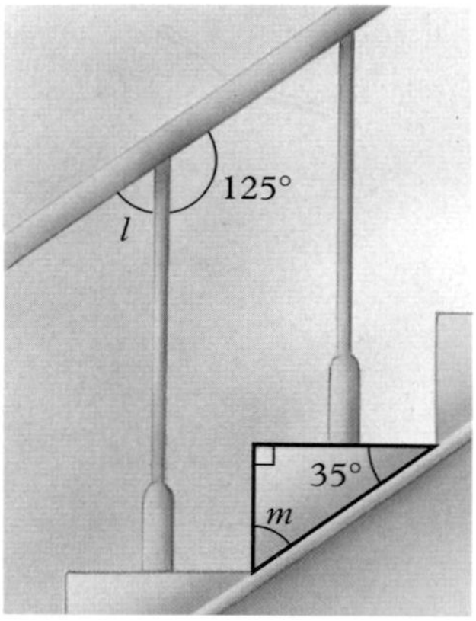

g The support for a hanging basket.

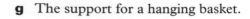

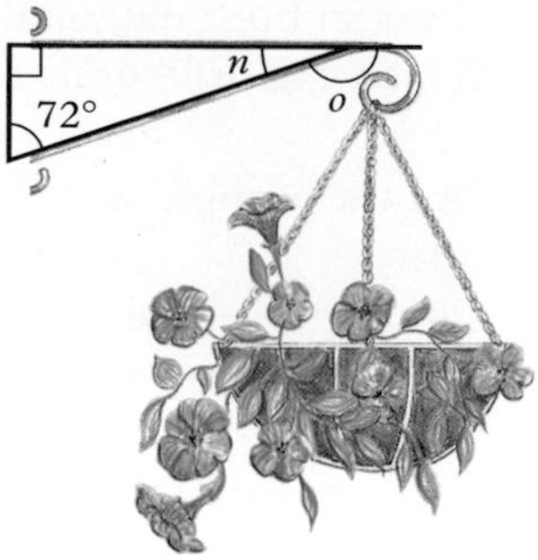

h A pair of tongs.

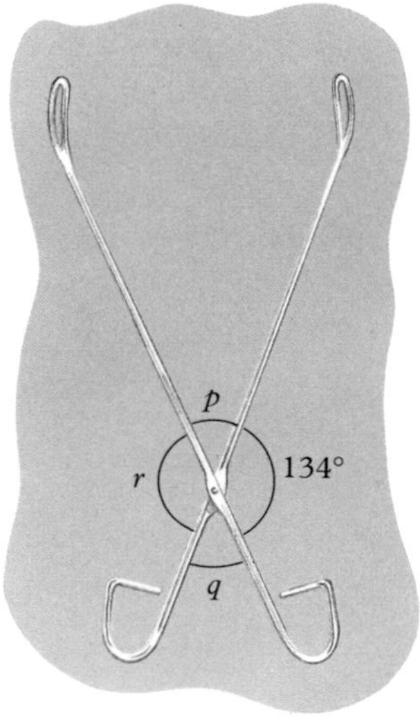

4 Write true or false for each of these.
- **a** A triangle may contain three acute angles.
- **b** A triangle may contain only one acute angle.
- **c** A triangle may contain only one obtuse angle.
- **d** The longest side of a triangle is opposite the largest angle.
- **e** The sides of a triangle could be 7 cm, 4 cm and 3 cm.

5 You need 9-point grids for this question.

These two triangles are congruent. (They would be the same if cut out.)

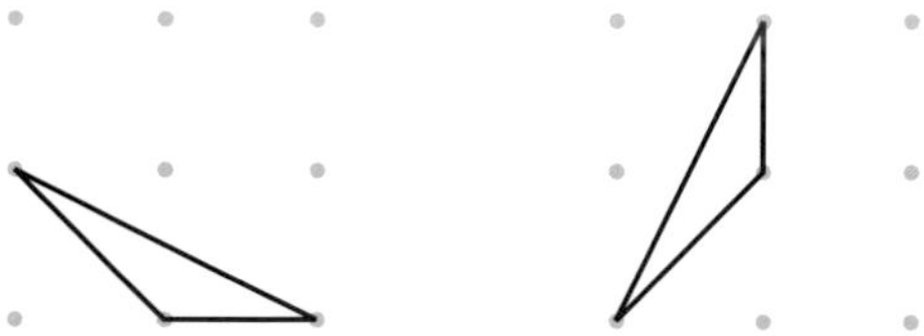

- **a** How many different triangles can you make using the grid?
- **b** How many triangles contain right angles?
- **c** How many triangles are isosceles?

- The **angles at a point** make a full turn. They add up to 360°

  The angles on a straight line add up to 180°

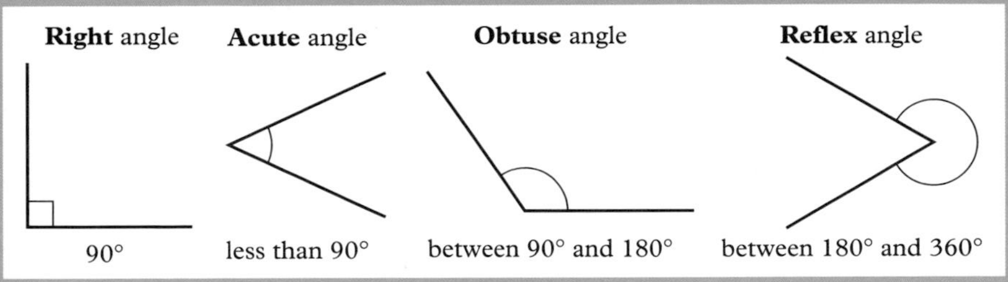

- Opposite angles are equal.

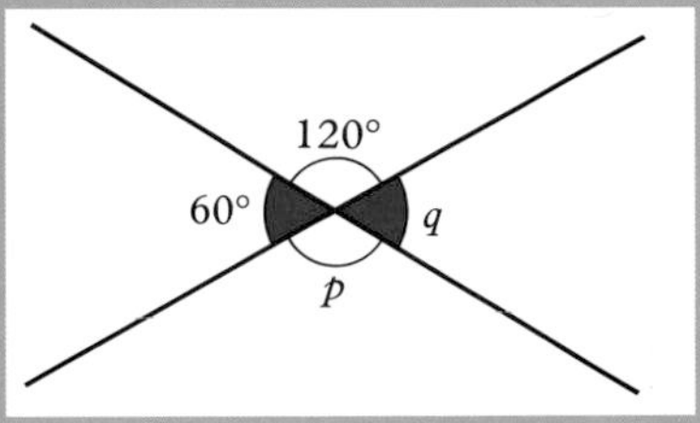

Example

p is opposite 120°
q is opposite 60°
p = 120°, *q* = 60°

- The angles of a triangle add up to 180°

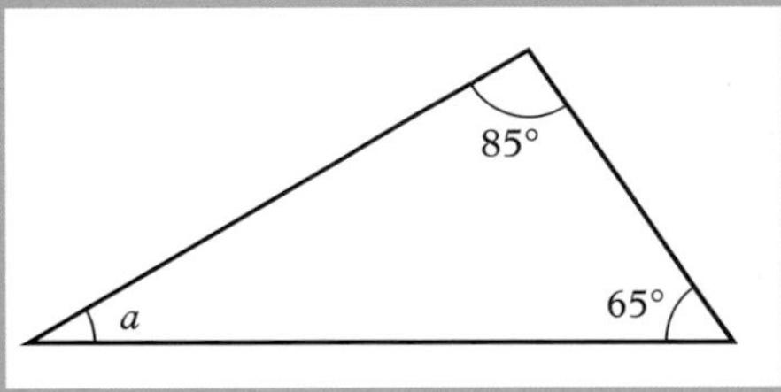

Example

Calculate angle *a*

$a = 180° - 85° - 65°$
$a = 30°$

- An isosceles triangle has two equal angles and two equal sides.

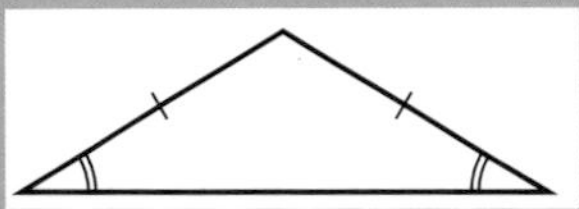

An equilateral triangle has three equal angles and three equal sides.

Each angle is 60°.

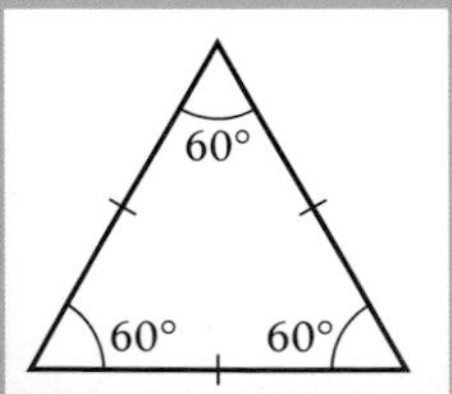

1 For each diagram write down:
a The fraction of a turn shown.
b If it is clockwise or anti-clockwise

(1)

(2)

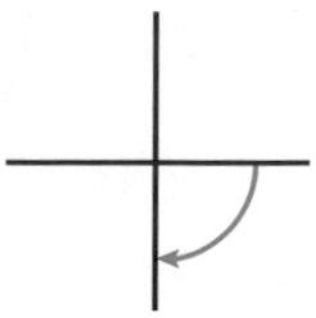

2 **a** Measure this angle.

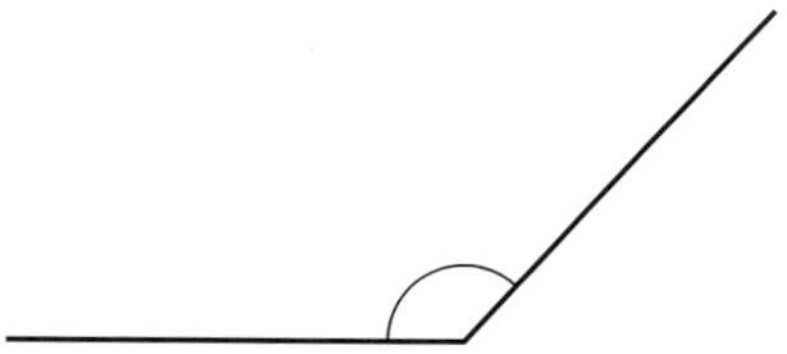

b Draw these angles.
(1) 54° (2) 237° (3) 126°

c For each part of **b** say whether each angle is acute, obtuse or reflex.

3 Calculate the angles marked with letters.

a

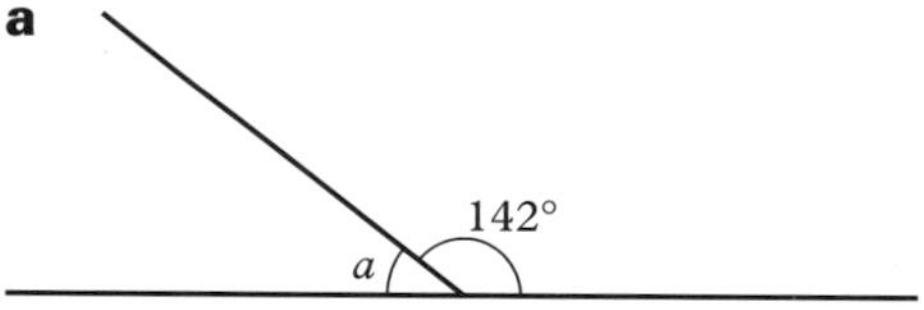

b

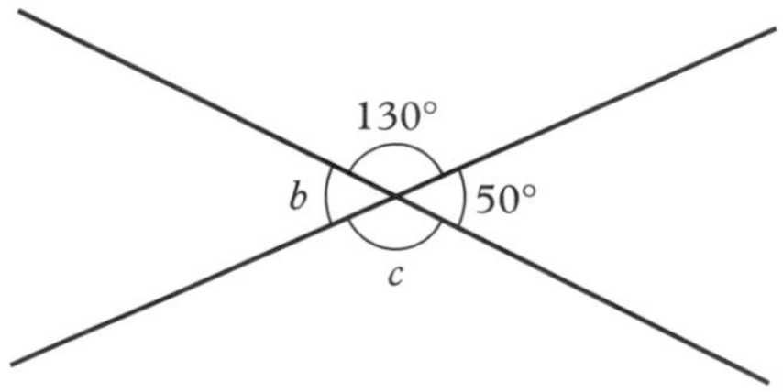

c

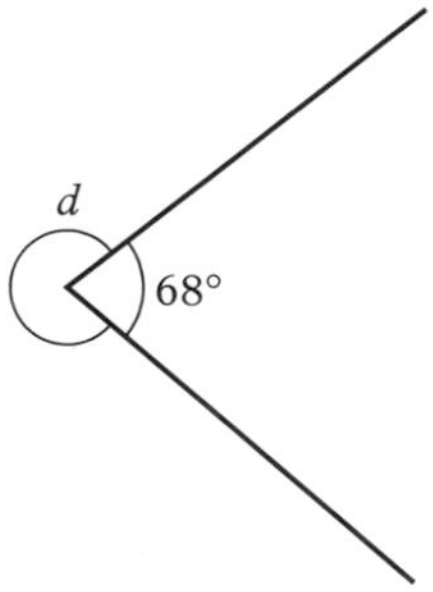

d

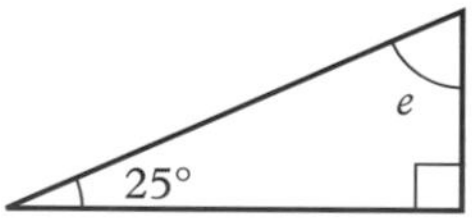

4 Measure angle Q.
Construct this triangle.

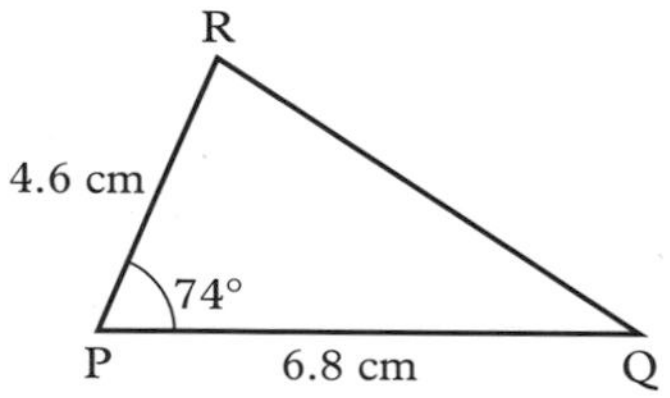

11 Extending the number line

CORE

1 **Introducing negative numbers**

2 **Co-ordinates in all four quadrants**

3 **Graphs of number patterns**

QUESTIONS

EXTENSION

SUMMARY

TEST YOURSELF

There are two common systems for measuring temperature.

Gabriel Daniel Fahrenheit (born in Prussia in 1686) put the freezing point of water at 32°F and its boiling point at 212°F.

Anders Celsius (born in Sweden in 1701) put the freezing point of water at 0°C and its boiling point at 100°C. The Celsius scale is sometimes called 'centigrade', meaning '100 degrees'.

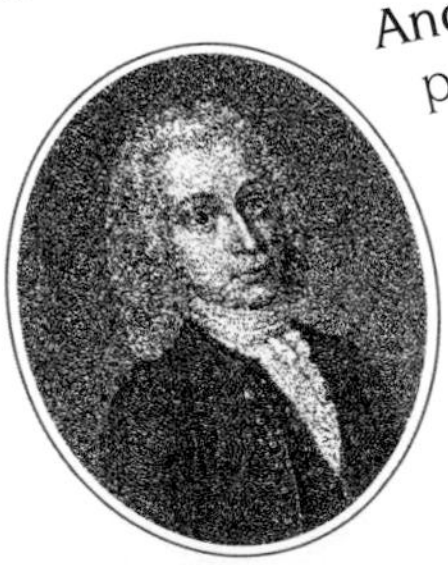

Fahrenheit called the coldest temperature he could find 0°F. The coldest temperature possible is approximately –273°C, although Celsius did not know this!

On a very frosty day we might say that it is '–5', using the Celsius scale. On a hot day we often use the Fahrenheit scale: 80°F sounds much hotter than 27°C!

1 Introducing negative numbers

Bill the ice-cream man has to keep his ice-cream cold.
He uses a Celsius thermometer.
The Celsius scale has the freezing point of water at 0 °C.
The temperatures below 0 °C have minus signs in front.
Bill's ice-cream is at −10 °C.

Negative numbers
Positive numbers

Numbers with minus signs in front are called **negative** numbers.
Other numbers except nought are **positive**. Positive numbers are sometimes written with a plus sign in front.
Nought is not positive or negative.

Examples Negative numbers −2, −5, −32. Positive numbers 7, +3, 25.

Exercise 11:1

1 From this list: −7, +3, −2, 0, −4, 5, +6, −9
 a Write down the negative numbers.
 b Write down the positive numbers.

2 Write down the temperatures in degrees Celsius (°C) on these thermometers.

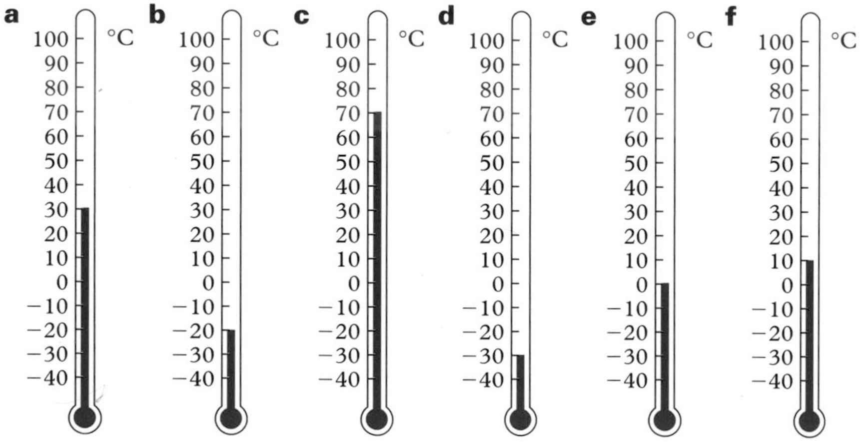

3 **a** Is 15 °C warmer than −10 °C?
b Is 10 °C warmer than −20 °C?
c Is −15 °C warmer than −5 °C?
d Is −10 °C colder than −2 °C?

4 **a** Which is warmer, 30 °C or −30 °C?
b Which is colder, −5 °C or −9 °C?
c Which is colder, −4 °C or 0 °C?
d Which is warmer, −14 °C or 4 °C?

● **5** Write down the temperatures in order, coldest first.
a 8 °C, −50 °C, 0 °C, −15 °C, −3 °C.
b −1 °C, 7 °C, −4 °C, 10 °C, −2 °C.

Example

One night the temperature is −4 °C. The next day the temperature is 8 °C.
What is the difference between the day and night temperatures?

The diagram shows part of a thermometer scale.
There are 12 spaces between −4 °C and 8 °C on the scale.
The difference between the temperatures is **12** °C.

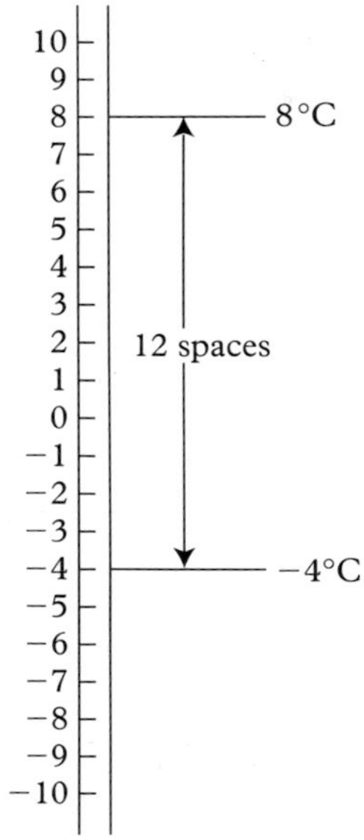

Exercise 11:2

1 What is the difference between these day and night temperatures?

a **b** **c** **d** **e** **f**

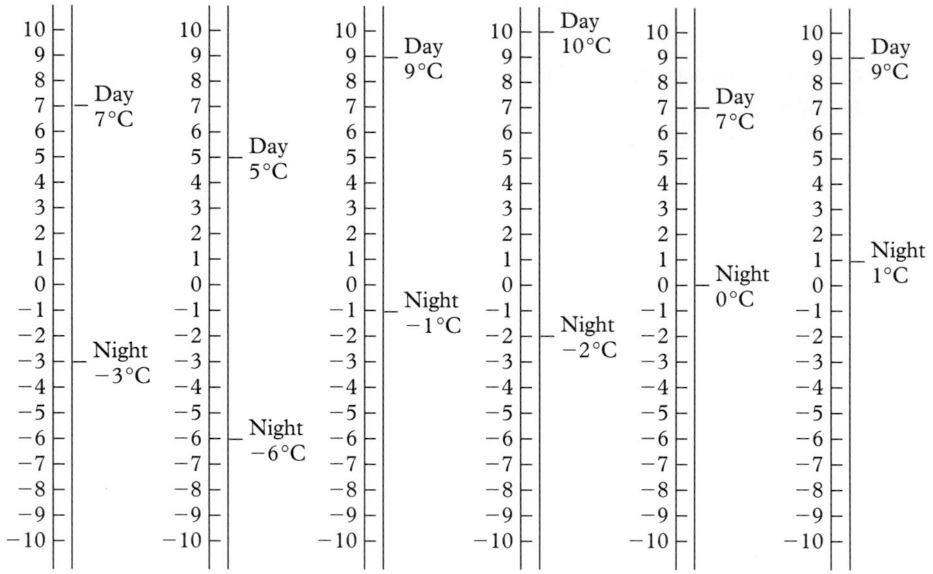

2 Draw a scale from −10 to 10 up the side of your page.
What is the difference between these night and day temperatures?
Use your scale to help you.

a night −4 °C, day 7 °C
b night −10 °C, day −1 °C
c night −9 °C, day −3 °C
d night −8 °C, day 2 °C
e night 2 °C, day 10 °C
f night −5 °C, day 0 °C

3 Calculators can show negative numbers.
Copy and complete this table to see which keys to use.

Press these keys	What is on the screen?
− 6	6
3 −	
+/− 2	
4 +/−	
2 +/−	

4 Which keys would you press to show these numbers? The first one is done for you.

	Number	Keys
a	−3	3 +/−
b	−5	
c	−8	
d	−12	

Example One day the temperature is 9 °C. That night the temperature is −3 °C.
What is the difference between the day and night temperatures?

Calculator: 9 − 3 +/− =

The answer is **12**°C.

---

5 Use your calculator.
Copy and complete the table.

Day temperature	Night temperature	Difference
5 °C	−2 °C	7 °C
6 °C	−3 °C	
3 °C	−5 °C	
7 °C	2 °C	
10 °C	−2 °C	
8 °C	3 °C	

6 One day the temperature is 6 °C. That night the temperature is −8 °C.
What is the difference between the day and night temperatures?

7 The temperature in a freezer is −18 °C.
A frozen chicken is thawed to room temperature. Room temperature is 20 °C.
By how many degrees does the chicken's temperature rise?

8 Wasim takes a coke from the fridge. The can is at 3 °C.
Claire's coke is not in the fridge. Her can is at 18 °C.
What is the difference in temperature between the cokes?

9 In deserts it can be very hot in the daytime but very cold at night. The day temperature in a desert is 44 °C and the night temperature is −3 °C.
By how many degrees does the temperature drop at night?

Negative numbers are not just found on thermometers. They have other uses.

Exercise 11:3

1 Here is the control panel of a lift.

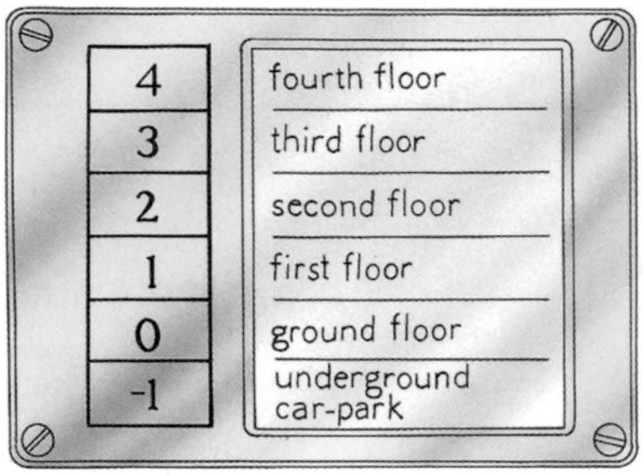

a What number is used for the ground floor?

b Where do you go if you press $\boxed{-1}$?

c You go from the first floor to the fourth floor.
How many floors do you go up?

d You go from the third floor to the car-park.
How many floors do you go down?

● **2** Mr Patel has a point system for his form 7P.
This is Dale's record for the week:

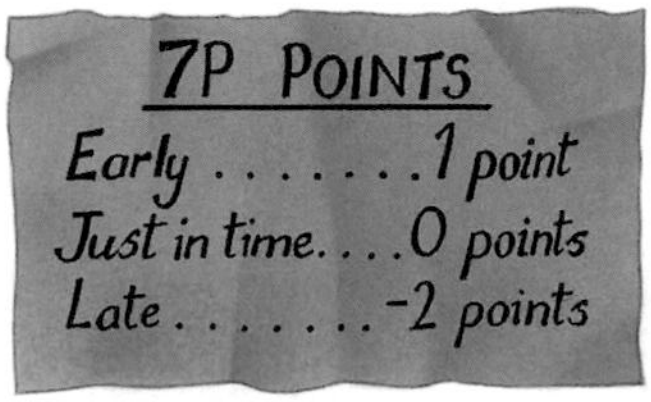
7P POINTS
Early .... 1 point
Just in time.... 0 points
Late .... -2 points

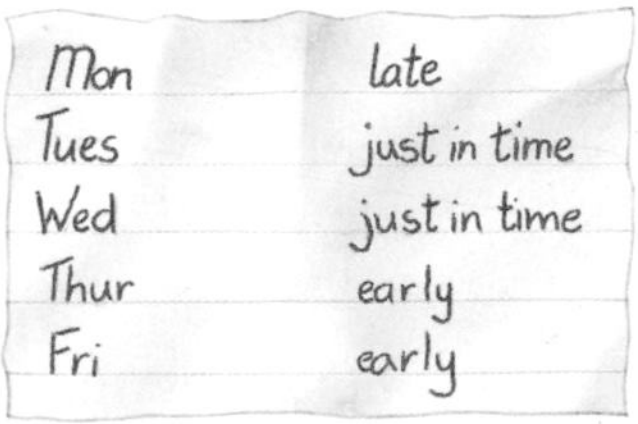
Mon late
Tues just in time
Wed just in time
Thur early
Fri early

a Write down Dale's score for each day.

b What is Dale's total for the week?

3 Melanie loses her bus pass. She borrows 75p from her friend. Melanie gives her friend 60p when they get home.

a How much does Melanie owe her friend now?

b Melanie takes £1 to school the next day. She pays her friend back.
How much does Melanie have left?

• **4** Use the time line to answer these questions.

a How old was Julius Caesar when he invaded Britain?

b How old was he when he was murdered?

c How many years after Julius Caesar died did the Romans conquer Wales?

d How many years after Julius Caesar died was Hadrian's Wall built?

e The Romans conquered Wales. How many years later did they build Hadrian's Wall?

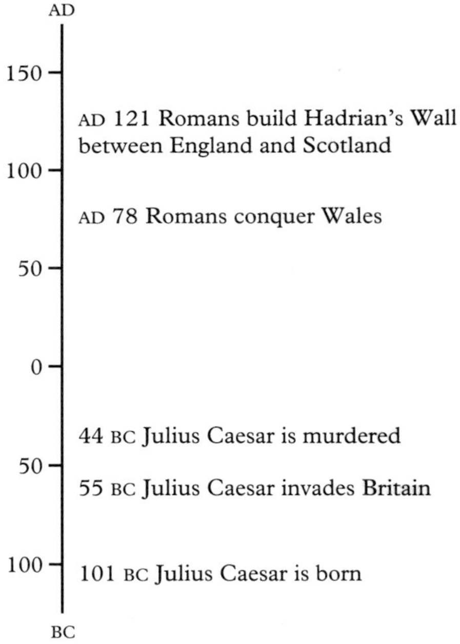

5 Sea-level is 0.
A wreck is at -21 m.
The diver is at -9 m.

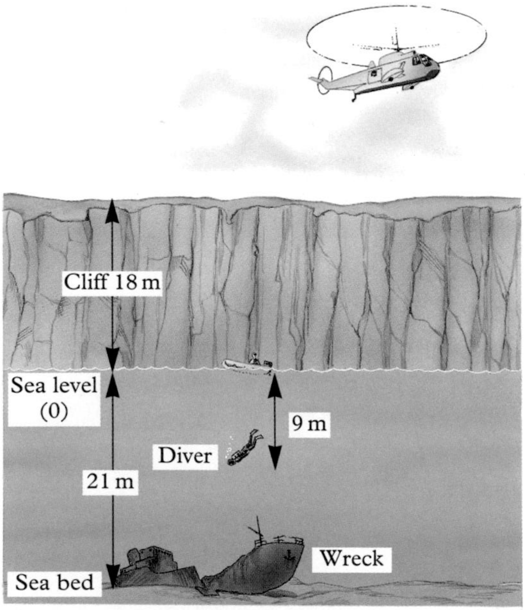

a How much further does the diver need to swim to reach the wreck?

b What is the distance between the top of the cliff and the sea-bed?

c A helicopter hovers at 30 m above sea-level.
(1) How high is the helicopter above the cliff?
(2) How high is the helicopter above the diver?

2 Co-ordinates in all four quadrants

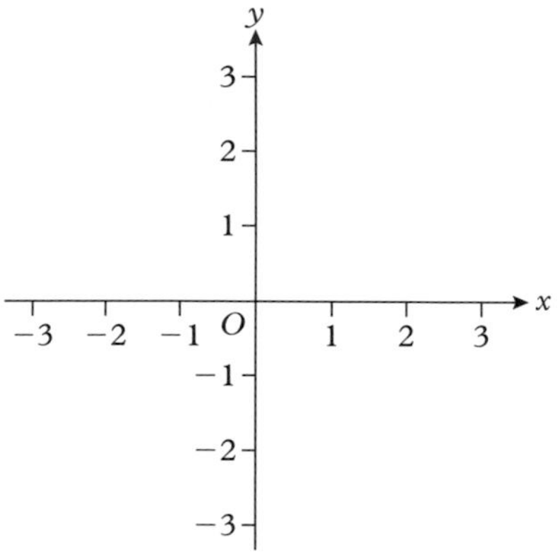

We can draw two number lines at 90° to each other. They can be used as an x axis and a y axis. The two lines cross at the zero value on each axis.

Origin

The point where the x axis and the y axis cross is called the **origin**. The co-ordinates of this point are (0, 0).

Quadrant

The x axis and the y axis divide the space into four **quadrants**. The quadrants are always numbered anti-clockwise.

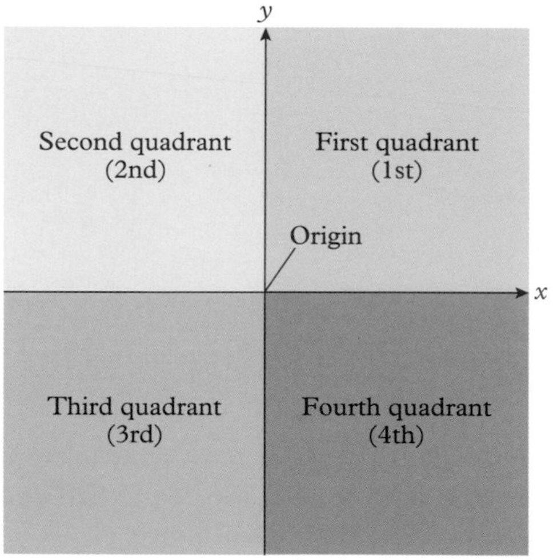

Exercise 11:4

1 Here are the co-ordinates of the points shown.

A (3, 0)
B (3, −2)
C (0, −3)
D (−3, 1)
E (−2, −1)
F (−1, −3)
G (−1, 3)
H (1, 2)

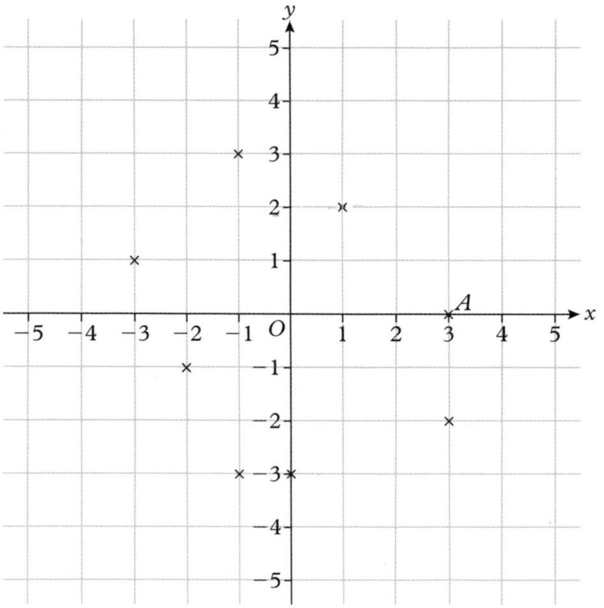

a Copy the diagram on to squared paper.
b Match the letters to the points.
The first one has been done for you.

2 Draw a table for the points A to H.
Write in the position of each point.
The table has been started for you.

Point	Position
A (3, 0)	*x* axis
B (3, −2)	4th quadrant
C (0, −3)	

3 Draw axes from −5 to 5 like those in Question **1**.
Plot these points in order.
Join them as you go.
a (5, 1) (4, 0) (2, 1) (2, 4) (0, 1)
b (0, 1) (−3, 0) (−4, −1) (0, −1)
c (0, −1) (2, −2) (2, −1) (4, −1) (5, −2) (5, 1)
d Eye (−2, 0)

4 Draw axes from −5 to 5.
Plot these points in order.
Join them as you go.

a (4, −1) (2, 1) (3, 1) (1, 3) (2, 3) (0, 5)
b (0, 5) (−2, 3) (−1, 3) (−3, 1) (−2, 1) (−4, −1)
c (−4, −1) (−1, −1) (−1, −3) (1, −3) (1, −1) (4, −1)

5 Draw axes from −5 to 5.
Plot these points in order.
Join them as you go.

a (4, 2) (3, 0) (−2, 0) (−2, 3) (−3, 2) (−5, 1)
b (−5, 1) (−5, 0) (−3, 0) (−3, −4) (−2, −2)
c (−2, −2) (−2, −4) (−1, −2) (2, −2) (2, −4)
d (2, −4) (3, −2) (3, −4) (4, −2) (4, 2)
e Eye (−3, 1)

6 Draw axes from −5 to 5.
Plot these points in order.
Join them as you go.

a (4, 0) (3, 2) (1, 2) (1, 3) (0, 3)
b (0, 3) (0, 2) (−3, 2) (−4, 0)
c (−4, 0) (−4, −3) (4, −3) (4, 0)
d (3, −1) (1, −1) (1, −2) (3, −2) (3, −1)
e (−2, −3) (−2, −1) (−1, −1) (−1, −3)

7 **a** Draw axes from −5 to 5.
b Plot these points and join them up in order: (4, 0), (4, 1), (1, 1), (1, 4), (0, 4)
c Reflect your drawing into the second quadrant.
d Reflect both sets of lines in the x axis.
You should have a cross.
e Copy this table and fill it in.
Go round the cross anti-clockwise.

Quadrant	Co-ordinates
First	(4, 1), (1, 1), (1, 4)
Second	(−1, 4), (…, 1), (−4, 1)
Third	(…, −1), (−1, …), (−1, …)
Fourth	(…, …), (…, …), (…, …)

● **8** **a** Draw a pair of axes from -5 to 5.

b Plot these pairs of points.

Join (1, 0) to (0, 4).
Join (2, 0) to (0, 3).
Join (3, 0) to (0, 2).
Join (4, 0) to (0, 1).

c Reflect the pattern into the second quadrant.
Copy these instructions for drawing the lines in the second quadrant.
Fill in the gaps.

Join (-1, 0) to (0, 4).
Join (-2, 0) to (0, 3).
Join (..., ...) to (..., ...).
Join (..., ...) to (..., ...).

d Copy these instructions for the third quadrant.
Use the number patterns to complete them.

Join (-1, 0) to (0, -4)
Join (-2, ...) to (..., -3).
Join (..., ...) to (..., ...).
Join (..., ...) to (..., ...).

Draw the pattern in the third quadrant.

e Complete the pattern in the fourth quadrant.
Write the set of instructions for the fourth quadrant:
Join (1, 0) to (0, -4).
...

3 Graphs of number patterns

Number patterns can be used to draw graphs.

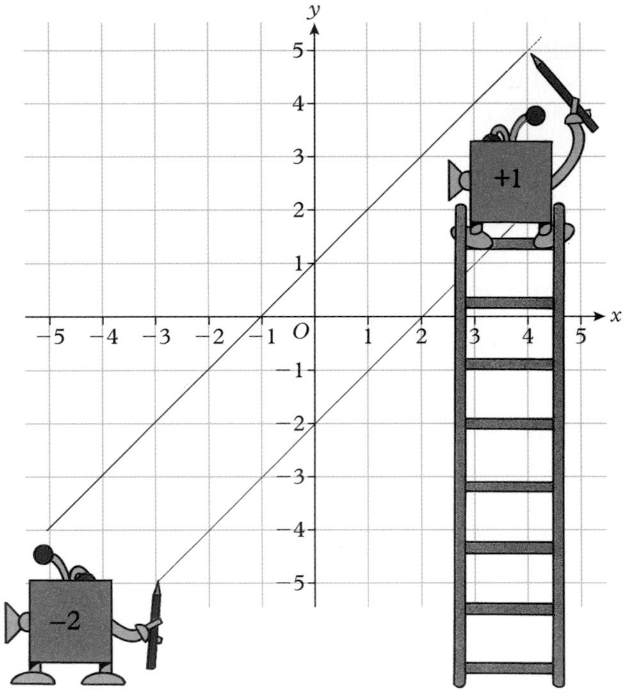

Exercise 11:5

Draw an x axis and a y axis from -5 to 5.

You only need one pair of axes for *all* the questions in this exercise.

1 **a** Plot the points (4, 4) (3, 3) (2, 2) (1, 1) and (0, 0).
b Place your ruler against the points.
Draw a line through the points. Extend the line into the third quadrant.
c Use your line to complete these co-ordinates. They are all on the line.
$(-1, ?)$ $(-2, ?)$ $(-3, ?)$
d Label your line $y = x$.
This is the rule for *any* point on the line.

2 **a** Copy and complete the number pattern and co-ordinates for $y = x + 1$.

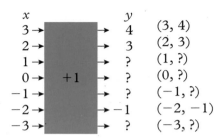

x		y	
3 →		→ 4	(3, 4)
2 →		→ 3	(2, 3)
1 →		→ ?	(1, ?)
0 →	+1	→ ?	(0, ?)
−1 →		→ ?	(−1, ?)
−2 →		→ −1	(−2, −1)
−3 →		→ ?	(−3, ?)

b Plot the points.
Join them up with a ruler.
Label your line $y = x + 1$.

3 **a** Copy and complete the number pattern and co-ordinates for $y = x + 2$.

x		y	
3 →		→ 5	(3, 5)
2 →		→ ?	(2, ?)
1 →		→ ?	(1, ?)
0 →	+2	→ ?	(0, ?)
−1 →		→ 1	(−1, 1)
−2 →		→ ?	(−2, ?)
−3 →		→ −1	(−3, −1)

b Plot the points.
Join them up with a ruler.
Label your line $y = x + 2$.

4 **a** Copy and complete this number pattern and co-ordinates for $y = x + 3$.

x		y	
2 →		→ ?	(2, ?)
1 →		→ ?	(1, ?)
0 →		→ ?	(0, ?)
−1 →	+3	→ 2	(−1, 2)
−2 →		→ 1	(−2, 1)
−3 →		→ ?	(−3, ?)

b Plot the points.
Join them up with a ruler.
Label your line $y = x + 3$.

Exercise 11:6 Naming lines of the grid

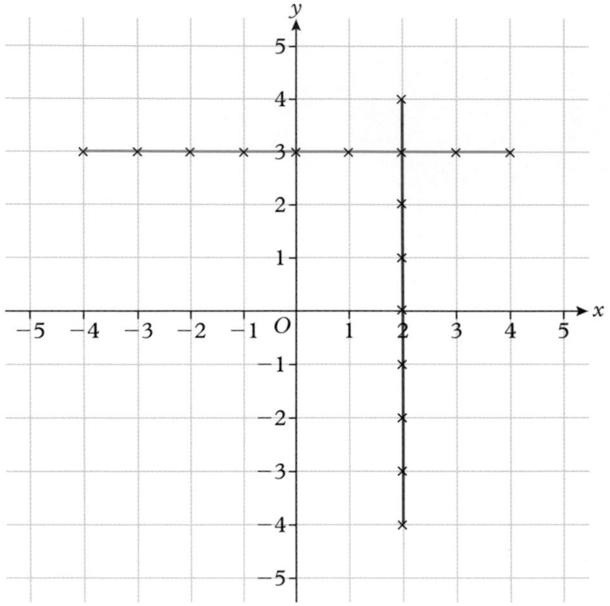

1 **a** Copy the diagram.
Draw the red line and the blue line.

b Copy and complete the co-ordinates.

Red line	Blue line
(…, 4)	(4, …)
(…, 3)	(3, …)
(…, 2)	(2, …)
(…, 1)	(1, …)
(…, 0)	(0, …)
(…, −1)	(−1, …)
(…, −2)	(−2, …)
(…, −3)	(−3, …)
(…, −4)	(−4, …)

c The rule for the red line is $x = 2$.
The rule for the blue line is $y = 3$.
Label your lines with these rules.

2 **a** Complete these co-ordinates for other rules.

$x = 1$	$x = -3$	$y = 2$	$y = -4$
(…, 4)	(−3, 4)	(4, …)	(3, …)
(…, 2)	(…, 1)	(2, 2)	(1, −4)
(1, 0)	(…, −1)	(−1, …)	(0, …)
(…, −2)	(−3, −4)	(−3, …)	(−2, …)

b Use the axes you drew for Question **1**.
Plot each set of co-ordinates.
Join each set to make a line.
Label each line with its rule.

1 Give the temperatures in °C on these thermometers.

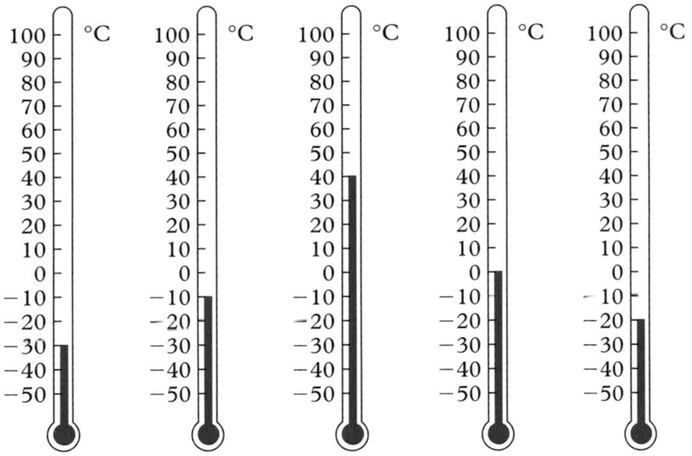

2 **a** Is 13 °C warmer than −20 °C?
b Is −12 °C warmer than −3 °C?
c Which is warmer, −14 °C or −6 °C?
d Which is warmer, −5 °C or 0 °C?
e Which is colder, −2 °C or 9 °C?
f Is −15 °C colder than −20 °C?

3

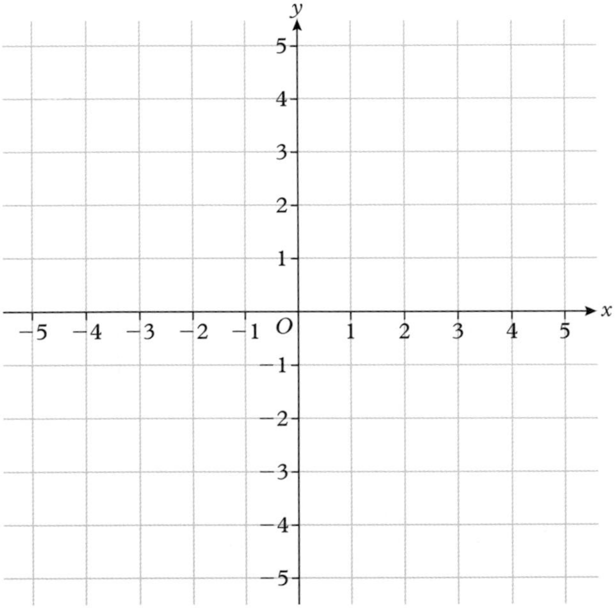

Draw axes from −5 to 5 like the ones shown.

Plot these points. Join them as you go.

a (2, 3) (2, 5) (−3, 5) (−3, −5) (2, −5)

b (2, −5) (2, −3) (−1, −3) (−1, −1) (1, −1)

c (1, −1) (1, 1) (−1, 1) (−1, 3) (2, 3)

4 **a** Draw a pair of axes from −5 to 5 like the ones in Question **3**.

b Plot these pairs of points.
Join each pair as you go.
Join (2, 0) to (0, −2).
Join (3, 0) to (0, −3).
Join (4, 0) to (0, −4).
In which quadrant is your pattern?

c Reflect your pattern into the third quadrant.

d Reflect both sets of lines in the x axis.
You should have three squares inside each other.

e Draw a small square in the middle of the pattern.
Write down the co-ordinates of the vertices (corners) of this small square.

5

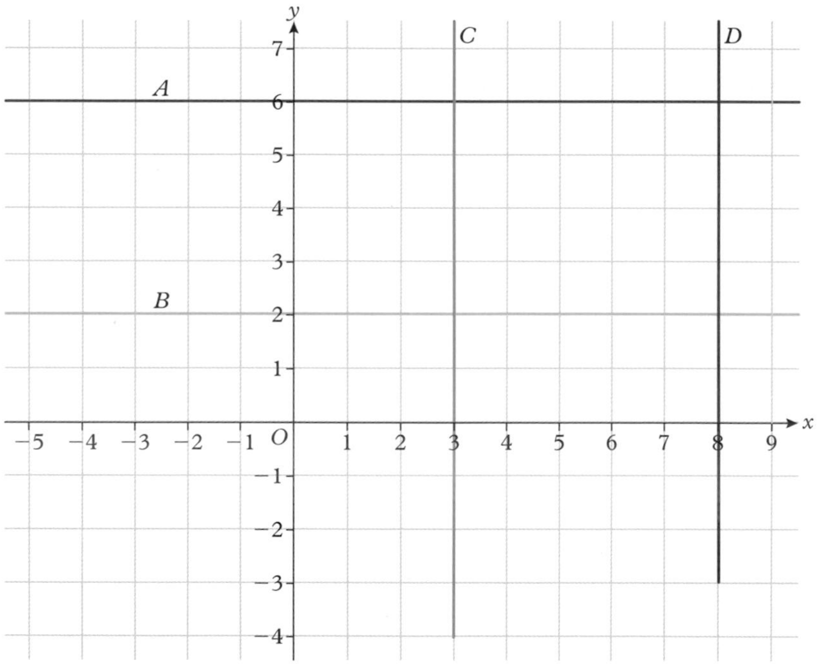

The rule for line A is $y = 6$.
Write down the rules for lines B, C and D.

1 Write down these temperatures in order, coldest first.
a 9 °C, −16 °C, 0 °C, −5 °C, 21 °C, −10 °C.
b −3 °C, −17 °C, 30 °C, −25 °C, 18 °C, 2 °C.

2 Here are some night and day temperatures.
Use **+/−** on a calculator to find the number of degrees difference between each pair.
a night −4 °C, day 9 °C
b night −2 °C, day 8 °C
c night −9 °C, day −2 °C
d night 1 °C, day 6 °C
e night −8 °C, day −3 °C
f night 0 °C, day 10 °C

3 **a** Mrs Smith buys some fish at 3 °C. She puts it in her freezer at −18 °C. By how many degrees is the fish cooled?
b Mrs Smith thaws the fish to a room temperature of 17 °C. By how many degrees does its temperature rise?

4 Sketch the thermometer. Mark on it approximately where you think the temperatures of the following will be:
a boiling point of water
b freezing point of water
c your body
d a warm spring day
e a very cold winter night in Britain
f the North Pole
g a can of cola out of the fridge
h a very hot summer day

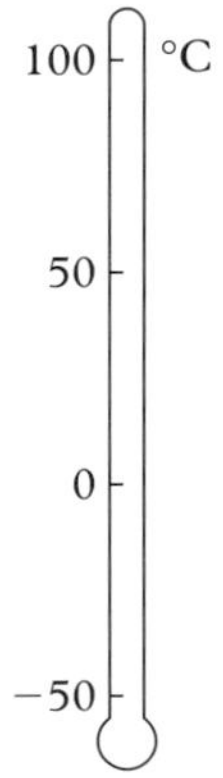

5 A crane is lifting gravel from a pit.
Ground level is 0.
The bottom of the pit is −8 m.

Copy and complete the number line.
Use the line to find:
a how far the bucket is below ground level.
b how high the crane's top is above ground level.

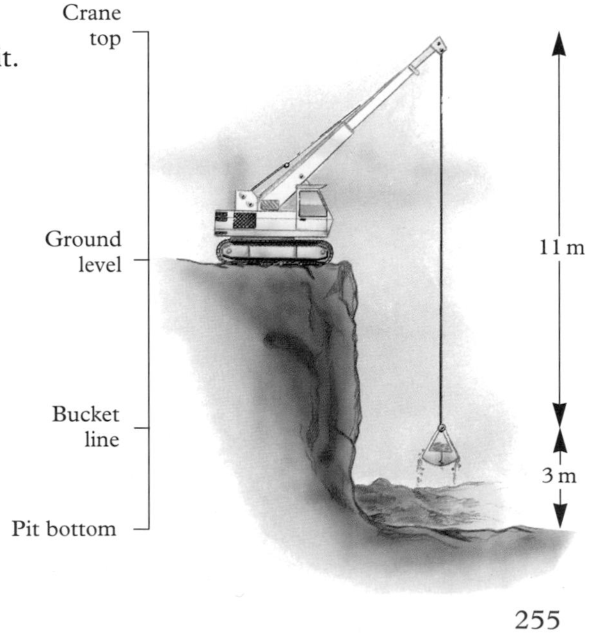

6 **a** Jo owes her father £34 for a broken window. She gives her father her savings of £22 and her father stops £5 from her pocket money. How much does Jo owe her father now?

b Jo gets paid £10 for baby-sitting. She finishes paying for the window. How much does Jo have left?

7 Draw an x axis and a y axis from -6 to 6.
Plot these points in order.
Join them up with a ruler as you go.

a $(-6, 6)$, $(-6, 3)$, $(-3, 3)$, $(-3, 6)$, $(-6, 6)$.
b $(2, 1)$, $(-3, -1)$, $(2, -3)$, $(2, 1)$.
c $(0, 2)$, $(-4, 2)$, $(-6, 0)$, $(-2, 0)$, $(0, 2)$.
d $(5, 1)$, $(3, 1)$, $(3, -5)$, $(5, -5)$, $(5, 1)$.
e $(1, 6)$, $(-1, 4)$, $(1, 2)$, $(5, 4)$, $(1, 6)$.
f $(2, -4)$, $(-2, -3)$, $(-6, -4)$, $(-2, -5)$, $(2, -4)$.
g Label the shapes with their names.
Choose from: rectangle, rhombus, kite, parallelogram, isosceles triangle, square.

8

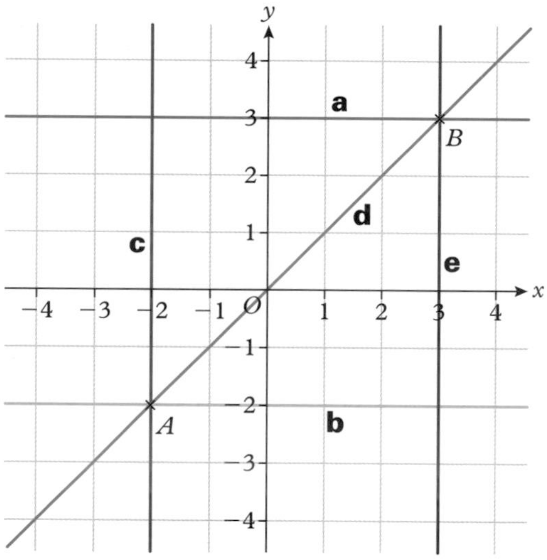

Five lines are drawn. The rules for the lines are $y = -2$, $x = 3$, $y = x$, $x = -2$, $y = 3$.

(1) Match the lines **a** to **e** with their rules.

(2) Point A is $(-2, -2)$ and point B is $(3, 3)$. For both the x number equals the y number.
Write down four more points which obey the same rule.

- **Negative numbers** / **Positive numbers** — Numbers with minus signs in front are called **negative** numbers. Other numbers except nought are **positive**. Positive numbers are sometimes written with a plus sign in front.
  Nought is not positive or negative.

  Examples — Negative numbers −2, −5, −32.
  Positive numbers 7, +3, 25.

- *Example* — One day the temperature is 9 °C. The next night the temperature is −3°C
  What is the difference between day and night temperatures?

  Calculator: 9 − 3 +/− =

  The answer is **12** °C.

- **Origin** / **Quadrant** — The point where an x and y axis cross is called the **origin**. The co-ordinates of this point are (0, 0). The two lines divide the space into four **quadrants**. The quadrants are always numbered anti-clockwise.

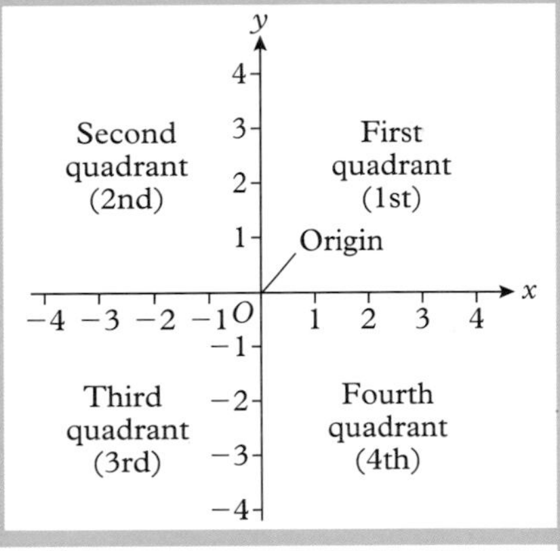

- A is the point (−2, 0), B is (−3, 2), C is −1, −3) and D is (1, −2).
  The lines $x = -3$ and $y = 2$ have been labelled with their rules.

  Number patterns can be used to give co-ordinates.

  Example $y = x + 1$

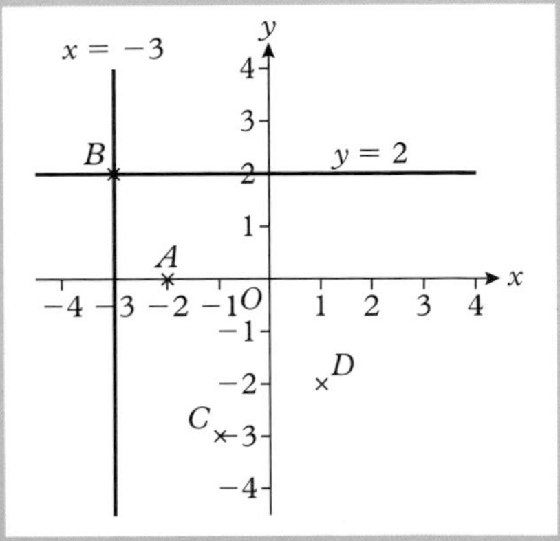

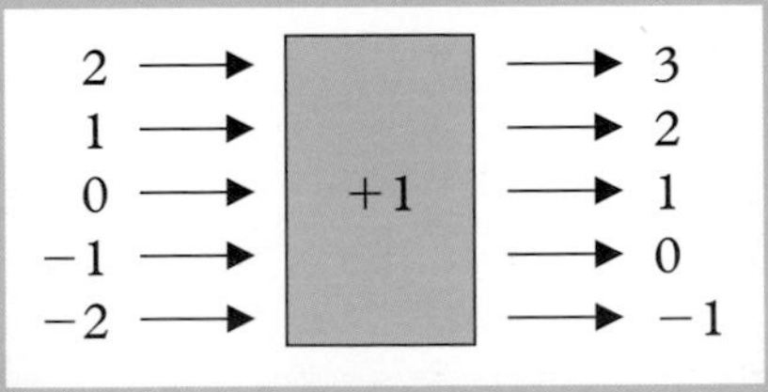

(2, 3)
(1, 2)
(0, 1)
(−1, 0)
(−2, −1)

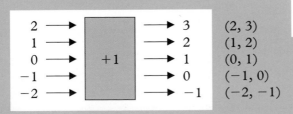

TEST YOURSELF

1 **a** Is 13 °C warmer than −18 °C?
b Which is colder, −5 °C or −8 °C?
c Is −14 °C colder than −20 °C?
d Which is warmer, −7 °C or 0 °C?

2 Use **+/−** on a calculator to complete this table.

Day temperature	Night temperature	Difference
4 °C	−6 °C	
7 °C	−1 °C	
10 °C	3 °C	
8 °C	−12 °C	

3 The temperature on a cold night is −8 °C. The next day the temperature rises to 3 °C.
By how many degrees has the temperature risen?

4 **a** Draw axes from −5 to 5.
b Copy and complete the number pattern and co-ordinates for $y = x + 4$.

x		y	
1 →	+4	→ ?	(1, 0)
0 →	+4	→ ?	(0, ?)
−1 →	+4	→ 3	(−1, 3)
−2 →	+4	→ ?	(−2, ?)
−3 →	+4	→ 1	(−3, 1)
−4 →	+4	→ 0	(−4, 0)
−5 →	+4	→ −1	(−5, −1)

c Plot the points.
Join them up with a ruler.
Label your line $y = x + 4$.
d On the same axes draw and label lines for the rules:
(1) $x = 3$ (2) $y = -4$ (3) $y = 2$

12 Units of length and scale drawing

CORE

1 **An introduction to units of length**

2 **Scale drawings**

3 **Finding lengths**

4 **Imperial to metric conversion**

QUESTIONS

EXTENSION

SUMMARY

TEST YOURSELF

The Romans measured in miles. 1 mile was 1000 paces. They counted two steps – left, right – as one pace.

But hands, feet and paces vary. Edward I was the first person in England to set out a system. In 1305, he had standard measures for people to compare, but the units were still complicated. Different measures were in use in different countries. Something better was needed.

In 1795, the French Academy of Science decided to solve the problem. A survey was made of the length of a line from the North Pole, through France to the Equator. This distance was divided into 10 million parts. Each part was called a metre. This was the start of the metric system.

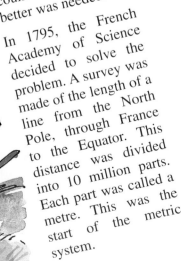

1 An introduction to units of length

In ancient times people used parts of the body to measure length.

thumb	(middle joint to tip)	1 inch
hand	(sideways across wide part)	4 inches
span	(hand stretched wide, thumb tip to little finger tip)	9 inches
cubit	(elbow to middle finger tip)	about 20 inches
foot	(length to tip of big toe)	12 inches
pace	(length of one step)	about 30 inches
yard	(length from nose to finger tip)	36 inches

Exercise 12:1

1 Make a table using the units listed above.

Name of unit	Sketch	Length (inches) (see table above)	My lengths (inches)	(cm)
thumb	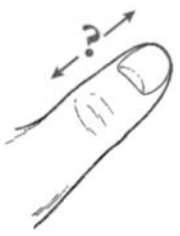	1 inch	…	…
hand	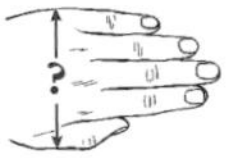	4 inches	…	…
span	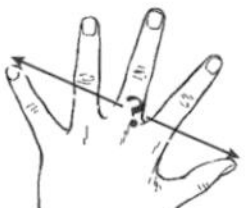		…	…

Common Imperial units of length

12 inches = 1 foot
12 in = 1 ft

3 feet = 1 yard
3 ft = 1 yd

36 inches = 1 yard
36 in = 1 yd

Examples

1 Convert 2 ft to inches

2 ft = 2 × 12 in
= 24 in

2 Convert 4 yd to feet

4 yd = 4 × 3 ft
= 12 ft

2 Convert these lengths to inches.

a 3 ft
b 5 ft
c 10 ft
d 8 ft
e 6 ft

3 Convert these distances to feet.

a 2 yd
b 6 yd
c 5 yd
d 10 yd
e 20 yd

● **4** **a** Saadiya is 4 ft 10 in tall.
She wants to know her height in inches.
Copy and complete:

4 ft = 4 × ? in
= ? in
? in + 10 in = ? in

b Gareth wants to know his height in inches.
He is 5 ft 3 in tall.
Copy and complete:

5 ft = 5 × ? in
= ? in
? in + 3 in = ? in

Examples

1 Convert 48 in to feet
48 in = 48 ÷ 12 ft
= 4 ft

2 Convert 15 ft to yards
15 ft = 15 ÷ 3 yd
= 5 yd

5 Convert these lengths to feet.

a 12 in
b 36 in
c 144 in
d 108 in
e 84 in

6 Convert these distances to yards.

a 6 ft
b 18 ft
c 30 ft
d 21 ft
e 39 ft

Common metric units of length

10 millimetres (mm) = 1 centimetre (cm)
100 centimetres = 1 metre (m)
1000 metres = 1 kilometre (km)

Example

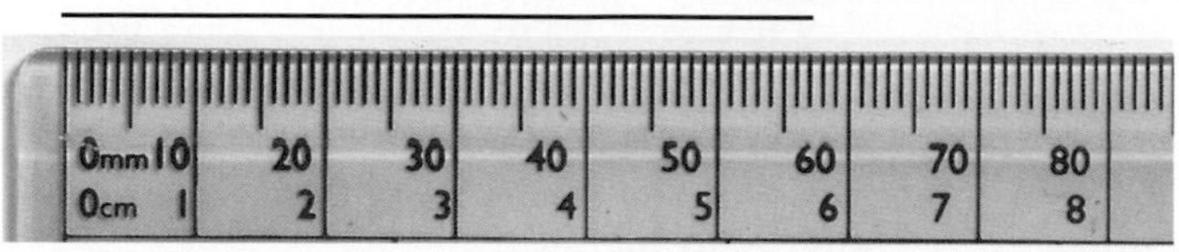

This line measures 5.7 cm (or 57 mm).

Exercise 12:2

1 Estimate the lengths of these lines in centimetres.

a

b

c

d

e

f

g

h

i

j

2 Measure the lines in Question **1** accurately.

3 Which units would you use to measure these?
Choose from mm, cm, m, km.

a The length of the wing of a fly.
b The length of the classroom.
c The length of a football pitch.
d The distance from London to Edinburgh.
e The width of this textbook.
f The height of the classroom.
g The width of a pencil.
h The length of a pencil.

4 Copy this table.
Estimate the length of each item.
Write your estimate in the table.

Add five more ideas of your own.

Complete the last column of the table by measuring.

Distance being measured	Estimate	Actual
Width of exercise book		
Length of classroom		
Height of door		
Length of blackboard		
Length of pen		
...		

Converting units within the metric system

Examples *Remember: there are 10 mm in 1 cm.*

1 Convert 6.9 cm to mm
$6.9 \text{ cm} = 6.9 \times 10 \text{ mm}$
$= 69 \text{ mm}$

2 Convert 65 mm to cm
$65 \text{ mm} = 65 \div 10 \text{ cm}$
$= 6.5 \text{ cm}$

Exercise 12:3

1 Copy and complete:
1 cm = ? mm
2 cm = ? mm
5 cm = ? mm
7.2 cm = ? mm
12.8 cm = ? mm

Write down the length and width of each rectangle in mm.

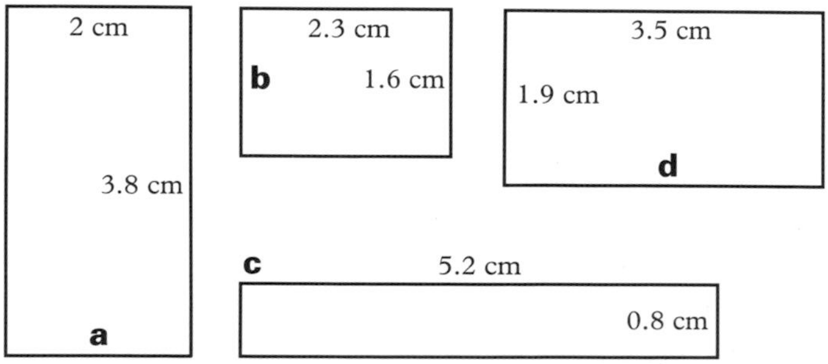

2 Copy and complete:

10 mm = ? cm
30 mm = ? cm
47 mm = ? cm
83 mm = ? cm
112 mm = ? cm

Work out the length of each line in cm.

a 50 mm
b 54 mm
c 75 mm
d 48 mm
e 87 mm

3 Give the length of each of these stamps in millimetres.

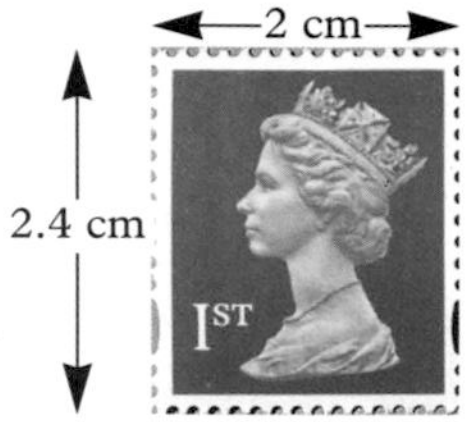

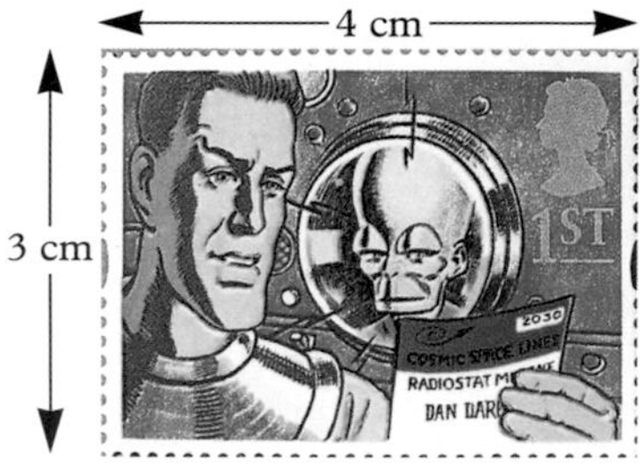

Examples *Remember: there are 100 cm in 1 m.*

1 Convert 5.34 m to cm

5.34 m = 5.34 × 100 cm
= 534 cm

2 Convert 148 cm to m

148 cm = 148 ÷ 100 m
= 1.48 m

---

4 Copy and complete:

1 m = ? cm	0.42 m = ? cm
5 m = ? cm	0.08 m = ? cm
1.24 m = ? cm	8.32 m = ? cm
0.75 m = ? cm	0.09 m = ? cm
6.8 m = ? cm	5.6 m = ? cm

5 Copy and complete:

100 cm = ? m	1250 cm = ? m
700 cm = ? m	1980 cm = ? m
650 cm = ? m	60 cm = ? m
220 cm = ? m	30 cm = ? m
875 cm = ? m	95 cm = ? m

6 Alex has measured her bedroom furniture. She used centimetres. She needs the lengths in metres. Alex has started a list. Copy and complete the list.

Length being measured	cm	m
Length of bed	190 cm	…
Width of bed	90 cm	…
Height of chest of drawers	…	…

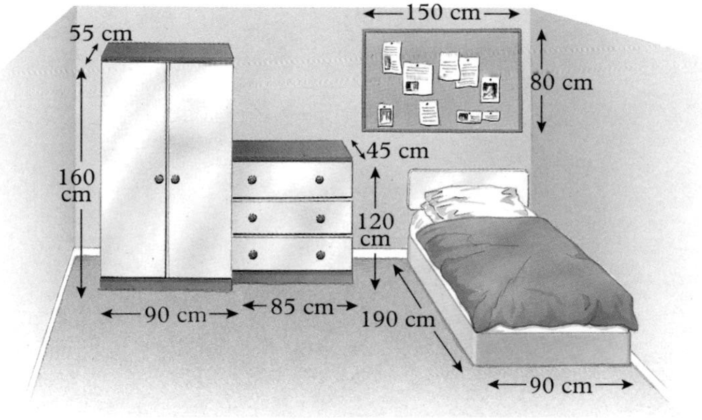

Examples *Remember: there are 1000 m in 1 km.*

1 Convert 7.3 km to m

7.3 km = 7.3 × 1000 m
= 7300 m

2 Convert 4500 m to km

4500 m = 4500 ÷ 1000 km
= 4.5 km

---

7 Copy and complete:

1000 m = ? km
8000 m = ? km
3500 m = ? km
7600 m = ? km
1700 m = ? km

650 m = ? km
900 m = ? km
600 m = ? km
405 m = ? km
2750 m = ? km

8 Copy and complete:

4 km = ? m
7 km = ? m
6.5 km = ? m
9.8 km = ? m

16.4 km = ? m
0.7 km = ? m
0.875 km = ? m
5.327 km = ? m

9 An athletics club competes in races over these distances:

100 m	400 m	1000 m	2000 m	5000 m
200 m	800 m	1500 m	3000 m	10 000 m

Change all these distances to kilometres.

2 Scale drawings

Actual lengths may not fit on to a sheet of paper. A scale drawing is the same shape as the original but different in size.

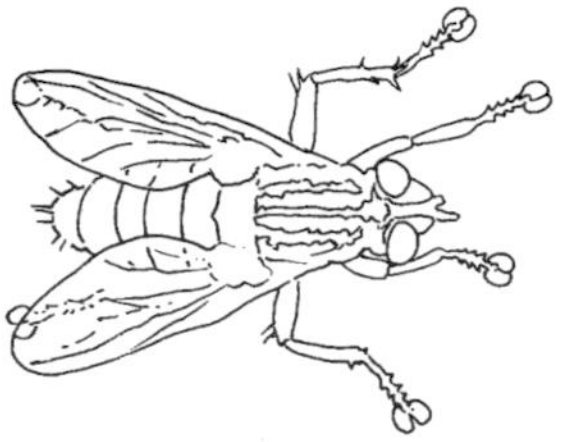

Scale The **scale** of a drawing gives the relative size of the actual length to the drawn length.

Exercise 12:4

1 Rowan makes a scale drawing of a room. The room is 6 m long.
Rowan uses 1 cm on his paper to represent 1 m.
So 6 cm represents 6 m.
He draws this rectangle to represent the floor of the room.

a Measure the width of the room on the drawing.

b What is the actual width of the room?

Rowan decides his drawing is too small.
He draws a new line of length 12 cm to represent the 6 m.

c How many centimetres represent one metre?
This is called the **scale** of his drawing.

d How many centimetres represent 5 m?

2 This is a scale drawing of a garden.

a Measure the length of the garden on the drawing.

b What is the actual length of the garden?

c Measure the width of the garden on the drawing.

d What is the actual width of the garden?

Scale: 1 cm represents 1 m

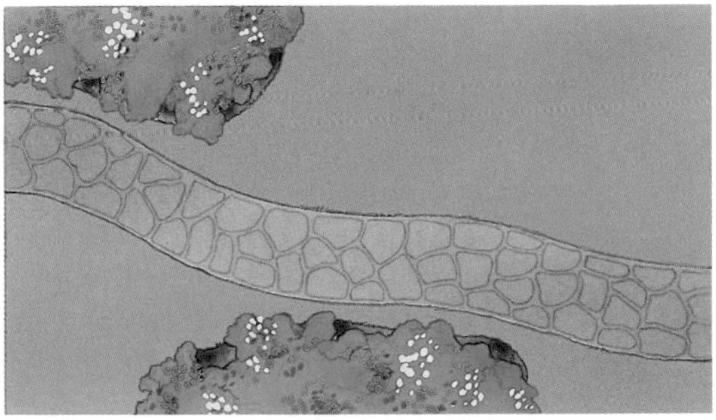

3 Charmaine makes a scale drawing of her village hall. She uses the scale '1 cm represents 1 m'.

a The hall is 10 m long.
How long is Charmaine's drawing?

b The hall is 8 m wide.
How wide is Charmaine's drawing?

4 The scale is 1 cm to 1 m.
Write down the length each line represents.

a

b

c

d

e

f

5 These lines were drawn using a scale of 1 cm to 4 m.
Write down the length each line represents.

a

b

c

d

e

f

6 These lines were drawn using a scale of 1 cm to 10 cm.
Write down the length each line represents.

a

b

c

d

e

f

7 Use a scale of 1 cm to 1 m.
Draw lines to represent these lengths.

a 4 m **c** 7 m **e** 3.5 m
b 2 m **d** 10 m **f** $6\frac{1}{2}$ m

8 Use a scale of 2 cm to 1 m.
Draw lines to represent these lengths.

a 5 m **c** 2 m **e** 1.5 m
b 6 m **d** 4 m **f** $3\frac{1}{2}$ m

● **9** These slippers have been drawn to scale.

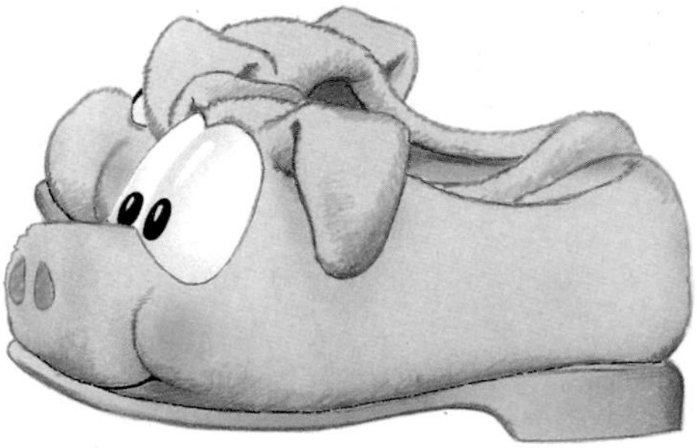

Which could be the scale used?

1 cm to 1 m 2 cm to 1 m
1 cm to 5 cm 1 cm to 1 km
1 cm to 20 cm

● **10**

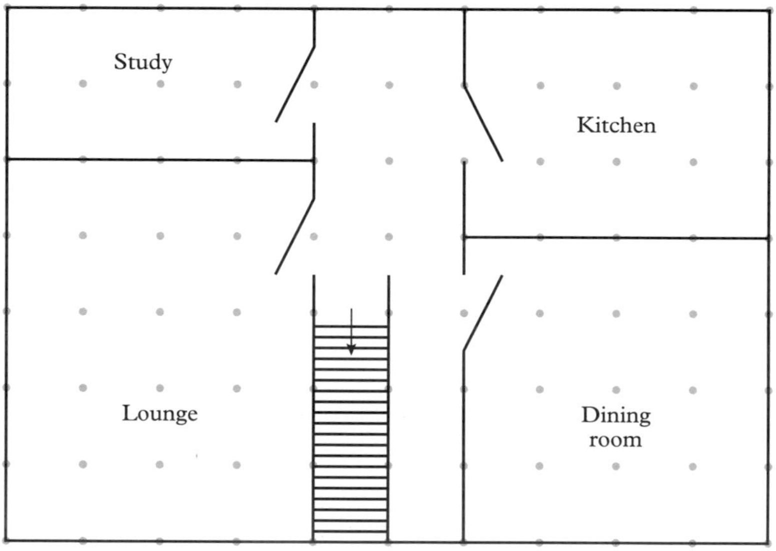

Scale:
1 cm to 1 m

This is a plan of the ground floor of a house.

a Copy this table and fill it in.

Room	Length (m)	Width (m)
Lounge		
Study		
Kitchen		
Dining room		

3 Finding lengths

Matthew and Kerry are finding out how far a plane travels between London and Paris.

We can use scale drawings to find lengths.

Exercise 12:5

1 This rectangle is a plan of a swimming pool.
The scale is 1 cm to 1 m.

a Measure the side of the rectangle.
Write down the length of the side in cm.
Use the scale to find the actual length of the swimming pool.

b Use the same method to find the actual width of the pool.

c What is the actual length of the diagonal of the pool?

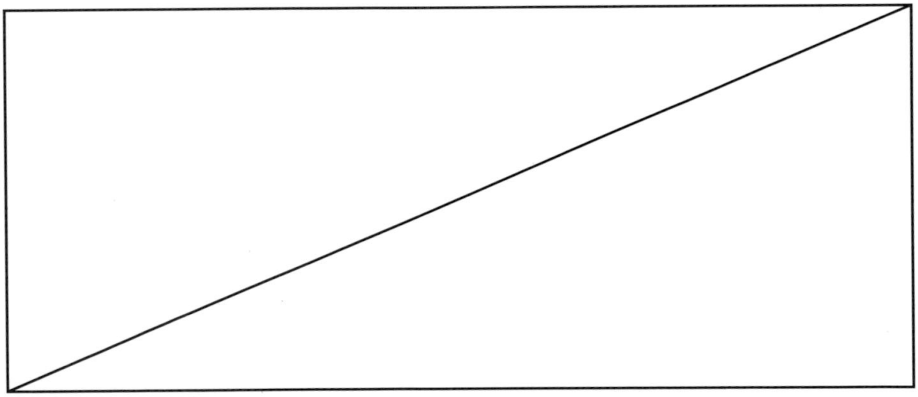

Scale: 1 cm to 1 m

2 A rectangular field has length 80 metres and width 60 metres.

a Make a scale drawing of the field.
Use a scale of 1 cm to 5 m.

b Use your scale drawing to find the length of the diagonal of the field.

3 A rectangular lawn is 2.5 metres by 6 metres.
Make a scale drawing of the lawn.
Use your drawing to find the length of the diagonal.

4 Make a scale drawing of this skating rink.
Use your drawing to find the length of the diagonal.

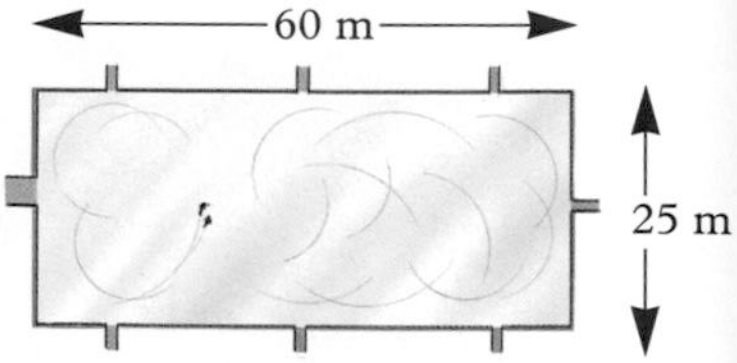

5 This triangle has been drawn to scale.
What is the actual length of the side AB?

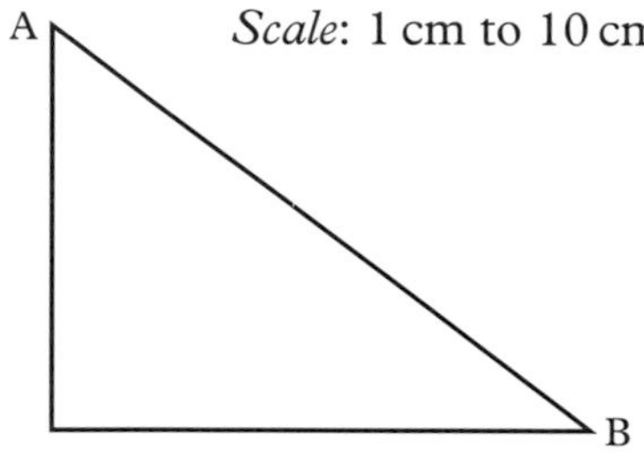

Curved lines

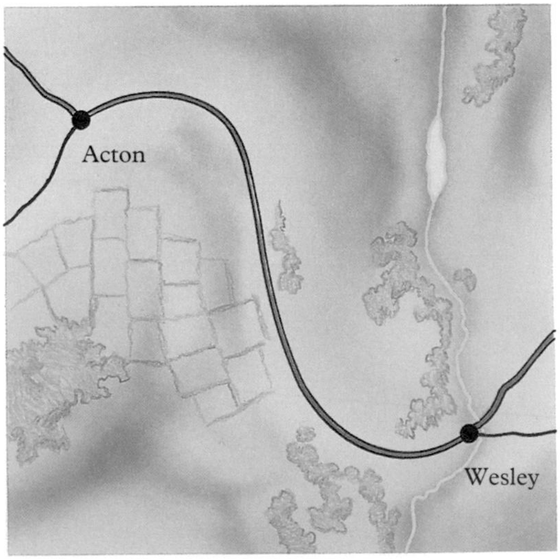

We can find the length of a curved line. We use a piece of string.

This map shows the footpath from Acton to Wesley.

Place the string on top of the curved path.

Start at Acton and mark the string when you get to Wesley.

Measure the marked length of the string.

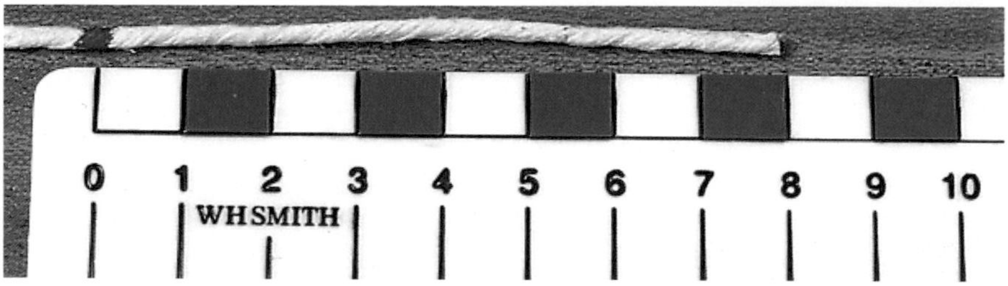

The string is 8 cm long. It represents 8 km.

Exercise 12:6

1 These lines are drawn to the scale 1 cm to 1 km.
Estimate the lengths they represent.

a

b

c

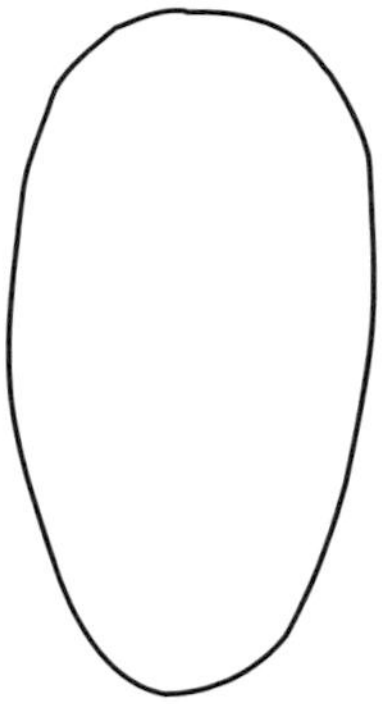

2 This is a scale drawing of a lake.

Estimate the length of the path around the lake.

Scale: 1 cm to 2 miles

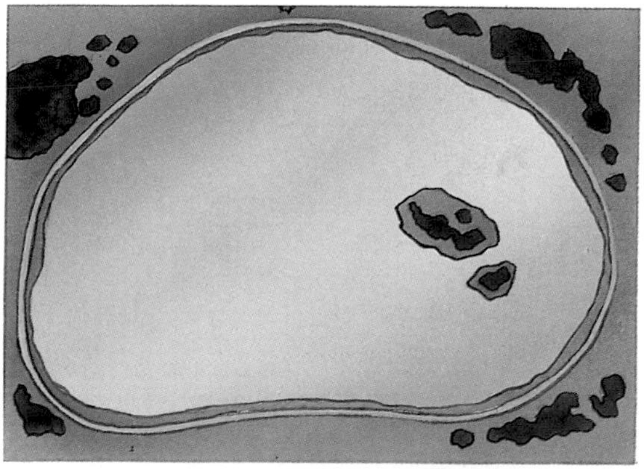

• **3**

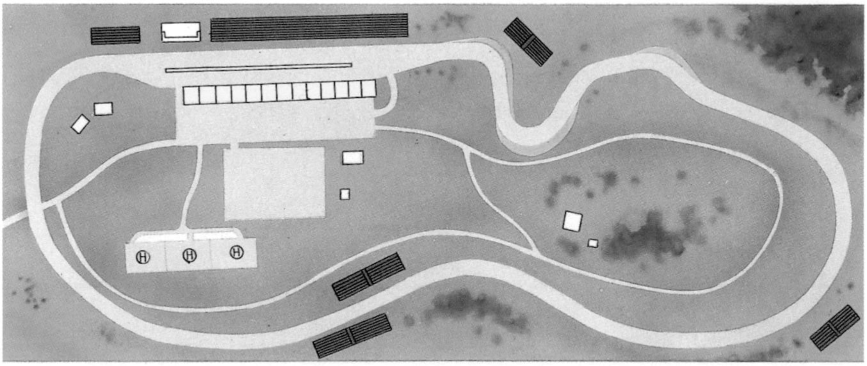

Scale: 2 cm to 1 km

This is a car race track.
Estimate the length of a complete circuit.
Give your answer in kilometres.

4 Imperial to metric conversion

Katie is 4 ft 11 in tall.
The minimum height for people allowed to use the ride is 120 cm.
Can Katie go on the ride?

Sometimes we need to convert lengths given in Imperial units to metric units. We can use estimates.

1 inch is about $2\frac{1}{2}$ cm
1 yard is a bit less than 1 metre
1 mile is a bit more than $1\frac{1}{2}$ km

Exercise 12:7

1 Estimate these in metric units:

a 2 inches
b 1 foot (12 inches)
c 6 inches
d 10 inches

e 2 yards
f 10 yards
g 50 yards
h 100 yards

i 2 miles
j 10 miles
k 50 miles
l 100 miles

Sometimes we need to be more accurate
1 in = 2.5 cm   1 yd = 0.9 m   1 mile = 1.6 km

Examples

1 Convert 9 in to cm

9 in = 9 × 2.5 cm
= 22.5 cm

2 Convert 4.5 yd to m

4 yd = 4 × 0.9 m
= 3.6 m

3 Convert 3.5 miles to km

3.5 miles = 3.5 × 1.6 km
= 5.6 km

---

2 Copy and complete:

a
1 in = 2.5 cm
2 in = ? cm
5 in = ? cm
10 in = ? cm
12 in = ? cm

b
1 yd = ? m
3 yd = ? m
5 yd = ? m
10 yd = ? m
15 yd = ? m

c
1 mile = ? km
3 miles = ? km
5 miles = ? km
8 miles = ? km
10 miles = ? km

3 A wren is 4 inches long.
Convert the lengths of all these birds to cm.

● **4** This chart shows the distances in miles.

Cardiff	393	392	152
	Edinburgh	45	403
		Glasgow	400
			London

a (1) How far is it in miles from Glasgow to Edinburgh?
(2) Convert this distance to kilometres.

b (1) How far is it in miles from Glasgow to Cardiff?
(2) Convert this distance to kilometres.

c (1) How far is it in miles from Edinburgh to London?
(2) Convert this distance to kilometres.

Exercise 12:8

Scales often have ten divisions between the labels.

1 Write down these lengths.

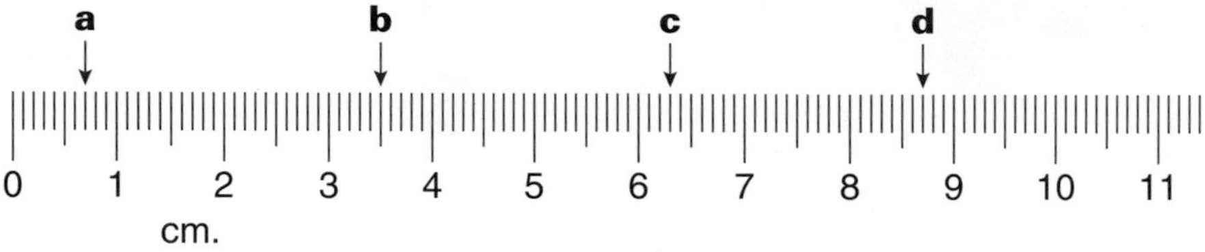

Write down the numbers the arrows are pointing to:

2

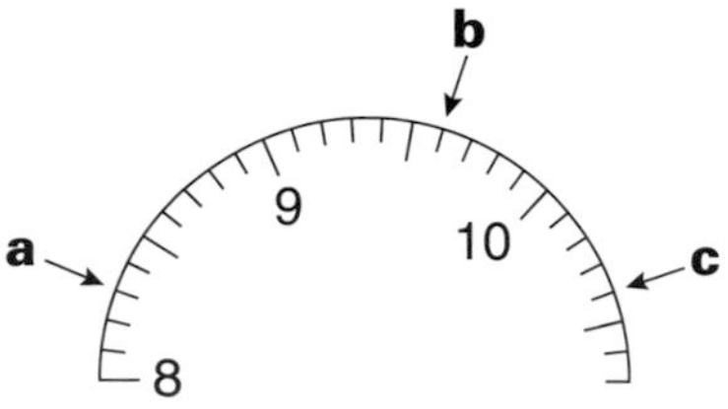

3

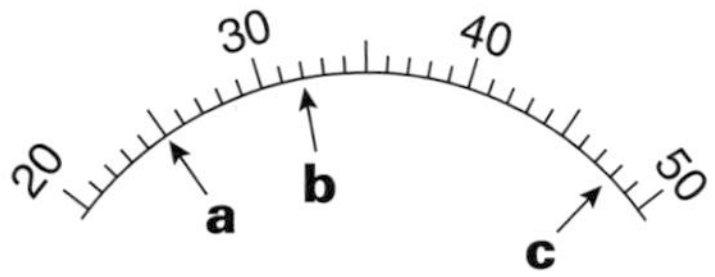

Some scales have five divisions.

Here each division is 2

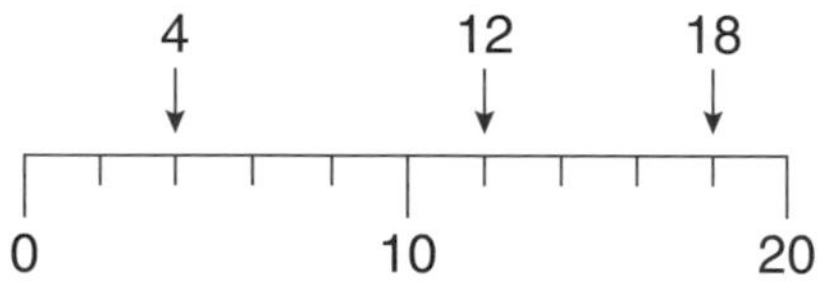

Here each division is 0.2

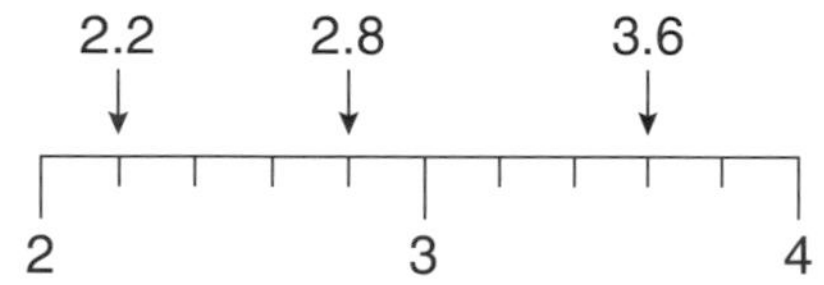

4

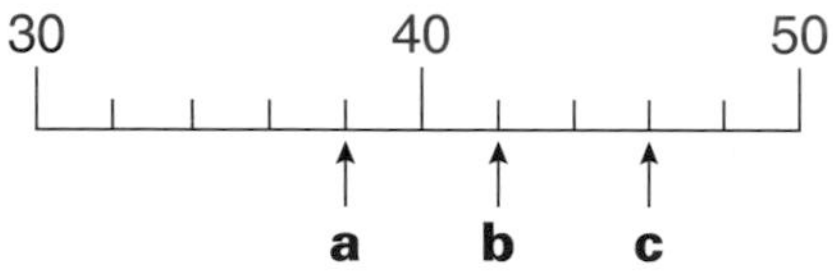

5

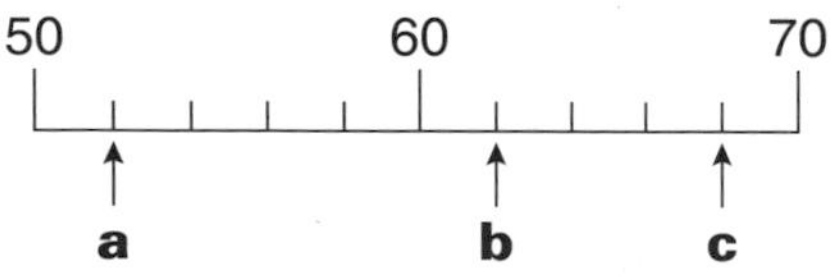

6

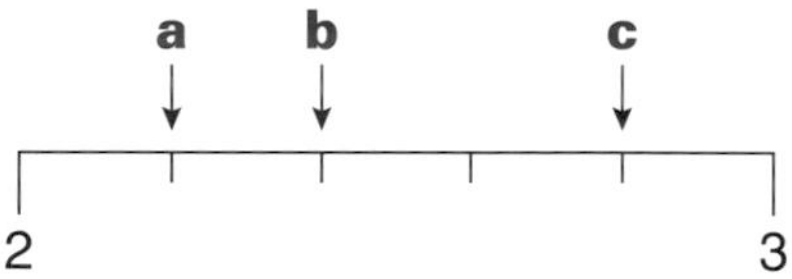

7

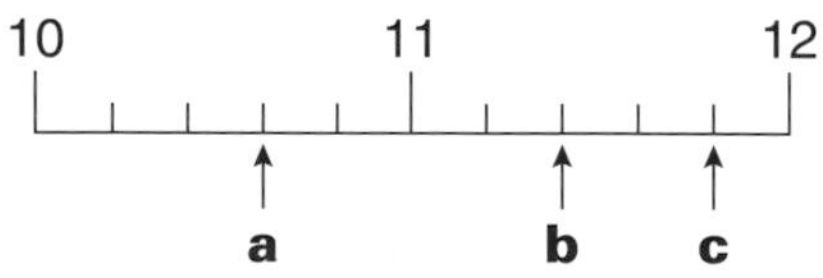

8

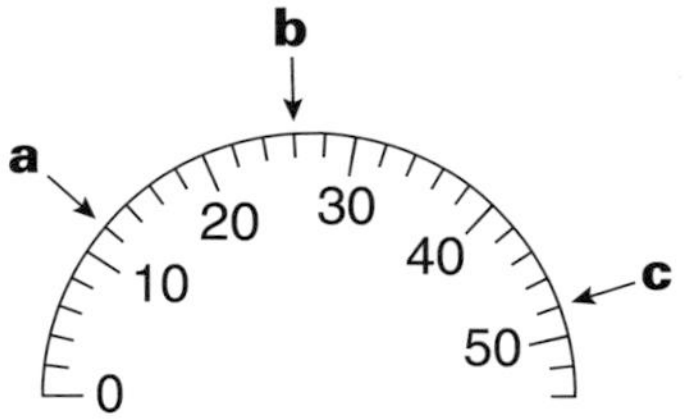

9

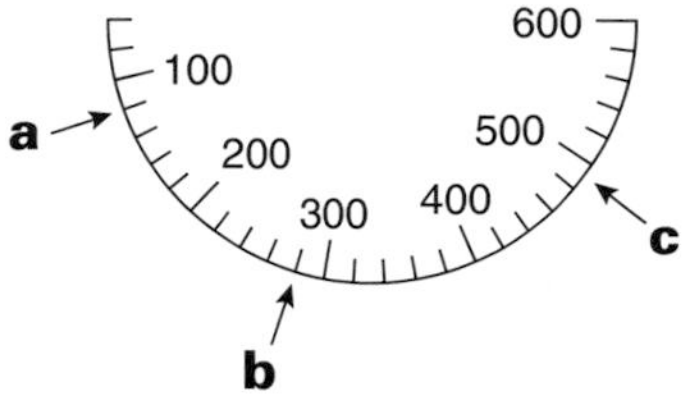

Some scales have other divisions.

10

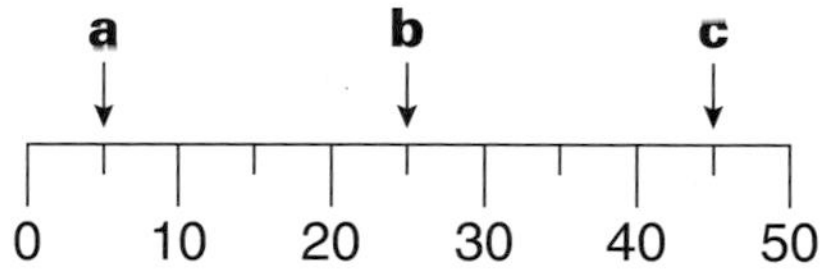

13

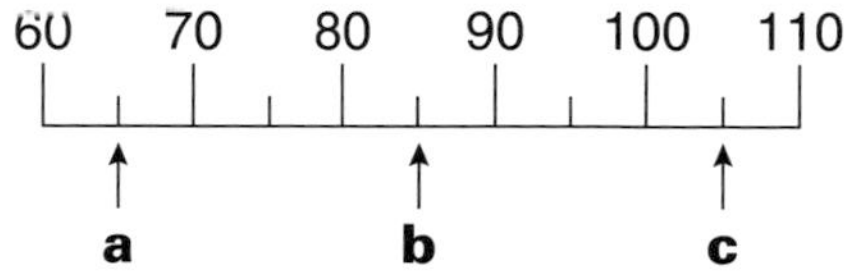

11

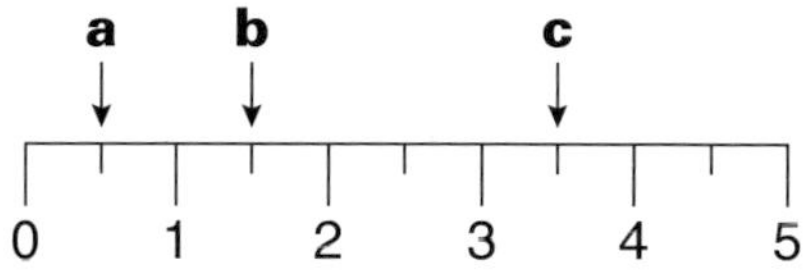

14

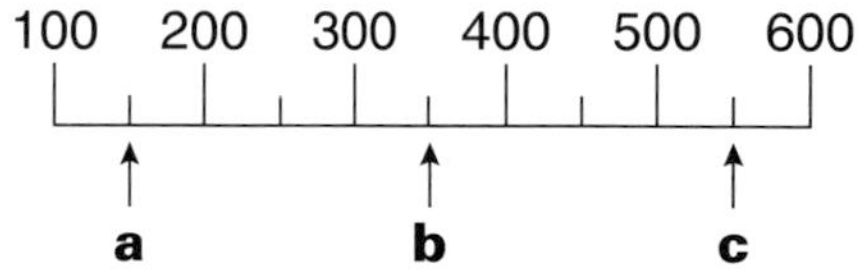

12

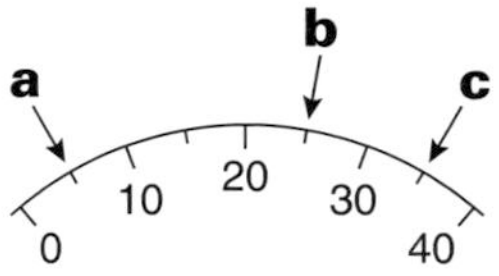

15

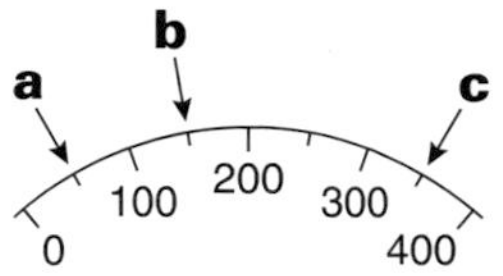

● **16**

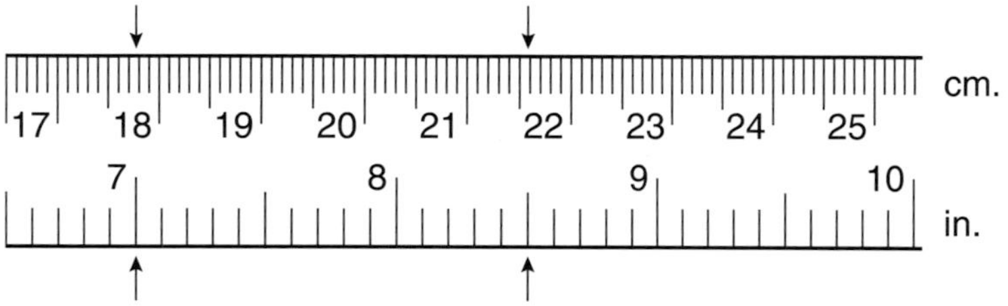

Copy and complete:

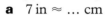

a 7 in ≈ … cm

b 8.5 in ≈ … cm

● **17**

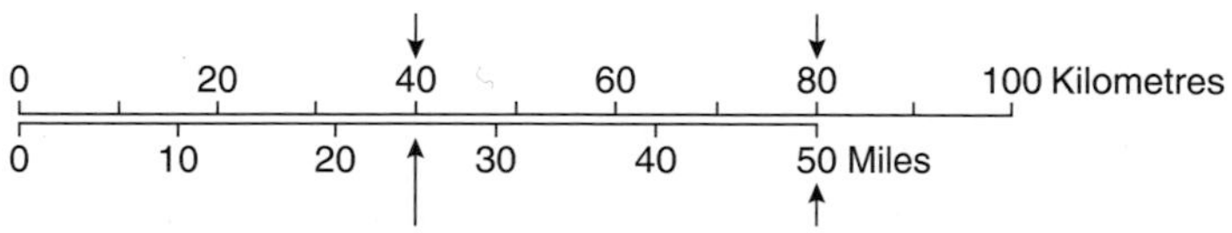

a 25 miles ≈ … km

b 50 miles ≈ … km

1 Copy and complete these. Choose from mm, cm, m, km.

a A tea-bag is about 7.5 … long.
b A bath towel is about 1.8 … long.
c The distance from London to Glasgow is about 650 … .
d A door is about 75 … wide.
e An exercise book is about 4 … thick.
f A small car is about 4 … long.

2 Copy and complete:

a	4 cm = ? mm	17 cm = ? mm	46 mm = ? cm
	3.8 cm = ? mm	50 mm = ? cm	125 mm = ? cm
b	3 m = ? cm	1.8 m = ? cm	450 cm = ? m
	25 m = ? cm	500 cm = ? m	1200 cm = ? m
c	7000 m = ? km	400 m = ? km	8.4 km = ? m
	2800 m = ? km	6 km = ? m	0.6 km = ? m

3 In this question each line is to the scale shown. Write down the length that each line represents.

a	____________________	1 cm to 2 m
b	_______________	1 cm to 5 km
c	_________________________	1 cm to 10 miles
d	__________	1 cm to 3 yd
e	________________	1 cm to 10 km
f	____________________________	1 cm to 4 miles
g	________	1 cm to 10 m
h	______________________	1 cm to 8 km

4 Draw lines to represent these lengths.
Use the scale given for each one.

a	6 m	1 cm to 1 m	**e**	400 miles	1 cm to 100 miles
b	$4\frac{1}{2}$ miles	1 cm to 1 mile	**f**	250 km	1 cm to 50 km
c	7 km	1 cm to 2 km	**g**	75 km	1 cm to 50 km
d	5 miles	1 cm to 2 miles	**h**	$3\frac{1}{2}$ km	1 cm to $\frac{1}{2}$ km

5 **a** Make a scale drawing of this rectangle.
Use a scale of 1 cm to 2 m.
b Use your drawing to find the actual length of the diagonal.

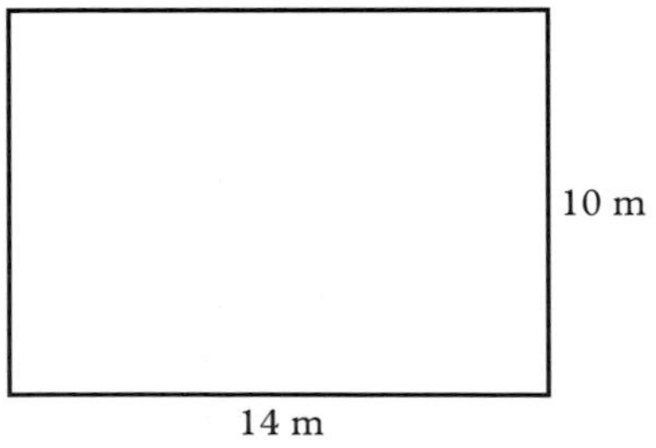

6 This is a floor plan of a one-bedroom flat.

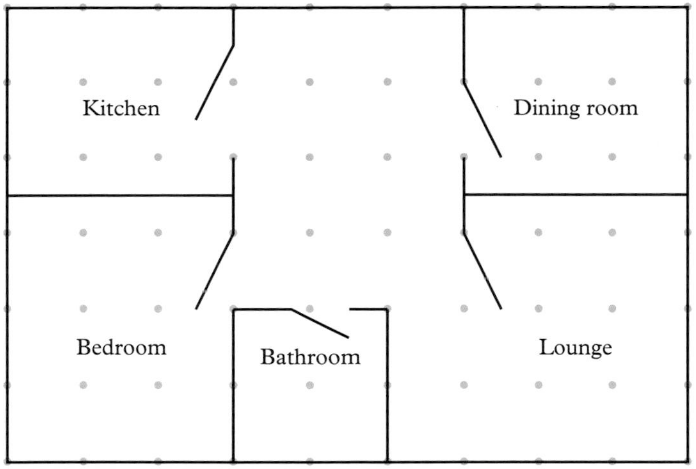

Scale:
1 cm to 1 m

Write down the actual length and width of each room.

7 The broken line shows the path of the pirate ship.

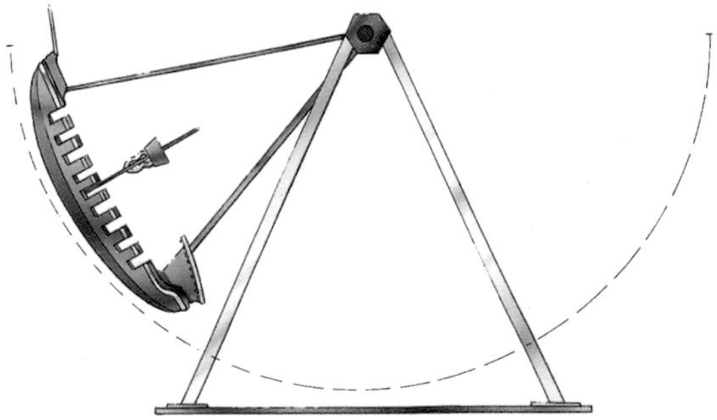

This pirate ship swings from side to side.

How far does it travel from this position …

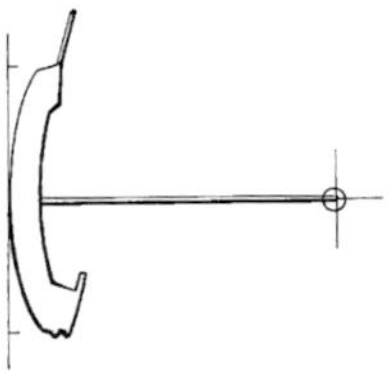

… to this position?

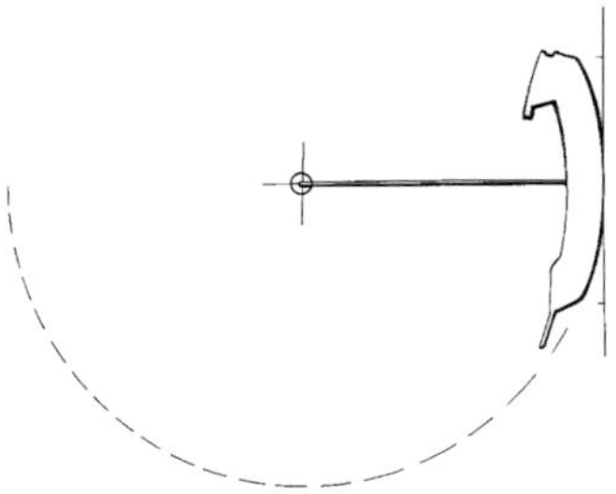

8 **a** Make a scale drawing of this triangle.
Use a scale of 1 cm to 2 miles.
b Use your drawing to find the actual length of AB in miles.

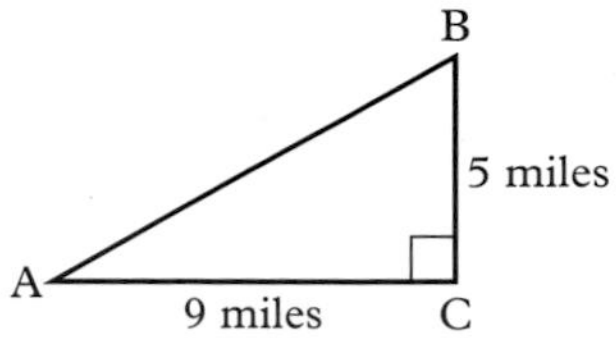

9 **a** Copy the pizza menu.
Convert the sizes to cm.

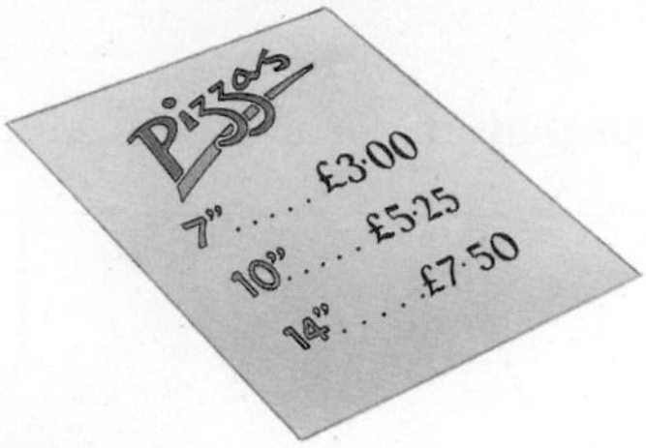

b Give the distance on this milestone in km.

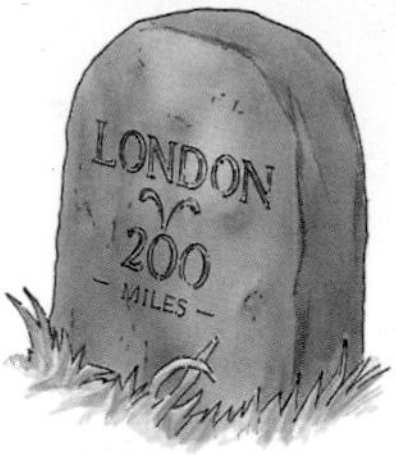

10 Write down the numbers shown by the arrows.

a

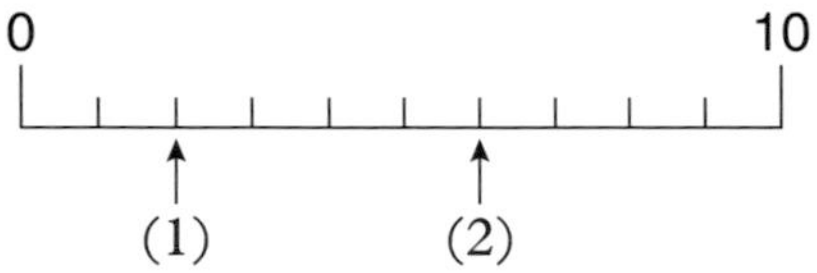

d

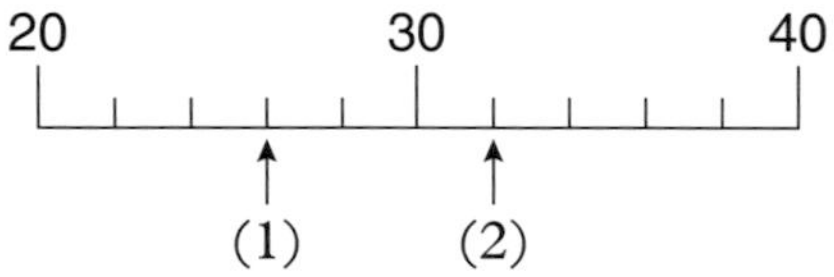

b

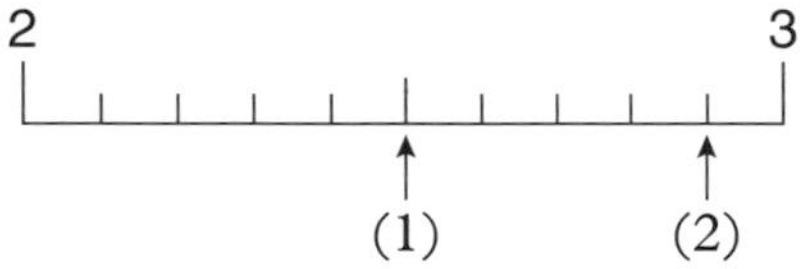

e

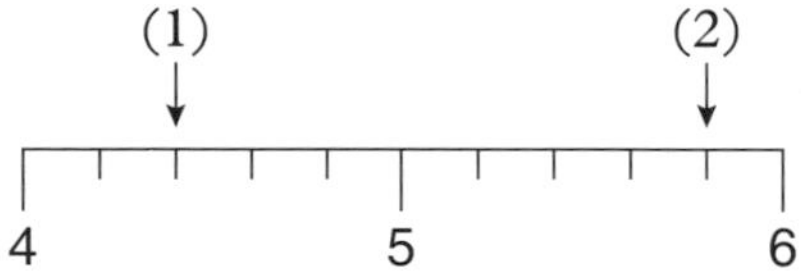

c

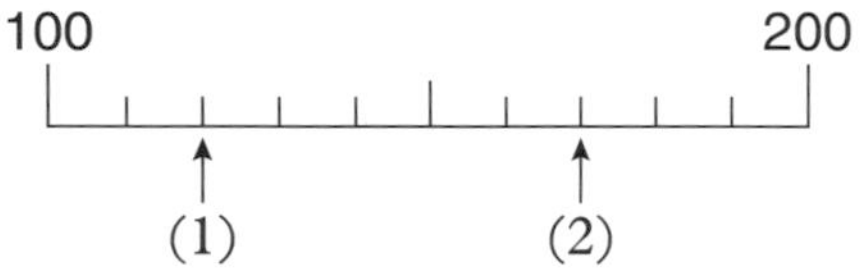

f

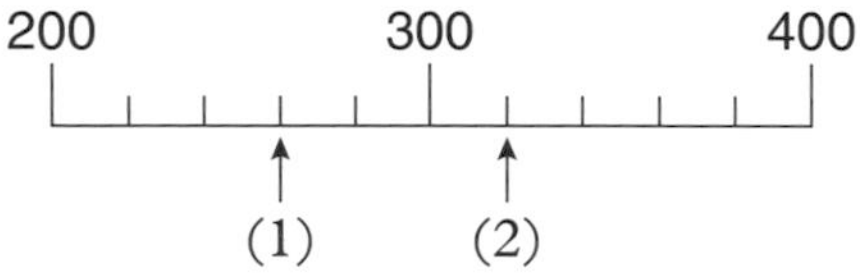

11 **a** 3.5 in = ? cm
4 in = ? cm
5 in = ? cm

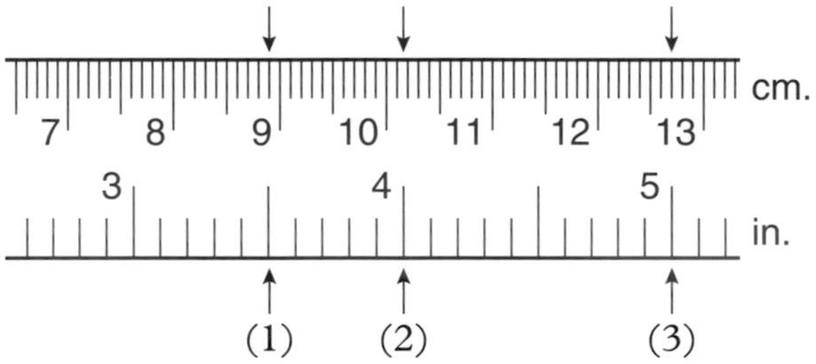

b

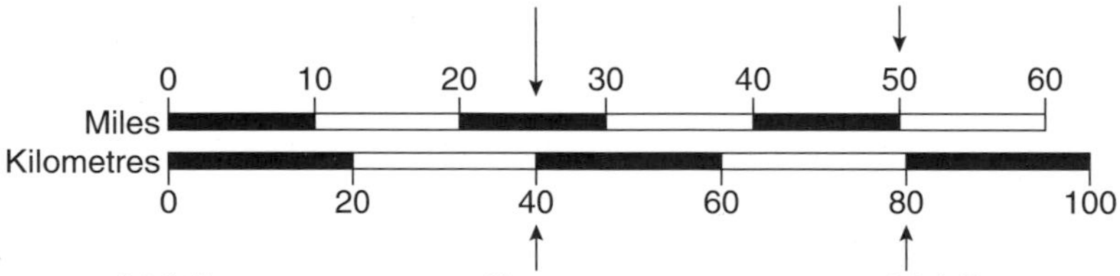

40 kilometres ≈ … miles   80 kilometres ≈ … miles

1 Change all these Imperial units to metric units.

Mr Smith bought an 8" pizza and a 12" pizza. He got into his 15 ft long car and drove the 3 miles to his home. He drove 20 yd along his drive to his house.

2 Furlong, chain and fathom are also imperial units. Find out what you can about them.

3 **a** The length of a pencil case is about:
(1) 2.5 cm (2) 2.5 m (3) 25 mm (4) 25 cm
b The length of a bus is about:
(1) 100 mm (2) 10 m (3) 100 cm (4) 100 m
c The length of the bristles on a toothbrush is about:
(1) 90 cm (2) 9 mm (3) 9 cm (4) 0.9 mm
d When a bus travels three stops it goes about:
(1) 100 m (2) 10 km (3) 1 km (4) 200 m

4 Copy and complete:

a 54 mm = ? cm	**e** 650 m = ? km	**i** 340 cm = ? m
b 1750 m = ? km	**f** 0.7 km = ? m	**j** 0.95 cm = ? mm
c 27 cm = ? mm	**g** 5400 m = ? km	**k** 85 cm = ? m
d 2.5 m = ? cm	**h** 8.5 km = ? m	**l** 132 mm = ? cm

5 This map has been drawn to a scale of 1 cm to 10 km.

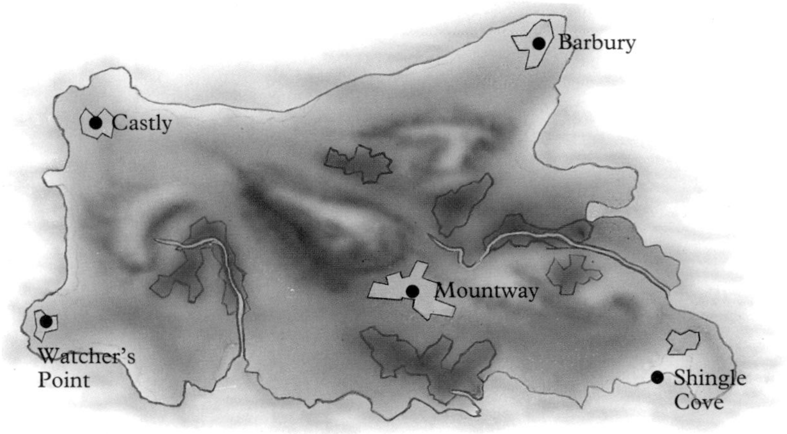

a Measure the distance between Castly and Barbury on the map in cm.
b Using the scale calculate the actual distance between Castly and Barbury.
c Using the same method, find the actual distance between:
(1) Watcher's Point and Mountway
(2) Watcher's Point and Shingle Cove
(3) Barbury and Mountway

6 A model of a Jaguar car is 13.2 cm long. The scale is 1 cm to 36 cm. What is the length of a real Jaguar car.

a In centimetres?

b In metres?

7 **a** What is the length of the space shuttle?

b What is the width of the space shuttle across the widest part including the wings?

Scale: 1 cm to 6 m

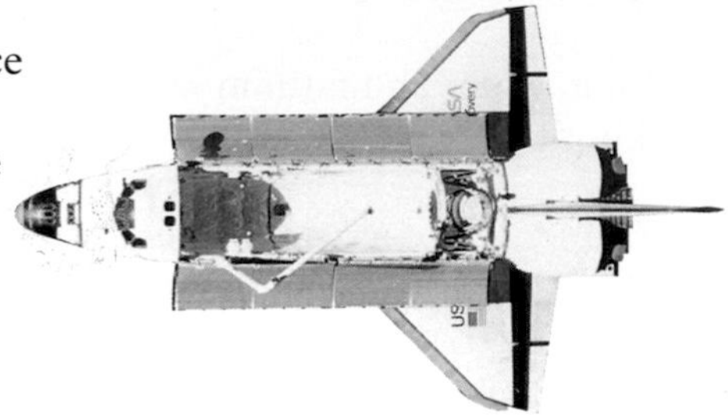

8 Write down the numbers shown by the arrows.

a

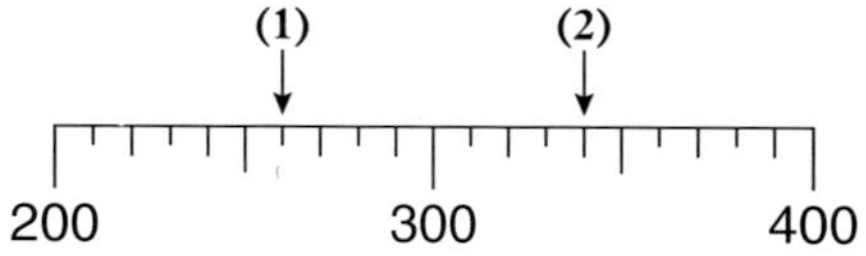

b

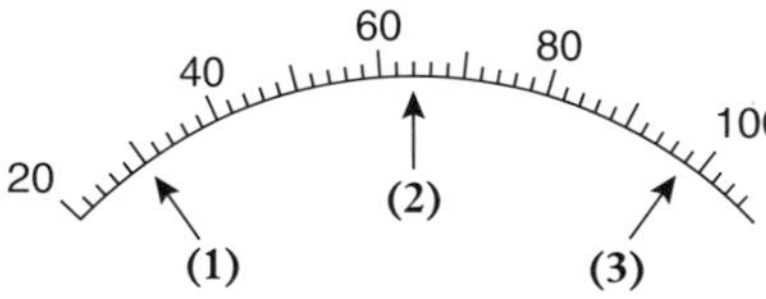

c

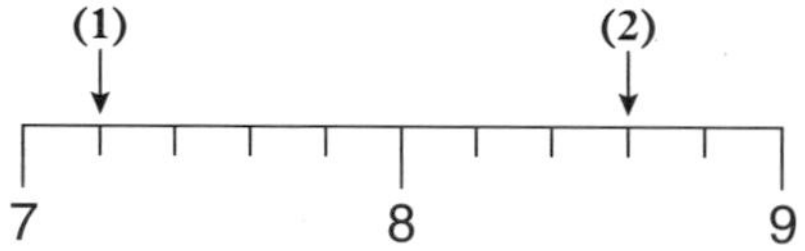

d

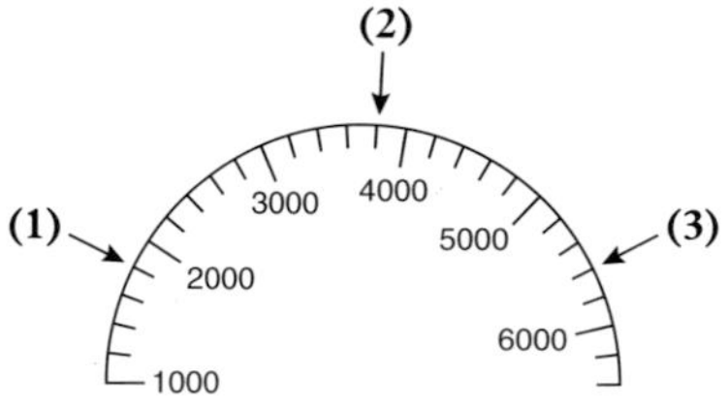

e

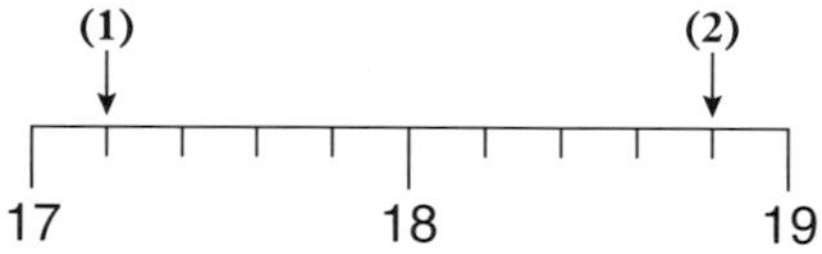

f

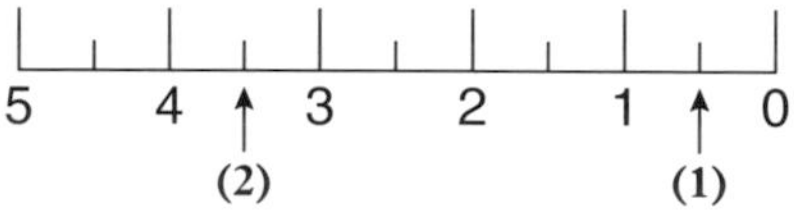

9 Copy and complete:

a … ft = … m

b … ft = … m

c … ft = … m

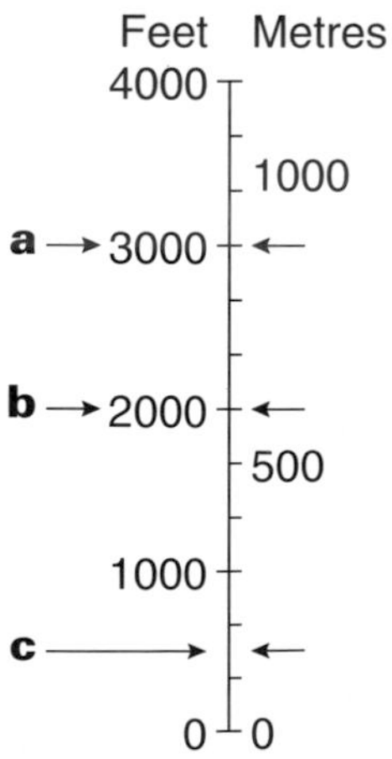

SUMMARY

- **Common Imperial units of length**
  12 inches = 1 foot   12 in = 1 ft   3 feet = 1 yard   3ft = 1 yd

- **Metric units of length**
  10 mm = 1 cm   100 cm = 1 m   1000 m = 1 km
  The thickness of a pencil lead is about 1 mm.
  The width of the nail on your middle finger is about 1 cm.
  A door is about two metres high.

- **Converting units within the metric system**

  1 Convert 6.9 cm to mm
  6.9 cm = 6.9 × 10 mm
  = 69 mm

  2 Convert 148 cm to m
  148 cm = 148 ÷ 100 m
  = 1.48 m

  3 Convert 7.3 km to m
  7.3 km = 7.3 × 1000 m
  = 7300 m

- A **scale drawing** is the same shape as the original but different in size.
  The scale of a drawing gives the relative size of the actual length to the drawn length.
  Examples of scales are: 1 cm to 1 km; 1 cm to 10 km.
  We can find lengths from scale drawings.
  We use string to measure the length of curved lines.

- **Imperial to metric conversion**
  1 inch is about $2\frac{1}{2}$ cm   1 in = 2.5 cm
  1 yard is a bit less than 1 metre   1 yd = 0.9 m
  1 mile is a bit more than $1\frac{1}{2}$ kilometres   1 mile = 1.6 km

  1 Convert 9 in to cm
  9 in = 9 × 2.5 cm
  = 22.5 cm

  2 Convert 4 yd to m
  4 yd = 4 × 0.9 m
  = 3.6 m

  3 Convert 3.5 miles to km
  3.5 miles = 3.5 × 1.6 km
  = 5.6 km

- **Scales** have different numbers of divisions.
  Start by working out what one division represents.

  Here each division is 2

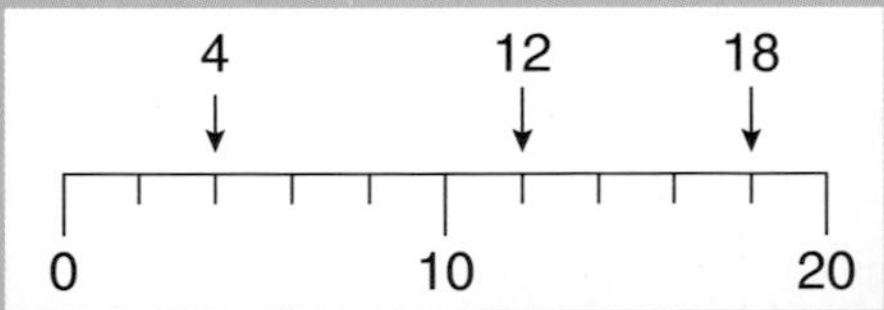

  Here each division is 0.2

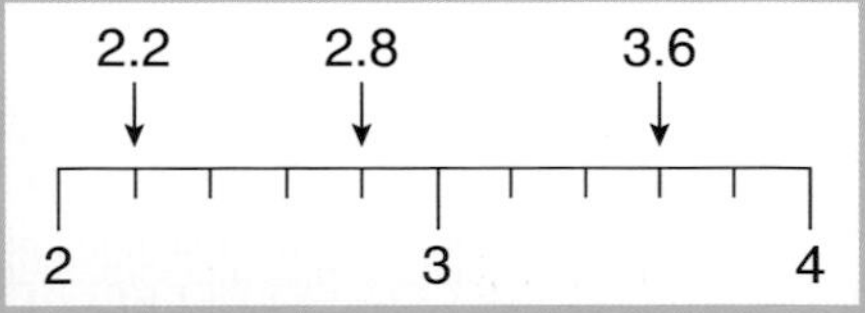

  Scales can be used to convert Imperial to metric units.

1 Convert these lengths into the units given.

a 2 ft to in **b** 36 in to ft **c** 4 yd to ft **d** 6 ft to yd

2 What units would you use to measure these?
Choose from mm, cm, m, km.

a The distance from London to New York.
b The width of your exercise book.
c The height of a tall tree.
d The length of a fly's leg.

3 Copy and complete:

a 20mm = ? cm
b 120 cm = ? m
c 5000 m = ? km
d 4.2 cm = ? mm
e 1.5 m = ? cm
f 3 km = ? m

4 These lines have been drawn using a scale of 1 cm to 2 km.
Find the length each line represents.

a ______________________ **b** ________________

c Give an estimate for this line.

5 Draw lines to represent these lengths.
Use the scale given for each one.

a A length of $5\frac{1}{2}$ miles using a scale of 1 cm to 1 mile.
b A length of 18 miles using a scale of 1 cm to 3 miles.

6 **a** Make a scale drawing of this rectangle.
Use a scale of 2 cm to 1 mile.
b Use your drawing to find the length of the diagonal in miles.

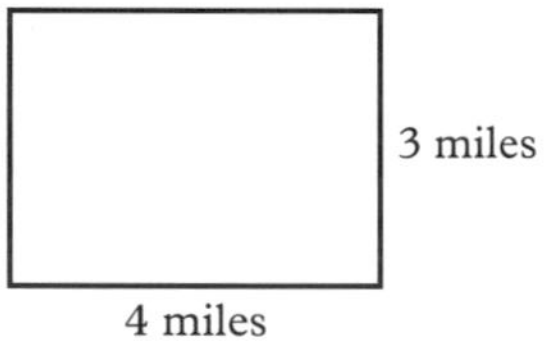

7 Estimate these in metric units:

a 4 inches **b** 5 yards **c** 4 miles

8 Write the numbers the arrows are pointing to.

a

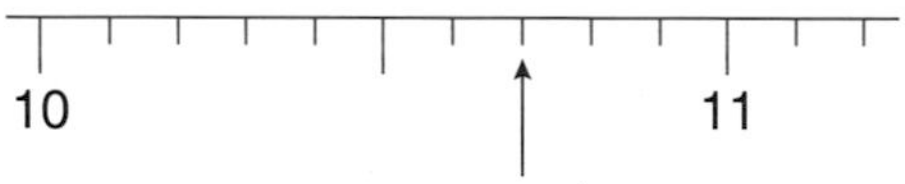

b

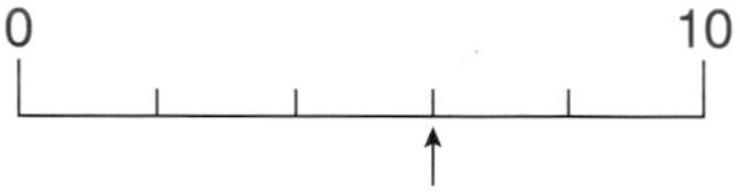

c

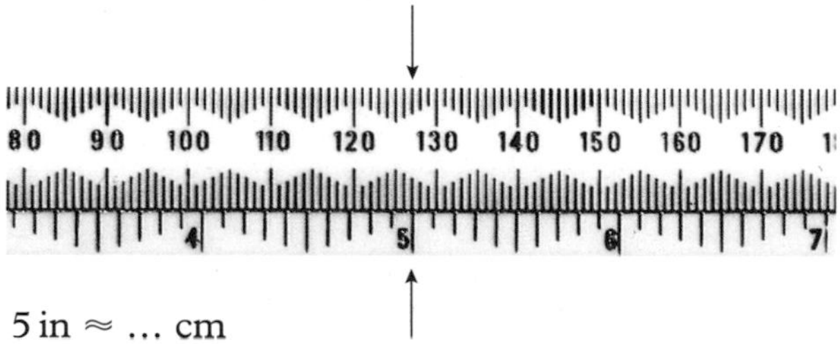

5 in ≈ … cm

13 Algebra: into the unknown

CORE

1 **Inverse operations**

2 **Equations**

3 **Trial and improvement**

QUESTIONS

EXTENSION

SUMMARY

TEST YOURSELF

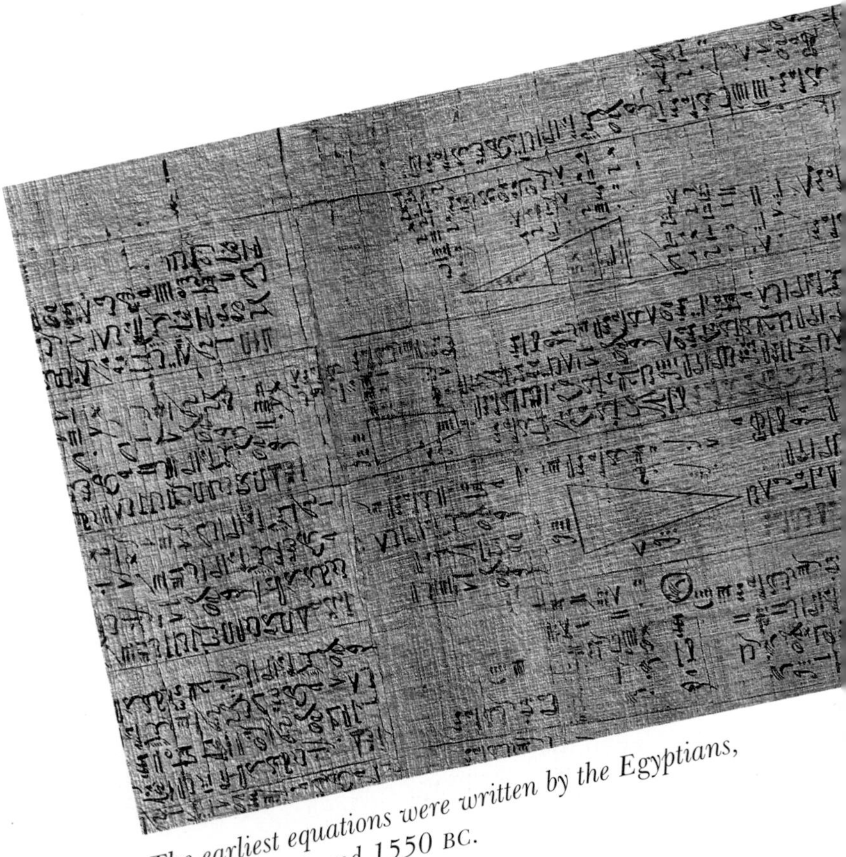

The earliest equations were written by the Egyptians, between 1650 and 1550 BC.

1 Inverse operations

Christopher has knitted a scarf.

His puppy undoes the scarf.

Christopher is back to where he started.
'Undoing the scarf' is called the inverse of 'knitting the scarf'.

Inverse An **inverse** returns you to where you started.

Exercise 13:1

Write down the inverse of:

1 open the door

2 walk up the stairs

3 turn left

4 walk backwards

5 turn the light on

6 turn 90° clockwise

• **7** reflection of the shape in the red line.

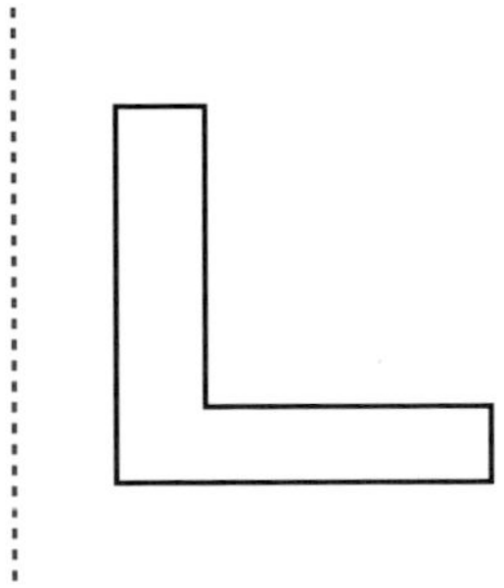

We can find inverses in mathematics.
Start with 3.
Add 4.
The answer is 7.

'Subtract 4' undoes the 'add 4'. It returns 7 to 3.

'Subtract 4' is the inverse of 'add 4'

Exercise 13:2

Write down the inverse of these:

1 + 6 **3** × 4 **5** add 2 **7** multiply by 3

2 − 9 **4** ÷ 7 **6** subtract 5 **8** divide by 10

Example We can use a **function machine** to represent 'add 10'.

Put 8 into this function machine.
You get the answer 18.

We can show the inverse by drawing the function machine backwards.

Put 18 into this function machine.
You get the answer 8.

We have returned to where we started.

Draw the inverse function machines.
We only draw the screen of the robot.

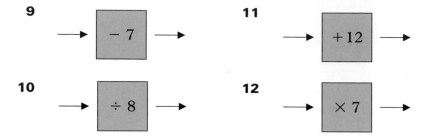

9 → [− 7] →

10 → [÷ 8] →

11 → [+ 12] →

12 → [× 7] →

Example

A function machine can have two steps.

→ [× 5] → [+ 6] →

The inverse machine is:

← [÷ 5] ← [− 6] ←

We can check our answer.
Put 10 into the first machine.

10 → [× 5] →(50) [+ 6] → 56

Put 56 into the inverse machine

10 ← [÷ 5] ←(50) [− 6] ← 56

You return to 10.

Exercise 13:3

Draw the inverse function machines.
Use the number 10 to check each machine.

1 → $\div 2$ → $+ 3$ →

The inverse machine is:

← … 2 ← … 3 ←

2 → $\times 10$ → $- 5$ →

The inverse machine is:

← …… ← …… ←

3 → $+ 8$ → $\times 3$ →

4 → $- 8$ → $\div 2$ →

5 → $\times 4$ → $+ 12$ →

6 → $+ 20$ → $\div 10$ →

2 Equations

How many chocolate bars has Bill's puppy eaten?
Find the missing number: $\square + 3 = 10$

We can use a letter instead of the $\square$ shape.

$x + 3 = 10$

These are equations.

Other examples of equations are:

$x + 8 = 34$ $\quad$ $x - 2 = 7$

$a + 4 = 1$ $\quad$ $y + 8 = 60$

Example

Solve the equation $x + 3 = 10$ using a function machine.

$x \longrightarrow \boxed{+3} \longrightarrow 10$

The inverse machine is:

$7 \longleftarrow \boxed{-3} \longleftarrow 10$

Answer: $x = 7$

Exercise 13:4

Copy and complete the function machines in Questions **1** and **2**.

1 $x + 4 = 7$

$x \longrightarrow$ [+ 4] $\longrightarrow 7$

...... $\longleftarrow$ [......] $\longleftarrow 7$

Answer: $x = \ldots$

2 $a - 5 = 11$

$a \longrightarrow$ [......] $\longrightarrow 11$

...... $\longleftarrow$ [... 5] $\longleftarrow$ ......

Answer: $a = \ldots$

Draw your own function machines to solve these equations.

3 $x + 8 = 15$

4 $x + 2 = 17$

5 $a - 4 = 10$

6 $x - 7 = 3$

7 $y + 6 = 14$

8 $x - 8 = 12$

9 $r - 3 = 8$

10 $x + 9 = 13$

Example

Solve the equation $3a = 12$

Remember: $3a$ means $3 \times a$

$a \longrightarrow$ [× 3] $\longrightarrow 12$

The inverse machine is:

$4 \longleftarrow$ [÷ 3] $\longleftarrow 12$

Answer: $a = 4$

Exercise 13:5

Solve these equations by drawing inverse machines.

1 $4x = 12$

x ⟶ [× 4] ⟶ 12

The inverse machine is:

⟵ [……] ⟵ 12

Answer: $x = \ldots$

2 $5x = 30$

3 $6y = 12$

Example

Solve the equation $\frac{x}{2} = 7$

Remember: $\frac{x}{2}$ means $x \div 2$

x ⟶ [÷ 2] ⟶ 7

The inverse function machine is:

14 ⟵ [× 2] ⟵ 7

Answer: $x = 14$

---

4 $\frac{a}{3} = 4$

a ⟶ [÷ 3] ⟶ 4

The inverse machine is:

…… ⟵ [……] ⟵ 4

Answer: $a = \ldots$

5 $\frac{x}{6} = 2$

6 $\frac{k}{5} = 6$

7 $3q = 21$

8 $\frac{x}{2} = 26$

9 $6x = 54$

10 $\frac{c}{4} = 20$

Example Solve the equation $2x + 4 = 14$

$x \longrightarrow$ [$\times 2$] $\xrightarrow{2x}$ [$+ 4$] $\longrightarrow 14$

The inverse machine is:

$5 \longleftarrow$ [$\div 2$] $\xleftarrow{10}$ [$- 4$] $\longleftarrow 14$

Answer: $x = 5$

Exercise 13:6

Copy these function machines. Fill them in.
Solve the equations.

1 $2x + 1 = 11$

$x \longrightarrow$ [$\times \ldots$] $\xrightarrow{?}$ [$+ \ldots$] $\longrightarrow 11$

$? \longleftarrow$ [$\div \ldots$] $\xleftarrow{?}$ [$- \ldots$] $\longleftarrow 11$

$x = \ldots$

Example Solve $3x - 5 = 19$

$x \longrightarrow$ [$\times 3$] $\xrightarrow{3x}$ [$- 5$] $\longrightarrow 19$

The inverse machine is:

$8 \longleftarrow$ [$\div 3$] $\xleftarrow{24}$ [$+ 5$] $\longleftarrow 19$

Answer: $x = 8$

2 $3x - 4 = 14$

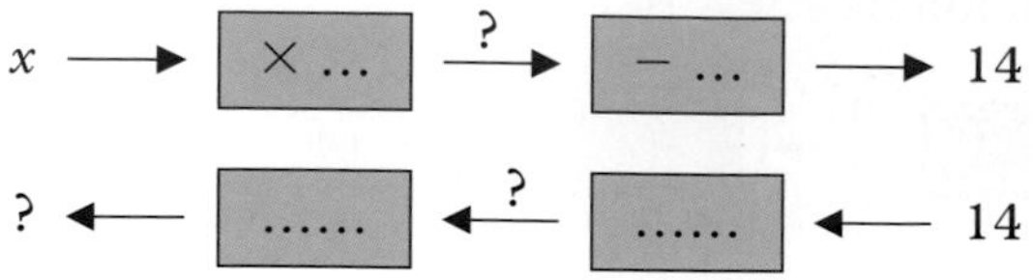

$x = \ldots$

3 $4r - 10 = 2$

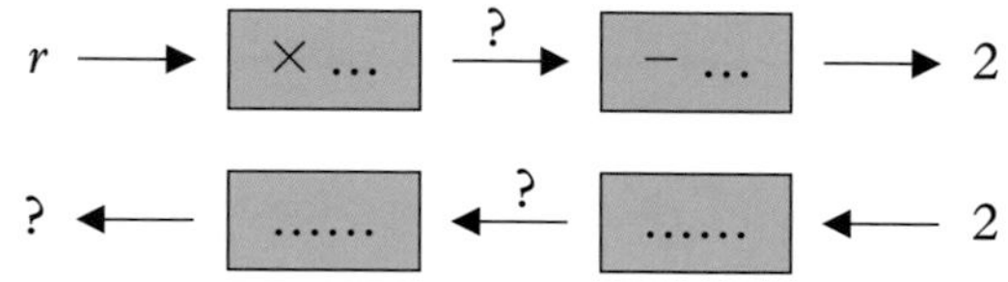

$r = \ldots$

4 $3p - 11 = 10$

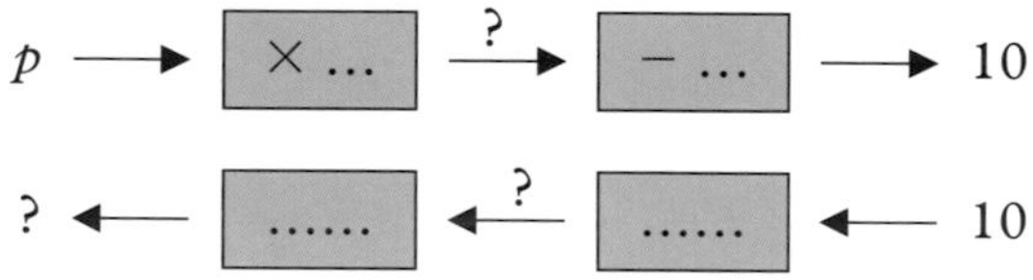

$p = \ldots$

Draw your own function and inverse function machines for these.
Solve the equations.

5 $2x + 7 = 19$

6 $5y - 3 = 37$

7 $8x + 3 = 59$

8 $7q - 11 = 10$

9 $3t + 4 = 13$

10 $4x - 3 = 21$

An equation can be given in words. You have to change the words into algebra.

Example

I think of a number and add 5.
The answer is 12.
What is the number?

Change the words into algebra.

Call the number x.	x
I think of a number and add 5.	$x + 5$
The answer is 12.	$x + 5 = 12$

Solve $x + 5 = 12$

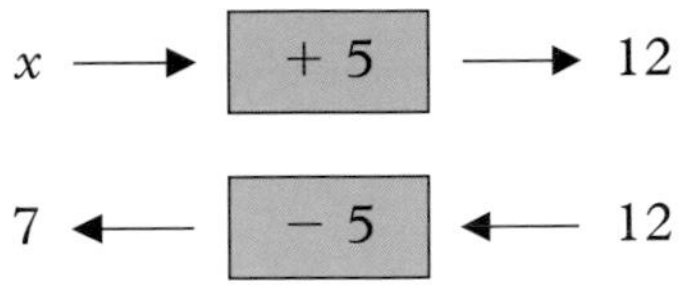

Answer: $x = 7$
The number is 7.

Exercise 13:7

In the questions change the words into algebra.
Solve the equation to find the number.

1 I think of a number and subtract 3. The answer is 12.

2 I think of a number and add 7. The answer is 13.

3 I think of a number and multiply it by 3. The answer is 18.

4 I think of a number and divide it by 2. The answer is 7.

5 I think of a number and add 8. The answer is 15.

6 I think of a number and multiply it by 4. The answer is 20.

7 I think of a number and subtract 10. The answer is 12.

8 I think of a number and add 6. The answer is 25.

9 I think of a number and divide it by 5. The answer is 3.

10 I think of a number and multiply it by 10. The answer is 200.

• **11** I subtract 6 from a number. The answer is 3.

• **12** When 6 is added to a number the answer is 9.

• **13** Paul has x sweets. Jane has 7 sweets. Together they have 19 sweets.
Find the value of x.

• **14** A class has 28 pupils. There are x boys and 15 girls.
Find the value of x.

Sometimes an equation is given as a diagram.

Example *Remember*: angles on a line add up to 180°

We can see that $x + 120 = 180$
We can now solve this equation.

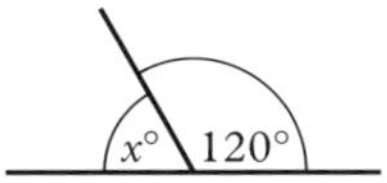

x ⟶ [+ 120] ⟶ 180

60 ⟵ [− 120] ⟵ 180

Answer: $x = 60$

Exercise 13:8

In each question write down an equation and solve it.

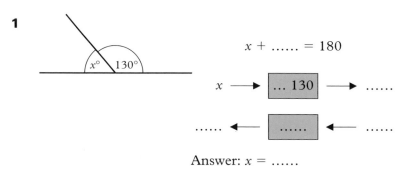

1

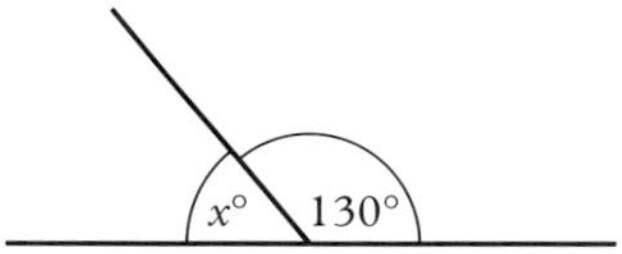

$x +$ …… $= 180$

x ⟶ [... 130] ⟶ ……

…… ⟵ [……] ⟵ ……

Answer: $x =$ ……

2

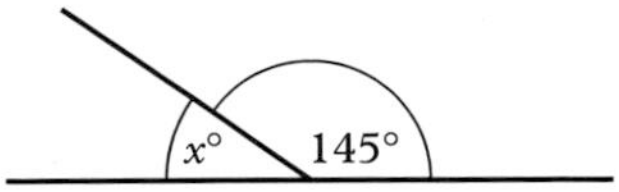

3

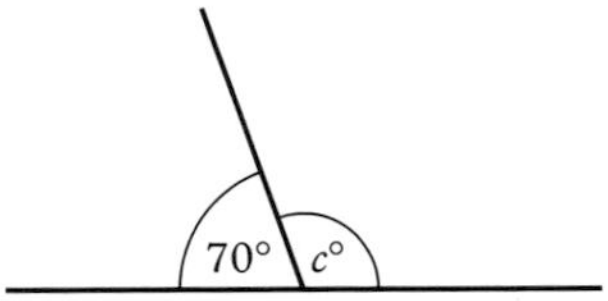

4 *Remember*: vertically opposite angles are equal.

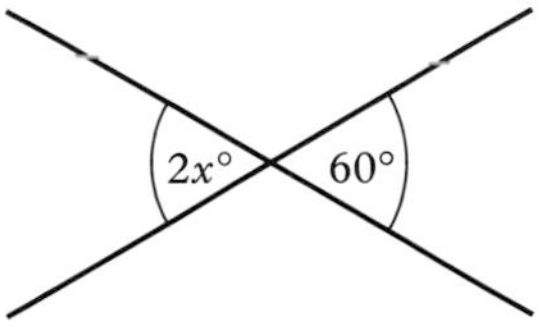

$2x =$ ......

x → [× 2] → ......

...... ← [......] ← ......

Answer: $x =$ ......

5

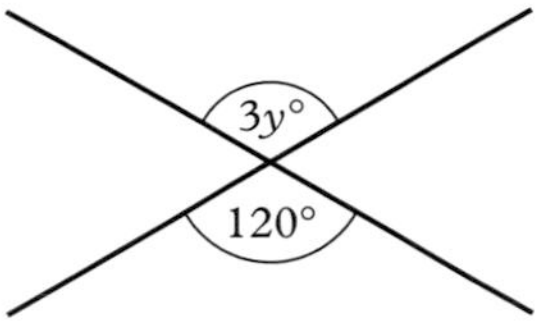

6

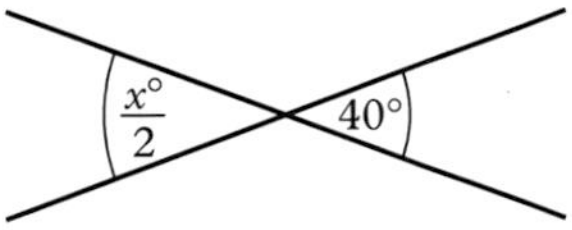

7 *Remember*: angles at a point add up to 360°.

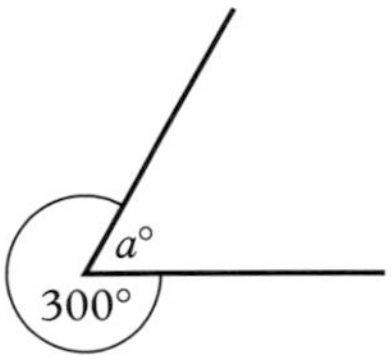

...... + 300 = 360

a → [+ 300] → ......

...... ← [......] ← ......

Answer: $a =$ ......

8

9

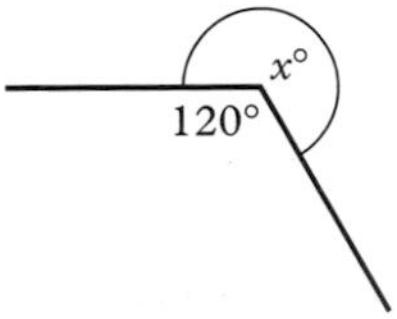

10

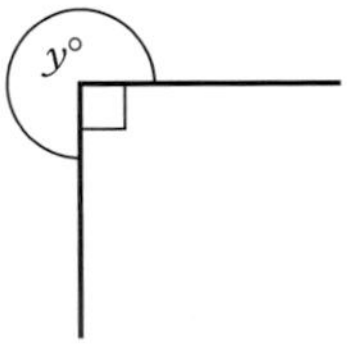

3 Trial and improvement

Aisha is unhappy.

She can't solve equations.

Aisha decides to solve her equation by guessing.
She has to solve $3x + 18 = 57$

Aisha's first guess is 10 .... $3 \times 10 + 18 = 48$..... This is too small.
Aisha tries 20 .... $3 \times 20 + 18 = 78$..... This is too big.
She tries a number between 10 and 20:
She tries 15 .... $3 \times 15 + 18 = 63$..... This is too big.
She tries 13 .... $3 \times 13 + 18 = 57$..... This is correct.

Answer: $x = 13$

Aisha's teacher tells her this method is called **trial and improvement**.
Aisha is happy and wants to solve another equation.

Example

Solve $a^2 = 81$ *Remember*: a^2 means $a \times a$

Aisha tries different numbers.
She writes her results in a table.

Value of a	Value of a^2	
4	$4 \times 4 = 16$	much too small
10	$10 \times 10 = 100$	too big
8	$8 \times 8 = 64$	too small
9	$9 \times 9 = 81$	correct

Answer: $a = 9$

Exercise 13:9

Solve these equations by trial and improvement.
Set out your work in a table.

1 $4x + 21 = 73$

Value of x	Value of $4x + 21$	
10	....	....
20	....	....
...	....	....

Continue the table until you find the answer.

Remember: $4x + 21$ means 'take a value for x, multiply it by 4 and then add 21.'

2 $27a - 36 = 261$

Value of a	Value of $27a - 36$	
18	....	....
15	....	....

Continue the table until you find the answer.

Remember: $27a - 36$ means 'take a value for a, multiply it by 27 and then subtract 36.'

3 $24x + 156 = 948$

Value of x	Value of $24x + 156$	
20	....	....
40	....	....

4 $57y - 129 = 954$

Value of ...	Value of	
10	....	....
20	....	....

• **5** $26x + 358 = 1294$

Value of ...	....	

• **6** $71c - 345 = 2637$

....	Value of	

• **7** $48x + 1235 = 8771$

8 $a^2 = 49$. *Remember* $a^2 = a \times a$

Value of a	Value of a^2	
15	....	....
10	....	....
...	....	....

9 $x^2 = 121$

Value of ...	Value of	

Now write your own table headings.

• **10** $y^2 = 576$

• **11** $a^2 = 1849$

• **12** $x^2 = 1225$

13 $4x + 15 = 83$

14 $7a - 21 = 140$

15 $13x + 120 = 588$

Write down the inverse of:

1 **a** add 23 **b** subtract 12 **c** multiply by 14 **d** subtract 5 **e** divide by 12 **f** multiply by 9

In Questions **2–5**, draw the inverse function machines.

2 **a** → -11 →

b → $\times 16$ →

c → $\div 5$ →

d → $+8$ →

3 **a** → $\times 4$ →

b → -16 →

c → $\div 10$ →

d → $+18$ →

4 **a** → $+5$ → $\times 8$ →

b → $\div 6$ → -3 →

5 **a** → -10 → $\times 9$ →

b → $\times 10$ → $+7$ →

Solve the equations in Questions **6–9**, by drawing inverse machines.

6 **a** $x + 7 = 19$ **b** $y - 5 = 4$

7 **a** $x + 13 = 24$ **b** $r - 12 = 30$

8 **a** $12p = 156$ **b** $\frac{x}{7} = 5$

9 **a** $\frac{x}{12} = 5$ **b** $7q = 28$

In Questions **10–14**, change the words into algebra.
Solve the equation.

10 I think of a number and add 9. The answer is 22.
What is the number?

11 I think of a number and subtract 12. The answer is 15.
Find the number.

12 I think of a number and multiply it by 10. The answer is 80.
Find the number.

13 When 21 is added to a number the answer is 35.
Find the number.

14 A class has x girls and 16 boys. There are 28 pupils in the class.
Find the value of x.

In Questions **15–20**, write down an equation and solve it.

15

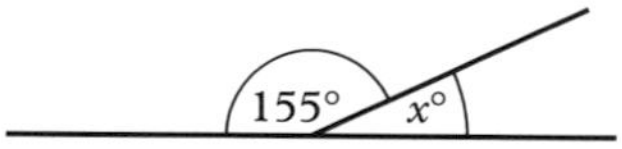

18

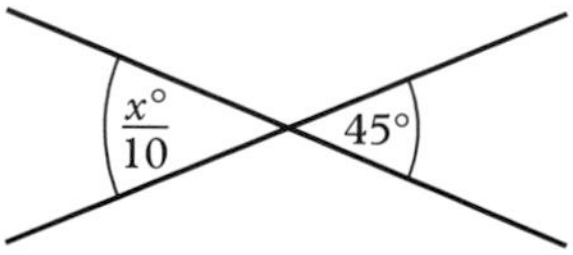

16

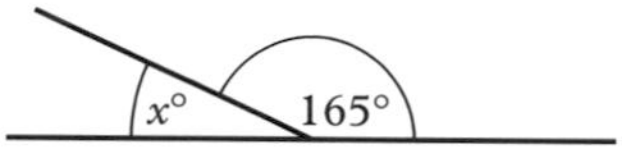

19

17

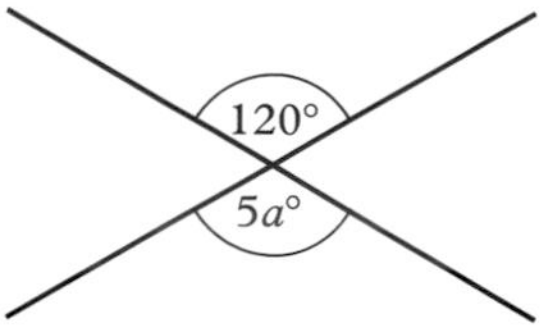

20

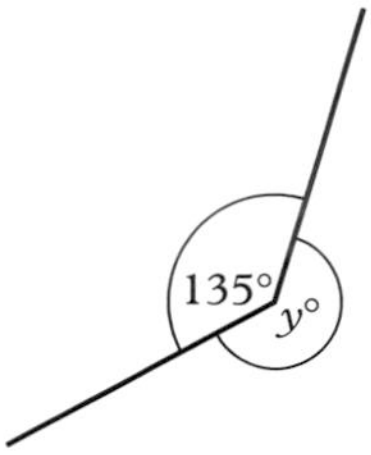

Solve the equations in Questions **21–24** by trial and improvement.

21 $4x + 41 = 197$

23 $y^2 = 361$

22 $5a - 64 = 76$

24 $x^2 = 24\,336$

Draw the inverse function machine for these:

1 → [$\times 5$] → [-7] →

2 → [$\div 2$] → [-8] →

Solve these equations:

3 $3x + 8 = 29$

4 $5y - 11 = 19$

5 $\frac{c}{5} + 10 = 16$

6 $8 + 2x = 20$

7 $10 + \frac{x}{3} = 16$

8 $3q + 11 = 11$

In Questions **9–12** change the words into algebra.
Solve the equation to find the number.

9 I think of a number and multiply it by 2. I then add 8.
The answer is 26.

10 I think of a number and divide it by 10. I then subtract 2.
The answer is 6.

11 I add 14 to a number. The answer is 41.

12 I think of a number, multiply it by 11 and then subtract 7.
The answer is 37.

Solve the equations in Questions **13–16** by trial and improvement.

13 $x^2 + 4x = 3965$

14 $x^3 = 512$ *Remember*: x^3 means $x \times x \times x$

15 $x^2 + 5x = 414$

16 $y^3 = 21\,952$

In Quesions **17–19** write down an equation and solve it.

17

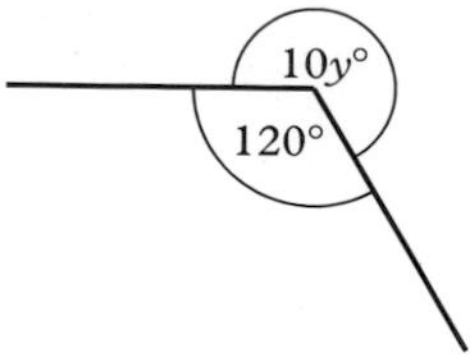

18

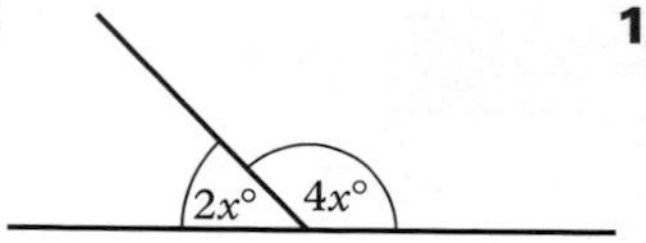

19

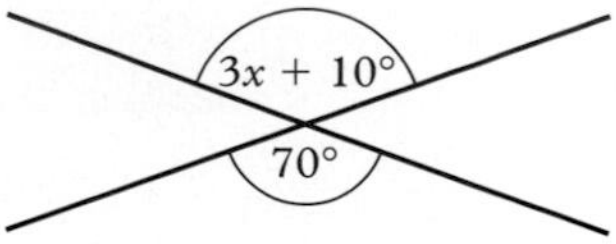

Crossnumber puzzle

Copy the crossnumber.
Solve each equation and put the answers in your crossnumber.

Across	Down
1 $\frac{x}{2} = 7$	**1** $x - 5 = 10$
2 $4x = 8$	**2** $x + 6 = 30$
3 $x - 5 = 7$	**4** $\frac{x}{5} = 4$
5 $\frac{x}{2} + 11 = 18$	**6** $\frac{x}{5} = 7$
7 $x - 6 = 10$	**7** $2x - 6 = 20$
8 $\frac{x}{5} = 3$	**8** $\frac{x}{3} - 4 = 2$
9 $x - 3 = 20$	**9** $3x + 5 = 80$
11 $4x + 2 = 50$	**10** $\frac{x}{11} + 6 = 8$
12 The value of $5x + 10$ when x is 9	**11** $5x - 60 = 20$
13 The value of $2x + 2$ when $x = 12$	

- The inverse returns you to where you started.

Operation	Inverse operation
$+3$	-3
-5	$+5$
$\times 4$	$\div 4$
$\div 2$	$\times 2$

- We can use a function machine to represent 'add 10'.

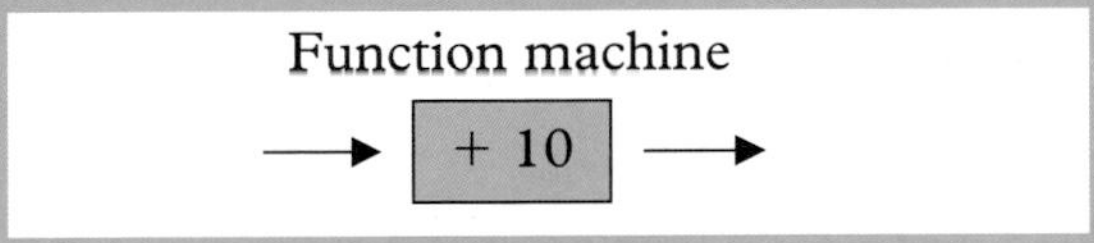

- We can show the inverse by drawing the function machine backwards.

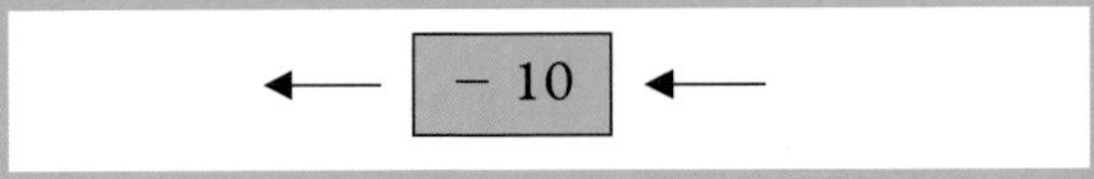

- A function machine can have more than one step.

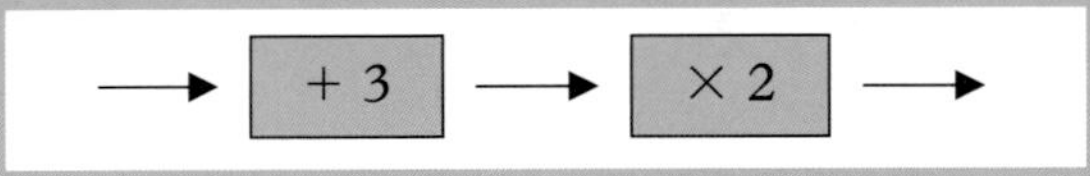

- The inverse function machine is:

- Function machines can be used to solve equations.

  Solve $x + 7 = 11$

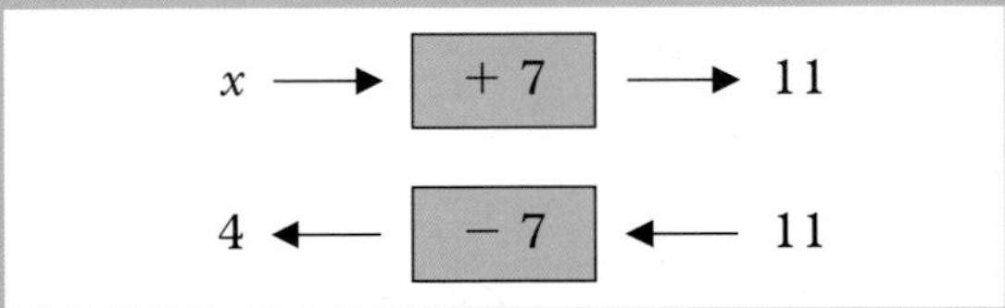

  Answer: $x = 4$

- Equations can be solved by trial and improvement.

  Guess what the answer is.
  Try a better guess.

Solve $2x + 14 = 50$

Value of x	Value of $2x + 14$	
10	$2 \times 10 + 14 = 34$	too small
20	$2 \times 20 + 14 = 54$	too big
19	$2 \times 19 + 14 = 52$	too big
18	$2 \times 18 + 14 = 50$	correct

Answer: $x = 18$

Write down the inverse of these operations.

1 add 3

2 multiply by 6

3 divide by 7

4 subtract 10

Draw the inverse function machines for these.

5 → [+ 2] → [× 10] →

6 → [÷ 8] → [− 2] →

Solve these equations by drawing inverse machines.

7 $x + 10 = 27$

8 $5y = 30$

9 $\frac{c}{4} = 8$

10 $2x - 13 = 17$

11 Change these words into algebra. Solve the equation.
I think of a number and divide it by 4. The answer is 8.
Find the number.

12 Solve this equation by trial and improvement:
$7x + 153 = 384$

In Questions **13** and **14** write down the equation and solve it.

13

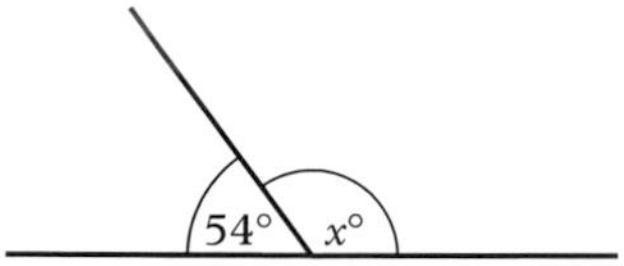

14

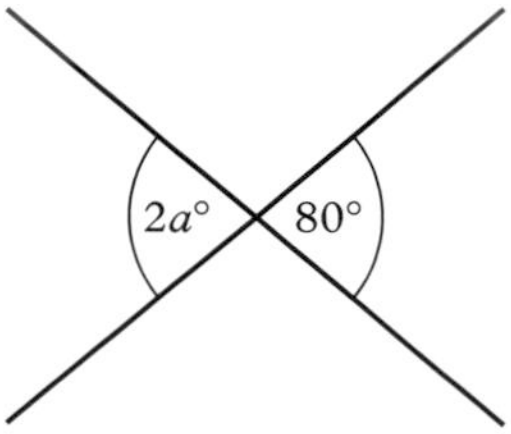

14 Area and perimeter

CORE

1 **Irregular shapes**

2 **Areas of rectangles**

3 **Perimeters of shapes**

4 **Areas of triangles and parallelograms**

5 **Compound shapes**

QUESTIONS

EXTENSION

SUMMARY

TEST YOURSELF

Four countries make up the United Kingdom. You may be surprised to see the area they cover compared with the number of people who live in each country:

- England has an area of 50 333 square miles and a population of 48.3 million
- Scotland has an area of 30 405 square miles and a population of 4.9 million
- Wales has an area of 8016 square miles and a population of 2.9 million
- Northern Ireland has an area of 5462 square miles and a population of 1.6 million.

But compare all these with Canada, which has an area of 3 851 800 square miles and a population of only 27.7 million.

1 Irregular shapes

Carpet-fitters are covering the floor space of this room. They are using square carpet tiles. Around the edges of the room is the skirting board.

The total distance around the room is the length of skirting board plus the width of the door. This distance is the perimeter of the room.

Perimeter

The total distance around the outside edges of a shape is its **perimeter**.

The perimeter of this shape is 14 cm.

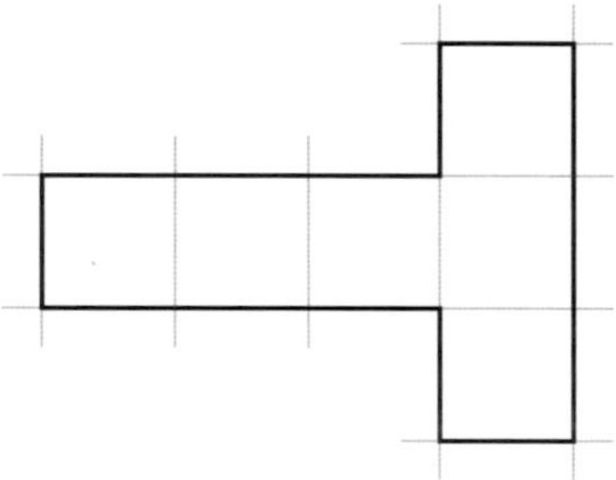

Exercise 14:1

You will need 1 cm squared paper for this exercise.

1 Copy these hexominoes on to squared paper.

a **b** **c** **d**

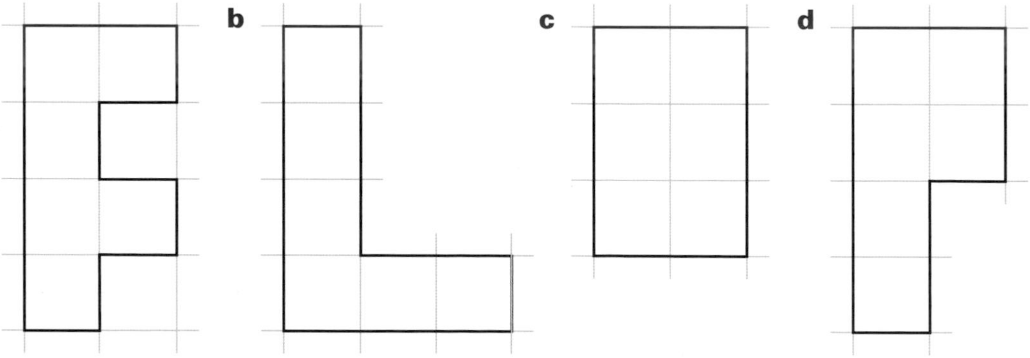

Write down the perimeter of each one.

2 **a** Draw a square of side 3 cm on squared paper.
b What is the perimeter of this square?
c Which hexomino in Question **1** has the same perimeter as this square?

3 **a** Copy this shape on to squared paper.
b Write down the perimeter of this shape.
c Which hexomino in Question **1** has the same perimeter?

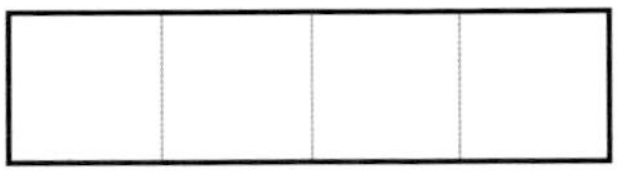

4 Copy these on to squared paper.

a

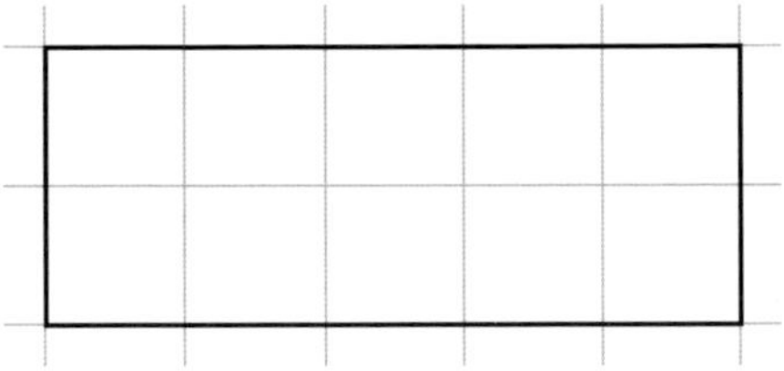

Number of squares = …
Perimeter = … cm

b

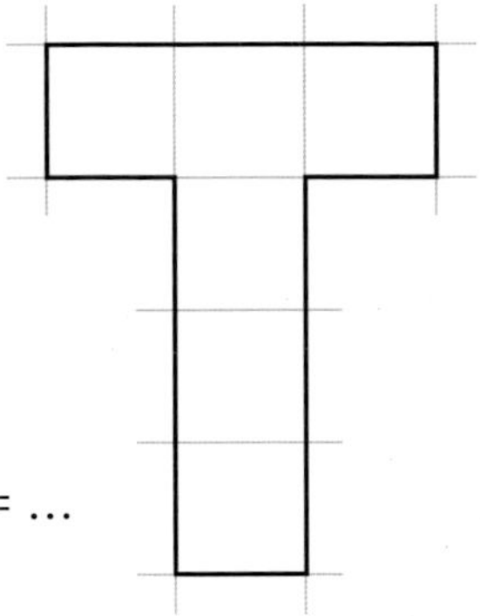

Number of squares = …
Perimeter = … cm

• **5** **a** Draw a new shape with a perimeter of 14 cm.
b Write down the number of squares inside your shape.

Area

The amount of space inside a 2-D shape is called the **area** of that shape.
Area is measured using squares.

The area of this shape is 6 cm^2.

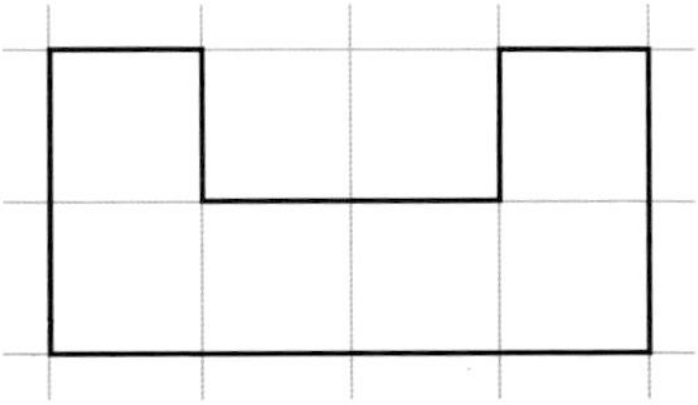

Area is measured in squares. Suppose you have to find the area of a leaf. Here is an easy way of counting bits of squares.

Count whole squares first. There are 30 whole squares.

Now count squares which lie more than half inside the outline. There are 10 of these.

An **estimate** of the area of the leaf is 30 + 10 = 40 squares.

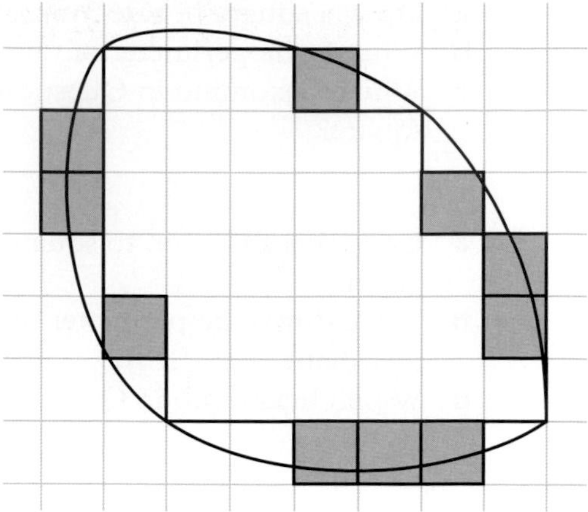

Exercise 14:2

1 Estimate the area of these leaves in cm^2 by counting squares.

Copy and complete:

a Number of whole squares ....
Number of part squares ....
Estimate of area .... cm^2

b Number of whole squares ....
Number of part squares ....
Estimate of area .... cm^2

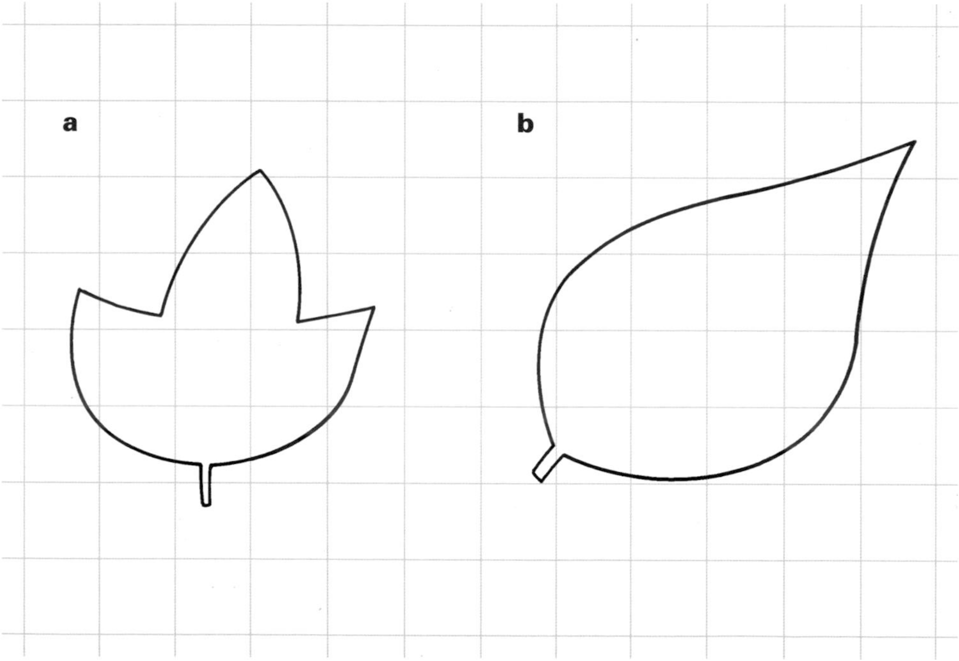

2 Areas of rectangles

Angela is painting a ceiling. The label on her tin of paint gives the area that the paint should cover.
Angela needs to know the area of the ceiling.

Exercise 14:3

1 **a** Write down the length of this rectangle.
b Write down the width of this rectangle.
c Write down the area of this rectangle.

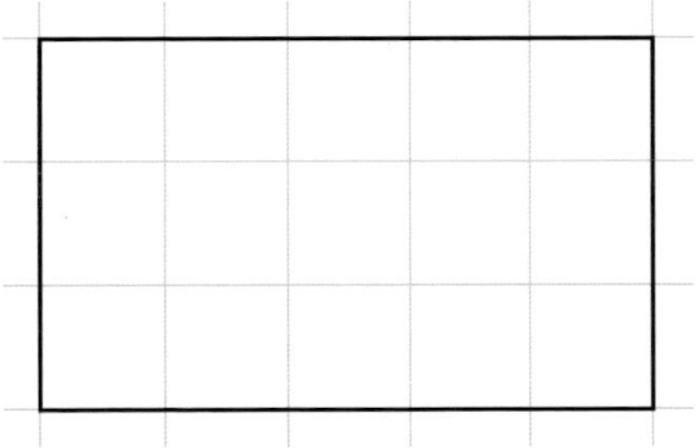

There is a rule for finding the area of a rectangle.

Area of a rectangle

Area of a rectangle = **l**ength × **w**idth
$A = l \times w$ or $A = lw$

Example

Calculate the area of this rectangle.

$A = lw$
$A = 5 \times 3$
$A = 15 \text{ cm}^2$

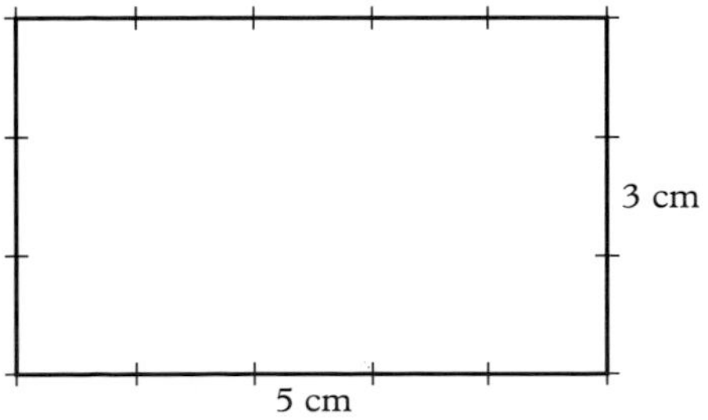

2 Use the formula $A = lw$ to find the areas of these rectangles.

a

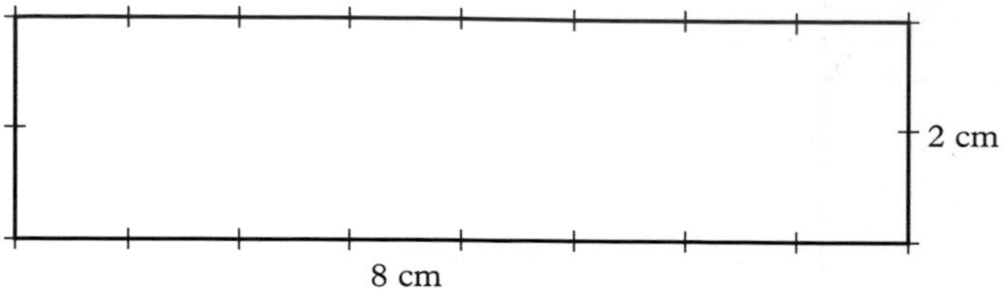

b

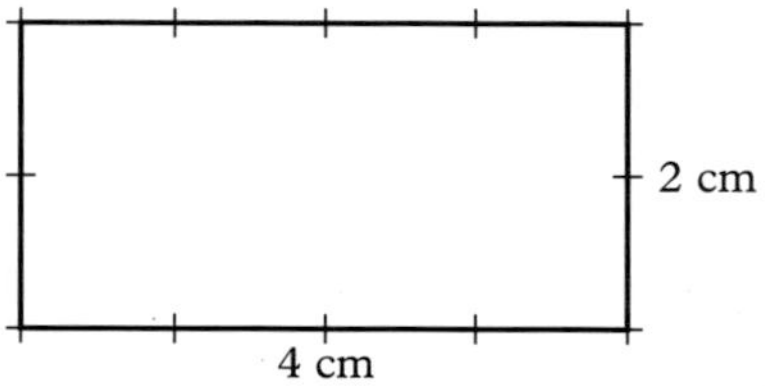

c

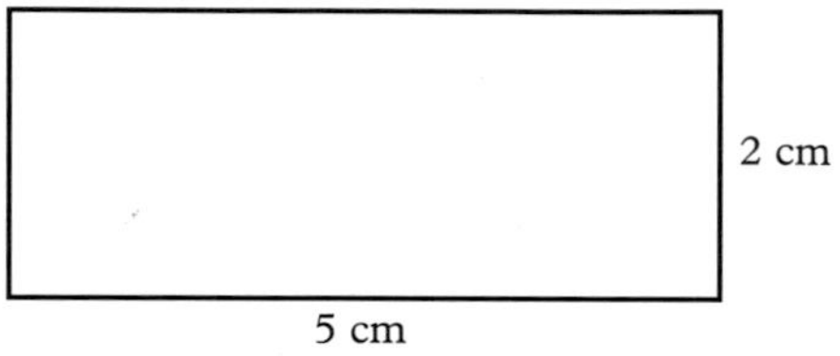

3 These rectangles have sides which are whole numbers of centimetres.
In each case, measure the length.
Measure the width.
Use the formula to calculate the area.

a

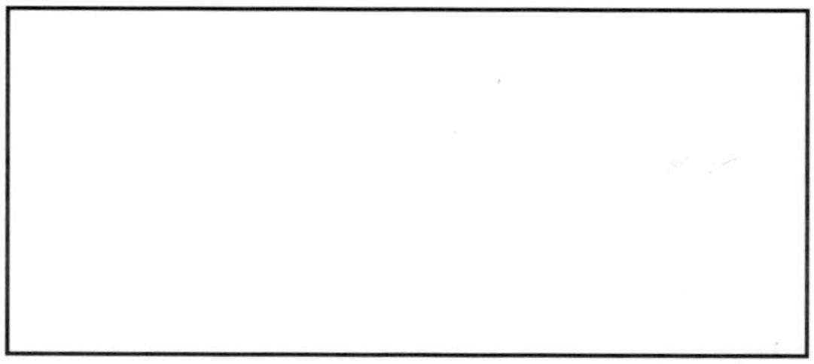

b

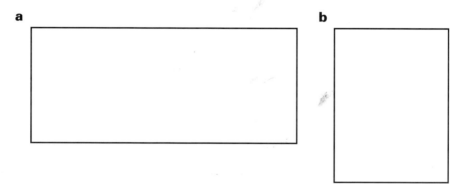

4 Use the formula $A = lw$ to calculate the areas of these rectangles.
You may need a calculator to help you.

a

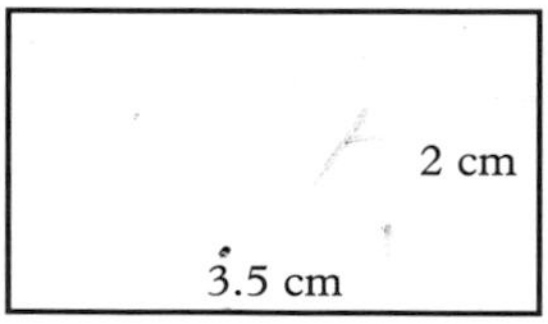

b

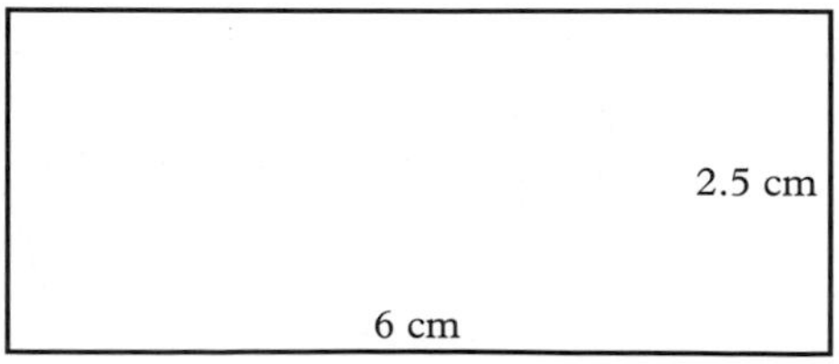

c

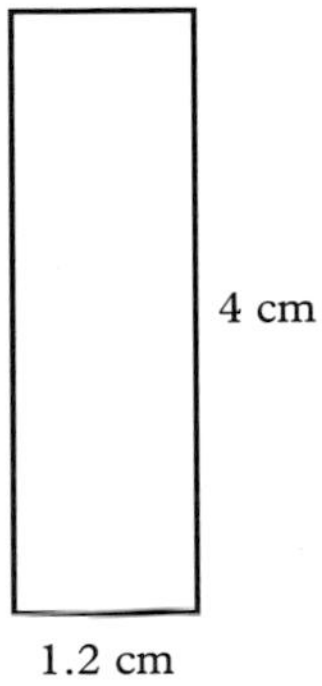

d

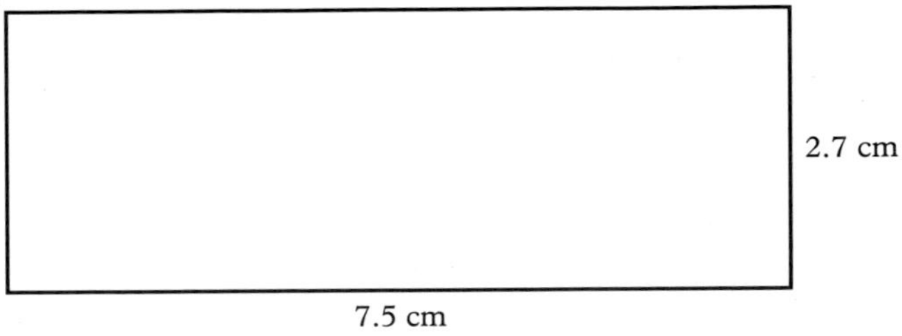

5 Squares are special rectangles.
Use the formula $A = lw$ to calculate the areas of these squares.

a

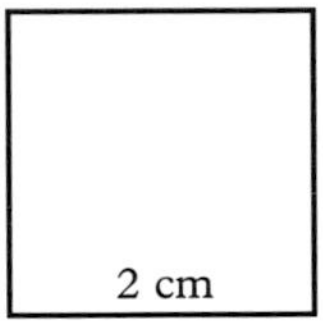

b

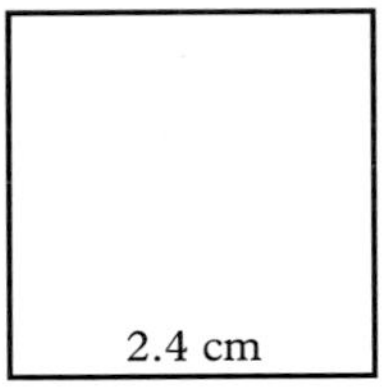

c

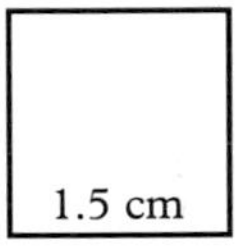

6 Here are some sketches of rectangles.
Calculate their areas.

a

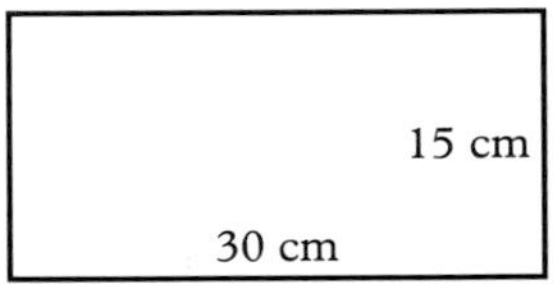

b

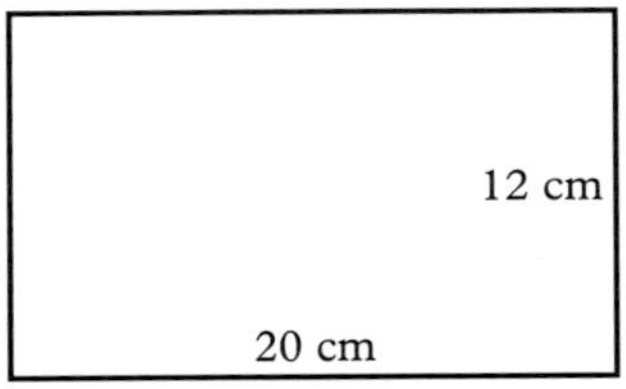

c

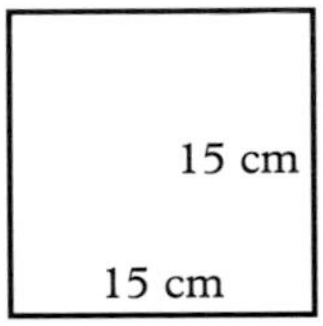

d

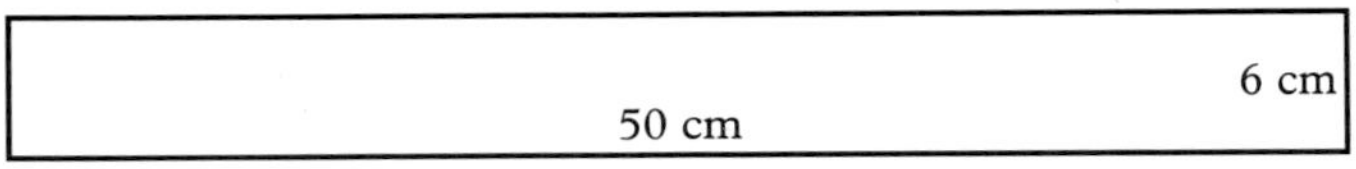

e

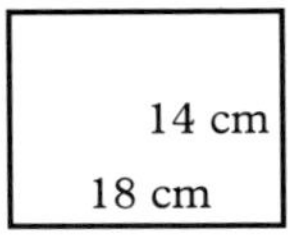

● **7** Draw a square. Make its sides 5 cm long.
- **a** What is the area of the square?
- **b** The square you have drawn is called a 5 cm square. Does this mean its area is 5 cm^2?
- **c** Draw a shape with an area of 5 cm^2.

Exercise 14:4 To find the largest area that will fit inside a loop of string

You need a piece of string and some 1 cm squared paper.

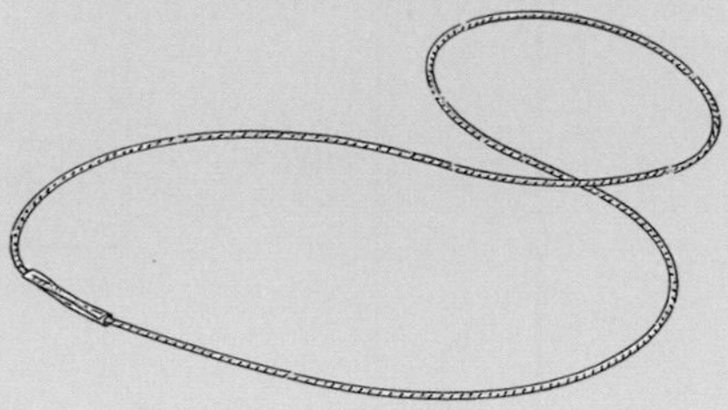

1 Cut a piece of string exactly 24 cm long. Sellotape its ends together like this.

2 Here are two rectangles inside the string. What are their areas?

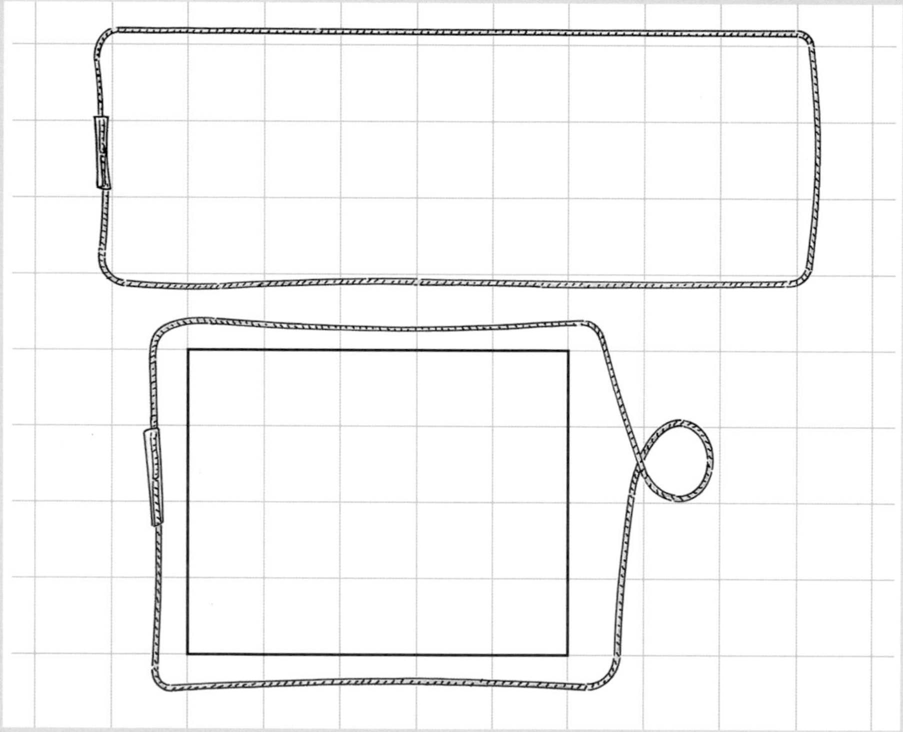

3 Copy this table for your results.

Length l	Width w	Area A
9	3	…
5	4	…

4 Find some more rectangles.

5 What is the largest rectangle that will fit inside the string?

6 Find some other shapes that fit inside.

7 What is the largest area that will fit?

Here are some very small leaves. We need to use very small squares to measure the area of these.

We need to use very large squares to measure the area of the classroom floor.

Units of area

Area is measured in square units. These can be **mm^2**, **cm^2**, **m^2** or **km^2**. Imperial units of in^2, ft^2, yd^2 or $miles^2$ can also be used. A postage stamp would be in mm^2 and a garden in m^2.

Exercise 14:5

1 Suggest units of area to measure these. Choose from mm^2, cm^2, m^2 or km^2.

a the page of an exercise book.
b the floor of your classroom.
c the çity of Liverpool.
d a fingernail.
e a television screen.
f a tennis court.
g the wing of a fly.
h the country of Wales.

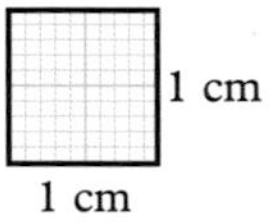

2 a What is the area of this square in cm^2?
b Write down the length of the square in mm.
c Write down the width of the square in mm.
d What is the area of this square in mm^2?
e Copy and complete $1\ cm^2 = \ldots\ mm^2$.

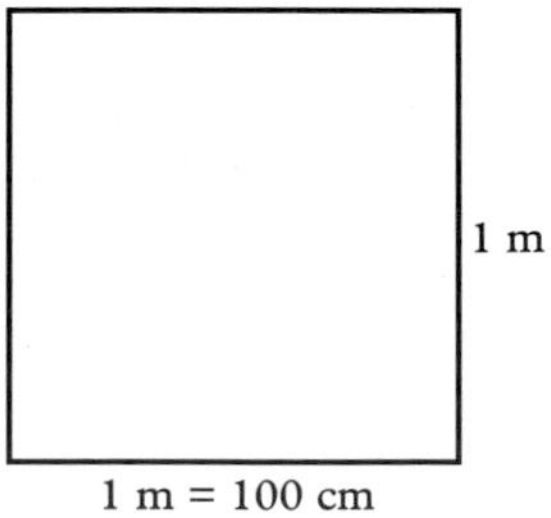

3 a What is the area of this square in m^2?
b Write down the length of the square in cm.
c Write down the width of the square in cm.
d What is the area of this square in cm^2?
e Copy and complete $1\ m^2 = \ldots\ cm^2$.

• **4** 12 in = 1 ft.

Copy and complete:

a The area of the square is … ft^2.
b The length of the square is … in.
c The width of the square is … in.
d The area of the square is … in^2.
e 1 ft^2 = … in^2.

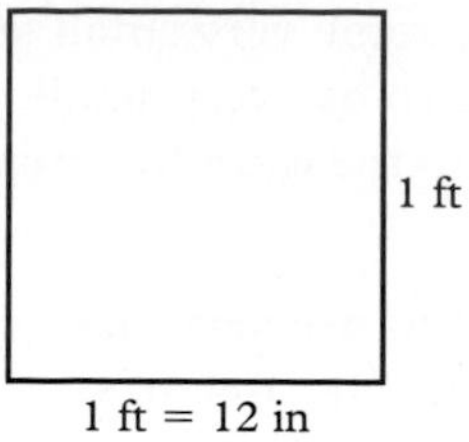

Exercise 14:6

1 A garage floor is a rectangle 5 m by 3 m.
Find the area of the floor.

2 A rug is a rectangle 2 m by 1.5 m.
Calculate the area of the rug.

3 A football pitch is 100 m by 72 m.
Calculate the area of the pitch.

4 A4 paper is 297 mm long and 210 mm wide.
Calculate the area of a sheet of A4 paper.

• **5** A classroom is 8 m by 6 m.
a What is the area of the classroom floor?
b To fit carpet costs £10 for 1 m^2.
How much would it cost to carpet the classroom?

• **6** First class stamps are 20 mm by 24 mm.
a What is the area of one stamp?
b Stamps are sold in sheets of ten stamps in a book.
What is the area of a sheet of ten stamps?

Example Find the width of this rectangle

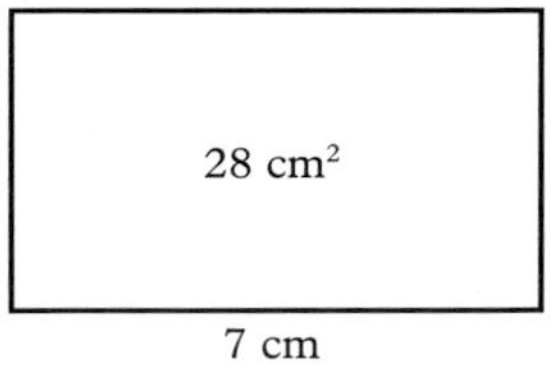

We know area = length × width

so 28 = 7 × width

We divide 28 by 7 to find the width.

$$\text{width} = \frac{28}{7}$$
$$= 4\text{ cm}$$

Exercise 14:7

Find the missing length or width of these rectangles:

1

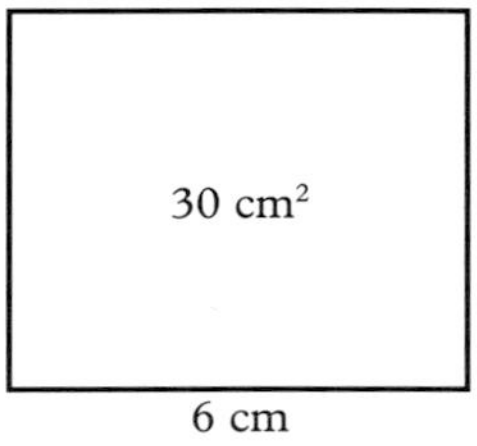

2

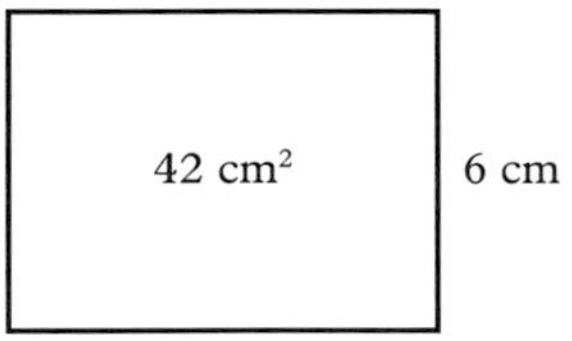

3

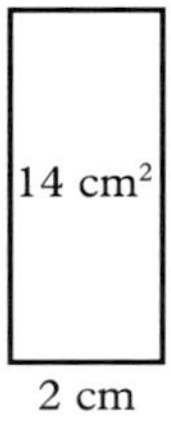

4

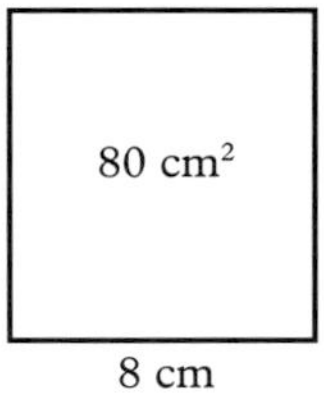

5

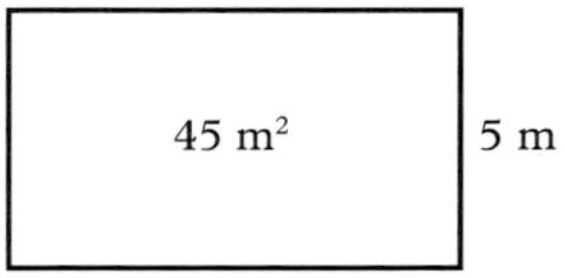

6

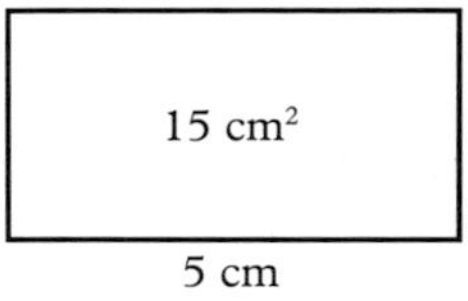

7 The area of a roller skating rink is 3000 m^2. The length is 100 m. What is the width?

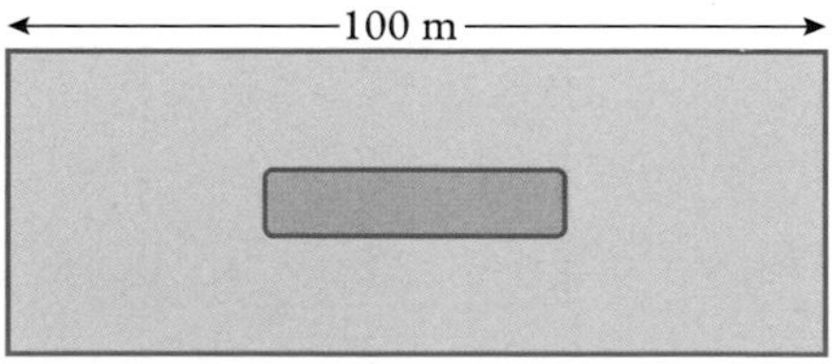

3 Perimeters of shapes

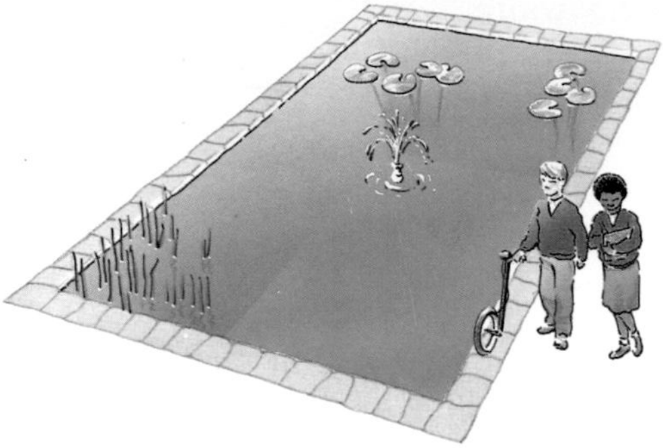

These pupils are measuring the distance around the Stanthorne High School pond.

The perimeter is the distance all the way round the outside of a shape.

Example

Find the perimeter of this rectangle.

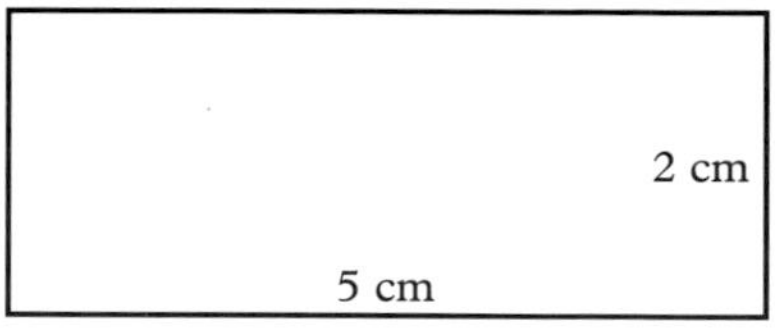

Perimeter $= 5 + 2 + 5 + 2$

$= 14$ cm

Exercise 14:8

1 Find the perimeters of these shapes.
You need to measure the sides.

a

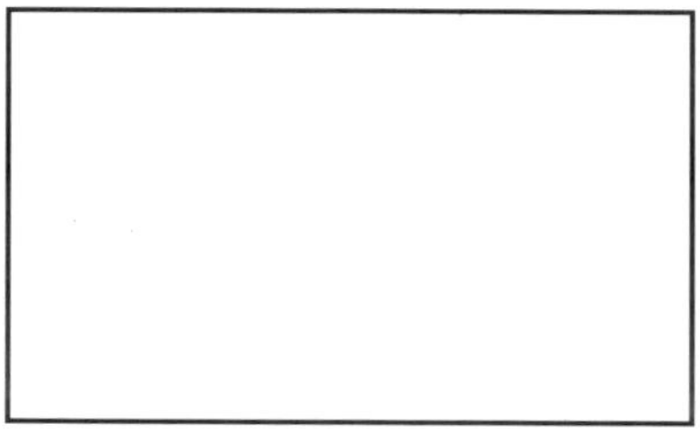

c

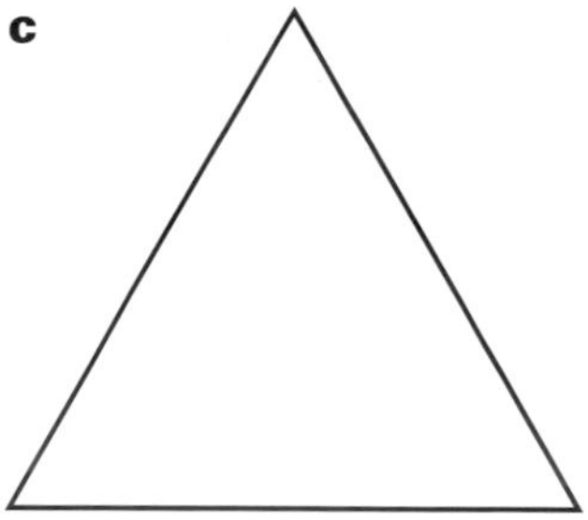

b

d

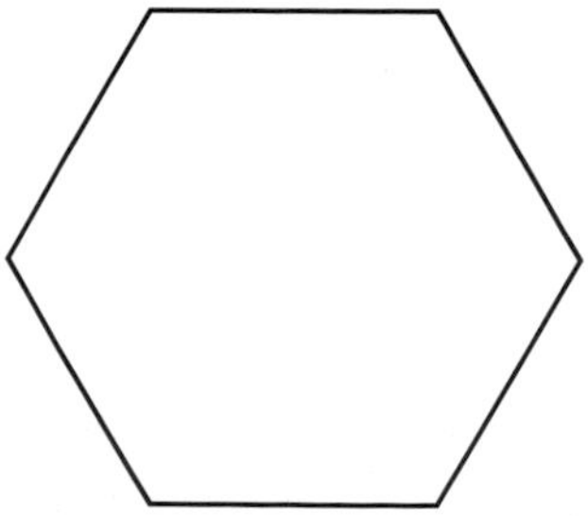

2 Here are some sketches of shapes.
Find the perimeters of the shapes.

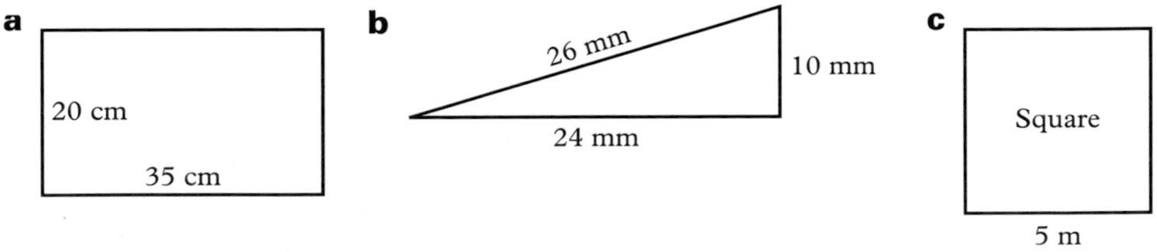

Exercise 14:9

1 A rectangle is 7 cm long and 4 cm wide.
What is its perimeter?

2 An equilateral triangle has each side 5 cm.
What is its perimeter?

3 A square has each side 10 cm.
What is its perimeter?

4 A rectangular bookmark has a gold edge. The bookmark is 14 cm by 4 cm.
How long is the gold edge?

5 Binding tape is put round the edge of a rug. The rug is 2 m by 3 m.
How much binding is needed?

● **6** A garden is 20 m by 15 m.
A fence is put round the outside of the garden. A 2 m gap is left for a gate.
What is the length of the fence?

7 Braid is put round the edge of the tablemat shown.
a What length of braid is needed for one mat?
b What length of braid is needed for a set of six mats?

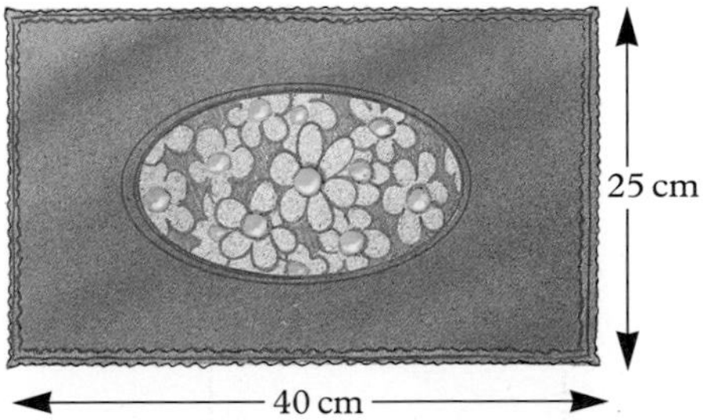

● **8** Skirting board is put round a room 6 m by 5 m. The door is 1 m wide.
What length of skirting board is needed?

4 Areas of triangles and parallelograms

Richard wants to grow grass on an old flower bed.

The bed is a triangle shape. Richard needs to know the area of the triangle.

He will then know how much grass seed to buy.

Exercise 14:10

1 Copy this table and fill it in.

	Area of rectangle	Area of triangle
a		
b		

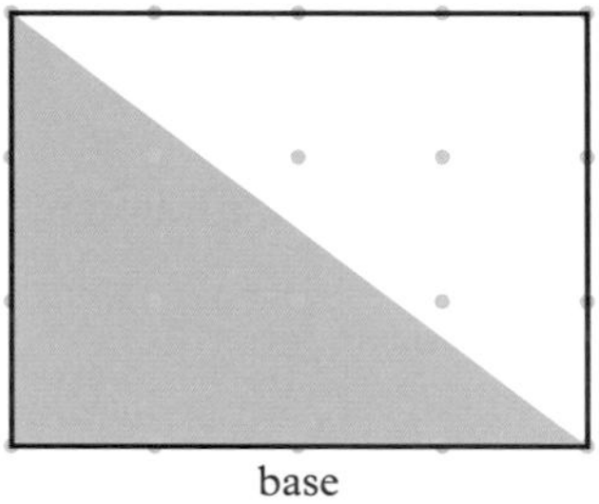

a

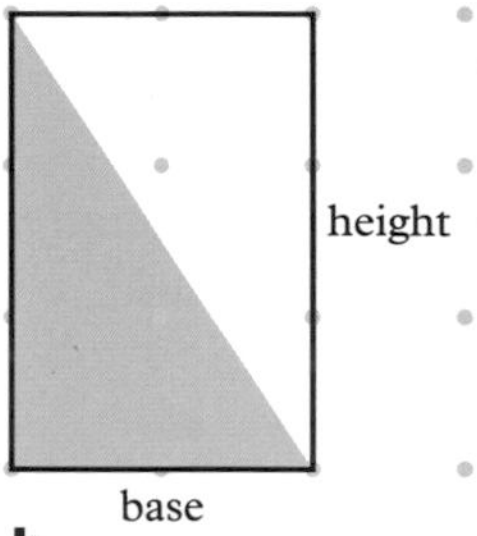

b

2 Draw some more rectangles and triangles of your own. Put these into your table. Can you find a rule for the area of a triangle from the area of its rectangle?

Here is a triangle.
We use **base** and **height** instead of length and width.

$$\text{Area of triangle} = \frac{\text{area of rectangle}}{2}$$

$$= \frac{\text{base} \times \text{height}}{2}$$

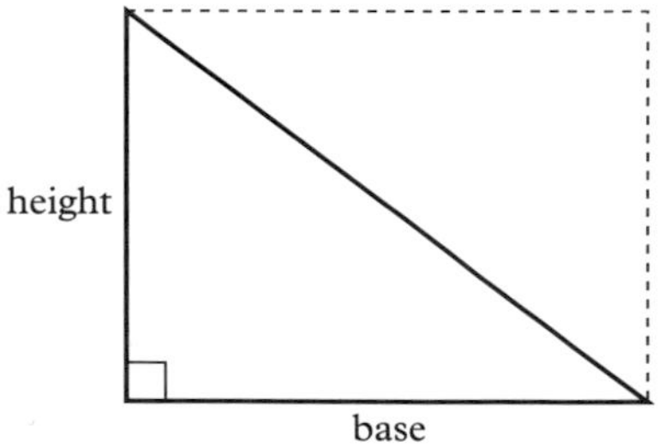

Example Find the area of this triangle.

$$\text{Area of triangle} = \frac{\text{base} \times \text{height}}{2}$$
$$= \frac{10 \times 8}{2}$$
$$= 40 \text{ cm}^2$$

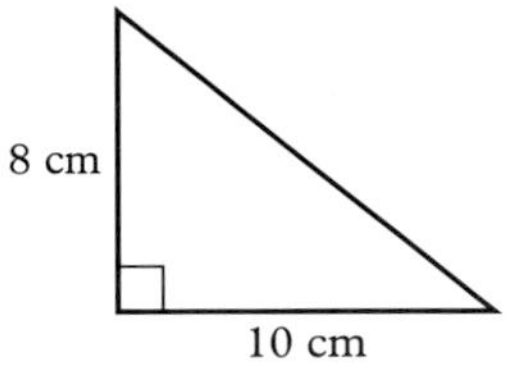

Exercise 14:11

Find the areas of these triangles.

1 Copy and complete:

$$\text{Area of triangle} = \frac{\text{base} \times \text{height}}{2}$$
$$= \frac{10 \times \ldots}{2}$$
$$= \ldots \text{ cm}^2$$

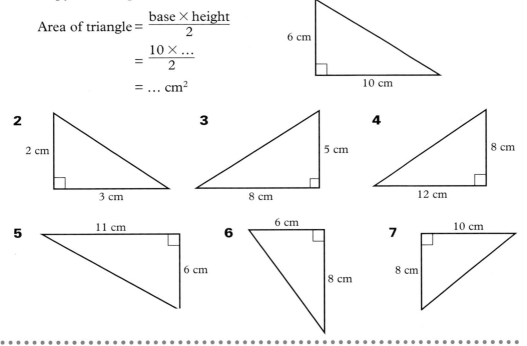

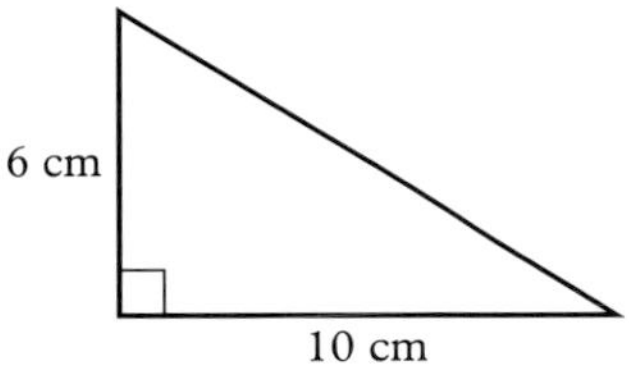

2

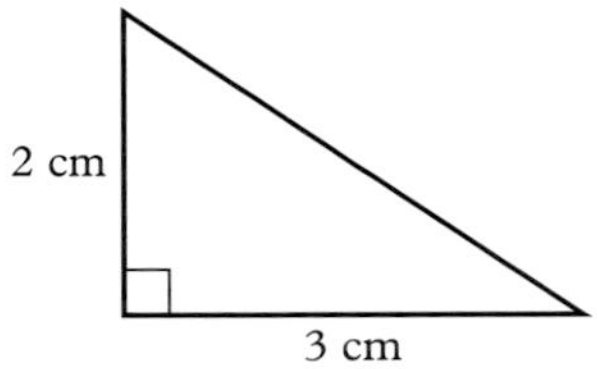

3

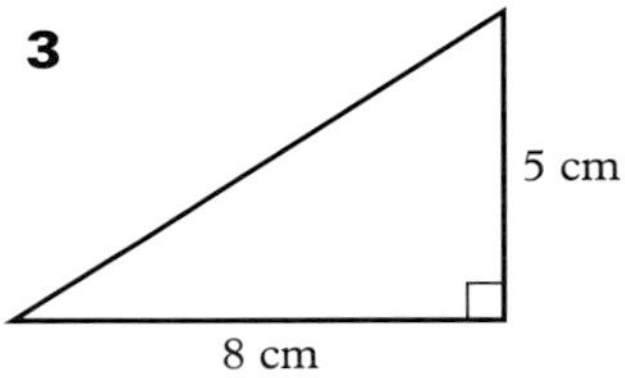

4

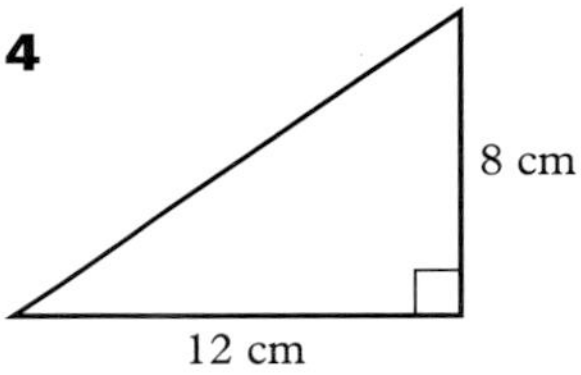

5

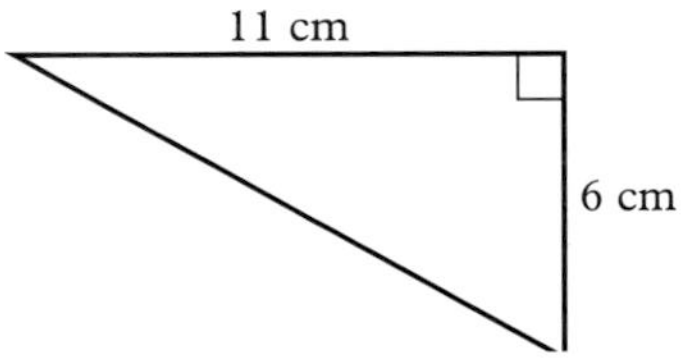

6

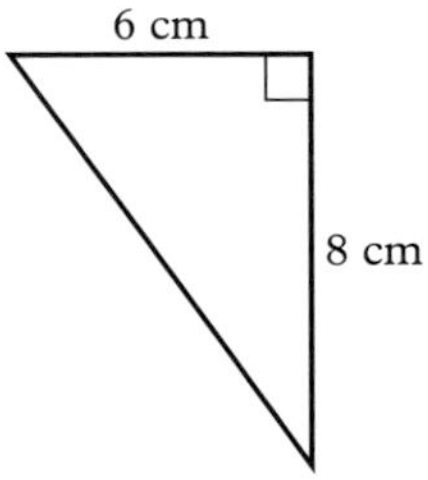

7

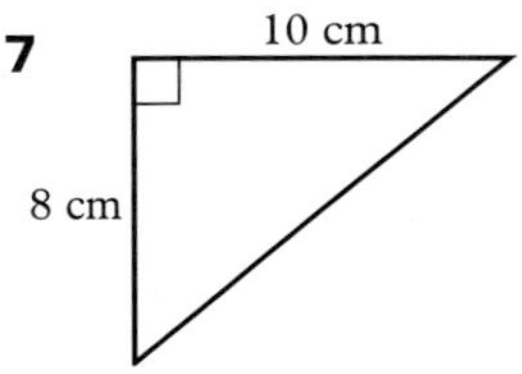

We can change the parallelogram to a rectangle by moving the triangle

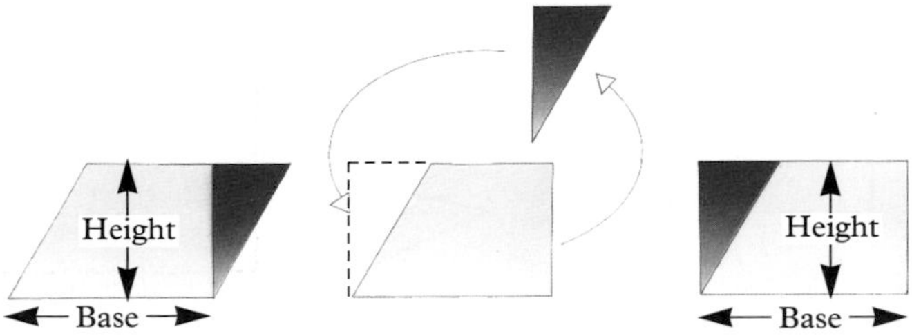

Area of parallelogram

Area of the parallelogram = Area of the rectangle
Area = base × height

Example Find the area of this parallelogram.

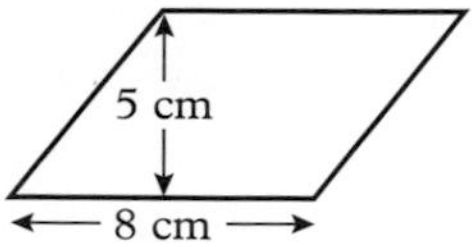

Area = base × height
$= 8 \times 5$
$= 40 \text{ cm}^2$

Exercise 14:12

Find the areas of these parallelograms.

1

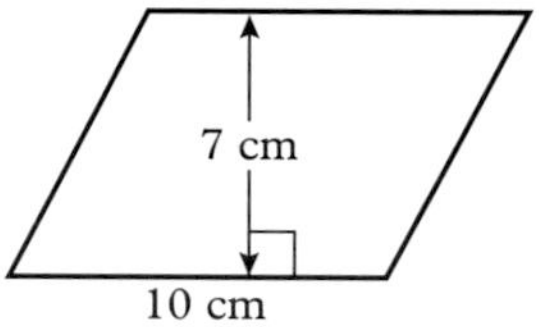

2

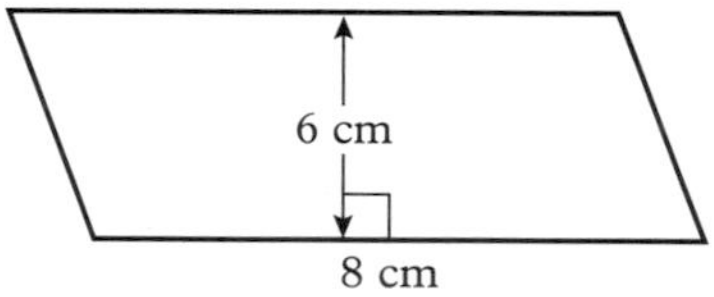

3

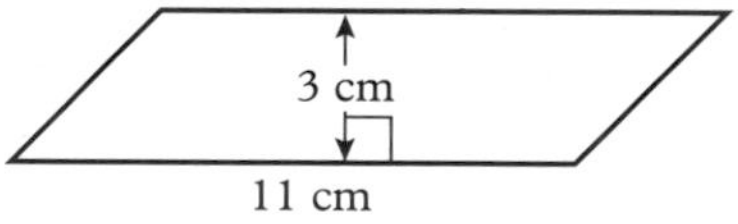

4

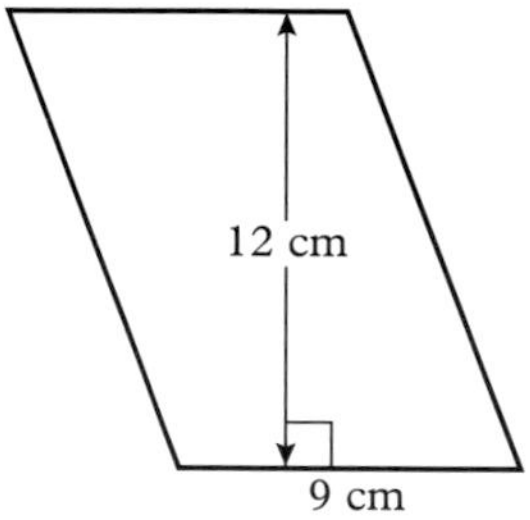

5

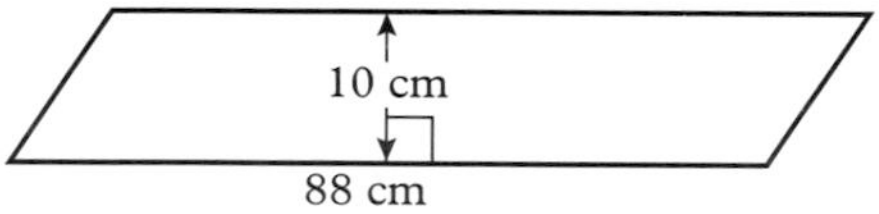

6

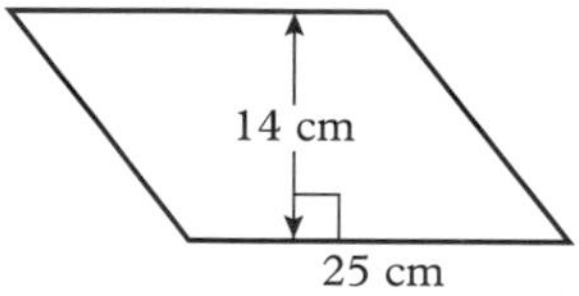

• **7** These parallelograms are drawn accurately.
Find their areas.

a

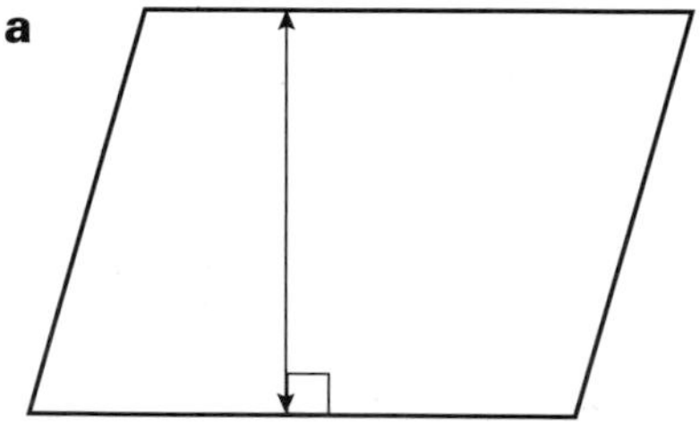

b

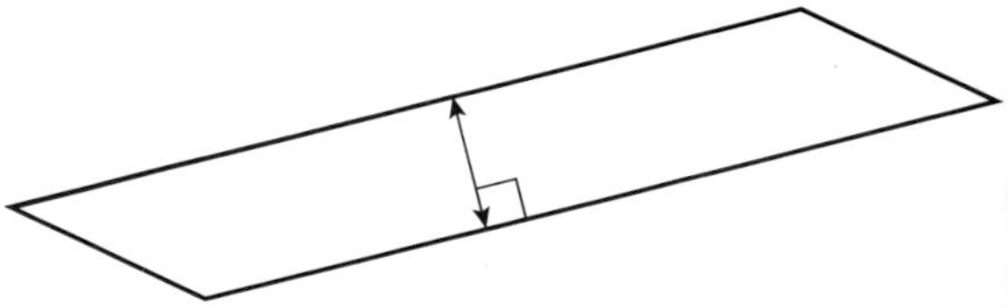

5 Compound shapes

Andrew is going to carpet a room. He needs to work out the area of the floor.
Andrew has a problem because the room is not a rectangle.

Example

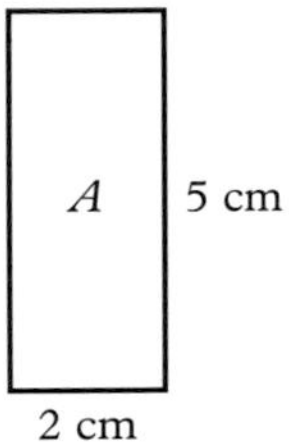

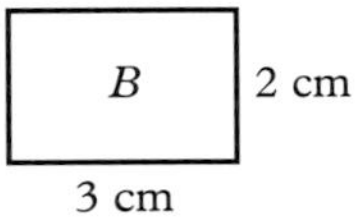

Area of rectangle A is $10\,\text{cm}^2$.

Area of rectangle B is $6\,\text{cm}^2$.

The two rectangles are joined.
The dashed line shows the join.

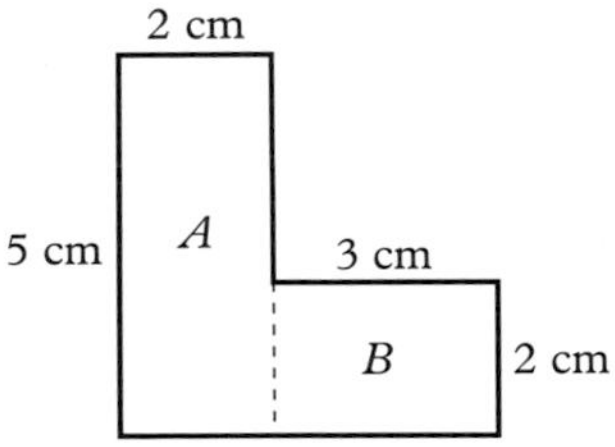

$$\begin{aligned}\text{Area of new shape} &= \text{area of } A + \text{area of } B \\ &= 10 + 6 \\ &= 16\,\text{cm}^2\end{aligned}$$

Exercise 14:13

1 **a** You can see the two rectangles that have been joined to make this shape.

Copy and complete:

Area of C = … cm^2
Area of D = … cm^2
Area of shape = … + …
= … cm^2

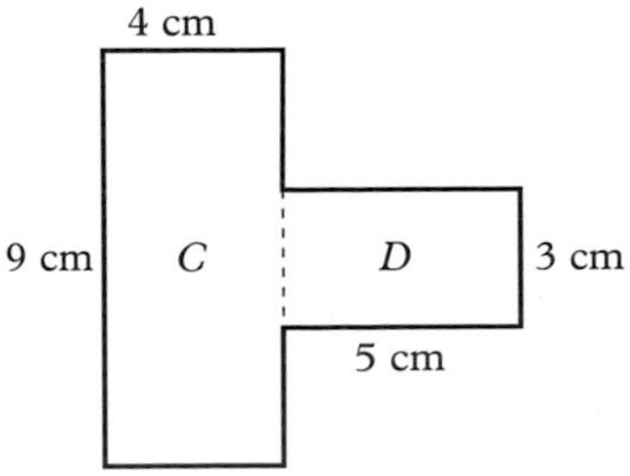

2 Find the area of this shape.

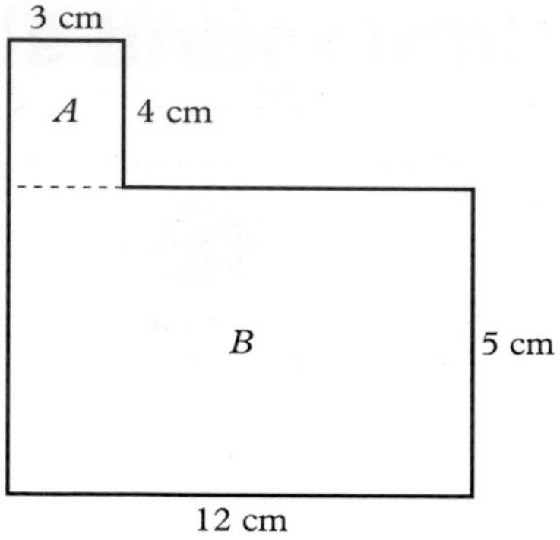

Copy and complete:

Area of A = … cm^2
Area of B = … cm^2
Area of shape = … + …
= … cm^2

Find the area of these shapes.

3

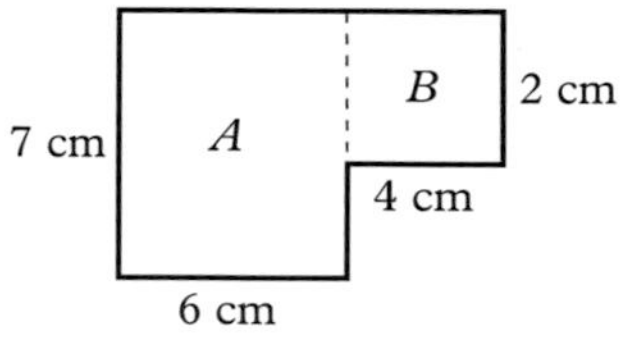

4

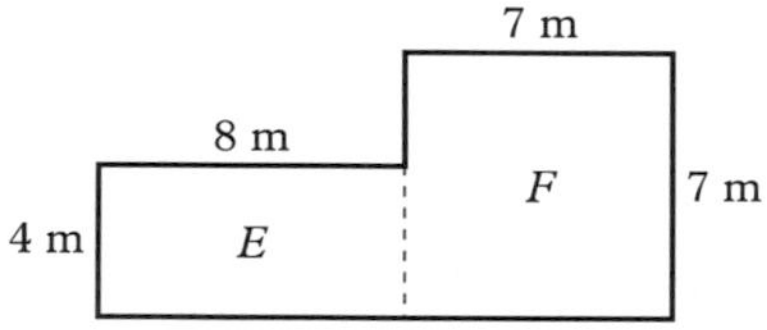

Example

Find the area of this shape.

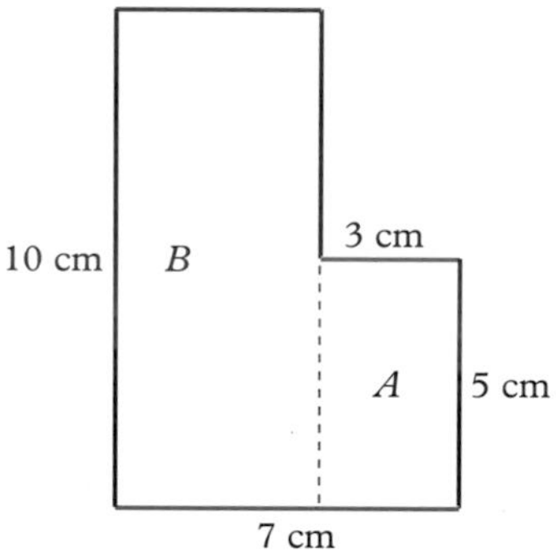

Area of $A = 3 \times 5\ cm^2$
$= 15\ cm^2$

The length of B is 10 cm.
We need to find the width.

red line + blue line = green line
red line + 3 = 7
so red line = 4 cm

Area of B = 4×10
= $40\ cm^2$

Area of shape = $15 + 40$
= $55\ cm^2$

---

5 Find the length of the blue lines in these shapes.

a

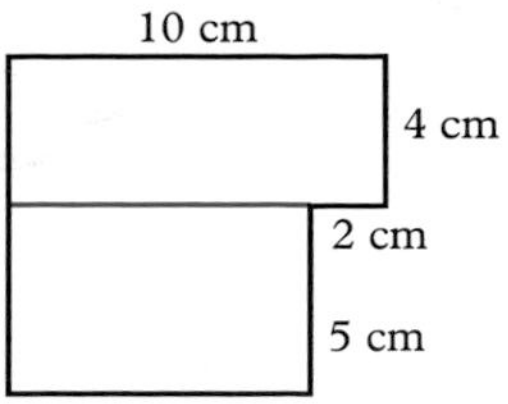

b

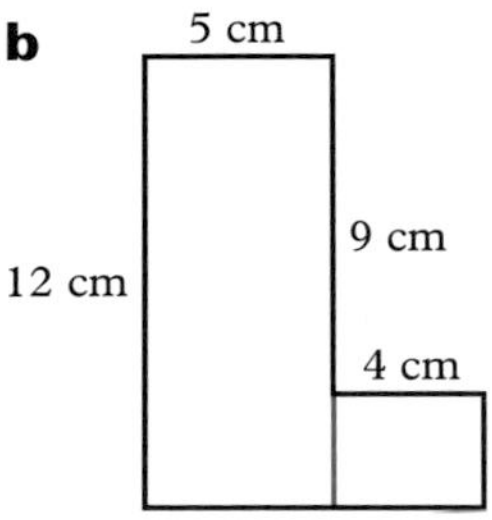

c

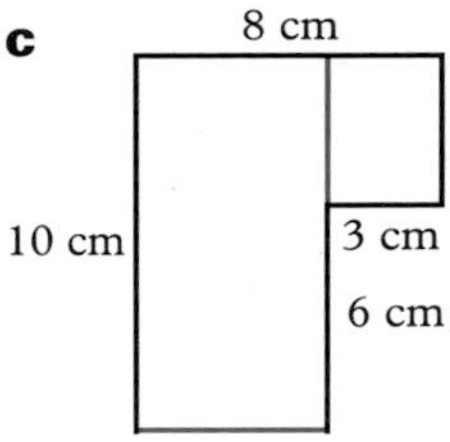

6 Find the area of each shape in Question 5.

Exercise 14:14

Use 1 cm squared paper for this exercise.

1 **a** Draw a rectangle 10 cm by 5 cm on squared paper.
Cut it out.
Work out the area of this rectangle.

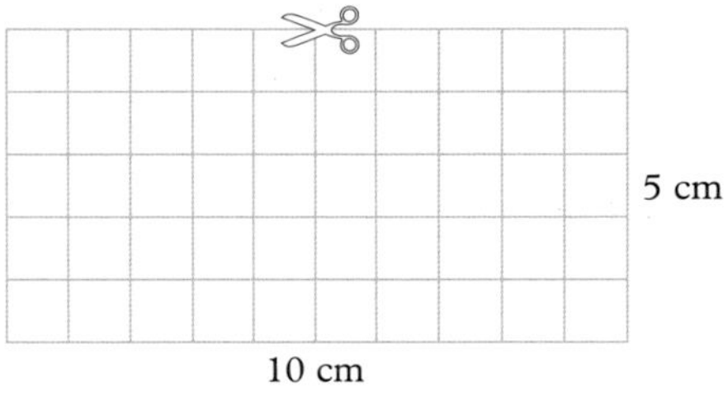

b Draw a rectangle 5 cm by 2 cm inside your rectangle.
Cut this out.
What is the area of the piece cut out?

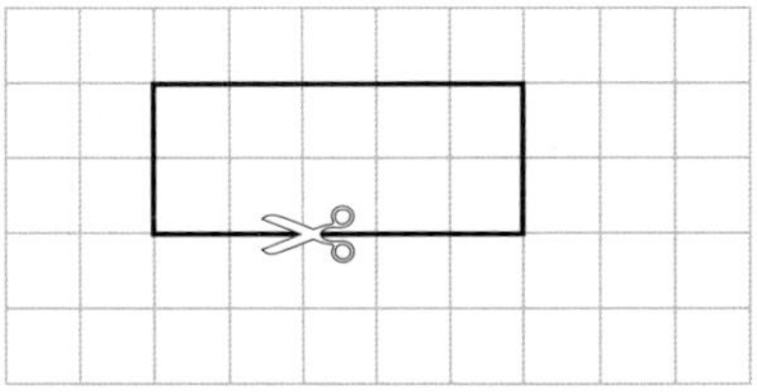

c The piece you have left looks like this:
what is the area of this piece?

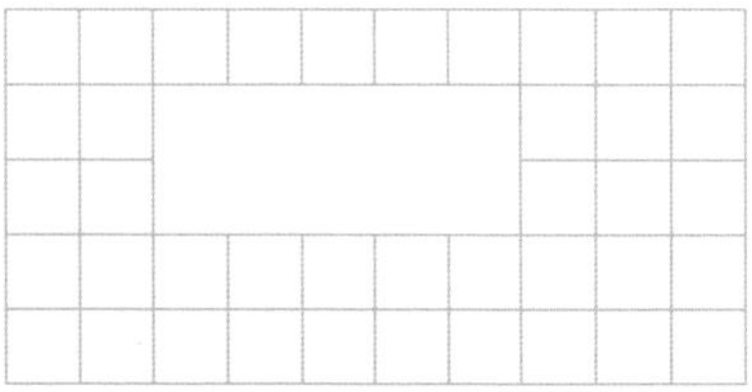

d Copy and complete:
Area of piece left = … − …
= … cm^2.

e Count the squares on the piece left to check your answer.

2 **a** Draw a new rectangle 6 cm by 8 cm.
Work out its area.

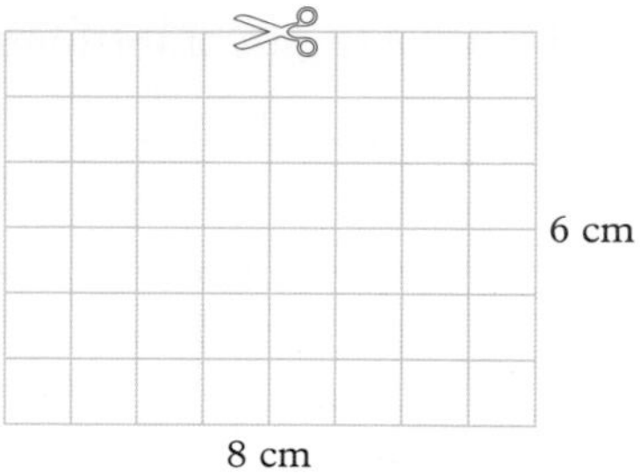

b Cut out a smaller rectangle 4 cm by 3 cm.
Work out its area.

c What is the area of the piece you have left?

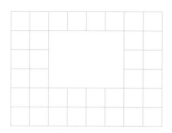

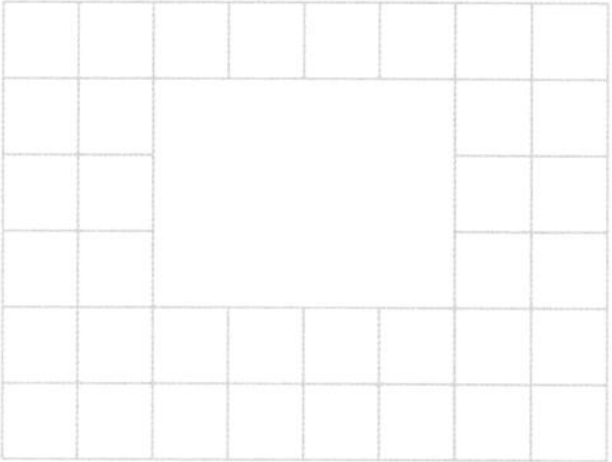

● **3** Laura wants to frame a picture. She has a piece of card 9 cm by 7 cm.

She cuts out a hole 5 cm by 3 cm to frame the picture.

What is the area of card left?

● **4** Look at this side of a house.

a What is the area of the big window?
b What is the area of a small window?
c What is the total area of the windows?
d What is the area of the whole side of the house?
e What is the area of the brickwork?

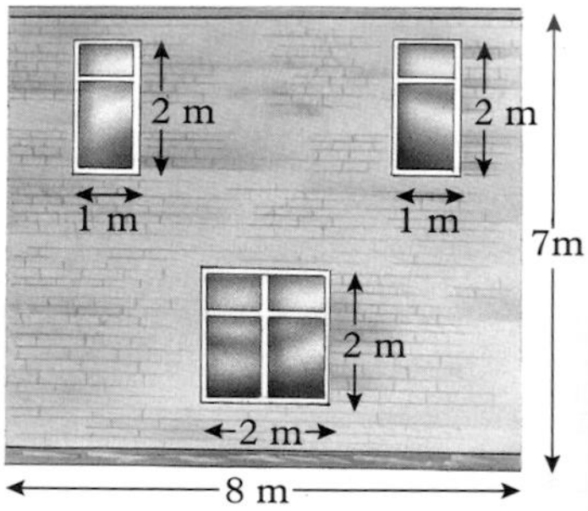

1 Here are three pentominoes.

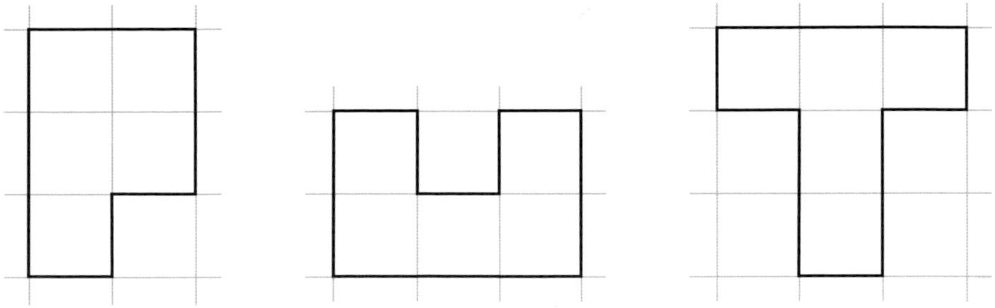

a Find the perimeter of each of the pentominoes.
b (1) What is the area of the 'P' pentomino?
(2) What is the area of the word 'PUT'?
(3) There are 12 pentominoes altogether.
What would be the area of all 12?

2 **a** What is the perimeter of this rectangle?
b What is the area of this rectangle?

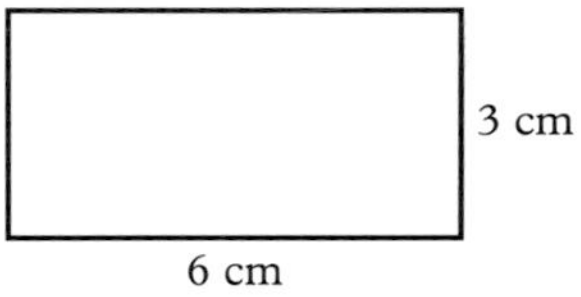

This is a special rectangle
The perimeter and area are the same number.
Only the units are different.

c Use 1 cm squared paper.
Draw these squares: 3 cm by 3 cm, 4 cm by 4 cm, 5 cm by 5 cm.
d Find the perimeter of each square.
Find the area of each square.
e Which square has the same number (but different units) for its perimeter and area?

3 Find the areas of these shapes.

a

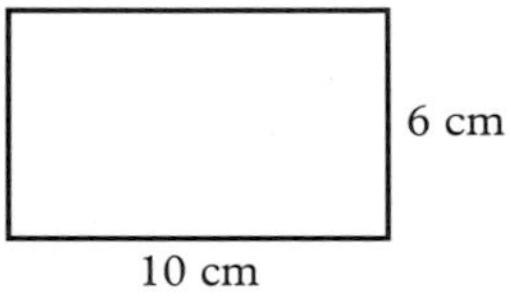

b

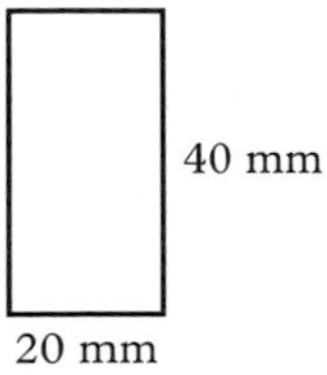

c

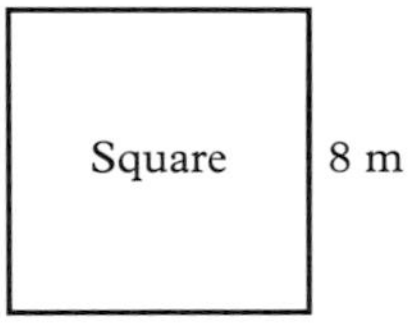

4 Find the perimeters of the shapes in Question **3**.

5 Find the areas of these triangles.

a

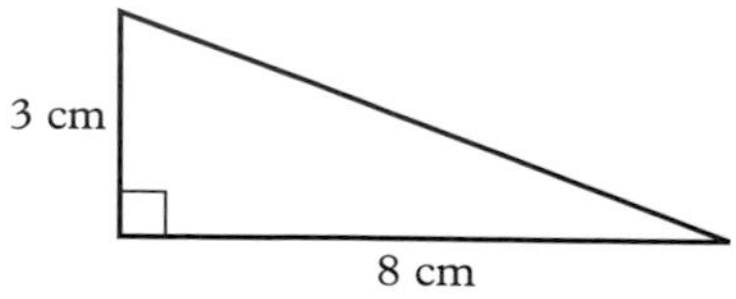

b

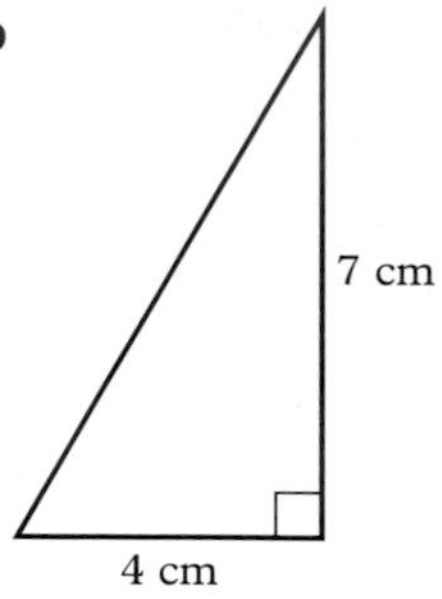

c

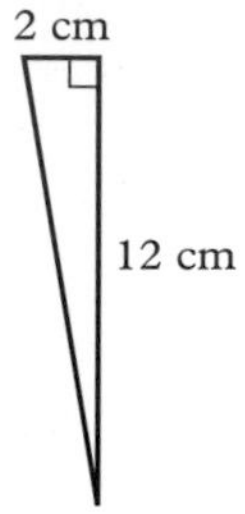

6 Find the areas of these parallelograms.

a

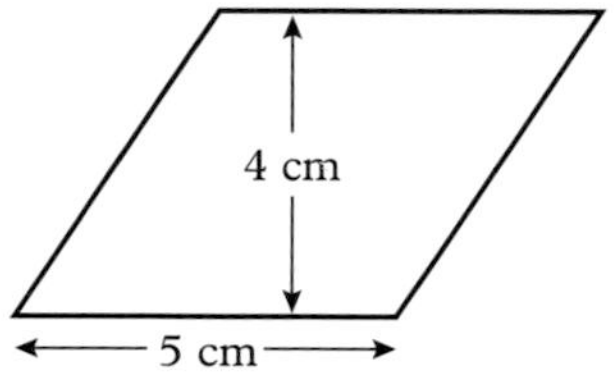

b

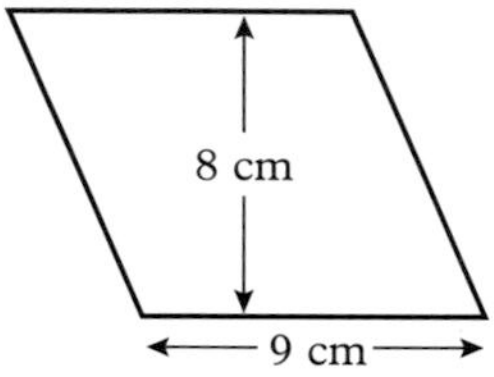

7 Find the areas of these shapes.

a

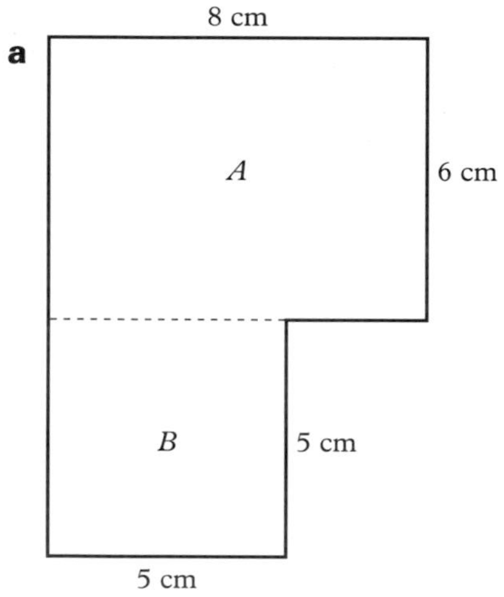

b

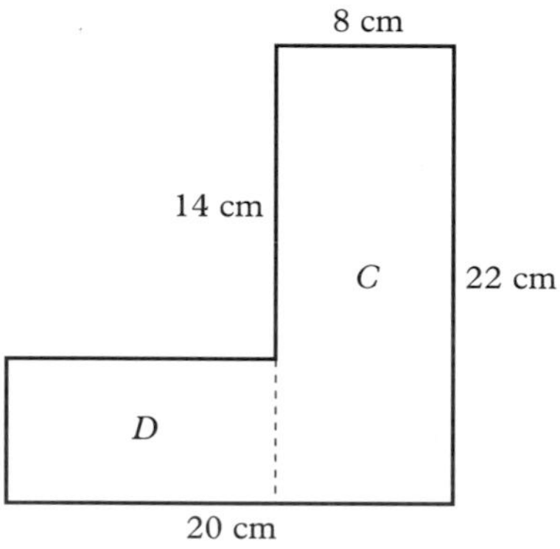

8 A pile of exercise books has been pushed over.

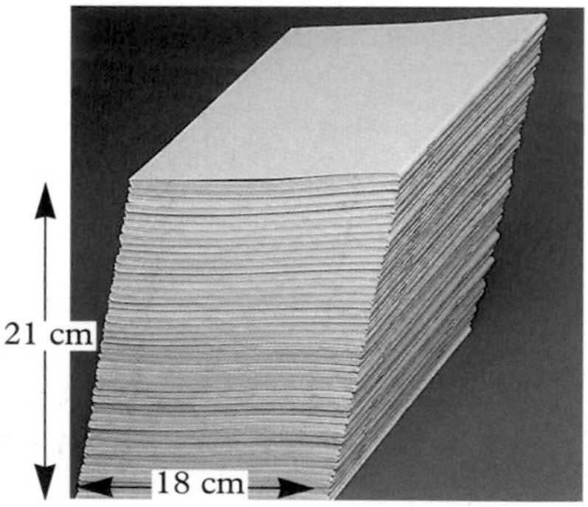

a The end of the pile forms a parallelogram. What is its area?

b The area of the front cover of one of the books is $396\,cm^2$. Its width is 18 cm. What is its length?

1 Here is a map of Tatton Park. It is just south of Manchester. Each square of the map represents 1 km^2 on the ground. Estimate the area of Tatton Park in km^2.

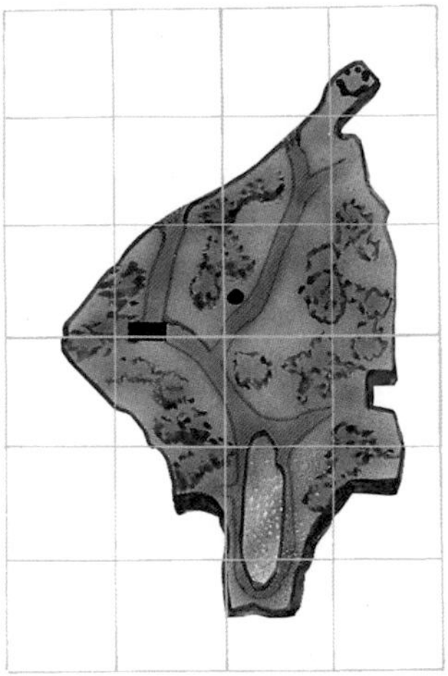

2 A stamp is 40 mm by 30 mm.

a Calculate the area of the stamp in mm^2.

b How many mm^2 are there in 1 cm^2?

c Find the area of the stamp in cm^2.

3 **a** A classroom is to have a carpet. The classroom is 7.5 m by 10 m. Calculate the area of carpet needed.

b The carpet costs £8 for 1 m^2. How much will it cost to buy the carpet for the classroom?

4 Use 1 cm squared paper to help you with this question. A rectangle of paper is 10 cm by 8 cm.

a What is its perimeter?

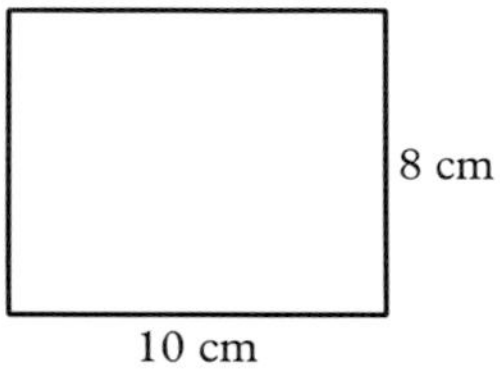

b A square 2 cm by 2 cm is cut from one corner. What is the perimeter of the shape that is left?

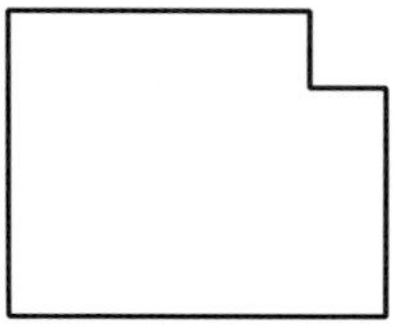

c Identical squares are cut from the other three corners. What is the perimeter of the shape that is left?

d What do you notice about the answers to parts **a**, **b** and **c**?

e How could you cut a square from the edge so that the perimeter changed?

5 Find the area of this stencil with the holes cut out.

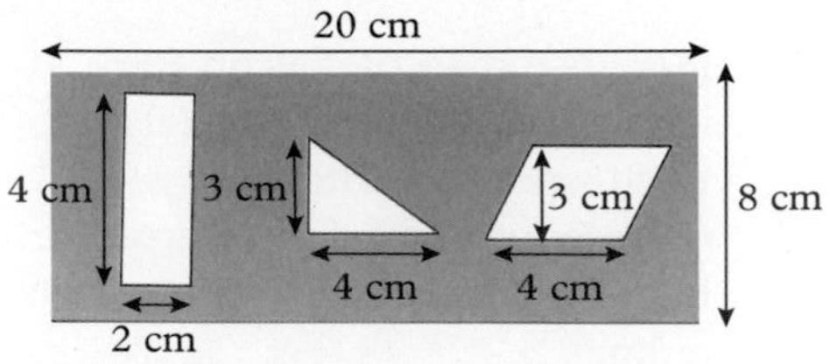

6 The picture shows a rug on a wooden floor.

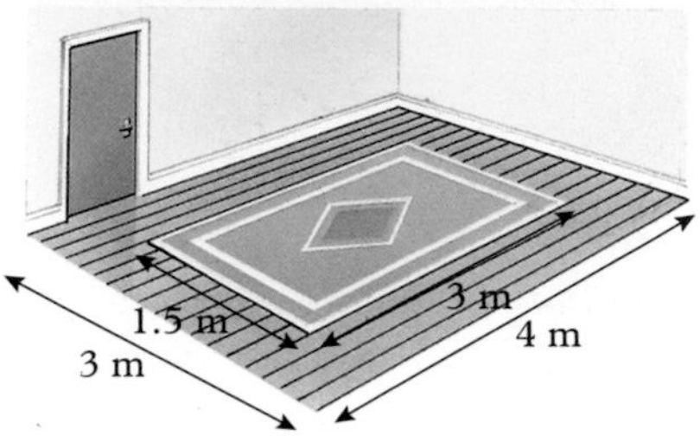

a What area of the floor is covered by the rug?
b What area of the floor is not covered by the rug?

7 What is the area of the shadow cast by the wall?

The wall has a length of 8 m.

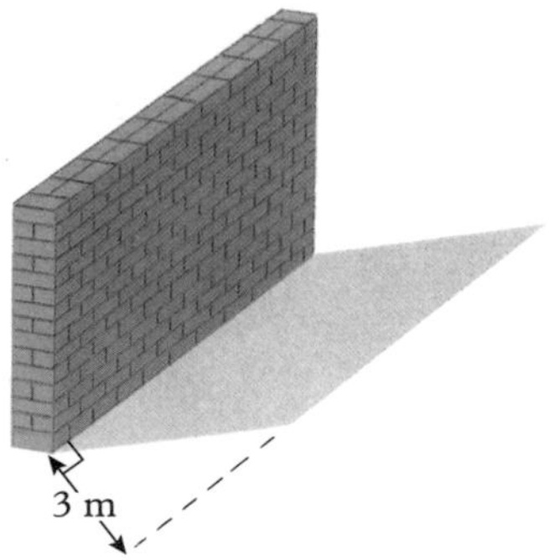

8 What is the area of this kite?

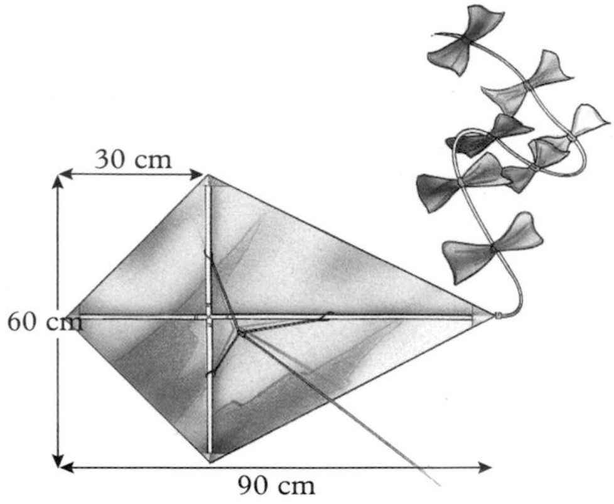

9 What is the area of the buckle of this belt?

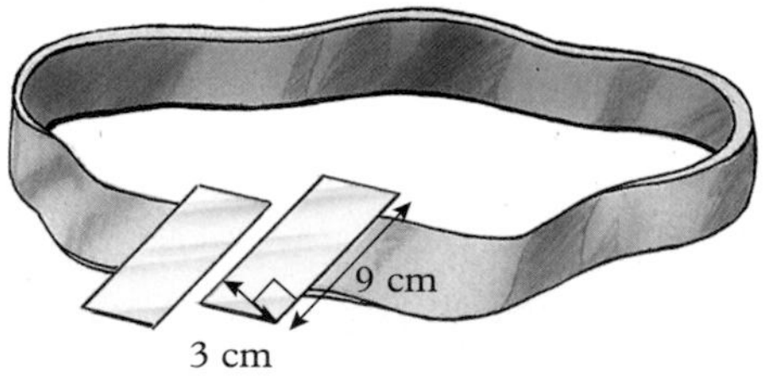

- Perimeter is the total distance around the outside edges of a shape.

- Area is the amount of space inside a shape.
  It is measured using squares.
  The size of squares you choose depends on the size of the area to be measured.

- Metric units of area are mm^2, cm^2, m^2, km^2
  Imperial units of area are in^2, ft^2, yd^2, $miles^2$

- Formulas: Area of rectangle = length × width
  = lw

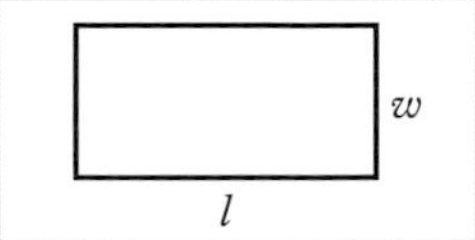

Area of triangle $= \dfrac{\text{base} \times \text{height}}{2}$

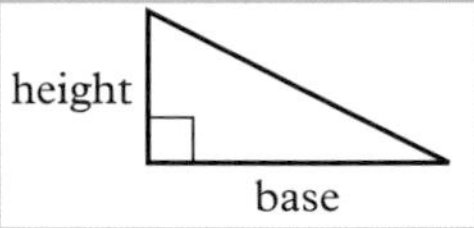

Area of parallelogram = base × height

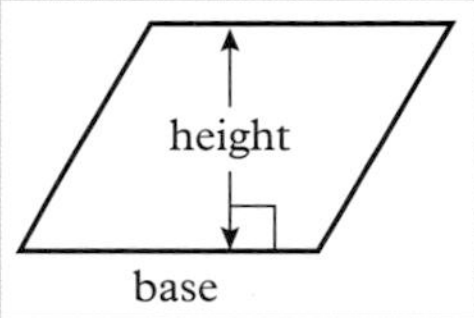

- To find the area of a compound shape we divide it up into simple shapes.

We can find this area by adding the areas of the two rectangles.

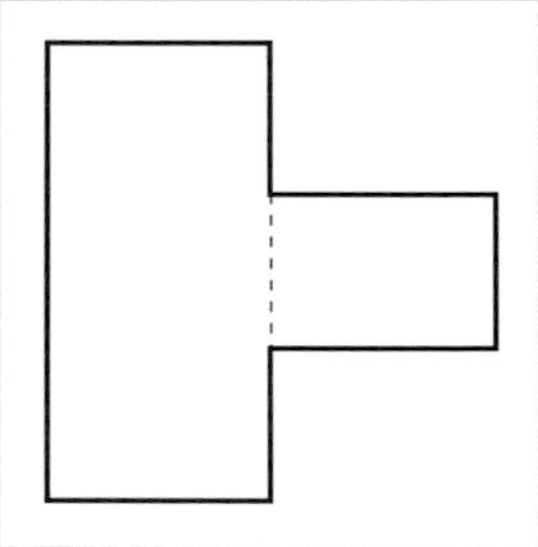

The green area can be found by subtracting the area of the cut out shape.

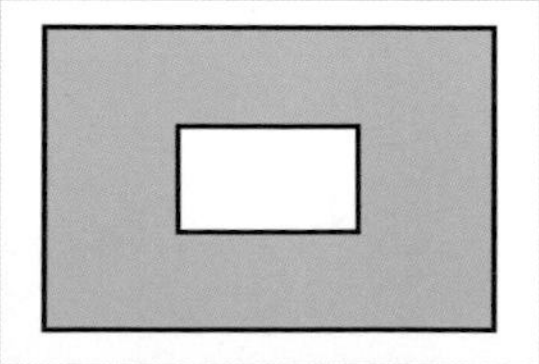

1 **a** What is the perimeter of this 'F' hexomino?

b What is the area of this 'F' hexomino?

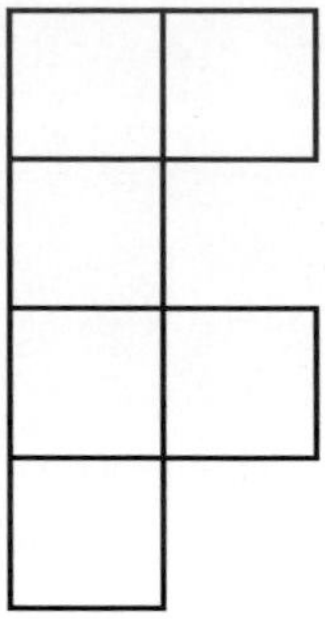

2 Measure the length and width of this rectangle.

a Calculate its area.

b Calculate its perimeter.

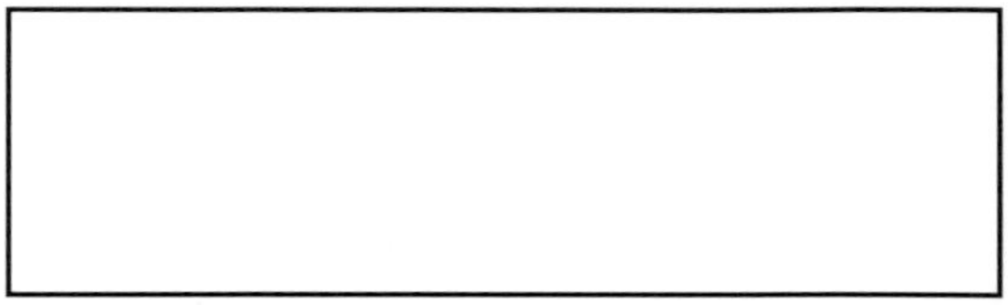

3 Give the units you would use to find the area of these.
Choose from cm^2, m^2, km^2.

a a lounge carpet

b a dolls' house carpet

c a magic carpet covering all of London

4 This rectangle has an area of $36\,cm^2$.
What is its length?

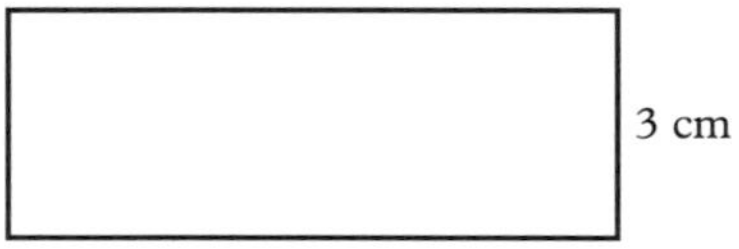

5 Find the areas of these shapes.

a

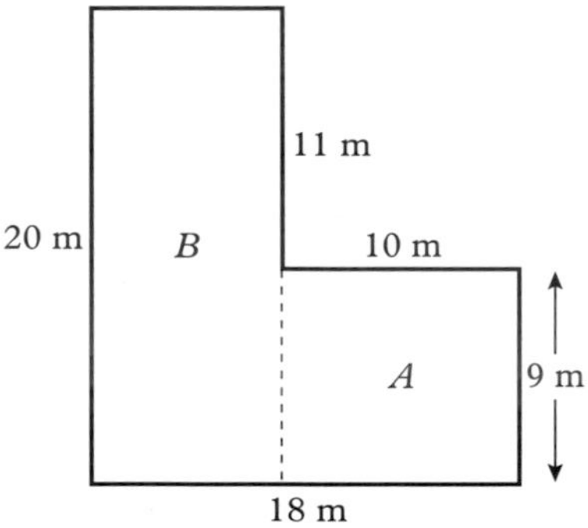

b

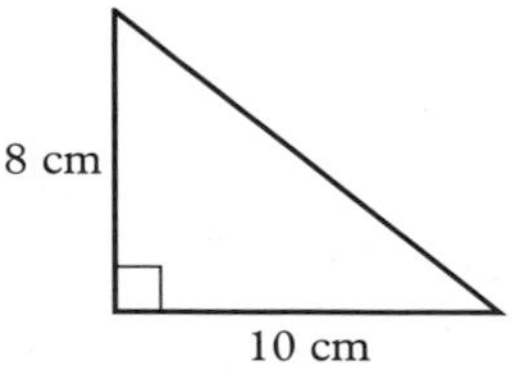

c

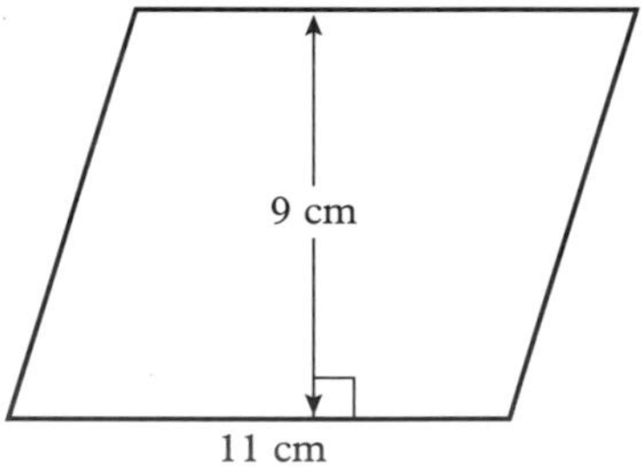

15 Small parts

CORE

1 **Introducing fractions**

2 **Working with fractions**

3 **Fractions, decimals and percentages**

4 **Ordering fractions**

QUESTIONS

EXTENSION

SUMMARY

TEST YOURSELF

In his will a man left his 17 camels to his three sons. He left $\frac{1}{2}$ of the camels to his oldest son, $\frac{1}{3}$ of them to his middle son and $\frac{1}{9}$ of them to the youngest son.

When the boys came to divide up the camels they found that 17 was a very awkward number!

The youngest boy who was the cleverest had a good idea. He borrowed a camel from their neighbour so that they now had 18.

They now split up the camels: $\frac{1}{2}$ of $18 = 9$
$\frac{1}{3}$ of $18 = 6$
$\frac{1}{9}$ of $18 = 2$

$9+6+2 = 17$ camels so they could return the last camel to their neighbour!!

Can you find out how this trick works?

1 Introducing fractions

Tim, Jane and Rachel are sharing a cake.

The cake has been cut into 8 equal parts. They have 1 piece each.

What fraction of the cake is left?

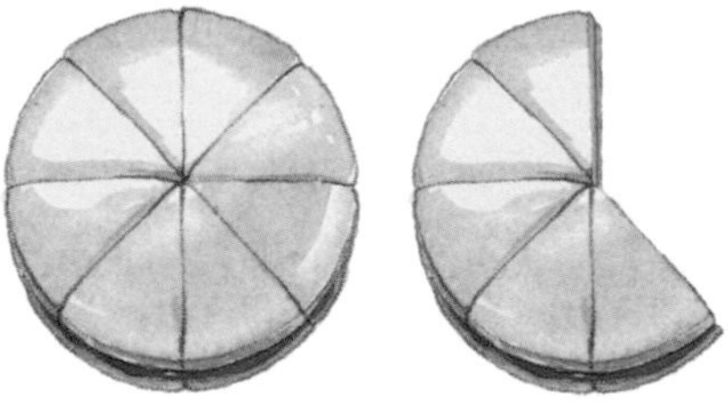

The cake has been cut into 8 pieces.

Each piece is **one** eighth. This is written $\frac{1}{8}$.

Five pieces are left. This is $\frac{5}{8}$.

So five-eighths of the cake is left.

Three pieces have been eaten. This is $\frac{3}{8}$.

So three-eighths of the cake has been eaten.

Numerator The top number of a fraction is the **numerator**. This tells you how many pieces you have to talk about.

Denominator The bottom number of a fraction is the **denominator**. This tells you how many pieces the whole was cut into.

Exercise 15:1

In questions **1–8**, write down:

a the fraction that is left
b the fraction that has been eaten.

Give both of your answers in words and in figures.

1

2

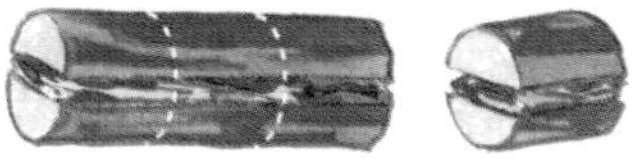

3

4

5

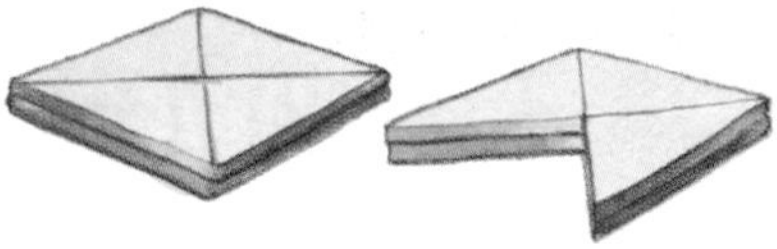

6

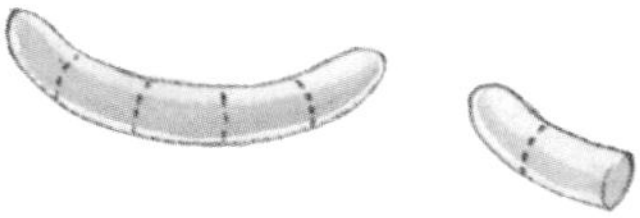

7

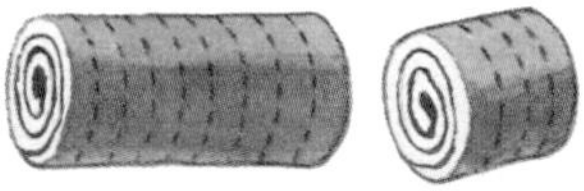

8

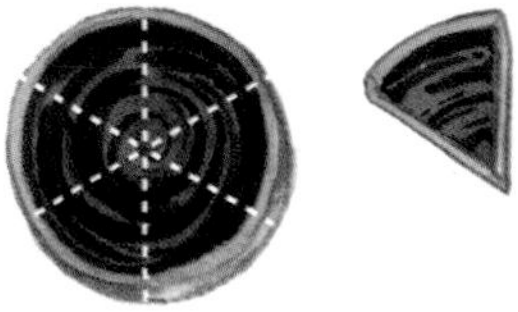

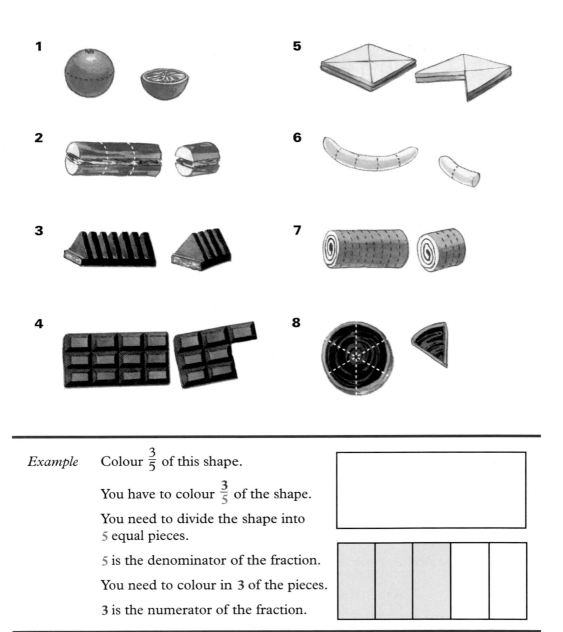

Example Colour $\frac{3}{5}$ of this shape.

You have to colour $\frac{3}{5}$ of the shape.

You need to divide the shape into 5 equal pieces.

5 is the denominator of the fraction.

You need to colour in 3 of the pieces.

3 is the numerator of the fraction.

Exercise 15:2

In questions **1–8**, colour in the fraction of each shape like this:

a Copy each shape and label it with the fraction that you have to colour.
b Split the shape into the number of equal pieces that the denominator tells you.
c Colour in the number of pieces that the numerator tells you.

1 $\frac{1}{2}$ of 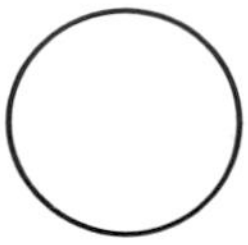

2 $\frac{2}{5}$ of 

3 $\frac{3}{4}$ of 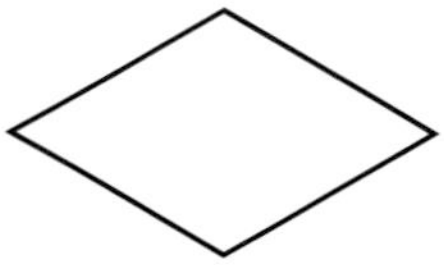

4 $\frac{3}{8}$ of 

5 $\frac{5}{6}$ of 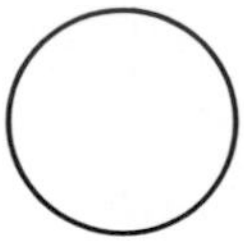

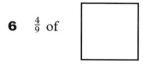

6 $\frac{4}{9}$ of 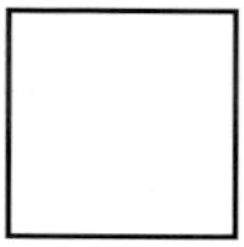

7 $\frac{3}{7}$ of 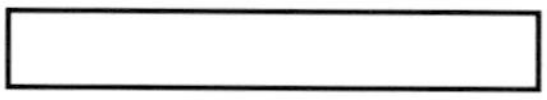

● 8 $\frac{2}{3}$ of 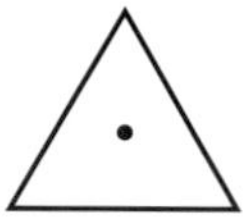

9 Copy and complete these sentences.
The first one has been done for you.

a **Two** halves make a whole.
b … thirds make a whole.
c … quarters make a whole.
d … tenths make a whole.
e … twentieths make a whole.
f … hundredths make a whole.

Writing one number as a fraction of another number

Make sure that the units are the same before you write down the fraction.

Example Write 10 minutes as a fraction of an hour.
1 hour = 60 minutes.

10 minutes as a fraction of an hour is $\frac{10}{60}$

---

10 Write the first amount as a fraction of the second amount.

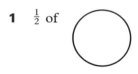

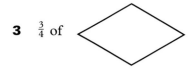

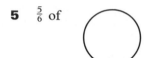

a 5 minutes, 1 hour
b 15 minutes, 3 hours
c 4 seconds, 2 minutes
d 23 seconds, 4 minutes
e 10p, £3
f 70p, £40
g 3 cm, 1 m
h 34 cm, 8 m
● **i** 12 g, 1 kg
● **j** 150 g, 3 kg

2 Working with fractions

Paul has 12 sweets. He is sharing them equally with his friends. The three boys get one third ($\frac{1}{3}$) each.

Example Find $\frac{1}{3}$ of 12 sweets.

$\frac{1}{3}$ of 12 sweets $= 12 \div 3$ (Divide by **3** to get $\frac{1}{3}$)
$= 4$ sweets

Exercise 15:3

Find:

1 $\frac{1}{2}$ of eight sweets (Divide by 2 to get $\frac{1}{2}$)

2 $\frac{1}{5}$ of ten sweets (Divide by 5 to get $\frac{1}{5}$)

3 $\frac{1}{3}$ of nine packets of crisps

4 $\frac{1}{4}$ of 20 p

5 $\frac{1}{5}$ of 15 marbles

6 $\frac{1}{6}$ of 24 biscuits

7 $\frac{1}{4}$ of £1 in pence

8 $\frac{1}{10}$ of £2 in pence

9 $\frac{1}{2}$ of an hour in minutes

10 $\frac{1}{4}$ of an hour in minutes

11 $\frac{1}{2}$ of a minute in seconds

• **12** $\frac{1}{10}$ of a centimetre in millimetres

Example Find $\frac{2}{3}$ of 12 sweets.

$\frac{1}{3}$ of 12 sweets $= 12 \div 3$
$= 4$ sweets

$\frac{2}{3}$ of 12 sweets $= 2$ lots of 4 sweets
$= 2 \times 4$
$= 8$ sweets

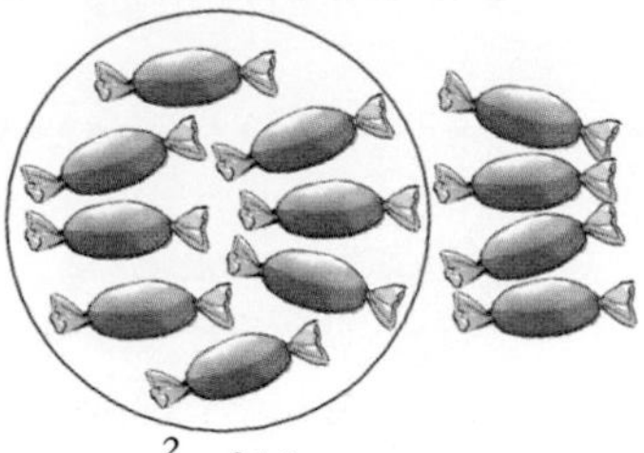

$\frac{2}{3}$ of 12 sweets

13 Find $\frac{2}{3}$ of 15 sweets.

Copy and complete:

$\frac{1}{3}$ of 15 sweets $= 15 \div ?$
$= ?$
$\frac{2}{3}$ of 15 sweets $= 2$ lots of 5 sweets
$= 2 \times ?$
$= ?$ sweets

14 Find $\frac{3}{4}$ of 8 sweets.

Copy and complete:

$\frac{1}{4}$ of 8 sweets $= 8 \div ?$
$= ?$
$\frac{3}{4}$ of 8 sweets $= 3$ lots of ? sweets
$= 3 \times ?$
$= ?$ sweets

Find:

15 $\frac{4}{5}$ of 10 p

16 $\frac{7}{10}$ of 20 counters

17 $\frac{5}{6}$ of 18 biscuits

You do not always get whole numbers as answers to these problems.

Ben, Ned, Kate and Emma have 7 cakes.
They want to share them out equally.
How many cakes will each person get?

They each take a whole cake.
There are only three cakes left. There are not enough cakes to have another whole cake each.

Because there are 4 of them, they cut the rest of the cakes into **quarters**

Each person gets 3 quarters.

Altogether, each person gets $1\frac{3}{4}$ cakes.

Exercise 15:4

1 Share 4 apples equally between 3 children.

Answer .... apples each.

2 Share 5 oranges equally between 4 children.

Answer .... oranges each.

3 Share these equally.
Draw diagrams to help you.

a 3 cakes between 2 children.
b 7 bananas between 4 children.
c 5 apples between 2 children.
d 7 cakes between 3 children.

4 Terry, Louise and Heidi cook 5 small pizzas.
They share the pizzas equally between them.
How many pizzas will each person get?

● **5** There 10 squares of chocolate in a bar.
Four friends share the bar equally between them.
How many squares will each person get?

6 Nine oranges are shared equally between 4 people.
How many oranges will each person get?

● **7** 30 cakes are shared equally between 8 people.
How many cakes does each person get?

Equivalent fractions

Half of each of these shapes is shaded.
Each shape also shows another fraction.
All these fractions must be the same as a half.

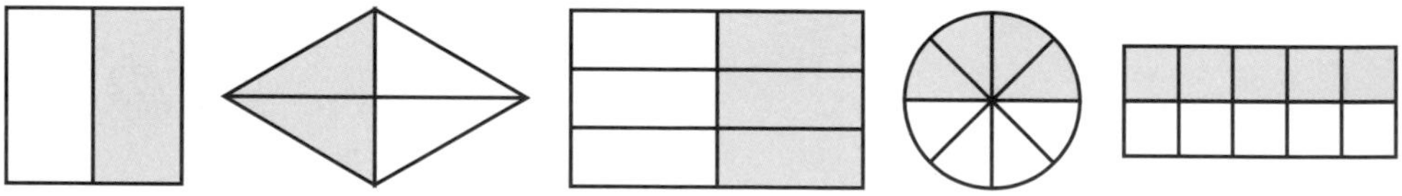

$\frac{1}{2} = \frac{2}{4} = \frac{3}{6} = \frac{4}{8} = \frac{5}{10}$

Equivalent fractions

Equivalent fractions are different ways of writing the same fraction.

Example

Write down 4 fractions which are equivalent to $\frac{1}{2}$.

Using the diagrams above, four equivalent fractions are

$\frac{2}{4}, \frac{3}{6}, \frac{4}{8}, \frac{5}{10}$

Exercise 15:5

Give each of these as two equivalent fractions.

1

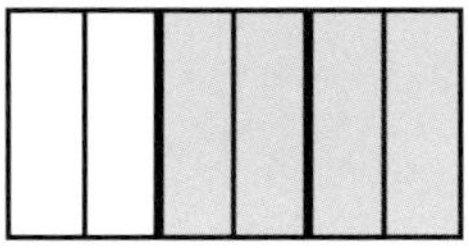

$\frac{4}{6} = \frac{?}{3}$

2

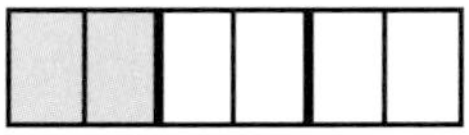

$\frac{?}{6} = \frac{?}{3}$

3

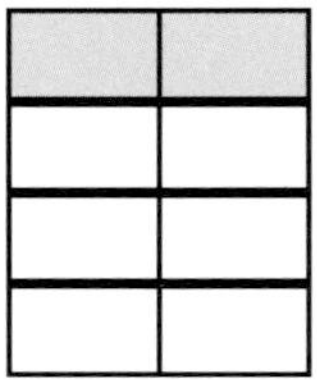

$\frac{?}{8} = \frac{?}{4}$

4

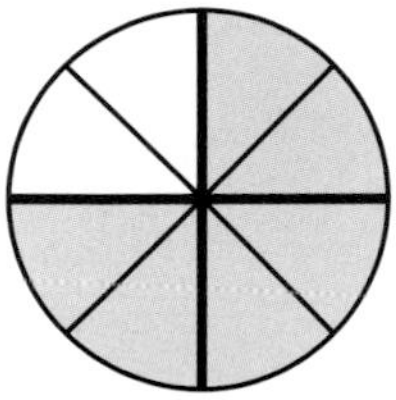

$\frac{?}{8} = \frac{?}{4}$

5

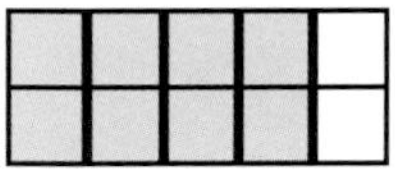

$\frac{?}{10} = \frac{?}{5}$

6

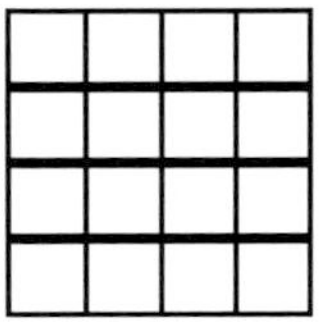

7

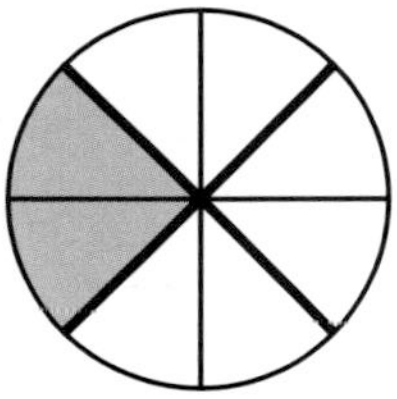

8

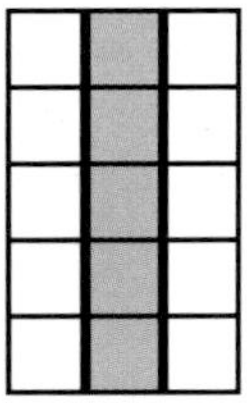

9

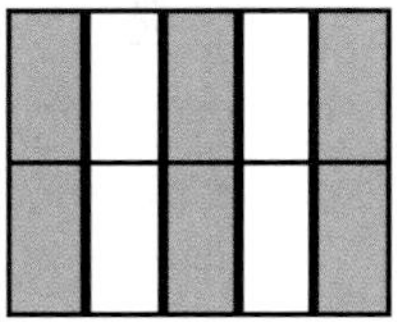

Simplifying fractions

Putting fractions into their simplest form is known as cancelling.

Example Write each of these fractions in their simplest form:

a $\frac{3}{6}$ **b** $\frac{8}{12}$

a Look for the biggest number that divides exactly into the numerator and the denominator. **3** divides exactly in to 3 and 6.

$$\frac{3}{6} \overset{\div 3}{=} \frac{1}{2}$$

(÷3 applied to both numerator and denominator)

$\frac{1}{2}$ is the simplest form of this fraction.

b 4 divides exactly in to 8 and 12

$$\frac{8}{12} \overset{\div 4}{=} \frac{2}{3}$$

(÷4 applied to both numerator and denominator)

$\frac{2}{3}$ is the simplest form of this fraction.

Exercise 15:6

Copy and complete these.
You will get each fraction in its simplest form.

1 $\frac{2}{4} \xrightarrow{\div 2} \frac{?}{?}$, top ÷2, bottom ÷2

2 $\frac{5}{10} = \frac{?}{?}$, top ÷5, bottom ÷5

3 $\frac{6}{10} = \frac{?}{?}$, top ÷2, bottom ÷2

4 $\frac{6}{8} = \frac{?}{?}$, top ÷2, bottom ÷?

5 $\frac{9}{12} = \frac{?}{?}$, top ÷3, bottom ÷?

6 $\frac{15}{20} = \frac{?}{?}$, top ÷5, bottom ÷?

Adding fractions

To add fractions the bottom numbers **must** be the same.

Example Work out **a** $\frac{1}{3} + \frac{1}{3}$ **b** $\frac{3}{5} + \frac{3}{5}$

a $\frac{1}{3} + \frac{1}{3} = \frac{2}{3}$

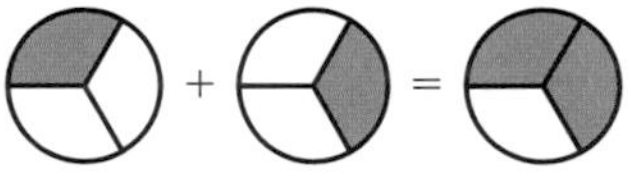

one third + one third = two thirds

b $\frac{3}{5} + \frac{3}{5} = \frac{6}{5} = 1\frac{1}{5}$

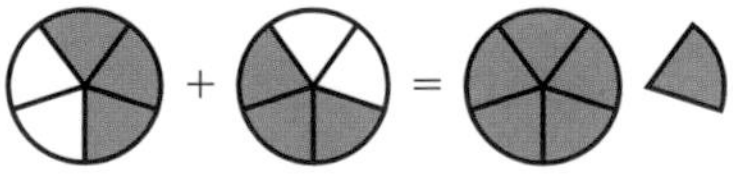

three fifths + three fifths = One and one fifth

Exercise 15:7

1 $\frac{2}{5} + \frac{1}{5}$

2 $\frac{3}{7} + \frac{1}{7}$

3 $\frac{4}{9} + \frac{2}{9}$

4 $\frac{3}{11} + \frac{2}{11}$

5 $\frac{4}{13} + \frac{6}{13}$

6 $\frac{5}{8} + \frac{2}{8}$

7 $\frac{3}{9} + \frac{4}{9}$

8 $\frac{7}{12} + \frac{3}{12}$

9 $\frac{7}{12} + \frac{5}{12}$

10 $\frac{3}{5} + \frac{4}{5}$

11 $\frac{5}{8} + \frac{7}{8}$

12 $\frac{10}{11} + \frac{4}{11}$

13 $\frac{8}{13} + \frac{9}{13}$

14 $\frac{5}{17} + \frac{12}{17}$

● **15** $\frac{3}{5} + \frac{1}{5} + \frac{2}{5}$

● **16** $\frac{6}{7} + \frac{2}{7} + \frac{3}{7}$

Sometimes the two bottom numbers are different.
Before you can add the fractions you **must** make the bottom numbers the same.
This is called finding a common denominator.

Example Work out $\frac{2}{3} + \frac{1}{6}$

You need to find a number that 3 and 6 both divide into exactly.

Numbers that 3 goes into exactly are:

3 (6) 9 12 ...

Numbers that 6 goes into exactly are:

(6) 12 18 ...

The first number that is in both lists is 6.

Now you need to write both fractions with 6 as the bottom number.

First change the $\frac{2}{3}$.

Ask yourself; 'What do I have to multiply the 3 by to get 6?' The answer is 2. You multiply the top and bottom of the fraction by 2.

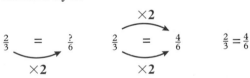

$\frac{2}{3} = \frac{?}{6}$ (×2) $\quad$ $\frac{2}{3} = \frac{4}{6}$ (×2, ×2) $\quad$ $\frac{2}{3} = \frac{4}{6}$

You can see this in a diagram.

The $\frac{1}{6}$ does not need changing.

So $\frac{2}{3} + \frac{1}{6} = \frac{4}{6} + \frac{1}{6} = \frac{5}{6}$

Exercise 15:8

1 $\frac{1}{4} + \frac{1}{2}$

2 $\frac{1}{6} + \frac{1}{12}$

3 $\frac{2}{5} + \frac{3}{10}$

4 $\frac{3}{8} + \frac{1}{4}$

5 $\frac{7}{12} + \frac{1}{6}$

6 $\frac{2}{9} + \frac{1}{3}$

7 $\frac{1}{3} + \frac{1}{4}$

8 $\frac{2}{7} + \frac{1}{3}$

9 $\frac{2}{5} + \frac{1}{3}$

10 $\frac{2}{7} + \frac{3}{5}$

11 $\frac{3}{8} + \frac{5}{7}$

12 $\frac{1}{6} + \frac{2}{7}$

13 $\frac{3}{5} + \frac{7}{10}$

14 $\frac{5}{9} + \frac{3}{11}$

• **15** $\frac{1}{2} + \frac{1}{3} + \frac{1}{4}$

• **16** $\frac{1}{3} + \frac{1}{4} + \frac{1}{5}$

Subtracting fractions

Subtracting fractions is very similar to adding.
Again you **must** make sure the bottom numbers of both fractions are the same.
Once you have done this, you take away the top numbers instead of adding them.

Example Work out $\frac{3}{8} - \frac{1}{4}$

You need to find a number that 8 and 4 both divide into exactly.

Numbers that 8 goes into exactly are:

(8) 16 24 ...

Numbers that 4 goes into exactly are:

4 (8) 12 16 ...

The first number that is in both lists is 8.

Now you need to write both fractions with 8 as the bottom number.

$\frac{1}{4} = \frac{?}{8}$ (×2 on the bottom) $\quad \frac{1}{4} = \frac{2}{8}$ (×2 on the top, ×2 on the bottom) $\quad \frac{1}{4} = \frac{2}{8}$

The $\frac{3}{8}$ does not need changing.

So $\frac{3}{8} - \frac{1}{4} = \frac{3}{8} - \frac{2}{8} = \frac{1}{8}$

Exercise 15:9

1 $\frac{5}{7} - \frac{2}{7}$	**5** $\frac{3}{8} - \frac{1}{4}$	**9** $\frac{4}{7} - \frac{1}{3}$	**13** $\frac{8}{9} - \frac{4}{7}$
2 $\frac{2}{3} - \frac{1}{3}$	**6** $\frac{5}{12} - \frac{1}{3}$	**10** $\frac{5}{7} - \frac{1}{4}$	**14** $\frac{7}{13} - \frac{1}{5}$
3 $\frac{6}{13} - \frac{2}{13}$	**7** $\frac{1}{3} - \frac{1}{4}$	**11** $\frac{7}{10} - \frac{1}{3}$	**15** $\frac{8}{9} - \frac{1}{4}$
4 $\frac{2}{3} - \frac{1}{6}$	**8** $\frac{3}{5} - \frac{1}{6}$	**12** $\frac{4}{7} - \frac{2}{5}$	• **16** $\frac{5}{13} - \frac{2}{11}$

You can check your answers to this section on your calculator.
Use the calculator help sheet on page 392.

3 Fractions, decimals and percentages

Parts of a whole can be shown as fractions.
They can also be written as a special fraction, called a percentage.

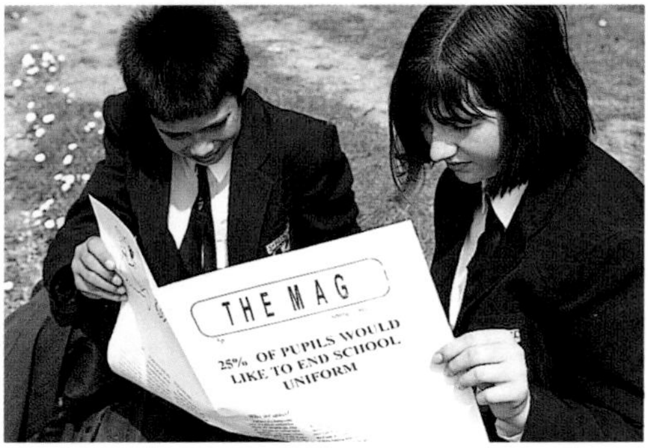

The large square has 100 small squares.
25 small squares are shaded.

25 out of 100 is the fraction $\frac{25}{100}$

25 out of 100 is 25 per cent.

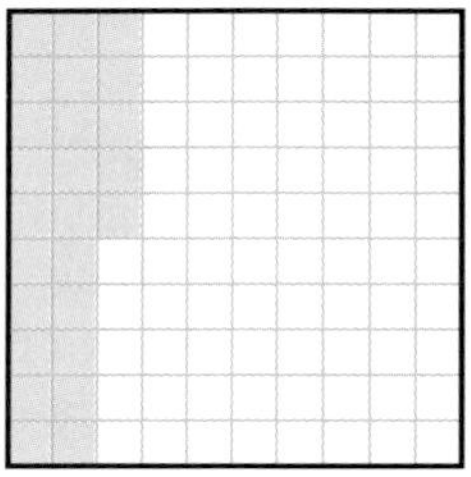

Percentage

A **percentage** is the same as a fraction out of 100.

There is a special symbol for percentages.
Instead of writing a fraction with a denominator of 100 you use the percentage symbol %.

This is a rearrangement of 100

25 out of 100 = $\frac{25}{100}$ = 25%

Exercise 15:10

1 Copy this table and fill it in for the grids **a** to **f**.

	Number of squares shaded	Fraction shaded	Percentage shaded
a	?	$\frac{?}{100}$	? %
b	?	$\frac{?}{100}$	? %
c	?		

a

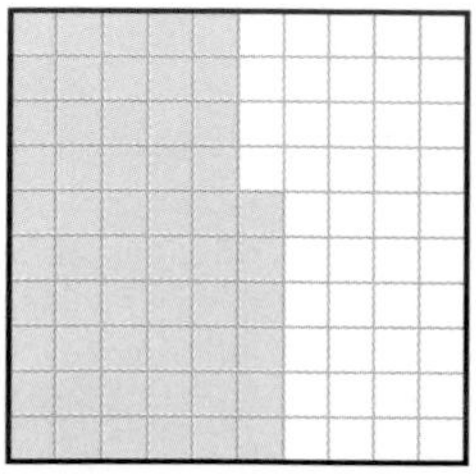

c

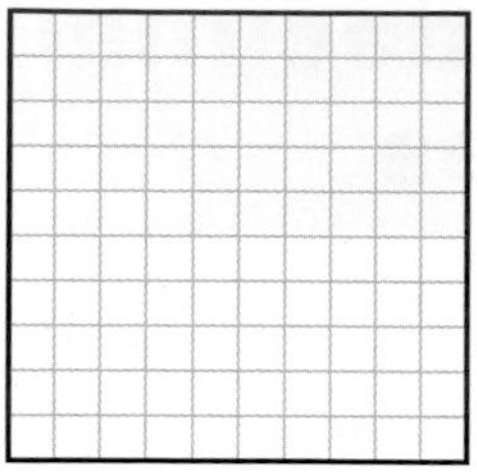

e

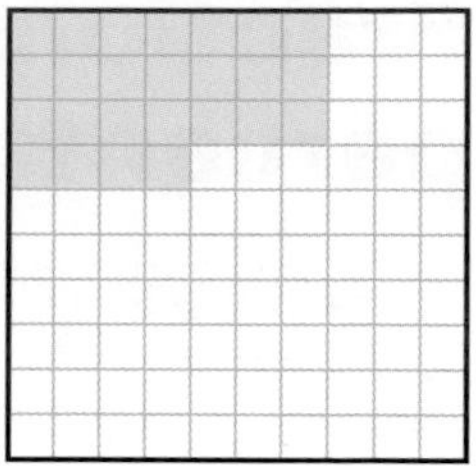

b

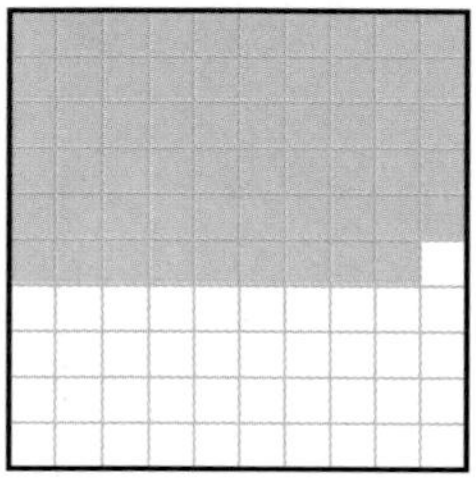

d

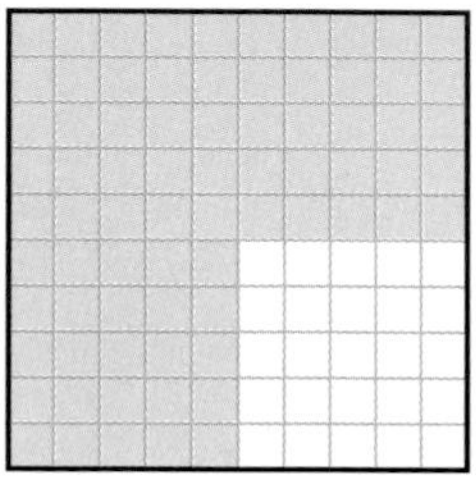

f

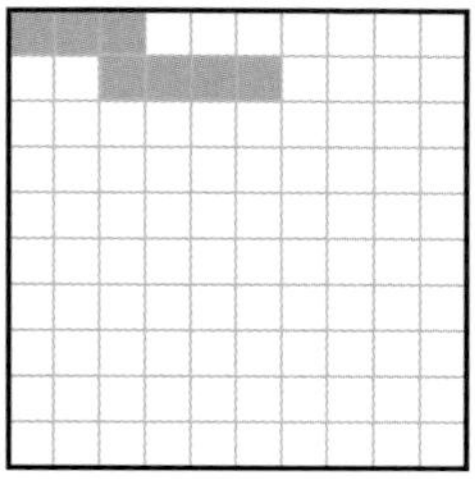

2 Write down:

a the percentage of this grid that is coloured green.

b the percentage of this grid that is coloured blue.

c the percentage of this grid that is coloured either blue or green.

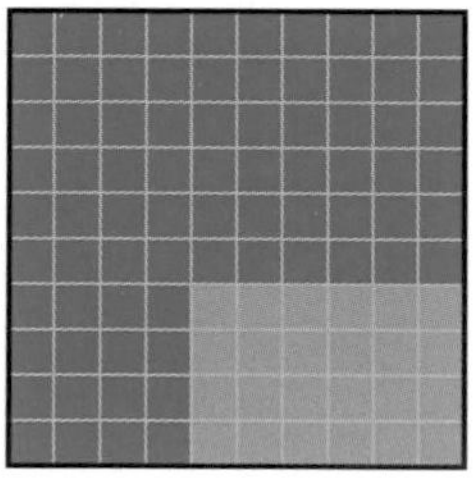

3 Write these percentages as fractions of 100.

a $42\% = \frac{?}{100}$ **c** 18% **e** 23% **g** 49% **i** 84%

b $93\% = \frac{?}{100}$ **d** 5% **f** 15% **h** 1% **j** 10%

4 Write these fractions as percentages.

a $\frac{16}{100} = ?\ \%$ **c** $\frac{18}{100}$ **e** $\frac{7}{100}$ **g** $\frac{31}{100}$ **i** $\frac{63}{100}$

b $\frac{74}{100} = ?\ \%$ **d** $\frac{96}{100}$ **f** $\frac{26}{100}$ **h** $\frac{4}{100}$ **j** $\frac{9}{100}$

5 20% of the pupils in 7M were absent on Monday.
Write down the percentage that were present.

6 6% of a box of light bulbs were faulty.
Write down the percentage that were not faulty.

7 71% of the Earth's surface is water.
Write down the percentage that is land.

Exercise 15:11

For questions **1–3** copy and complete the lists. Use the diagrams to help you.

1 Copy and complete:

a $25\% = \frac{25}{100} = \frac{1}{4}$

b $75\% = \frac{?}{100} = ?$

c $50\% = \frac{?}{100} = ?$

2 Copy and complete:

a $10\% = \frac{?}{100} = \frac{1}{10}$

b $30\% = \frac{?}{100} = \frac{?}{10}$

c $70\% = ? = ?$

d $90\% = ? = ?$

3 Copy and complete:

a $20\% = \frac{?}{100} = \frac{1}{?}$

b $40\% = \frac{?}{100} = \frac{?}{5}$

c $60\% = ? = ?$

d $80\% = ? = ?$

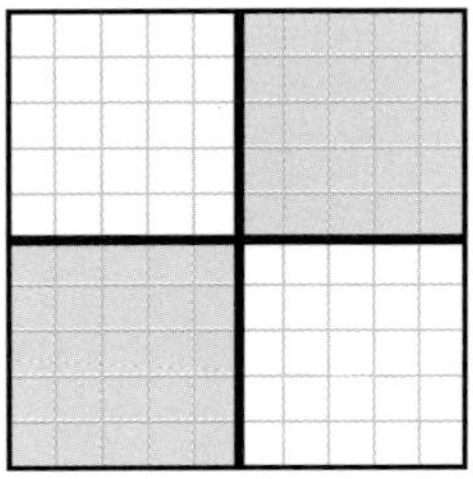

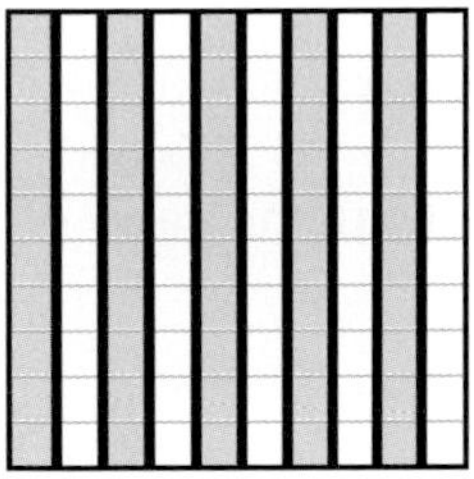

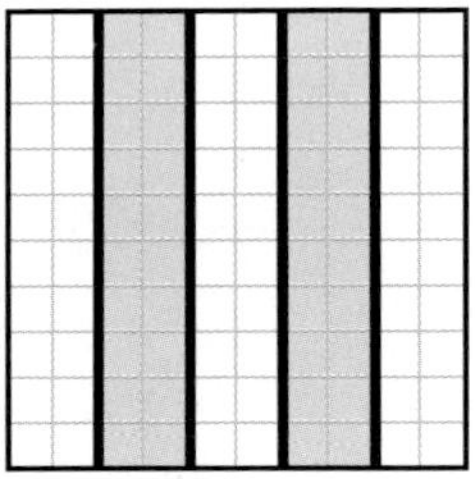

4 The milkman delivers these bottles.
The red tops are semi-skimmed milk.
Write down:

a the fraction that are semi-skimmed.

b the percentage that are semi-skimmed.

5 Write down:

a the fraction of the hot-air balloons that are striped.

b the percentage that are striped.

c the fraction that are yellow.

d the percentage that are yellow.

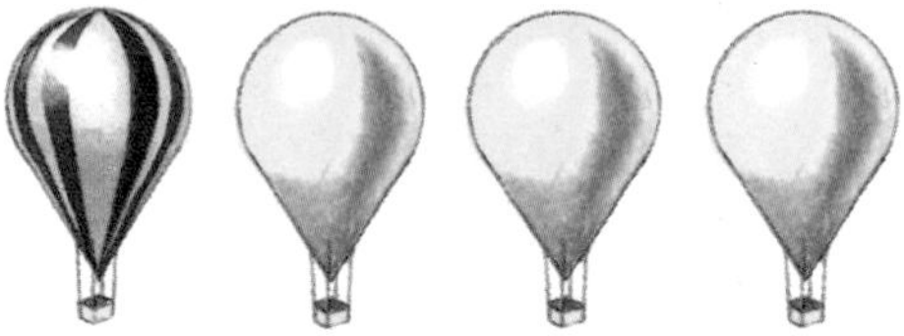

6 Write down:

a the fraction of the counters that are red.

b the percentage that are red.

c the fraction of the counters that are blue.

d the percentage that are blue.

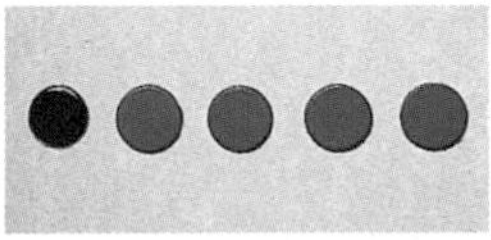

7 **a** What fraction of the cubes are blue?

b What percentage of the cubes are blue?

c What percentage of the cubes are red?

Fractions and percentages are parts of a whole.
You have already seen decimals. They are also part of a whole.

Changing fractions to decimals

A fraction is another way of writing a divide question.

$\frac{3}{5}$ is **three fifths** but it is also 3 divided by 5.

You change this to a decimal by dividing.

3 divided by 5 is 0 with 3 to carry.

$$\begin{array}{r} 0.\ 6 \\ 5\overline{)\,3.{}^{3}0} \end{array}$$

Add a decimal point and a nought and carry on.

So $\frac{3}{5} = 0.6$

You can turn any fraction into a decimal like this.

Exercise 15:12

1 Change each of these fractions to decimals.

a $\frac{1}{2}$	**c** $\frac{2}{5}$	**e** $\frac{1}{10}$	**g** $\frac{7}{10}$
b $\frac{1}{5}$	**d** $\frac{4}{5}$	**f** $\frac{3}{10}$	**h** $\frac{8}{10}$

Sometimes you need to add more than one nought.

$\frac{3}{4}$ is 3 divided by 4.

3 divided by 4 is 0 with 3 to carry.

$$\begin{array}{r} 0.\ 7 \\ 4\overline{)\,3.{}^{3}0} \end{array}$$

Add a decimal point and a nought.

Now do $30 \div 4$. This is 7 with 2 to carry.

$$\begin{array}{r} 0.\ 7\ 5 \\ 4\overline{)\,3.{}^{3}0{}^{2}0} \end{array}$$

Add another nought $20 \div 4 = 5$. So $\frac{3}{4} = 0.75$

2 Change each of these fractions to decimals.

a $\frac{1}{4}$	**c** $\frac{3}{8}$	**e** $\frac{3}{20}$	● **g** $\frac{1}{16}$
b $\frac{1}{8}$	**d** $\frac{1}{20}$	**f** $\frac{7}{20}$	● **h** $\frac{7}{16}$

Changing decimals to fractions

You need to remember the values of the decimal places to do this.
Look at the column that the last digit is in to see what fraction you need.

units	.	tenths	hundredths	thousandths	
0	.	6			means 6 tenths which is $\frac{6}{10}$ as a fraction.
0	.	2	4		means 24 hundredths which is $\frac{24}{100}$ as a fraction.
0	.	2	7	2	means 272 thousandths which is $\frac{272}{1000}$ as a fraction.

Don't forget that you should cancel the fractions when you can.
Look for a number that divides into the top number and the bottom number.
Don't worry if you need to cancel more than once.
Keep going until you cannot cancel any more.

$$\frac{6}{10} \overset{\div 2}{=} \frac{3}{5} \qquad \frac{24}{100} \overset{\div 4}{=} \frac{6}{25} \qquad \frac{272}{1000} \overset{\div 2}{=} \frac{136}{500} \overset{\div 2}{=} \frac{68}{250} \overset{\div 2}{=} \frac{34}{125}$$

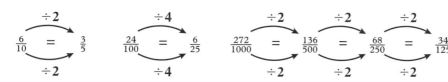

You could do this in one go if you divide by 8.

3 Write each of these as a fraction.

a 0.3 **c** 0.13 **e** 0.169 ● **g** 0.2341
b 0.7 **d** 0.27 **f** 0.499 ● **h** 0.7911

4 Write each of these as a fraction.
Cancel the fraction down as much as you can.

a 0.4 **e** 0.66 **i** 0.56 **m** 0.875
b 0.5 **f** 0.24 **j** 0.245 **n** 0.625
c 0.8 **g** 0.52 **k** 0.125 ● **o** 0.1875
d 0.42 **h** 0.32 **l** 0.375 ● **p** 0.8125

4 Ordering fractions

Get in order you 'orrible lot!!!

It can be quite difficult to get fractions into the right order!

It is best to use a number line to help you.

Exercise 15:13

1 **a** Draw a line 12 cm long.
Split your line into thirds.
Leave 4 cm between each mark

b Mark the numbers 0 $\frac{1}{3}$ $\frac{2}{3}$ 1 on the number line.

2 **a** Draw another line 12 cm long.
Line it up exactly under your first line.
Split your line into quarters.
Leave 3 cm between each mark

b Mark the numbers 0 $\frac{1}{4}$ $\frac{1}{2}$ $\frac{3}{4}$ 1 on the number line.

3 **a** Draw another line 12 cm long.
Line it up exactly under your other lines.
Split your line into sixths. Leave 2 cm between each mark.

b Mark the numbers 0, $\frac{1}{6}$, $\frac{2}{6}$, …, etc. on the number line.

4 **a** Draw another line 12 cm long.
Line it up exactly under your first line.
Split your line into eighths. Leave 1.5 cm between each mark.

b Mark the numbers 0, $\frac{1}{8}$, $\frac{2}{8}$, …, etc. on the number line.

5 Use your number lines to help you with this question.
Write down each pair of fractions.
Circle the bigger of the two fractions.

a $\frac{1}{2}$ $\frac{1}{3}$ **c** $\frac{2}{3}$ $\frac{1}{2}$ **e** $\frac{7}{8}$ $\frac{4}{6}$ **g** $\frac{7}{8}$ $\frac{5}{6}$

b $\frac{1}{4}$ $\frac{1}{3}$ **d** $\frac{5}{8}$ $\frac{1}{3}$ **f** $\frac{2}{3}$ $\frac{7}{8}$ **h** $\frac{1}{4}$ $\frac{3}{8}$

6 Use your number lines to help you with this question.
Rewrite each set of fractions in order.
Start with the **smallest**.

a $\frac{1}{2}$ $\frac{1}{3}$ $\frac{1}{6}$ $\frac{1}{8}$ $\frac{1}{4}$

b $\frac{2}{3}$ $\frac{1}{6}$ $\frac{5}{8}$ $\frac{5}{6}$ $\frac{2}{4}$

c $\frac{7}{8}$ $\frac{2}{3}$ $\frac{3}{8}$ $\frac{2}{6}$ $\frac{3}{4}$

Sometimes, you can estimate where fractions are on the number line.

Example Which fraction is bigger, $\frac{4}{7}$ or $\frac{5}{11}$?

$\frac{4}{7}$ is bigger than $\frac{1}{2}$ because 4 is more than half of 7.

$\frac{5}{11}$ is smaller than $\frac{1}{2}$ because 5 is less than half of 11.

On the number line they would look like this.

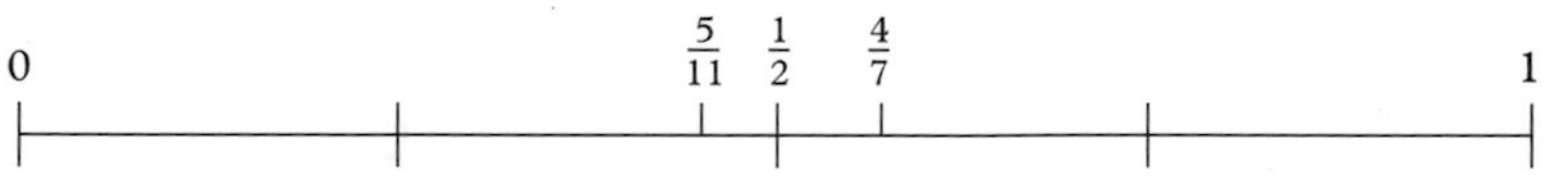

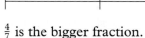

$\frac{4}{7}$ is the bigger fraction.

Exercise 15.14

1 In each part write down the pairs of fractions.
Circle the bigger fraction.
Use a number line to help you.

a $\frac{3}{5}$ $\frac{3}{7}$ **d** $\frac{1}{3}$ $\frac{4}{7}$ **g** $\frac{2}{5}$ $\frac{4}{7}$

b $\frac{4}{9}$ $\frac{6}{11}$ **e** $\frac{2}{3}$ $\frac{5}{12}$ **h** $\frac{8}{15}$ $\frac{9}{19}$

c $\frac{1}{4}$ $\frac{3}{5}$ **f** $\frac{1}{2}$ $\frac{7}{13}$ ● **i** $\frac{11}{20}$ $\frac{9}{16}$

Sometimes it is helpful to think about moving back from the other end of the number line.

You can think of $\frac{8}{9}$ as $\frac{1}{9}$ back from 1

You can think of $\frac{7}{8}$ as $\frac{1}{8}$ back from 1

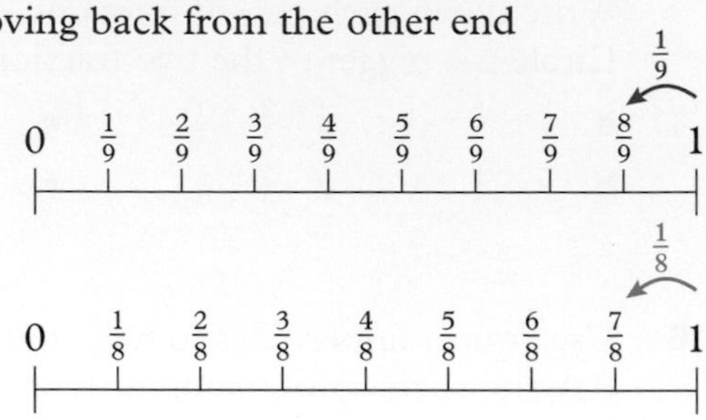

$\frac{1}{9}$ is smaller than $\frac{1}{8}$ so $\frac{1}{9}$ is a smaller step back from 1.

This means that $\frac{8}{9}$ is the bigger fraction.

2 In each part write down the pairs of fractions. Circle the bigger fraction. Use a number line to help you.

a $\frac{5}{6}$ $\frac{4}{5}$ **d** $\frac{8}{9}$ $\frac{7}{8}$ **g** $\frac{3}{5}$ $\frac{4}{6}$

b $\frac{8}{9}$ $\frac{9}{10}$ **e** $\frac{10}{11}$ $\frac{12}{13}$ **h** $\frac{11}{13}$ $\frac{12}{14}$

c $\frac{4}{5}$ $\frac{3}{4}$ **f** $\frac{5}{6}$ $\frac{7}{8}$ ● **i** $\frac{17}{20}$ $\frac{16}{19}$

The other way to order fractions is to change them so that they all have the same bottom number. This is called finding a common denominator. It is the method you used in addition and subtraction.

Example

a Write $\frac{3}{5}$ and $\frac{4}{7}$ as fractions with a common denominator.

b Use your answer to **a** to say which is the bigger fraction.

a You need to find a number that 5 and 7 both divide into exactly. 5 and 7 both go into 35.

$$\frac{3}{5} \xrightarrow{\times 7} = \frac{21}{35} \qquad \frac{4}{7} \xrightarrow{\times 5} = \frac{20}{35}$$

b $\frac{21}{35}$ is bigger than $\frac{20}{35}$ so $\frac{3}{5}$ is the bigger fraction.

3 In each part:

(1) Write the fractions with a common denominator.

(2) Use your answer to (1) to say which is the bigger fraction.

a $\frac{1}{3}$ $\frac{1}{2}$ **d** $\frac{3}{8}$ $\frac{2}{5}$ **g** $\frac{3}{5}$ $\frac{4}{6}$

b $\frac{5}{6}$ $\frac{11}{12}$ **e** $\frac{3}{5}$ $\frac{5}{8}$ **h** $\frac{1}{4}$ $\frac{2}{7}$

c $\frac{4}{5}$ $\frac{3}{4}$ **f** $\frac{5}{6}$ $\frac{7}{8}$ ● **i** $\frac{7}{12}$ $\frac{3}{5}$

1 $\frac{1}{4}$ of the cubes are showing.

Write down:

a the fraction of the cubes that are hidden.

b the number of cubes under the book.

2 Half of this shape is shaded.
How many ways can you do this?
Use squared paper to investigate.

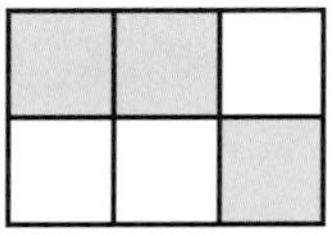

3

Write down the fraction of the cubes that are:

a red **b** yellow **c** blue.

4 Copy and complete these fraction lines.

a

0	$\frac{1}{4}$	$\frac{?}{4}$	$\frac{?}{4}$	$\frac{4}{4}$	$\frac{?}{4}$	$\frac{?}{4}$	$\frac{?}{4}$	$\frac{8}{4}$
0	$\frac{?}{4}$	$\frac{?}{2}$	$\frac{?}{4}$	1	$1\frac{1}{4}$	$1\frac{?}{2}$	$1\frac{?}{4}$	?

b

0	$\frac{?}{5}$	$\frac{?}{5}$	$\frac{?}{5}$	$\frac{?}{5}$	$\frac{?}{5}$	$\frac{?}{5}$	$\frac{?}{5}$	$\frac{?}{5}$	$\frac{?}{5}$	$\frac{10}{5}$
0	$\frac{?}{5}$	$\frac{?}{5}$	$\frac{?}{5}$	$\frac{?}{5}$	?	$1\frac{?}{5}$	?	?	?	?

5 Work out:

a $\frac{1}{3} + \frac{1}{3}$ **c** $\frac{4}{7} + \frac{4}{7}$ **e** $\frac{1}{4} + \frac{3}{8}$ **g** $\frac{7}{10} + \frac{3}{5}$

b $\frac{3}{5} + \frac{2}{5}$ **d** $\frac{1}{3} + \frac{3}{6}$ **f** $\frac{2}{5} + \frac{3}{10}$ **h** $\frac{3}{7} + \frac{2}{5}$

6 Work out:

a $\frac{2}{3} - \frac{1}{3}$ **c** $\frac{7}{9} - \frac{4}{9}$ **e** $\frac{1}{4} - \frac{1}{8}$ **g** $\frac{7}{10} - \frac{2}{5}$

b $\frac{4}{5} - \frac{2}{5}$ **d** $\frac{1}{3} - \frac{1}{6}$ **f** $\frac{2}{5} - \frac{3}{10}$ **h** $\frac{3}{7} - \frac{1}{5}$

7 Mr Smith is a builder.
Here is his plan for a square building plot.

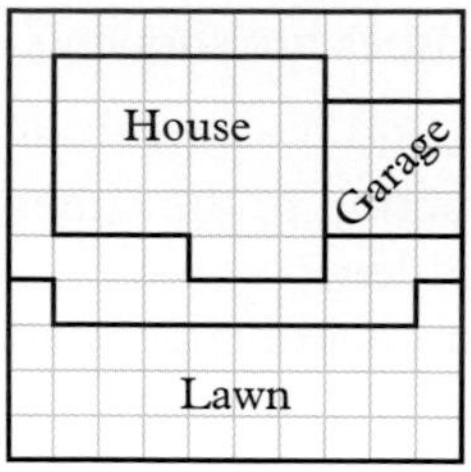

What percentage of the plot is:

a the house?
b the garage?
c the lawn?

8 Copy this table. Fill it in.

Fraction	Percentage
$\frac{42}{100}$	
	29%
	60%
$\frac{56}{100}$	

9 **a** Write 25% as a fraction.
b Write your answer to **a** in its simplest form.

10 Change these fractions to decimals.

a $\frac{3}{5}$ **c** $\frac{1}{4}$ **e** $\frac{7}{8}$
b $\frac{9}{10}$ **d** $\frac{3}{4}$ **f** $\frac{7}{20}$

11 Change these decimals to fractions.

a 0.9 **c** 0.479 **e** 0.44
b 0.23 **d** 0.6 **f** 0.625

12 In each part write down the pairs of fractions. Circle the bigger fraction. Use a number line to help you.

a $\frac{3}{7}$ $\frac{4}{9}$ **d** $\frac{1}{3}$ $\frac{2}{5}$
b $\frac{4}{9}$ $\frac{5}{10}$ **e** $\frac{2}{3}$ $\frac{11}{12}$
c $\frac{3}{5}$ $\frac{5}{11}$ **f** $\frac{5}{7}$ $\frac{7}{9}$

13 In each part:
(1) Write the fractions with a common denominator.
(2) Use your answer to (1) to say which is the bigger fraction.

a $\frac{2}{3}$ $\frac{1}{2}$ **d** $\frac{3}{8}$ $\frac{3}{7}$
b $\frac{1}{6}$ $\frac{3}{12}$ **e** $\frac{4}{5}$ $\frac{7}{8}$
c $\frac{3}{5}$ $\frac{1}{2}$ **f** $\frac{5}{6}$ $\frac{7}{9}$

1 **a** How many degrees are there in a full turn?

Work out the number of degrees in:

b

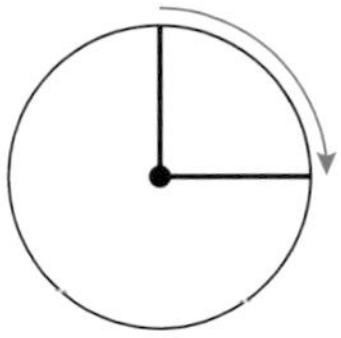

$\frac{1}{4}$ turn

d

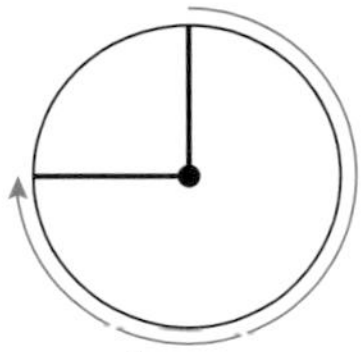

$\frac{3}{4}$ turn

f

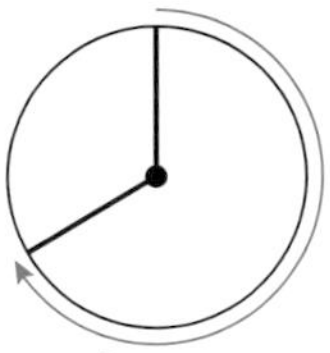

$\frac{2}{3}$ turn

c

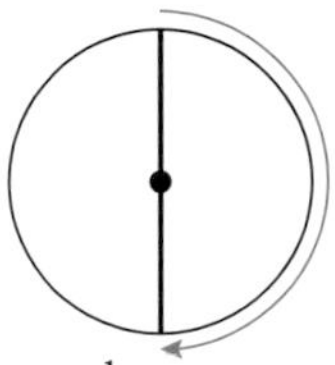

$\frac{1}{2}$ turn

e

$\frac{1}{3}$ turn

g

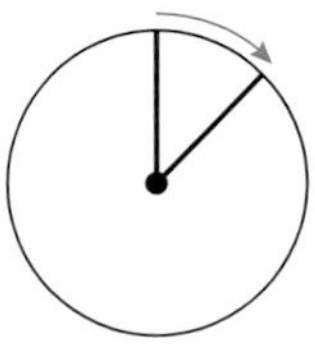

$\frac{1}{8}$ turn

2 **a** Copy the diagram.
b Shade $\frac{1}{4}$ of the diagram.

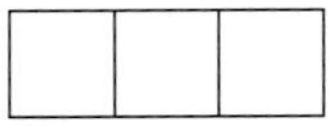

3 True or false?
a $\frac{9}{16}$ is less than one half.
b If the denominator and the numerator are equal, the fraction is 1.
c If the denominator is twice the numerator, the fraction is equal to a half.
d If you add 1 to the denominator you make the fraction larger.
e If the denominator is more than the numerator, the fraction is less than 1.

4 Give the first quantity as a fraction of the second.
Give your answer in its simplest form.
a 1 day, 1 week
b 3 days, 1 week
c 1 week, 1 year
d 30 seconds, 1 minute
e 10 seconds, 1 minute
f 50 cm, 1 metre
g 2 mm, 1 cm
h 1 metre, 1 km
i 100 m, 1 km
j 40 p, £1
k 90 p, £1
l 75 p, £1

5 Work out:
a $\frac{2}{3} + \frac{3}{7}$
b $\frac{4}{9} + \frac{2}{5}$
c $\frac{5}{6} - \frac{4}{7}$
d $\frac{2}{3} - \frac{5}{13}$
e $\frac{1}{2} + \frac{1}{3} + \frac{1}{4}$
f $\frac{2}{3} + \frac{3}{4} + \frac{4}{5}$

6 Rebecca and Julia did a traffic survey.
They recorded the colour of 100 cars.
Here are their results.

Colour of car	Tally
White	卌 卌 卌 卌 卌
Black	卌 卌
Blue	卌 卌 卌 卌 I
Silver/Grey	卌 卌 II
Yellow	II
Red	卌 卌 卌 卌 卌 II
Green	III

a Which colour is the most popular?
b What percentage of the cars were yellow?
c Write the percentage in **b** as a decimal.
d What percentage of the cars were blue?
e Write the percentage in **d** as a fraction of a hundred.
f What percentage of the cars were black?
g Write the percentage in **f** as a fraction of 100.
Simplify your fraction.

7 Write each of these decimals as fractions.
Cancel the fraction down as much as you can.

a 0.1805 **c** 0.3125 **e** 0.488 88
b 0.9755 **d** 0.130 25 **f** 0.428 46

8 Howard has been trying to change $\frac{1}{3}$ to a decimal.
Here is his working.

$$\begin{array}{r} 0.\,3\,3\,3\,3\,3 \\ 3\,\overline{)\,1.\,{}^{1}0\,{}^{1}0\,{}^{1}0\,{}^{1}0\,{}^{1}0} \end{array}$$

a What will happen if Howard continues this division?
b Find out the quick way of writing the answer to this division.
c Use your answer to **b** to write $\frac{2}{3}$ as a decimal.

9 Rewrite each set of fractions in order.
Start with the **smallest**.

a $\frac{1}{3}$ $\frac{2}{5}$ $\frac{4}{7}$ $\frac{5}{11}$
b $\frac{4}{5}$ $\frac{9}{12}$ $\frac{8}{11}$ $\frac{9}{17}$
c $\frac{5}{9}$ $\frac{6}{11}$ $\frac{7}{15}$ $\frac{9}{17}$

- **Numerator** The top of a fraction is the **numerator**. This tells you how many pieces you have to talk about.
  Denominator The bottom of a fraction is the **denominator**. This tells you how many pieces the whole was cut into.
  Shading $\frac{3}{5}$ of  gives 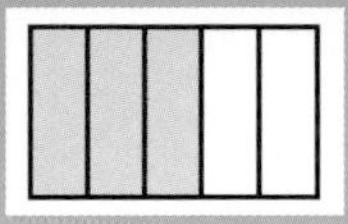 The shape is divided into 5 pieces. 3 pieces have been shaded.

- *Example* Find $\frac{2}{3}$ of 12 sweets

  $\frac{1}{3}$ of 12 $= 12 \div 3$ (Divide by 3 to find $\frac{1}{3}$)
  $= 4$
  $\frac{2}{3}$ of 12 $= 4 \times 2$ (Multiply by 2 to find $\frac{2}{3}$)
  $= 8$

- **Equivalent fractions** Equivalent fractions are different ways of writing the same fraction.
  $\frac{2}{4}$ $\frac{3}{6}$ $\frac{4}{8}$ $\frac{5}{10}$ are all equivalent to $\frac{1}{2}$

- **Simplifying fractions** Simplifying fractions is also known as cancelling. Look for the biggest number that will divide exactly into the top and bottom numbers.
  $\frac{8}{12} = \frac{2}{3}$ (÷4 top and bottom)

- **Adding fractions** To add fractions the bottom numbers of both fractions must be the same.
  $\frac{2}{3} = \frac{?}{6}$ (×?) $\quad \frac{2}{3} = \frac{4}{6}$ (×2) $\quad \frac{2}{3} = \frac{4}{6}$

  The $\frac{1}{6}$ does not need changing.
  So $\frac{2}{3} + \frac{1}{6} = \frac{4}{6} + \frac{1}{6} = \frac{5}{6}$

  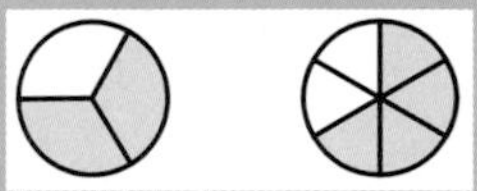

- **Percentage** A **percentage** is a fraction out of 100.
  25 out of 100 $= \frac{25}{100} = 25\%$

- **Fraction to decimal** To change a fraction to a decimal, divide the top number by the bottom number.
  $\frac{3}{5} = 3 \div 5 = 0.6$ $\quad$ $5\overline{)3.{}^{3}0}$ = 0.6

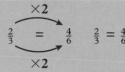

- **Decimal to fraction** $0.6 = \frac{6}{10}$ $\quad 0.24 = \frac{24}{100}$ $\quad 0.272 = \frac{272}{1000}$

- **Ordering fractions** $\frac{2}{3}$ is the same as $\frac{8}{12}$. $\frac{3}{4}$ is the same as $\frac{9}{12}$
  So $\frac{2}{3}$ is smaller than $\frac{3}{4}$

TEST YOURSELF

1 **a** Write down the fraction three fifths.
b Label the numerator.
c Label the denominator.

2 Copy this rectangle.
Shade $\frac{2}{5}$ of your rectangle.

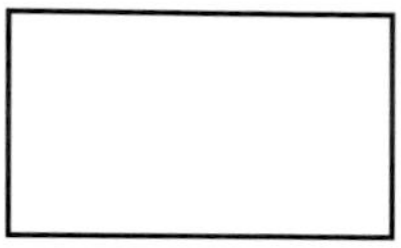

3 **a** Find $\frac{1}{3}$ of 15
b Find $\frac{2}{5}$ of 20

4 Share 5 cakes equally between 3 children.

5 Write $\frac{4}{6}$ as a fraction in its simplest form.

6 **a** Write down the fraction of squares that are shaded.
b Write down the percentage of squares that are shaded.

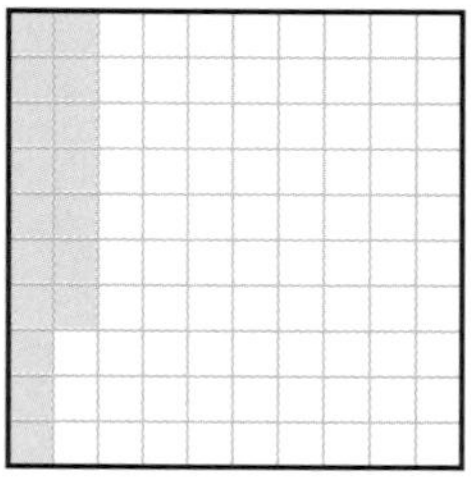

7 **a** Write 10 minutes as a fraction of 1 hour.
b Write your answer to **a** in its simplest form.

8 Work out
a $\frac{2}{5} + \frac{2}{5}$ **b** $\frac{2}{5} + \frac{1}{10}$ **c** $\frac{5}{6} - \frac{1}{3}$

9 **a** Change $\frac{4}{5}$ to a decimal.
b Change $\frac{5}{8}$ to a decimal.

10 Write each of these as fractions.
Cancel the fraction down as much as you can.
a 0.4 **b** 0.56 **c** 0.175

11 Write down the bigger of these two fractions.
$\frac{1}{3}$ $\frac{1}{4}$

12 Rewrite these fractions in order of size.
Start with the smallest.
$\frac{2}{3}$ $\frac{1}{2}$ $\frac{3}{4}$ $\frac{1}{5}$

16 Statistics: what does it all mean?

CORE

1 The mean

2 Other types of average

3 The range

4 Misleading statistics

QUESTIONS

EXTENSION

SUMMARY

TEST YOURSELF

An average puzzle to start this chapter:

A stick is broken into two pieces at random. What is the average length of the shorter piece?

1 The mean

Football clubs like to know how many people are likely to come to watch each game. They record the number of tickets sold for each match and then work out the average.

If they play 21 home games in one season, then the average number of tickets sold is the total number of tickets sold divided by 21.

Example

In the 1994/5 season, the total number of tickets sold at Matlock Town was 8100. They played 27 home games.

So the average attendance was $8100 \div 27 = 300$

This type of average is called the **mean**.

Exercise 16.1

1 Copy this table and fill in the mean attendance for each club.

Club	Total attendance (home matches only)	Number of home matches	Mean
Liverpool	808 584	21	
Middlesbrough	239 200	23	
Tottenham Hotspur	570 360	21	
Celtic	514 000	20	
Altrincham	18 312	21	

Example

You may have to work out the total before you can work out the mean.

For example, the heights of five pupils in centimetres are:
132, 143, 129, 140 and 136.

So the total is:

$132 + 143 + 129 + 140 + 136 = 680$

The mean is $680 \div 5 = 136$ cm

Mean

To find the mean of a set of data:

1 Find the total of all the data values.

2 Divide by the number of data values.

2 The heights, in centimetres, of 12 children are:

132	148	141	136	134	129
146	132	137	118	150	141

a Add up all the heights and write down the total.
b Copy and complete: Mean height = ... ÷ 12 = ...

put your total here

3 The cost of a week's shopping for 15 families is:

£45	£56	£53	£32	£56
£48	£34	£64	£71	£49
£61	£41	£29	£61	£65

a Find the total amount spent by the 15 families.
b Divide this total by 15 to find the mean amount spent.

4 The amounts collected for *Children in Need* by the 8 Year 7 classes were:

£12	£16	£18	£19
£14	£21	£22	£24

a How much was collected altogether?
b Find the mean amount collected.

5 The times taken, in seconds, for the girls in class 7M to run the 100 m race were:

14.1	15.3	15.5	15.6	15.0	14.7	13.9
16.1	15.8	14.5	15.7	14.6	16.3	15.7

a Find the mean time taken to run the race.
b Write down all the times that are faster than the mean (the numbers that are smaller).

6 The weekly wages of 21 people chosen at random from a factory are:

£120	£115	£90	£120	£128	£120	£110
£550	£115	£130	£120	£95	£250	£130
£550	£110	£115	£120	£90	£105	£140

a Find the mean wage.
b Write down the number of people who earn less than the mean wage.
● **c** Explain why so many people earn less than the mean.

Sometimes data is given in a table.

Class 7M counted the number of Smarties found in 100 tubes chosen at random.
Many tubes contained the same number of Smarties.
They put their data in a table.

Number of Smarties in a tube	Number of tubes
34	13
35	24
36	27
37	22
38	14

This row shows that 13 of the tubes had 34 Smarties in them. This is a total of $13 \times 34 = 442$ Smarties

To work out the total number of Smarties they need to find the total for each row. They add another column to the table so it looks like this:

Number of Smarties in a tube	Number of tubes	Number of Smarties
34	13	$13 \times 34 =$ 442
35	24	$24 \times 35 =$ 840
36	27	$27 \times 36 =$ 972
37	22	$22 \times 37 =$ 814
38	14	$14 \times 38 =$ 532
		Total = 3600

Mean number of Smarties $= 3600 \div 100 = 36$

Exercise 16:2

1 Here are 6 piles of Smarties.

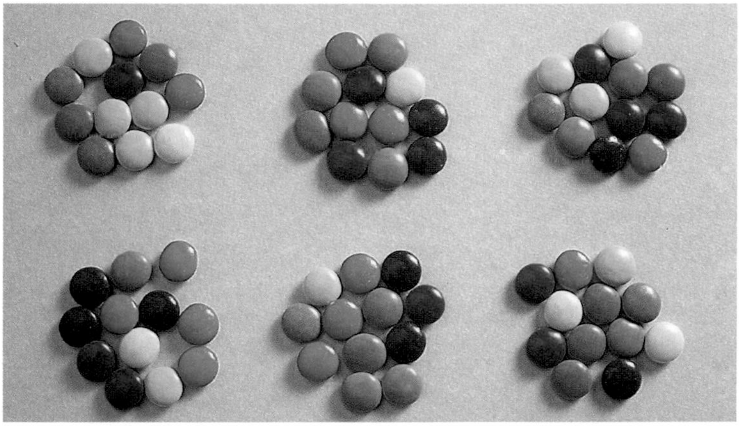

Each pile has 12 Smarties.
Write down the total number of Smarties.

2 Here are 8 packets of chocolates.
a Write down the number of chocolates in each packet.
b Write down the total number of chocolates.

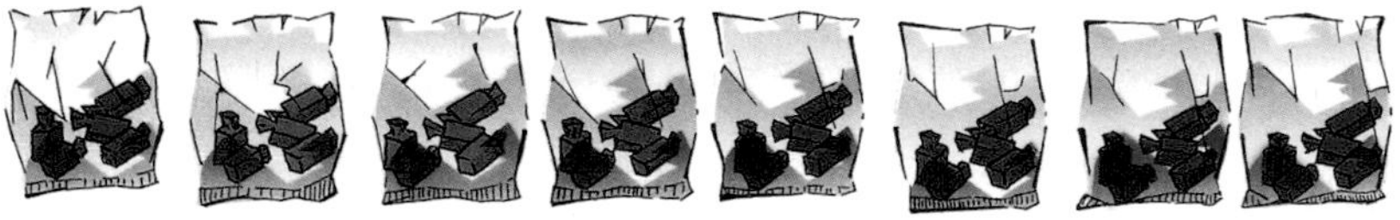

3 Janine has 5 packets of M&Ms. Each packet has 40 sweets.
a Copy and complete:
Janine has $40 + 40 + 40 + 40 + 40 =$ .... M&Ms altogether.
b Copy and complete:
Janine has $40 \times 5 =$ .... M&Ms altogether.
c Which is the quicker way of working out the total number of M&Ms?

4 David has 20 tubes of Rolos. Each tube has twelve sweets.
Copy and complete:
David has a total of $20 \times 12 =$ .... Rolos.

5 Majid has 7 packets of Polos. Each packet contains 20 mints.
Write down the total number of Polos.

6 Sandra has ten packets of Maltesers.

a 6 packets contain 25 sweets.
How many sweets is this?

b The other 4 packets contain 24 sweets.
How many sweets is this?

c Write down the total number of Maltesers.

7 7M chose another 100 tubes of Smarties at random. The number of Smarties in each tube is shown in the table.

a Copy this table and fill in the answers in the last column.

Number of Smarties in a tube	Number of tubes	Number of Smarties
35	14	$35 \times 14 =$
36	24	$36 \times 24 =$
37	26	$37 \times 26 =$
38	20	$38 \times 20 =$
39	16	$39 \times 16 =$
		Total =

b Copy and complete:
The mean number of Smarties in a tube is
.... ÷ 100 = ...

8 The number of matches in 60 boxes is shown in the table.

a Copy the table and fill in the last column.

Number of matches in a box	Number of boxes	Number of matches
46	6	$46 \times 6 =$
47	10	$47 \times 10 =$
48	27	$48 \times 27 =$
49	12	$49 \times 12 =$
50	5	$50 \times 5 =$
		Total =

The makers claim that the average contents is 48.

b Find the mean number of matches in a box.

Do you think the makers are telling the truth?
Write down your reasons.

2 Other types of average

The manager of this shoe shop wants to know the most popular size of shoe sold, so that she doesn't run out of stock.
She decides to work out the average for a month's sales.
The mean shoe sizes are 5.8 for women and 9.2 for men.
She realises that this is not helpful and decides to use a different type of average.
She looks at how many shoes are sold in each size. She writes down the size that sells the most.
For women this is 5 and for men it is 9.
This type of average is called the **mode**.

Mode The **mode** is the most common or the most popular data value.
This is sometimes called the **modal value**.

Exercise 16:3

1 A dice was thrown 100 times. The results were recorded in a tally-chart.

Score	Tally	Total
1	卌 卌 卌 |	16
2	卌 卌 卌	
3	卌 卌 ||||	
4	卌 卌 |||	
5	卌 卌 卌 卌	
6	卌 卌 卌 卌 ||	

a Copy the table and fill in the totals.
b Write down the score which happened the most. This is the mode.

2 These are the numbers of hours of sunshine on each day in August.

5	8	7	6	8	7	3	10	5
7	6	7	8	9	10	4	6	7
6	3	0	10	7	5	8	7	6
5	7	6	5					

a Make a tally-chart for this data.
b Write down the mode.

3 This graph shows the favourite colours of class 7B.

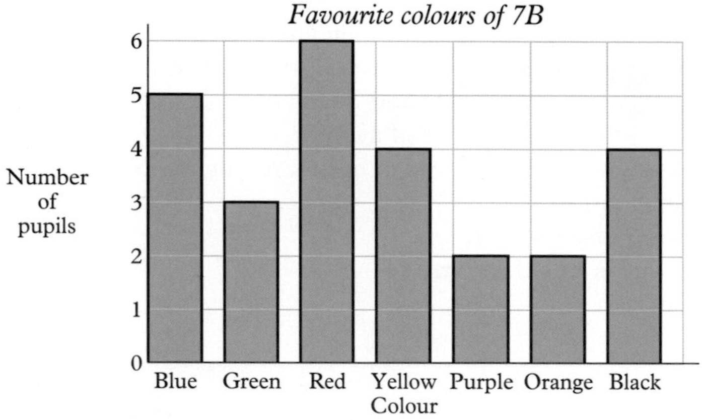

a Write down the modal colour.
b Why is it impossible to work out the mean colour?

4 This pie-chart shows the banks used by 60 people.

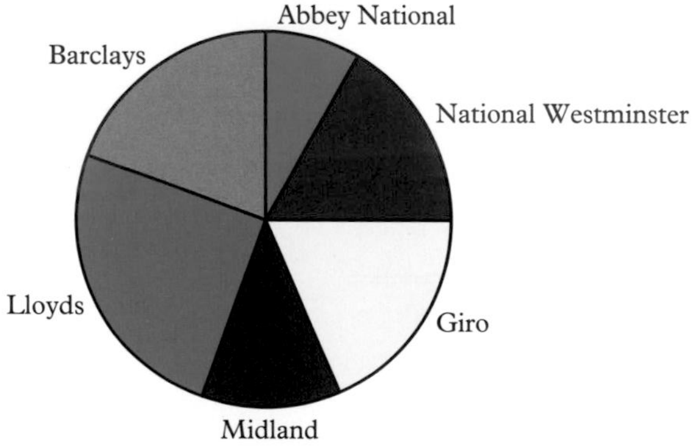

a What is the mode?
b Explain how you can find the mode from the pie-chart.

Median

There is a third type of average called the **median**. The median is the middle value of the data.

Of course you must make sure that your data is in order from smallest to largest. It wouldn't make sense just to find the middle value if the data hadn't been sorted – you might get the smallest value!

These were the wages in a question that you saw earlier:

£120	£115	£90	£120	£113	£120	£110	£550	£115
£130	£120	£95	£250	£130	£550	£110	£115	£120
£90	£105	£140						

You need to re-write this data in order of size to find the median.

£90	£90	£95	£105	£110	£110	£113	£115	£115
£115	£120	£120	£120	£120	£120	£130	£130	£140
£250	£550	£550						

There are 21 values so the middle one is the 11th. There are 10 on either side.
The middle value is £120 so this is the **median**.

This is quite different from the mean which is £158.
Next time you hear people arguing about average wages remember that they may have worked out the average in different ways to make their point.

Exercise 16:4

1 Copy these numbers.
Circle the middle number in each list. This is the **median**.

a 2 3 4 8 12 13 14 18 19

b 3 8 8 9 10 12 14 18 21 23 25

2 Write out these lists in order of size, starting with the **smallest**.
Circle the median of each list.

a 16 12 8 3 4 9 16 1 8

b 2.9 2.4 1.6 2.2 8.6 9.1 0.7 8.1 7.3 6.2 5.3

3 Here are the heights of the 27 pupils in 7R.

Height in cm	Number of pupils
120	3
125	10
130	6
135	4
140	4

a List all 27 heights in order of size, starting with the smallest.
120 120 120 125 ....

b Circle the median height.

So far we have found the median when there is an odd number of data values. If there is an even number of values we must look at the middle pair of values.

Example Find the median of the numbers

3 6 8 9 12 14 16 17

The median is half-way between the middle two numbers. Sometimes this is easy to spot but if not add the two numbers together and divide by 2.

So median $= \frac{9 + 12}{2} = 10.5$

Like the mean, the median does not have to be one of the data values.

4 Find the median of each of these sets of numbers.

a 6 8 9 10 11 13 14 15 17 20

b 4 8 12 14 14 15 17 18

c 2 6 7 8 9 9 10 11

• **d** 14 12 2 8 6 14 23 17 6 23 4 5 9 15 18 16

3 The range

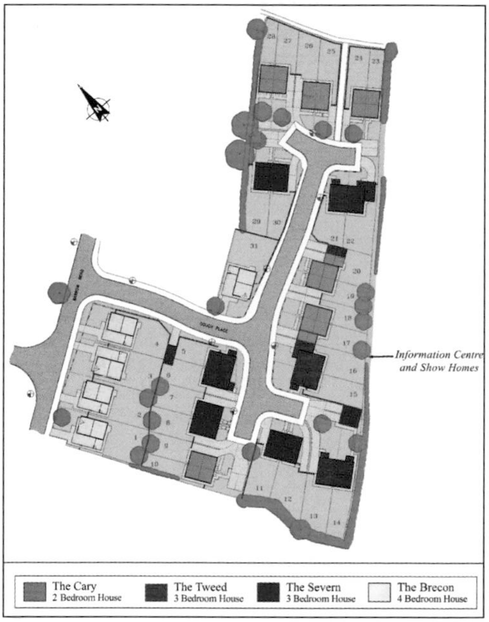

The prices of houses on this new estate start at £56 000 and go up to £90 000.

The difference in price between the cheapest and the most expensive house is
£90 000 − £56 000 = £34 000

This difference is called the **range**.

Range For any set of data, the **range** is the biggest value take away the smallest value.

Exercise 16:5

1 **a** Copy each of the following sets of data.
b Draw a circle around the biggest value.
c Draw a square around the smallest value.
d Find the range.

(1)	4	8	9	10	11	15	16	
(2)	1	2	4	8	16	17	19	22
(3)	10 800		15 000		15 500		18 300	21 300
(4)	2.8	3.1	4.9	8.6	14.3	21.6		
(5)	7.2	1.3	8.4	2.1	3.6	4.7	9.3	8.4

2 The range of a set of data is 16. The biggest data value is 26.
Find the smallest value.

3 Look at the data for hours of sunshine during the year in two different countries.

Month	Jan	Feb	Mar	Apr	May	Jun	Jul	Aug	Sep	Oct	Nov	Dec
Country 1	154	161	165	170	173	185	190	198	187	164	153	140
Country 2	50	80	120	165	190	236	260	301	276	197	101	64

a Work out the total number of hours of sunshine for each country.
b Work out the mean number of hours of sunshine for each country.
c Write down the biggest value for Country 1.
d Write down the smallest value for Country 1.
e Work out the range for Country 1.
• **f** Work out the range for Country 2.

4 When you call a taxi you don't usually wait a long time before the taxi arrives. The time it takes for the taxi to arrive is called the response time.
Here are some response times in minutes for Carol's Cars.

12 15 9 17 8 13 16 19 10 7 13

a Add up all the times for Carol's Cars.
b Divide by 11 to find the mean response time.
c Copy and complete:
The slowest time for Carol's Cars was .... mins.
The quickest time for Carol's Cars was .... mins.
The range in response times is .... − .... = ... mins.

Alan's Autos is a rival firm.
Some of their response times in minutes are:

14 12 11 14 12 10 13 12 13 14 14

d Work out the mean.
e Work out the range.
f How many times did Carol's Cars take more than 14 minutes?
g How many times did Alan's Autos take more than 14 minutes?
h How many times did Carol's Cars take less than 11 minutes?
i How many times did Alan's Autos take less than 11 minutes?
j Mr Jones has an important meeting at another office in 30 minutes. The journey will take 15 minutes.
Which taxi company should he use? Explain why.
k Mr Jones would like a chance for a quick cup of coffee before the meeting starts.
Which taxi company should he use? Explain why.

Exercise 16:6 Simulation

Sometimes it is easier to do experiments than to collect data directly. These experiments are often called **simulations.**

Cereal packets often have cards or models to collect.

You can use dice to do an experiment to simulate how many boxes you would need to buy to collect the whole set.

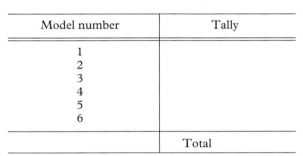

Six model cars are being given away inside Corn Crunchies packets.

Take an ordinary dice. Each number on the dice represents one of the models.

Draw a table like this to record your results:

Model number	Tally
1 2 3 4 5 6	
	Total

Roll the dice and record the number you score in the tally column.
Each time that you roll the dice it is like buying a packet of Corn Crunchies.
Keep rolling the dice, but stop as soon as you have rolled all the numbers.

Now add up the total number of rolls. This is the number of packets you would have to buy to get all six models.

Repeat the experiment at least ten times.

Find the mean number of packets you would have to buy.

Find the range of the number of packets you would have to buy.

● What would happen if there were 8 or 10 models to collect?
Change the experiment and try it for one of these.
Is the range different?

4 Misleading statistics

The Minister of Health and Social Security is presenting information during an election campaign. His charts show increases in spending on the National Health Service.
Do the charts give a fair picture of the figures?

Changing the scale of a diagram can have a big effect on its appearance. When you read statistical diagrams, you should always look carefully at the scale or the key.

Look at the two diagrams below.
The one on the left was drawn by a record company that specialises in selling singles.
The one on the right was prepared by a company that sells CDs of chart hits.

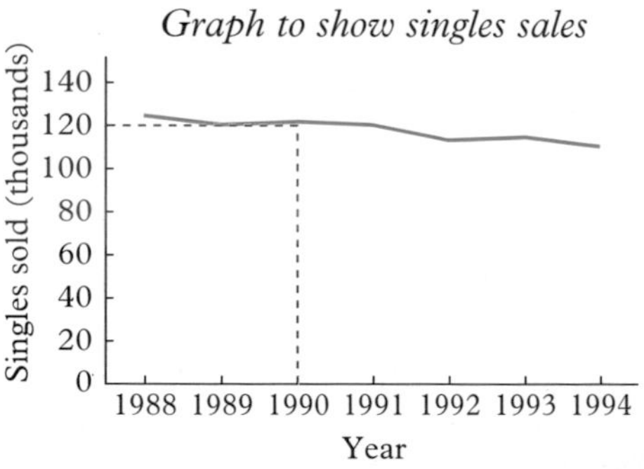

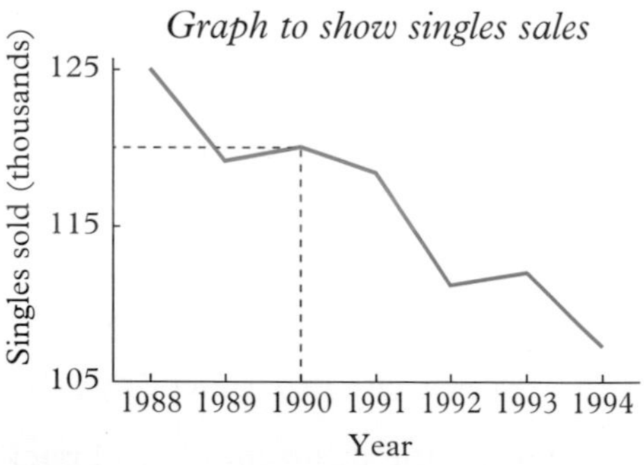

The two graphs show exactly the same information. They look very different because the scales are different.
Read off the figure for 1990 on each graph, shown by the red dotted line.
You will see that they both give the same figure.

Exercise 16:7

1 For each of the following questions there are two graphs. They show the same information but look different because of the scales.
Read the explanation that goes with each pair.
Say which graph each person would choose and why.

a A car sales manager is trying to prove to one of the sales staff that he is not selling enough cars and that he is in danger of losing his job.
The salesperson is trying to show that he is doing well.

Graph A

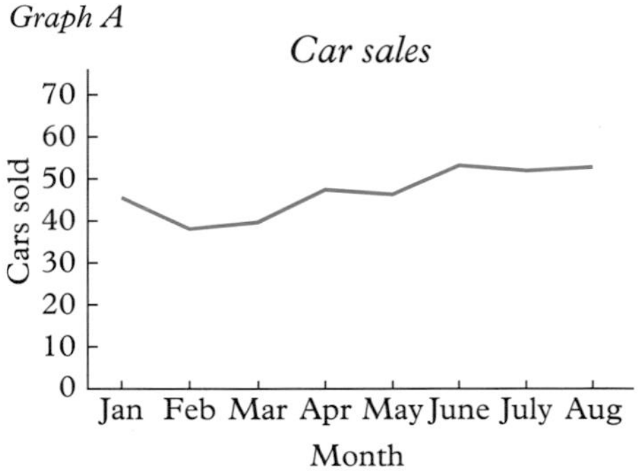

Graph B

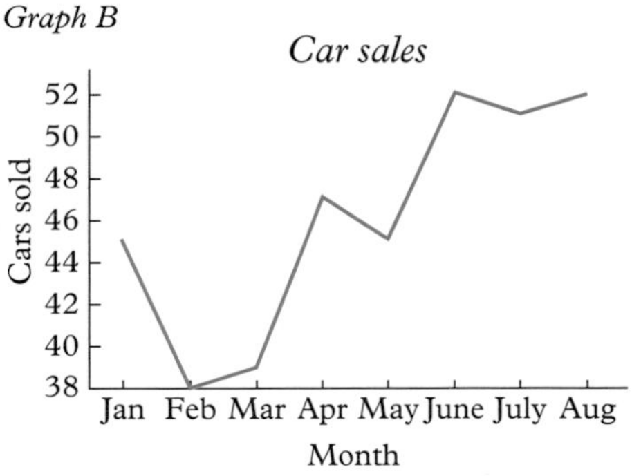

b The government is trying to prove to the voters that unemployment is holding steady.
The opposition wants to show that it is rising steeply.

Graph C

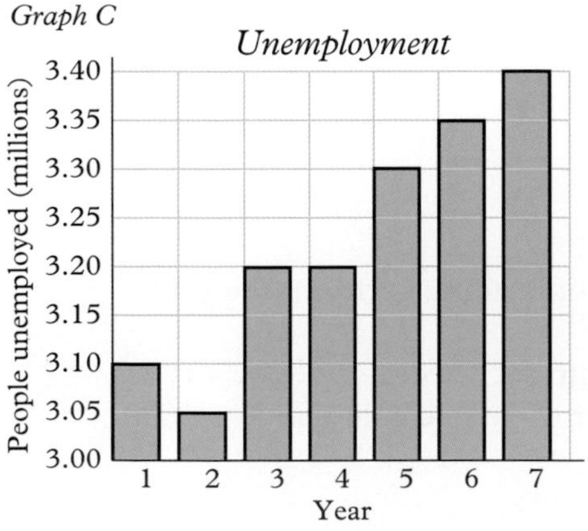

Graph D

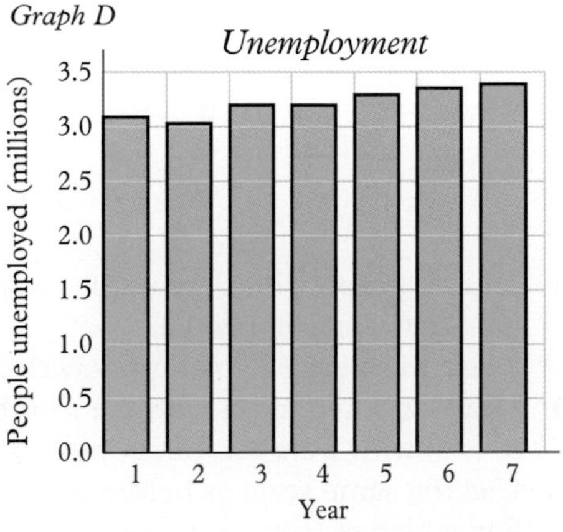

c A new DJ has taken over the breakfast show on a local radio station and wants to show that the audience figures have gone up.
The station manager is not impressed. She thinks that the new DJ is not doing a good job.

Graph E

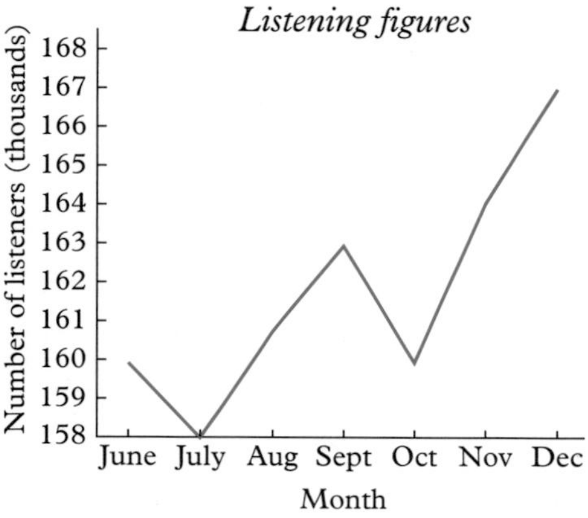

Graph F

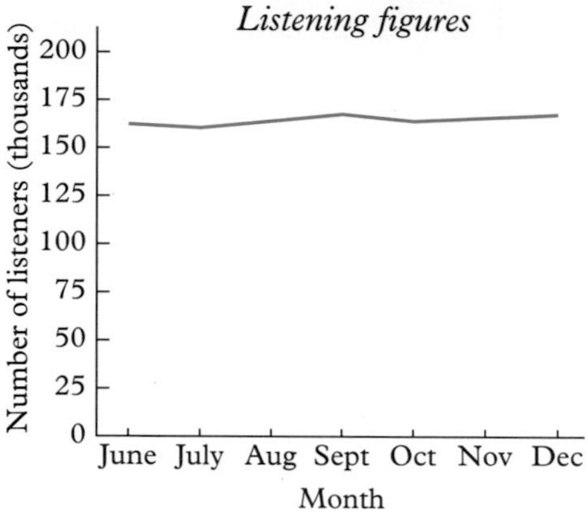

2 The audience figures for a theatre over a period of eight weeks are shown below.
The person in charge of the box office wants to show that the audiences are increasing because she wants some extra staff.
The manager does not want to pay any more staff and so he wants to show that the audiences are staying at about the same level.

Week 1	840	Week 5	870
Week 2	860	Week 6	870
Week 3	855	Week 7	875
Week 4	867	Week 8	878

a Draw a graph with the number of people going up from 0 to 900.
Use 2 cm for 100 people.
Mark the weeks going across with 2 cm for 1 week.

b Draw another graph with the number of people going up from 830 to 880 with 2 cm for 10 people.
Use the same scale as before going across.

c Say which person would use each graph and why.

Exercise 16:8

You are now going to use all the statistics skills you have learned to produce a new advertising campaign.

You are going to advertise a new breakfast cereal.

You will need to show how good it is compared with another breakfast cereal that you can already buy. You will need the details from the panel at the side of a cereal packet showing the energy, fibre and vitamin contents.

Below are the details of your new cereal:

Nutritional Content (per 100 g)		
Energy	320 Kcal	Vitamins:
Protein	8 g	B6 1.6 mg
Fat	1.6 g	B2 1.7 g
Carbohydrate	68 g	B1 0.8 μg
Fibre	9.8 g	D 2.3 μg
		B12 1.8 μg
		Iron 7.3 μg

Look at these details carefully and compare them with your cereal packet. You need to pick out the things in this new cereal that are better and produce some diagrams to make it look really good by choosing your scale carefully.

If the things in the new cereal are not as good then alter the scale on the graph so that it looks as if there is very little difference.

Produce an advertisement for a magazine and a more detailed information sheet to be sent to shop managers to tell them about the new product.

Remember that you must not lie, but you must use your skill to make the new cereal look as good as possible. You will also need to give it a name and decide on the price.

W To see how the Government produces its statistics, ask your teacher for the '*Social Trends*' worksheets.

1 The pocket money given to 12 pupils in 7B is:

60 p   70 p   80 p   90 p   95 p   £1.30   £1.40
£1.45   £1.55   £1.60   £1.75   £2

a Find the total amount of pocket money given to these 12 pupils.
b Find the mean amount of pocket money given to these pupils.

2 Chenise waits for the school bus outside her house.
These are the times she had to wait in one week.

2 mins   3 mins   5 mins   6 mins   8 mins

a Find the mean waiting time.

Over the next 9 weeks Chenise collected data and drew this table to tally her results.

Number of minutes to wait	Tally	Total
1	||	
2	||	
3	𝍸 |||	
4	𝍸 |||	
5	𝍸 |	
6	𝍸 𝍸	
7	|||	
8	|||	
9	||	
10	|	

b Copy the table and fill in the total column.
c Find the mode.

3 **a** Find the median of these wages.

£100   £110   £120   £120   £130   £140
£160   £160   £160   £400   £600

b Find the mean wage.
c Which average do you think is the best? Explain why.

4 Find the range of each set of data.

a 8   16   21   24   29   30   32
b 4   8   6   1   3   19   12   18
c 20 000   20 001   20 010   20 020   20 025

5 This graph shows how much time Saleem spent helping his Mum around the house over the last 4 weeks.
Saleem says that he should have more pocket money because the amount of time he has spent helping has shot up.

a Does Saleem deserve a big rise? Explain your answer.

b Draw a graph using the same numbers on a different scale to help his Mum.

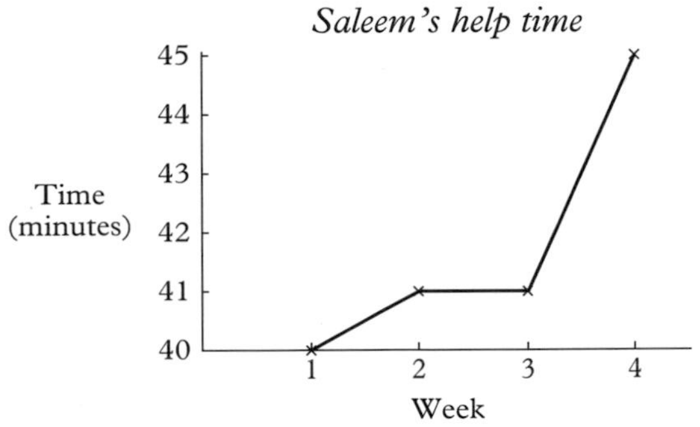

6 This pie-chart shows the favourite TV programmes of the 30 children in 7M.

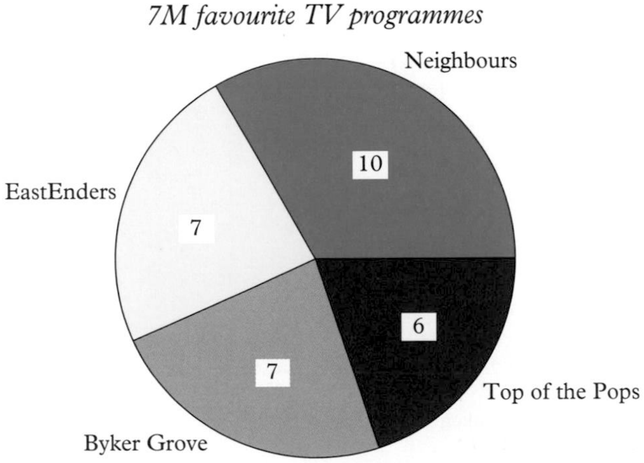

a Which is the mode? Explain how you can tell.
b Draw a bar-chart to show the same data.

1 The weekly wages of 20 people chosen at random from a factory are:

£135	£119	£113	£135	£113	£135	£110
£490	£119	£130	£135	£127	£245	£130
£490	£110	£119	£135	£105	£160	

a Find the mean wage.
b Write down the number of people who earn below the mean wage.

2 Bags of sweets are labelled 'Average contents 100'. A random sample of 50 bags was tested.
The results are shown in the table.

Number of sweets in each bag	Number of bags
98	𝍸 I
99	𝍸 𝍸 II
100	𝍸 𝍸
101	𝍸 𝍸 III
102	𝍸 IIII

a Work out the mean and the mode for these bags of sweets.
b Is the statement 'Average contents 100' true for both types of average? Explain your answer.

3 The times taken by 90 snails to finish a race are shown below.

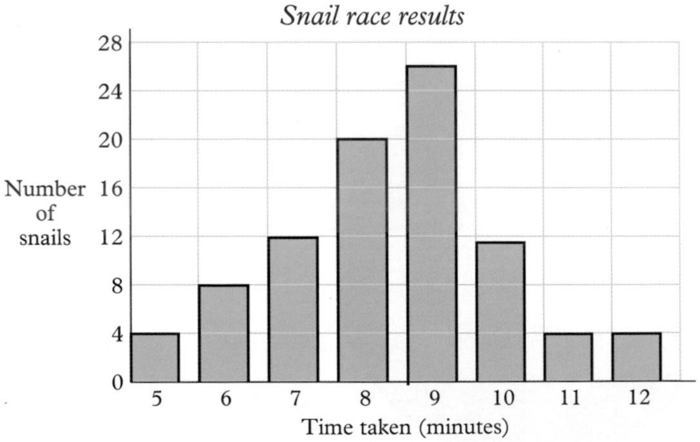

a What is the modal time taken?
b Calculate the mean time taken.
c How many snails took more than the mean time to finish the race?

4 Find the median of each set of data.

a 23 28 34 27 31 30 42 34 39

b 24 28 37 40 24 26 29 31 35 38

5 The owner of a small shop is applying for a bank loan. She sends the bank manager this graph to show her profits over the past 6 months.

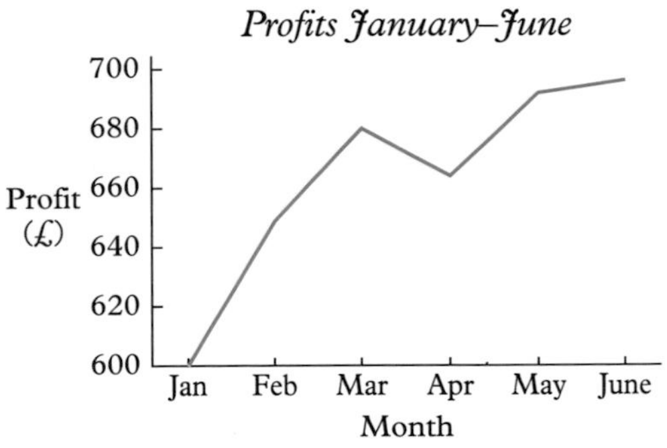

a What has the shop-owner done to the graph to make her profits look very good?

b This is the data she used:

Jan	Feb	Mar	Apr	May	Jun
£600	£650	£680	£670	£690	£695

Plot another version of the graph with the profits starting at 0 on the side scale.

c Describe how the profits look on your graph compared with the first one.

6 These are the heights in centimetres of 10 pupils in Sally's class:

124	136	118	127	143
131	129	122	138	134

Sally works out the mean height and gets 102.3 cm.

Explain why Sally must be wrong. Do not work out the mean.

- To find the **mean** of a set of data:
  1 Find the total of all the data values.
  2 Divide by the number of values.

  For example, the mean of the numbers 2, 4, 7, 9 and 13 is

  $$\frac{2 + 4 + 7 + 9 + 13}{5} = \frac{35}{5} = 7$$

- When data is in a **table**, add another column to work out the total.

  Example
  Number of Smarties in 100 tubes.

Number of Smarties in a tube	Number of tubes	Number of Smarties
34	13	13 × 34 = 442
35	24	24 × 35 = 840
36	27	27 × 36 = 972
37	22	22 × 37 = 814
38	14	14 × 38 = 532
		Total = 3600

  Mean number of Smarties $= \frac{3600}{100} = \mathbf{36}$

- The **mode** is the most common data value – the one which appears the most.
  The **median** is the middle value of the data when it is in order from smallest to largest.
  For an even number of values find the middle two. Then find the number in the middle of these by adding them and dividing by 2.

  For example, the mode of 2, 4, 6, 7, 8, 7, 5, 9, 6, 4, 8, 5, 8 is **8** because there are more 8s than anything else.

  To find the median, write the data out again in order:
  2, 4, 4, 5, 5, 6, **6**, 7, 7, 8, 8, 8, 9
  The median is 6 as this is the middle number.

- The range is the biggest value take away the smallest value.
  The range tells us how spread out the data is. The bigger the range the more spread out the data.

  The range of 2, 4, 6, 7, 8, 7, 8, 5, 9, 6, 4, 8, 5, 8 is 9 − 2 = 7

- Statistics can be **misleading** if you draw axes which do not start at 0. Always look very carefully at the scale when you are reading any type of diagram.

1 The cost of a week's shopping for 12 families is:

£45	£54	£29	£32	£39	£42
£78	£47	£23	£46	£76	£29

a Find the total amount spent by these 12 families.
b Find the mean amount they spend.

2 Packets of crisps are marked 30 g **e** which means that 30 g is the average contents.

Here are the weights of 30 packets of crisps, chosen at random from the production line.

Weight	Number of packets	Weight of crisps
28 g	4	$4 \times 28 =$
29 g	5	$5 \times 29 =$
30 g	11	$11 \times 30 =$
31 g	7	$7 \times 31 =$
32 g	3	$3 \times 28 =$
		Total =

a Copy the table and fill in the last column.
b Find the total weight of all the packets.
c Find the mean weight of these 30 packets.

3 These are the totals obtained by throwing two dice and adding the scores together.

12	7	4	9	11	6	8	7	7
3	9	10	12	3	5	7	6	8
9	12	11	3	6	8	7	9	4
10	6	8	9	11	7	8	7	5

a Copy and complete this tally-chart of these results.

Score	Tally	Total
2		
3		
4		
5		
6		
7		
8		
9		
10		
11		
12		

b Write down the mode of these scores.

4 Howard is testing his reaction times using a computer program. His times in seconds are:

0.23	0.24	0.29	0.24	0.34	0.25	0.34	0.23	0.27
0.34	0.23	0.29	0.34	0.32	0.41	0.39	0.21	

a Write down his slowest time.
b Write down his quickest time.
c Find the range of these reaction times.
d Re-write the results in order and circle the median time.

5 The sales figures for eight weeks in a furniture shop are:

Week	Sales (£)
1	8500
2	8800
3	8650
4	9200
5	9000
6	9400
7	9550
8	9400

The figures are shown in these two graphs:

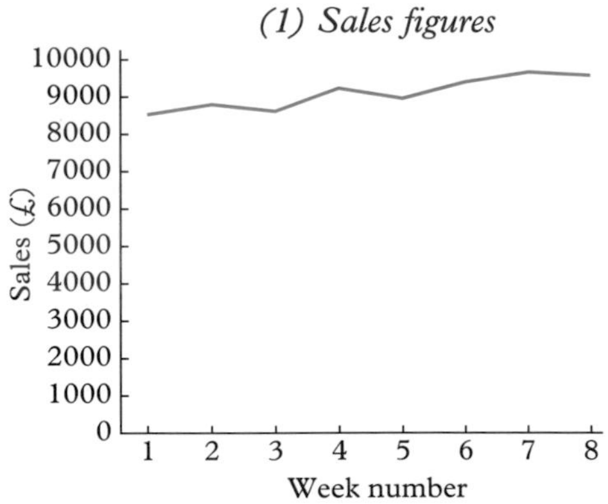

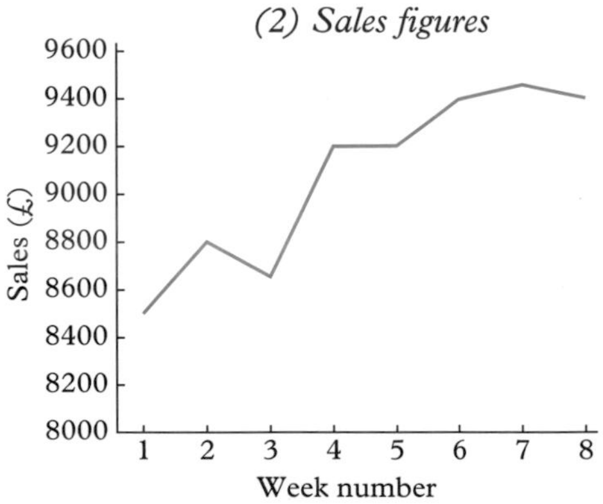

a Which graph makes the sales figures look best? Explain why.
b Which graph would the shop manager want to use? Explain why.
c If you were in charge of a rival firm, which graph would you like to see? Explain why.

Help yourself

1 Adding

You should set out additions in columns.

Example

13 + 2 should be set out like this:

$$\begin{array}{r} 13 \\ +\ \ 2 \\ \hline 15 \end{array}$$

Here are some more examples.

27 + 21 431 + 26 542 + 136

$$\begin{array}{r} 27 \\ +\ 21 \\ \hline 48 \end{array} \qquad \begin{array}{r} 431 \\ +\ \ 26 \\ \hline 457 \end{array} \qquad \begin{array}{r} 542 \\ +\ 136 \\ \hline 678 \end{array}$$

Sometimes we need to 'carry'. This happens when a column adds up to 10 or more.

Example

13 + 9

$$\begin{array}{r} 13 \\ +\ \ 9 \\ \hline 22 \\ {}_{1}\ \ \end{array}$$

Here are some more examples.

27 + 29 246 + 28 558 + 67

$$\begin{array}{r} 27 \\ +\ 29 \\ \hline 56 \\ {}_{1}\ \ \end{array} \qquad \begin{array}{r} 246 \\ +\ \ 28 \\ \hline 274 \\ {}_{1}\ \ \end{array} \qquad \begin{array}{r} 558 \\ +\ \ 67 \\ \hline 625 \\ {}_{1\,1}\ \end{array}$$

Exercise 1

Copy these into your book.
Work out the answers.

1 $\begin{array}{r} 16 \\ +\ \ 3 \\ \hline \end{array}$

2 $\begin{array}{r} 24 \\ +\ 32 \\ \hline \end{array}$

3 $\begin{array}{r} 36 \\ +\ 12 \\ \hline \end{array}$

4 $\begin{array}{r} 431 \\ +\ 134 \\ \hline \end{array}$

5 $\begin{array}{r} 621 \\ +\ \ 48 \\ \hline \end{array}$

6 $\begin{array}{r} 27 \\ +\ 632 \\ \hline \end{array}$

7 $\begin{array}{r} 5042 \\ +\ \ 627 \\ \hline \end{array}$

8 $\begin{array}{r} 3609 \\ +\ 4290 \\ \hline \end{array}$

9 11 + 6

10 32 + 26

11 542 + 37

12 541 + 126

Exercise 2

Copy these into your book.
Work out the answers.

1 $\begin{array}{r} 18 \\ +\ \ 6 \\ \hline \end{array}$

2 $\begin{array}{r} 38 \\ +\ 27 \\ \hline \end{array}$

3 $\begin{array}{r} 178 \\ +\ 219 \\ \hline \end{array}$

4 $\begin{array}{r} 324 \\ +\ 167 \\ \hline \end{array}$

5 $\begin{array}{r} 435 \\ +\ 175 \\ \hline \end{array}$

6 $\begin{array}{r} 423 \\ 122 \\ +\ \ 48 \\ \hline \end{array}$

7 $\begin{array}{r} 397 \\ +\ 483 \\ \hline \end{array}$

8 $\begin{array}{r} 1476 \\ +\ \ 646 \\ \hline \end{array}$

9 36 + 27 **11** 2488 + 512

10 243 + 361 **12** 7959 + 929

Other words

All these words can also mean **add**.

plus **sum** **total**

Examples
Work out 24 **plus** 13
Find the **sum** of 24 and 13
Find the **total** of 24 and 13

all mean $\begin{array}{r} 24 \\ +\ \underline{13} \\ \underline{37} \end{array}$

---

2 Subtracting

Subtractions should also be set out in columns.

Example

28 − 10 should be set out like this:

$$\begin{array}{r} 28 \\ -\ \underline{10} \\ \underline{18} \end{array}$$

Here are some more examples.

29 − 16 436 − 25 587 − 226

$$\begin{array}{r} 29 \\ -\ \underline{16} \\ \underline{13} \end{array} \qquad \begin{array}{r} 436 \\ -\ \underline{25} \\ \underline{411} \end{array} \qquad \begin{array}{r} 587 \\ -\ \underline{226} \\ \underline{361} \end{array}$$

Exercise 3

Copy these into your book.
Work out the answers.

1 $\begin{array}{r} 56 \\ -\ \underline{23} \\ \underline{} \end{array}$ **7** $\begin{array}{r} 3861 \\ -\ \underline{510} \\ \underline{} \end{array}$

2 $\begin{array}{r} 368 \\ -\ \underline{144} \\ \underline{} \end{array}$ **8** $\begin{array}{r} 6213 \\ -\ \underline{102} \\ \underline{} \end{array}$

3 $\begin{array}{r} 469 \\ -\ \underline{135} \\ \underline{} \end{array}$ **9** 648 − 26

4 $\begin{array}{r} 864 \\ -\ \underline{41} \\ \underline{} \end{array}$ **10** 493 − 281

5 $\begin{array}{r} 643 \\ -\ \underline{102} \\ \underline{} \end{array}$ **11** 193 − 181

6 $\begin{array}{r} 1826 \\ -\ \underline{405} \\ \underline{} \end{array}$ **12** 4291 − 1111

Sometimes we need to 'borrow'. This happens when the number on the bottom of a column is bigger than the one on the top.

Example

42 − 19

The 4 is worth 4 lots of 10. We can 'borrow' → one of these 10s. We change it into ten ones.

$\begin{array}{r} \mathbf{42} \\ -\ \underline{19} \\ \underline{} \end{array}$ ← The 9 is bigger than the 2.

Our working now looks like this:

$$\begin{array}{r} \overset{3}{\not4}\,\overset{1}{}2 \\ -\ 1\ 9 \\ \hline 2\ 3 \end{array}$$

← We can now take the 9 away from the 12.

Here is another example:

64 − 28

$$\begin{array}{r} 6\,4 \\ -\ 2\,8 \\ \hline \end{array} \rightarrow \begin{array}{r} \overset{5}{\not6}\,\overset{1}{}4 \\ -\ 2\,8 \\ \hline \end{array} \rightarrow \begin{array}{r} \overset{5}{\not6}\,\overset{1}{}4 \\ -\ 2\,8 \\ \hline 3\,6 \end{array}$$

Here are some more difficult examples:

82 − 67   231 − 119   623 − 487

$$\begin{array}{r} \overset{7}{\not8}\,\overset{1}{}2 \\ -\ 6\,7 \\ \hline 1\,5 \end{array} \quad \begin{array}{r} 2\,\overset{2}{\not3}\,\overset{1}{}1 \\ -\ 1\,1\,9 \\ \hline 1\,1\,2 \end{array} \quad \begin{array}{r} \overset{5}{\not6}\,\overset{11}{\not2}\,\overset{1}{}3 \\ -\ 4\,8\,7 \\ \hline 1\,3\,6 \end{array}$$

Exercise 4

Copy these into your book.
Work out the answers.

1 $\begin{array}{r} 32 \\ -\ 18 \\ \hline \end{array}$

2 $\begin{array}{r} 42 \\ -\ 27 \\ \hline \end{array}$

3 $\begin{array}{r} 217 \\ -\ 123 \\ \hline \end{array}$

4 $\begin{array}{r} 642 \\ -\ 329 \\ \hline \end{array}$

5 $\begin{array}{r} 842 \\ -\ 791 \\ \hline \end{array}$

6 $\begin{array}{r} 911 \\ -\ 635 \\ \hline \end{array}$

7 $\begin{array}{r} 643 \\ -\ 257 \\ \hline \end{array}$

8 $\begin{array}{r} 1423 \\ -\ 979 \\ \hline \end{array}$

9 83 − 29

10 432 − 86

11 521 − 156

12 1240 − 736

You cannot borrow from the next column if there is a zero in it.
You may need to borrow across more than one column.

Example

$$\begin{array}{r} 3\,0\,0 \\ -\ 1\,9\,6 \\ \hline \end{array} \rightarrow \begin{array}{r} \overset{2}{\not3}\,\overset{1}{}0\,0 \\ -\ 1\,9\,6 \\ \hline \end{array} \rightarrow \begin{array}{r} \overset{2}{\not3}\,\overset{9}{\not\overset{1}{}0}\,\overset{1}{}0 \\ -\ 1\,9\,6 \\ \hline 1\,0\,4 \end{array}$$

Exercise 5

Copy these into your book.
Work out the answers.

1 $\begin{array}{r} 300 \\ -\ 174 \\ \hline \end{array}$

2 $\begin{array}{r} 406 \\ -\ 138 \\ \hline \end{array}$

3 $\begin{array}{r} 5000 \\ -\ 287 \\ \hline \end{array}$

4 $\begin{array}{r} 6000 \\ -\ 5246 \\ \hline \end{array}$

Other words

All these words can also mean **subtract**.

take away	**take**
minus	**difference**

Examples
Find 73 **take away** 24
Work out 73 **take** 24
Find 73 **minus** 24
Find the **difference** between 73 and 24

Checking

You can always check a subtraction by adding.

Example

256 − 183

$$\begin{array}{r} \overset{1}{\not{2}}\,\overset{1}{5}\,6 \\ -\ 1\,8\,3 \\ \hline 7\,3 \\ \hline \end{array} \qquad \text{check} \qquad \begin{array}{r} 1\,8\,3 \\ +\ \ 7\,3 \\ \hline 2\,5\,6 \\ \hline \end{array}$$

Go back to your answers for Exercise 5. Check each of them by adding.

3 Multiplying

When we are adding lots of the same number it is quicker to multiply.

Example

$$\begin{array}{r} 3\,1 \\ 3\,1 \\ 3\,1 \\ 3\,1 \\ +\ 3\,1 \\ \hline 1\,5\,5 \\ \hline \end{array} \quad \text{is the same as} \quad \begin{array}{r} 3\,1 \\ \times\ \ 5 \\ \hline 1\,5\,5 \\ \hline \end{array}$$

To do $\begin{array}{r} 3\,1 \\ \times\ \ 5 \\ \hline \\ \hline \end{array}$ first do 5 × 1 $\begin{array}{r} 3\,1 \\ \times\ \ 5 \\ \hline 5 \\ \hline \end{array}$

then do 5 × 3 $\begin{array}{r} 3\,1 \\ \times\ \ 5 \\ \hline 15\,5 \\ \hline \end{array}$

Remember to keep your numbers in columns.

Here are some more examples:

$$\begin{array}{r} 6\,2 \\ \times\ \ 4 \\ \hline 2\,4\,8 \\ \hline \end{array} \qquad \begin{array}{r} 5\,1 \\ \times\ \ 9 \\ \hline 4\,5\,9 \\ \hline \end{array}$$

Exercise 6

1 $\begin{array}{r} 3\,2 \\ \times\ \ 4 \\ \hline \\ \hline \end{array}$ **3** $\begin{array}{r} 4\,2 \\ \times\ \ 4 \\ \hline \\ \hline \end{array}$

2 $\begin{array}{r} 4\,3 \\ \times\ \ 3 \\ \hline \\ \hline \end{array}$ **4** $\begin{array}{r} 4\,2\,3 \\ \times\ \ 3 \\ \hline \\ \hline \end{array}$

Sometimes we need to carry.

Example

$$\begin{array}{r} 2\,6 \\ \times\ \ 3 \\ \hline 8 \\ \hline {\scriptstyle 1} \end{array} \quad \rightarrow \quad \begin{array}{r} 2\,6 \\ \times\ \ 3 \\ \hline 7\,8 \\ \hline {\scriptstyle 1}\ \ \end{array}$$

3 × 2 = 6
Then add the 1 to give 7

Exercise 7

1 $\begin{array}{r} 2\,6 \\ \times\ \ 2 \\ \hline \\ \hline \end{array}$ **6** $\begin{array}{r} 6\,2\,7 \\ \times\ \ 3 \\ \hline \\ \hline \end{array}$

2 $\begin{array}{r} 3\,5 \\ \times\ \ 2 \\ \hline \\ \hline \end{array}$ **7** $\begin{array}{r} 5\,6 \\ \times\ \ 7 \\ \hline \\ \hline \end{array}$

3 $\begin{array}{r} 4\,6 \\ \times\ \ 3 \\ \hline \\ \hline \end{array}$ **8** $\begin{array}{r} 7\,8 \\ \times\ \ 6 \\ \hline \\ \hline \end{array}$

4 $\begin{array}{r} 1\,2\,4 \\ \times\ \ 4 \\ \hline \\ \hline \end{array}$ **9** $\begin{array}{r} 2\,4\,7 \\ \times\ \ 5 \\ \hline \\ \hline \end{array}$

5 $\begin{array}{r} 2\,5\,3 \\ \times\ \ 3 \\ \hline \\ \hline \end{array}$ **10** $\begin{array}{r} 6\,0\,5 \\ \times\ \ 4 \\ \hline \\ \hline \end{array}$

Other words

These words can also mean **multiply**.

times **product** **of**

Examples

Find 24 **times** 16
Find the **product** of 24 and 16
Find one half **of** 24

4 Multiplying by 10

When we multiply by 10, all the digits move across one column to the **left**.
This makes the number 10 times bigger.
We can use the headings **Th H T U** to help.
They mean **Th**ousands, **H**undreds, **T**ens and **U**nits. Units is another way of saying 'ones'.

Example

$23 \times 10 = 230$

H T U

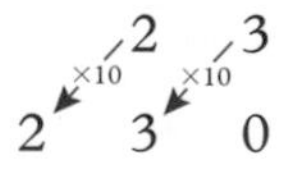

Here are some more examples:

Th H T U

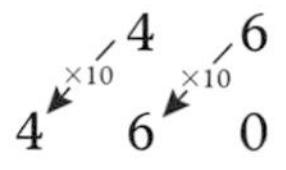

$46 \times 10 = 460$

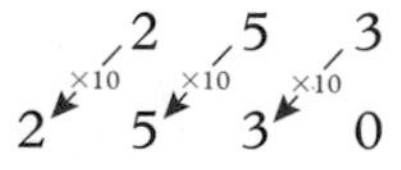

$253 \times 10 = 2530$

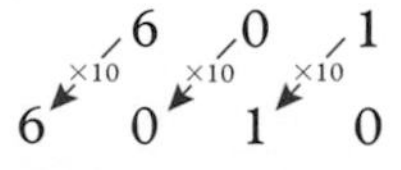

$601 \times 10 = 6010$

Exercise 8

Multiply each of these numbers by 10.

1 27 **4** 823 **7** 8000

2 36 **5** 635 **8** 9001

3 326 **6** 7426

5 Multiplying by 100, 1000, ...

When we multiply by 100, all the digits move across two columns to the left.
This makes the number 100 times bigger.
This is because $100 = 10 \times 10$. So multiplying by 100 is like multiplying by 10 twice.

Example

$74 \times 100 = 7400$

Th H T U

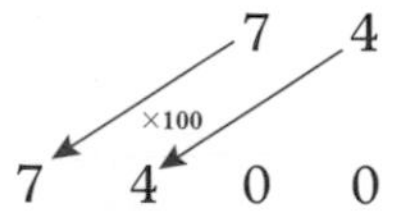

When we multiply by 1000 all the numbers move across three columns to the left.

This is because $1000 = 10 \times 10 \times 10$. This means that multiplying by 1000 is like multiplying by 10 three times.

Example

$74 \times 1000 = 74\,000$

TTh Th H T U

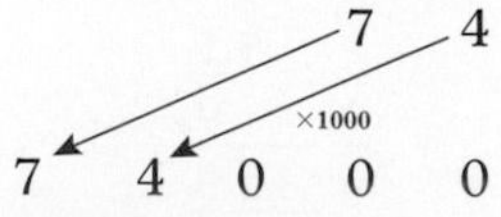

Exercise 9

Write down the answers to these questions.

1 63×100

2 91×100

3 42×1000

4 873×100

5 2770×100

6 605×1000

7 4321×100

8 400×1000

9 2001×1000

10 $634 \times 10\,000$

11 $206 \times 10\,000$

12 $435 \times 100\,000$

6 Multiplying by 20, 30, ...

When we multiply by 20 it is like multiplying by 2 then by 10. This is because $20 = 2 \times 10$.

Example

To do 18×20:

first do

$$\begin{array}{r} 18 \\ \times \quad 2 \\ \hline 36 \\ \hline {\scriptstyle 1} \end{array}$$

Then do $36 \times 10 = 360$

So $18 \times 20 = 360$

In the same way multiplying by 30 is the same as multiplying by 3 and then multiplying by 10.

Example

To do 26×30:

first do

$$\begin{array}{r} 26 \\ \times \quad 3 \\ \hline 78 \\ \hline {\scriptstyle 1} \end{array}$$

Then do $78 \times 10 = 780$

So $26 \times 30 = 780$

Exercise 10

Work out:

1 23×20

2 26×20

3 17×30

4 32×30

5 18×30

6 26×30

7 12×40

8 23×50

9 42×50

10 123×20

11 247×30

12 132×70

7 Long multiplication

When we want to multiply two quite large numbers we have to do it in stages.
Here are two methods. You only have to know one of them.

Method 1

Example 146×24

First do 146×4

$$\begin{array}{r} 146 \\ \times \quad 4 \\ \hline 584 \\ \hline {}_{1\,2} \end{array}$$

Then do 146×20

$$\begin{array}{r} 146 \\ \times \quad 2 \\ \hline 292 \\ \hline {}_{1} \end{array}$$

$292 \times 10 = 2920$

Now add the two answers together.

$$\begin{array}{r} 584 \\ + \; 2920 \\ \hline 3504 \\ \hline \end{array}$$

Usually the working out looks like this:

$$\begin{array}{r} 146 \\ \times \quad 24 \\ \hline 584 \\ 2920 \\ \hline 3504 \\ \hline \end{array}$$

Here is another example.

$$\begin{array}{rl} 223 & \\ \times \quad 36 & \\ \hline 1338 & \leftarrow (223 \times 6) \\ 6690 & \leftarrow (223 \times 30) \\ \hline 8028 & \\ \hline {}_{1\,1} & \end{array}$$

Method 2

Example 125×23

First set out the numbers with boxes, like this:

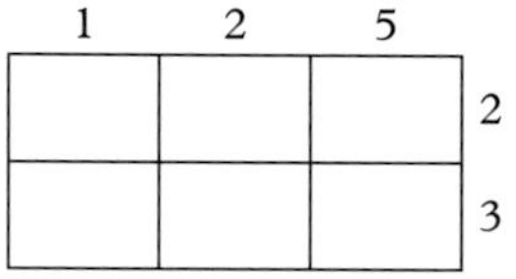

Now draw in the diagonals like this:

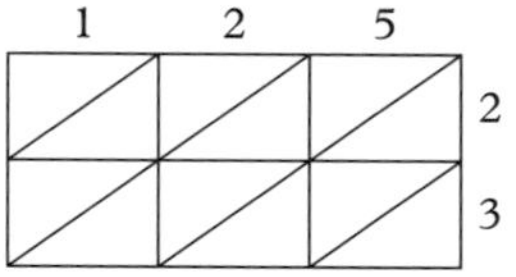

Fill in like a table square then add along the diagonals like this:

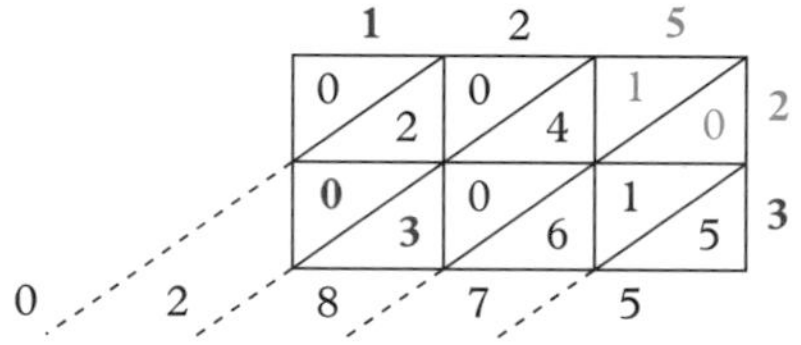

$1 \times 3 = 3$

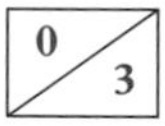

Notice the 0 in the top box when the answer is a single digit.

So the answer is **2875**

Here is another example.
When the diagonal adds up to more than 10, we carry into the next one.

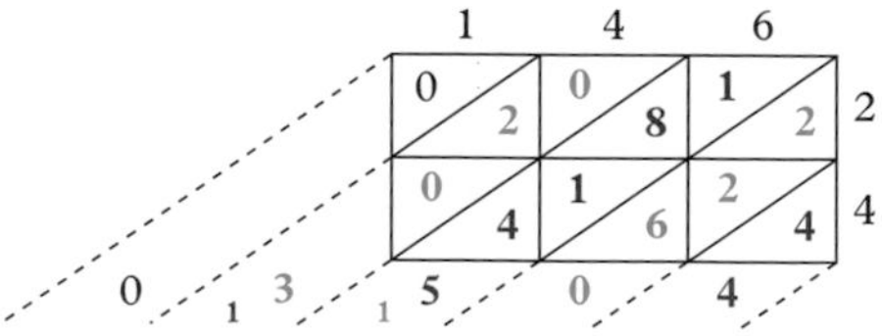

So $146 \times 24 = 3504$

Exercise 11

Use the method you prefer to work these out.

1 43×25

2 56×32

3 123×32

4 241×37

5 361×25

6 248×73

7 481×52

8 572×64

9 634×33

10 721×56

11 863×74

12 999×99

8 Dividing

Multiplying is like doing lots of additions. In the same way dividing is like doing lots of subtractions.

To find out how many 4s make 12 we can see how many times we can take 4 away from 12.

$12 - 4 = 8$ (once)
$8 - 4 = 4$ (twice)
$4 - 4 = 0$ (three times)

So there are 3 lots of 4 in 12.

We can say 12 divided by 4 is 3

or $12 \div 4 = 3$

Example

$15 \div 3 = ?$
$15 - 3 = 12$ (once)
$12 - 3 = 9$ (twice)
$9 - 3 = 6$ (three times)
$6 - 3 = 3$ (four times)
$3 - 3 = 0$ (five times)

So $15 \div 3 = 5$

Exercise 12

Work these out.

1 $18 \div 3$

2 $16 \div 4$

3 $24 \div 6$

4 $25 \div 5$

5 $28 \div 4$

6 $28 \div 7$

7 $36 \div 9$

8 $50 \div 10$

9 $18 \div 2$

10 $30 \div 6$

11 $56 \div 8$

12 $63 \div 9$

When the numbers get bigger, this method takes too long. We need a new way to work it out.

Example

$68 \div 2$

$$2\overline{)68}$$

First work out $6 \div 2 = 3$. Put the 3 above the 6:

$$\begin{array}{r} 3 \\ 2\overline{)68} \end{array}$$

Now work out $8 \div 2 = 4$. Put the 4 above the 8:

$$\begin{array}{r} 34 \\ 2\overline{)68} \end{array}$$

So $68 \div 2 = 34$

Here is another example: $84 \div 4$

$$\begin{array}{r} 21 \\ 4\overline{)84} \end{array}$$

So $84 \div 4 = 21$

Exercise 13

Work these out.

1 $2\overline{)46}$

2 $3\overline{)96}$

3 $6\overline{)66}$

4 $69 \div 3$

5 $82 \div 2$

6 $448 \div 4$

Sometimes we need to 'carry'. This happens when a number does not divide exactly.

Example

$72 \div 4$

$4\overline{)72}$

First do $7 \div 4$. This is 1 with 3 left over.
Put the 1 above the 7 and carry the 3 like this.

$$\begin{array}{r} 1 \\ 4\overline{)7{}^{3}2} \end{array}$$

Now do $32 \div 4$. This is 8. Put the 8 above the ${}^{3}2$ like this

$$\begin{array}{r} 18 \\ 4\overline{)7{}^{3}2} \end{array}$$

So $72 \div 4 = 18$

Here is another example: $85 \div 5$

$$\begin{array}{r} 17 \\ 5\overline{)8{}^{3}5} \end{array}$$

So $85 \div 5 = 17$

Exercise 14

Work these out.

1 $2\overline{)36}$

2 $3\overline{)48}$

3 $96 \div 4$

4 $52 \div 4$

5 $91 \div 7$

6 $68 \div 4$

7 $90 \div 6$

8 $96 \div 8$

9 $436 \div 4$

10 $256 \div 2$

11 $387 \div 3$

12 $294 \div 7$

9 Dividing by 10

When we divide by 10, all the digits move across one column to the **right**. This makes the number smaller.

Example

$230 \div 10 = 23$

H	T	U
2	3	0
	2	3

($\div 10$: each digit moves one column to the right)

Here are some more examples.

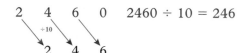

Th	H	T	U	
	5	8	0	$580 \div 10 = 58$
		5	8	
2	4	6	0	$2460 \div 10 = 246$
	2	4	6	

Exercise 15

Divide each of these numbers by 10.

1 630

2 70

3 4960

4 740

5 9010

6 2900

7 3000

8 400 000

10 Dividing by 100, 1000, ...

When we divide by 100, all the digits move across **two** columns to the **right**. This is because 100 = 10 × 10. So dividing by 100 is like dividing by 10 twice.

Example

7400 ÷ 100 = 74

Th H T U

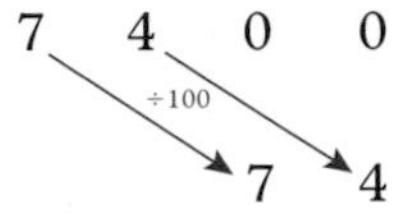

When we divide by 1000, all the numbers move across **three** columns to the **right**.

Example

74 000 ÷ 1000 = 74

TTh Th H T U

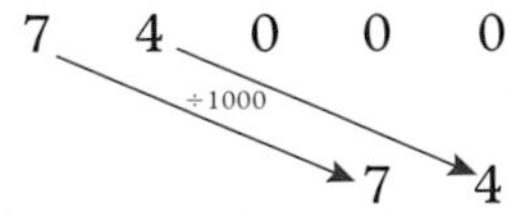

11 Dividing by 20, 30, ...

When we divide by 20, it is like dividing by 2 then by 10. This is because 20 = 2 × 10.

Example

To do 360 ÷ 20

first do $\begin{array}{r} 180 \\ 2\overline{)3^{1}60} \end{array}$

Then do 180 ÷ 10 = 18

So 360 ÷ 20 = 18

In the same way dividing by 30 is the same as dividing by 3 then by 10.

Example

To do 780 ÷ 30

first do $\begin{array}{r} 260 \\ 3\overline{)7^{1}80} \end{array}$

Then do 260 ÷ 10 = 26

So 780 ÷ 30 = 26

Exercise 16

Work these out.

1 6300 ÷ 100
2 6700 ÷ 100
3 8600 ÷ 100
4 24 000 ÷ 1000
5 87 000 ÷ 100
6 87 000 ÷ 1000
7 800 000 ÷ 1000
8 800 000 ÷ 10 000

Exercise 17

Work these out.

1 520 ÷ 20
2 720 ÷ 30
3 2080 ÷ 40
4 1450 ÷ 50
5 1320 ÷ 20
6 1740 ÷ 30
7 3240 ÷ 90
8 16 160 ÷ 80

These words can also mean **divide**.

share **quotient**

Share 240 by 12
Find the **quotient** of 240 and 12 } both mean 240 ÷ 12

To enter a fraction on your calculator use the **ab/c** key.

To enter $\frac{1}{2}$ key in **1** **ab/c** **2**

Your display should show 1┌2

To enter $1\frac{3}{4}$ key in **1** **ab/c** **3** **ab/c** **4**

Your display should show 1┌3┌4

Example Find $\frac{2}{3}$ of 12 sweets.

You want to find $\frac{2}{3} \times 12$

Key in **2** **ab/c** **3** **×** **1** **2** **=**

The answer is 8 sweets.

You can also use the **ab/c** button to work out sharing problems.

Example Share 5 oranges equally between 3 children.

Key in **5** **ab/c** **3** **=**

Your display should show 1┌2┌3

The answer is $1\frac{2}{3}$ oranges.

Examples

1 $\frac{3}{4} + \frac{1}{2} =$ **3** **ab/c** **4** **+** **1** **ab/c** **2** **=** 1┌1┌4
Answer is $1\frac{1}{4}$

2 $2\frac{1}{3} - 1\frac{5}{6} =$ **2** **ab/c** **1** **ab/c** **3** **−** **1** **ab/c** **5** **ab/c** **6** **=** 1┌2
Answer is $\frac{1}{2}$

3 $\frac{2}{3}$ of $4\frac{1}{2} = \frac{2}{3} \times 4\frac{1}{2} =$ **2** **ab/c** **3** **×** **4** **ab/c** **1** **ab/c** **2** **=** 3
Answer is 3

4 $6\frac{3}{4} \div 9 =$ **6** **ab/c** **3** **ab/c** **4** **÷** **9** **=** 3┌4
Answer is $\frac{3}{4}$

CHAPTER 1

1 Half the 28 pupils stayed in the UK.
Half of 28 is $28 \div 2 = 14$.

USA and Europe are each half the UK.
Half of 14 is $14 \div 2 = 7$.

7P on holiday	UK	USA	Europe
Number of pupils	14	7	7

2

7P's holidays

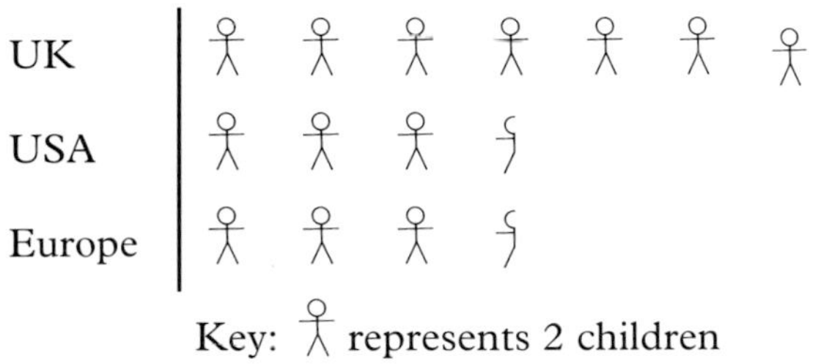

3 a

Results	Tally	Total
1–20	𝍸 |	6
21–40	|||	3
41–60	𝍸 𝍸	10
61–80	𝍸 |||	8
81–100	𝍸	5
	Total	32

b

Pupils' results in the Science exam

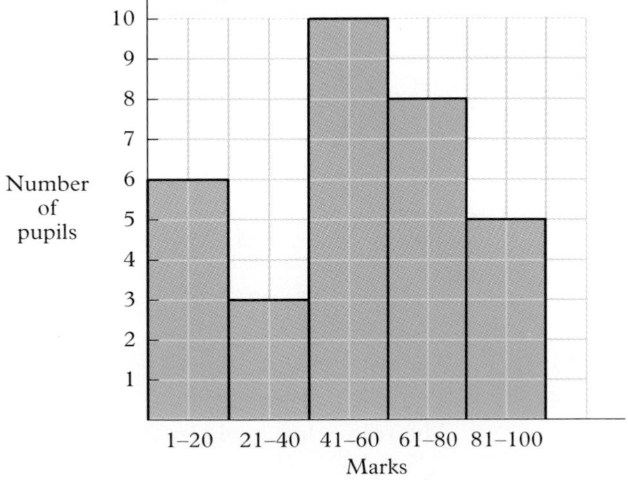

4 Graph A shows correlation. In graphs B and C the points are scattered all over the place.

CHAPTER 2

1 **a**

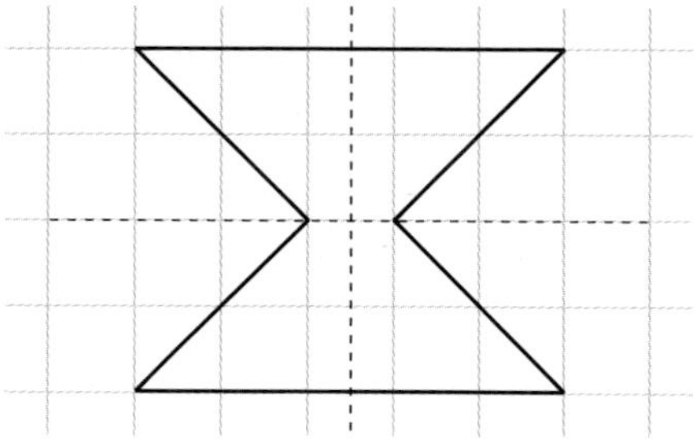

b

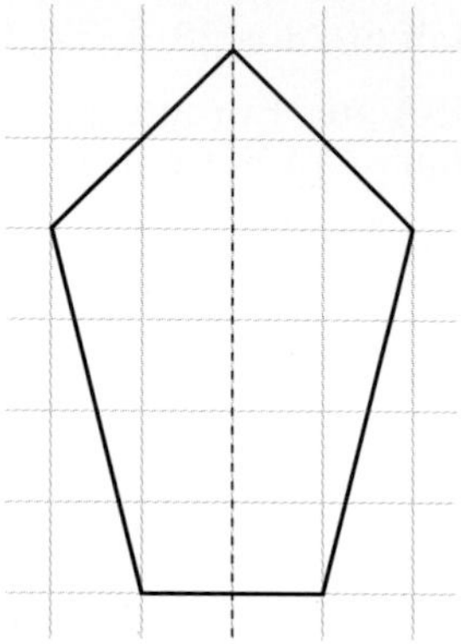

2 **a**

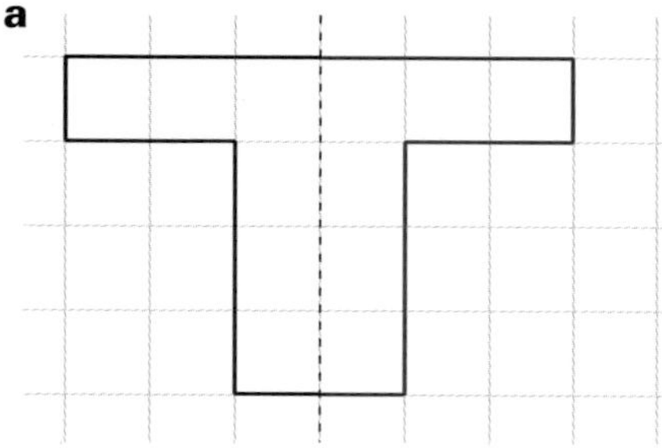

b

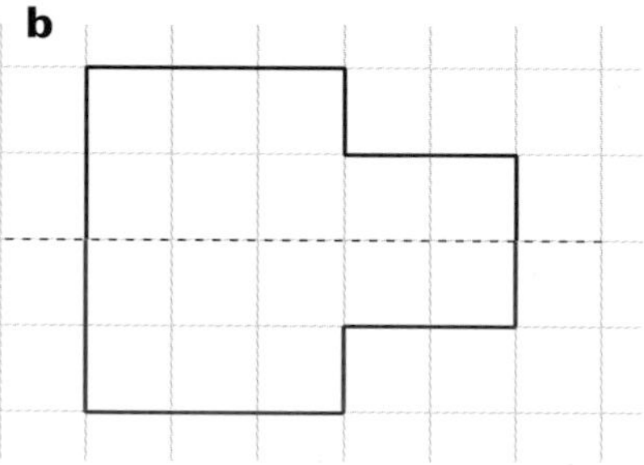

3 **a** **A W Y** **b** **C D** **c** **J S**

4 **a** and **c**

5 Rotational symmetry of order:
a 2 **b** 3 **c** 7

CHAPTER 3

1 **a** 18, 28, 228, 320 **b** 15, 23, 125

2 **a** 8, 10, 12, **14**, **16**, 18 The rule is 'add 2' or '+2'.
b 26, 23, 20, **17**, 14, **11** The rule is 'subtract 3' or '−3'.
c 1, 2, 4, **8**, **16**, 32 The rule is 'multiply by 2' or '×2'.

3 4, 8, 12, 16, 20, 24

4 **a** 1, 2, 4, 8 **b** 1, 3, 5, 15

5 **a** The rule is 'add 4' or '+4'.
b 5, 13, 17
c 1, 21
d 1, 9, 25

6 **a**

Input	Rule	Output
2	+4	6
3		7
5		9

b

Input	Rule	Output
3	×4	12
5		20
6		24

c

Input	Rule	Output
16	−5	11
7		2
21		16

7 The rule +8 belongs on the screen.
$4 + 8 = 12$
$7 + 8 = 15$
$12 + 8 = 20$

8

Input	Rule		Rule	Output
1	+3	4	×4	16
3		6		24
5		8		32

CHAPTER 4

1 **a** 40 since 38 is closer to 40 than to 30.
b 90 since 85 is half-way between 80 and 90, so we choose the higher.
c 250 since 253 is closer to 250 than to 260.

2 **a** 400 since 449 is closer to 400 than to 500.
b 700 since 681 is closer to 700 than to 600.
c 300 since 250 is half-way between 200 and 300.

3 **a** We need to add $25 + 3 = 28$
b We need to multiply $25 \times 3 = 75$

4 **a** We need to subtract £12 − £7 = £5
b We need to divide £24 ÷ 2 = £12

5 **a** $20 \div 2 - 8 = 10 - 8$ Do the division first.
$= 2$
b $24 + 2 \times 4 = 24 + 8$ Do the multiplication first.
$= 32$
c $24 - 2 \times 7 = 24 - 14$ Do the multiplication first.
$= 10$

6 **a** $(5 + 4) \times 2 = 9 \times 2$ Do the bracket first.
$= 18$
b $(16 - 11) \times 3 = 5 \times 3$ Do the bracket first.
$= 15$
c $60 \div (7 + 5) = 60 \div 12$ Do the bracket first.
$= 5$

7 **a** $5 \times 6 + 7 \times 8 = 30 + 56$ Do the multiplication first.
$= 86$
b $9 \times 3 - 3 \times 5 = 27 - 15$ Do the multiplication first.
$= 12$
c $15 + 10 \div 5 = 15 + 2$ Do the division first.
$= 17$

8 **a** $3^3 = 3 \times 3 \times 3$
$= 27$
b $5^4 = 5 \times 5 \times 5 \times 5$
$= 625$
c $2^3 + 8^2 = 2 \times 2 \times 2 + 8 \times 8$ Do the powers first.
$= 8 + 64$ Do the addition next.
$= 72$

CHAPTER 5

1 **a** **B** is isosceles. It has two equal sides.
b **C** is equilateral. It has three equal sides.
c **A** is scalene. It has no equal sides.

2 **A** trapezium
B rectangle
C kite
D parallelogram
E rhombus
F trapezium
G arrowhead
H square

3 **a**

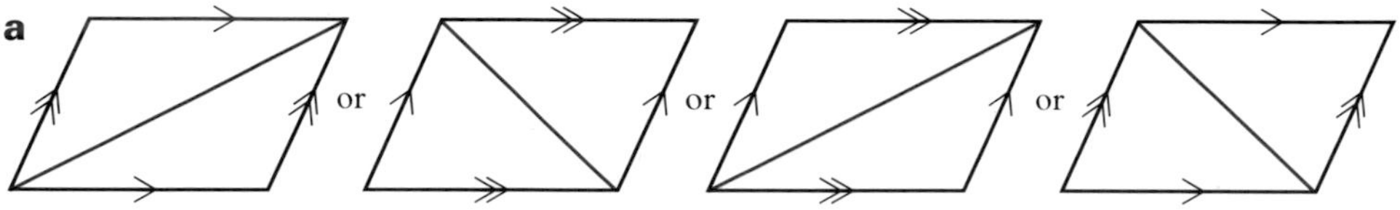

b The parallelogram has four vertices (corners).
c The diagonals are shown in red.

4 **a** (1) **A** and **B** are regular.
(2) **A** and **B** are convex.
(3) **C** is concave.

b (1) **C** is an octagon (8 sides).
(2) **A** is a pentagon (5 sides).
(3) **B** is a hexagon (6 sides).
(4) **D** is not a polygon (it has a curved side).

5 **a** (1) DE (or ED) is a chord (misses the centre).
(2) AB (or BA) is a diameter (through the centre).
(3) OC (or CO) is a radius (centre to circumference).
b (1) All the way round the outside of a circle is the **circumference**.
(2) An **arc** goes part of the way round the outside.
(3) Half a circle is called a **semicircle**.

6

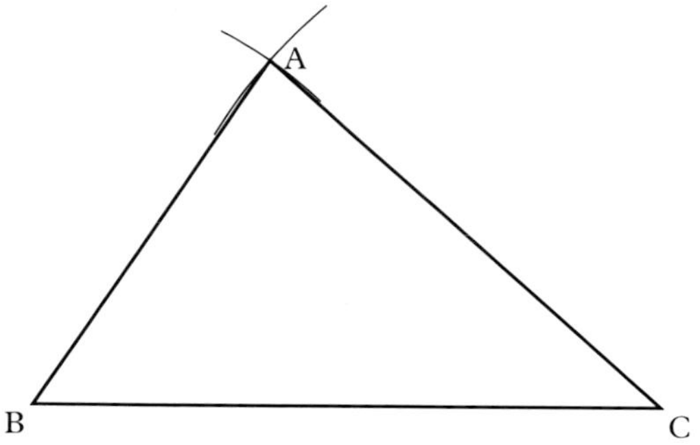

7 **a** (1) **B**
(2) **B**
b Here are two tessellations.
The pattern must be regular.
There must not be any gaps.

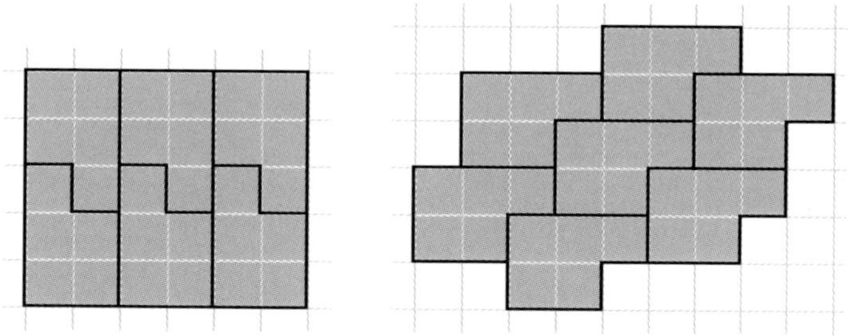

CHAPTER 6

1 **a** The 4 is multiplied by 10×10 or 100.
b The four has moved two columns.

2 **a** Five point six three
b 0.079

3 a

	thousands	hundreds	tens	units	.	tenths	hundredths	thousandths
(1)			6	5	.	3	1	9
(2)	8	1	0	4				
(3)				7	.	0	9	6
(4)		1	0	4	.	5	7	
(5)				0	.	4	2	3

b (1) six tens
(2) eight thousands
(3) nine hundredths
(4) five tenths
(5) three thousandths

4 3.42, 4.414, 4.42 (4.414 is smaller than 4.42 as 1 is smaller than 2. The numbers in front of the 1 and 2 are the same, 4.4).

5 a 3.6, 3.8, **4.0**, 4.2, 4.4, 4.6, **4.8** The rule is add 0.2 each time.
b **9.0**, 8.5, 8.0, 7.5, 7.0, **6.5**, 6.0 The rule is subtract 0.5 each time.

6 a $\begin{array}{r} 4.51 \\ +\ 6.20 \\ \hline 10.71 \end{array}$ **b** $\begin{array}{r} 9.50 \\ -\ 5.38 \\ \hline 4.12 \end{array}$ **c** $\begin{array}{r} 6.05 \\ +\ 7.00 \\ \hline 13.05 \end{array}$ **d** $\begin{array}{r} 29.0 \\ -\ 8.7 \\ \hline 20.3 \end{array}$

7 a $\begin{array}{r} 3.4 \\ \times\ 5 \\ \hline 17.0 \end{array}$ **b** $\begin{array}{r} 0.16 \\ \times\ 3 \\ \hline 0.48 \end{array}$ **c** $3\overline{)8.4}$ = 2.8 **d** $4\overline{)17.04}$ = 4.26

8 a (1) 4.9 is closer to 5.
(2) 8.5 is halfway so it rounds to 9.
(3) 13.3 is closer to 13.
b (1) 3.79 rounds to 3.8
(2) 4.62 rounds to 4.6
(3) 6.35 rounds to 6.4 (halfway so round up)

9 a £3.752 rounds to £3.75
b £25.609 rounds to £25.61
c £0.875 rounds to £0.88 (halfway so round up)

CHAPTER 7

1 a A pyramid has a base.
Opposite the base all the edges meet at a point.
A prism is the same all the way through.
Both ends of a prism are the same.
b A square pyramid **c** 8 edges **d** 5 faces **e** 5 vertices

2 **a** Length 4 cm, width 2 cm, height 2 cm.
b The smallest numbers of cubes needed are
(1) 6 cubes (2) 7 cubes (3) 6 cubes.

3 **c** is not a net. You can test this by cutting out the patterns and folding.

4 **a** Length 3 cm, width 2 cm, height 1 cm.
b Tetrahedron or triangular pyramid.

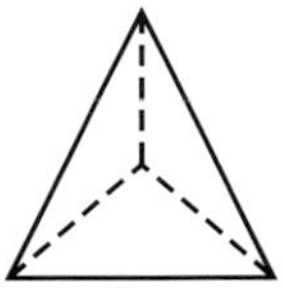

CHAPTER 8

1

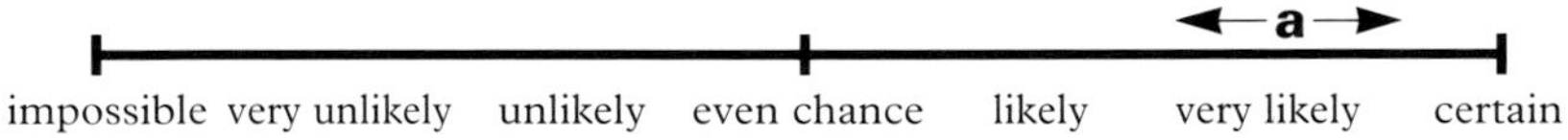

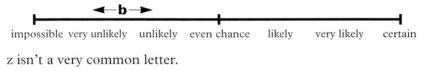

e is the most common letter in the alphabet so it is fairly certain to occur.

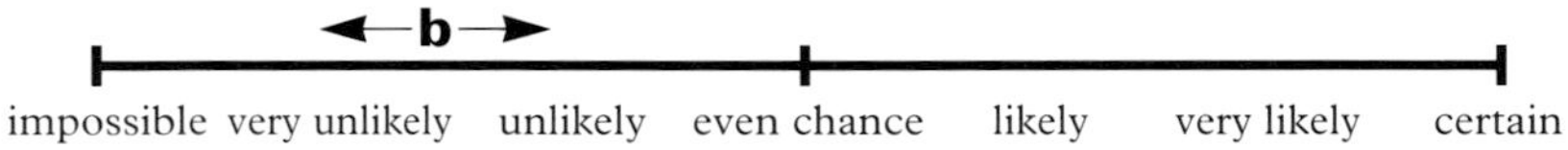

z isn't a very common letter.

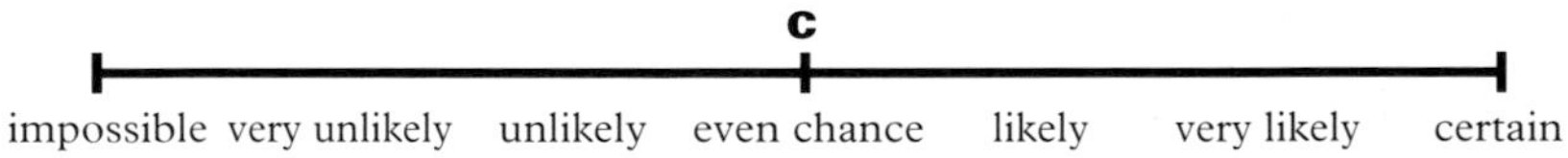

Getting an even number is as likely as not getting an even number.

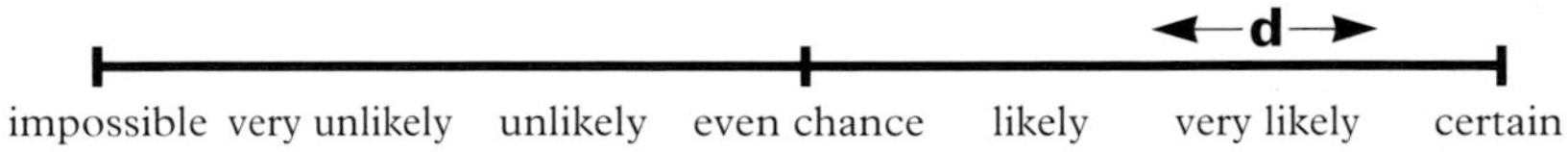

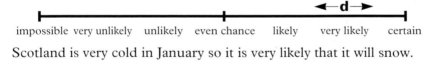

Scotland is very cold in January so it is very likely that it will snow.

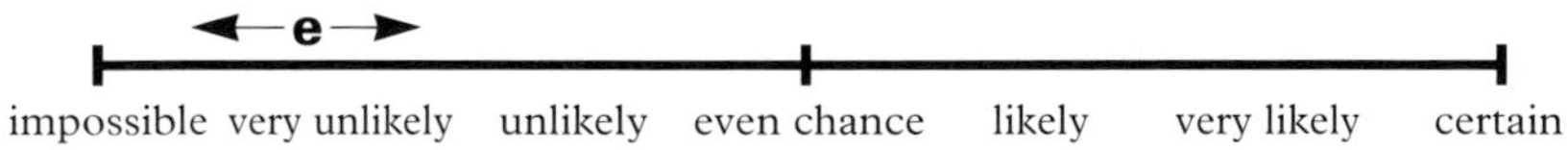

It is not impossible but it's very unlikely.

2 **a** $\frac{1}{6}$ Getting any single number on a dice is equally likely. So it is a $\frac{1}{6}$ probability for every score on a dice
b $\frac{1}{6}$ Getting any single number on a dice is equally likely. So it is a $\frac{1}{6}$ probability for every score on a dice
c $\frac{1}{325}$ One ticket out of 325
d $\frac{5}{325}$ or $\frac{1}{65}$ Five tickets out of 325

e $\frac{1}{2}$ Getting a head or a tail is equally likely. Then it is a $\frac{1}{2}$ probability for a head or a tail

f $\frac{1}{12}$ One 6 out of 12 faces altogether

3 **a** $\frac{3}{10}$ There are 10 cubes (3 + 2 + 5) altogether and 3 of them are red.

b $\frac{2}{10}$ or $\frac{1}{5}$ 2 are green

c $\frac{5}{10}$ or $\frac{1}{2}$ 5 are blue

d 2 **e** 3 **f** 5 **g** 6 **h** 9 **i** 15

The answers for **d** to **i** are what you would expect. If you did the experiment it may not turn out this way.

4 **a**

Score on dice	1	2	3	4	5	6
Estimate of probability	$\frac{80}{600}$	$\frac{110}{600}$	$\frac{170}{600}$	$\frac{80}{600}$	$\frac{70}{600}$	$\frac{90}{600}$

You get these answers by putting the frequency on the top of the fraction with the total number of throws on the bottom.

b 100 each A fair dice should give equal numbers of each score. So for 600 throws you should get 600 ÷ 6 = 100 of each score.

c Biased The 170 scores of 3 looks like this dice is biased. The others are close enough to 100 but the 170 is very much bigger than it should be.

CHAPTER 9

1 **a** $t = 4 \times m$ or $t = m \times 4$ or $t = 4m$

b $t = 8 + e$ or $t = e + 8$

c $a = 25 - p$

d $a = p \div 4$

2 **a** $C = 3r$ **b** $t = p - w$ **c** $a = \frac{b}{c}$ **d** $h = 3r + 4$

3

Number of shirts *S*	Cost of shirts (£)	Cost of postage and packing (£)	Total cost *T* (£)
1	10	3	13
2	20	3	23
3	30	3	33
4	40	3	43
5	50	3	53
6	60	3	63

To find the total cost multiply the number of shirts by 10 and add three.

$T = S \times 10 + 3$ or $T = 10S + 3$

4 **a** $5n$ **d** $7 + 5e$
b $13g$ **e** $2a + 3b$ (terms are all different so we cannot collect)
c $6r + 7s$ **f** $2s + t$

5 **a** $g^2 = g \times g$
$= 5 \times 5$
$= 25$

b $g + h = 5 + 2$
$= 7$

c $g - h = 5 - 2$
$= 3$

d $gh = g \times h$
$= 5 \times 2$
$= 10$

e $2g + h = 2 \times 5 + 2$
$= 10 + 2$
$= 12$

f $\frac{g}{5} = \frac{5}{5}$
$= 5 \div 5$
$= 1$

CHAPTER 10

1 **a** $\frac{1}{2}$ turn anti-clockwise

b $\frac{1}{4}$ turn clockwise

2 **a** 133°, obtuse (You can have 132° or 134°)

b and **c** (1)

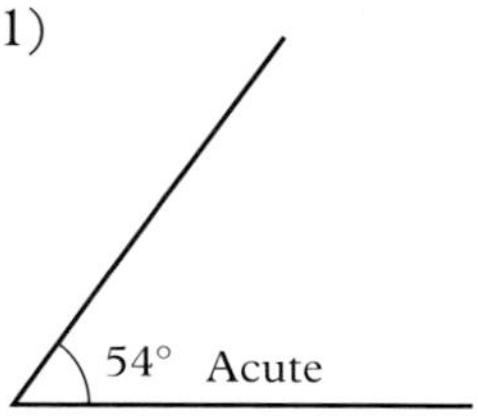

(2)

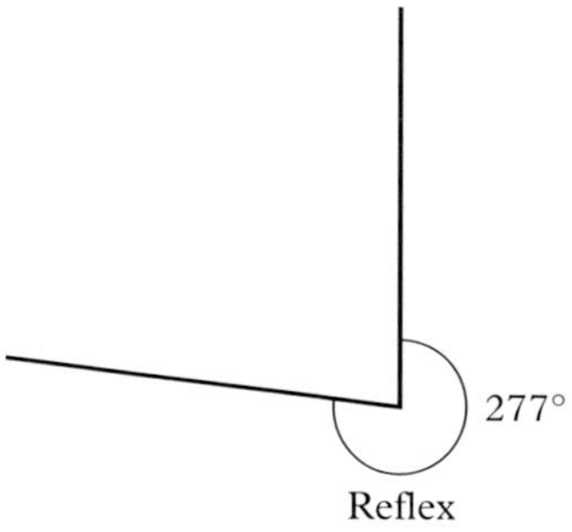

(3)

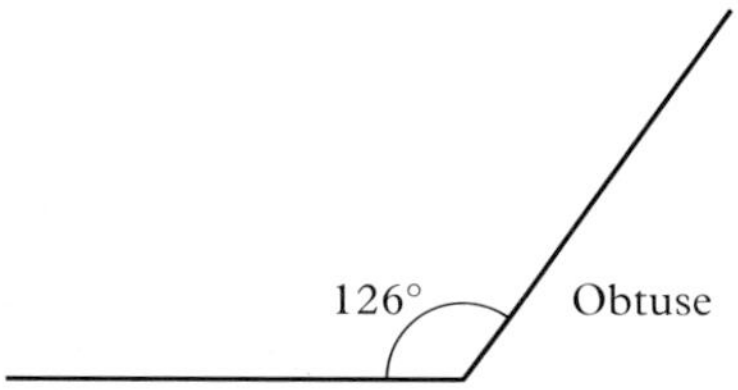

3 **a** $a = 180° - 142°$
$= 38°$

b $b = 50°$
$= 130°$

c $d = 360° - 68°$
$= 292°$

d $e = 180° - 90° - 25°$
$= 65°$

4

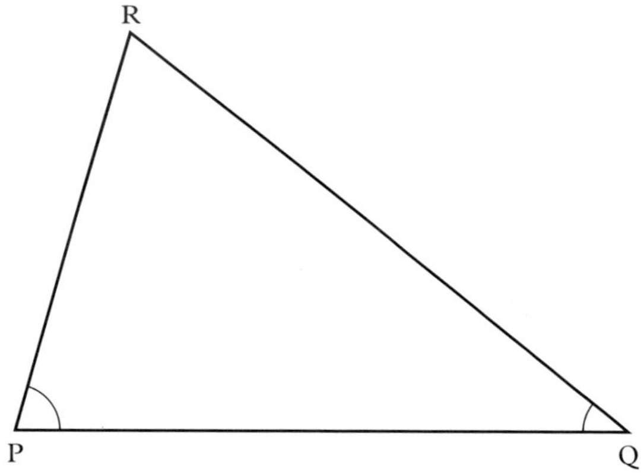

$\angle Q = 39°$ (You can have 38° or 40°)

CHAPTER 11

1 Find the temperature on the thermometer scale. Warmer temperatures are higher up the scale.

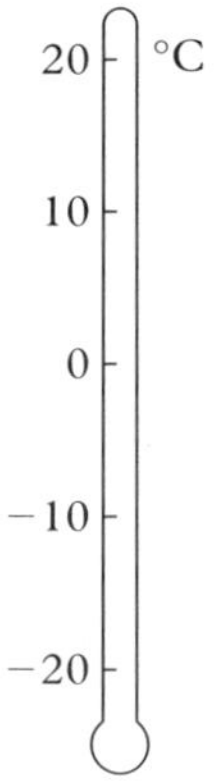

a Yes, 13 °C is warmer than −18 °C.

b −8 °C is colder than −5 °C.

c No, −14 °C is not colder than −20 °C.

d 0 °C is warmer than −7 °C.

2

Day temperature	Night temperature	Difference	Keys to press
4 °C	−6 °C	10 °C	4 − 6 +/− =
7 °C	−1 °C	8 °C	7 − 1 +/− =
10 °C	3 °C	7 °C	1 0 − 3 =
8 °C	−12 °C	20 °C	8 − 1 2 +/− =

3 −8 °C to 3 °C goes up the scale 11 °C.
This can be done on a calculator 3 − 8 +/− =

4 b $y = x + 4$

x		y	
1 →	+4	→ 5	(1, 5)
0 →		→ 4	(0, 4)
−1 →		→ 3	(−1, 3)
−2 →		→ 2	(−2, 2)
−3 →		→ 1	(−3, 1)
−4 →		→ 0	(−4, 0)
−5 →		→ −1	(−5, −1)

c and **d**

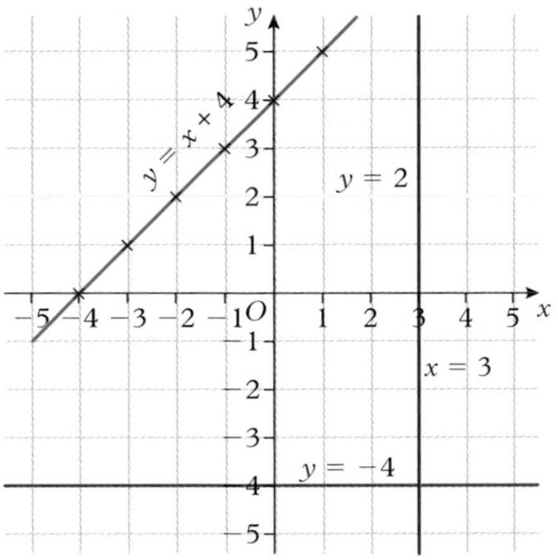

CHAPTER 12

1 **a** 2 ft = 2 × 12 in
= 24 in

b 36 m = 36 ÷ 12 ft
= 3 ft

c 4 yd = 4 × 3 ft
= 12 ft

d 6 ft = 6 ÷ 3 yd
= 2 yd

2 **a** The distance from London to New York would be in km.
b The width of your exercise book would be in cm.
c The height of a tall tree would be in m.
d The length of a fly's leg would be in mm.

3 **a** 20 mm = 2 cm
b 120 cm = 1.2 m
c 5000 m = 5 km
d 4.2 cm = 42 mm
e 1.5 m = 150 cm
f 3 km = 3000 m

4 **a** Length of line = 5 cm. It represents 5 × 2 km = 10 km.
b Length of line = 3.5 cm. It represents $3\frac{1}{2}$ × 2 km = 7 km.
c Any answer between 11 km and 15 km.

5 **a** The line should be $5\frac{1}{2}$ cm long.

b $18 \div 3 = 6$ The line should be 6 cm long.

6 **a**

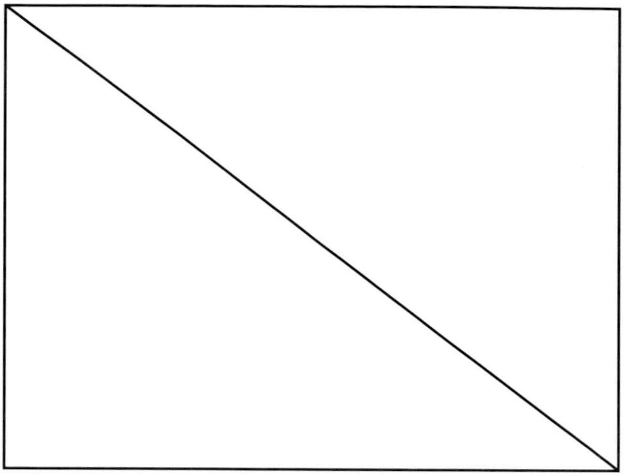

b Diagonal is 10 cm long. 10 cm ÷ 2 cm = 5 cm. Distance is 5 miles

7 **a** 4 inches is $4 \times 2\frac{1}{2}$ cm = 10 cm.

b 5 yards is a bit less than 5 metres.

c 4 miles is a bit more than $4 \times 1\frac{1}{2}$ km = 6 km.

8 **a** 10.7 **b** (Scale goes up in twos) 6 **c** 5 in ≈ 12.7 cm

CHAPTER 13

1 Subtract 3

2 Divide by 6

3 Multiply by 7

4 Add 10

5 → [+ 2] → [× 10] → Inverse is: ← [− 2] ← [÷ 10] ←

6 → [÷ 8] → [− 2] → Inverse is: ← [× 8] ← [+ 2] ←

7 x → [+ 10] → 27 Inverse is: 17 ← [− 10] ← 27

Answer: $x = 17$

8 $y \longrightarrow \boxed{\times 5} \longrightarrow 30$ Inverse is: $6 \longleftarrow \boxed{\div 5} \longleftarrow 30$

Answer: $y = 6$

9 $c \longrightarrow \boxed{\div 4} \longrightarrow 8$ Inverse is: $32 \longleftarrow \boxed{\times 4} \longleftarrow 8$

Answer: $c = 32$

10 $x \longrightarrow \boxed{\times 2} \xrightarrow{2x} \boxed{-13} \longrightarrow 17$

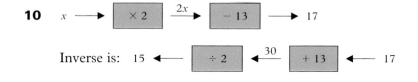

Inverse is: $15 \longleftarrow \boxed{\div 2} \xleftarrow{30} \boxed{+13} \longleftarrow 17$

Answer: $x = 15$

11 Let the number be x. $\frac{x}{4} = 8$

$x \longrightarrow \boxed{\div 4} \longrightarrow 8$ Inverse is: $32 \longleftarrow \boxed{\times 4} \longleftarrow 8$

Answer: $x = 32$

12 $7x + 153 = 384$

Value of x	Value of $7x + 153$	
20	$7 \times 20 + 153 = 293$	too small
30	$7 \times 30 + 153 = 363$	too small
40	$7 \times 40 + 153 = 433$	too big
35	$7 \times 35 + 153 = 398$	too big
34	$7 \times 34 + 153 = 391$	too big
33	$7 \times 33 + 153 = 384$	correct

Answer: $x = 33$

13 $x + 54 = 180$

$x \longrightarrow \boxed{+54} \longrightarrow 180$ $126 \longleftarrow \boxed{-54} \longleftarrow 180$

Answer: $x = 126$

14 $2a = 80$

$a \longrightarrow \boxed{\times 2} \longrightarrow 80$ $40 \longleftarrow \boxed{\div 2} \longleftarrow 80$

$a = 40$

CHAPTER 14

1 **a** The perimeter of F hexomino is 14 cm.
This is the distance around the outside of the shape.
You find it by counting the squares.
b The area of the F hexomino is 6 cm.
You find this by counting the squares inside the shape.

2 Length 7 cm width 2 cm
a Area = length × width
$= 7 \times 2$
$= 14\ \text{cm}^2$
b Perimeter $= 7 + 2 + 7 + 2$
$= 18$ cm

3 **a** You would measure a lounge carpet in m^2.
b You would measure a dolls' house carpet in cm^2.
c You would measure a magic carpet covering London in km^2.

4 Area = length × width
36 = length × 3

$$\text{length} = \frac{36}{3}$$
$= 12$ cm

5 **a** Area of A $= 9 \times 10$
$= 90\ \text{m}^2$
Width of B $= 18 - 10$
$= 8$ m
Area of B $= 20 \times 8$
$= 160\ \text{m}^2$
Area of shape $= 90 + 160$
$= 250\ \text{m}^2$

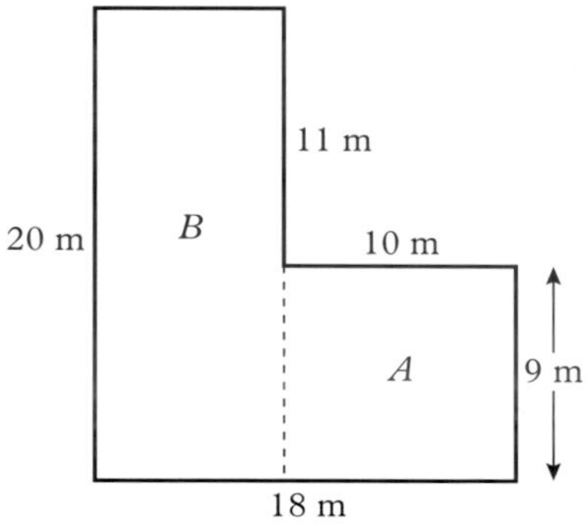

b Area of triangle $= \dfrac{\text{base} \times \text{height}}{2}$
$= \dfrac{10 \times 8}{2}$
$= 40\ \text{cm}^2$
c Area of parallelogram = base × height
$= 11 \times 9$
$= 99\ \text{cm}^2$

CHAPTER 15

1 **a, b, c** $\frac{3}{5}$ $\begin{matrix} 3 \leftarrow \text{numerator} \\ 5 \leftarrow \text{denominator} \end{matrix}$

2 **a, b** $\begin{matrix} 2 \leftarrow \text{shade 2 pieces} \\ 5 \leftarrow \text{split into 5 pieces} \end{matrix}$

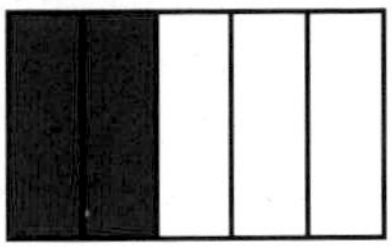

3 **a** To find $\frac{1}{3}$, divide by 3. $\frac{1}{3}$ of $15 = 15 \div 3 = 5$

b To find $\frac{2}{5}$, divide by 5 then multiply by 2.

$\frac{1}{5}$ of $20 = 20 \div 5 = 4$

$\frac{2}{5}$ of $20 = 4 \times 2 = 8$

4 Each child gets $1\frac{2}{3}$ cakes.

5 $\frac{4}{6} \overset{\div 2}{=} \frac{2}{3}$ (numerator $\div 2$, denominator $\div 2$) $\quad \frac{4}{6} = \frac{2}{3}$ in its simplest form

6 17 out of 100 squares are shaded **a** $\frac{17}{100}$ **b** 17%

7 **a** 1 hour = 60 minutes so 10 minutes = $\frac{10}{60}$ of an hour

b $\frac{10}{60} = \frac{1}{6}$ in its simplest form.

8 **a** $\frac{2}{5} + \frac{2}{5} = \frac{4}{5}$

b $\frac{2}{5} + \frac{1}{10} = \frac{4}{10} + \frac{1}{10} = \frac{5}{10} = \frac{1}{2}$

c $\frac{5}{6} - \frac{1}{3} = \frac{5}{6} - \frac{2}{6} = \frac{3}{6} = \frac{1}{2}$

9 **a** $\frac{4}{5}$ as a decimal = $\begin{array}{r} 0.8 \\ 5\overline{)4.{}^40} \end{array}$

b $\frac{5}{8}$ as a decimal = $\begin{array}{r} 0.625 \\ 8\overline{)5.{}^50{}^20{}^40} \end{array}$

10 **a** $0.4 = \frac{4}{10} = \frac{2}{5}$ **b** $0.56 = \frac{56}{100} = \frac{14}{25}$ **c** $0.175 = \frac{175}{1000} = \frac{7}{40}$

11 $\frac{1}{3} = \frac{4}{12}$ $\quad \frac{1}{4} = \frac{3}{12}$

So $\frac{1}{3}$ is the bigger.

12 $\frac{1}{5}$ $\quad \frac{1}{2}$ $\quad \frac{2}{3}$ $\quad \frac{3}{4}$

CHAPTER 16

1 **a** £540 **b** £45

2 **a**

Weight	Number of packets	Weight of crisps
28	4	$4 \times 28 = 112$
29	5	$5 \times 29 = 145$
30	11	$11 \times 30 = 330$
31	7	$7 \times 31 = 217$
32	3	$3 \times 32 = 96$
		Total = 900

b 900 g **c** 30 g

3 **a**

Score	Tally	Total
2		0
3					3
4				2
5				2
6						4
7	~~||||~~ ||	7
8	~~||||~~	5
9	~~||||~~	5
10				2
11					3
12					3

b 7 is the mode.

4 **a** 0.41
b 0.21
c $0.41 - 0.21 = 0.20$
d 0.21, 0.23, 0.23, 0.23, 0.24, 0.24, 0.25, 0.27, (0.29), 0.29, 0.32, 0.34, 0.34, 0.34, 0.34, 0.39, 0.41.

5 **a** Graph (2). It looks as if they are increasing quickly.
b Graph (2). It looks as if the sales are very high and increasing.
c Graph (1). The figures look as if they are staying the same.

Exercise 1

1	19	**5**	669	**9**	17
2	56	**6**	659	**10**	58
3	48	**7**	5669	**11**	579
4	565	**8**	7899	**12**	667

Exercise 2

1	24	**5**	610	**9**	63
2	65	**6**	593	**10**	604
3	397	**7**	880	**11**	3000
4	491	**8**	2122	**12**	8888

Exercise 3

1	33	**5**	541	**9**	622
2	224	**6**	1421	**10**	212
3	334	**7**	3351	**11**	12
4	823	**8**	6111	**12**	3180

Exercise 4

1	14	**5**	51	**9**	54
2	15	**6**	276	**10**	346
3	94	**7**	386	**11**	365
4	313	**8**	444	**12**	504

Exercise 5

1	126	**3**	4713
2	268	**4**	754

Exercise 6

1	128	**3**	168
2	129	**4**	1269

Exercise 7

1	52	**6**	1881
2	70	**7**	392
3	138	**8**	468
4	496	**9**	1235
5	759	**10**	2420

Exercise 8

1	270	**5**	6350
2	360	**6**	74 260
3	3260	**7**	80 000
4	8230	**8**	90 010

Exercise 9

1	6300	**7**	432 100
2	9100	**8**	400 000
3	42 000	**9**	2 001 000
4	87 300	**10**	6 340 000
5	277 000	**11**	2 060 000
6	605 000	**12**	43 500 000

Exercise 10

1	460	**5**	540	**9**	2100
2	520	**6**	780	**10**	2460
3	510	**7**	480	**11**	7410
4	960	**8**	1150	**12**	9240

Exercise 11

1	1075	**5**	9025	**9**	20 922
2	1792	**6**	18 104	**10**	40 376
3	3936	**7**	25 012	**11**	63 862
4	8917	**8**	36 608	**12**	98 901

Exercise 12

1 6
2 4
3 4
4 5
5 7
6 4
7 4
8 5
9 9
10 5
11 7
12 7

Exercise 13

1 23
2 32
3 11
4 23
5 41
6 112

Exercise 14

1 18
2 16
3 24
4 13
5 13
6 17
7 15
8 12
9 109
10 128
11 129
12 42

Exercise 15

1 63
2 7
3 496
4 74
5 901
6 290
7 300
8 40 000

Exercise 16

1 63
2 67
3 86
4 24
5 870
6 87
7 800
8 80

Exercise 17

1 26
2 24
3 52
4 29
5 66
6 58
7 36
8 202